Failure of Em

The Joan Palevsky  Imprint in Classical Literature

In honor of beloved Virgil—

"O degli altri poeti onore e lume . . ."

—Dante, *Inferno*

Failure of Empire

*Valens and the Roman State
in the Fourth Century A.D.*

Noel Lenski

Constantius II — 337 – 361)
Julian — 361 – 363
Jovian — 363 – 364

Valentinian I — 364 – 375

Valens — 364 – 378

Gratian — 367 – 383

Valentinian II — 375 – 392

UNIVERSITY OF CALIFORNIA PRESS
Berkeley   Los Angeles   London

The publisher gratefully acknowledges the generous
contribution to this book provided by Joan Palevsky.

University of California Press
Berkeley and Los Angeles, California

University of California Press, Ltd.
London, England

© 2002 by The Regents of the University of California

First Paperback Printing 2014

Library of Congress Cataloging-in-Publication Data

Lenski, Noel Emmanuel, 1965–
    Failure of empire : Valens and the Roman state in the fourth
century A.D. / Noel Lenski.
        p.   cm.
    Includes bibliographical references and index.
    ISBN 978-0-520-28389-3 (pbk.: alk. paper)
        1. Valens, Emperor of the East, ca. 328–378.   2. Byzantine
Empire—History—Valens, 364–378.   3. Valentinian I, Emperor
of Rome, 321–375.   4. Rome—History—Valentinian I, 364–
375.   I. Title.

DF559 .L46   2002
949.5'9013—dc21   2002009716

Manufactured in the United States of America

19 18 17 16 15 14

10 9 8 7 6 5 4 3 2 1

Ausoniae
amoribus meis

CONTENTS

vii

ILLUSTRATIONS

ACKNOWLEDGMENTS

By some turn of fate, I was inspired to work on Valens while watching Donizetti's *L'elisir d'amore* at the Metropolitan Opera. Valens would not have approved. After all, he and his brother killed people for dabbling in love philters. Of course, I am well aware that Valens is not a person to whom many would choose to be wedded for eight years. Indeed, I did not begin my study believing that our relationship would last so long, nor did I pursue it because my feelings for the man grew as I worked. Even so, I hardly regret my choice to investigate his life and times in such lavish detail. I have always found misfits fascinating, and I find Valens's peculiarities and peccadilloes particularly attractive for their complexity and pathos. His humanity has not been entirely obscured by the thick shroud of rhetoric that envelops so many late Roman rulers. Though the shroud is certainly present, Valens's failures have left a large rent in its fabric, giving us a fairly clear picture of the man underneath. For this reason, Valens makes an excellent case study in how an ordinary man confronted an extraordinary challenge—the challenge of empire—and ultimately failed to meet it.

This book grew out of a Princeton dissertation, which I completed in 1995. That work, which included the material found here in chapters 1 through 4 and chapter 7, was substantially rewritten. To it were added chapters 5 and 6 and the appendices. As this book owes much to its previous incarnation, I owe much to my dissertation advisors, Peter Brown, Ted Champlin, and Bob Lamberton. Each has fostered my work and my career with incomparable generosity and intellect. The numismatic work in the book was done on fellowship at the American Numismatic Society under the direction of Bill Metcalf, whose graciousness and acumen merit the highest praise. Much of the dissertation was written while I held a Donald and Mary Hyde Foundation Fellowship at Oxford in 1993–94. There Peter Heather, Roger Tomlin, and

Charlotte Roueché were especially generous in sharing their time and knowledge. Above all, however, John Matthews offered unstinting support and advice. I owe a heavy debt not just to his encouragement but also to his scholarship, which has, more than anyone's, influenced my own work.

As I began to revise, Craige Champion read and commented on the entire dissertation with admirable care. Individual chapters and sections were read by Jacques Bailly, Tim Barnes, Glen Bowersock, Garth Fowden, Mike Gaddis, Cathy King, John Ma, and Brent Shaw. My learned wife Alison Orlebeke patiently read at least one draft of everything I wrote and proved to be my best critic of style and logic. Eventually, Hal Drake and Peter Heather read the manuscript I sent to Berkeley and helped me clear away several hurdles I had left standing. I am particularly grateful to Heather, who has been involved in this project since 1993 and who has treated me and my work with the utmost respect, despite our differences on matters Gothic.

The University of Colorado granted me a teaching release in the spring of 1998, and Dumbarton Oaks awarded me a fellowship for that summer, part of which I used for this book. CU also funded two undergraduate research assistants, Joanna Koutsis, who helped me assemble Theodosian Code laws, and Leanne Smoot, who prepared the maps. Jim Robb of CU cartography did final revisions on those maps, Dave Underwood in CU graphics did much of the work for my images, and the CU interlibrary loan staff have been amazingly efficient in helping me find resources. As editor, Kate Toll has combined equal measures of patience and pressure into a remarkably effective elixir, which has finally helped me break the spell of Valens.

More than anyone, however, I must thank my family: my parents and brothers, who have always supported my endeavors with encouragement; my children Paul and Helen, who have had to share daddy with a long-dead emperor since they were born; and above all my true love Alison, whose charms offer the only real antidote for my labors.

ABBREVIATIONS

Abbreviations for ancient sources follow the conventions of either *The Proso-pography of the Later Roman Empire*, vol. 1: A.D 260–395, ed. A. H. M. Jones, J. R. Martindale, and J. Morris (Cambridge, 1971), or *The Oxford Classical Dictionary³*, ed. S. Hornblower and A. Spawforth (New York, 1996). Abbreviations for periodical titles follow *L'Année philologique*. Note also the following:

AM   Ammianus Marcellinus, *Rerum gestarum libri qui super-sunt*, ed. C. U. Clark (Berlin, 1910)

ASX   *The Geography of Ananias of Sirak (Asxarhac'oyc')*, trans. R. H. Hewsen (Wiesbaden, 1992)

BP   *Buzandaran Patmut'iwnk'*, *Epic Histories attributed to P'awstos Buzand*, trans. N. Garsoïan (Cambridge, Mass., 1989)

Chron. Edes.   *Chronicon Edessenum*, ed. I. Guidi (Paris, 1903)

CSCO   *Corpus scriptorum Christianorum orientalium* (Paris, 1903–)

DRB   *De rebus bellicis*, ed. R. I. Ireland (Leipzig, 1984)

Ephrem   Ephrem Syrus *(CJ = Contra Iulianum; CN = Carmina Nisibena)*

Epit.   *Epitome de Caesaribus*, ed. F. Pichlmayr (Leipzig, 1966)

Exc. Val.   *Excerpta Valesiana*, ed. J. Moreau (Leipzig, 1968)

Exp. tot. mun.   *Expositio totius mundi et gentium*, ed. J. Rougé (Paris, 1966)

Fest. Ind.   *Festal Index*, eds. A. Martin and M. Albert (Paris, 1985)

Gnecchi   *I medaglioni romani*, ed. R. Gnecchi (Milan, 1912)

GNO   *Gregorii Nyseni opera*, ed. W. Jaeger et al. (Leiden, 1952–)

Itin. Eg.	*Itinerarium Egeriae,* eds. A. Franceschini and R. Weber (Turnhout, Belgium, 1965)
Josh. Styl.	*The Chronicle of Pseudo-Joshua the Stylite,* trans. and comm. F. R. Trombley and J. W. Watt (Liverpool, 2000)
MX	*Moses Khorenats'i History of the Armenians,* trans. R. W. Thomson (Cambridge, Mass., 1978)
Nagl "Val."	A. Nagl "Valens 3" *RE* II.7.2 (Stuttgart, 1948)
Nagl "Vt."	A. Nagl "Valentinianus 1" *RE* II.7.2 (Stuttgart, 1948)
Paschoud	*Histoire nouvelle,* ed., trans. and comm. F. Paschoud (Paris, 1971–89)
Pass. Artemii	*Passio Artemii,* in *Philostorgius Kirchengeschichte,* ed. J. Bidez and F. Winkelmann (Berlin, 1972)
Pass. S. Sabae	*Passio Sancti Sabae,* ed. H. Delehaye (Paris, 1912)
Philostorg.	Philostorgius, *Historia Ecclesiastica: Kirchengeschichte,* ed. J. Bidez and F. Winkelmann (Berlin, 1972)
RGDS	*Res gestae Divi Saporis,* ed. E. Honigmann and J. Maricq (Brussels, 1953)
RRMAM	*Roman Roads and Milestones of Asia Minor,* ed. D. French (Oxford, 1988)
Seeck, *Briefe*	O. Seeck, *Die Briefe des Libanius zeitlich geordnet* (Stuttgart, 1906)
Seeck, *Regesten*	O. Seeck, *Regesten der Kaiser und Päpste* (Stuttgart, 1919)
Seeck, *Untergang*	O. Seeck, *Geschichte des Untergangs der antiken Welt,* vol. 5 (Stuttgart, 1913)
VM Thecla	*Vie et miracles de Sainte Thecle,* ed. G. Dagron (Brussels, 1978)

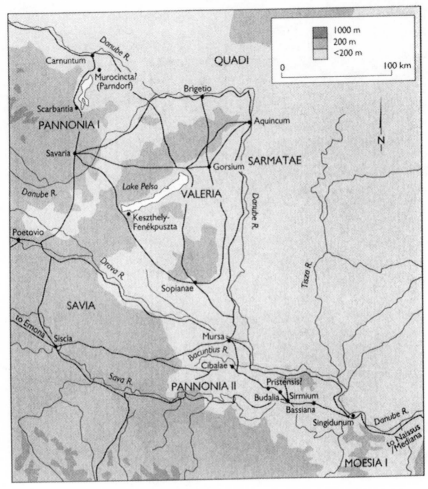

Map 1. Pannonia in the Fourth Century

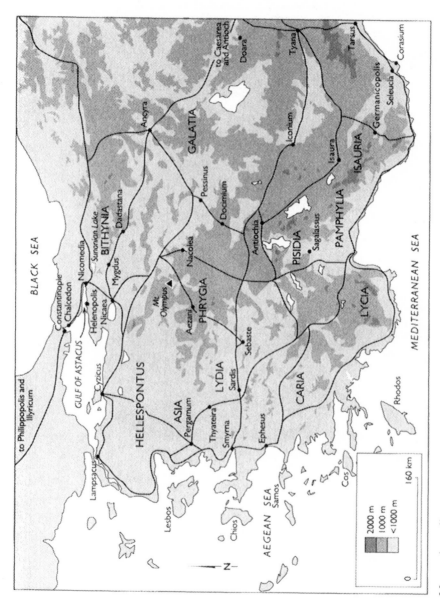

Map 2. Anatolia

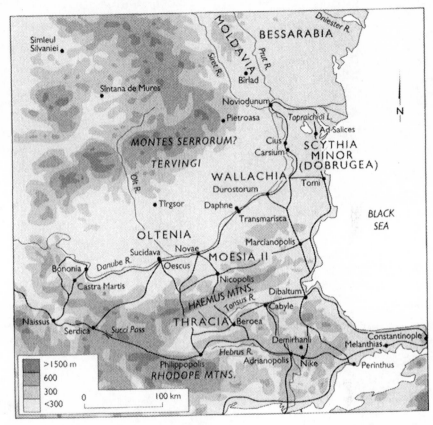

Map 3. Thrace and Gothia

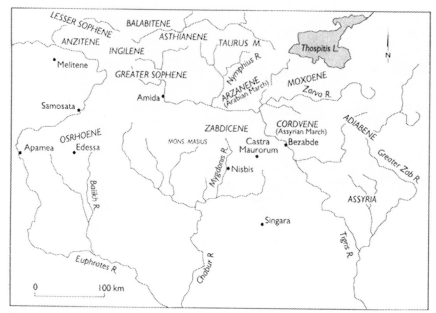

Map 4. Armenian Satrapies

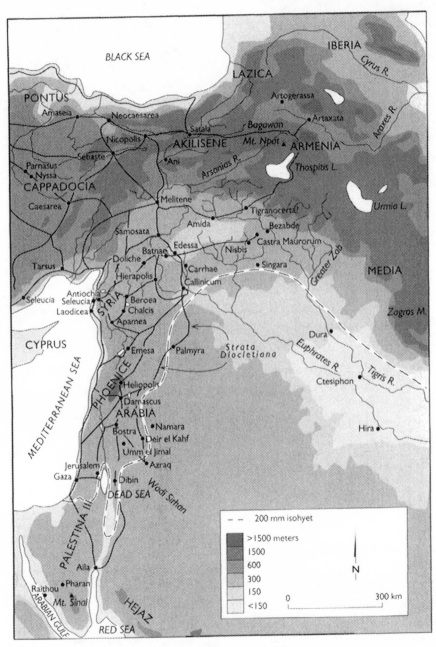

Map 5. The Eastern Roman Empire and Western Persia

Introduction

The late-fourth-century historian Ammianus Marcellinus tells us that his contemporary the emperor Valens was "a man with an equal amount of outstanding and awful qualities."[1] He was neither a hero nor a monster, but rather very much an ordinary human faced with a superhuman task. This book is about both the man and the task, about Valens and his empire. It aims to set Valens in his context and show how a person of unremarkable talents faced the demands of a remarkably complex world. My object is not to denigrate Valens. The ancient sources have gone quite far enough to blacken the man's reputation for all ages to come. Nor, however, do I seek to rehabilitate him. Such efforts are invariably reductive and predictable. At this remove I neither despise Valens nor particularly admire him. He did the best he could to live up to what was undoubtedly the biggest job in the world of his day, and his ultimate downfall is as much a testament to the difficulty of ruling the empire as it is to the failings of the emperor.

Unfortunately for Valens, and indeed for his empire, he was what contemporary Americans might refer to with duly sterile bureaucratic sympathy as "imperially challenged." He was not handsome, he was not educated, he was not well born, he was not charismatic, he was not particularly brave, and he was not especially intelligent. Then, as now, a ruler was evaluated by the impression he or she created, and Valens's made—and still makes—a rather poor impression. He thus cuts a distinctly underwhelming figure in Roman history. None of this means, however, that Valens was, like some other emperors, malevolent or even obtuse. On the contrary, he was well-intentioned and had much to recommend him, which he put to work as best he

---

1. AM 30.7.4: "inter probra medium et praecipua."

I

could for the benefit of the empire. He was a good farmer and good administrator, he was sympathetic to his subjects, particularly to commoners,
and he was adamant about the territorial integrity of his realm and the importance of upholding the military glory of Rome. Thus Ammianus seems
bang on in his assessment of Valens as a man of both good and bad qualities. In his case, though, both stand out more starkly than those of other emperors, precisely because his image has not been polished up for contemporaries and posterity by our sources. For this reason, even if he was no great
emperor, Valens makes for a great study.

This book attempts to present what Germans would call *Kaisergeschichte*,
or "emperor history." It is not quite biography, in large part because we do
not have adequate sources to write a true biography of Valens the man. It is
also much more than biography, for Valens, like any emperor, lived in far
too intricate a world for any portrait of him to be drawn without copious ac-
companying detail in the fore, middle, and background. In this sense, I would
hope that this book resembles something like a northern Renaissance painting, in the manner, say, of Hugo van der Goes's Portinari altarpiece. As is
typical of such paintings, Valens is foregrounded in all of his earthy simplicity.
Surrounding him in the middle ground are the characters who advised him
and implemented his policies and the adversaries he faced at home and
abroad. Receding into the background, I have tried to paint representative
scenes that bring the portrait to life in all of its dimensions and details. Such,
in my estimation, is the essence of *Kaisergeschichte*.

This genre has in some sense always been fashionable. Even in an era when
one is more likely to find synchronic and synthetic investigations of a specific
theme or motif, we have seen a steady stream of excellent biographical work
on major and minor emperors in the past decade. Even Valens has won attention in two recently published German dissertations, one on Valens's
Gothic wars by Ulrich Wanke (1990) and the second on Valens's persecution of pagans by Franz Josef Wiebe (1995). Up until the present, though,
no one has undertaken a full-length biography of all aspects of Valens and
his reign.[2] This is a pity, for a number of reasons. Not least, Valens provides
a marvelous case study in the stresses and strains of empire. Things hardly
turned out well for him; crisis piled onto crisis in a steady crescendo that culminated in his disastrous defeat at Adrianople. Only by looking at all of the
problems that Valens faced—natural disasters, usurpation and assassination
attempts, barbarian incursions, treaty violations, economic shortfalls, religious infighting, and military catastrophe—can we begin to see how the demands placed on this emperor were literally overwhelming. By undertaking
an omni-comprehensive study of all aspects of this troubled reign, we can

---

2. Köhler 1925 is quite primitive and omits many subjects. Nagl, "Val.," is useful, but only
in the manner of an encyclopedia article.

see the stress points of power, the fissures in the imperial façade, and how these affected the fate of the emperor and his empire.

An investigation of Valens can also provide a fairly clear outline of what was expected of a fourth-century emperor. Many of Valens's problems arose precisely because he did not live up to the expectations set for him by his world. He thus provides an excellent example—often a negative example—of what a late Roman emperor was supposed to be like. Much of this study is concerned with this question. What did contemporaries want from Valens? What did they find in him to satisfy or disappoint their expectations? What were the pressures on an emperor: social, cultural, religious, economic, administrative, and military? How did these interact, and how did the emperor himself react to their combined effects? In the end, these questions can only be answered by looking at all of the evidence synthetically. Much of what this book entails, then, is the rebuilding of a giant puzzle, whose thousands of pieces have been scattered by time, and above all by the nature of our sources, into sterile discontinuity from one another. By recombining nearly all of them, I have attempted to provide a satisfying reconstruction of the man and his times. The result, I hope, should be a three-dimensional matrix of interlocking elements, each of which pulls on the next in tension and reflexion.

Through a fortunate coincidence of historical accident, we still have many, many pieces with which to recreate this portrait. The reign of Valens has left a uniquely well developed source record, better than for nearly any emperor in the fourth century except Julian and perhaps Constantine. It is thus worthwhile to lay out in brief the nature of these sources so that readers may be familiar with how they affect our understanding of this fascinating emperor.

Pride of place surely goes to Ammianus Marcellinus (ca. 330–95).[3] This accurate and faithful guide to fourth-century political and military history covers the entire reign of Valens in his twenty-sixth through thirty-first books.[4] He provides a precise and detailed narrative for Valens's accession, his civil war with the usurper Procopius, his first Gothic war, his Persian war, his magic trials in Antioch, and his spectacular defeat by the Goths at Adrianople. Ammianus did not compose his narrative until the early 390s, but he lived through Valens's reign and was witness to many of the events he describes, including the Persian war that immediately preceded Valens's rule and the magic trials that shook Antioch during Valens's residence there in the early 370s.[5] Ammianus had also visited Thrace, where Valens died at

3. Among the many recent studies on Ammianus, I single out Sabbah 1978, Matthews 1989, and Barnes 1998.
4. For Ammianus's shift in intention and technique beginning at bk. 26, see Matthews 1989, 204–7.
5. For Ammianus's presence in Antioch in 372, see AM 29.2.4; cf. Matthews 1989, 48–66, 131–79.

Adrianople, and had close contacts in Armenia, where Valens's forces fought for many years.[6]

Despite his accuracy and detail, Ammianus has come in for some well-deserved criticism in recent studies.[7] No historian is perfect, even one as intelligent and multidimensional as Ammianus. He is thus demonstrably guilty of some factual errors in his report of Valens's rule.[8] More important, though, his are generally sins of omission rather than commission. This is certainly true in the realm of Christianity, where Ammianus, a pagan, maintains a studied reserve that occasionally leads to misunderstanding and even distortion.[9] Ammianus's failure, for example, to discuss the murder of the Christian Patriarch Nerses by the Armenian king Pap during Valens's reign is misleading, for Nerses's murder helped provoke Valens in turn to have Pap murdered.[10] Even more surprising, Ammianus omits mention of three major uprisings in the final years of Valens's reign, one by the Isaurians, one by the Saracens, and a third in Gothic territory.[11] At least two of these—those of the Saracens and Goths—involved Christianity. One begins to suspect that, to snub Christianity, our pagan historian has deliberately left us with a skewed impression of even the political forces affecting the history of his times.

Fortunately, there are other good sources, which serve as controls on the narrative of Ammianus. We can only regret the loss of a history by Ammianus's younger contemporary Eunapius of Sardis (ca. 345–ca. 415).[12] Eunapius was also a witness to events in Valens's reign and composed two versions of a full-length history in Greek, which, while disorganized and tendentious, was filled with important information. Unfortunately, the original text is no longer extant, but useful fragments survive in Constantine Porphyrogenitus.[13] Then, too, Eunapius's other major work, the *Lives of the Sophists,* also offers biographies of many philosophers contemporary with Valens, some of whom were attacked by the emperor at various points in his reign. More-

6. On Thrace, see AM 18.6.5, 22.8.1, 27.4.2; cf. Sabbah 1978, 115; Wolfram 1988, 70–71. On Armenia, see Sabbah 1978, 235–36.

7. Esp. Barnes 1998 and 1990b, with earlier bibliography.

8. Thus AM 27.5.2 locates Daphne on the wrong side of the Danube (cf. Wanke 1990, 91–94); AM 31.11.2 implies that Beroea and Nicopolis were near each other, when in fact they are separated by the Shipka pass; AM 31.11.2 and 12.1 appear to be doublets for the same event.

9. See Barnes 1998, 79–94, and 1990b. For earlier bibliography on the question, see Neri 1985a.

10. See Baynes 1910, Garsoïan 1969, and pp. 177–81.

11. On the Isaurian uprisings, see Lenski 1999a. On the Saracen uprising, see pp. 204–9. On the Gothic civil war, see Lenski 1995.

12. On Eunapius, see Blockley 1981–83, 1: 1–26; Penella 1990, 1–38. It has been posited, most strongly by Paschoud 1971–89 and 1975, that Ammianus and Eunapius shared a common source in the *Annales* of Nicomachus Flavianus. The question remains vexed. For recent discussion, see Bleckmann 1995.

13. I follow the order of the fragments laid out in Blockley 1981–83, vol. 2.

over, the late-fifth-century pagan Greek writer Zosimus composed an apologetic history of his own, which draws almost exclusively on Eunapius for its useful account of Valens's reign.[14] We thus have an alternative—if more abbreviated—narrative with which to supplement and partially critique Ammianus's much fuller and generally more accurate version of events.

We also have no fewer than five ecclesiastical histories that treat the reign of Valens in some detail. Because Valens was—even in his own lifetime—branded an arch-persecutor of Christians, he drew considerable attention from ecclesiastical historians, who provide us with considerable information on major events related to the church and the government of his day. We thus have good accounts in the ecclesiastical histories of Rufinus (ca. 403),[15] Philostorgius (ca. 425),[16] Socrates (ca. 446),[17] Sozomen (ca. 448/49), and Theodoret (449/50).[18] In many instances, the material in these histories overlaps, for Socrates used Rufinus as a source for some of his narrative, Sozomen then used Socrates, and Theodoret seems to have used both Socrates and Sozomen.[19] This does not mean, however, that they merely copied one another. Sozomen often corrects and supplements the material of Socrates, and, while Theodoret is generally less reliable than his two predecessors, he too adds new documentary material from contemporary sources, which can be quite useful.[20] In addition, Rufinus and Socrates had access to an ecclesiastical historian contemporary with Valens, Gelasius of Caesarea.[21] Finally, while our other ecclesiastical sources generally present information from a Nicene position, the copious fragments of Philostorgius's *Ecclesiastical History* offer a radical Arian view of Valens's reign; and Philostorgius himself drew on a history written by an anonymous Arian historiographer who, like his contemporary Valens, was a semi-Arian Homoian.[22] There is thus ample material with which to reconstruct church affairs under Valens from a variety of doctrinal standpoints.

Even more important, we have a remarkable wealth of material by contemporaries of Valens, much of it written for Valens. Themistius (ca. 317–88) composed no fewer than nine political orations during Valens's lifetime, seven

14. I follow the text and translation of Paschoud 1971–89. See Paschoud 1971, ix–xcvi, for background on Zosimus.

15. On Rufinus, see also Thelamon 1981. For the—much disputed—dates of all these authors, see Lenski 2002; cf. Leppin 1996, 273–82.

16. On Philostorgius, see Bidez and Winkelmann 1972, cvi–cxlii.

17. On Socrates, see Urbaincyzk 1997b.

18. On Valentinian and Valens in the ecclesiastical historians, see Leppin 1996, 91–104.

19. I summarize the literature on the interdependence of these sources at Lenski 2002.

20. See esp. Urbaincyzk 1997a and Barnes 1993, 209–11.

21. On the contentious question of Gelasius, see Winkelmann 1966.

22. The fragments are collected in appendix VII of the edition of Philostorgius edited by Bidez and Winkelmann (1972, 202–41).

of which survive, and six of which were delivered to Valens himself.[23] These provide not only extremely valuable information about the events of Valens's reign but the official perspective on those events as presented by the court orator.[24] From the west, we have fragments of six political orations of Symmachus (ca. 340–402) written during Valens's lifetime, three of which were written for Valentinian and Gratian and another for Gratian alone.[25] The poet and orator Ausonius also flourished under Valentinian and Gratian and wrote a number of works, mostly in verse, with direct relevance to the emperors for whom he worked.[26] Moreover, the historians Festus and Eutropius both wrote abbreviated accounts of Roman history at Valens's request while serving in succession as his *magistri memoriae*, and although they do not cover Valens's own reign, their highly selective and politically charged narratives of the past offer unique insights into the contemporary political situation.[27] Finally, the common consensus among English-speaking scholars is that the peculiar military and economic treatise called the *De rebus bellicis* also seems to have been written for Valens.[28] The anonymous author offers unique advice to the emperor on economic management, which Valens actually followed.

Some of our contemporary material comes not from those connected with the court but from people distinctly outside it. This is often quite useful because of the "unofficial" perspective it provides on Valens and the events of his reign. The brilliant but stodgy orator Libanius (314–ca. 393) lived through Valens's reign with some trepidation. He had been a fawning supporter of Julian and thus came in for some harassment under Valens, leading him to curtail his previously copious correspondence during the Pan-

---

23. Themistius wrote the extant orations 6–11 for Valens. Lib. *Ep.* 1495 indicates that he also delivered a speech, now lost, to Valens on January 1, 365 (see p. 28). Soc. 4.32.2–5 and Soz. 6.36.6–37.1 confirm that another nonextant speech was offered ca. 375/76. The extant Latin [*Or.* 12] purports to be this last, but is obviously a forgery (Foerster 1900; contrast Ando 1995, 180, with unconvincing arguments for authenticity). For Themistius, see the recent translations of Heather and Matthews 1991 (orations 8 and 10 only), Maisano 1995, and Leppin and Portmann 1998. For secondary work, see esp. Dagron 1968, Vanderspoel 1995, and Errington 2000.

24. On the relationship between panegyric and imperial policy, see Nixon and Rodgers 1994, 26–33.

25. On Symmachus, see esp. Matthews 1975 and Pabst 1989.

26. See esp. Sivan 1993, with earlier bibliography.

27. On these authors, see also Boer 1972; Bird 1986 and 1993.

28. See the helpful translation and commentary of Thompson 1952. On the date, Cameron 1985 is most convincing with 367/69 (see Cracco-Ruggini 1987 and Chauvot 1998, 219–22). Even so, Giardina 1989, xxxvii–lii, abides by ca. 360, proposed by Mazzarino 1951, 72–109. Brandt 1988 argues for a fifth-century date but has not won wide acceptance (see Liebeschuetz 1994, 132–34).

nonian emperor's rule.[29] The only oration he delivered to Valens is no longer extant, but a number of letters from the first two years of the reign have found their way into the extant corpus and provide priceless insights into the fate of Julian's supporters in the early years of the Valentiniani.[30] Saint Basil (ca. 330–79), bishop of Cappadocian Caesarea, was nearly an exact contemporary of Valens: he was born some two years after Valens and seems to have died less than two months after him.[31] Of his 234 authentic letters, all but the first 19 were written under Valens.[32] These provide a wealth of information, not just about ecclesiastical affairs but also about political, military, and even economic matters. A handful of Basil's sermons are also quite useful for events during Valens's reign. So, too, are about 70 of the letters by Basil's friend and compatriot Saint Gregory of Nazianzus (329–89) that were written under Valens. Although the letters are less rich in political details, Gregory's orations, many written under Valens or shortly after his death, are invaluable for their wealth of material on Valens and his ministers.[33] Finally, Saint Gregory of Nyssa (ca. 330–95), Basil's younger brother, offers some useful contemporary information, particularly in his massive polemical treatise *Contra Eunomium* and his sermons.

Also contemporary with Valens are some other, less helpful but nonetheless significant authors, including Saint Epiphanius of Salamis (ca. 315–403).[34] Epiphanius was a staunch defender of Nicene orthodoxy who managed to write a compendious heresiology called the *Panarion* ("Medicine Chest") during the latter years of Valens's reign (374–77). It occasionally reports the author's quirky but useful perspective on the religious persecutions worked by Valens and his circle. Saint John Chrysostom (ca. 345–407) began his career as a golden-mouthed orator under Valens, and some of his works from this early period, when he lived alongside Valens in Antioch, survive to give us insights into Valens's activities.[35] Saint Ambrose (ca. 339–397) also began his career as bishop of Milan in the last years of Valens's rule and reports some interesting perspectives on Valens and his brother.[36]

29. I follow H. Foerster's text (1903–23). On Libanius, see esp. Petit 1955, Liebeschuetz 1972, and the translation with commentary of A. F. Norman (1969–77, 1992).

30. On the oration, see Lib. *Or.* 1.144. For the letters datable to 364–65, see Seeck, *Briefe,* 418–42.

31. On the date of Basil's death, see Pouchet 1992.

32. On Basil, see esp. Rousseau 1994.

33. *Or.* 43, the "Encomium of Basil," edited by J. Bernardi, is especially useful.

34. The translation of Williams 1987–94 has a useful introduction.

35. On Chrysostom's early years under Valens and the works he produced then, see Kelly 1995, 1–82.

36. On Ambrose in his early years, see McLynn 1994, 31–78, and Williams 1995, 104–27.

And the mellifluous Syrian Saint Ephraem (d. 373) lived under Valens and wrote some material interesting for political and religious history. There are thus abundant contemporary sources, both from those connected with Valens and those detached from him, to provide a very full picture of his reign.

Documentary sources are also plentiful. Chief among these, the Theodosian Code offers over 450 laws from the years between 364 and 378. I shall not offer a catalog of these in what follows, chiefly because Federico Pergami already provides one.[37] I shall, however, treat themes in these laws extensively in chapter 6, where I also discuss further the problems of this source. Suffice it to say here that although most of the material in the Theodosian Code comes from the western court, much of it applied to Valens's territory in the east as well. The Codex Justinianus, a sixth-century counterpart to the Theodosian Code, corrects this picture somewhat, for although it offers fewer laws from the period, these are more evenly balanced between eastern and western issues. In addition, I have examined over 170 Greek and Latin inscriptions from the reigns of Valentinian, Valens, and Gratian. Here again, I do not discuss each in detail but focus on the scores of inscriptions that can teach us about the extensive building and fortification programs of the two emperors. In addition, three major inscriptions—two from Ephesus and a third from Canusium in Apulia—provide remarkable insights into the workings of certain administrative structures under the Valentiniani.[38] Finally, I have examined over sixty contemporary papyri, some of which offer quite useful insights into administrative questions and particularly the recruitment of troops under Valens.

Among the many advantages of working in late Roman history is that we begin to get sources from cultures other than Rome. These are the stories from the other side, outsiders' perspectives that help round out what for early periods is necessarily a two-dimensional picture. For Valens's reign, such sources are crucial. We get some of our first insights from inside Gothic territory in a group of martyrologies written during the reign of Valens—particularly the martyrdom of Saint Saba the Goth—which survive from the persecutions carried out in the early 370s by the Gothic chieftain Athanaric.[39] These open a tantalizing window into cultures that had previously been obscured by the one-sided nature of our records. Even more important, from Armenia, where Valens's forces struggled from 369 until the end of his reign, we have the late-fifth-century *Epic Histories (Buzandaran Patmut'-iwink')*, which preserve considerable information about events in Valens's

37. Pergami 1993.

38. For these texts, see Schulten 1906 and Giardina and Grelle 1983.

39. I follow the texts at Delehaye 1912. These accounts are conveniently assembled and translated at Heather and Matthews 1991, 103–31.

reign.[40] Although this work drew primarily on oral sources, and thus contains numerous chronological inaccuracies, when checked against the Greek and Roman sources, it appears surprisingly reliable on questions of local and international politics. The *Epic Histories* offer a unique window into the workings of Armenian society and thus a chance to assess Valens's perspective from inside a world he could only partially understand.

Finally, we have a number of chronographers who help us to pinpoint events in Valens's reign with incredible precision. Jerome, who began his career as an administrator under Valentinian in the 360s, eventually moved east to Syria under Valens and later composed his *Chronicle* in Constantinople, shortly after Valens's death.[41] For the period of Valens's reign, he drew heavily from the so-called *Consularia Constantinopolitana*, which includes a number of detailed entries on events in and around the eastern capital in the period of Valens's reign. Many of these are also repeated and supplemented by the seventh-century *Chronicon paschale*.[42] There are also other accurate and reliable local chronicles, like the *Historia acephala* and *Festal Index*, which describe and date the major events in the life of Saint Athanasius of Alexandria, and the *Chronicon Edessenum* (ca. 540), which lists important dates for events in Valens's reign at the city of Edessa. John Malalas, who composed his world chronicle in the sixth century, also offers useful material drawn from contemporary sources in Antioch.

Before I leave off introducing this book, it is worthwhile to outline briefly the major topics covered in the pages to come. In chapter 1, I treat the accession of Valentinian and Valens and the establishment of their administrations. I argue that Jovian, their immediate predecessor, was promoted to the purple against the will of the consistory by a group of his fellow imperial guardsmen who were disgruntled with the emperor Julian's cutbacks in their ranks. This laid the groundwork for the election of Valentinian, who was also in the guards, and Valentinian's promotion of his brother Valens, another guardsman. Valentinian, as we shall see, chose his brother to be co-emperor in large part because he knew he could trust and, to some extent, even control him. Stepping back in time and place, I then look at the territory of Pannonia out of which the two emperors sprang. Their background as soldiers and farmers was in many ways dictated by their homeland, the development of which under imperial sponsorship probably encouraged both to turn to imperial service. We shall then examine the early careers of both

40. For the *Buzandaran Patmut'iwnk' (BP)*, I follow the translation of Garsoïan 1989. See the introduction to this translation and Baynes 1910 on the value of this source for the reign of Valens. The eighth-century Armenian Moses Xorenatc'i is also used, although his material is of much lower value (see Thomson 1978, 1–61).

41. For Jerome in these years, see Kelly 1975, 25–67; Booth 1981.

42. See the introduction at Whitby and Whitby 1989.

emperors and that of their father Gratian. All were guardsmen, but Valens was less like his father in that he remained a farmer until quite late into his life before turning to the military. This experience sharpened his administrative skills, but at the same time it probably dulled his martial prowess. Finally, we shall look at the officials both emperors chose to staff their administrations. These included several fellow Pannonians, although their numbers and influence have often been exaggerated. More important for both Valens and Valentinian were seasoned administrators, especially lawyers, whom both kept in office for extremely long tenures. This was particularly true of Valens, who relied heavily on his advisors because of his inability to speak Greek and his lack of legal and liberal learning.

In chapter 2, I turn to the revolt of Procopius, a frightening upheaval that snatched much of Asia, Bithynia, and Thrace from Valens's control from late 365 until early 366. Procopius was a relative of Julian's and capitalized on his connections to the dynasty of Constantine to win support from a populace already aroused to anger by the stiff exactions levied in Valens's early years. Valens upset his subjects on other scores as well. His lack of an imperial pedigree, education, and previous distinction made him vulnerable to Procopius's dynastic attacks. In the years that followed Valens's suppression of the revolt, both he and his brother made stronger efforts to forge links to the Constantinians in order to secure their own dynasty. I also look briefly at the way Valens and Valentinian provoked the revolt by their own harsh treatment of those who had supported Julian. While it would be wrong to see in the Procopius revolt a pagan reaction to the new Christian administration, it is certainly fair to say that Valens had disappointed and even incited his foes with his ill-timed harshness. This he toned down considerably in the immediate aftermath of the uprising.

Procopius had attempted to enlist a number of Gothic auxiliaries against Valens in his unsuccessful bid for power. In chapter 3, we shall see how Valens, in consultation with his brother, determined to launch a major expedition against the Goths to retaliate for this. In a three-year campaign (367–69), Valens succeeded in defeating the Goths but did little significant damage to their forces. By the time he arranged a peace in 369, he was thus forced to close off what had been a flexible frontier between Goths and Romans along the Danube. In so doing, he probably lost the right to draft Gothic auxiliaries into his forces, a serious impediment to his future military plans. I devote some time to examining further how the ideals of triumphal rulership affected Valens's choice to campaign against the Goths. Indeed, there is very little evidence to prove that the Goths had done anything so grievous as to merit a full-scale assault like that undertaken by Valens. Rather, they provided a seemingly easy target for an emperor in serious need of a victory to boost his flagging reputation in the years after the Procopius revolt.

Perhaps the most complex chapter in the book, chapter 4, treats Valens's interactions with the peoples of the eastern frontier: the Persians, the Armenians, the Georgians, the Saracens, and the Isaurians. These peoples formed a complicated web of interrelationships, which could only be negotiated by the most skillful politician and general. To Valens's credit, he actually achieved some success—albeit fleeting—in this arena. Valens had been left with a shameful and devastating treaty by his predecessor, which ceded half of Rome's territorial claims in upper Mesopotamia to the Persian empire. He used chinks in the wording of that treaty to insinuate his forces back into some of the satrapies his predecessor had abandoned and to regain control of the Armenian throne. This his generals defended in a successful engagement against the Persian Shahanshah Shapur in a battle at Bagawan in the summer of 371. A truce, more like a peace, was settled, which allowed Valens a chance to consolidate his gains. Unfortunately, although Valens's court historians Eutropius and Festus bolstered his claims to Armenia and upper Mesopotamia with slanted accounts of Roman history, these gains began to disintegrate toward the end of his reign, when multiple military crises forced Valens to withdraw his forces to other hot spots. This was in part because Valens faced other threats in the region, particularly from the Isaurian mountaineers, who struck in 367 and again in 375, and the Saracens, who completely derailed his efforts to address the Gothic crisis he faced in 377 and 378.

Chapter 5 turns from military and political history to the question of religion. Proceeding on the assumption—established in chapter 1 and further substantiated in chapter 6—that Valens largely followed the lead of his brother on internal policy, it presents Valentinian's and Valens's attitudes toward pagans as a unified whole. Both emperors were largely indifferent to the diversity of religious belief in their worlds, and both tried primarily to maintain the status quo by privileging Christianity while not attacking paganism. Chapter 5 investigates the dramatic magic and treason trials that have often been used to brand both emperors as persecutors of pagans. In both instances, however, the emperors were attacking "magic," not paganism as such, and even contemporaries regarded their actions—and particularly those of Valens—as justified, albeit extreme. I then turn to Christian religion to see how Valens differed from his brother, primarily because of the differing circumstances in which the two operated. Valentinian maintained a detached indifference to the doctrinal debates of his day, a luxury he was allowed by the much calmer atmosphere in the churches of the west, where he ruled. Valens, by contrast, was forced to clean up the mess Julian had created by forcibly applying the doctrines of the Council of Constantinople (360), which had imposed Homoian Christianity in the east and deposed some of the most important Homoiousian bishops there. Having done this,

Valens was able to operate with much the same indifference as his brother during the middle years of his reign, when he aimed primarily at achieving peace and concord in the church. Only at the end of his reign did Valens turn to the scorching persecutions that have left him with the reputation of a religious persecutor.

Chapter 6 addresses administrative and economic questions. The tone is set with a brief examination of how Valentinian's and Valens's laws can often be shown to dovetail perfectly. I examine four areas of administration on which both emperors concentrated: eliminating corruption, shoring up the fabric of the cities, benefiting the masses, and strengthening agriculture. Many of these concerns stemmed from their own agricultural experience, and many of their solutions reflect their deep knowledge of household management. The same experience and knowledge are reflected in their economic measures. Valentinian and Valens spent the first years of their administration crawling out from under the economic problems bequeathed them by Julian. Their extreme exactions in this period helped provoke the Procopius revolt but eventually gave way to policies much more beneficial to the taxpaying masses. Valens, in particular, cut the tribute by one-quarter and planned even deeper cuts, which he seems not to have been able to implement. This was in part because of a major coinage reform that the two undertook, which purified the gold and silver coinage to the advantage of their subjects, but in the process compromised the already tight money supply. Valens, in particular, who felt compelled to abide by his tax cuts, eventually had to resort to intensified mining, confiscations, and even the sale of imperial estates to meet expenses. He was thus overjoyed when he learned that a group of Goths hoped to enter his empire as soldiers and farmers. These would simultaneously provide recruits for his armies, populate his tax rolls and allow him to commute his expensive recruitment tax into gold for diversion to other necessities.

This Gothic migration in 376 and the military problems it precipitated form the subject of the seventh and final chapter. Valens had good reason to believe that his migration scheme could benefit the empire, for he had enjoyed previous contact with the group of Goths he planned to import. Unfortunately for the empire, however, he was not well enough aware that these Goths were only the first arrivals in the much larger flood of peoples that poured across the Danube fleeing the Huns in the years after 375. Thus, when Valens's own commanders provoked a revolt among the Goths whom he had authorized to enter the empire, these quickly joined forces with other migrating Goths, Huns, and Alans to form a nearly invincible if highly volatile roving army. Because of his distractions in the east, Valens was unable to move against these Goths until the late spring of 378, after already having lost significant advance forces sent the previous summer. Valens moved out to the city of Adrianople to await reinforcements from his younger western colleague Gratian—Valentinian had died in 375—but he was disappointed in his hopes of linking up with a western army. Angry with his impudent nephew and determined to win the victory for himself, Valens then plunged his troops into the fateful battle of Adrianople, a military disaster that shook the foundations of the Roman empire for decades to come, some would say forever. Adrianople not only ended Valens's life but sealed his reputation as a deeply flawed and tragically failed emperor. I hope to show that this impression is certainly exaggerated, while avoiding the implication that it is entirely wrong.

Chapter 1

The Pannonian Emperors

On the afternoon of June 26, 363, the emperor Julian was pierced through the side with a spear in combat.[1] His troops carried him back to his camp, where later that night he died.[2] There was no time to waste in grieving. Julian had been leading his army in retreat north along the Tigris after his grandiose expedition into Persia had gone totally wrong. Roman supplies were dangerously low, and the Persians had been threatening the faltering Roman lines with constant attacks. On the morning of June 27, the coterie that had assembled around Julian's deathbed the previous evening convened to choose a successor.[3] The sources agree that these electors consisted of the top military commanders and civilian bureaucrats, the *consistorium*.[4] Ammianus offers the most detail. He informs us that the group was split along party lines: the generals Arinthaeus and Victor led a group of easterners, former subordinates of Constantius, who, less than two years earlier, had marched against Julian and his Gallic army; opposed to them were the representatives of that army, headed by two commanders from Gaul, Nevitta and Dagalaifus. In the face of the present danger, the two groups united to offer the empire to the revered bureaucrat Saturninius Secundus Sallustius, a Gaul placed

---

1. For the date, see *Cons. Const.* s.a. 363; Soc. 3.21.17; AM 25.3.9, 5.1. See also *Chron. Edes.* s.a. 674 (with month but not year) and *Hist. aceph.* 4.1, reporting August 19 as the day when Julian's death was announced in Alexandria.

2. Zos. 3.29.1; AM 25.3.7–10, 15–23. For the time, see AM 25.3.23: "medio noctis horrore"; Zos. 3.29.1: μέχρι τε νυκτὸς μέσης.

3. On the date, see *Cons. Const.* s.a. 363; AM 25.5.1; Malalas 13.23 (p. 333); *Chron. pasch.*, p. 551; cf. Philostorg. 8.1; Soc. 3.22.1; Jer. *Chron.* s.a. 363.

4. AM 25.5.1; Zos. 3.30.1; Theod. *HE* 4.1.1.

above partisanship by his equal distinction in east and west and by his unimpeachable equanimity. Pleading old age, however, Sallustius declined.[5]

As the *consistorium* continued to debate, Jovian, a *primicerius domesticorum*, or lieutenant in the corps of the imperial guards—the Protectores Domestici[6]—was promoted from outside their circle. Ammianus writes of the event in disparaging terms: "During these delays, which were slight considering the importance of the matter, before the various judgments had been weighed, a few rabble-rousers *[tumultuantibus paucis]*—as often happens in extreme crises—chose an emperor in the person of Jovianus, a commander of the household troops."[7] Later, Ammianus refers to the same men as a "an excited throng of camp-followers,"[8] a phrase that drives home the point: Jovian was foisted onto the *consistorium* by a small clique of subordinate soldiers.[9] Unfortunately, Ammianus is not entirely clear on precisely which group of soldiers this was. A closer look at the new emperor's connections can, however, give us some indication). A number of sources report that Jovian was promoted above all because of the reputation of his father, Varronian, who had held the post of *comes domesticorum*—or commander of the Protectores Domestici—up until 361. Themistius actually said as much to Jovian's face: "[T]he kingship was owed to you even before because of your father's virtue (πατρῷας μὲν ἀρετῆς ἕνεκεν)."[10] Jovian's father-in-law, Lucillianus, had also served as *comes domesticorum* in the early 350s.[11]

The most obvious group to have been aware of Varronian's virtues—and thus Jovian's—were, then, the Protectores Domestici. It is thus entirely reasonable to assume that they nominated the new emperor. This conjecture gains credibility when we consider that the Protectores Domestici had ample motives for promoting one of their own. Together with the Scholae Palatinae, they formed a sizeable body of elite guardsmen,—by the mid fourth century, their combined total reached several thousand men—and

5. AM 25.5.3, on which see Lenski 2000, 496 n. 19.

6. Amm. 25.5.4: "domesticorum ordinis primus"; cf. 25.5.8; Eutr. 10.17; Jer. *Chron.* s.a. 363; Them. *Or.* 5.66b; cf. Jord. *Rom.* 305; Joh. Ant. fr. 179.

7. AM 25.5.4.

8. AM 25.5.8: "turbine concitato calonum."

9. Further sources are discussed in Lenski 2000, which argues against those who have questioned Ammianus's credibility on this event, e.g., Haehling 1977; Wirth 1984, 355–57; Brennecke 1988, 160–61; Barnes 1998, 138–42. Esp. useful are Theod. *HE* 4.1.1–2; Malalas 13.23–25 (pp. 334–35); cf. *Chron. pasch.*, pp. 551–52, which support Ammianus's version of events. Indeed, Them. *Or.* 9.124d–125a, and Symm. *Or.* 1.8 already confirm Ammianus's account.

10. *Or.* 5.65b; cf. AM 25.5.4; *Epit.* 44; Eutr. 10.17; Joh. Ant. fr. 181; Zon. 13.14.

11. On Lucillianus, see *PLRE* I, Lucillianus 3, esp. AM 14.11.14. On Varronian as *comes domesticorum*, see Zos. 3.30.1 with AM 25.5.4 and Zon. 13.14. See also Lenski 2000, 507 n. 89, contra Woods 1995a, 43, 53–54, who argues that Varronian was rather *comes Iovianorum et Herculianorum*.

both divisions were commanded by the *comes domesticorum*.[12] Because the Protectores Domestici had been heavily involved in the plot that resulted in the execution of Julian's half-brother Gallus in 354 under Constantius II, however, Julian reduced their ranks to a mere rump when he became Augustus.[13] This would have been devastating to these ambitious climbers, for normally a posting to the guards led to important promotions within five years.[14] Moreover, Jovian's family had suffered directly from Julian's wrath. His father-in-law Lucillianus, who as *comes domesticorum* had been implicated in Gallus's execution, was forced into retirement.[15] And his father Varronian, who had subsequently been Constantius's *comes domesticorum*, also saw his career cut short by Julian.[16] It is thus reasonable to assume that Julian's cuts provoked a response among the remaining or former guards that led them to agitate for their corps after the emperor's death. It was apparently they who foisted Jovian—the poster boy for their plight—on the *consistorium*.

Jovian was hardly the first *protector* to ascend the throne: Diocletian, Constantius I, Maximin Daia, and the mid-fourth-century pretenders Magnentius and Marcellus had all served as *protectores* as well. Indeed, prior to the rise of Constantine the pattern of selecting guardsmen for emperor had been quite pronounced. With the death of the last Constantinian dynast in 363, the pattern was once again resumed when the upper tiers of the imperial apparatus gave way, leaving the imperial guards to fill the throne.[17] Nor do the similarities with late-third-century patterns of imperial election stop here. Jovian was not just an imperial guardsman, he was an Illyrian, from Singidunum (Belgrade) in Moesia Superior.[18] Since the mid third century, Illyricum had been the prime cradle of emperorship; even the house of Constantine, which had become international with the assumption of empire, originated in this region. Moreover, it can be said that Illyrians and guardsmen were in many ways synonymous. Illyrians constituted far and away the most common ethnic group from which *protectores* were drawn through the

---

12. *Not. dign. or.* 11.4–10, 15; *oc.* 9.4–8, 13. On the Protectores, see Mommsen 1884; A. H. M. Jones 1964, 53; 636–40; Diesner 1968; Frank 1969, 81–97; Matthews 1989, 74–79. On the Scholae Palatinae, see Mommsen 1889, 230–34; A. H. M. Jones 1964, 613–14; Frank 1969; Hoffmann 1969–70, 1.279–303; Woods 1997; Barlow and Brennan 2001. For the de facto command of the *comes domesticorum* over the Scholares, see Frank 1969, 88–90, and Lenski 2000, 502–3.

13. *CTh* 6.24.1 (Aug. 18, 362), with Lenski 2000, 504–5. Julian seems to have had this reduction in mind several months earlier, as indicated at *Pan. Lat.* 3[11].24.7.

14. E.g., *P Abinn.* 1.9–10; *ILS* 2781–83, 2788; cf. Lenski 2000, 504.

15. AM 21.9.5–10.1; cf. 25.8.9. On Lucillianus's dealings with Gallus, see AM 14.11.14.

16. AM 25.5.4, with Lenski 2000, 507.

17. Sivan 1996 has argued that Theodosius was also promoted by an army clique, although not the Protectores Domestici. A different assessment is offered at Errington 1996a.

18. On Jovian's birthplace, see *Epit.* 44.1. Alföldi 1952, 13, and Soraci 1968, 23, also believe that Jovian's promoters were Illyrian.

Figure 1. Jovian ensures the SECVRITAS REIPVBLICAE. Solidus of Sirmium, *RIC* 8.393.111. Courtesy American Numismatic Society.

third and fourth centuries.[19] Thus, when the *consistorium* was presented with a guardsman and an Illyrian in Jovian, they must have recognized that in some sense they were faced with an inevitability.

There was no time to celebrate Jovian's proclamation. He and his army trudged north along the Tigris and, after further skirmishes and four days of marching without supplies, came to a place called Dura.[20] There, faced with exhaustion and the prospect of annihilation, Jovian was forced to agree to a devastating treaty that ceded to Persia much of Roman Mesopotamia, including the impregnable city of Nisibis.[21] This agreement brought to an end the military nightmare that Julian's expedition had become. Jovian's men scuttled across the Tigris and began a very slow retreat to Antioch, which they first reached only in October of 363.[22] Jovian was aware that his position as emperor was far from secure and that under the circumstances, propaganda was extremely important to his success. Already at Ur, shortly after crossing the Tigris, the new emperor had sent forth a legation to announce his election in the west.[23] Ammianus tells us that they were commanded to test support for the new emperor and to put the best light on the disastrous treaty with which he had inaugurated his reign. Their success is apparent in the milestones we find proclaiming Jovian VICTOR AC TRIUMFATOR as far afield as Africa.[24] We also find Jovian's coins produced in most of the mints of the empire, proclaiming SECURITAS REIPUBLICAE and VICTORIA RO-MANORUM (figs. 1 and 2).[25]

The dissonance between propaganda and reality was not lost on the An-

19. See Lenski 2000, 509.

20. AM 25.6.1–9; Zos. 3.30.2–4.

21. On the treaty of 363, see pp. 161–67.

22. AM 25.8.2–3. Jovian is attested in Antioch from October 22, see *CTh* 10.19.2; cf. Theoph. a.m. 5856: μηνὶ ὑπερβερεταίῳ. See also AM 25.10.1, 4; Zos. 3.34.3, 35.3; Zon. 13.14; Soc. 3.26.1.

23. AM 25.8.8–12. Zos. 3.33.1, 35.1–2 offers an extremely confused account of this legation, on which see Paschoud 2.1:235 n. 103.

24. On African milestones, see *AE* 1981, 905b; *CIL* 8.4647, 10266, 10237, 10472. On milestones in Italy, see *CIL* 5.8037 = *ILS* 757; *CIL* 9.6057; 10.6844.

25. *RIC* 8.196 (Lyon); 229–31 (Arles); 304–5 (Rome); 338 (Aquileia); 381 (Siscia); 393–94 (Sirmium); 242–45 (Thessalonica); 438–39 (Heraclea); 463–65 (Constantinople); 484–85 (Nicomedia); 501 (Cyzicus); 532–33 (Antioch); 546 (Alexandria). It is interesting that no coins are known for Trier (169). Cf. Ehling 1996.

Figure 2. Jovian proclaims
VICTORIA ROMANORVM. *RIC*
8.465.176. Aes of Constantinople.
Courtesy American Numismatic
Society.

tiochenes, with whom Jovian spent the last days of October. These lampooned the new emperor and his army with insults, graffiti, and *famosi*—nameless bills circulated against him. Hecklers are reported to have posted notices like the following paraphrase of Odysseus's insult to the low-born Thersytes:

> So help me if I don't take you and strip off your dear clothing,
> your mantle and tunic that cover the bits of which you are ashamed,
> and send you straight back to the Persians howling![26]

This eastern disdain of the upstart Illyrian would reecho in similar bills posted against his Illyrian successor Valens just two years later. The animosity it reflected was not, however, a simple matter of prejudice but above all of fear. The memory of the Persian attacks on Antioch in the third century was still very much alive.[27] By amputating half of the Roman defenses in the east, Jovian had rekindled anxieties and violated the prime mandate of all fourth-century emperors, the maintenance of territorial security.[28] The anger this generated in Antioch became so fevered that Jovian is reported to have ordered the burning of the library recently established there by Julian.[29] Further pandemonium was on the verge of breaking out when Jovian's prefect Sallustius, the boon companion of Julian, intervened and reminded Jovian how crucial it was for him to continue west in order to secure his shaky hold on the throne.[30] After only a month in Antioch, in the midst

26. Suid. *I* 401; cf. *Φ* 64 and Joh. Ant. fr. 181. The hexameters adapt *Il.* 2.261–63, a passage with obvious relevance to an emperor whose claims to the throne were regarded as presumptuous.

27. For sources on the third-century sacks of Antioch, see Dodgeon and Lieu 1991, 51–54. For analysis and dating, see Potter 1990, 290–97; 300–303. On the ongoing fear of a Persian invasion in the fourth-century east, see Them. *Or.* 4.56a; Lib. *Or.* 12.71–72; 24.38.

28. Joh. Ant. fr. 181; AM 25.9.3–5; Zos. 3.34.1–3.

29. Joh. Ant. fr. 181; Suid. *I* 401 with Downey 1961, 398–99; Petit 1955, 227. Wirth 1984, 381–83, offers a much different assessment.

30. The anger lived on in Antioch. When news of Jovian's death reached the city, its inhabitants rioted and devastated the estates of Datianus, whose career Jovian had recently revived, Lib. *Ep.* 1184, 1186, 1259.

of blustery November weather, Jovian left the city. He hoped to reach Constantinople with his army and then continue to his native Illyricum, which he no doubt planned to mine to fill the ranks of his administration and army with friends.[31]

By late December, he had reached Galatian Ancyra (Ankara). There, on January 1, Themistius met him and delivered a speech on the occasion of his first consulship.[32] Jovian shared the honor with his son, a boy named after his grandfather Varronian. The younger Varronian, still an infant, put up a rather unpropitious fuss when he was forced to sit on a curule chair in keeping with the solemnity of the ceremony.[33] The consulship was probably a preparation for the child's proclamation as co-emperor, which would have helped secure the fragile new dynasty.[34] Before this could take place, however, Jovian was dead. He had continued on from Ancyra despite the winter weather. When he reached the road station of Dadastana, about 100 miles to the west, the emperor went to bed and never reawakened.[35] Although a few contemporaries speculate about conspiracy, it seems likely that he suffocated in the night when a smoky brazier leached toxic fumes from the newly painted walls of his bedchamber.[36]

For the second time in less than a year, the empire was without an emperor, although not quite without a dynasty. When the next emperors came

---

31. AM 25.10.4: "flagrante hieme die"; *Epit.* 44.4: "hieme aspera"; Suid. *I* 401: χειμῶνος ὄντος; cf. Malalas 13.28 (p. 337); Joh. Ant. fr. 181; *Chron. pasch.*, pp. 554–55; Theod. *HE* 4.5.1. Eutr. 10.17 alone records that Jovian hoped to reach Illyricum.

32. On the speech, *Or.* 5, see Vanderspoel 1995, 137–54; Errington 2000, 873–78. Jovian is attested at Ancyra on December 28 at *CJ* 1.40.5, with Seeck, *Regesten*, 84.

33. AM 25.10.11; cf. 25.10.17. Contrast the optimism of Them. *Or.* 5.64d–65a and 71b, where Themistius calls the boy: τὸν ἐν ἀγκάλαις ὕπατον, τὸν ἐκ τοῦ μαστοῦ πατρωΐζοντα ἤδη; cf. Sabbah 1978, 358–59; Vanderspoel 1995, 153. See also Philostorg. 8.8; Theoph. a.m. 5856. Zon. 13.14 confuses grandfather and grandson when he asserts that the boy failed to reach Jovian in time to see him as emperor. Soc. 3.26.2–3 wrongly locates Jovian's assumption of the consulate in Dadastana, but he alone tells us that Themistius was present to deliver the consular address, along with "others of the senatorial order."

34. See p. 90.

35. On Dadastana's location, see *It. Ant.* p. 92 (Cuntz).

36. Eutr. 10.18, our best source given that he was probably present, offers three explanations: (1) the vapors from the newly painted walls; (2) the fumes of the brazier; and (3) overeating. AM 25.10.13 repeats these. They also appear in different combinations at Soz. 6.6.1 (1 and 3); Philostorg. 8.8 (1); Jer. *Chron.* s.a. 364 (1 and 3); *Ep.* 60.16 (2); Prosper *Chron.* 1125 (1 and 3); Oros. 7.31.3 (1); Jord. *Rom.* 306 (1). Soc. 3.26.3 reports that Jovian died of an illness caused by an obstruction. Four sources contend that he was poisoned: Joh. Chrys. *In Epist. ad Philipp. Hom.* 15.5 (*PG* 62.295) (in his drink); Joh. Ant. fr. 181 (poison mushrooms); Cedrenus p. 540; Zon. 13.14 (either poison mushrooms or 1 and 2 above). No cause is reported at Ruf. *HE* 11.1; Theod. *HE* 4.5.1; Zos. 3.35.3; *Chron. pasch.*, p. 539; *Cons. Const.* s.a. 364; Malalas 13.28 (p. 337); Theoph. a.m. 5856; *Chron. pasch.*, p. 555. Julian *Mis.* 340d–342a reports that he almost suffered the same fate in Gaul.

to power, they granted the title *divus* to their predecessor and buried his body in Constantine's imperial mausoleum in Constantinople, the church of Holy Apostles.[37] Nevertheless, while paying their respects to their fellow Illyrian, Valentinian and Valens carefully disposed of any possible threat posed by the minor remnants of dynasty Jovian had left behind. Jovian's father, Varronian, apparently died before he could reach his son to congratulate him on his accession.[38] Jovian's wife, Charito, survived into the reign of Theodosius, but John Chrysostom tells us that she lived in constant fear for her own life and the life of her son.[39] Her fears were not groundless, for although the boy Varronian was spared, his eye was gouged out to ensure he could never assume the throne.[40] The budding imperial family was thus pruned back to harmless sterility.

Jovian's death fell on February 17, 364.[41] The following day, the army advanced from the tiny *statio* of Dadastana to the metropolis of Nicaea. Once there, the top commanders and civilian officials met once again to choose a successor.[42] This time not only were the circumstances not so volatile, but also, it would seem, the consistory was better prepared to satisfy the ranks of the guards. A number of candidates were debated, most of them with qualifications remarkably similar to those of Jovian. Sallustius was once again offered the throne and once again declined.[43] Three more candidates came

37. Eutr. 10.18: "benignitate principum, qui ei successerunt, inter Divos relatus est." Cf. *CTh* 1.6.2: "Divo Ioviano et Varroniano consul(ibus)." The title was standard even after the Christianization of the empire and continued to be conferred down to Anastasius (see Cagnat 1914, 171). For Jovian's burial at Holy Apostles, see Philostorg. 8.8; Zon. 13.14; AM 26.1.3; cf. Grierson 1962, 3 and 42.

38. AM 25.10.16.

39. Joh. Chrys. *Ad vid. iun.* 4 (a. 380/81): ἡ μὲν παῖδα ἔχουσα ὀρφανὸν τρέμει καὶ δέδοικε μή τις αὐτὸν τῶν κρατούντων φόβῳ τῶν μελλόντων ἀνέλῃ must refer to Charito. The only source for Jovian's wife's name is Zon. 13.14.

40. Joh. Chrys. *In epist. ad Philip.* 15.5 (*PG* 62.295): καὶ ὁ υἱὸς αὐτῷ τὸν ὀφθαλμὸν ἐξωρύττετο φόβῳ τῶν μελλόντων, οὐδὲν ἠδικηκώς. Philostorg. 8.8 reports that Varronian was the elder of two sons, but no other source confirms this. Note that Licinius did much the same with Maximin Daia's family (Lactant. *De mort. pers.* 50.5–6).

41. Different dates are reported in the sources, but Feb. 17 is the most reliable. It is found at Eutr. 10.18; AM 26.1.5 with 14; Soc. 3.26.5; 4.1.1. cf. Seeck, *Regesten* 214.

42. On the location of Valentinian's election, see AM 26.1.3 with 7; 30.7.4; Zos. 3.36.3–4.1.2; Eunap. *Hist.* fr. 31 (Blockley); Soc. 4.1.1; Soz. 6.6.2; Jer. *Chron.* s.a. 364; Prosper *Chron.* 1125; *Cons. Const.* s.a. 364; Philostorg. 8.8; *Pass. Artemii* 70; Zon. 13.14; *Chron. pasch.*, p. 555; Oros. 7.32.1.

43. Zos. 3.36.1–2 and Zon. 13.14 report that Sallustius was offered the purple after Jovian's death, and that when he declined it, it was offered to his son and again declined. Paschoud 2.1: 210–2; 238–39, and Neri 1985b, 157 n. 19, argue that Sallustius was considered twice. Neither notice Them. *Or.* 9.125a, which may clench the case for Sallustius's candidacy in 364 (cf. Maisano 1995, 418 n. 22). *PLRE* I makes no mention of Sallustius's son but Lib. *Ep.* 1467 appears to refer to him.

up in turn, all of them, like Jovian, Illyrians, and two of them junior commanders in the imperial guards.[44] The first of these, Aequitius, was then serving as tribune of the Prima Schola Scutariorum, a unit of the Scholares. When he was rejected as too boorish, an in-law of Jovian's named Ianuarius was proposed. He too was quickly passed over, because he was then in Illyricum, too far to summon quickly. Finally, they settled on Valentinian, a native of Cibalae in Pannonia.[45] Like Jovian, Valentinian caught people's attention as the son of a distinguished Illyrian commander and former *protector domesticus*.[46] Also like Jovian, Valentinian was himself serving in the imperial guard, as tribune of the Secunda Schola Scutariorum.[47]

Valentinian had joined Jovian's father-in-law on his mission into Gaul and had, remarkably, survived the mutiny of Julian's supporters there. This good fortune had won him his tribuneship from Jovian and no doubt numbered among his qualifications for empire. Like Jovian, Valentinian represented the middle ranks of the soldiers. He was a man with considerable military experience,[48] but he had not yet advanced far enough to pose a threat to either of the factions bickering over Julian's successor. Several sources, following Eunapius, report that Valentinian won special recommendation from his rival candidate the praetorian prefect Sallustius, and Philostorgius indicates that the patrician Datianus, a close ally of Jovian's, and the generals Arinthaeus and Dagalaifus supported him as well.[49] All probably realized that, as in Jovian's case, the election of an Illyrian and a guardsman was something of an inevitability. Valentinian was chosen as a man remarkably like his predecessor, although, unlike his predecessor, he was promoted by the *consistorium* rather than the guards themselves.

Valentinian was an ideal candidate, but for the fact that he was at Ancyra,

---

44. AM 26.1.4–5.

45. On Valentinian's election, see Heering 1927, 12–18; Straub 1939, 15–17; Nagl, "Vt.," 2161–63; Alföldi 1952, 10–12; Soraci 1971, 29–34; Tomlin 1973, 23–34; Fasolino 1976, 7–12; Neri 1985b; Matthews 1989, 188–89.

46. AM 30.7.4: "cuius [Gratiani] meritis Valentinianus ab ineunte adulescentia commendabilis."

47. On Valentinian's rank, see AM 25.10.9; 26.1.5; Jer. *Chron.* s.a. 364; Prosper *Chron.* 1125; cf. Oros. 7.32.2; Jord. *Rom.* 307. Scholares often had very close access to the emperor and his court; see AM 16.12.2; 29.1.6; 31.10.3, 20.

48. AM 30.7.11: "usuque castrensis negotii diuturno firmatus"; Soc. 4.1.2: τάξιν δὲ στρατιωτῶν ἐγχειρισάμενος, πολλὴν ἐπεδείξατο τῶν τακτικῶν ἐπιστήμην; Soz. 6.6.2: ἄνδρα ἀγαθὸν καὶ τῆς ἡγεμονίας ἄξιον; Theod. *HE* 4.6.1. Cf. Symm. *Or.* 1.2: "privatae hoc industriae tuae debes, quod te dignum reddidit principatu."

49. On Sallustius, see Philostorg. 8.8; Suid. Σ 64; Malalas 13.29 (p. 338); *Chron. pasch.*, p. 555; Zon. 13.14; cf. AM 26.2.1. On Datianus, Arinthaeus and Dagalaifus, see Philostorg. 8.8. Valentinian sent messengers to Rome that May ordering a statue to be dedicated to Sallustius *pleno aequitatis ac fidei* (*CIL* 6.1729 = *ILS* 1254). This was probably in thanks for his role in helping Valentinian to secure the throne.

some 160 kilometers from the imperial entourage.[50] After the *consistorium* had made its choice, a messenger was quickly dispatched to fetch him, and a group of fellow Pannonians went to work enlisting support among the ranks in the days before he arrived.[51] Within a week, Valentinian had reached Nicaea, as it happened on the bisextile day—leap year—an inauspicious time for such beginnings.[52] There was no hurry, as there had been the summer before, and Valentinian wisely postponed his proclamation. The following day, February 25,[53] a tribunal was erected and Valentinian ascended it and received the purple robe and diadem. In keeping with the protocols of late antique ceremony, he was acclaimed unanimously by the assembled troops and, at some point, was probably raised on a shield by some of them.[54] Following the custom, the event culminated in his delivery of a prepared *adlocutio*, during which he promised the usual accession donative of one solidus and a pound of silver to each of the soldiers.[55] Such were the formalities of imperial proclamation.[56]

In this case, however, when the new emperor began to speak, the soldiers grew restless and demanded that he appoint a co-Augustus. The fourth-century empire was large and dangerous, too much so to be governed by one man. The troops knew this well. In a period of less than a year, Julian's fool-hardy charge to his death and Jovian's freak suffocation had taught them how fragile a thing an emperor could be.[57] Prior to that, they had witnessed,

50. AM 26.1.5. Jord. *Rom.* 307 wrongly states that Valentinian was acting as tribune in Nicomedia.

51. AM 26.1.6.

52. Nicaea capitalized on its good fortune as the place of Valentinian's promotion by persuading the emperor to assert its status as metropolis, a coup that greatly bothered its rival Nicomedia. This we learn from two laws preserved in the Acts of the Council of Chalcedon (Actio XIV.27–30: Schwartz *ACO* I.3.61 [420]), one datable to February 364, and both previously unnoticed—even by Pergami 1993.

53. On Valentinian's *dies Imperii*, see AM 26.1.7, 2.1–2; *Cons. Const.* s.a. 364; Soc. 4.1.1 with Heering 1927, 13–15; Tomlin 1973, app. 2. Contrast Seeck, *Regesten*, 214 (Feb. 26) followed by Chastagnol 1987, 255. *Pass. Artemii* 70 wrongly states that the empire remained without an emperor for forty days.

54. AM 26.2.2–4; cf. Symm. *Or.* 1.7–10. Symm. *Or.* 1.10 (cf. AM 26.2.6) indicates that Valentinian initially resisted the appointment, but this can be dismissed as a topos (Beranger 1948; Straub 1939, 62–63). On Valentinian's acclamation by the troops and its unanimity, cf. AM 26.1.5, 2.6–7, 11, 4.3, 27.6.6; Them. *Or.* 9.124d–125a; Philostorg. 8.8; Soz. 6.6.7; Soc. 4.1.1; Theod. *HE* 4.6.2; Oros. 7.32.1. On the shield, see Philostorg. 8.8; cf. AM 20.4.17. For acclamations in late Roman ceremonial, see Roueché 1984; Matthews 2000, 35–49.

55. AM 26.2.6–10; Philostorg. 8.8; Soz. 6.6.8; Theod. *HE* 4.6.2; Zon. 13.15. On the accession donative, see AM 26.2.10; cf. 26.8.6 with Bastien 1988; Kent 1956, 192–24. The most complete account of the ceremony of late Roman imperial accessions comes at Const. Porph. *De caeremoniis* 1.91–95 (*PG* 112.745–69, esp. § 91, Leo's election).

56. Straub 1939, 7–35; MacCormack 1981, 160–266, esp. 196–205.

57. AM 26.2.3–4: "multitudinis . . . documento recenti fragilitatem pertimescentis sublimium fortunarum"; Zos. 4.1.2: μὴ ταὐτὰ πάθοιεν οἷς ἐπὶ τῆς Ἰουλιανοῦ πεπόνθασι τελευτῆς.

not to say sanctioned, a phenomenon that had recurred time and again since the third century: usurpation. Julian's unsanctioned assumption of full power as Augustus in the west while Constantius was occupied in the east had brought the two halves of the empire to the brink of mutual annihilation. If properly engineered, however, shared power could stave off similar conflicts in the future. Moreover, by 364, shared rule had been common for over a century, some would say two. Only the three-year period under Julian and Jovian had significantly interrupted this pattern in the past seventy years.[58] The troops thus insisted that Valentinian appoint a co-ruler. Ammianus records his response:

> The task that was placed in your hands before a fashioner of empire was chosen, you carried out expediently and gloriously. Now I ask you to listen calmly while I explain in simple words what I think is best for us all. That to meet all chances, necessity demands the choice of a colleague with common powers . . . I neither doubt nor dispute. . . . But with all our strength we must strive for concord . . . and this will easily be attained, if your forebearance, combined with fairness, willingly allows me what belongs to my position.[59]

Nothing better illustrates the power of the military in influencing the creation of fourth-century emperors. Although the decision rested with Valentinian, he could not refuse the request. Nor did he try.

On the same day he was proclaimed, Valentinian assembled his chief marshals and ministers to consult on the issue. Most were reluctant to speak, but Dagalaifus, the *comes domesticorum*, broke the silence with gnomic frankness: "If you love your relatives, most excellent emperor, you have a brother; if it is the state that you love, seek out another man to invest."[60] Valentinian had to restrain his anger at this insult to his only sibling, Valens. Moreover, it became clear immediately that he did not intend to follow Dagalaifus's advice. The day after his election, Valentinian moved the army to Nicomedia, where he promoted Valens to the post of *tribunus stabuli*—tribune of the imperial stable—on March 1.[61] This post put Valens close to the emperor while he waited in the wings to be appointed. Valentinian must have known that his own election represented a compromise. The factions formed around the courts of Julian and Constantius had used him as a candidate who, as a soldier would satisfy the ranks, but as a junior officer would pose little threat

58. Seeck, *Untergang*, 5; Valensi 1957, 102–6; Pabst 1986, passim.
59. AM 26.2.7–8. This *vox* recurs in the Eunapian source tradition as well, cf. Philostorg. 8.8; Zon. 13.15. See also Soz. 6.6.8, who also used Eunapius (Schoo 1911, 80–83), and was followed by Theod. *HE* 4.6.2. The same incident may also be referred to at Eunap. *Hist.* fr. 31 (Blockley) and Symm. *Or.* 1.9 (cf. Pabst 1989, 188–89). The implications are thoughtfully treated at Neri 1985b, 169–74.
60. AM 26.4.1; cf. Cedrenus p. 541.
61. AM 26.4.2.

to rivals in the highest echelons. Valentinian knew better than to upset this precarious balance once he was emperor by choosing a colleague from one faction or another. What Valentinian needed was a junior partner, someone whom he could trust with power and, above all, whom he could control. Valens would fit the bill perfectly.

From Nicomedia, Valentinian continued to Constantinople. There the usual embassies poured in, bearing congratulations and crown gold *(aurum coronarium)*, some of which had initially been sent to honor Jovian.[62] But Valentinian did not bask in this glory alone for long, for before the winter was out, he moved to appoint his brother as colleague. On March 28, one month after his own election when reckoned by Roman time, Valentinian set out with his brother for the Hebdomon, seven miles west of the city.[63] This was the site of the imperial military camp, a place that after this date would become the standard locus of Byzantine imperial proclamations.[64] Once again to the unanimous acclamation of the troops, Valentinian hailed his brother not as Caesar but as Augustus.[65] He had probably learned from Constantius's difficulties with the Caesars Gallus and Julian that restricting the power of imperial colleagues could be more dangerous than sharing full dominion. Because he trusted Valens and assumed his brother's subordination to himself, he willingly granted full powers.[66] Valentinian placed a dia-

---

62. On Valentinian's journey to Constantinople, see AM 26.4.3; Zos. 4.1.2; Theoph. *Chron.* a.m. 5856; Philostorg. 8.8; Soc. 4.1.4; Soz. 6.6.9. On crown gold, see p. 289 .

63. I accept Ammianus's account, although the sources in fact give two dates: (1) *quintum Kalendas Aprilis*, thirty days after Valentinian's election (AM 26.4.3; cf. Soc. 4.1.4), and (2): *die IIII k. Apr.* (Cons. Consp. s.a. 364; cf. *Chron. pasch.*, p. 556). Pass. *Artemii* 70 mistakenly offers: τῇ πρὸ πέντε καλανδῶν μαρτίων and tells us that Valens's election occurred thirty-two days after Valentinian's. Malalas 13.29 (p. 338) wrongly offers: μηνὶ ἀπριλίῳ πρώτῃ. Seeck, *Untergang*, 6, first noted that Valens and Valentinian were both proclaimed on the same day one month apart, "ante diem quintum." On the location, see *Cons. Const.* s.a. 364: "in miliario VII"; *Chron. pasch.*, p. 556: ἐν τῷ Ἑβδόμῳ; cf. AM 26.4.3: "in suburbanum"; Them. *Or.* 6.82a: εἰς τὸ προαστεῖον.

64. Dagron 1972, 87–8; 100–101. Themistius was especially concerned to promote his native Constantinople by emphasizing the role it played in Valens's election (see *Or.* 6.82a, 9.128b, 11.150d, 13.168a). Valens himself referred to Constantinople as the "mother of emperorship" (μῆτερ τῆς Βασιλείας; cf. Them. *Or.* 6.82d), apparently alluding to his own election there. The proclamation of co-emperors in military camps had been standard since the third century, and the practice stretched back before that (cf. Straub 1939, 17–21).

65. AM 26.4.3. On Valentinian's and Valens's equal powers, see Them. *Or.* 6.76a–b; Symm. *Or.* 1.11–13. For additional sources on Valens's proclamation, see Them. *Or.* 9.128b; AM 30.7.4, 9.2; Zos. 4.1.2; Philostorg. 8.8; Jer. *Chron.* s.a. 364; Prosper *Chron.* 1125; Theoph. a.m. 5856; Zon. 13.15; Oros. 7.32.4; *Epit.* 45.4; Jord. *Rom.* 307; Soz. 6.6.9; Ruf. *HE* 11.2; Theod. *HE* 4.6.3. For secondary work, see Köhler 1925, 8–13; Nagl, "Val.," 2097–98; Fasolino 1976, 13–18; Pabst 1986, 56–7; 1989, 208–18; Matthews 1989, 190.

66. Zos. 4.1.2: πιστότατον αὐτῷ πάντων ἡγησάμενος ἔσεσθαι; cf. AM 30.7.4; Symm. *Or.* 1.11. AM 27.6.16 stresses the irregularity of appointing a co-Augustus, but ignores the third-century precedents stretching up to Diocletian's appointment of Maximian. On Valentinian's reasons

dem on Valens's head and probably reaffirmed the promise of a donative to the troops, which he had not yet fulfilled.[67] The ceremony culminated in Valentinian's acceptance of his brother into his imperial chariot and their joint procession back into the city. This sign of Valens's new status would have been readily understood by contemporaries.[68] Valentinian was displaying his brother as a full sharer in his power. Themistius evoked the scene a year later when he told Valens, "Having gone out to the suburb a king and a private citizen, you returned shortly as a double-yoke chariot of emperors (ξυνωρὶς αὐτοκρατόρων)."[69]

During their sojourn in the eastern capital, Valentinian and Valens fell sick with fever. Their illnesses were serious enough that when they recovered, they initiated a series of investigations into the cause of their infirmity under the direction of two Pannonian compatriots, Ursacius and Viventius. Ammianus tells us that their inquests revealed no wrongdoing, but that the emperors used them to stir up resentment against Julian's confidants, as if they had caused the fever through sorcery.[70] In a related account, Zosimus, relying on Eunapius, tells us that Valentinian's suspicions were laid to rest by the mitigating influence of Sallustius.[71] The Eunapian tradition even reports that Sallustius himself fell under suspicion and was temporarily dismissed. More than likely, this anticipates the temporary dismissal of Sallustius, which Ammianus locates a year later.[72] In fact, the letters of Libanius from the period indicate that, at least in 364, Sallustius was still able to mollify the zeal of the new emperors against Julian's friends.[73] How far he was successful is difficult to gauge. Ammianus implies that the investigations ended for lack of credible evidence. Even so, we shall see that a number of sources report prose-

---

for choosing Valens as full Augustus, see Köhler 1925, 9–10; Heering 1927, 16–18; Matthews 1989, 190; Pabst 1989, 208–14.

67. See pp. 290–91.

68. AM 26.4.3. Ammianus (16.10.12) tells us that Constantius refused the privilege of riding in the imperial chariot to any but emperors. Thus he granted the right to Julian on his accession in 355, AM 15.8.17. Cf. *Pan. Lat.* 10 [2].13.2 and 11 [3].11.3 of Diocletian and Maximian.

69. Them. *Or.* 6.82a; cf. 84a and the much greater elaboration of this metaphor at 76a–b, esp.: ἀλλ' ἄγουσιν ἄμφω ταῖς αὐταῖς ἡνίαις. See Them. *Or.* 5.64d, 15.198b for the same rhetoric.

70. AM 26.4.4. Them. *Or.* 6.72b–c seems to confirm that the investigations ended without bloodshed. On the illness, see Köhler 1925, 12; Nagl, "Vt.," 2166–67; Clauss 1981, 73. On Valentinian's and Valens's recovery, see Seeck, *Regesten*, 109.

71. Zos. 4.1.1. Zosimus differs from Ammianus in reporting that Valentinian alone fell ill while still in Nicaea. His account is apparently confused although he does share with Ammianus the contention that the fever was believed to be caused by the sorcery of Julian's friends; cf. 4.2.1–4. On these passages, see Paschoud 2.2:331 n. 106–7.

72. Zos. 4.2.4; Suid. Σ 64; contrast *Chron. pasch.*, p. 556; Zon. 13.15. See the discussion at Paschoud 2.2:333 n. 109, which argues against *PLRE*'s acceptance of Zosimus. On Sallustius's dismissal, see p. 106 above.

73. See p. 105.

cutions against Julian's former officials.[74] Times were tense, even if the tension had not yet reached a breaking point.

Sometime in the spring, Valentinian and Valens left Constantinople for the west. They are attested in the city as late as April 364, but by May 8, they had reached Adrianople (Edirne),[75] and they continued at a measured pace to the city of Naissus (Niš) in Moesia.[76] Outside that city, at a villa called Mediana, where they are attested in a law of June 8, the two emperors split the army between them,[77] along lines that had existed before Julian marched east in 361: Julian's former troops and commanders from the west were assigned to Valentinian, while Valens received Constantius's former eastern troops and generals. From Naissus, the paired Augusti moved on to Sirmium (Sremska Mitrovica), the capital of their home province of Pannonia Secunda, which they had reached by July. There they split the administrative personnel along similar lines, with westerners tending to fall to Valentinian and easterners to Valens.[78] At Sirmium, they also divided the jurisdictions of the empire. Zosimus provides the fullest description: "Valentinian decided to divide up the empire with his brother and to hand over to him the east as far as Egypt and Bithynia and Thrace. Having assigned himself the cities in Illyria, he crossed over to Italy and reserved for his own jurisdiction the cities there together with the trans-Alpine provinces, Spain, Britain and the whole of Libya."[79]

The only peculiarity in Zosimus's notice is his use of the word "Libya" to describe the limit of Valentinian's jurisdiction in North Africa. With this name, he must be retaining the archaic usage that associated Libya with Carthage, for we have solid evidence that Valens held all of the diocese of Oriens, including Libya Cyrenaica. If we accept this proviso, we can see that Zosimus's division effectively gave Valens control of only one-third of the dioceses in the empire, or one of the empire's three prefectures, essentially what Constantius II had received in 337.[80] This left Valentinian indisputably in the domi-

---

74. See pp. 107–8.

75. Seeck, *Regesten*, 215, with 84 and 109.

76. On the slowness of their journey, see Seeck, *Untergang*, 12.

77. AM 26.5.1–3. Valentinian and Valens are attested at Naissus in several constitutions from June 8–11, 364, see Seeck, *Regesten*, 215. On June 8 and 19, 364, they are attested at "Med" (*CTh* 1.6.2; 15.1.13), not "Mediolanum," as assumed by Mommsen and Seeck, but "Mediana," as indicated by Petrovic 1993, 73, and Barnes 1998, 248. On the division of the army, see also Zos. 4.6.3 and pp. 308–9.

78. AM 26.5.4; Philostorg. 8.8. On the date, see Seeck, *Regesten*, 216.

79. Zos. 4.3.1; cf. 4.2.3. On the division, see also Them. *Or.* 6.74b, 82a–b; Symm. *Or.* 1.14, 3.11; Philostorg. 8.8; Soz. 6.6.9; Ruf. 11.2; Theod. *HE* 4.6.3; Zon. 13.15; Theoph. a.m. 5856; Jord. *Rom.* 307.

80. The most telling evidence that Valens controlled Libya is the inclusion of Cyrenaica in the list of eastern provinces prepared for Valens by Festus (§ 13). Valens's contemporary Gregory of Nyssa (*Eun.* 1.143) also lists Libya among the provinces that experienced Valens's per-

nant position in terms of territorial, military, and administrative control. Valentinian thus directed the weight of his superiority westward. This would be the last time in Roman history that the west was given precedence over the east.

In August, Valentinian and Valens left Sirmium for the west and east respectively.[81] They would never see each other again. We can trace Valentinian's progress in the constitutions he issued as he slowly worked his way from Emona to Aquileia, Altinum, Verona, and finally Milan, which he reached late in October.[82] The imperial ceremonies of accession and *adventus,* both inextricably intertwined in the fourth century, dictated the august pace of this grand procession. Entire populations would have traveled outside their walls to greet the emperor as he approached, and once he reached the city, panegyrics were delivered in his honor, and acclamations made.[83] Rewards for this enthusiasm were distributed in the form of $1\frac{1}{2}$ solidus "Fest-aurei" that Valentinian issued from the mints of Aquileia and Milan on his way westward (fig. 3).[84] These bore an image of the emperor as he would have appeared on his arrival, riding on horseback in military garb, with his right hand raised in greeting.

After reaching Milan, Valentinian made this Italian city his capital for the first year of his reign. From there, he issued a hoard of laws setting out the administrative policies that he had planned while still with Valens the previous summer.[85] Valens, meanwhile, had made his way eastward, perhaps to less fanfare than his brother was receiving, given that he was passing back through cities that had previously experienced his *adventus.* He had reached Constantinople certainly by December, and probably much earlier.[86]

On January 1, 365, Valens and Valentinian inaugurated their reign with

secutions. Them. *Or.* 7.92a states that Libya sent an embassy to Constantinople in 365/66; Theod. *HE* 5.1.2 reports that Gratian regained the rest of Africa (Λίβυη) on Valens's death; and Syn. *Ep.* 66 indicates that Valens sent troops to Libya. The problem is discussed by Paschoud 2.2: 335–6 n. 110, who fails to note these sources but accepts Valens's retention of Cyrenaica. On the split, see Köhler 1925, 12–13; Heering 1927, 20–24; Straub 1939, 34–38; Nagl, "Vt.," 2167–68; Gaudemet 1956; Pabst 1986, 83–85. Philostorg. 8.8 understood the implications of the division quite clearly.

81. AM 26.5.4; Soc. 4.2.1–2; and Soz. 6.7.8, which incorrectly reports that Valentinian went to Rome.

82. Seeck, *Regesten,* 216, 218.

83. Millar 1977, 31–32; MacCormack 1981, 17–89.

84. Three Aquileia medallions bear the legend FELIX ADVENTUS AUG N (Gnecchi 1.34–35.2 pl. 14 no. 6; Jameson 1913, vol. 2 no. 537 = Ulrich Bansa 1949, 15–18 pl. A.f). One Milan medallion bears the legend FELIX ADVENTUS AUG M *[sic]* (Gnecchi 1.34–35.1 = *RIC* 9.75.1 pl. V.15). See also the *adventus* medallions minted in Trier for Valentinian's arrival there in 367 (Gnecchi 1.35.3 = *RIC* 9.15 [Trier 8a]; Gnecchi 1.36.2 = *RIC* 9.15 [Trier 8b]). On *adventus* coinage, see Toynbee 1944, 107–9; Bastien 1988, 25–26.

85. Seeck, *Regesten,* 218, 220, 222, 224, 226.

86. Ibid., 217, 219, 221.

Figure 3. Valentinian celebrates his *adventus* into Milan. "Fest-Aureus" of Milan. *RIC* 9.75.1. Courtesy British Museum.

the first of what would be four shared consulships.[87] Themistius offered a speech on the occasion. This we know only from a letter of Libanius, which also mentions another speech, one that Themistius had delivered earlier in the winter of 364. The latter, apparently the speech that survives in the Themistian corpus as oration 6, was given in response to an address that Valens himself had delivered before the Senate of Constantinople; it represents the first of eight orations Themistius is known to have offered to Valens over the next thirteen years.[88] The theme of Themistius's address was the brotherly concord shared by the two new emperors and the way it would bring peace and prosperity to the earth. The speech is hardly unique, and neither was its theme new. Fraternal concord already dominates the rhetoric of the earliest extant panegyrics from Late Antiquity. The two orations delivered to Maximianus are replete with references to the *concordia* shared between that emperor and his co-Augustus, Diocletian.[89] This rhetoric is enhanced by the introduction of a fictitious fraternal relationship between the two rulers, whose mutual *pietas* is said to serve as an example of cooperation for all the world.[90]

Although the spirit and rhetoric of concord was more muted under Constantine and his successors,[91] Themistius easily revived it when he prepared his address for the new brother rulers. His sixth oration, entitled "Beloved Brothers, or, On Brotherly Love," takes as its starting point the very fact that the new Augusti were indeed siblings. Themistius claims that their harmo-

87. See Bagnall et al. 1987, 264–65, 270–71, 274–75, 280–81.

88. Lib. *Ep.* 1495 makes reference to two λόγοι and the influence they had already won for Themistius. Vanderspoel 1995, 157–58, argues that the first (*Or.* 6) came in early winter 364 and the second was offered when Valens asumed the consulship. Valens's speech to the Senate is mentioned at *Or.* 6.81a–c, 82d.

89. *Pan. Lat.* 10[2].9.1–10.1, 11.1–7, 13.1–5, 11[3].6.3–8.5, 11.1–12.5, 19.4. Cf. Aur. Vict. *Caes.* 39.28; Lactant. *De mort. pers.* 8.1. See esp. Straub 1939, 40–43 and now Leadbetter 1998, 224–27 against Corcoran 1996, 265–68.

90. *Pan. Lat.* 10[2].1.5, 4.1, 9.2–3, 10.6, 13.2, 11[3].7.5–7; cf. *ILS* 646. See Straub 1939, 42–45; Nixon and Rodgers 1994, 45–51.

91. Straub 1939, 52–56; MacCormack 1981, 111–13; Pabst 1986, 80–82. But see also, e.g., Lib. *Or.* 59.152–54, 171–73.

nious fraternal relationship was made clear when the one who had been elected emperor appointed the other to equal honors; the mutual love gave their subjects confidence that all would experience similar goodwill from the emperors, and would themselves use the emperors as models for mutual cooperation.[92] Symmachus echoed many of the same strains in a quinquennial speech he delivered to Valentinian at Trier three years later. There, the orator used a cosmic metaphor, asserting that the two brothers surpassed the moon and the sun, because the one did not depend on the other for brilliance.[93] The similarities between the two orations should come as no surprise. These addresses were only a small part of a much greater effort to propagate the message of imperial *concordia* in both halves of the empire.

We must not forget that, even in his first address to the troops, Valentinian is said to have assuaged their passion for a second Augustus by claiming that his primary concern was to preserve *concordia*.[94] Once he had chosen his brother, whose goodwill he could trust,[95] the two emperors openly advertised their *concordia* and *pietas* on the coinage, in constitutions, and in public inscriptions. Coins were issued from all mints with the images of both Augusti, each bearing equal symbols of status. One remarkable medallic type whose obverse features the two emperors enthroned side by side, each with his right hand raised and a globe in his left hand, would have conveyed the shibboleth of unity and parity well (fig. 4).[96] Imperial constitutions always bore the names of both reigning Augusti in order of seniority, as did public inscriptions, which sometimes openly heralded imperial *concordia*.[97] When inscriptions listed victory titles, both of the emperors shared these, regardless of which enemies each had personally conquered,[98] and panegyrics like those mentioned above also lauded the *concordia* or ὁμόνοια of the emperors.[99]

The rhetoric of fraternal relationship, so important in the Latin panegyrics and again recycled in Themistius's sixth oration, was likewise part of a broader

92. *Or.* 6.77b, 82a; cf. 9.127b. On *concordia* as a theme under Valentinian and Valens, see Nagl, "Vt.," 2165–66; Soraci 1971, 34–36, with n. 85; Tomlin 1973, ch. 4; Pabst 1986, 83–89.

93. *Or.* 1.11–14, esp. § 13. On the date, see Chastagnol 1987.

94. AM 26.2.8: "sed studendum est concordiae viribus totis."

95. AM 30.7.4: "ut germanitate ita concordia sibi iunctissimum"; cf. 26.5.1: "concordissimi principes."

96. Gnecchi 1.37.10 pl. 18.1 = *RIC* 9.116.1.

97. On the presence of all Augusti in inscriptions and law codes, see Gaudemet 1979, 21–4; Parsi 1963, 69–74; Mommsen 1882, 314–20. On *concordia*, see *AE* 1895, 108: CONCORDIAE DD NN VALENTINIANI ET VALENTIS PERPETUORUM AUGG; *CIL* 3.10596 = *ILS* 762: FRATRES CONCORDISSIMI; cf. *CIL* 6.31402 = *ILS* 769: OB PROVIDENTIAM QUAE ILLI SEMPER / CUM INCLYTO FRATRE COMMUNIS EST and *IRT* 472–73.

98. E.g., *CIL* 6.1175 = *ILS* 771. This had long been common, see Barnes 1982, 27, 254–58.

99. Them. *Or.* 9.127c: τὴν πρὸς ἀλλήλους ὁμόνοιαν; cf. 6.74b: ἡ πρὸς ἀλλήλους εὔνοια καὶ σπουδή.

Figure 4. Valentinian and Valens enthroned in equal glory. *RIC* 9.116.1. Medallion of Rome. Courtesy Kunsthistorisches Museum, Vienna.

campaign to honor the *divinis fratribus et semper Augustis*.[100] Otto Seeck first noticed that Libanius often refers to Valentinian and Valens not by their names but simply as "the brothers" in the dual. He felt that this shorthand showed Libanius's contemptuous refusal to mention these two Pannonians explicitly, but a closer inspection of the imperial panegyrics of Themistius and Symmachus reveals that such usage was common currency in imperial propaganda.[101] In an empire too large for a single Augustus, *concordia* was crucial for imperial security. Shared strength, guaranteed by fraternal good-will, was both an asset against the external threats of an extensive frontier and a surety against the omnipresent danger of usurpation from within. For this reason, the brother emperors did not hesitate to advertise their mutual goodwill, and Libanius did not fail to take the hint.

This rhetoric was carried over to the imperial children as well. When Valentinian appointed his son Gratian as a third Augustus, he joined his prede-

100. *CIL* 5.8031 = *ILS* 760. Note also the interesting image at Lib. *Ep.* 1225: κοινοὶ τῶν ἀρ‑ χομένων πατέρες.

101. Lib. *Or.* 24.10: τοῖν ἀδελφοῖν; *Or.* 19.15: τοῖν ἀδελφοῖν Παιόνιοιν; *Or.* 30.7: παρὰ τοῖν ἀδελφοῖν; cf. duals at *Ep.* 1223–25, 1235, 1263, 1336, 1467. See Seeck, *Briefe*, 404. Festus 2: "quo prosperius fratrum imperium Roma sortita est"; Symm. *Or.* 1.11: "germanum"; 22: "germani"; cf. *Or.* 2.31: "geminis custodibus" (of Gratian and Valentinian). Themistius later uses

cessors on the coinage, inscriptions, and constitutions in both east and west, and once again the familiar theme was sounded in panegyric. In a speech of 370, Symmachus applies the same notion of shared empire, the same praise of dual power and the same emphasis on fraternal piety he had used of Valentinian and Valens when he describes Valentinian's relationship with his son.[102] Themistius had aired similar notions the year before in a consular address he delivered to Valens's son, Valentinian Galates. Although the boy had not yet been appointed emperor, Themistius set the stage for his antic-ipated election by resurrecting the message he had emphasized in 365. In his speech, he claims that the rulers who shared the empire, older brother, younger brother, and son, would soon grant another share to the other son, Galates. In so doing, they would revive the spirit that prevailed at Valens's election by showing the world "[a] four-part yoke of emperors, two teams [ξυνωρίδας] composed of members of almost the same age and contempo-raneous, each walking the same, thinking the same, equaling the ends of the earth they guard."[103] This desire to cover the four corners of the world with

the dual to refer to Valens and Gratian, see p. 360. See also the image at Malalas 13.30 (p. 338): εἶχε γὰρ πᾶσαν ἐξουσίαν εἰς πρόσωπον τοῦ ἰδίου ἀδελφοῦ.

102. Symm. *Or.* 2.31–32: "sciet res publica, geminis se custodibus esse munitam sed quasi uni esse munificam, sub communi stipendio duos principes militare."

103. Them. *Or.* 9.128a; cf. 127c. For the image of the ξυνωρίς, see p. 25. Themistius also draws other parallels between Galates and the three Augusti; see *Or.* 9.120c, 125a, 125d.

a quadripartite team of emperors was also an ideal harkening back to the tetrarchy.[104] The harmony guaranteed by family ties would gain strength as it expanded into the next generation and across the limits of the empire.

Even so, the power relationship was never one of complete equality, not even between Valentinian and Valens. In his Easter Verses, the poet-*cum*-politico Ausonius offers another cosmic metaphor in a bizarre but revealing instance of the deeper meaning behind the rhetoric of concord and fraternity. In this poem, addressed to Valentinian, Ausonius compares the three co-Augusti—Valentinian, Valens, and Gratian—to the holy Trinity by laying out the relationship between the members of the imperial triune in a remarkably Arian-sounding scheme:

> Even on this earth below, we behold an image of this mystery,
> where is the emperor, the father, begetter of twin emperors,
> who in his sacred majesty embraces his brother and his son,
> sharing one realm with them, yet not dividing it,
> alone holding all, although he has all distributed.[105]

The two Augusti appointed by Valentinian were, in Ausonius's terms, his creatures and thus his subordinates. Their dependence on Valentinian for their appointments left no question about their inferiority to him in power. This principle, sanctified in Ausonius's peculiar marriage of Christian imagery and imperial propaganda, was not unique to the western perspective. Valens's subordination to his brother was clear from the beginning of the reign. Already in 365, Themistius introduced this theme in his sixth oration, and he would return to it as a leitmotiv in later speeches: Valentinian's election, claimed the rhetorician, had come from the empire at large, but Valens was dependent on his brother for rule.[106] In Themistius's terms, Valentinian was to Valens not just his brother, but his father, the origin of his reign.[107]

In fact, although Valens was granted full imperial powers from the start, the official propaganda of the joint administration distinguished him as *iunior*, reserving for his brother the title of *senior* Augustus. Thus, when the

104. *Pan. Lat.* 8[5].4.2. Contrast the image of Constantine riding in a chariot pulled by his four Caesars in Eus. *Laudatio Constantini* 3.4. On the image, see also Pabst 1986, 95–96.

105. Aus. IV *Versus paschales* ll. 24–28; cf. XIII *Epig.* 4.7 with Green 1991, 380. For analysis, see Pabst 1986, 90–93; Sivan 1993, 109. See a similar image at Eus. *VC* 4.40.

106. Them. *Or.* 6.74a: καὶ νικᾷ τῷ πλήθει μὲν ἅτερος (Valentinian) τῷ κρατοῦντι δὲ σύ (Valens); cf. 75a–c, 83a, 9.124d, 128a; AM 26.5.1: "unus nuncupatione praelatus, alter honori specie tenus adiunctus."

107. *Or.* 6.76b: ἀδελφὸς καὶ πατήρ, τὸ μὲν ἐκ τῆς φύσεως, τὸ δὲ αὐτὸν ποιήσας. Note the rhetoric at *Or.* 9.120c, 125a, which describes both Valentinian and Valens as the "fathers" of Valentinian Galates. For similar rhetoric in earlier periods, see Parsi 1963, 63–68. The same was applied to Gratian, Pabst 1989, 227–32.

two Augusti split the army in 364, the units the emperors divided between them were given the added titles of Iuniores and Seniores to distinguish Valens's men from Valentinian's.[108] The titles *senior* and *iunior* even filtered into Libanius's prose and into the historiography of the day. Valens's *magister memoriae* and court historian Festus, for example, anachronistically applied the title *iunior* to Lucius Verus, half brother and co-emperor to Marcus Aurelius, in the history he composed for Valens.[109]

The titles *senior* and *iunior* were applied, not just to distinguish the older brother from the younger, but to distinguish the supreme from the subordinate Augustus. Above all, they marked a distinction in power. This was not lost on Ammianus, who, in his description of Valens's election noted that Valentinian had chosen his brother as "his legitimate partner in power, but one who was in fact more like an obsequious lieutenant *(apparitor)*."[110] Ammianus's use of the word *apparitor* is significant. In other places, he employs it of subordinate officers, men detailed to senior commanders, and especially to describe the status of Gallus and Julian, appointed *caesares* by the Augustus Constantius.[111] Indeed, Valentinian broadcast his brother's inferiority with subtle hints in his numismatic propaganda. A series of gold multiples was minted by Valentinian's mint at Thessalonica in two types, both bearing the reverse legend VICTORIA DN AVGVSTI and featuring a winged Victory writing VOT / V / MVLT / X on a shield in honor of the quinquennalia of the two emperors in 368. Extant exemplars differ, however, in that those with obverses of Valentinian feature a victory seated—in honor—on the reverse, while those with obverses of Valens have a Victory who stands—in deference (figs. 5–6).[112] So, too, the solidus reverse with legend VOTA-PV-BLICA, first minted in 368, shows the two emperors nimbate, wearing consular robes, and enthroned side by side as a sign of unanimity. This message breaks down slightly, however, when we compare eastern and western issues of the type. On the eastern coins—those minted by Valens—both emperors raise a *mappa* (racing flag) in their right hand as a gesture of power; on those of the west, however, only the emperor on the left, the *senior* Valentinian, raises his *mappa*

---

108. On the application of the titles to the army, see p. 308. Symm. *Or.* 1 title: "Laudatio in Valentinianum Seniorem Augustum"; Jord. *Get.* 131: "Valentiniani imperatoris senioris"; cf. Them. *Or.* 6.75b: μέγαν δὲ σὺ βασιλέα πεποίκας. On these titles more broadly, see Straub 1939, 44–50.

109. Lib. *Or.* 1.145, 24.12: ὁ πρεσβύτερος; *Or.* 19.15, 20.25, 24.13: ὁ νεώτερος. On Lucius Verus, see Festus 21; cf. Eutr. 8.9: "reverentia tamen fratris nihil umquam atrox ausus."

110. AM 26.4.3; cf. Straub 1939, 68.

111. On *caesares* as *apparitores*, see AM 14.11.10, 16.7.3, 17.11.1, 20.8.6; Straub 1939, 56–57. On the word *apparitor* in Ammianus, see Chiabò 1983, 64; cf. Pabst 1986, 326 n. 433.

112. Four exemplars exist for Valentinian: (1) Gnecchi 1.35.10 pl. 14.11 (Paris) = *RIC* 9.177 (Thessalonica 20); (2) Gnecchi 1.35.10 (Vienna); (3) Gnecchi 1.35.10 (collection Trau); (4) J. Schulman catalog (Mar. 9–12, 1959) no. 1429. Two for Valens: (1) Gnecchi 1.37.13 pl. 18.3 (Vienna) = *RIC* 9.177.21; (2) Gnecchi 1.37.13 (Quellen collection).

Figure 5. Valentinian's *Victoria* seated in honor. Medallion of Thessalonica. *RIC* 9.177.20. Courtesy Bibliothèque nationale de France.

Figure 6. Valens's *Victoria* standing in deference. Medallion of Thessalonica. *RIC* 9.177.21. Courtesy Kunsthistorisches Museum, Vienna.

(figs. 7–8).[113] Valentinian was thus at pains to make clear that, although he had shared full power, it was not quite equal power.

Most of our evidence indicates that this inferior position did not bother Valens. On the contrary, he seems willingly to have taken orders from Valentinian and to have implemented policies at his behest. Thus, when the army and later the provinces and administration were divided in 364, it was done according to the designs of Valentinian alone, "by whose judgement affairs were managed."[114] And when Valens defeated the usurper Procopius, he sent his head to Valentinian and ceded to his brother jurisdiction over some of the rebels of western origin.[115] Shortly thereafter, Valens consulted Valentinian on whether to undertake his first Gothic war, and he only did so with Valentinian's consent.[116] The appointment of consuls was also apparently determined by Valentinian: although candidates were drawn equally in almost patterned fashion from the east and west, in 375, a year that was due to see eastern consuls, military affairs preoccupied Valentinian, and new consuls were simply not chosen.[117] The law codes reveal that many of the policies im-

113. Woloch 1966, 171–78. On the consular *mappa*, see Grierson and Mays 1992, 75.

114. AM 26.5.2, 4. See Pergami 1993, xxvii–xxix.

115. AM 26.20.6, 8; see pp. 81 and 113.

116. AM 27.4.1: "ut consulto placuerat fratri"; cf. 27.5.1, where the plural *principibus* implies that the Gothic attack was regarded as affecting both emperors.

117. Jer. *Chron.* s.a. 375: "quia superiore anno Sarmatae Pannonias vastaverant, idem consules permansere"; cf. Prosper *Chron.* 1155; see Bagnall et al. 1987, 285; Piganiol 1972, 216–17. For the consuls under Valentinian and Valens, see Bagnall et al. 1987, 264–85. Note that in

Figure 7. Solidus of Constantinople with both emperors raising their *mappae*. *RIC* 9.217.29a. Courtesy American Numismatic Society.

Figure 8. Solidus of Trier with only the left emperor raising his *mappa. RIC* 9.17.18b. Courtesy Kunsthistorisches Museum, Vienna.

plemented by Valens, from standardizing weights and measures to marriage laws, from fortification efforts to curial protection, were implemented on the initiative of Valentinian. Valens was thus subordinate in both name and deed. Though he was granted the title Augustus, his authority was always contingent so long as his brother lived. Valens's policies and their motivation must thus be approached with caution. Although he was a full sharer in his brother's power, he was always made aware of its source, and with very few exceptions, we find that he kept that awareness in the forefront of his mind.

"PANNONIA . . . STRONG IN MEN AND PROSPEROUS IN LAND"

Solinus knew well what sort of stock Pannonia produced when he called it "strong in men."[118] Like all late Romans, he was keenly aware of origins: who a man was depended not just on his birth and education, but on his *patria*. Pannonians were people like Martin of Savaria,[119] known to us as Saint Martin of Tours: stout and stubborn, endowed with a keen sense of justice and an irascibility prone to violence. Like so many Pannonians, Martin was the son of a soldier, a common man who had worked his way up from the ranks to become a petty officer. Again like his fellow countrymen, the future saint

---

the years when Valentinian and Valens did not hold the consulate, the consuls alternated in a fairly regular pattern: 366, two western consuls; 367, one western and one eastern; 369, two eastern; 371, two western; 372, two eastern; 374, two western; 375, postconsulate.

118. Solinus 21.2: "Pannonia . . . viro fortis et solo laeta"; cf. Isidore *Etymol.* 14.4.16. The best surveys of Pannonian history and archaeology are Mócsy 1974; Lenyel and Radan 1980; Srejović 1993b.

119. Sulpicius *Vita Martini* 2.1. For the dispute over the birthplace of Martin, see Zeiller 1918, 297 n.4; Fontaine 1967–69, 2: 432–5; Tóth 1973, 121 n.40.

followed in his father's footsteps, entered the army, and eventually won his way into the imperial guards (Scholares). He held this position for five years before renouncing worldly service to become a "soldier of God."[120] Despite this success, Martin's hagiographer Sulpicius Severus firmly insists that the future saint served against his will, and he even foreshortens Martin's term of service in his biography to diminish the taint of a career that the holy man never fully succeeded in living down.[121] In this sense, Martin's Pannonian origins marked him through the rest of his life. Indeed, his Pannonian background not only pushed him toward a military career, it also in some sense shaped who he was. From his spirited destruction of polytheist temples and his superhuman battles with demons to his bold defiance of the emperor Julian and the usurper Maximus, Martin was of a character that all late Romans would readily have recognized as Pannonian.

The territory of Pannonia (see map 1) fell under the Roman heel in the first century B.C. when Augustus extended the borders of Illyricum to the Danube.[122] Trajan divided the province into Pannonia Superior in the west and Pannonia Inferior in the east, and in the late third century, Diocletian split the two provinces again, into four: Pannonia Superior was divided along the river Drava into Pannonia I in the north and Savia in the south, and Pannonia Inferior became Valeria north of the Drava and Pannonia II to its south. These late Roman provinces had their capitals at Savaria, Siscia, Sopianae, and Sirmium respectively.[123] It was in Pannonia II, near Sirmium, in the city of Cibalae (Vinkovci), that Valentinian and Valens were born.

Like Martin's, theirs was a military family. Their father, Gratian the elder, had exploited his strength and bravado to win his way up to the command of the imperial guards, and his career had already advanced well beyond this by the time he had his two sons. This illustrious trajectory was not atypical of men from these parts. Pannonia had been notorious for producing military men for centuries,[124] and Cibalae itself enjoyed a rich tradition of spawning imperial guards.[125] Gratian and his sons Valentinian and Valens were thus

120. Sulpicius *Vita Martini* 2.2, 5–6. Woods 1995c holds that Martin actually served under Valentinian in the Schola Gentilium. This hypothesis is problematic for several reasons; see Lenski 2002; cf. Barlow and Brennan 2001, 250.

121. This hypothesis was first put forward by Babut 1912; cf. Fontaine 1967–69, 2: 436–44. The veracity and chronology of the life are much disputed. See now Barnes 1996 against Stancliffe 1983, 111–33.

122. Augustus *Res gestae* 30 with Nagy 1991.

123. On the history of this administrative division, see Fitz 1983, 11–19, who holds that Pannonia Superior was actually first divided ca. 314.

124. E.g. *Pan. Lat.* 10[2].2.2: "Quis enim dubitat quin . . . Italia quidem sit gentium domina gloriae vetustate, sed Pannonia virtute?"; cf. 10[2].2.4; Veget. 1.28; AM 21.12.22, 29.6.13; Dio Cass. 49.3.1–6.

125. *CIL* 6.2833.9, 12, 17, 2385.1, 13, 32536.28, 32542 passim; 32624.14. In general, Pannonia had become a major supplier of Praetorians after Septimius Severus's reform of the guards.

carrying on a local tradition. Nor would their exposure to military men have been limited to imperial officers, for all would have grown up with locally based military units stationed close at hand. The *Notitia Dignitatum* records that Pannonian cities housed a number of riparian garrisons that dated back to the reign of Diocletian.[126] The Danube bend, which cradled Pannonia, created a treacherous reentry into the territory of the barbarian Quadi and Sarmatians; this location necessarily demanded formidable defenses and equally formidable men to man them. Pannonia was thus a seminary for soldiers, out of which Gratian and his sons naturally sprang.

With the growing importance of military prowess as an essential quality of imperial rule, Pannonia had also become a fertile producer of emperors. Decius had been born in Budalia, a village located on the road between Cibalae and Sirmium. He lasted less than three years (249–51) before suffering a crushing defeat at the hands of the Goths in Thrace, where he disappeared in battle. His fate anticipated that of his fourth-century compatriot Valens, a point not lost on the contemporary Ammianus.[127] In the years that separated the two, Pannonia became a launchpad for emperors as a succession of men either born or promoted there laid claim to the throne.[128] Aurelian (r. 270–75), to whom Valentinian was often compared, may have been born in Sirmium and was certainly chosen to the purple there.[129] So, too, Probus (r. 276–82) was born near Sirmium and eventually assassinated there, and Maximianus (r. 286–305) was from the area around Sirmium.[130] The latter two later developed their family estates in the territory in a fashion that—as we shall see—became characteristic of emperors from the region.

To understand better how Valentinian's and Valens's *patria* might have affected the future emperors, we must look more closely at the history and archaeology of the area. Cibalae had become a *colonia* in the second century.[131] Given that the city occupied fifty-six hectares, it must have been of some importance even in the fourth century, but the site has not been systematically

126. *Not. dign. oc.* 32.26, 35 (Aquincum); 32.49–50, 54 (Sirmium); 32.52 (Mursa); 32.56–57 (Siscia). The Lanciarii Sabarienses, *Not. dign. oc.* 5.9, 152, 7.82, must originally have been a Pannonian garrison unit as well. Cf. Hoffmann 1969–70, 1: 517–19; Fitz 1980, 131–39; Poulter 1992, 108–9.

127. Aur. Vict. *Caes.* 29.1–4; *Epit.* 29.1–5; Eutr. 9.4; cf. Kienast 1996, 204. The comparison between Valens and Decius is noted at AM 31.13.13. More on Sirmium's connections with late Roman emperors at Mirković 1971, 34–41; cf. Syme 1971, 194–220; Mócsy 1974, 266–96.

128. For emperors promoted in or around Pannonia, see Septimius Severus, Ingenuus, Regalianus, and Vetranio (Kienast 1996, 156, 223–24, 321).

129. Kienast 1996, 234; *PLRE* I, L. Domitius Aurelianus 6. SHA *Aurel.* 3.1–2 offers several possible birthplaces, including Sirmium. Eutr. 9.13 and *Epit.* 35.1 report Dacia Ripensis. For comparisons between Valentinian and Aurelian, see AM 30.8.8; Jerome *Chron.* s.a. 365.

130. Kienast 1996, 253, 272; *PLRE* I, M. Aurelius Probus 3; M. Aur. Val. Maximianus Herculius 8.

131. *AE* 1980, 724–25; *CIL* 3.2388, 14038. See also *CIL* 6.2833.9, 12, 17; cf. *CIL* 3.3267.

excavated to confirm this.[132] It was situated eighty kilometers east of Sirmium, where the road forked westward to Emona via Siscia and northward to Sopianae and Aquincum. It sat near the river Bacuntius (Bosut) in the rich valley between the Sava and Drava. Zosimus describes it as "a city of Pannonia resting on a hill; the road leading up to the city is narrow, and a deep swamp five stades wide extends along most of it, but the remainder is mountainous; here is the hillside where the city is located; below this a vastly spreading plain extends as far as the eye can see."[133] Across this plain, the estates of the wealthier citizens of Cibalae, men like Valentinian's and Valens's father Gratian, would have been scattered.

Solinus characterized Pannonia as a region of strong men but also of great fertility. His testimony finds confirmation in the *Expositio totius mundi*, which calls Pannonia "a land rich in all things, produce and horses and trade and partly also in slaves."[134] The archaeological record adds color and complexity to this picture. Pannonia had traditionally manufactured few wares for export, and what little manufacturing capacity it had dropped off after the third century.[135] Trade had also declined in the late empire, although Pannonia's proximity to the Sarmatians along the Danube did continue to encourage considerable exchange in barbarian amber, brooches, and slaves.[136] In the early fourth century, as in earlier periods, the primary engine of the Pannonian economy was rather the land, and this remained a source of magnificent wealth throughout Valentinian's and Valens's lifetimes. As in other parts of the west, large estates came to predominate in central Pannonia in the later empire. Their grain, livestock, and wool cloth generated such abundant capital for the region that its effects are still reflected in the rich archaeological and numismatic record from Pannonia. Indeed, late Roman Pannonia was awash in money, particularly in coins of Balkan or eastern manufacture.[137] From this evidence, it has become clear that grain from Pannonian estates was being shipped down the Danube and paid for by eastern provinces or armies in gold.[138]

Gratian the elder no doubt hoped to capitalize on this source of wealth when he acquired his estate near Cibalae. It is unlikely that a soldier of common birth *(ignobili stirpe)* like Gratian would have inherited a family villa, yet some time before 351, he owned a farmstead, to which he retired after serv-

132. Patsch 1899; Soproni 1968, 46, s.v. Cibalae; Mócsy 1962, 644; 1974, 143, 152, 225–26.

133. Zos. 2.18.2; cf. 48.3–4. *Epit.* 41.5 names the swamp "Hiulca."

134. *Exp. tot. mun.* 57: "terra dives in omnibus, fructibus quoque et iumentis et negotiis, ex parte et mancipiis." Rougé 1966, 9–26, dates the work to 359.

135. See Mócsy 1962, 687, on export trade.

136. Lányi 1972, 69–96, 135–37; Mócsy 1974, 319–20. The few luxury goods uncovered from grave sites were imported (Lányi 1972, 80–82). On amber, see esp. Solinus 20.10.

137. Lányi 1974, 91–92, 136; Duncan 1993, 20–23.

138. Mócsy, 1962, 693; 1974, 321–22.

ing in Britain in the 340s.[139] Here again, he followed a path typical of Illyrian commanders.[140] Even today, abundant remains of estates like the one Gratian owned offer stubborn testimony to the lifestyle Valentinian and Valens grew up with. After the mid third century, a new class of fortified and fully independent villas sprang up in the countryside of central Pannonia, especially in the area around Lake Pelso (Balaton).[141] These had vast expanses of fortification walls equipped with multiple towers, which enclosed self-supporting estates. One such villa, at modern Keszthely-Fenékpuszta, sat on the southwest corner of Lake Pelso between Sopianae and Savaria. Its central complex had a square circuit of walls enclosing an area of fourteen hectares. These surrounded a vast series of buildings, including a large *horreum*, a central palace with bath complex, and, from early in the fourth century, a Christian basilica.[142] Such estates constituted islands of wealth, which could remain independent of the markets generated by cities and the duties imposed by urban centers on their wealthier citizens.

The sort of wealth these plantations attracted can be seen in a recently discovered hoard of fourteen silver vessels given to an otherwise unknown man named Sevso between the mid fourth and mid fifth centuries. The prize piece in the hoard, a large, engraved platter, depicts a *déjeuner champêtre* along the shores of a lake teeming with fish and labeled PELSO by an inscription below it. The master reclines at a sumptuous feast, while his horse, identified as INNOCENTIUS, rests nearby. Around the border of the platter an inscription reads:

> May these, O Sevso, yours for many ages be,
> Small vessels fit to serve your offspring worthily.[143]

This was a mentality that Gratian must have shared. His military accomplishments had put him in a position to acquire what he hoped would be a self-perpetuating source of felicity for his posterity.

There are strong indications that many of the Pannonian *villae* attested in the archaeology were in the possession of the imperial *res privata*, or privy

139. AM 30.7.3.

140. *PLRE* I, Marcellus 3; Lucillianus 3; and Varronianus 1 all returned to property in their homeland after being forced into retirement. After serving in Ticinum, St. Martin's father also retired to his home town of Savaria, perhaps to an estate like Gratian's; see Sulpicius *Vita Martini* 5.3; Fontaine 1967–69, 2: 432–33. One wonders if Gratian bought the estate using the money with which he had absconded while serving as *comes per Africam* in the 330s (AM 30.7.3). Here too he would not have been atypical; cf. A. H. M. Jones 1964, 644–45.

141. Thomas 1964, 18, 389; Mócsy 1974, 299–308; Biró 1974.

142. Thomas 1964, 60–68. See Sági 1961 on the basilica. Mócsy 1974, 300–307, argues that this and five other square fortified villae were imperial latifundia, but although Pannonia was filled with imperial estates, we have nothing connecting this or the other five with the emperor.

143. Mundell Mango and Bennett 1994, 55–97. Mundell Mango's contention (p. 78) that the "Pelso" in question is not Lake Pelso seems like special pleading designed to sidestep the tender question of the hoard's proper country of origin, surely Hungary; cf. Landesman 2001.

purse. Emperors had owned estates in Illyricum since the second century, and the third-century concentration of rulers from the region greatly increased the number of properties that accrued to the imperial fisc.[144] Galerius, for example, developed the territory where he was born in Dacia Ripensis, three hundred kilometers east of Pannonia, into an elaborate imperial theme park, which he named Romuliana after his mother. After Galerius's death, the villa devolved to the *res privata,* and, in the course of the fourth century, it was reconstructed under imperial auspices.[145] Similarly, the family of Constantine, themselves good Moesians, added what was probably their homestead at Mediana (outside Niš) to the *res privata.* This villa had originally been owned by Constantius I, but, after devolving to the imperial estates, it played host regularly to any and all reigning emperors. In June 364, Valentinian and Valens used Mediana as the staging place to divide their imperial army.[146] Valentinian also had the use of another lavishly appointed imperial villa, called Murocincta, probably modern Parndorf, south of Carnuntum. His younger son, Valentinian II, was staying there in 375 when the emperor died at Brigetio, a hundred and sixty kilometers to the east.[147]

Yet another imperial villa, called Pristensis and located twenty-six Roman miles west of Sirmium, was where the princess Constantia, daughter of the deceased Constantius II, was nearly captured by the Quadi in 374. She had stopped there to rest on her way to marry Valentinian's son, the fifteen-year-old Gratian, in Trier.[148] She cannot have been far from a rather more recently acquired imperial estate, the former property of Gratian the elder. In the summer of 351, Cibalae hosted Constantius II as he prepared for battle against the usurper Fl. Magnus Magnentius.[149] On September 28, in a no-

144. Decius presumably had estates near Sirmium, and Probus and Maximianus certainly did (see p. 37). For Galerius's and Constantius I's estates in Dacia, see what follows.

145. Srejović 1993a, 29–33. The site is mentioned at *Epit.* 40.16 (Romulianum); cf. Proc. *Aed.* 4.4 ('Ρωμυλίανα). The identification of Gamzigrad with Galerius's villa is confirmed by the discovery of an inscription identifying the site as "FELIX ROMULIANA"; see Srejović 1985, 551, with fig. 1. The more recent discovery of the dual mausolea of Galerius and Romula (Srejović and Vasic 1994) and of a porphyry head of Galerius (Srejović 1992–93) have put to rest the stubborn skepticism of Duval (1987) about the villa's identification.

146. Mócsy 1974, 302, conjectures that Mediana was the villa of Constantius I, although Petrovic 1993, 57–75, is more cautious. Petrovic 1993, 73–74, offers a full list of constitutions issued from Mediana. On Valentinian's and Valens's stay there, see p. 26. Matthews 1989, 401, catalogs other imperial villae mentioned by Ammianus, most of them in Pannonia. See also the villa of Mursella (Mórichida-Kisárpás) where Constans stayed in 339 (*CTh* 16.8.1, 6, 9.2, with Seeck, *Regesten,* 48, 106).

147. AM 30.10.4, with Mócsy 1970, 583. On the remains of the villa, see Thomas 1964, 177–92; Saria 1966, 268–71. The villa has also been suggested as the meeting place for the tetrarchic congress of 308.

148. AM 29.6.7. Imperial properties are also attested outside Savaria: *CIL* 3.4219 was dedicated there by the *ex p(rae)p(osito) si[l]varum domnicarum.*

149. Zos. 2.48.3.

toriously bloody battle, Constantius defeated Magnentius outside Mursa.[150] In the wake of this massacre, Gratian the elder, who was suspected of supporting the usurper, paid with the loss of his villa.[151]

The location of Cibalae at the bottleneck in east-west routes through the northern Balkans had always rendered it a hot spot in regional military conflicts,[152] and emperors seem to have taken advantage of the mayhem this created to expand their vast holdings in Pannonia through confiscations. Such was the fate of Gratian's villa: the nest egg into which he had sunk his fortune was gulped into the belly of the largest leviathan of fourth-century Pannonia, the imperial *res privata*. The estate where Valentinian and Valens had grown up was lost, at least temporarily, to the family.

There is no firm evidence as to where Gratian and his sons lived after they lost the estate. It is certainly possible, however, that the family moved back into Gratian's native city of Cibalae. Later, Valentinian apparently spent time in Sirmium, because his first son, the younger Gratian, was born there.[153] Given these contacts, it is clear that not just the rural but also the urban environment of Pannonia affected our future emperors. The cities thus bear examining.

No one would dispute that in the fourth century, the great cities of second-century Pannonia, all of them lined up along the Danube, failed to maintain the standard of prosperity that they had once enjoyed.[154] Of the 650 inscriptions surviving from the city of Carnuntum (Petronell), for example, only three are fourth-century.[155] The city saw only one new building erected in the fourth century, a tetrapylon monument, one of whose arches still stands,[156] and, although it continued to be inhabited, its private houses ceased to be well maintained.[157] The baths were closed and a baptistery was attached to the civil am-

---

150. *Epit.* 42.4; cf. Jer. *Chron.* s.a. 351; Zos. 2.49.4, with Mócsy 1974, 286.

151. AM 30.7.3's "per agrum suum ad proposita festinantem" would indicate that Gratian allowed Magnentius to pass through his land on his way to the battle of Mursa. This seems like a minor offense given that Gratian would have had trouble denying right of way to a full army. One can thus assume that he offered active support to Magnentius in the days before the battle. Unfortunately, Zosimus's intricate narrative of the campaign (2.49.3–50.1) is filled with geographical impossibilities that prevent an accurate reconstruction of Magnentius's route and thus preclude a closer estimate of the location of Gratian's villa. See Paschoud 1: 253–59 nn. 59–65; cf. Barnes 1993, 105–6.

152. In A.D. 7: Dio Cass. 55.32.3; Vell. 2.112.3–6. In 258/59: Aur. Vict. *Caes.* 33.2; Eutr. 9.8; Zon. 12.24. In 314: *Epit.* 41.5; Eutr. 10.5; *Exc. Val.* [5]16; Zos. 2.18.2–19.1, 48.3; Jer. *Chron.* s.a. 314; cf. Di Maio 1990.

153. *Epit.* 47.1. On the date, see Jer. *Chron.* s.a. 359; *Cons. Const.* s.a. 359; *Chron. pasch.*, p. 543.

154. Póczy 1980, 244–45; Poulter 1992, 112–13. On the prosperity of the riparian cities of the second century, see Mócsy 1974, 112–40.

155. Swoboda 1964, 74–75. For the scale of second- and third-century Carnuntum, see the striking aerial photographs in Vorbeck and Beckel 1973.

156. Swoboda 1964, 171, gives a Constantian date for the famous "Heidentor von Petronell," but Stiglitz, Kandler, and Jobst 1974, 617–18, argues for a third-century date.

157. Stiglitz, Kandler, and Jobst 1977, 593–613.

phitheater, indicating that it ceased to be used for performances.[158] Valentinian visited Carnuntum in 375 but found it "quite deserted now and in ruins."[159] Similarly, Aquincum (Budapest), once the capital of Pannonia Inferior, saw its former public buildings converted into apartments and its houses fall into disrepair.[160] Decline had weakened the city to such a point that Valentinian did not consider it an appropriate place to winter in 375.[161] These riparian cities had thus lost the luster they had enjoyed under the high empire.

The situation was considerably different in the cities of central Pannonia, particularly Sopianae, Siscia, Savaria and Sirmium, the capitals of the four late Roman provinces created by Diocletian. Their status as administrative centers brought them a new degree of prestige and, along with it, prosperity. Sopianae (Pécs) had witnessed a period of rapid growth funded at imperial expense when it became the capital of Valeria after 296. Buildings were radically reconstructed along a new street grid, and a huge structure with a bath complex, possibly a *palatium*, was added.[162] Siscia (Sziszek), which has been less systematically excavated, likewise expanded when it became the capital of Savia. An imperial mint had been in operation there since the 260s, and it remained the center of western Balkan coin production throughout the fourth century.[163] When Savaria (Szombathely) was made the capital of the new province of Pannonia I, it too witnessed a period of building and rebirth.[164] It housed an imperial treasury and, according to Ammianus, boasted a palace with a "royal bath-chamber."[165] This last has been identified with an apsidal *aula* equipped with hypocaust heating, mosaic floors, and marble revetment, a structure built in the first half of the fourth century.[166]

A similar situation prevailed at Sirmium, in Valentinian's and Valens's home province. The *Expositio totius mundi* singles out Sirmium, which occupied 120

158. Ibid., 608–16; Swoboda 1964, 181, 204.

159. AM 30.5.2: "desertum quidem nunc et squalens." He remained there through the summer and apparently rebuilt the camp and fortifications (AM 30.5.11; Swoboda 1964, 74–75; Stiglitz, Kandler, and Jobst 1977, 660).

160. Mócsy 1974, 310.

161. AM 30.5.13–15. Brigetio's decline can also be charted in the shrinkage of its boundaries in the fourth century, although excavation has yet to reveal details.

162. Fülep 1984, 33–4, 274–79, even speculates on building activity under Valentinian based on brick stamps (cf. Fülep 1977, 9–10). An increase in coin circulation from the period of Constantine and Constantius also points to the wealth of the early fourth-century city (Fülep 1984, 278–79).

163. *Not. dign. oc.* 11.24, 39; *RIC* 8.339–347; *RIC* 9.137–140.

164. Mócsy and Szentléleky 1971, 32–33; Pócsy 1980, 265.

165. AM 30.5.16: "regii lavacri" with Balla 1963. On the *thesauri Savarienses*, see *Not. dign. oc.* 11.25.

166. Tóth 1973. See also the *horrea* built by Constans (*CIL* 3.4180 = *ILS* 727) and the arch of Constantius II (Pócsy 1980, 265).

hectares, as Pannonia's "greatest city."[167] It hosted not only the governor of Pannonia II, but also, at various points, the praetorian prefect of Italy, Africa, and Illyricum and the master of the cavalry for Illyricum.[168] It had an imperial arms factory and cloth works and, for parts of the fourth century, an imperial mint.[169] Between 316 and 324, a massive hippodrome complex extending 470 meters was constructed, parts of which were then rebuilt later in the course of the fourth century.[170] Here Julian witnessed publicly funded games during his brief stay in the city in 361. He would have lodged in the *palatium* that Ammianus tells us was near the forum and *curia*, which excavations have provisionally identified.[171] Two bath complexes in the city have been uncovered, the larger of which was built between 308 and 314 under Licinius, and large *horrea* were also constructed near the hippodrome, probably to serve the imperial *officia*.[172] Thus outfitted, there is little wonder that Sirmium more than any Pannonian city gave credence to the claim of the *Expositio* that Pannonia was "always the domicile of emperors."[173] Even more than the other capitals of Diocletian's new Pannonian provinces, late Roman Sirmium had grown by leaps and bounds thanks to the beneficence of the emperors.

Even so, these impressive catalogs mask a situation that quickly became less prosperous than might appear. All of Savaria's new structures, for example, were constructed by the first half of the fourth century, and all were built by the imperial treasury, not with local wealth. Later in the century, the town began to decline. During his Quado-Sarmatian campaign of 375, Valentinian considered Savaria the only suitable place in Pannonia I to winter, but even it was "weak at that time and plagued with relentless afflictions." Valentinian had first learned this during a visit earlier in the year, when he found the city gate through which he tried to exit blocked with rubbish. Although he had it cleared, the people were still unable to raise its iron portcullis, which neglect had left jammed shut.[174] Sirmium had also witnessed a tapering off of imperial investment in the latter half of the cen-

---

167. *Exp. tot. mun.* 57. Cf. Popović 1971, 119–33, on size and topography.

168. On Sirmium as a military and administrative center in the fourth century, see Mirković 1971, 41–42.

169. On the *fabrica* and *gynaeceum*, see *Not. dign. oc.* 9.18, 11.47. The mint was intermittently active in the 350s (*RIC* 8.382). After 364, when Valentinian and Valens met in Sirmium, minting ceased, and Sirmium's *officinae* were apparently transferred to the mint of Siscia (*RIC* 9.156), which is the only mint in the region listed in the *Notitia dignitatum*.

170. Popović and Ochenschlager 1976, 156–72.

171. AM 21.10.1–2, 30.5.16; Popović and Ochenschlager 1976, 172–75; Popović 1993, 21.

172. On the Licinian baths, see Mirković 1971, 37, with reference to *CIL* 3.10107. On the second group of Baths, see Duval and Popović 1977, 75–78; Bavant 1984, 250. On the *horrea*, which may date to Constantine and were perhaps expanded under Constantius, see Duval and Popović 1977, 29–73.

173. *Exp. tot. mun.* 57: "et semper habitatio imperatorum est"; cf. Mirković 1971, 33–45.

174. AM 30.5.14, 17; cf. Matthews 1989, 395–96.

tury. When the Quadi invaded Pannonia in the summer of 374, Petronius Probus was residing at Sirmium as praetorian prefect and was faced with the task of clearing out a moat piled with garbage and rebuilding crumbling fortifications. For this, he used material that had been collected some time before in the vain hope of building a theater.[175] Evidently, Sirmium, indeed all of Pannonia, was losing its grip on the prosperity it had enjoyed in the first half of the century.[176]

Between the high empire and the later empire, then, the locus of urban power in Pannonia had moved from periphery to center and the source of urban wealth had shifted from a private to an imperial origin. The tetrarchs had rearranged the provincial structure of Pannonia and relocated the capitals from the cities along the Danube to urban centers deeper inside provincial territory. In doing so, they built these new capitals into magnificent showpieces of grandiose proportion.[177] Unlike in earlier periods, however, the urban prosperity of the fourth century was funded almost exclusively through imperial initiative rather than with local wealth. Furthermore, the prime beneficiaries of this new prosperity were above all imperial officials. Most of the new structures, from city walls, to *horrea*, to palaces, to baths, were built for the advantage of soldiers and praesidial bureaucrats, not the indigenous inhabitants.[178] Moreover, even imperial expenditures fell off after the mid fourth century, leading inexorably to the beginnings of decay.[179] It is indicative that the stones assembled for the construction of a theater in Sirmium were eventually used in 374 to repair its crumbling fortifications.[180]

---

175. AM 29.6.11.

176. Many of the cities of the Pannonian interior that were not imperial capitals also experienced a rebirth in the early fourth century, followed by a gradual slide into decline. Gorsium (Tác): Fitz and Fedak 1993; Fitz 1976. Bassiana (Gradina): Grbic 1936. Scarbantia (Sopron): Póczy 1977, 32–40; Gömörri 1986, 379–82.

177. This is the picture presented by Mócsy 1974, 308–19; cf. Balla 1963.

178. Poulter 1992. This trend can be seen more broadly in cities across the empire (Ward Perkins 1998).

179. Among the cities I have treated, the only identifiable building activity after 337 was the remodeling of the *spina* in the hippodrome of Sirmium (Popović and Ochenschlager 1976, 181); the construction of the *horrea* of Savaria (*ILS* 727); and the triumphal arch of Savaria, possibly built under Constantius (Pócsy 1980, 264). Brick stamps may indicate new building in Sopianae in the 370s, but their exact use is uncertain (Fülep 1984, 279). Villae also bear little evidence of new construction or rebuilding after the first part of the fourth century; see Keszthely-Fenékpuszta at Thomas 1964, 60; Tác-Fenékpuszta, ibid., 299–325, 314–324; Parndorf, ibid., 177–92; and Mursella and Triciana at Mócsy 1974, 302–6.

180. The only indicator of extensive imperial expenditure in the second half of the fourth century comes in Valentinian's massive outlays on the Danube to rebuild the system of fortifications; see Soproni 1969; Lanyi 1969; Duncan 1993, 15–17; cf. Nixon 1983. Even here, Valentinian's imposition of heavy taxes to fund the project probably hastened the decline of an already weak urban economy; cf. AM 30.5.3–10 and app. A. These taxes, combined with the

Out of this world came Valentinian and Valens. Born in the 320s, the two spent their early years in the golden age of late Roman Pannonia: the tetrarchs and then Constantine had lavished their favor on the region, and this was reflected in the monuments that would have surrounded the future emperors as young men. During the course of their early careers, in the 340s and 350s, however, Valentinian and Valens would have witnessed the beginnings of regional decline. The imperial superstructure that had showered wealth on the territory failed to continue its largesse, and this began to take its toll by midcentury. The power of imperial favor thus greatly affected the region, for both better and worse. Nor did it fail to affect the household of the two future emperors more personally: the imperial hand that had outfitted their father so handsomely had then taken away the very estate he had acquired through service. In this atmosphere, Valentinian and Valens must have recognized early on that imperial connections dictated individual prosperity. Their father had certainly proven this to be the case, and the evidence lay before them in the buildings that adorned their homeland. Because of this, they would have had good reason to turn to imperial service after the loss of Gratian's estate in 351. To be sure, as the sons of a veteran, they were legally obliged to serve. But more than this, Valentinian and Valens were pushed toward a military career both by the example of their father and by their own ambitions to make good on his losses.

PANNONIAN BEGINNINGS

Next to his family connections, Jovian's greatest asset as a soldier must have been his size. After he was chosen emperor, some of the troops in the lines misunderstood when his name was proclaimed and thought "Julian" had revived. They had only to see him, tall and ungainly, to realize that he was not the short and stocky man they had expected.[181] He was so tall that the men who proclaimed him were at a loss to find an imperial robe large enough to cover his prodigious frame.[182] When he was staying in Antioch, an old woman angered with his shameful Persian treaty taunted him with the contrast between brain and body: "My but stupidity is big and tall."[183] He also had a voracious appetite to accompany his massive bulk. Rumor had it that overeating

---

depredations of the Quado-Sarmatian invasions, dealt the teetering province a blow from which it would never recover. After Valentinian's death in 375, monetary flow into the province ground to a halt; cf. Fitz 1990; Lányi 1993; Duncan 1993, 17–19. On Pannonia after 375, see Varady 1969; Eadie 1982; Bavant 1984; Wellner 1990; Christie 1996.

181. AM 25.5.6.

182. AM 25.10.14. See also *Epit.* 44.3, "fuit insignis corpore"; Theod. *HE* 4.1.2; Greg. Naz. *Or.* 5.15; Zon. 13.14; Eunap. *Hist.* fr. 29 (Blockley).

183. Suid. *I* 401: ὅσον μῆκος καὶ βάθος ἡ μωρία.

contributed to his mysterious death.[184] This gargantuan stature was typically Illyrian. It was something Jovian shared with another Illyrian *protector domesticus,* a man of his father's generation, Gratian the elder.

Gratian was born in Cibalae possibly in the 280s.[185] Like so many Pannonians before him, he embarked on a military career. Because he lacked political connections, any advancement he hoped for had to be obtained through personal achievement. In Gratian's case this was not lacking. He was a scrappy character with a reputation for toughness that went back to his childhood. As a boy, he had won the nickname Funarius when he was able to keep five soldiers from wresting a rope *(funis)* from his iron grip.[186] He cultivated this strong man image by imitating the famous wrestler Milo of Croton, who used to invite challengers to try to extract apples from his clenched fist.[187] Gratian's bodily strength and experience in wrestling won him a wide reputation, and this reputation no doubt helped secure him a post among the Protectores Domestici.

Despite his extraordinary strength, it would likely have taken Gratian at least twenty years to win his way up the ranks and into this elite corps.[188] He had perhaps just made it when Valentinian was born in the early 320s. As noted above, *protectores domestici* rarely went long before enjoying a promotion, and Gratian's came with his appointment as count of Africa, a post he must have won after Valentinian was old enough to travel, since Symmachus reports that the future emperor accompanied his father there. Symmachus does not mention Valens's presence in Africa, and it seems improbable that he too went. His birth in Cibalae in late summer 328 may provide a termi-

184. AM 25.10.13; cf. 15 and Lib. *Or.* 18.279; Zon. 13.14.

185. On Gratian, see Seeck 1912, 1831; id., *Untergang,* 2; Solari 1932b; Tomlin 1973, 1–12. Gratian's age may be estimated based on the year of Valentinian's birth. Valentinian was thirty-eight or thirty-nine when his first son was born in 359; Valens was thirty-eight when Valentinian Galates was born in 366 and thus younger when his daughters were born; Jovian was thirty-one when Varronian was born ca. 362. Based on this pattern, we might assume that Gratian was also in his thirties when his first son, Valentinian, was born in 321 and was thus himself born ca. 281–91. This coincides well with what we know about the average age of Romans males at marriage (see Saller 1987).

186. AM 30.7.2–3; cf. *Epit.* 45.2 with Lippold 1991, 376–77. For nicknames, see Kempf 1901, 354–57.

187. *CIL* 3.3676 = *ILS* 2558 records the feats of another self-made Pannonian strongman. Similar stories, generally told of Balkan emperors, recur in the *Historia Augusta;* see SHA *Tyr. trig.* 8.5–6, *Clod.* 15.5–8, *Aurel.* 5.4, *Max.* 2.1, 3.1–5, 6.8–9, 8.5; cf. Lippold 1991, 251–56, 301–4, 317–32, 371–77; Lendon 1997, 245.

188. Mommsen 1884, 435–37; cf. Lenski 2000, 504 n. 62. A dedication in Salona may mark his posting there while still a Protector Domesticus: *CIL* 3.12900: "[Gr]atiani pr[otectoris / d]omestici / . . . festi." Following *PLRE* I, Vanderspoel 1995, 156 n. 7, misreads *prae]fecti* for the last word and suggests the inscription confirms *Epit.* 45.3: "usque ad praefecturae praetorianae potentiam conscendit." Recourse to *CIL* 3 shows that the editors cautioned against just such a reading.

nus post quem for Gratian's departure.[189] Valentinian would have been seven when his brother was born, old enough to withstand the "Gaetulian swelters" in which Symmachus claimed he was raised, and despite his youth, the opportunity would have given him valuable military experience.[190] Ammianus tells of a *protector domesticus* named Masaucio who was sent to Africa on a sensitive assignment precisely because he had been raised in the province while his father served as count there.[191]

Unfortunately, Gratian's term in Africa ended with his dismissal on suspicion of peculation, and he returned to his native Pannonia, where he bought his estate. This was probably before 337, given that he was back in favor after Constans came to power that year.[192] In the early 330s, though, Gratian experienced a hiatus in his career, which provided him the chance to establish his estate back in Cibalae. His next post, that of count in Britain, probably began in 343, when Constans visited the province in response to raiding along the northern frontier. Constans's visit was brief, and he apparently left Gratian behind with an ad hoc command over comitatensian forces to finish the work of rebuilding fortifications and patrolling the frontier.[193] There is no clue as to whether Valentinian or Valens accompanied their father on this mission. We know only that sometime before 351, Gratian had retired honorably from the army and returned to Pannonia to enjoy his estate, "far from the hubbub."[194] To his misfortune, the civil war between Constantius II and Magnentius that swept through Pannonia that year swept away the family property. Precisely what happened in the decade that followed is a mystery. If Gratian lived to see his sons on the throne, it was not long afterward that he died, because the vicar of Africa dedicated a statue to his *memoria* before late 367.[195]

189. Valens's birthdate in late summer 328 is deduced from AM 31.14.1: "perit autem hoc exitu Valens quinquagesimo anno contiguus, cum per annos quattuor imperasset et decem, parvo minus"; cf. Soc. 4.38.11; Soz. 6.40.5. He actually ruled for fourteen years and five months from March 28, 364, to August 9, 378. Cf. *Epit.* 46.1, thirteen years and five months; Soc. 4.38.11 and Soz. 6.40.5, thirteen years with Valentinian and three years after Valentinian's death.

190. *Or.* 1.2, quoted on p. 48.

191. AM 26.5.14.

192. AM 30.7.3 says that there was a long gap between his service as *comes per Africam* and *comes Britanniae* in 343 (?).

193. See Frere 1987, 225, 337–39; cf. Salway 1981, 351–52; 1993, 245. For the visit of Constans, see Lib. *Or.* 59.139–41; Firm. Mat. *Err. prof. rel.* 28.6; AM 20.1.1 with date from *CTh* 11.16.5 (a. 343). Ammianus's description of Gratian's position is elliptical and confusing. At 30.7.3 he says: "comes praefuit rei castrensi per Africam, unde furtorum suspicione contactus, digressusque multo postea pari potestate Brittanicum rexit exercitum." Ammianus's failure to specify Gratian's exact title in Britain has led to dispute over the origins of the office of *comes Britanniarum* and thus over the earliest date for the permanent posting of comitatensian forces in Britain. See the conflicting arguments of A. H. M. Jones 1964, 124; Hoffman 1969–70, 1: 166–67, 350; Martin 1969, 408–28.

194. AM 30.7.3: "procul a strepitu."

195. *CIL* 3.7014 = *ILS* 758.

Valentinian took after the elder Gratian: Themistius called him the "living image" of his father.[196] Like his father, he had a powerful build and cut a striking figure. Ammianus noted that "his frame was strong and muscular" and that "he was of good height, perfectly well-built and presented a splendid figure of imperial majesty."[197] Like Jovian, he had a healthy appetite,[198] and like Martin, a stubborn irascibility, marking him as a true son of Pannonia. In keeping with the traditions of panegyric, those who wished to praise him took account of his background and personality by making a virtue of his rustic and martial origins. In an epigram to Valentinian and Gratian the Younger, Ausonius has the Danube salute her nurslings:

> I bid the emperors hail, father and son,
> whom I have nurtured amid the weapon-bearing Pannonians.[199]

Symmachus also paid honor to Valentinian's birth and upbringing in his first address to the emperor:

> Gaetulian swelters made you accustomed to summer heat, and Illyrian frosts made you tolerant of winter cold, you who were born into a frigid world and raised in a sunny one.[200]

Valentinian was the product of both Illyrian cold and African heat because, above all, he was the product of the camp.[201] He and his court gladly played to the rhetoric stereotyping his background. In the same speech, Symmachus praised Valentinian for his ability to endure the rugged camp life, and Ammianus confirms that this was more than rhetoric, noting that a rug sufficed for the emperor's tent while he campaigned.[202] In the speech he delivered at the younger Gratian's accession, Valentinian supposedly excused his son's lack of military experience, saying: "[H]e has not, like us, had a harsh up-

196. *Or.* 6.81d: ἔμψυχος εἰκών. For similar comparisons between Constantine and his father, see *Pan. Lat.* 6 [7].4.3–6. On the early career of Valentinian, see *PLRE* I, Flavius Valentinianus 7; Alföldi 1954, 9–12; Nagel, "Vt.," 2159–60; Tomlin 1973, 13–21; Lenski 2000.

197. AM 30.9.6; cf. Zon. 13.15.5: ἰσχὺν γενναιότατος; Theod. *HE* 4.6.1: μεγέθει σώματος διαπρέποντα; Cedrenus, p. 541: ἦν δὲ τῷ σώματι εὐμεγέθης. For the glorification of this type of physique and physiognomy in late imperial art and panegyric, see R. R. Smith 1997.

198. *Epit.* 45.9 says overeating contributed to Valentinian's death as well.

199. Aus. XIII *Epig.* 3 ll. 3–4; cf. XIII *Epig.* 4 l. 4 and XVIII *Cent. Nupt.* ll. 1–11.

200. Symm *Or.* 1.2; cf. 1.1. See the similar praise of Maximianus's Pannonian *patria* at *Pan. Lat.* 10 [2].2.2, 4, 11 [3].3.8–9. The panegyrist was, of course, obliged to praise the origin of the emperor, as Menander Rhetor 2.369 insists. Menander specifies, however, that praise should concentrate on the virtues common to the people of the region and specifically mentions ἀν-δρεῖον as a quality of Gauls and Pannonians.

201. Cf. *Pan. Lat.* 6 [7].4.2 and 12 [2].8.3–5 for similar praise of Constantine's and Theodosius's upbringing in the camps of their fathers.

202. Symm. *Or.* 1.14: "et regalis aula sub pellibus, somnus sub caelo, potus e fluvio, tribunal campo"; AM 29.4.5: "cui tapete . . . suffecerat pro tentorio."

bringing from his very cradle and been inured to the endurance of hardship."[203] Valentinian and his contemporaries thus conspired in the glorification of his Illyrian and by extension his military past.

Valentinian was born in Cibalae in 321.[204] As we have seen, his first taste of military life came in the 320s and 330s, when his father took him to Africa. By 357, he was serving as tribune of a cavalry unit in Gaul.[205] He had come north as one of the 25,000 troops sent by Constantius under the *magister peditum* Barbatio to aid Julian against the Alamanni. Unfortunately for Valentinian, Barbatio was waging an open vendetta with the Caesar, and Valentinian found himself caught in the middle. Barbatio ordered him to stand down from a roadblock Julian had organized against a group of raiders, with the result that they escaped, and Valentinian was blamed for the bungled mission, dismissed, and sent home.[206] This incident was probably at the root of the legend that Julian had persecuted Valentinian for confessing Christianity. The story was apparently propagated by Valentinian and his successors, both to cover up the former tribune's mishap and to glorify him as a defender of the faith. It is first mentioned by Ambrose in a letter of 386 and again in his lament over the death of Valentinian's son, Valentinian II, in 392. In the latter instance, Ambrose describes the prince's entry into heaven, where "[a]lso present is your father, who scorned military service and the honors of the tribunate for love of the faith."[207] Ambrose's vague allusion to the incident dates a generation after the fact, long enough that religion could be offered as a plausible cause for Valentianian's dismissal. In the following century, various historians and epitomators embellished the story and muddled it with bogus details, leaving us with four different accounts of what happened, involving four different military units to which Valentinian was supposedly assigned and four different places where he was supposedly exiled. Ammianus's simplicity is to be preferred: caught in a power play between Julian and Barbatio, Valentinian botched a mission and was discharged.[208]

According to Ammianus, Valentinian's dismissal in 357 was followed by his

203. AM 27.6.8; cf. Them. *Or.* 7.99d: ὑμεῖς οἱ τοῖς ὅπλοις ἐντεθραμμένοι and 6.81b cited p. 283.

204. On Valentinian's birthplace, see AM 30.7.2; Philostorg. 8.16; Soc. 4.1.2; Zos. 3.36.2; Lib. *Or.* 20.25; Jer. *Chron.* s.a. 364. His birthdate can be deduced from AM 30.6.6, which reports that he died on November 18, 375: "aetatis quinquagesimo anno et quinto imperii (minus centum dies) secundus et decimus"; cf. *Epit.* 45.8; cf. Seeck, *Untergang,* 2, 5, 421, 423; Heering 1927, 7.

205. AM 16.11.6–7. Perhaps the Equites Cornuti, named at Philostorg. 7.7, a unit serving in Gaul in 357 (AM 16.11.9). Woods 1995c has recently attempted to flesh out this period in Valentinian's career, not entirely successfully. See Lenski 2002.

206. Cf. AM 30.7.5: "Valentinianus post periculorum molestias plures dum esset privatus emensas." The incident is mentioned at Lib. *Or.* 18.49–51.

207. Ambrose *De obit. Val.* 55; *Ep.* 75[21].3.

208. For extended treatment of the question, see Lenski 2002, which refutes Woods 1995c; 1995a, 32–33, 54; 1997, 281 and Nixon 1998.

return to Pannonia. As noted above, he must still have been in Sirmium around 359, because his son Gratian was born there in that year.[209] He was definitely there in 363 when Jovian came to power. Immediately after his election, Jovian sent envoys to his father-in-law Lucillianus in Sirmium informing him that he had been appointed *magister equitum et peditum* and requesting that he select a few trusted aides and travel west to proclaim the new emperor.[210] One of the confidants Lucillianus chose was Valentinian.[211] Valentinian had thus used the years after he was cashiered to insinuate himself into the good graces of one of the most powerful generals from the region, a man who, like him, was experiencing a lull in his career thanks to Julian. Valentinian had apparently courted other Pannonian notables as well. By the time he left Sirmium as emperor in 364, he must have known many local grandees, because when he returned a decade later, he could rattle off their names as personal friends during an inquest.[212] The years between 357 and 363 would thus have given him ample time to strengthen his Pannonian connections.

Valentinian's military career was, as noted, resurrected through Lucillianus. With Lucillianus, he made the journey west in 363 to proclaim Jovian in Italy and Gaul. When they reached Rheims, in the heart of territory still very much enamored of Julian, they met with serious resistance. An *exactuarius* convinced the Gallic armies that Julian was still alive and provoked them to kill the *magister equitum et peditum*. Valentinian was saved by his host in Rheims, a man named Primitivus, perhaps a friend from Valentinian's tour in Gaul.[213] After the troubles had died down, Valentinian returned east and met the emperor in Tyana. His faithfulness and good fortune on the Gallic mission won him command of a guard unit, the Secunda Schola Scutariorum.[214] He continued with the imperial court to Ancyra, where he was left behind with instructions to follow later.[215] Before he could comply, news reached him that Jovian was dead and that he was the designated successor.

Born seven years after his brother in late summer 328, Flavius Valens was every bit as much a Pannonian as his brother and father. In fact, he and his brother were Pannonian down to their names.[216] "Valens" and its cognates

---

209. See p. 41.

210. AM 25.8.7–10, esp. "monens ut quosdam lectos exploratae industriae fideique duceret secum adminiculis eorum usurus"; cf. Zos. 3.35.1–2, with the cautions mentioned on p. 17.

211. AM 25.10.6–7.

212. AM 30.5.10.

213. AM 25.10.7. The incident is alluded to at Symm. *Or.* 1.6. Julian's forces were stationed at Rheims when Valentinian served under him, AM 16.11.1.

214. AM 25.10.9. For the unit, see *Not. dign. or.* 11.5; *oc.* 9.4. On the Scholae Palatinae, see pp. 15–16.

215. AM 26.1.5.

216. See p. 47 n. 189 on Valens's birth year. On Valens's early career, see Nagl, "Val.," 2097; Tomlin 1973, 56–58.

were among the most common *cognomina* in Illyricum. Inscriptions from the region account for over 70 percent of the instances of the name cited in one empirewide onomastic study.[217] The cognate "Valentinus" is the most frequently occurring *cognomen* on inscriptions from the area around Sirmium, and "Valentinianus" uses a suffix that was also typically Illyrian. "Valens" is apparently a translation of a typically Illyrian name, Licca, meaning something like "strongman."[218] This made it a favorite choice for the sons of soldiers like Valens's father.[219] The *gentilicium* "Flavius" was also commonplace, not just in Illyricum but throughout the fourth-century empire. Beginning under the Flavii Constantini, officers and administrators acquired the name as a function of their imperial service, so that by the late fourth century, it had taken on a blandness akin to the modern "Mr."[220] Any upper-level officeholder, civilian or military, was entitled to use the *gentilicium*. Even so, while it is common on inscriptions and in the headings of official documents, it was rarely used by aristocrats when they referred to themselves or to one another. A man who called himself Flavius Valens was clearly marked as Illyrian, but also as a servant of the Constantinian dynasty.

Although every bit a Pannonian, Valens was in many respects not like his father or brother. He was not a great soldier; he did not grow up in the camp; he was not well built. Ammianus tells us he was pot-bellied, bowlegged, and had a bad eye.[221] There is very little evidence that he was even born in Cibalae.[222] Yet he remained a quintessential Pannonian, even if of a different ilk. In the same way that Gratian and Valentinian were men of the camp,

217. Dean 1916, 54–56. See also the more comprehensive analysis of Mócsy 1985, 94, which demonstrates that "Valens" was only the ninth most popular cognomen in Pannonia, but that its cognate Valentinus was the second. Valens ranked first in Moseia Inferior and Superior and second in Dacia. Cf. Kajanto 1965, 247.

218. Barkóczi 1964, 295, 326. The suffix -*ianus* was particularly common in Pannonia, Moesia, and Dacia; see Mócsy 1985, 45.

219. See Rendić-Miočević 1964, 109–10; Dean 1916, 9. Valens had already been the name of two and possibly three "emperors" in the third and fourth centuries: Iulius Valens Licinianus, Valens [?], and C. Aurelius Valerius Valens; see Kienast 1996, 208, 227, 296.

220. On the "Flaviate," see Bagnall, Cameron, and Schwartz 1987, 36–40; Salway 1994, 137–40. There were, of course, already Flavii Valentes in Illyricum from the first century. Dean 1916, 302–3 lists nine dating from A.D. 134–253. For second-century Flavii around Sirmium, see Barkóczi 1964, 284–85, 326.

221. AM 31.14.7. For portraits of Valens—which reflect his corpulence but not the eye—and of other members of the dynasty, see Delbrueck 1933, 178–99; Floriani Squarciapino 1946–48; 1949–50; Von Sydow 1969, 73–81; Von Heintze 1984; Meischner 1992; 1993; cf. Staesche 1998, 57–58. Valens's obstructed pupil would have constituted a significant deficiency in the mind of contemporaries. Late panegyrists and artists elevated the *fulgor oculorum* to a prominent imperial attribute; cf. R. R. R. Smith 1997, 198–200.

222. In contrast with the numerous sources testifying to Valentinian's birthplace, there are only three confirmations of Valens's: Philostorg. 8.16: ὅτι Οὐαλεντινιανὸν καὶ Οὐάλεντα τὴν

Valens was a man of the country. While his father and brother were campaigning, Valens apparently stayed on the family estate, which accounts for
what Ammianus calls his "rustic nature" (an attribute that the historian uses
to characterize all Pannonians).[223] Any military service Valens saw before 363
was without distinction. Zosimus tells us that empire came as a great shock
to him, because he had led an inactive life before he shouldered its burdens;
Ammianus confirms this, saying that Valens was "schooled in neither military nor liberal disciplines."[224]

Valens's only attested military post before 364 was that of imperial guardsman, *protector domesticus*. Testimony comes in two passages in Socrates and
one in John of Antioch, which claim that Valens, like his brother and indeed
Jovian, suffered at the hands of Julian for confessing the Christian faith while
a guardsman.[225] The story is, as we have seen in the case of Valentinian, suspect, and this naturally calls Valens's service into question. But other indications hint that Valens was indeed in the army prior to 364. He was in Nicomedia on March 1, 364, when his brother appointed him tribune of the
stable.[226] This was too soon after Valentinian's proclamation, five days earlier, for Valens to have made the journey from his home around Sirmium.
Since there was no reason for him to have been in or near this part of Asia
unless he were following the imperial *comitatus,* one can assume that he was
in the army. Valens also seems to have been acquainted with the count of
the *domestici* Dagalaifus, who knew him well enough to question his qualifications for empire from the outset of his brother's rule.[227] It is thus likely that
Socrates and John of Antioch were right. Indeed, of all the accounts on the
confession of the future emperors, the tradition reported by these two seems
closest to some reality. Valens and even Jovian—although not Valentinian—
seem to have resisted an order by Julian to sacrifice in Antioch, without, however, suffering serious consequences.[228]

If we accept that Valens was indeed a *protector domesticus,* we might speculate that he was recruited in 359, when Constantius, then at Sirmium, was
mustering huge numbers of troops in preparation for an eastern expedi-

---

Κίβαλιν λαχεῖν ἀναγράφει πατρίδα; Jord. *Rom.* 307: "nam Pannones erant Cibalenses utrimque
germani"; Lib. *Or.* 20.25: τοῖν ἀδελφοῖν οἷς πόλις ἡ Κίβαλις ὁ νεώτερος. Cf. Lib. *Or.* 19.15:
τοῖν Παιόνοιν; *Or.* 46.30: ὁ Παίων Βασιλεύς.

223. See pp. 86–87.

224. Zos. 4.4.1: πρότερον μὲν ἀπράγμονα τρίψαντα βίον ἄφνω δὲ βασιλείαν παραλαβόντα καὶ
τὸν τῶν πραγμάτων ὄγκον οὐ φέροντα; AM 31.14.5: "nec bellicis nec liberalibus studiis eruditus."

225. Soc. 3.13.3–4, 4.1.8; Joh. Ant. fr. 179.

226. AM 26.4.2. Theod. *HE* 4.6.3 states directly that Valentinian sent to Pannonia for Valens,
but his account here is probably, as often, unreliable.

227. AM 26.4.1; see p. 23.

228. See Lenski 2002 for further arguments.

tion.[229] This would explain both the testimony that Valens had little military experience—four and a half years—and the implication that he was with the eastern army in early March 364. It certainly seems reasonable that Gratian could have helped Valens to win a place in his old unit. The sons of veterans were in any case legally obliged to serve, but influential fathers could lighten the burden by winning fashionable positions for their children.[230] If Valens was so fortunate, he is unlikely to have survived Julian's cuts in the guard corps in 362. Even so, dismissal from the guards would not have meant expulsion from the army. In fact, neither John of Antioch nor Socrates say that Valens was expelled for confessing the faith. Julian had a war to fight, and every available man was retained. Later, Valens and his court probably glossed this demotion as the outcome of his defense of the faith. Ultimately, it was simply a demotion.

At some point, Valens married a soldier's daughter named Domnica. She bore him three children, two daughters, Anastasia and Carosa, and a son, whom Valens named after his brother. We have no *terminus post quem* for the date of the marriage nor any evidence for the birth dates of the daughters, although the boy is known to have been born in 366.[231] We can assume that Valens was married before he took the throne, because he appointed his father-in-law, an ex-legionary commander named Petronius, to the rank of *patricius* at the start of his reign. Domnica was a Christian and, like Valens, an "Arian."[232] A few fourth-century inscriptions indicate that Christians named Petronia, Petronilla, and Petronius lived in Sirmium.[233] Since the names are not typical of Pannonia, it is tempting to associate Domnica's family with these Sirmians. Valentinian certainly had connections in that city, and, as we have seen, there is reason to suspect that he may have moved there after the loss of Gratian's estate. Valens may have as well. Domnica outlived her husband, and she is mentioned as alive by Chrysostom still in 381.[234] She had come a long way from soldier's daughter to empress, but she never lost touch with her family's military background. After Valens's death at Adrianople, we meet her distributing arms to volunteers in Constantinople to help defend the city against the Goths.[235]

Although he had been compelled to service, Valens's heart was on the farm. He probably never forgot Constantius's appropriation of his family's estate. Ammianus's obituary of him is hardly glittering, but the one virtue

229. AM 19.11.17; cf. 20.8.1. On Constantius's presence in Sirmium, see Seeck, *Regesten*, 206.
230. Valentinian and Valens were certainly aware of the phenomenon and did little to discourage it; see *CTh* 6.24.2–3; cf. 6.23.3–6, 7.21.1–3, with Mommsen 1884, 438.
231. On the boy, see p. 91. On the daughters, see *PLRE* I, Anastasia 2; Carosa.
232. See pp. 241 and 243–44.
233. *CIL* 3.9576, 14304, 14622.
234. Joh. Chrys. *Ad vid. iun.* 4.
235. Soc. 5.1.3; Soz. 7.1.2; Theoph. a.m. 5870; Jord. *Rom.* 314.

that he extols unreservedly in Valens is his dedication to fair administration: "[H]e was an extremely just guardian of the provinces, each of which he kept free from harm as if it were his own household."[236] Themistius understood perfectly why Valens was so solicitous of landholders. In 368, he explained that Valens's generous tax relief measures were rooted in the emperor's past:

> Shall I tell you the reason for this? It is because you had charge of a household before a palace and transferred your experience from the lesser to the greater field. [They say] . . . one should first hold the oar before taking the helm in hand. But there is no need for you to seek men to teach you with how much sweat farmers earn a *hemiekton*, an *amphiekton*, and an *amphoreus*, a single bronze coin or a stater of silver or—what most men dearly love to see—of gold.[237]

The orator goes on to compare Valens to "Numa"—a mistake for Cincinnatus— whom "the Roman senate snatched from his team as he ploughed in his shirt and clothed in the purple." As we shall see in chapter 6, this agricultural expertise gave Valens distinct advantages when it came to managing the empire.

Valentinian had this in mind when he awarded his brother the post of tribune of the stable. It has been argued that this job was little more than a sinecure. Eight *tribuni* or *comites stabuli* are securely attested for the fourth century. Four of these were under the Valentiniani, and three were somehow connected with the family: Valens was the first, followed by Cerealis and Constantianus, brothers of Valentinian's second wife, Justina.[238] These fairly clear-cut cases of nepotism have led to speculation that the only qualification one needed to be *tribunus stabuli* was the right family.[239] Yet *tribuni stabuli* were charged with important responsibilities. They ranked with the tribunes of the Scholae Palatinae and had regular contact with these.[240] This meant that *tribuni stabuli* were at the emperor's side in peace and war—at least two were slain in the line of duty in the fourth century.[241] They were also charged with overseeing the collection of horses not only for the imperial court but for the entire cavalry. If nothing else then, a *tribunus stabuli* had to know something about horses.[242]

---

236. AM 31.14.2; cf. *Epit.* 46.3: "fuit possessoribus consultor bonus." See pp. 283–84.

237. Them. *Or.* 8.113d–114b. In his first address to the Constantinopolitan Senate, Valens apparently played up his own agricultural and martial experience; cf. Them. *Or.* 6.81b.

238. *PLRE* I, Cerealis 1; Constantianus 1; cf. Scharf 1990, 144–47.

239. A. H. M. Jones 1964, 625–26; Tomlin 1973, 56, 75. The case of Stilicho, appointed *comes stabuli* around the time he married Theodosius's niece Serena, would seem to confirm this (*PLRE* I, Flavius Stilicho).

240. E.g., AM 20.2.5, 4.3, 5.1; Jul. *Ep. ad Ath.* 282d; cf. Scharf 1990, 142–44.

241. AM 28.2.10, 31.13.18.

242. A. H. M. Jones 1964, 372, 625–26. If, as Milner 1993, xxii–xxv argues, Vegetius held the post—upgraded to *comes Stabuli*—he must have had real equestrian expertise, because he composed a *De mulomedicina*. The same had already been suggested by Goffart 1977; cf. Scharf 1990.

Valens, and indeed Valentinian, apparently did. From the beginning of their administration, they overhauled the levying of horses from the provinces, and Valens later refined the process even further. He also divided the province of Cappadocia to rein in control of the imperial horse ranches there.[243] A quaint passage from Theodoret even tells us that Valens had a favorite horse, which, when it fell ill with a urinary problem, caused great grief to the emperor. Valens's *tribunus stabuli* summoned veterinarians, and when these failed to cure the beast, he was forced to pay a secret visit to the Nicene ascetic Aphraates, who effected a miraculous cure. When Valens learned of this during his regular visit to the stable that evening, he was too elated to attack his officer for consulting the troublesome monk.[244] Of course, none of this proves that Valens had raised horses, but it would not be surprising if he had. Pannonia was after all rich in *iumenta*, as the *Expositio totius mundi* reveals.[245] Illyricum was famous for producing cavalry detachments in the fourth century, and Valentinian himself served in a cavalry unit of the palatine guards.[246] Some Pannonian *villae*, most notably Parndorf, played host to horse breeders, and the Sevso platter, whose inscription is translated above, prominently features a prize horse.[247] The evidence is not conclusive, but it points in a general direction. Themistius tells us certainly that Valens had experience as an estate manager, and other evidence may pinpoint his expertise even further as an equestrian specialist.

Valens and Valentinian were thus products of their background. Pannonia, "strong in men and prosperous in land," had nursed the one to be a soldier and the other to be a farmer. Valentinian, like his father, had experienced the ups and downs of imperial military service, for which his very fiber seemed to have been formed. Ultimately, it was this service that carried him to the throne. Valens, by contrast, had only served under compulsion and without great success. His strength was in the management of land, and he would put this to good use when he took control of the east. Unfortunately, his rustic background was not quite adequate to empire. The virtues required of an emperor were many, and the very rural simplicity that was his strong suit would prove a liability when he faced the urbane refinement of the eastern aristocracy and the hazardous complications of imperial rule.

243. See p. 285.

244. Theod. *HR* 8.11–12, esp.: κατὰ τοῦτον γὰρ ὁ βασιλεὺς τὸν καιρὸν εἰώθει παρὰ τὸν ἱππῶνα φοιτᾶν. Valentinian himself displayed marked sympathy for retired racehorses (*CTh* 15.10.1; cf. Aus. XIII *Epig.* 7). On imperial horse obssession, see Staesche 1998, 194–98.

245. *Exp. tot. mun.* 57. Constantius deliberately chose the plain north of Cibalae for battle with Magnentius because its open terrain favored his cavalry forces; cf. Zos. 2.48.3.

246. On Illyrian cavalry, see Claud. *Carm. min.* 30.61–62: "dat Gallia robur / militis, Illyricis sudant equitibus alae."

247. On Parndorf, see Saria 1966, 268. On Sevso, see p. 39.

THE IMPERIAL COURTS: ILLYRIANS AND PROFESSIONALS

When Julian went east in 361, Valentinian was only one of a host of Illyrians whom the brash new emperor had dismissed or kept from office. We have seen that the casualties also included Jovian's father, Varronian, and his father-in-law, Lucillianus.[248] Marcellus, another Illyrian who had served as *magister equitum et peditum* in Gaul during the first year of Julian's residence there, had also provoked the Caesar's wrath and was eventually sent home to Serdica.[249] Nor had this extinguished Julian's animosity toward Marcellus, for once he became Augustus, he targeted the ex-general's son and executed him for conspiracy.[250] Serenianus, another Illyrian who, like Lucillianus, was implicated in the murder of Julian's half-brother Gallus, was also being held in "retirement" when Jovian came to power.[251] Many Illyrians had been kept down under Julian, and these men had cause to rejoice when the Apostate was replaced by a ruler of their own stock.

Their sense of optimism was not ill-founded. As we would expect, Jovian quickly began appointing his fellow countrymen to positions of power.[252] Some of these were relatives, men like Lucillianus and another in-law named Ianuarius—both given military commands—and Jovian's own son, Varronian, consul in 364.[253] It is probable that Jovian also appointed the Pannonian Viventius of Siscia as his *quaestor* and almost certain that he named Ursacius, a Dalmatian, to the key post of *magister officiorum*.[254] Both positions were extremely close to the emperor, the one controlling the drafting of constitutions, the other coordinating the various palatine offices and access to

---

248. See p. 16. See also the prosopographical analysis of Valens's reign at Tritle 1994.

249. *PLRE* I, Marcellus 3, with Woods 1995b.

250. AM 22.11.2; Eunap. *Hist.* fr. 25.5 (Blockley) = Suid. *Σ* 63.

251. *PLRE* I, Serenianus 2, esp. AM 26.5.3

252. Them. *Or.* 5.67a–b praises Jovian's restoration of those who had been out of favor; cf. Vanderspoel 1995, 147. Nor was it only Illyrians who experienced better treatment under Jovian, Valentinian, and Valens than under Julian. Compare the careers of *PLRE* I, Flavius Saturninus 10, Florentius 3 (to be identified with Florentius 5), Lupicinus 6, Nebridius 1, Romanus 2 (to be identified with Romanus 3), Vincentius 3 (to be identified with Vincentius 4), and Vitalius. *PLRE* I, Flavius Taurus 3, who had been exiled by Julian, was not given an office but was honored posthumously with a gold statue in the Roman forum in the first years of Valentinian's and Valens's reign (*AE* 1934, 159).

253. On Ianuarius, see *PLRE* I, Ianuarius 5, citing AM 26.1.4–5.

254. *PLRE* I, Viventius and Ursacius 3, to which add Himerius *Or.* 23.5; cf. Barnes 1987, 214–15. It is not certain that either was appointed under Jovian. Ursacius is first attested as *magister officiorum* under Valentinian and Valens in early 364 (AM 26.4.4) but was probably appointed by Jovian to replace Julian's *magister officiorum*, Anatolius, who had died in Persia (AM 25.3.14, 21; Zos. 3.29.3). Viventius is also first attested in office at AM 26.4.4 (a. 364). He replaced Iovius, who was last attested as *quaestor* by a law of March 362 (*CTh* 11.39.5) and was certainly urban prefect of Constantinople by March of 364 (*CTh* 14.17.1); cf. Tomlin 1973, 25.

them.[255] With these two installed at the gates of power, it is little wonder that Illyrians soon began to populate high offices.

As we might expect, with the installation of Valentinian and Valens, this new tide from the Balkans continued to rise. We have already seen that when Jovian expired, three more Illyrians were on the short list to fill his position, Aequitius, Ianuarius—just mentioned—and Valentinian.[256] When Valentinian was selected, the same Aequitius, who knew Valentinian as a fellow *scutarius* (guardsman), and another Pannonian, the *numerarius* (accountant) Leo, quickly stepped in "as Pannonians and supporters of the emperor designate" to secure approval for Valentinian from the troops in Nicaea.[257] Both were duly rewarded, Leo with a promotion to *notarius* (stenographer) and later *magister officiorum* and Aequitius with command of the troops in Illyricum.[258] Valentinian also retained the Illyrians Viventius and Ursacius in the posts Jovian had assigned them, *quaestor* and *magister officiorum*. He later promoted Viventius to urban prefect of Rome and praetorian prefect of Gaul. Viventius's nephew Faustinus was also given a post under Valentinian as a *notarius*.[259] From the very beginning, then, Valentinian enlisted a considerable crop of compatriots to serve his administration.

The trend continued when, in the late spring of 364, Valentinian and Valens marched all the way to Sirmium to apportion the empire and its administrators between them. To be sure, Sirmium had also hosted the division of empire between the sons of Constantine, if for nothing else than because it constituted the center point on the east-west axis of the empire. But Valentinian and Valens apparently chose it as the locus for their own imperial division, largely in order to recruit compatriots to their service. It made sense to surround oneself with men one knew and could trust, who shared a common background and value system. Jovian had hoped for the same reason to reach his home in Illyricum in the first year of his rule, and Theodosius would similarly take an entourage of Nicene Spaniards east with him after his election in 379.[260] Thus, beginning in 364, Illyrian administrators began to crop up in unusual places all across the empire.[261]

In the west, these administrators stood out most clearly against the land-

255. On the *quaestor*, see A. H. M. Jones 1964, 504–5; Honoré 1986, 189–216; Harries 1988. On the *magister officiorum*, see A. H. M. Jones 1964, 368–69, 575–84; Clauss 1981.

256. AM 26.1.4–5.

257. AM 26.1.6: "ut Pannonii fautoresque principis designati." With Aequitius came Gaudentius, a man whose origins are unknown but who had also served in the Scutarii and thus befriended Valentinian, AM 26.5.14.

258. *PLRE* I, Leo 1, with Clauss 1981, 165–66; Flavius Equitius 2.

259. *PLRE* I, Faustinus 3.

260. Matthews 1967; 1975, 94–96, 108–15.

261. Alföldi 1952, 13–27; Matthews 1975, 32–55.

scape of Italy, which had generally been dominated by Italian aristocrats.[262] For example, some time in the first year of Valentinian's administration, the Pannonian Maximinus of Sopianae was appointed to the governorship of Corsica.[263] Over the next five years, he continued to climb the ladder of office as governor of Sardinia, governor of the senatorial province of Tuscia, prefect of the Roman grain supply, vicar of Rome, and, eventually, praetorian prefect of Gaul, where his tenure lasted through the end of the reign. These were no small achievements for a man of "the most insignificant birth" whose father, of barbarian descent, had been a mere secretary in the office of the governor of Valeria.[264] Maximinus brought with him Illyrian friends and family. During his tenure in Rome, he secured marriage into a senatorial family for his son, Marcellianus, and later won the post of duke of Valeria for the young man.[265] In addition, a certain Valentinianus, no relation to the emperor but rather a brother-in-law of Maximinus, was appointed consular governor of Picenum.[266]

Maximinus apparently also initiated into Italian politics another Pannonian, Leo, the same man whose canvassing had helped hold down the throne for Valentinian in 364. When Valentinian promoted Maximinus to vicar of Rome, Leo was dispatched to assist him, and he was later appointed *magister officiorum* from 371 until 376. By 375, he was powerful enough to make a bid, albeit unsuccessful, to snatch the praetorian prefecture of Italy, Illyricum, and Africa from the senatorial grandee Petronius Probus.[267] The fact that Leo had been seconded to Maximinus in Rome, that he later moved to Trier around the same time as Maximinus, and that he held his post as master of the offices for almost the same tenure that Maximinus was praetorian prefect implies that the two enjoyed a bond of friendship.[268] This they shared with another man from the region, Simplicius of Emona (Ljubljana), just west of the Pannonian border. Simplicius's association with Maximinus

262. Matthews 1975, 39; Chastagnol 1982, 186.

263. *PLRE* I, Maximinus 7, with revisions suggested at Barnes 1998, 241–43.

264. AM 28.1.5. To replace Maximinus as vicar of Rome, Valentinian appointed *PLRE* I's Ursicinus 6. Although there is no proof that Ursicinus was Illyrian, his name is typical of the region (Mócsy 1985, 63), and Valentinian seems to have had a propensity for promoting Illyrian vicars of Rome in the 370s. *PLRE*'s Paulus Constantius 11, Valentinian's *proconsularis Africae* in 374, may also have been Illyrian, given that he was buried at Salona (*CIL* 3.9506 = *ILS* 1287).

265. AM 28.1.34–35 with *PLRE* I Marcellianus 2. The son married the stepdaughter of Maximinus's friend *PLRE* I Victorinus 5, the daughter of *PLRE* I Anepsia (which misprints Maximinus as the name of the bridegroom).

266. The identification between the *consularis Piceni*, *PLRE* I, Valentinianus 2, and the rebel, *PLRE* I, Valentinus 5 (*Maximini coniugis frater*), is plausibly conjectured at Demandt 1972, 90, and Matthews 1975, 38 n. 6, the former of whom correctly identifies the correct spelling of the name.

267. AM 30.5.10, with *PLRE* I, Leo 1.

268. Ammianus frequently associates the two (28.1.12, 41, 30.2.10–11).

dated at least to the first years of the new administration when he served as Maximinus's *consiliarius*. It may have gone back even further if it was Simplicius, a former *grammaticus*, who provided Maximinus with the "moderate study of liberal learning" that Ammianus ascribes to him.[269] Simplicius's career included the governorship of Numidia Constantina and the vicariate of Rome, positions normally reserved for Roman senatorials. The western court was thus not wanting for men from the region of Valentinian's birth.

This is not, however, to say that there was an ironclad contingent of Illyrians. Maximinus, for example, won his son's appointment as duke of Valeria by carping at his fellow Pannonian, Aequitius.[270] Leo's bid for the praetorian prefecture was eventually dismissed by Valentinian.[271] Faustinus, the nephew of the prefect Viventius, was executed at Carnuntum for magic in 375, and Maximinus's in-law Valentinianus faced exile to Britain and later execution when he raised a revolt there.[272] Such incidents clearly demonstrate that there was never a seamless Illyrian front; such were not the terms of fourth-century politics. Any imperial appointment was precarious, and one could fall from favor as fast as one had gained it. More important, there is no evidence that Valentinian walled himself in with Illyrians in the first place. Rather, he introduced a number of men from his homeland into positions they might not otherwise have enjoyed. In so doing, he changed the quality of western government, in some places profoundly, in others very little.

If it is difficult to speak of an "Illyrian front" in the western empire, it is even more so in the case of the east. There are simply fewer known Illyrians in the eastern administration.[273] Here again, this comes as no surprise. The part of the east that Valens controlled constituted only one of the three praetorian prefectures common in the fourth century, and it was the one where Illyrians, as Latin speakers, were of least use. Furthermore, with the exception of Constantinople, the east had its own traditions of local and regional office-holding, which were not as pliant to the introduction of outsiders as were those in regions like Gaul or Spain. Finally, if we are to believe Ammi-

---

269. AM 28.1.45: "Maximini consiliarius ex grammatico"; 28.1.52: "et consiliario suo et amico," with AM 28.1.6: "mediocre studium liberalium doctrinarum"; cf. 28.1.46. See also Tomlin 1973, 263–65, on the relationship between Maximinus, Simplicius, and Leo.

270. AM 29.6.3. Aequitius's career did not, however, suffer a setback, for he remained in office at least until Valentinian's death in 375 (see AM 30.6.2; *Epit.* 45.10; Zos. 4.19.1).

271. AM 30.5.10. Probus remained praetorian prefect after the incident (AM 30.5.4, 11) and until after Valentinian's death (see Ruf. *HE* 2.12; Tomlin 1973, 39 n. 47).

272. On Faustinus, see AM 30.5.11–12. On Valentinianus, see AM 28.3.4–6, 30.7.10; Jer. *Chron.* s.a. 371, misdated for 369; Zos. 4.12.2; Jord. *Rom.* 308.

273. Tomlin 1973, 63–65. Contrast Alföldi 1952, 17: "If men from Pannonia and the neighboring lands swarmed round Valentinian, such friends and relatives seem to have been present in even greater numbers in the entourage of Valens," an unsupported pronouncement that is patently wrong.

anus, Valens was attentive and eager to ensure that people should not win promotions because of their "relations" (*propinquitas*).[274]

This last statement seems odd, given the evidence. Although few Pannonians are registered in Valens's court, most of those we know of were his relatives. Ammianus tells us that a certain Aequitius, Valens's *cura palatii* in 378, was "related" (*propinquus*) to the emperor, probably by blood.[275] We can also document a concentration of officials drawn from the family of Valens's wife, Domnica. Her father, Petronius, although never assigned to an official post, was granted the title *patricius* early on and placed in charge of important operations.[276] Ammianus has it that Petronius was also at the center of a larger *factio* that engineered the replacement of Julian's comrade Sallustius Secundus as praetorian prefect in the late summer of 365.[277] We might suspect that this group consisted largely of Pannonians, although proof is lacking. Petronius was an old soldier, an ugly man with a disposition to match his appearance and a love of money unrivaled by his son-in-law. Unfortunately, his personality made the ex-tribune a liability, and his harsh exactions at the beginning of the reign set the stage for the revolt of the usurper Procopius. In its aftermath, Valens was forced to diminish his father-in-law's role.[278] Even so, Petronius's family was not entirely removed from the circle of power. In the 370s, a man named Eusebius, who was serving as the vicar of Pontica, attempted to have Basil of Caesarea flogged. A late commentator claims that he was the uncle of Valens's wife, Domnica.[279] Perhaps another in-law finds mention in Libanius, who refers to a Domnicus among a group of Valens's officers, whose visits he was at pains to avoid in the 370s.[280] Yet another relative by marriage, a different Procopius, was apparently prefect of the city of Constantinople in 377 and remained in the political limelight into the

274. AM 31.14.2: "pervigil et anxius semper ne quis propinquitatem praetendens altius semet efferret." The same is said of Valentinian, AM 30.9.2; cf. Tomlin 1973, 270.

275. AM 31.12.15. He died at Adrianople (AM 31.13.18). For *propinquus* as "kinsman," see *OLD* s.v. *propinquus* 4.

276. AM 26.6.7: "socer Petronius, ex praeposito Martensium militum, promotus repentino saltu patricius, animo deformis et habitu." He is attested as *patricius* from at least April 365 (*CTh* 7.22.7), although one can assume from "repentino saltu" that the title was probably granted a year earlier. On his position in the Martenses, see Hoffmann 1969–70, 1: 356–57. From the reign of Constantine, the title *patricius* had been used to distinguish the nearest friends of the emperor and highest officials of his court; cf. Enßlin 1934; A. H. M. Jones 1964, 106, 528, 534, 1225 n. 28; Piganiol 1972, 346–47.

277. AM 26.7.4.

278. Petronius's role was reduced at the same time that Valens called Sallustius back into office, perhaps as early as summer 366; see p. 106.

279. The incident is mentioned at Greg. Naz. *Or.* 43.55–57. The commentator Nicetas of Serra provided the name of the governor and his relation to Domnica; see Prunaeus 1571, *Or. XXX In laudem Basilii* p. 522 n. 77. Cf. *PLRE* I, Eusebius 19.

280. Lib. *Or.* 2.9 (a. 381).

390s.[281] Despite Petronius's early setback, then, his family retained some influence.[282] Given this, we must concede that Valens was not entirely innocent of appointing people based on *propinquitas*. But Ammianus was also not entirely wrong to assert that he avoided nepotism. With the exception of Petronius and the prefect Procopius, none of Valens's relations was assigned a particularly powerful post, and even Petronius did not hold an actual office. The others of whom we know held jobs in the middle or lower ranks of the imperial bureaucracy. This is neither unusual nor disturbing. Not even the emperor was above taking care of family;[283] on the contrary, as Valentinian considered when he made his brother Valens Augustus, family could be trusted.

The same was true of fellow countrymen more broadly. Like Valentinian, Valens was naturally eager to enlist compatriots. His first count of the *domestici*, the Pannonian Serenianus, appealed to Valens precisely "because of his similarity of character and common homeland."[284] Another local, Flavianus, prefect of Egypt from 364 until 366, stands out as the only Illyrian known to have held the Egyptian prefecture since before Constantine.[285] Valens's confidant Festus of Tridentum (Trent), although not of Pannonian descent, might also be listed among the circle. He had served with Valentinian's henchman Maximinus in the office of the praetorian prefect at Sirmium.[286] And Festus apparently brought with him another Tridentine, Fidelius, who served with him in Syria as well.[287] These, together with the relatives listed above, formed a notable, although far from overwhelming, coterie from the area around Pannonia.

Nevertheless, with the exception of these and a few other westerners,[288]

---

281. *PLRE* I, Procopius 9, referring to Zos. 5.9.3–5: τοῦ μὲν βασιλέως ... Οὐάλεντος κηδεστής. Seeck, *Briefe*, 247 argues that the Procopius mentioned in Zosimus is probably to be associated with the Procopius of *CJ* 12.1.11 of 377, apparently addressed to a an urban prefect of Constantinople (= *PLRE* I, Procopius 5). This Procopius is possibly also to be identified with *PLRE* I, Procopius 6, mentioned at Greg. Naz. *Epp.* 129, 130 (a. 382) in a post that might be the *vicarius Ponticae;* cf. Hauser-Meury 1960, s.v. Procopius II.

282. The predominance of Greek names in the family—Domnicus(a), Petronius, Eusebius, Procopius, and Valens's daughter Anastasia—may imply that it numbered among the Greek-speaking Christian families common in fourth-century Sirmium; cf. Barkóczi 1964, 285; Balla 1989. If Valens had married into a Greek family, it would have added to his qualifications for eastern rule and would help to explain why so many of his in-laws held eastern posts.

283. Valentinian also appointed his in-laws Cerealis and Constantianus, not to mention his brother, to the post of *tribunus stabuli;* see p. 54. Cf. Julian's praise at *Or.* 2.116a–c of Eusebia for finding positions for her relatives.

284. AM 26.10.2: "ob similitudinem morum et genitalis patriae vicinitatem."

285. *PLRE* I, Flavianus 3.

286. *PLRE* I, Festus 3; AM 29.2.22: "in nexum germanitatis a Maximino dilectus ut sodalis et contogatus." Cf. Tomlin 1973, 264.

287. *PLRE* I, Fidelius, with Lib. *Or.* 1.163: ἦν μὲν Φήστου πολίτης.

288. There were also two Italians (*PLRE* I, Nebridius 1 and Auxonius 1) and two Gauls who had come east with Julian in 361 (*PLRE* I, Saturninius Salutius Secundus 3 and Theodorus 13).

Valens's court was largely run by men from the east. Valens's provincial governors were, as we would expect, largely of eastern origin, and, because Valens never returned to the west after 364, his palatine officials were drawn increasingly from the east as well. This meant that, with the passing of time, the eastern emperor became increasingly isolated in his own empire. Given that, as we shall see, he did not speak Greek, he was dependent on bilingual staff to communicate with his own government, and these tended to be native Latin speakers from the west. As a result of the Procopius revolt in 365–66, he lost his two closest Pannonian aides, his father-in-law Petronius and his Pannonian *comes domesticorum*, Serenianus. As time passed and further westerners fell away, Valens must have felt even more isolated. This sense of isolation probably helped push him to focus elsewhere for allies.

These he found in the tight circle of professional bureaucrats he used to fill important offices in the latter part of his reign. The most striking thing about this group is not just that most were bureaucrats, rather than aristocrats, but that all held office for unusually long tenures. The proconsulship of Asia, for example, a post that had often crowned the career of eastern aristocrats, was tied down from 366 until 378 by just three of Valens's men, two of them bureaucrats and one of these a westerner of low birth.[289] Valens's *magister officiorum* Sophronius held his post from 369 until 378;[290] the *comes rei privatae* (count of the imperial privy purse) Fortunatianus remained in office from 370 until 377; and the praetorian prefect Domitius Modestus kept his office from 370 until 377.[291] Similarly, the bureaucrat Flavius Eutolmius Tatianus held a continuous string of offices from 367 until after Valens's death in 378, including a combined post that simultaneously occupied the positions of consular governor of Syria and *comes orientis* (count of the east) in the early 370s. His tenure as *comes sacrarum largitionum* (count of the imperial treasury) lasted through the last four years of Valens's reign.[292] Tatianus's friend Aburgius would also have been the subject of envy,

289. For Clearchus, Eutropius, and Festus, see Malcus 1967, 109–16. Clearchus's dates as *proconsul Asiae* are uncertain. *PLRE* is mistaken in associating Clearchus with the proconsul (Anonymus 44) mentioned at Eunap. *Hist.* fr. 29.2 (Blockley), which it misdates from 363 to 367/68; cf. Blockley 1981–83, 2: 137 n. 69. On the importance of the proconsular governorship of Asia in the senatorial careers of eastern aristocrats, see Malcus 1967, 143–54; Chastagnol 1982, 181–82.

290. *PLRE* I, Sophronius 3, with Clauss 1981, 190–1.

291. *PLRE* I, Fortunatianus 1; cf. Delmaire 1989, 57–59. *PLRE* I, Domitius Modestus 2, is surely wrong to move Modestus's appointment as praetorian prefect to August 369 on the strength of an emendation to *CTh* 11.30.35. Modestus was in fact urban prefect of Constantinople at the time, as *Cons. Consp.* s.a. 369 reveals. On this question, see Dagron 1974, 246; Pergami 1993, 476–77, 516–17; Errington 2000, 902–3.

292. *PLRE* I, Fl. Eutolmius Tatianus 5; cf. Delmaire 1989, 62–67; Roueché 1989, 50–52. Compare the western senatorial *PLRE* I, Sex. Claudius Petronius Probus 5, who tied up key offices in a similar fashion.

given that he seems to have served as *quaestor* from 369 until 374.[293] Thus between Sophronius, Fortunatianus, Modestus, Tatianus, and Aburgius, Valens filled his top five palatine offices with the same five men for most of the latter half of his reign.[294]

Indeed, both Valentinian and Valens were notorious among contemporaries for retaining officials for long tenures. Ammianus called the latter "excessively slow in proffering and taking away offices."[295] Indeed for Valens, the restriction of access to office seems to have been a matter of stated policy. In this vein Themistius trumpeted:

> It is for this reason that you have brought about a dearth of office seekers; now no market for offices is open, nor are governorships announced for sale like market goods, but the ancient dignity has returned to justice and experience. And if anyone is found to possess these qualities, he will have no need to petition for codicils of appointment but will serve the common good even against his inclination.[296]

Although the orator lauded Valens's circumspection, office seekers would have been less quick to praise, especially because this slowness to shuffle replacements into the administration was part of a broader trend that favored professional bureaucrats and soldiers over arisocrats.[297] To be sure, some measure of efficiency was gained, but those of senatorial background, who expected high office almost as a birthright, would have been downright indignant. Valentinian and Valens gummed up the patronage machine and in so doing won the wrath of the traditional elite.

Undaunted by aristocratic discomfiture, Valentinian imposed on Rome a series of nonsenatorial urban prefects and vicars who dominated these strongholds of the senatorial career.[298] He and Valens also reserved the consulship for themselves, their sons, and their generals, excepting one western sena-

---

293. *PLRE* I, Aburgius. Aburgius's exact title and the dates of his administration are not certain; cf. Delmaire 1989, 61–62. Pergami 1993, xxxii, even questions whether Valens had a *quaestor*, which seems unnecessarily speculative.

294. Haehling 1978, 561, points out that Valens and Arcadius ruled the east for the same number of years, but that whereas fifty-five holders of high office are known under Arcadius, only thirty-nine are known under Valens, despite the fact that the sources for Valens's reign are far better; see ibid. 557 on the same trend under Valentinian, and see also Clauss 1981, 108–9. Under most fourth-century emperors, offices were normally held for much shorter tenures (Kelly 1998, 153; Heather 1998, 195–96).

295. AM 31.14.2; cf. *Epit.* 46.3: "mutare iudices rarius."

296. Them. *Or.* 8.117a–b.

297. For laws favoring imperial bureaucrats, see *CTh* 6.35.1, 7–8; *CTh* 8.1.11 = *CJ* 12.49.3; *CTh* 8.4.11 = *CJ* 12.57.3; *CTh* 9.40.11, 12.1.74.

298. See Chastagnol 1962, 159–94, nos. 66–76, with the cautions of Barnes 1998, 237–40. Matthews 1975, 15–17, describes how tight a hold the senatorial aristocracy normally maintained on the urban prefecture.

tor, Petronius Probus in 371, and one eastern bureaucrat, Modestus in 372.[299] Aristocratic resentment would also have been aroused when Valentinian and Valens enacted a law in 372 to equate high-ranking bureaucratic and military officials with their senatorial counterparts. *Magistri militum* and praetorian prefects were equalized in status with the prefect of Rome and the top four palatine posts, together with the *comites rei militaris,* were ranked above senatorial proconsuls.[300] Even military *duces* were granted senatorial status as *clarissimi.*[301] None of these measures would have sat well with an elite anxious to preserve its status by monopolizing offices and honors.

The senatorial elite felt particularly threatened by a notoriously ambitious group of climbers, the lawyers. The primary springboard for launching a lawyer's career in the imperial service was the legal office of the *sacra scrinia,* especially the key position of the *magister memoriae* and the related post of *quaestor* in the consistory. These jobs required juristic knowledge, which was best sought among bureaucrats, and, though emperors did not always look to such bureaucrats, Valentinian and Valens usually did. Because the holders of these posts acted as mouthpieces of imperial policy, they often won both rank and influence quickly. Indeed, many professionals appointed by Valentinian and Valens, usually men of modest provincial backgrounds, experienced meteoric rises.[302] Under Valentinian, for example, the Mauretanian lawyer Eupraxius went from *magister memoriae* to *quaestor,* to urban prefect of Rome.[303] Sextius Rusticus Julianus, a new man from Gaul, began his career as *magister memoriae* and went on to enjoy prestigious senatorial posts as proconsul of Africa and, after Valentinian's reign, urban prefect. In the process, he amassed wealth enough to make him the equal of the Roman elite, but he could never escape the censure of elitists like Ammianus.[304] The most obvious example

---

299. Bagnall et al. 1987, 264–91. The emperor's regular assumption of the consulship in quinquennial years was of course normal; see Burgess 1988, esp. 84.

300. *CTh* 6.7.1 + 9.1 + 11.1 + 14.1 + 22.4, all part of the same original constitution of 372; cf. *CTh* 12.7.3 and 6.5.2 = *CJ* 12.8.1. Symm. *Or.* 1.23 and Them. *Or.* 8.114b both praised Valentinian's and Valens's equalization of military and civilian officers already in 368. On these laws, see Andreotti 1931, 464–65; A. H. M. Jones 1964, 142–43; Matthews 1975, 39–40; 2000, 221–23; Chastagnol 1982, 176–77, 184; Heather 1994, 13–14, 18–21.

301. Hoffmann 1969–70, 1: 313–5, 2: 132. See Ammianus's acid criticism of this policy at 27.9.4; cf. 21.16.2 and Lendon 1997, 222–35.

302. On the offices of *quaestor* and *magister memoriae,* see A. H. M. Jones 1964, 367–68, 504–5; Vogler 1979, 169–82; Harries 1988; 1999, 42–47; Honoré 1998, 11–23. On the importance of legal education in advancing bureaucratic careers, see Gaudemet 1979, 86–89. Corcoran 1996, 92–94, points out that legal and literary talent were not mutually exclusive.

303. *PLRE* I, Flavius Eupraxius; cf. Honoré 1986, 189–203. See A. H. M. Jones 1964, 576 on careers in the *sacra scrinia.*

304. *PLRE* I, Sextius Rusticus Iulianus 37, esp. AM 27.6.1: "quasi adflatu quodam furoris bestiarum more humani sanguinis avidus." Cf. Symmachus *Or.* 7 recommending Julianus's son for adlection to the Senate.

of such arrivistes was once again the Pannonian Maximinus, who rose from the depths of obscurity to the heights of power, taking as his starting point his mastery of the law. He, too, despite the attainment of the highest offices and the arrangement of an aristocratic marriage for his son, became a target of abuse from the aristocrats whose status he threatened.[305]

Similar criticisms were lodged against the professionals used by Valens. Lawyers were extremely important to Valens, whose inability to speak the lingua franca of the east was compounded by his lack of legal learning. Early in his reign, he compensated for these handicaps with the aid of an easterner who had acquired Latin while studying in Rome, Eutropius.[306] Eutropius, who was probably first promoted to *magister memoriae* by Valens,[307] eventually became proconsul of Asia, and although he was dismissed during the magic trials of 372, he later won his way back into imperial service as praetorian prefect and consul under Gratian. Valens's close confidant Festus offers an even more striking story. Like his comrade Maximinus, Festus came "of the lowest and most obscure parentage," studied law, and used his training as a barrister to win promotion to a senatorial position, consular governor of Syria.[308] From this post, Festus was promoted to *magister memoriae* in succession to Eutropius and eventually followed Eutropius as proconsul of Asia, ca. 372. Eunapius tells us that he was not dismissed from this post until after Valens's death in 378.[309] His six-year term in this coveted senatorial position was unprecedented and galled eastern aristocrats: the Sardian philosopher and historian Eunapius regarded Festus's freak death, which followed shortly after his dismissal, as a punishment by Nemesis for his bad behavior toward revered easterners such as Julian's court philosopher Maximus.[310]

Festus, a western careerist, probably assumed the post of governor of Syria in 365 from Marcianus, an easterner who, according to Libanius, had won office under Julian because of "his rhetorical talent."[311] This was an attribute that Festus did not enjoy. He had never learned Greek, a disadvantage that

---

305. See esp. Symm. *Or.* 4.11–14; AM 28.1.5–7, 12, 31, 33, 41, 29.2.23. Szidat 1995 puts too much weight on Maximinus's literary education and not enough on his legal background.

306. *PLRE* I, Eutropius 2. For Eutropius's background, see Bird 1988; 1993, vii–viii; Ratti 1996, 11–13. For law as entrée into senatorial positions, especially senatorial governorships, see Wolf 1952, 83–87.

307. Bird 1988, 55–56.

308. AM 29.2.22: "Ultimi sanguinis et ignoti." The date of his governorship of Syria depends on *CTh* 8.4.11 (365 or 368). Norman 1958, 74–75, favors 365. For more on Festus, see Baldwin 1978.

309. Eunap. *VS* 7.6.9. Malcus 1967, 114, does not accept Eunapius's contention, although he offers no explanation for his skepticism. Given that administrative sclerosis was typical of Valens's reign, there is no reason to doubt Eunapius, who lived in Sardis and experienced Festus's administration at firsthand.

310. Eunap. *VS* 7.6.11–13. Cf. Eunap. *Hist.* fr. 39.8 (Blockley); AM 29.2.23.

311. Lib. *Ep.* 1282: ἐκ τοῦ δύνασθαι λέγειν; *PLRE* I, Marcianus 7, with Norman 1958, 74–75.

elicited sarcasm from Libanius, whom Festus had tormented while serving in Syria.[312] Festus's Tridentine friend and fellow bureaucrat Fidelius also provoked Libanius, who called him a "country bumpkin."[313] Ammianus likewise described Valens's praetorian prefect Domitius Modestus as "of a boorish nature refined by no reading of the ancient writers."[314] Such was the eastern aristocratic assessment of these upstart careerists. Libanius had always been grumpy about such types, especially when they had studied law rather than rhetoric. In his judgment, such narrow-minded professionals had bypassed the traditional pursuit of *paideia*, formerly the hallmark of aristocratic power.[315] Similar hauteur had led Julian to take direct action against the tendency to hire bureaucrats. As Libanius crowed: "Seeing that men full of poetry, prose, and subjects from which the art of government could be learned had been slighted, [Julian] once more put them in charge of the provinces."[316] The problem, in Libanius's eyes, was that Valentinian and Valens once again replaced them with "savages who, for all their skill in shorthand, had not a scrap of sense."

Indeed, the Pannonian emperors made public their interest in dredging law schools to fill their pool of administrative talent. In his edict laying out guidelines for the conduct of students at Rome, Valentinian specifically demanded that a list of the best and brightest be submitted to his *sacra scrinia* annually in order to facilitate recruiting.[317] In so doing, he continued a trend characteristic of the fourth century by filling posts with men of talent and ambition, even if their backgrounds and professional training were unacceptable to pedigreed notables.[318]

Of course, Valens's administration was no more composed solely of professional bureaucrats than of Pannonians. The imperial government was far too large and lumbering for Valentinian and Valens to pack it exclusively with men cast from a single mould. Indeed, many positions were simply filled by those who were closest to hand and capable of serving. These often included precisely the traditional aristocrats who could be so indignant when the

---

312. Lib. *Or.* 1.156: ὁ μὲν οὖν φωνῆς Ἑλλάδος ἄπειρος ἦν, ὁ Φῆστος, παραπαίων ἄνθρωπος.

313. *PLRE* I, Fidelius. Lib. *Or.* 1.163–65: ἄγριος ἄπνθρωπος.

314. AM 30.4.2. Libanius was more charitable; see references in Seeck, *Briefe*, 213–18.

315. Lib. *Or.* 2.43–46; cf. 49.29, 52.10–16, 62.8, 10, 51; *Ep.* 1224. For a full catalogue of such passages, see Festugière 1959, 410–12; Teitler 1985, 24–29. For analysis, see esp. Brown 1992, 35–70.

316. Lib. *Or.* 18.157–8; cf. *Pan. Lat.* 3 [11].21.2. See also Lib. *Or.* 42.23–25 for a vitriolic catalogue of the "low-born" sorts of men Constantius employed; cf. *Pan. Lat.* 3 [11].20.1–4, 25.1–5. For more on the problems created by the redefinition of elite status in late antiquity, see Rapp and Salzmann 2000.

317. *CTh* 14.9.1.

318. On the creation of the bureaucratic career in the fourth century, see Chastagnol 1982, 174–80; Heather 1994; 1998; Kelly 1998, 171–75; Garnsey and Humfress. 2001, 36–49.

offices they sought were assumed by less well-heeled professionals. Thus, a circle of local notables from Gaul blossomed in Valentinian's court at Trier and came to flourish under Gratian,[319] and similar regional entourages evolved around Valens. In passing through Cappadocia in 365 and several more times between 370 and 378, Valens came into contact with the burgeoning crop of qualified men that province produced in the fourth century. His *magister officiorum* for the better part of his reign was a Cappadocian from Caesarea, Sophronius. With Sophronius came his fellow Caesarean Aburgius, quaestor around 369 and perhaps Valens's last praetorian prefect in succession to Modestus.[320] Another friend of Sophronius's, Caesarius—brother of Gregory of Nazianzus—served as a court doctor and later on the staff of the governor of Bithynia under Valens.[321] Sophronius's successor as *magister officiorum*, Himerius, may also have been Cappadocian.[322] Finally, Fortunatianus, Valens's *comes rei privatae*, has been identified as a Cappadocian.[323] Naturally, our information about Cappadocian officials is colored by the fortunate survival of the massive corpora of the Cappadocian Fathers. One can imagine that if Libanius had not systematically destroyed his correspondence for the period, we might find that more of his Syrian friends also held office under Valens than his disdain would lead us to expect.[324] Indeed, for all his foibles, Valens was an eminently practical man, and one can only imagine that in his quest for efficiency, he assigned offices to those closest to hand and best qualified for the job.

319. Matthews 1975, 51, 56–87; Sivan 1993, 97–114.

320. *PLRE* I, Sophronius 3 and Aburgius.

321. *PLRE* I, Caesarius 2; Calvet-Sebasti 1995, 49.

322. *PLRE* I, Himerius 5. Basil *Ep.* 274 implies that Himerius was a fellow Cappadocian.

323. *PLRE* I, Fortunatianus 1; identified by Sievers 1868, 131 n. 38, with the Cappadocian who saved Libanius from charges of excessively praising Julian (cf. *Or.*1.138).

324. In fact, Valens's praetorian prefect Domitius Modestus, his *comes rei privatae* Fortunatianus, and his *comes sacrarum largitionum* and prefect of the city of Constantinople Vindaonius Magnus were all friends of Libanius's, and the last was a former pupil.

Chapter 2

The Revolt of Procopius

PROCOPIUS'S UPRISING

Valens faced a major challenge to his power as early as the second year of his reign. A usurper named Procopius, who claimed blood relations with the house of Constantine, had himself proclaimed in Constantinople and quickly assembled an army large enough to pose a serious threat. Over the next eight months, from late 365 until mid 366, Valens was forced to turn all of his attention to this problem. In a century filled with usurpation attempts, that of Procopius stands out as perhaps the least typical. It was unusual both because it arose in the east and because it did not germinate in the ranks of the military. It is also distinctive in that abundant sources survive to help reconstruct both the events of the revolt and how they were portrayed at the time. Narrative accounts in Ammianus and Zosimus are supplemented by fragments of Eunapius, brief notices in the ecclesiastical sources, and, most important, two contemporary panegyrics, by Themistius and Symmachus.[1] These last give us a window into the propaganda generated in the aftermath of the revolt and the way it affected contemporary and therefore modern understandings of what happened. The attitudes that later sources take and the ambiguities that they leave unanswered are, as we shall see, rooted in contemporary discourse.[2]

---

1. AM 26.5.8–10.19; Zos. 4.4.2–8.4; Eunap. *Hist.* fr. 34–37 (Blockley); Philostorg. 9.5–8; Soc. 4.3, 5; Soz. 6.8.1–4; *Epit.* 46; Joh. Ant. fr. 184; Oros. 7.32.4; Them. *Or.* 7; Symm. *Or.* 1. See also *Cons. Const.* s.a. 365–66; Jer. *Chron.* s.a. 366; Prosper *Chron.* 1131; Jord. *Rom.* 308; *Chron. pasch.* p. 556–57; Cedrenus, p. 542–43; Zon. 13.16; Theoph. a.m. 5859.

2. For secondary work, see Seeck, *Untergang*, 46–58; Köhler 1925, 13–24; Solari 1932d; 1933; Nagl, "Val.," 2100–2106; Ensslin 1957, 252–56; Kurbatov 1958; Stein 1959, 175–76; Piganiol 1972, 171–74; Salamon 1972; Austin 1972b; 1979, 88–92; Blockley 1975, 55–61; Grattarola 1986; Matthews 1989, 191–205; Wiebe 1995, 3–85.

Procopius was a relative of Julian's, although it remains uncertain precisely what his ties were. Otto Seeck contended that he was a maternal cousin. Seeck built his argument on silence: since the sources mention a blood relationship only to Julian, we can assume that there was none to the Constantines.[3] The case is strengthened by a passage from Themistius that makes a point of deriding Procopius's "pretense" to Constantinian ancestry and by Ammianus's reference to Procopius as a *cognatus* of the Apostate, a maternal relation.[4] Thus, while there is no doubt that Procopius was kin to Julian, it seems likely that he had no connection to the agnatic family of the emperor.[5] This did not, of course, deter him from asserting one. On the contrary, his supposed Constantinian connections became a cornerstone in the fabric of his revolt.

This was not Procopius's only pretense. There was also a rumor circulating that Julian had already invested his cousin with the symbols of empire prior to Valentinian's and Valens's accession. Before he set off down the Euphrates on his Persian expedition, Julian had left Procopius with a reserve force in Mesopotamia,[6] and some said that he had even consigned to him a purple imperial robe *(paludamentum purpureum)* with the understanding that Procopius should take over the empire if he perished. Zosimus reports the story as a simple fact, but the more reliable accounts in both Philostorgius and Ammianus are careful to distance themselves from this "quite shadowy rumor."[7] In fact, a number of sources—including Julian's admirer Libanius—make it explicitly clear that, when Julian was asked to name a successor on

---

3. Seeck, *Untergang*, 443. Seeck cites AM 26.7.10, but he fails to mention that this passage actually does imply that Procopius claimed *(praetendebat)* relations with Constantius. Even so, because Ammianus portrays the claim as a pretense, Seeck's argument remains valid. It is accepted at Ensslin 1957, 252–53; *PLRE* I, Procopius 4. For other sources on Procopius's relationship to Julian, see AM 23.3.2, "propinquo suo ... Procopio"; cf. 26.6.18, 7.10, 16, 9.3; Lib. *Or.* 24.13: οἰκεῖος ...Ἰουλιανῷ; Philostorg. 9.5: εἰς τὸ τοῦ Ἰουλιανοῦ γένος ἀναφέρετο; Eunap. *Hist.* fr. 34.3 (Blockley): τοῦ συγγενοῦς Ἰουλιανοῦ; Zos. 3.35.2, 4.4.2, 7.1; Zon. 13.16: ὁ ἀνεψιὸς Ἰουλιανοῦ; cf. Symm. *Or.* 1.22, "usurpator tanti nominis."

4. Them. *Or.* 7.92b; AM 26.6.1.

5. Despite her name, Julian's mother, Basilina had no royal blood (*PLRE* I, Basilina). If *PLRE* I is correct that Procopius 1 = Procopius 2 was a relative, the case would be strengthened, since Procopius's 1 position as *praeses Ciliciae* was hardly worthy of imperial blood and Libanius's mentions of Procopius 2 at *Ep.* 194 and 319 also indicate circumscribed authority.

6. AM 23.3.5, 6.2, 24.8.16–17; Zos. 3.12.5, 4.4.2; Lib. *Or.* 18.214, 260; Malalas 13.21 (p. 329). On this division of forces, see pp. 161 and 308.

7. AM 23.3.2: "*dicitur... nullo arbitrorum admisso* occulte paludamentum purpureum propinquo suo tradidisse Procopio ... "; 26.6.2: "mandaratque *(ut susurravit obscurior fama, nemo enim dicti auctor extitit verus)* ... si subsidia rei Romanae languisse sensisset, imperatorem ipse se provideret ocius nuncupari"; Philostorg. 9.5: καὶ πολλοὶ ἀνεκινοῦντο λογισμοὶ τὴν βασιλείαν αὐτῷ περιάπτοντες, καὶ τοὺς λογισμοὺς καὶ λόγοι διέφερον; cf. Zos. 4.4.2–3. For a similar assessment of this rumor, see Wiebe 1995, 11–20, with bibliography at n. 107, to which add Bowersock 1978, 109. Procopius himself gave a purple robe to his relative Marcellus (Zos. 4.8.4).

his deathbed, he flatly refused.[8] It seems likely that, here too, Procopius and his confidants invented the story to invest the usurpation with a patina of the legitimacy that it lacked at its core.

To say that Procopius's claims to empire were dubious does not deny that he had enjoyed successes under the patronage of his Constantinian relatives. Under Constantius, Procopius served in the east as a *tribunus et notarius,* a high-level secretary. As an imperial favorite, he quickly advanced to the top ranks of this corps, and he was eventually sent on a crucial embassy to Persia in 358. The assignment certainly indicated a measure of advancement, but Procopius's position at this point was hardly exalted. Indeed, Themistius would later poke fun of his job "in the eternal post of a secretary, eking out his living from pen and ink."[9] Only with the advent of his cousin did Procopius's career take off.

Julian promoted him to *comes* and gave him joint command of his reserve army in Mesopotamia. Ammianus tells us that it was then that this normally morose and taciturn character began to aim at greater things.[10] During his command, Procopius made some forays into Persian-controlled Media, but he never linked up with the expeditionary army until after Julian's death and the installation of Jovian.[11] By this time, the new emperor was firmly enough ensconced that any hopes, not to say claims, that Procopius may have had had become moot. He had little choice but to accept the election of the Illyrian from Singidunum. Perhaps as a reward for his cooperation—or simply to get him as far from the army as possible—Jovian charged Procopius with transporting Julian's body to Tarsus and burying it there.[12] This was his last official duty.

What exactly became of Procopius in the following year and a half is not entirely clear and must be pieced together from contradictory sources. Procopius was certainly in a dangerous position. Being a relative of Julian's, he was naturally suspected of being a rival for the throne. If, as has been argued, he had also been considered as a candidate for the purple before Jovian ac-

---

8. Lib. *Or.* 18.273; AM 25.3.20; *Epit.* 43.4. AM 26.6.3 reports that, in the period after Julian's death, a *falsus rumor* was spread that Julian had named Procopius to succeed him with his dying breath. See esp. Béranger 1972, 77, 87–92.

9. Them. *Or.* 7.86c: ἐν ὑπογραφέως ἀεὶ μοίρᾳ διαβιοὺς ἐκ τοῦ μέλανος καὶ τῆς καλαμῖδος; cf. *Or.* 7.90b; AM 26.6.1. On the embassy to Persia, see AM 17.14.3, 18.6.17–19. On the post of *notarius et tribunus,* see A. H. M. Jones 1964, 572–75; Teitler 1985, passim, esp. 27–29 for carping at *notarii.*

10. AM 26.6.1. On Procopius's morose nature, cf. Them. *Or.* 7.90b–c, with Sabbah 1978, 362.

11. AM 25.8.16; cf. 24.7.8, 25.8.7; Lib. *Or.* 18.260, with Barnes 1998, 205.

12. AM 25.9.12–13. *Pace* Curran 1998, 79, Zos. 3.34.3 is wrong to assert that most of the army accompanied Julian's funeral cortege to Tarsus; cf. Paschoud 2.1: 233 n. 102.

ceded to the throne in 363,[13] his situation would have been doubly precarious, especially since Jovian had just executed another such rival, also a *notarius*. Jovian does not, however, seem to have driven Procopius into hiding, although this is far from evident from Ammianus's account. According to Ammianus, Jovian made attempts to arrest Procopius following the obsequies for Julian but could not locate him.[14] Zosimus reports conversely that, once he had buried Julian, Procopius renounced his office as count and judiciously retreated with his family to their estates near Cappadocian Caesarea (see map 2). By his account, the order to arrest Procopius only came after the accession of Valentinian and Valens, who sent men to capture him there. In the event, Procopius narrowly escaped by intoxicating his would-be captors and fleeing, eventually to the Tauric Chersonese. Zosimus's details about Procopius' retirement seem convincing, but the story of wily escape and flight to the barbarians smacks of the Greek novel.[15] If it is difficult to determine which account to believe, it must in part be credited to Procopius's own skill in evading those who wished to eliminate him. Our ancient sources were probably as uncertain of Procopius's movements in this period as were his hunters.

Moreover, very early on, the propaganda that colors all that we learn of Procopius affected the historiography. Ammianus reports that Jovian was already concerned about a usurpation by Procopius in 363, and that he hastened to strike his disastrous Persian treaty in order to forestall this.[16] His account of Jovian's motivations, however, appears to be based on the version of events propagated by Valens's own court historians, Eutropius and Festus. In the epitomated Roman histories they wrote for Valens, both also charged that Jovian's fear of Procopius drove him to agree to the Persian treaty.[17] Whether Jovian's usurpation worries were actually to blame for the giveaway of 363 thus becomes murky. Valens and his ministers—who themselves faced Procopius and then Jovian's problematic treaty—certainly wanted to link the two, but more than likely, they were retrojecting their own anxieties onto Valens's predecessor after vaguer fears of a usurpation became reality.

This is not to deny that both Valentinian and Valens feared Procopius and

13. Neri 1985b, 157–63.

14. AM 26.6.3–4 is explicit that Procopius went into hiding for fear of *Jovian*, but the chronology seems shaky, since it implies that Procopius had already reached Chalcedon while Jovian was still alive. Cf. Philostorg. 9.5.

15. Zos. 4.4.3–5.2. Zosimus is favored over Ammianus at Piganiol 1972, 172, but the scholarship has tended to prefer Ammianus's version, as in Köhler 1925, 18–20; Ensslin 1957, 253; Paschoud 2.2: 340 n.114; Grattarola 1986, 88; Matthews 1989, 191. *Pace* Paschoud, Philostorg. 9.5 does not offer enough detail to determine precisely when Procopius was driven underground.

16. AM 25.7.10–11; cf. 25.9.8, esp.: "dum extimescit aemulum potestatis."

17. Eutr. 10.17, esp.: "dum aemulum imperii veretur"; cf. Festus 29.

other supporters of Julian's from the beginning. We have already seen that they undertook investigations during their initial stay in Constantinople that were directed against Julian's men. Perhaps at this point, the soldiers Zosimus speaks of were sent to capture Procopius. His escape was followed by over a year of life on the run, "in fear and hiding and in daily expectation of arrest, fleeing from the death he anticipated."[18] Finally, in desperation, the fugitive betook himself to Chalcedon, across the Bosporus from Constantinople.[19] There he remained in hiding on the estates of friends, who sheltered him as he sounded out the situation in the capital, at times making his way furtively into the city disguised by his squalor. There he learned that Constantinople had been suffering in the iron grip of Valens's father-in-law, Petronius, who was engaged in the relentless collection of debts.[20] Petronius's unmitigated extraction of money had created considerable unrest, uniting the masses and the elite in their openness to a change of administration. When he became aware of the opportunity created by this disquiet, Procopius decided it was time to "throw the dice" in a bid for the throne.[21]

Valens was, at the time, on his way to Antioch, where he hoped to secure the tenuous situation on the Persian frontier. On his way east, he had learned that a band of Goths was preparing an attack on the territory of Thrace, and he accordingly dispatched a pair of units, the Divitenses et Tungrecani Iuniores, to supplement forces already in the region.[22] When these reached Constantinople on their way to Thrace and took up quarters there for two days' rest, Procopius contacted their commanders and contrived to get the units to come over to his cause. He did so by promising a massive donative, paid by the eunuch and former court official Eugenius.[23] By this time, Procopius had already assembled a considerable circle of confidants, which was soon to grow. On the night of September 28, in the Baths of Anastasia,[24] he was brought

18. Lib. *Or.* 24.13; cf. AM 26.6.4,12; Philostorg. 9.5; Symm. *Or.* 1.17: "rebellis exul."

19. AM 26.6.4–6; Philostorg. 9.5, 8. Zos. 4.5.2 implies that he returned directly to Constantinople.

20. AM 26.6.6–9; cf. pp. 291–92.

21. This trope recurs in the sources; cf. Lib. *Or.* 24.13: ἀνέρριψε τὸν κύβον; Philostorg. 9.5: ἀναρρίπτει κύβον; AM 26.6.12: "aleam periculorum omnium iecit abrupte." It no doubt traces to Julius Caesar's bon mot, Suet. *Iul.* 32: "[I]acta alea est."

22. AM 26.6.11. On this Gothic threat, see p. 116.

23. AM 26.6.12–13. On Eugenius and his funding for the revolt, see Zos. 4.5.3–4; cf. AM 26.6.13, 16. Zosimus reports that Eugenius paid off "the garrison of Constantinople, which consisted of two units" (τὴν ἐν τῇ πόλει καθεσταμένην φρουράν, ἣν τάγματα στρατιωτῶν δύο ἐπλήρου). As Dagron 1974, 108–13, notes, Constantinople lacked a permanent garrison, thus Zosimus must be referring confusedly to the two mobile units mentioned by Ammianus. Constantinople's lack of a garrison to defend the interests of the emperor rendered the city all the more suitable as a staging point for the revolt.

24. For the date, see *Cons. Const.* s.a. 365; cf. Theoph. a.m. 5859. For the place, see AM 26.6.14; cf. Them. *Or.* 7.91c. See p. 399. AM 26.6.14 reports that the proclamation occurred

before the troops for what was, inevitably, a makeshift proclamation. Because a purple robe could not be found—the possession of imperial accoutrements was strictly forbidden—he was draped in a gold-bordered tunic like those of palace attendants and presented to the troops with a pair of purple slippers, a spear and a scrap of purple cloth in hand.[25] Despite his motley appearance, the troops, acting on cue, promptly hailed their new emperor. They then marched him out onto the streets, with shields clanging above their heads as they attempted to protect their new ruler against potential tile throwers.[26]

The Constantinopolitans met this late-night procession with bleary-eyed confusion rather than hostility, and when the gaunt, timid new emperor mounted the imperial tribunal near the palace and delivered a half-hearted harangue, the dumbfounded crowd, prompted by criers, played along by hailing him with acclamations.[27] In his speech, Procopius concentrated on his relationship to the imperial house, a theme that became a rallying cry in his power play. After this address, he was whisked on to the Senate, and, when no senators of high standing assembled for him, back to the palace.[28]

The account is largely that of Ammianus, who paints the whole picture in explicitly theatrical terms.[29] At one point, he even mocks Procopius's farcical appearance, "just as sometimes on the stage you might think that a splendidly decorated figure was suddenly made to appear as the curtain was raised or through some mimic deception."[30] As with the story of Jovian's dread of a Procopian revolt, Ammianus's imagery is rooted in contemporary discourse. Themistius had already portrayed the whole affair as a "comedy" gone wrong, a "multiform and variegated tragedy" whose lead character would have succeeded in his plot but for Valens, who stepped into the role of deus ex machina to foil him.[31] The fact that Ammianus's narrative is filtered

---

"ubi excanduit radiis dies," i.e., at daybreak. Other sources, especially the eyewitness Themistius, indicate that it was still night, Them. *Or.* 7.91a–b: μεσούσης τῆς νυκτός; 92 b:μέχρι τῆς ἑσπέρας ἐκείνης; Zos. 4.5.5: νυκτὸς ἀωρί; *Cons. Const.* s.a. 365: "latro nocturnus."

25. AM 26.6.15; cf. Them. *Or.* 7.91a–c, esp.: κἄπειτα ἐπόμπευεν ἐκ βαλανείου ἐν ἀσπίδι καὶ δορατίῳ περιδέραια περικείμενος. On purple imperial garments, see *CTh* 10.20.18, 10.21 with Steigerwald 1990, esp. 218–19.

26. AM 26.6.16. On the urban masses using tiles as weapons, see Barry 1996.

27. AM 26.6.17–18; Zos. 4.5.5, 6.3. The *tribunal* at AM 26.6.18, described at Zos. 4.6.3 as τὸ πρὸ τῆς αὐλῆς βῆμα was probably the "tribunal purpureis gradibus extructum in regio" of *Not. urb. Consp.* 3.9.

28. AM 26.6.18.

29. Matthews 1989, 193–95, "a ridiculous piece of burlesque." Matthews's account is a masterful analysis of Ammianus's historiography. Blockley 1975, 55–61, treats many of the same themes. Straub 1939, 22–25, also emphasizes theatricality and regards Ammianus's account "fast als Musterbeispiel für die literarische Darstellung einer Usurpation."

30. AM 26.6.15; cf. 26.6.19; Zos. 4.5.5.

31. Them. *Or.* 7.91a–c is filled with new comic elements: note esp. 7.91a: καὶ οὐδ' ἂν τὸν Δία ἴσως ἡ κωμῳδία τοῦ τηνικαῦτα ἀποδρασθεῖν ὑπεξείλετο, 92c: ταύτην τοίνυν τὴν οὕτω

through the accounts offered by Valens's own propagandists should alert us that we are hearing what the court would have wished. We should not let the contemporary rhetorical strategy of dismissing Procopius's revolt as farcical lead us to underestimate its sophisticated organization.

Although Procopius was now "emperor," much had to be done to keep him in power. His activities over the days and weeks following September 28 give us an interesting picture of the steps he took to secure his position. The key to his progress was above all his careful control of information, which he used to assemble the money and military manpower that rapidly made him a formidable opponent for the weak new emperor.[32] The very night he was proclaimed, Procopius issued a series of arrest warrants for Valens's officials in the city.[33] Of particular importance was his arrest of Valens's new praetorian prefect, Nebridius, and the urban prefect of Constantinople, Caesarius. These were imprisoned and replaced by Procopius's own men, Phronimius and Euphrasius.[34] Nebridius was eventually done in, but Procopius apparently kept him alive long enough to make him compose a missive—as if from Valens—ordering the *comes* Julius to proceed to Constantinople with the forces he was commanding in Thrace. On arrival, Julius was easily arrested and Procopius thereby won control of the "warlike peoples of Thrace."[35] Procopius also closed the harbors of Constantinople to traffic, ordered the garrisoning of the city fortifications and unleashed spies throughout the capital. This gave him effective control of the Bosporus and drove a wedge into the communication routes between Valens and his brother.[36]

Once he had gained control of communications, Procopius arranged for a series of embassies from eastern provinces and client territories offering him congratulations and thereby lending him an air of legitimacy. He also received "legates from Italy, Illyricum and the provinces of the western Ocean."[37] These latter, certainly impostors, were part of a larger effort to circulate the rumor that Valentinian was dead. It was clear to all that Valentinian

---

πολυειδῆ καὶ ποικίλην τραγῳδίαν μικροῦ μὲν ἔτι μέλλουσαν προαπέκλεισας τῆς ἐξόδου, 86c. Cf. Sabbah 1978, 362–63, on these images.

32. On the importance of information and propaganda, see Austin 1972b, 1979, 90; Matthews 1989, 198–99; cf. Elton 1996b, 230, on the control of information during all usurpations.

33. See the vivid description at Them. *Or.* 7.91a–b.

34. AM 25.7.4; Zos. 4.6.2; Them. *Or.* 7.91b.

35. AM 26.7.5; cf. Zos. 4.6.2. Them. *Or.* 7.92c implies that Nebridius was killed or died in captivity but Caesarius survived. Procopius took over the entire Thracian diocese and eventually appointed Andronicus as vicar; cf. Lib. *Or.* 62.59.

36. Them. *Or.* 7.91d–92a.

37. On embassies, see Them. *Or.* 7.92a. On legates, see AM 26.7.3; Them. *Or.* 7.91d. Procopius may even have circulated coinage with phony mint marks of Arelate (Arles: CONST and SCONST) to bolster his pretense of western support (Pierce *RIC* 9.215 n. 18, followed by Wiebe 1995, 76; cf. Kent 1957).

was the senior Augustus, and Procopius must have known that if people believed he were dead, they would be much more inclined to support his own bid against the junior colleague. To guarantee the neutralization of Valentinian, Procopius sent men to distribute money in Illyricum in hopes of buying support. Here, Procopius did not anticipate the alacrity of Valentinian's Pannonian compatriot, the *comes per Illyricum* Aequitius, who captured Procopius's agents and tortured them to death.[38] Aequitius then fortified the three passes that would have allowed access to Illyricum and thus blocked any further encroachment on the west.[39]

The loss of Illyricum was important for Procopius, not just because it sealed off his access to the other half of the empire, but also because it closed a potential recruiting ground for troops. This failure set the stage early for what would be an ongoing problem for the usurper, military manpower. Even so, Procopius did a remarkable job of compensating for his deficit, given that he began with only 2,000 men. We have seen that he soon added the Thracian units formerly under the *comes* Julius, and Ammianus indicates that other cavalry and infantry units that were marching through Thrace joined as well.[40] He also apparently drafted the urban rabble and slaves into his army in the early days of his venture.[41] In gaining control of the Bosporus, Procopius acquired naval forces, which he would use in a siege of Cyzicus, and he later persuaded an advance army of Valens's, the paired Iovii et Victores Iuniores, to join his cause.[42] Finally, he had a number of foreign auxiliaries available already in 365, and the Goths sent 3,000 more men, although these arrived only after his death.[43] A number of sources agree that Procopius assembled a sizeable force in remarkably short order.[44] By the time he engaged Valens's advance forces in late 365, only months after the start of the revolt, his fledgling army was nearly able to overwhelm the emperor's men. Pro-

38. Even so, at least some of Procopius's gold eventually reached as far west as Vindobona (Vienna); cf. Polascheck 1925, 127–29.

39. AM 26.7.11–12. See pp. 81–82.

40. AM 26.7.9.

41. AM 26.7.1, 5, 7, 14; Zos. 4.5.5; Them. *Or.* 7.86d. It is difficult to know how to assess these passages, since it was a historiographical topos to assert that the slaves and urban rabble had been drafted into the army of a rebel. Even so, they have led some to adopt a Marxist interpretation of the usurpation as a popular revolt (e.g., Hahn 1958). Such arguments are countered at Salamon 1972.

42. On naval forces, see AM 26.8.8; Zos. 4.6.5. On the Iovii et Victores, see AM 26.7.13–17; cf. Zos. 4.7.1.

43. On the Goths, see pp. 116 and 151. On the other auxiliaries, AM 26.8.5 tells us that Hyperechius commanded *auxilia*, although it is not clear from where. Zos. 4.7.1 also indicates that barbarian auxiliaries were actually available and not just on their way, as with the Goths.

44. AM 26.7.8; Zos. 4.6.4, 7.1; Eunap. *VS* 7.5.2; Soz. 6.8.1; Soc. 4.3.1. Themistius *Or.* 7.85d–86a, 97d. *Or.* 8.111a also implies that large numbers of commanders and troops sided with Procopius.

copius was thus remarkably resourceful at manufacturing an army almost out of thin air.

Procopius's undertaking was also bolstered by the absence of a decisive reaction from the reigning emperors. When we last saw Valentinian, he had gone west in the late summer of 364 to establish his first capital at Milan.[45] There he had remained until autumn of the following year, when Alamannic invasions across the Rhine forced him to move north into Gaul. By the time he arrived there, the Germans had crushed his advance force and killed its commander. As Valentinian was approaching Paris, around the first of November, he was apprised of the defeat of these forces and the revolt of Procopius on one and the same day.[46] This double blow forced him to a decision, to defend the western provinces against the barbarians or to protect his brother's and, by extension, his own position against the usurper.

By restricting the flow of information, Procopius had engineered the single biggest impediment to this decision. Western reports on the revolt were thirdhand and extremely vague. Initially, Valentinian did not even know whether his brother was still alive.[47] In the event, he wavered, at first deciding to return to Illyricum and later determining to press on against the Alamanni. He made this final choice on the advice of close advisers and at the request of urban provincials, who, Valentinian must have known, would have been tempted to appoint their own usurper to face the Alamanni if he departed. Ultimately, then, Valentinian did little more than secure his own position. He quickly promoted the Illyrian commander Aequitius from *comes* to *magister militum* and probably ordered him to continue his blockade of the passes on the military roads westward.[48] He also sent trusted confidants to Africa to hold that crucial province.[49] Aside from this, Valens was left to fend for himself.

Ammianus tells us that, in justifying his decision to abandon his brother, Valentinian often said that "Procopius was only his own and his brother's enemy, but the Alamanni were enemies of the whole Roman world."[50] We hear much the same sentiment in Symmachus's first oration, delivered to Valentinian in 368. Symmachus presents an elaborate explanation of Valentinian's conduct in which his failure to aid his brother is excused as a sign of his

45. See p. 27.

46. AM 26.5.7–8, 27.1; Zos. 4.9. On the chronology, see Baynes 1928, 222–24. Cf. Tomlin 1973, 496.

47. AM 26.5.9–10. Symm. *Or.* 1.17 implies that a decision was postponed until reliable information became available. Zos. 4.7.3 does indicate that Valens made an effort to communicate with Valentinian.

48. AM 26.5.11–12; cf. 10.4. On Aequitius's initial rank as *comes*, see AM 26.5.3.

49. AM 26.5.14. This precaution was standard; cf. AM 21.7.2; SHA *Pesc. Nig.* 5.4.

50. AM 26.5.13: "hostem suum fratrisque solius esse Procopium, Alamannos vero totius orbis Romani."

confidence in Valens's capacities and Procopius is portrayed strictly as a personal enemy. Valentinian, Symmachus says, often replied to those who insisted that he attack Procopius: "[T]hese [the Alamanni] are our common enemy; that one is only my private foe. Our first concern must be public victory; then we can worry about my private revenge."[51] Once again, contemporary propaganda has set the tone for later historiography.[52]

Valens was thus left to face this first challenge of his rule alone, and he did not immediately rise to the occasion. After inaugurating his first consulship at Constantinople in January 365, Valens had remained in the city until the late summer, when he set out for Antioch. After he had reached Cappadocian Caesarea, however, he stopped to wait out the stifling heat, and before he could resume his journey, his *notarius* Sophronius arrived with word of the revolt, probably in early October.[53] Upon receiving the news, Valens is said to have considered renouncing his imperial robes, and he may even have considered suicide.[54] Fortunately, his ministers were available to steady his shaky hand and help him begin to make efforts to rescue the situation. His first action was to dispatch an advance force consisting of the Iovii et Victores to confront Procopius's fledgling army when it crossed the Hellespont into Bithynia. He also sent his *comes domesticorum*, Serenianus, to secure Cyzicus and its mint.[55] Valens himself returned northwest to Ancyra, where he established his base.[56]

In the meantime, Procopius's successes continued unabated. The usurper met the Iovii et Victores at Mygdus, east of Nicaea on the road to Ancyra,

---

51. Symm. *Or.* 1.17–22, esp. 19: "hic communis hostis est, ille privatus; prima victoriae publicae, secunda vindictae meae causa est." Zos. 4.7.4 offers a much harsher, but perhaps more realistic explanation: ἀλλὰ Οὐαλεντινιανὸς μὲν ἀπέγνω μὴ βοηθεῖν ἀνδρὶ πρὸς φυλακὴν οὐκ ἀρκέσαντι τῆς αὐτῷ παραδεδομένης ἀρχῆς.

52. I withhold judgment on the advisability of Valentinian's choice, on which, see Seeck, *Untergang*, 51; Nagl, "Vt.," 2169–70; Paschoud 2.2: 347 n. 120; cf. Austin 1979, 88.

53. AM 26.7.2; cf. Greg. Naz. *Or.* 43.21–23. The heat wave is confirmed at Them. *Or.* 7.86c; Lib. *Ep.* 1524. Valens issued *CTh* 12.6.5 from Caesarea on Nov. 2, 365; cf. Seeck, *Regesten*, 227, with 33. Letters from Libanius in Antioch to Valens's court at Caesarea are catalogued at Seeck, *Briefe*, 440–41. Other sources confirm Valens's intention of reaching Antioch; cf. Zos. 4.4.1; Philostorg. 9.5. Zos. 4.7.3 mistakenly places Valens in Galatia when he learned of the revolt.

54. AM 26.7.13; Zos. 4.7.3; Soc. 4.3.2; Theoph. a.m. 5859. Zos. 4.7.3's notice that Arbitio encouraged Valens in Galatia is apparently to be connected with Eunap. *Hist.* fr. 34.4 (Blockley). It does not, however, apply to Valens's initial reaction, since Arbitio did not join Valens until later (AM 26.8.13–14). No source testifies that Valens contemplated suicide, but Eutropius was especially careful to catalog instances when great leaders had; cf. *Brev.* 6.12 Mithradates; 6.23 Cato, Scipio, Petreius, Iuba; 6.24 Caesar; 7.7 Antony; 7.17 Otho. Perhaps he was responding to his patron's experience in 365. Them. *Or.* 7.86b is naturally obliged to paint a more sanguine picture. See Staesche 1998, 105–8, on imperial suicide.

55. On the Iovii et Victores, see AM 26.7.13. On Cyzicus, see AM 26.8.7; Zos. 4.6.4. Two milestones of Valentinian and Valens from around Cyzicus may trace to this period (*RRMAM* 214, 218).

56. AM 26.7.2–3, 13.

and easily persuaded them to desert.[57] He also secured Nicaea itself, along with Chalcedon, Nicomedia, and Helenopolis.[58] He had already won the diocese of Thrace in the first days of his revolt, and with these acquisitions, he expanded his control into Bithynia. In the weeks that followed, the prize would be the wealthy diocese of Asiana.

As winter set in, Valens marched west to challenge Procopius personally. He left a force under Vadomarius to besiege Nicaea and himself continued past Nicomedia and on to Chalcedon, which he besieged.[59] Here his efforts proved fruitless, indeed dangerous. Procopius's garrison commander at Nicaea, Rumitalca, successfully broke out of the city, defeated Vadomarius, and moved up the peninsula toward Chalcedon in an effort to trap Valens. The emperor, who had learned of Rumitalca's advance, narrowly managed to escape with a maneuver around the Sunonian Lake.[60] With these victories, Procopius secured his claim to Bithynia. He then continued his successes by taking the city of Cyzicus by siege, and with it Valens's count of the *domestici*.[61] This victory, which quickly became a rallying cry for the rebels, gave Procopius control over Hellespontus, from which he expanded southward through the diocese of Asiana.[62]

After his close call at Chalcedon, Valens beat a retreat to Ancyra. The fact that a mere garrison commander had worsted his general at Nicaea and nearly captured the emperor himself implies that, in this early stage, Valens's available forces were exiguous. Prior to this, his use of the commander of his bodyguard to garrison Cyzicus and of only two field units against Procopius's initial eastward march both point to the same problem.[63] In fact, it is likely that the emperor had sent much of his army ahead to Antioch before he learned of the revolt.[64] His initial efforts to block Procopius's ex-

57. AM 26.7.14–17.

58. AM 26.8.1–2. Procopius probably won support in Chalcedon early on given that it was from this city that he had planned the revolt.

59. This march may be marked by a series of five milestones of Valentinian and Valens found along the road between Dadastana and Nicaea (*RRMAM* 222, 227, 245, 250, 262).

60. AM 26.8.2–3. A law received by Sallustius on Dec. 1, 365, at Chalcedon may attest Valens's presence in the area at this late date; cf. *CTh* 7.4.14, with Seeck, *Regesten*, 33. On the lake, see Pliny *Ep.* 10.41, 61.

61. AM 26.8.7–11; Zos. 4.6.4–5, with Paschoud 2.2: 344–45 on discrepancies.

62. On Cyzicus as a rallying cry, see Them. *Or.* 7.87b: οἱ τὴν Κύζικον αὐχοῦντες; cf. AM 26.8.13; Zos. 4.7.1. On Procopius's control of Asiana, see AM 26.8.14. Procopius must have acquired Asia when Valens's *proconsul Asiae*, *PLRE*'s Helpidius 6, deserted to him. Procopius apparently replaced him with Hormisdas, AM 26.8.12. He also appointed governors for the Aegean islands (Philostorg. 9.6) and probably a *vicarius Asiae* in succession to Valens's vicar, *PLRE* I's Clearchus 1.

63. AM 26.7.13, 26.8.6–7; Zos. 4.6.4: Σερηνιανοῦ καὶ τῶν σὺν αὐτῷ βασιλικῶν ἱππέων.

64. Valens had sent Petronius to assemble recruits in Antioch by April 365 (*CTh* 7.22.7) and preparations were being made for his own arrival there (Lib. *Ep.* 1499, 1505). Soc. 4.2.6–3.1,

pansion into Bithynia and Asia were thus hindered by the lack of available troops. This situation changed only at the very end of 365, when the master of the cavalry, Lupicinus, got troops back to Valens in Ancyra.[65] Once these had swelled his ranks, the emperor sent them with Arinthaeus up to the border of Galatia and Bithynia, where they met a force under the command of the completely inexperienced Hyperechius at Dadastana. Arinthaeus easily persuaded Hyperechius's men to desert and thus finally put a halt to the eastward advance of the usurper's army.[66] He dared not, however, continue the pursuit since by now cold weather prevented further action. Both sides fell back to winter quarters, Valens to Ancyra and Procopius apparently to Cyzicus.[67]

Thus far, Procopius had met almost entirely with success. By now he would also have sensed that Valentinian did not intend to take direct action against him. He was thus free to concentrate his attention east of the Bosporus.[68] It was perhaps this confidence that led Procopius to dally in Asia into the following spring trying to win support from hesitant *poleis* there and money from their wealthy aristocrats.[69] Those who refused to cooperate were punished. Maximus of Ephesus was apparently penalized, and Procopius confiscated the estates of Constantius's former commander, Arbitio. These heavy handed tactics drove Arbitio to Valens, who appointed him ad hoc *magister militum*.[70]

This last move on Procopius's part proved entirely unadvisable. Arbitio, a venerable senior officer dearly loved by the soldiery, was able to shore up Valens's sagging support among the troops and rally them against the usurper. Boosted by this good fortune and by the arrival of the auxiliaries from Syria, Valens finally began taking decisive action. He advanced from Ancyra to Pessinus, in western Galatia and, after fortifying this town as his new base, set off through Phrygia to intercept Procopius's army. Ammianus's notice that he moved toward "Lycia" should probably be emended to "Lydia,"

5.2 and Soz. 6.7.10–8.2 actually report that Valens was already in Antioch when he learned of the revolt, clearly a mistake, but perhaps based on the presence of comitatensian forces there already in 365. This appears to be born out by Theod. *HR* 13.15, which describes the general Lupicinus's provisioning efforts in Antioch.

65. AM 26.8.4, 9.1–2. Valens even drafted into his comitatenses former garrison units like the I Isaura (*Not. dign. or.* 7.56), on which, see Lenski 1999a, 313 n. 21.

66. AM 26.8.4–5.

67. On Valens at Ancyra in winter 365/66, see AM 26.8.4. See Mitchell 1993, 2: 84–95, on Ancyra in this period. On Procopius at Cyzicus, see AM 26.8.11; cf. Philostorg. 9.6.

68. AM 26.10.4: "conversam molem belli totius in Asiam"; cf. 26.8.14.

69. AM 26.8.14–15. Eunap. *Hist.* fr. 34.1 (Blockley) may be related; cf. Blockley 1981–83, 2: 137 n. 72.

70. On Maximus, see Them. *Or.* 7.99c, 100b–c. Maximus is not named directly but must be the referent of καθηγητὴς τοῦ ἐκείνου τοῦ αὐτοκράτορος. Cf. Eunap. *VS* 7.4.14–15, 5.7–8. See Seeck, *Briefe*, 209, Maximus X. On Arbitio, see AM 26.8.13–14, 9.4–5; Zos. 4.7.4. On his office, see Demandt 1970, 705.

since Zosimus and Eunapius indicate that he eventually reached that province. Eunapius's rather jejune fragments even give us some clue about Valens's route: "[T]he emperor moved into Lydia, Procopius into upper Phrygia," and "Procopius and the emperor Valens, mistakenly taking different roads, missed each other."[71] From Galatia and upper Phrygia, there were, in fact, three major routes Valens could have taken to Lydia, and, *per contra,* three Procopius could have taken in the opposite direction. A milestone of Valens's near Docimium may mark his route along the easternmost of the three, the most direct road to Lydia from his base in Pessinus.[72] Procopius, who had split his forces and left half in Asia under Gomoarius and Hormisdas,[73] must have taken one of the other two into Phrygia, perhaps that leading directly to Nacoleia, where he would confront Valens's army a few weeks later.[74]

Because the two did not cross paths, Valens made it into Lydia undeterred. After passing through Sardis, he first met resistance around the town of Thyateira, perhaps in early April.[75] There, he came up against Procopius's Asian division led by the master of the cavalry Gomoarius and the governor-*cum*-general Hormisdas. Fortunately for the emperor, Gomoarius was easily persuaded by Arbitio, an old friend, to desert to Valens with all his men.[76] Hormisdas, however, seems to have resisted and, after being narrowly routed, fled through Phrygia and escaped captivity.[77] With this success, Valens had neutralized half of Procopius's army. It remained for him to pursue the rest, whose plans he had discovered from the captured Gomoarius.[78] After regrouping in Sardis, Valens marched back toward Phrygia and Galatia and eventually met Procopius and his master of the infantry, Agilo, outside Nacoleia.[79] Like his counterpart Gomoarius, Agilo and his men deserted with-

71. AM 26.9.1–2; cf. Eunap. *Hist.* fr. 34.6–7 (Blockley); Zos. 4.8.1. Seeck, *Untergang,* 446, first argued that Ammianus's "Lycia" should be read as "Lydia." Eunapius—a native of Lydia and contemporary of these events—should be trusted here.

72. *CIL* 3.7172 = *RRMAM* 33 (a. 364/67).

73. Seeck, *Untergang,* 53–55, with 446.

74. Procopius may have hoped to win support from troops permanently garrisoned in this city (Drew-Bear 1977, 269 n. 60).

75. Seeck, *Regesten,* 229, with 109, referring to *CTh* 4.12.6 (Apr. 4, 366). Cf. *CIL* 3.475 = *RRMAM* 477 (a. 364/367) and *AE* 1995, 1465d, two milestones of Valentinian and Valens from Smyrna and *RRMAM* 694 and 711, two more from around Thyateira on the road between Pergamum and Sardis.

76. AM 26.9.5–6; Zos. 4.7.4–8.2. Zosimus is the only source to name the battle site, although AM 26.9.2 says that Valens approached Gomoarius *praeter radices Olympi montis excelsi,* only 50 km to the northwest.

77. Zos. 4.8.1; Eunap. *Hist.* fr. 34.8 (Blockley). Ammianus does not mention Hormisdas in the context of Thyateira, although 26.8.12 appears to describe the aftermath of the battle.

78. Zos. 4.7.4.

79. Zos. 4.8.3 indicates that Valens regrouped at Sardis, an assertion borne out by a milestone of Sardis dating from 364/67 (*AE* 1995, 1465d). Valens's route may be marked by a mile-

out a fight.[80] Both seem to have arranged in advance to surrender, and the lives of both were spared.[81] Procopius, now utterly helpless, took refuge in the nearby woods, where he remained overnight. The following morning, May 27, his attendants, Florentius and Barchalba, bound him and turned him over to Valens.[82] These betrayers, unlike their higher-ranking counterparts, were quickly executed.[83] So too Procopius. The tradition that he was tied to two trees that had been flexed to the ground and then split apart when the trees were released is a fanciful invention of ecclesiastical historians eager to make Valens look gruesome. As Ammianus tells us, he was simply beheaded and his head sent to Valentinian in Gaul.[84]

On its way west, the head was shown at the walls of cities still loyal to Procopius to convince the inhabitants that the usurper was no more. This had been the practice for centuries and proved particularly useful in persuading the citizens of Thracian Philippopolis to abandon the hopes they had placed in the rebel.[85] The city had been under siege by Valentinian's master of the soldiers, Aequitius, for some time. Once Aequitius learned that the center of action had shifted east of the Bosporus, he advanced from his defensive position at the Succi pass and laid siege to the town.[86] While he was engaged

---

stone (a. 364/67) near ancient Aezanoi (*AE* 1989, 699), along the most direct road between Thyateira and Nacoleia.

80. AM 26.9.7; Zos. 4.8.3; Them. *Or.* 7.87b, which implies that Valens was still some way off when Agilo's forces surrendered. Nacoleia is also named at Joh. Ant. fr. 184; Soz. 6.8.2; Soc. 4.5.2; *Cons. Const.* s.a. 366; *Chron. pasch.*, p. 557; Theoph. a.m. 5859; cf. Jer. *Chron.* s.a. 366 (*apud Phrygiam Salutarem*) followed by Prosper *Chron.* 1131; Jord. *Rom.* 308. Julian had spent considerable time in the area of Pessinus and Nacoleia only four years earlier (Christol and Drew-Bear 1986, 53–55; Mitchell 1993, 2: 89).

81. Agilo was certainly spared (AM 26.10.7); Gomoarius probably was (AM 26.9.6). Agilo cannot have lived too long after the revolt, however, because Gregory of Nyssa (*Vita Macrinae* 988) tells us that his wife, Vetiana, was widowed after only a short marriage.

82. AM 26.9.8–9. Philostorg. 9.5 claims that Procopius took refuge in Nicaea and that Florentius, who was garrison commander there, betrayed him. This seems unlikely, since AM 26.10.1 reports that Marcellus commanded the garrison at Nicaea when Procopius was killed. The date is given at *Cons. Const.* s.a. 366. I take "VI kal Iun." to refer to the day of Procopius's death rather than the day of the surrender at Nacoleia; cf. Soc. 4.9.8. *Chron. pasch.*, p. 557, mistakenly reports the date as μηνὶ δαισίῳ πρὸ ιβ καλανδῶν ἰουλίων.

83. AM 26.9.10; Philostorg. 9.5 reports that the army burned Florentius alive. Some ecclesiastical sources, confusing the paired betrayers Florentius and Barchalba with Gomoarius and Agilo, charge that these latter were sawn in two (Soc. 4.5.4; Soz. 6.8.3; Theoph. a.m. 5859).

84. AM 26.9.9; Philostorg. 9.5. Zos. 4.8.4 says only that Procopius was killed. Soc. 4.5.4; Soz. 6.8.3; Joh. Ant. fr. 184; Zon. 13.16; and Theoph. a.m. 5859 claim that Procopius was split in two. Seyfarth 1968–71, 4: 311–2 n. 114, points out that this mode of execution is a topos in folklore and also recurs in the SHA.

85. AM 26.10.6. Valentinian received the head in Paris (AM 27.2.10). For other instances of this gruesome practice, see Elbern 1984, 136. On the practice in subsequent centuries, see McCormick 1986, 57, 60, 134, 180–81, 235.

86. AM 26.10.4.

in the assault, Procopius was killed, and the news reached Aequitius before the town had fallen. Nevertheless, the revolt was not yet over. Earlier, Procopius had invested a relative named Marcellus with the tokens of empire, and when Marcellus learned what had happened at Nacoleia, he continued the fight from Chalcedon.[87] He had no idea that Aequitius was at his back in Thrace and hoped he could resist Valens by turning to the Gothic auxiliaries who had been sent at Procopius's request. Aequitius, however, sent agents to arrest the rebel and had him tortured and executed.[88] Only eight months after it had started, the revolt was at an end. Oddly, however, the final blow had been struck by a general of Valentinian's who had earlier refused any aid. In his panegyric congratulating Valens on the victory, Themistius does not mention Marcellus and concludes with the mass desertion at Nacoleia.[89] His silence may reflect Valens's vexation that Aequitius had stolen the finale to a revolt that the emperor had otherwise single-handedly quashed without western aid.

Although usurpation attempts were common in the fourth-century empire,[90] Procopius's had been far from typical. Because usurpations usually took place where troops were available, mobile, and isolated from imperial power, every major fourth-century usurpation except that of Procopius occurred in the western half of the empire. The east, which lacked large numbers of mobile units and rarely went without the presence of legitimate emperors, was not as conducive an environment to revolt. Procopius's power grab was thus unusual in its location.[91] It was also unusual in that Procopius held no official military command at the time of his rebellion. The army was the ultimate arbiter of imperial power and had repeatedly proclaimed emperors illegally, mostly from its own ranks; it was, in fact, inconceivable for an emperor to be made without its approval.[92] Even Procopius, whose military career had been quite limited, felt obliged to engineer his proclamation by a body of soldiers, albeit a mere 2,000 men. For any pretender to make a bid for power without the force of arms was suicide. It seems strange, then, that Procopius rose up with what was initially only a handful of soldiers.

The strains of undertaking a revolt from outside the army are especially

---

87. AM 26.10.1 reports Marcellus was Procopius's relative *(cognatus)* but not that he was named successor. This notice comes in Zos. 4.8.4. AM 26.10.3 does say that he claimed the throne; cf. Joh. Ant. fr. 184.2.

88. AM 26.10.3, 5; Zos. 4.8.3–4. Eunap. *Hist.* fr. 34.10 (Blockley) may refer to the period after Procopius's death, Blockley 1981–83, 2: 138 n. 78.

89. Them. *Or.* 7.87a–b.

90. On fourth-century usurpations, see Wardman 1984; Elbern 1984; Elton 1996b, 193–98, 227–33; Paschoud and Szidat 1997; Shaw 1999, 147–50.

91. AM 18.9.3 describes the Oriens as a place "ubi nihil praeter bella timetur externa"; cf. Crump 1975, 55; Elbern 1984, 38–41; Lee 1998, 225–26.

92. Elbern 1984, 61–63; cf. Straub 1939, 8–10.

clear at the command level of Procopius's forces. He faced serious difficulties coordinating his army under the direction of experienced leaders. Aside from his *magister equitum,* Gomoarius, and his *magister peditum,* Agilo, most of his leaders lacked military experience, and many were asked to double up in both civilian and military positions.[93] Rumitalca served him as both *cura palatii* and military tribune; Hyperechius, who was given command of some auxiliaries, had formerly risen only to *castrensianus,* a "servant of his commander's belly and gullet"; and Hormisdas, Procopius's proconsul of Asia, was given a military command along with his civilian capacities.[94] In this last instance, the piggybacking of functions does not reflect a nostalgic return to the days of combined military and civil posts.[95] Rather, it represents a lack of support from the upper echelons of the army. Procopius had never been a military man until Julian's reign and, although he had no trouble assembling a following among civilian aristocrats, his lack of backing from the military brass always proved an impediment.

Despite this crucial weakness, though, Procopius had a number of other advantages to fall back on. We have already seen that discontent with Valens ran high and that Procopius was a master at capitalizing on this with his manipulation of the lines of communication and his skilled deployment of propaganda. These issues will be treated in more detail in what follows. For now, it is important to look only at a single element, which was key to every usurpation, money.[96] Procopius wisely understood that if his revolt was to make any headway, it would need large amounts of capital, and from the outset, he acted on this knowledge. He began with the suborning of the Divitenses et Tungrecani, using money provided by the eunuch Eugenius.[97] Next, he occupied the treasury and mint of Constantinople and began minting coins in his own name.[98] With these he paid to recruit troops from among the urban masses, to buy officials over to his side, and to co-opt other army units.[99] With the acquisition of Thrace, he took the mint of Heraclea, which also issued his coins, and he later acquired the mints and treasuries of Bithynia and Hellespontus at Nicomedia and Cyzicus.[100] In the end, this "counterfeit emperor," as Themistius calls him, struck coins in his name from four of the

---

93. AM 26.7.4; cf. 9.6–8. On Gomoarius and Agilo, see also Zos. 4.8.2; Soz. 6.8.1; Soc. 4.5.3; Philostorg. 9.5; Theoph. a.m. 5859. All Greek sources give the name Γομάριος rather than Ammianus's *Gomoarius.* See Demandt 1970, 703.

94. AM 26.8.1–3, 5, 12.

95. *Pace* AM 26.8.12.

96. MacMullen 1985, 70–72.

97. AM 26.6.13–14: "spe praemiorum ingentium"; "vendibilium militum"; 16: "opesque pollicitus amplas"; 18: "paucorum . . . pretio inlectorum"; Zos. 4.5.4.

98. Them. *Or.* 7.91c–d: θησαυροφυλάκια μὲν ἀνεπετάννυντο.

99. AM 26.7.8, 11; Zos. 4.6.4.

100. Cyzicus was especially flush at the time (AM 26.8.6).

five eastern mints that issued gold in the late fourth century.[101] Procopius also obtained money through confiscations and by accepting payment for offices, practices used by all rulers, legitimate and illegitimate.[102] Moreover, he exacted a double levy on the senators of Constantinople in the winter of 365/66 and used the grain stores of Constantinople to supply his own troops.[103] In all, then, Procopius was a remarkably resourceful financier.

This adroit use of money nearly helped Procopius to buy his way out of his military deficit. In the end, however, his need to collect money from wealthy aristocrats in Asia during the spring of 366 impeded the speed of his response to Valens's counterattacks and contributed to his defeat. After the revolt, this scramble for funds encouraged the tendency of contemporary sources—here again following Valens's court—to refer to Procopius as "the criminal," and "the late night burglar" and to portray him as a Spartacus redivivus leading a gaggle of misfits and brigands.[104] Although it was common to deride usurpers as "robbers of power,"[105] contemporary propagandists probably found the stereotype particularly useful against a usurper who, because he initially lacked the force of arms, was compelled to fall back on the strength of money. In what follows, we shall see that this was far from his only resource.

VALENS AND THE IDEAL EMPEROR

The later empire is rich in models for rulership. In contemporary panegyrics, epitomized imperial biographies, coins, and inscriptions, we find catalogs of stock virtues by which an emperor could be measured. These attributes had been codified already in the second century, and by the fourth century, they were so fixed as to seem immovable.[106] By these standards, the ideal ruler

101. Them. *Or.* 7.91c: παράσημος αὐτοκράτωρ. On Procopius's minting, see pp. 99–100.

102. On confiscations, see AM 26.8.13; Them. *Or.* 7.86c; cf. 91c. On money for offices, see AM 26.7.6.

103. Them. *Or.* 7.92b. This was presumably the *collatio lustralis*, normally collected every five years.

104. Themistius is particulary harsh on Procopius, calling his men a group of "ruffians" (7.91b κάκουργοι) and never referring to Procopius by name, but only as "the criminal" (ὁ παλαμ-ναῖος), in his speeches to Valens (7.90a, 8.111a, 9.122c, 11.148c); cf. MacCormack 1975, 160 n. 97, on this commonplace. Themistius (*Or.* 7.86b–87a) also compares Procopius (and Marcellus?) to Spartacus and Crixus. Ammianus portrays Arbitio using this rhetoric already in the height of the rebellion; cf. 26.9.5: "publicum grassatorem"; cf. 26.7.1, 9.10, 10.3, 5. It also recurs in Symmachus's oratory (*Or.* 1.21: "illius latronis iustus occasus") and in the *Cons. Const.* (s.a. 365: "latro nocturnus hostisque publicus; s.a. 366: idem hostis publicus et praedo"), in passages compiled in Constantinople contemporaneously with the unfolding of the revolt.

105. MacMullen 1963.

106. Wallace-Hadrill 1981; 1983, 142–74; Kelly 1998, 145–50; Noreña 2001. On Valens and Procopius specifically, see Wiebe 1995, 23–35.

would spring from a famous homeland, his family would be noble, he would be well educated, he would demonstrate martial valor and achieve victories, and he would show clemency, justice, and equity in his affairs. Although the perfect emperor was never a reality, the model itself was very real, and it was probably evident to all in what respects a particular ruler achieved or fell short of it. Unfortunately for modern historians, contemporary rhetoric tended to gloss over a ruler's shortcomings and thus to obscure candid assessments until after he had died. Because of this, we are often ill informed about how an emperor's failure to match the ideal affected public opinion during his lifetime. One point where we can catch a glimpse into the dissatisfaction of subjects with their less than ideal rulers is, however, during revolts. How, then, did Valens measure up to the standards of ideal rulership? To what extent did his evident mediocrity affect reactions to him during his lifetime?

When a fourth-century orator set out to compose an imperial panegyric, a *basilikos logos,* he fully expected to focus on the themes of ideal rulership. This is clear from the late third-century rhetorical handbook attributed to Menander Rhetor.[107] Menander provides a formula for the *basilikos logos,* following which the panegyrist would map out his address along two broad structural axes—character attributes *(ēthē)* and actions *(praxeis).* Building on this grid, the speaker would fill in his oration with details of a particular emperor's attributes and accomplishments: in the first part, focusing on character, he retailed the ruler's native land *(patris),* his family background *(genos)* and birth *(genesis),* and his upbringing *(anatrophē)* and education *(paideia);* in the second, he enumerated the emperor's deeds according to which of the four canonical virtues—courage, justice, temperance, and wisdom—each best reflected.[108] Menander thus offered a template by means of which any rhetor could highlight the deeds and attributes of any ruler so as to make him reflect the "ideal." Of course, Menander knew that not all emperors were possessed of all the virtues he identified. Keeping this in mind, and remaining aware of the delicacy with which one handled a monarch, he counseled wisely that a *basilikos logos* should "embrace a generally agreed amplification of the good things attaching to the emperor but allow no ambivalent or disputed features."[109] If the orator could find nothing positive to say on a particular theme, Menander advised that he refrain from discussing it altogether. In this sense, Menander's template constituted a sort of checklist of possible subjects, which could either be glorified as examples of virtue or omitted as silent testimonies of shortcomings.[110]

---

107. Russell and Wilson 1981, with xxxiv–xl on date and authorship.
108. Men. Rhet. 2.369–76. See pp. 137–38 and 264.
109. Ibid., 368.
110. Each panegyric was naturally unique to its author and circumstances. Many extant panegyrics follow Menander's model, but many others obviously do not (cf. Russell and Wilson

When Valens arrived in Caesarea the summer before the revolt, he was probably greeted with a panegyric much like the one that Menander describes. This was the first time he had passed through the city as emperor, and his arrival would have been celebrated with the ceremonies of *adventus*—including a panegyric—which were as formulaic as Menander's *basilikos logos*.[111] At this early date, Valens had yet to fight a war, he had yet to put down a usurpation, he had yet to institute any political or legal reforms, and he had only just begun his major building program. In other words, he had yet to accomplish any of the sorts of "actions" *(praxeis)* that would have redounded to his glory. Whoever delivered the panegyric in Caesarea would thus have been forced to concentrate on Valens's "qualities of character" *(ēthē)*. Even here, however, he would have found it difficult to offer the unqualified praise that Menander prescribes.[112] Valens simply did not have much to recommend him.

Whoever undertook the task would have begun, as Menander advises, with Valens's native land *(patris)*. As we have seen, little is now known of Cibalae, and even in Valens's day, it was hardly renowned. Pannonia, however, and by extension Illyricum would have offered a broader canvas with which to work. Here our hypothetical panegyrist could have praised Valens as the son of a region noted for producing men of a strong, martial nature. Indeed, we have already seen that both Valentinian and Valens received precisely such accolades, and that they themselves propagated the stereotype of their warlike Pannonian origins.[113] Pannonian birth was not, however, a distinction that brought unambiguous acclaim. The counterpoint to the courageous Pannonian was the brutish Pannonian, a stereotype applied in antiquity to all Illyrians. Ammianus, for example, characterizes the Pannonian Aequitius, Valentinian's master of the cavalry, as "rude and rather boorish" ("asper et subagrestis" [AM 26.1.4]). He uses the same word to describe Valens's "boorish character" ("subagrestis ingenii") and Valentinian's "boorish manner of speech" ("subagresti verbo"),[114] and he attributes a similar lack of culture to Valentinian's first *magister officiorum*, the Dalmatian Ursacius.[115] Ammianus's fellow Antiochene John Chrysostom, who evidently accepted the same stereo-

---

1981, xi–xxxiv, esp. xxv–xxix; MacCormack 1975, passim, esp. 144–46; id. 1981, passim, esp. 1–14; Nixon and Rodgers 1994, 10–13, 21–35). On panegyrics and ideal rulership more broadly, see Straub 1939, 149–60; L'Huillier 1992, 325–60.

111. See p. 27.

112. Cf. Lib. *Or.* 18.7 and Blois 1986 for rhetorical aporia in the face of emperors with similarly undistinguished backgrounds.

113. See pp. 48–49.

114. AM 31.14.5, 29.3.6; cf. 29.1.11: "Valentem, subrusticum hominem"; cf. 27.5.8: "imperator rudis." For *subagrestis* in AM, usually used for soldiers, especially of barbarian origin, see Chiabó 1983, 750.

115. AM 26.4.4: "Delmatae crudo"; cf. 26.5.7: "iracundo quodam et saevo."

type, alludes to Valens a "rustic tyrant."[116] Julian, himself of Illyrian background, was also aware of what Balkan origins meant to contemporaries. In his *Misopogon,* he argued that "those who dwell between the Thracians and Pannonians, I mean the Moesians, on the very banks of the Danube, from whom my own family is derived, [are] a stock wholly boorish, austere, awkward, without charm, and abiding immovably by its decisions; all of which qualities are proofs of terrible boorishness."[117] Aurelius Victor and the anonymous author of the *Epitome de caesaribus* applied the same stereotypes to the Illyrian emperors of the third century. The latter described the emperor Maximianus, for example, as "wild by nature, burning with lust, stupid in counsels, of rustic *[agresti]* and Pannonian birth."[118] "Of Pannonian birth" thus encoded a series of associations readily decipherable to the fourth-century audience.[119]

As the last quotation implies, the stereotype extended from the presumption of brutish manners to that of savage behavior. Leo, Valentinian's master of the offices, was attacked by Ammianus as a "Pannonian, a robber of tombs *[bustuarium latronem],* snorting forth cruelty from the gaping maw of a wild beast *[ferino rictu]* and no less insatiable for human blood [than Maximinus]."[120] Maximinus, himself a Pannonian, was savaged as a "brigand with the heart of a wild beast *[spiritus ferini latronem]*", and Valens's father-in-law, Petronius, was "inexorable, cruel and fearlessly hard-hearted."[121] Serenianus, Valens's Pannonian *comes domesticorum,* was described as a "man of rude nature, burning with a cruel desire to hurt," qualities that Ammianus tells us appealed to Valens as a fellow countryman.[122] This is not to say that Pannonians alone came in for such slurs,[123] or that we can speak of evidence for "racial" prejudice as we now understand it.[124] However, the evidence in-

---

116. Joh. Chrys. *Adv. opp. vit. mon.* 1.7 (*PG* 47.328–29).

117. *Mis.* 348c–d.

118. *Epit.* 20.10; cf. Aur. Vict. *Caes.* 40.17, "agrestibus ac Pannonicis parentibus."

119. Aur. Vict. *Caes.* 39.17, 26, 40.12–13, 17, 41.26. The same stereotype is found in Dio Cass. (49.36.1–6), who served as governor of Pannonia. Eutropius, writing for Valens, tends not to mention an emperor's country of origin unless he was Illyrian. Other than Trajan, Hadrian, and Septimius Severus (8.2, 6, 18), all provincials, he reports only on Illyrians (e.g., 9.4, 13, 19, 22; 10.4) and then avoids the disparaging stereotypes in Aurelius Victor. Where, for example, most sources savage Maximinus Thrax, Eutr. 9.1 has none of this.

120. AM 28.1.12.

121. On Maximinus, see AM 28.1.38; cf. Symm. *Or.* 4.13, "externis moribus." On Petronius, see AM 26.6.8.

122. AM 26.10.2: "incultis moribus homo, et nocendi acerbitate conflagrans, Valentique ob similitudinem morum et genitalis patriae vicinitatem acceptus"; cf. 26.10.5. On Valens's own cruelty, see p. 231.

123. See Ammianus's stereotyping of Gauls as rough and rude (15.12.1, 19.6.3–4, 27.6.1, 27.9.2, 28.1.53) and Egyptians as unruly and dirty (22.6.1, 11.4–5, 16.23; cf. Eunap. *VS* 6.3.1–3; *Hist.* fr. 71.2). See also Jul. *Con. Gal.* 116a, 138b. On the stereotyping of Illyrians, see Straub 1939, 29–30; cf. Barnes 1998, 109–11, on the problem in Ammianus.

124. Thompson 1989; Amory 1997, 13–42; Hall 1997.

dicates that regional stereotyping, a phenomenon deeply rooted in the Greek and Roman intellect, informed people's understanding of the world out of which Valentinian and Valens sprang. A Syrian like Ammianus, an African like Aurelius Victor, and even a man of Illyrian background, Julian, all readily accepted the assumption that Illyrians were savage brutes.

If we accept that the stereotype was widely held and played a role in forming preconceptions, we must still ask whether it affected people's reactions to Valens as emperor. It is difficult to imagine that the depth of distaste found in the writings of people like Ammianus did not manifest itself in their dealings with real people. We have already seen that abundant evidence exists that such judgments influenced relations between the Pannonian ministers of Valentinian and Valens and the Italian, Asian, and Syrian aristocrats with whom they had dealings.[125] But there is also good evidence that similar assessments affected attitudes to the emperor himself, and that Procopius, skilled propagandist that he was, harnessed these attitudes to his advantage. Seeking to persuade the Iovii et Victores to desert to his side, Ammianus reports, he harangued them, demanding: "Can it be your wish, my brave men, that our people should draw their swords in such numbers for strangers, and that we should have to groan under your and my wounds to enable a degenerate Pannonian [*Pannonius degener*] who ruins and tramples everything to win a throne for which he never dared to entertain the faintest hope?"[126] This rhetoric evidently achieved the desired effect, for the units defected. The same rhetoric apparently formed a broader motif in Procopius's campaign for power. When Valens laid siege to Chalcedon, Ammianus tells us, the inhabitants insulted him as a *sabaiarius* from their walls, *sabaia* being a beer commonly drunk by Illyrian peasants.[127] Insults in the face of siege were, of course, common, but in this case, they were directed specifically at Valens's origins. Similar insults were publicly posted on bills (*famosi*) in Constantinople at the instigation of Procopius, Libanius reports.[128] The previous winter, such *famosi* had been forbidden by Valens on pain of death.[129] By blatantly denying the order, the Constantinopolitans drove home the pointed nature of their attacks: in their judgment, Valens was by his very origin disqualified for rule.[130]

---

125. See pp. 63–66.

126. AM 26.7.16.

127. AM 26.8.2; cf. Soc. 4.8.1. Jerome, himself an Illyrian, confirms the name's origins and its "barbarous" connotations in *Comm. ad Isaiam* 7.19.11-15 (*CCSL* 73.280). On Illyrian beer drinking, see Dio Cas. 49.36.2–3. Julian himself had composed an epigram in mockery of beer (*Anth. pal.* 9.368).

128. Lib. *Or.* 19.15, 20.25–26.

129. *CTh* 9.34.7 (Feb. 16, 365) with Seeck, *Regesten,* 33, on the date. Valens's law against *famosi* is much harsher than those of previous emperors (*CTh* 9.34.1–6). Cf. Wiebe 1995, 68–69; Matthews 2000, 193–95.

130. On the power of the mob to adjudicate imperial legitimacy, see Lendon 1997, 120–29.

If country of origin provided the raw material for empire, good birth could shape it into recognizably regal form. Our hypothetical panegyrist would have turned to this topic next, and here too, his task would have been complicated. In any period, dynastic claims rendered an emperor's position more secure by providing a guarantee of inherited authority. Of course, by the fourth century, many rulers had come and gone who could hardly have claimed distinguished birth, but when Valens came to power in 364, the sons of emperors had ruled for nearly six decades. The unbroken chain of Constantines had habituated the empire to dynasties, such that, for Valens to have conformed to the ideal, he would have had to be born to the purple.

Because he and his brother did not spring from an imperial family, every effort was made to create an aura of dynasty to strengthen their tenure. Even Constantine, who could claim imperial birth,[131] felt compelled to invent a longer dynastic pedigree for himself at one point by pretending descent from Claudius Gothicus.[132] In the section which follows, we shall see that Valentinian was similarly manipulative in his attempts to graft his own house onto that of his predecessors. Here, however, it suffices to examine how even their father, Gratian, a man of low birth,[133] was magnified as a dynastic forebear. At the celebration of his first consulship in Constantinople, Valens dedicated a statue of his father and delivered a speech in praise of his virtues, which Themistius duly echoed.[134] About the same time, across the empire in Africa, a similar statue was raised in Numidian Cirta "to a man of most blessed memory who should be celebrated through all ages, Gratian, father of our emperors."[135] By 367, the troops were familiar enough with Gratian that, when his grandson and namesake was promoted to Augustus, Valentinian could recommend the boy on the basis of the "honors of his family and the outstanding deeds of his ancestors."[136] The troops played along, readily acclaiming: "The family of Gratian merits this!" ("familia Gratiani hoc meretur!" [AM 27.6.14]). Resonances of the same acclamation occur in a speech of Symmachus the following year: "You merited, O renowned

131. Indeed, *Pan. Lat.* 6 [7].2.5–4.6 obsesses on Constantine's imperial pedigree.

132. First mentioned in 310 at *Pan. Lat.* 6 [7].2.1–2; Julian perpetuated the myth, *Or.* 1.6d–7a, 3.51c. On the fabrication of the claim, see Syme 1971, 204, 234; 1974, 240–42; contrast Lippold 1992a. Eutr. 10.2 is quick to impugn this pseudo-geneology, no doubt to please his patron.

133. AM 30.7.2; cf. *Epit.* 45.2. Of course, Valentinian and Valens never attempted to portray their father as anything but a civilian (cf. Them. *Or.* 9.124b–c), but the rhetoric implied that his achievements merited the reward of empire.

134. On the statue, see Them *Or.* 6.81d. On Valens's speech, see Them. *Or.* 6.81a–b, 82d.

135. *CIL* 8.7014 = *ILS* 758. The date can be inferred from a law received at Cirta by its dedicant, Dracontius, on Aug. 31, 365 (*CTh* 12.6.9). Similar statues were dedicated by Theodosius I to his father; cf. *CIL* 9.333 = *ILS* 780 (Apulia); Symm. *Rel.* 9.4 (Rome); *AE* 1966, 435 (Ephesus).

136. AM 27.6.8–9.

Gratian *[meruisti . . . inclute Gratiane]*, you merited that at some point, you would generate imperial offspring, that you would be a seedbed of the principate, that you would become a royal vein."[137] In 379, Ausonius sounded the same theme once again with Gratian's homonymous grandson: "You, Gratian, who have merited *[meruisti]* your name not by isolated deeds but by the continual kindliness of your gracious life, you who would have received this as a surname by general consent had you not inherited it from your grandfather."[138] As time passed, then, the empire grew accustomed to acknowledging the name Gratian as a dynastic title.

In 365, by contrast, the message may not have been so clear. At this early date, Valens's position in the east was quite wobbly, especially with Julian's cousin Procopius still on the loose. Valens not only lacked regal ancestors but had as yet no male offspring, another essential element of dynastic security. Jovian, whose own claims to empire were extremely tenuous, had taken steps to remedy his dynastic weaknesses by naming his infant son consul for 364 and according him the title *nobilissimus puer,* an indication that the boy was slated to be proclaimed emperor.[139] Valentinian followed suit when he named his own son consul for 366 and granted him the same title at age seven.[140] He then sealed the case by proclaiming Gratian Augustus in Ambiani (Amiens) on August 24, 367.[141] This proclamation secured the family's claim to the empire by binding empire and family as one. In this sense, the boy became the repository of hopes both for dynastic continuity and for the continued strength of Rome: "the exuberance of things present and the guarantee of things to come."[142] The connection is clear in the stereotyped propaganda of coins that associated Gratian with the "Glory of the New Age"

137. Symm. *Or.* 1.3. Cf. Aus. XVIII *Cento nup.* l. 9: "nomine avum referens." On these parallels between Ammianus and Symmachus, see Sabbah 1978, 340–42.

138. Aus. XXI *Grat. act.* 8 [39].

139. On Varronian's consulate, see p. 19 and esp. Them. *Or.* 5.71b. See also Them. *Or.* 5.64r–65a, which implies the intent to make Varronian Caesar. On Varronian as *nobilissimus puer,* see Philostorg. 8.8. On the title *nobilissimus puer* and its connotations, see Instinsky 1952, 98–103; Pabst 1986, 57–58.

140. For evidence of Gratian's consulship and the title *nobilissmus puer,* see Bagnall et al. 1987, 266–67, to which add *AE* 1955, 52. See also Pabst 1989, 218–23, and Doignon 1966, which, however, builds on the incorrect assumption that Gratian was the first to receive the title.

141. For the date, see *Cons. Const.* s.a. 364; Soc. 4.11.3; *Chron. pasch.,* p. 557. For other sources on the proclamation, see AM 27.6.1–16, 30.7.7; Symm. *Or.* 1.3, 2.31–32, 3.1–6; Soz. 6.10.1; *Epit.* 45.4; Zos. 4.14.4; Jer. *Chron.* s.a. 367; Prosper *Chron.* 1135; Philostorg. 8.8; Theoph. a.m. 5857; Zon. 13.15. The sources agree that Gratian's mother played a role in influencing Valentinian's decision to make Gratian Augustus; cf. AM 27.6.1; Zos. 4.12.2; *Epit.* 45.4. On Gratian's proclamation, see esp. Seeck, *Untergang,* 37; Straub 1939, 17–19, 67; Fortina 1953, 19–32; Pabst 1986, 94–97.

142. Symm. *Or.* 3.2: "laetitia praesentium, securitas posterorum"; cf. Pabst 1989, 223–26, with Del Chicca 1987 on the date (a. 370). It also initiated the practice of appointing child em-

Figure 9. Gratian, the SPES R(ei) P(ublicae), between Valentinian and Valens. Solidus of Antioch. *RIC* 9.277.20b. Courtesy American Numismatic Society.

(*GLORIA NOVI SAECVLI*) and the "Hope of the State" (*SPES R*[ei] P[ublicae]) (Fig. 9).[143]

Not until after he had quashed Procopius's revolt could Valens have hoped for similar security. His first son, Valentinian Galates, was born in the midst of the rebellion on January 18, 366.[144] At that point, Valens and his army were waiting out the winter in Galatian Ancyra before moving to face the usurper. Imperial propaganda later played up the connection between the boy's birth and the revolt by hailing him with his topographical nickname— taken from Valens's winter headquarters—and by heralding the felicitous co- incidence between Valentinian's birth and the suppression of the usurper.[145] The latter was emphasized in Themistius's oration 9, delivered on the occa- sion of Galates' first consulship in 369. His appointment to this office at the age of three and designation in his turn as *nobilissimus puer* make it clear that, but for his untimely death ca. 372, Galates would soon have followed in his cousin's footsteps.[146] Gregory of Nazianzus tells us that Galates' fatal illness

---

perors with full honors as Augustus, a practice that, like the use of the Hebdomon for Valens's proclamation, became standard in the Byzantine empire.

143. These epithets were heralded on the coinage (GLORIA NOVI SAECVLI = *RIC* 9.45 [Lug- dunum 15]; 64, 66 [Arelate, 10, 15]; SPE-SRP = *RIC* 9.277 [Antioch 20]) and in panegyric (Symm. *Or.* 3.2: "novi saeculi spes sperata"; 4: "spe electus es"; 9: "novo saeculo"; 12; cf. *Or.* 2.31 and Aus. XVIII *Cent. nupt. praef.* 7).

144. *Cons. Const.* s.a. 366; *Chron. pasch.*, p. 556. Soc. 4.10, followed by Soz. 6.10.1, mistak- enly claims that Valentinian's second son, Valentinian II, was born in 366. In his edition of Themistius 1965–74, 1: 181–82, Downey is misled by this notice and assumes that *Or.* 9 was ad- dressed to "Valentiniano Valentiniani filio, annos tres nato." In fact, Valentinian II had not been born when the oration was delivered in 369. His birth must have fallen in 371, because a num- ber of sources claim that he was four years old when he came to the throne in 375 (AM 30.10.4; *Epit.* 45.10; Philostorg. 9.16; Zon. 13.17; Theoph. a.m. 5867; cf. Oaks 1996).

145. Them. *Or.* 9.121a, 122c. On the other side of the empire, Symmachus *Or.* 3.7 offered similar praise to Gratian, whose consulship coincided with Procopius's defeat.

146. For evidence of Galates's consulship and designation as *nobilissimus puer*, see Bagnall et al. 1987, 272–73, to which add *P Oxy* 4377–80. Themistius *Or.* 9, esp. 128a–c, also spread the word that Galates's proclamation was in the offing. On the death of Galates, see Greg. Naz. *Or.* 43.54; Ruf. *HE* 11.9; Soc. 4.26.22–24; Soz. 6.16.8–9; Theod. *HE* 4.19.8–10; *BP* 4.5; Theoph. a.m. 5868. The exact date is not secure. Galates was alive when Themistius addressed him in 369, but not in 373, when Them. *Or.* 11.153c asked Zeus for a son for Valens, imply- ing that his first was no longer alive. Greg. Naz. *Or.* 43.54 implies that Galates's death fell af-

nearly crushed his father, literally bringing the emperor to his knees in tears.[147] Valens's grief must have been heightened by his awareness that the boy's death ended his hopes for dynastic security.[148] The failure to produce another male descendant continued to weaken Valens's position through-out his rule and no doubt increased fears of challenges to his power.

Having covered Valens's homeland and birth, our panegyrist would have turned to his education, and, once again, the Pannonian would have fallen short of the ideal. Fourth-century panegyrics and epitomized histories were insistent on the importance of education and rhetorical skills to the ideal ruler.[149] More important for Valens, during the half century prior to his ac-cession, the Constantinian emperors had come reasonably close to achiev-ing this ideal. Constantine was a man of considerable learning and rhetori-cal ability. Above all, his knowledge of both Latin and Greek helped him to communicate with all his subjects, in west and east.[150] Constantius II was, like his father, bilingual and was reputed to be quite learned. He placed great personal stock in *paideia* and, *pace* Ammianus, was praised as a man of con-siderable rhetorical talent.[151] Julian, of course, carried imperial learning to precipitous new heights. In his reign, the significance of *paideia* hypertro-

---

ter Valens's encounter with Basil at the feast of Epiphany, which we have dated to 372. The boy's death probably occurred later that year; cf. Seeck, *Untergang,* 460, which misdates Them. *Or.* 11 to 374.

147. Greg. Naz. *Or.* 43.54.

148. In keeping with the customary rhetoric, contemporaries portrayed Galates's birth as guaranteeing the well-being of the state (Them. *Or.* 8.120a; *DRB praef.* 8). See similar rhetoric of Gratian, pp. 90–91. Valens's "dynasty" seems not to have survived his death; it is unknown whether his daughters, Anastasia and Carosa, married. Valentinian's was subsumed by that of Theodosius. Neither of Valentinian's sons bore children, but his daughter Galla married Theo-dosius, and their daughter Galla Placidia eventually gave birth to the emperor Valentinian III.

149. For panegyrics, see *Pan. Lat.* 9[4] passim, esp. 9[4].2.3–4, 19.1–4; Lib. *Or.* 59.32–38; cf. Straub 1939, 174–94; Lendon 1997, 117; Staesche 1998, 236–65. See Bird 1984, 71–80, on the great importance of education in Aurelius Victor's epitomated history. No similar study exists for the *Epitome de caesaribus,* but see 1.16–17, 24, 2.4, 8.6, 10.2, 13.8, 14.2, 16.6, 20.8, 29.2, 40.15, 18, 41.8–9, 14, 25, 42.7, 10, 18–19, 43.5, 44.3, 45.5, 47.4, 48.9, 11. Similar praise in SHA *Hadr.* 14.8–9, 15.10–13, 20.6–7; *Marc.* 27.6–7; *Gall.* 11.4–9; *Carus* 11.1–3. Bird 1993, xliii, notes that education was largely neglected by Eutropius in his epitome for Valens, but see 7.21, 8.7, 11–12, 19, 10.7, 10, 16.

150. On Constantine's education, see Corcoran 1996, 259–60, 263–64. Eus. *Vit. Const.* 4.8, 29, 32, 47 tells us that Constantine had speeches translated into Greek and delivered them thus and *Vit. Const.* 3.13 compliments him on his efforts to use Greek. He seems to have understood Greek but to have spoken it with diffidence, as the interesting court case at *CTh* 8.15.1 would indicate. See Millar 1977, 205–6; Barnes 1981, 73–75; Corcoran 1996, 260–65.

151. On Constantius's interest in education, see Zon. 13.11; *CTh* 14.1.1 (a. 360); Them. *Or.* 3.45b; *Constantiou demegoria* passim, esp. 20d (*Themistii orationes* 3: 121–28). On his rhetor-ical skill, see Jul. *Or.* 1.32a, 3.75b–d; Them. *Or.* 2.29a, 34b, 37a–b, 3.45c, 4.54a; Aur. Vict. *Caes.* 42.1–4, 23; Lib. *Or.* 59.97; cf. AM 21.16.4; *Epit.* 42.18. On Constantius's education more broadly, see Teitler 1992, 119–20.

phied into an obsession so large that volumes have been written on it.[152] Here it suffices to recall the respect that the emperor's learning commanded in precisely the region of Procopius's greatest support, Asia Minor. Asians honored Julian in inscriptions as the "emperor revered for his *philosophia*,"[153] and their *philosophoi* welcomed his invitation to join the imperial court.[154] After his death, many of the same cities that so admired his abilities must have been correspondingly dismayed at the rise of a new crop of Illyrians whose meager scholastic attainments rendered them much less amenable to the values they cherished. In a world where "learning" in the broadest sense provided those in authority not just with the proper refinement but with a veritable code of conduct, an undereducated emperor was both unseemly and threatening.[155]

Of course, Valentinian and Valens enjoyed some education, and both seem to have agreed that *paideia* should number among the qualities of a good ruler. Both undertook educational reforms, and both proved remarkably generous to teachers.[156] Valentinian in particular is portrayed as a man of moderate learning and considerable talent—a sculptor, painter, and armorer.[157] In the introduction to his *Cento nuptialis*, Ausonius, the erudite Bordelais who served Valentinian as court poet, called his patron a "learned man, in my estimation."[158] Indeed, Ausonius composed his *Cento* in an effort to match Valentinian's ability to quote Vergil, which has tempted some to credit the emperor with great erudition. The contents, however, raise doubts. As its name implies, the *Cento nuptialis* is a wedding poem, a genre that calls for ribaldry. In this case, however, Ausonius reshapes Vergil's lines into an epyllion so sodden with violent, pornographic images that one questions his purported admiration of Valentinian's cultural attainments.[159] As we have seen, from a young age, Valentinian spent much of his life in military camps, where

152. Esp. Lib. *Or.* 12.27–31, 18.11–30; Soc. 3.1. See Bowersock 1978, 21–32; Athanassiadi 1981, esp. 13–51; R. B. E. Smith 1995, 23–36.

153. *IEph.* 313a: "philosophiae princeps venerandus"; 3021; Μουσείον καὶ βιβλιοθήκη 5.1 (1885) 61 n. υν̀: (Iasos) τὸν ἐκ φιλοσοφίας βασιλεύοντα; *CIL* 3.14218 (near Smyrna): "filosofiae m[agi / stro veneran]do"; *CIL* 3.7088 = *ILS* 751 (near Pergamum): "filosfi[ae] magistro / venera[nd]o."

154. Jul. *ELF* 26–39; Eunap. *VS* 7.3.10–4.10; Greg. Naz. *Or.* 5.20; cf. Penella 1990, 119–21.

155. On the culture of *paideia* in the east and its social and political function, see Straub 1939, 146–74; Wolf 1952, 75–92; Brown 1992, 35–74; Gleason 1995.

156. See pp. 269–70.

157. AM 30.9.4; *Epit.* 45.6; but see Zos. 3.36.2: παιδεύσεως οὐδεμιᾶς μετεσχήκει. An assessment of Valentinian's education and interest in culture is not easy to arrive at, given the contradictory sources. See the varied assessments in Seeck, *Untergang*, 2–3, 15–16, 41; Stein 1959, 173; Tomlin 1973, 42–47; Matthews 1975, 49–55.

158. Aus. XVIII *Cento nupt.* heading: "vir meo iudicio eruditus."

159. Green 1991, 518–19: "[N]otwithstanding the thin veil of allegory, it is one of the most detailed descriptions of sexual intercourse in Latin Literature, and also one of the most vio-

he is unlikely to have been steeped in books. Unlike his Constantinian predecessors, too, he never learned Greek.[160] In his native Latin, Valentinian's manner of speech was vigorous but laconic, approaching eloquence without, apparently, attaining it.[161] He was thus moderately learned. To judge by contemporary sources, however, he fancied himself more a soldier than a scholar, and, if Ammianus can be believed, he even harbored active resentment of the erudites.[162]

Valens was even less well trained.[163] In terms of positive evidence for his education, we know only that he could write.[164] Like his brother, he spoke scant Greek, a great disadvantage to the ruler of the eastern empire. This difficulty was already clear in the first words that Themistius addressed to him, an elaborate apology for the orator's inability to communicate in his native tongue. In subsequent speeches, Themistius repeated similar apologies for addressing philologically fine-tuned speeches to a man who could not understand them.[165] When Libanius delivered such a panegyric to Valens, imperial ministers actually cut him off in mid speech, perhaps a reflection of Valens's distaste for such exercises.[166] Valens was certainly no orator himself. He seems to have been extremely diffident about delivering public addresses, given that we hear of only one occasion on which he did so.[167] Themistius marveled that Valens matched Pericles as a mediator, even though he was "not of equal ability with Pericles as a demagogue."[168] Valens

---

lent. The frankness is found in some of [Ausonius's] epigrams; the violence, which is not, could have been a concession to Valentinian's tastes." Contrast Sivan 1993, 105–6.

160. AM 30.5.9–10 indicates that Valentinian spoke only Latin, *pace* Tomlin 1973, 43, 253, and Vanderspoel 1995, 157 n. 10. Them. *Or.* 6.71c, although probably delivered only to Valens, implies the same with: ὑμῖν. Sotiroff 1972, who charges that both Valentinian and Valens knew Latin, Greek, and "Pannonian," is not at all careful with the evidence. The author of SHA *Aurel.* 24.2–4 certainly assumed that Pannonians knew only Latin, although epigraphy around Sirmium confirms that some at least spoke Greek (Balla 1989). On fourth-century bilingualism, see Matthews 1989, 67–74.

161. AM 30.9.4: "memoria sermoneque incitato quidem sed raro, facundiae proximo vigens"; cf. *Epit.* 45.5; Symm. *Or.* 2.29–30.

162. AM 30.8.10.

163. AM 31.14.5: "subagrestis ingenii, nec bellicis nec liberalibus studiis eruditus"; cf. 27.5.8: "imperator rudis"; 31.14.8: "ut erat inconsummatus et rudis"; Zos. 4.4.1.

164. Theod. *HE* 4.19.15.

165. Them. *Or.* 6.71c–d. Cf. 8.105c–d, 9.126b, 10.129c, 11.144c–d.

166. Lib. *Or.* 1.144. Valens's impatience with court oratory may be alluded to at Them. *Or.* 10.129a, 11.144a. Contrast the positive reactions of Constantine (Eus. *Vit. Const.* 4.33) and Julian (Lib. *Or.* 15.7) to lengthy oratorical displays. More on proper imperial behavior on such occasions at L'Huillier 1992, 116–20.

167. See p. 28. AM 31.11.1 implies that Valens spoke to troops individually in 378 but does not mention a general harangue.

168. Them. *Or.* 7.94b; cf. 7.93b, 9.123c, 10.134b. Valens's ministers were also derided for their inability to speak Greek or to speak it properly; see Lib. *Or.* 1.156 (Festus); AM 30.4.2

was also short on historical knowledge, leading both Eunapius and Ammianus to lament the mistakes he could have avoided with a modicum of learning.[169] Even so, in keeping with the protocol of empire, few hesitated to flatter the emperor's wisdom. In nearly every speech he made to Valens, Themistius gushed with praise for the "true philosopher," and Valens's praetorian prefect, Modestus, went so far as to call Valens's "rough, crude words 'choice Ciceronian posies.'"[170]

With such wheedling, Modestus and Themistius did little more than confirm the inadequacy of Valens's education by drawing attention to it. Even Valens and Valentinian would have been aware that they fell short of the ideal. The fact that they both engaged the most learned of tutors for their children indicates that they felt compelled to make up for their own deficiencies in the next generation. Valentinian enlisted Ausonius to teach his son from a very early age, winning for the boy the highest praise in subsequent panegyrics.[171] In the east, Themistius was slated to fill the same role for Galates had the child survived: he actually told the three-year-old in 369 that he already surpassed his father in the teachers he had at his disposition.[172] A similarly learned tutor was engaged for Valens's daughters.[173] This interest in retaining great scholars as imperial tutors offers a clear sign that the Pannonian brothers accepted the ideal of the educated emperor, while no doubt remaining aware that they themselves fell short of it. Their subjects probably understood the same. The late fourth-century "Life of Maximinus" in the *Historia Augusta* mocks the stereotypically rough-hewn Illyrian emperor for engaging great minds to teach his son, perhaps an allusion to the rustic Valentinian and his overeducated son Gratian.[174]

(Modestus); Greg. Naz. *Or.* 43.47 (Demosthenes), followed by Theod. *HE* 4.19.12 and Theoph. a.m. 5868. Cf. Zos. 5.9.3–5 (Valens's relative Procopius).

169. Eunap. *Hist.* fr. 44.1 (Blockley); AM 26.10.12, 29.2.18; cf. AM 30.8.4–6, 9, of Valentinian. Contrast Julian's good use of historical knowledge once he was emperor (Lib. *Or.* 18.53, 233, 245–46; Jul. *Or.* 4.244c–246a). Like Valentinian and Valens, Jovian was far from a model of the educated emperor (cf. AM 25.10.15; Joh. Ant. fr. 177, 181).

170. On Modestus, see AM 29.1.11: "horridula eius verba et rudia, flasculos Tullianos appellans." On Themistius, see *Or.* 8.105c–d, 110d–111a, 11.144d–145a, 146d–147a. The author of *DRB* also seems to have regarded Valens as a man of limited intellect (cf. 1.10, 3.4, 5.2, 6.5).

171. Sivan 1993, passim, esp. 101–6. Sivan contends that Ausonius began tutoring Gratian in 367. For praise of Gratian's education, see Symm. *Or.* 3.7; *Ep.* 1.20.2, 10.2.5; Them. *Or.* 9.125c; Aus. XXI *Grat. actio* 15 [68–71]; XX *Prec. var.* 1; AM 27.6.9, 31.10.18; cf. Pabst 1989, 200–202.

172. Them. *Or.* 8.120a, 9.122d–124b, 125d–126d. In both cases, Themistius prays that he may play the role of Aristotle to Galates's Alexander. Themistius had similar aspirations with Arcadius, *Or.* 16.204b–d, 212c–213b, 18.224b–225b; cf. Dagron 1968, 11–12.

173. Soc. 4.9.5; Soz. 6.9.3.

174. SHA *Max.* 27.2–5. Like Gratian, Maximinus's son was supposed to have been granted a dynastic marriage (to the sister of Severus Alexander [SHA *Max.* 29.1–3]). More on the younger Maxim[in]us's education at Lippold 1991, 593–605.

Valens would certainly have felt the scrutiny of an eastern public that had known educated emperors for forty years before he came to power. Indeed, as with his birthplace and family background, Procopius drew attention to Valens's educational deficiencies by emphasizing his own superiority in this arena. Ammianus tells us that Procopius was "born in Cilicia of distinguished family and correspondingly educated."[175] Having been raised in the east, Procopius naturally spoke Greek, and Ammianus indicates that he knew Latin as well.[176] Ammianus also transmits an encrypted message sent by Procopius in the wake of his embassy to Persia, which is larded with allusions to historical literature, again implying considerable learning.[177] Well aware of the advantages of his education, Procopius apparently put these to work in his propaganda war against Valens. His wish to advertise his philosophical pose is nowhere more evident than in his coinage, where he had himself portrayed wearing a philosopher's beard (fig. 10). This attribute is unusual in the fourth century and was certainly meant to evoke memories of Procopius's cousin, Julian, who advertised his own philosophical pretensions with a studiously overgrown beard (fig. 11).[178] For this reason, after the end of the revolt, Themistius was anxious to praise Valens, "who had been raised among weapons," as a true devotee of philosophy by contrasting him with that ruler, "who grew out his beard and laid claim to being the most philosophical of kings" but ultimately proved reluctant to defend *philosophia*.[179] Nor would Procopius's philosophical posturing have been lost on his eastern supporters. This was a world where a man's worth was judged by his education, where aristocrats, pagan or Christian, strove above all to be considered *philosophoi*, where the culture of Hellenism, a culture founded on the Greek language, was the primary guarantor of unity among a vast sea of peoples.[180] To this audience, Procopius was much more palatable than Valens, and it was with this in mind that Procopius scripted his performance.

Thus, on three counts, Valens and his brother were not ideal emperors. As men of Pannonian origin, they could be praised for their martial background but also derided as stereotypically brutish. This latter is precisely what happened when Procopius revolted. As men of common birth, their right to rule could also be challenged, and, as we shall see in what follows, Valens's actually was. As men of little education, they could be scorned as

175. AM 26.6.1: "insigni genere Procopius in Cilicia natus et educatus."

176. AM 26.7.15: "latine salute data."

177. AM 27.6.15, 18.6.17–19.

178. On Julian's beard, see Jul. *Mis.* 355d; cf. AM 25.4.22; Soc. 3.17.4. For the beard as an attribute on obverses, see Kent 1959, 109–17; Bastien 1992, 36–37.

179. Them. *Or.* 7.99c–d, esp. ὁ τὸν πώγωνα καθειμένος καὶ τοῦ φιλοσοφωτάτου τῶν Βασιλέων ἀντιποιούμενος. Here Themitius is referring to Julian but must also intend a double allusion to his cousin Procopius.

180. See esp. Bowersock 1990, 29–33, 61–68.

Figure 10. A bearded Procopius proclaims the REPARATIO FEL(icium) TEMP(orum). Solidus of Cyzicus. *RIC* 9.239.1. Courtesy American Numismatic Society.

Figure 11. Bearded Julian. Solidus of Antioch. *RIC* 8.530.196. Courtesy American Numismatic Society.

unworthy of the responsibilities of empire and upstaged by a man who deliberately played up his cultural attainments. We have seen that in each of these "qualities of character," Valentinian's and Valens's cognition of the dissonance between ideal emperorship and the reality of their own rule led them to compensate, to mould themselves to an ideal that they did not entirely represent. These efforts helped them over time to strengthen their claims to legitimacy. During this early period, however, these claims were still dangerously tenuous.

THE LONG SHADOW OF CONSTANTINE

A dynasty had a life of its own. Once a family had secured for itself the prize of empire, the aura of power continued to surround its members until their dying days. This had been true since the first century, and even in the chaos of the mid third century, rulers generally took faltering steps to ensure dynastic succession. The webs of interrelation established by Diocletian and his fellow tetrarchs, following the former's stabilization of the empire, continued to affect dynastic links through the first quarter of the fourth century. Thus, when Constantius I died in 306, it seemed natural that his son would be promoted to fill his place. Constantine's accession marked the first in a series of dynastic proclamations that would dominate much of the fourth century. Even after his death, Constantine's name continued to command respect among the troops, and some people even came to worship him as a virtual deity despite his Christianity.[181] By the time his nephew Julian died

181. Jul. *Or.* 1.8a. On worship paid to Constantine's statue at his porphyry column, see Philostorg. 2.17; Malalas 13.8 (p. 322); *Chron. pasch.*, p. 530; Cedrenus, p. 518; Theod. *HE* 1.34.3;

in 363, the "New Flavian" dynasty, the second longest to rule Rome up to that day, had acquired an indelible glow of empire.[182]

Julian's successors were aware of the importance of dynasty and thus anxious to glorify their own families and highlight their connections to the imperial family that had preceded them. Even when racing west to shore up his position, Jovian was careful to make a stop in Tarsus and pay his respects at Julian's tomb.[183] This gesture was especially important because Julian's remains had been deposited there only a short while earlier by his cousin, which would have strengthened public awareness that the family lived on.[184] When Valentinian and Valens succeeded Jovian, they must have kept this in mind, for they too "showed great concern about [Julian's] tomb and for the expense it involved."[185] They could not afford to ignore the respect owed to the last member of a dynasty that had defined emperorship since before their birth.

When Procopius revolted, he was certainly aware that claiming the Constantinian name offered him his strongest argument for legitimacy. From the beginning, he played this trump card, boasting of his "relationship with the imperial family" (AM 26.6.18) and giving out that Julian had named him as his successor. Neither claim being entirely justified, however, Procopius needed further evidence. This he obtained through Constantius's former wife, Fausta, and baby daughter, Constantia. Early on, he garnered support among the troops by carrying the baby about in his arms and boasting of his familial connection to her. He also saw to it that Fausta was present at a ceremony during which he received some of the imperial emblems.[186] In the field, Procopius harangued his troops to the effect that he was fighting on behalf of the "imperial stock," using Fausta and Constantia, who followed him as living emblems of his dynastic claim, to drive home the point.[187]

In the speech during which he mocked Valens as a "base Pannonian," Procopius stressed the same connections: "Nay, follow rather the offspring of the loftiest royal line, one who has taken up arms with the greatest justice,

cf. Fowden 1991, 125–31. See Corcoran 1996, 68–69, on Constantine's normative role in later imperial law.

182. On the importance of dynastic propaganda in cementing the authority of Constantine's family, see MacCormack 1981, 185–88.

183. AM 25.10.4; Soc. 3.26.1–2; Zon. 13.14.

184. AM 25.9.12; cf. 23.2.5. Zos. 3.34.4 and Zon. 13.13 record the epigram on Julian's tomb. See also Lib. *Or.* 1.132, 15.4–5, 77, 16.53, 18.306, 24.8; Greg. Naz. *Or.* 5.18, 21.33. Philostorg. 8.1 tells us that Julian's tomb was next to that of Maximin Daia.

185. Lib. *Or.* 24.10. Greg. Naz. *Or.* 21.33 states that Julian's tomb was destroyed in an earthquake, perhaps the earthquake of 365. If so, Libanius may imply that Valentinian and Valens had it rebuilt. Julian's remains were later transferred to Constantinople; cf. DiMaio 1978.

186. AM 26.7.10. Eunap. *Hist.* fr. 34.2 (Blockley) may be related to the same claims, see Blockley 1981–83, 2: 137 n. 73.

187. AM 26.9.3.

not in order to seize what belongs to another, but to restore himself to the possession of his ancestral majesty."[188] Zosimus confirms that such claims won support among the soldiery.[189] They certainly struck a chord with the Divitenses et Tungrecani—the first units to join the revolt—and their commanders, who knew Procopius personally. These had initially been formed as crack mobile units by Constantine and thus owed their existence and allegiance to Procopius's "family."[190] The connection to Constantine also enabled Procopius to persuade the Goths to send him auxiliaries. As we shall see, these firmly believed that they owed the usurper the same loyalty that they had accorded his "family" ever since they struck a treaty with Constantine in 332.[191] Procopius's Constantinian connections also apparently played a role in winning over high-level commanders. His purported relations probably helped secure the support of his *magistri militum*, Gomoarius and Agilo; the careers of both had been advanced in the reign of Constantius. Once in office under Procopius, Agilo also won the praetorian prefecture for his father-in-law, Araxius, another man who owed his career to Constantius.[192] So, too, Rumitalca, whose acuity won Procopius a foothold in Asia, was probably the son of a Thracian with long-standing connections to Constantine's house, and Vitalianus, a tribune who had probably served under Julian in Gaul, transferred his loyalty and his units to Procopius as a personal friend.[193] Procopius's dynastic claims thus constituted one of his chief weapons in the war to assemble an army from scratch.

These claims were, of course, built around the successful use of propaganda. Here, as we have seen, the usurper's skill was uncanny. Further evidence is readily available in Procopius's coinage. He was undoubtedly aware that coins offered the quickest way to reach the largest audience with physical confirmation of his rule, and having seized control of most of the eastern mints, he sent men to distribute coins "bearing the image of the new

188. AM 26.7.16. Ironically, the latter part of this passage has a tenuous textual pedigree of its own. Them. *Or.* 2.33d–34a, 3.43a–c used similar rhetoric to justify Constantius's defense of his ancestral rights to the throne against Magnentius; cf. Lib. *Or.* 59.10–28, 30, 49–55.

189. Zos. 4.7.1; cf. Them. *Or.* 7.90a, 92b. For further examples of dynastic loyalty among the soldiery, see Lendon 1997, 254.

190. AM 26.6.12–13: "per quosdam ex isdem numeris notos." On the formation of the Divitenses et Tungrecani under Constantine, see Hoffmann 1969–70, 1: 177–79.

191. AM 26.10.3, 27.5.1; Eunap. *Hist.* fr. 37 (Blockley); Zos. 4.7.1; see pp. 147–52.

192. *PLRE* I, Gomoarius; Agilo. Both Gomoarius and Agilo appear to have been dismissed by Julian. Gomoarius had actually been sent by Constantius to halt Julian's advance through Moesia in 361. On Araxius, see AM 26.7.6, 10.7; and see *PLRE* I on his earlier career.

193. On Rumitalca, see *PLRE* I, which associates Procopius's tribune Rumitalca with Val. Rometalca, DUX AEG ET THEB UTRAMQUE LIBB under Constantine, *CIL* 3.12073 = *ILS* 701. His family may also be attested in a dedication at the Moesian villa of Mediana, often associated with the family of Constantine (Petrovic 1993, 72–73). On Vitalianus, see AM 26.7.15, if this Vitalianus is to be associated with the one mentioned at AM 25.10.9, as at *PLRE* I, Vitalianus 3.

Figure 12. Aes of Procopius holding a *labarum* with Chi-Rho in field. Double-sized. *RIC* 9.215.17a. Courtesy British Museum.

emperor" into Illyricum.[194] These would have carried messages that reinforced his dynastic propaganda with their reverse legend REPARATI-O FEL(icium) TEMP(orum), a patent evocation of the famous legend of Constantius's prolific bronze type, FEL(icium) TEMP(orum)-REPARATIO (figs. 10, 12–13).[195] To drive home the link, Procopius also shifted his bronze denominations back to a standard initiated under Julian.[196] Furthermore, as noted earlier, his obverses portrayed him with a beard, an attribute meant simultaneously to evoke Procopius's own philosophical pretensions and his dynastic connections with the Apostate. Unlike Julian, however, Procopius was apparently Christian— a fact also advertised on his coinage with the labarum. By juxtaposing these seemingly contradictory symbols, Procopius played all available angles of dynastic politics, concurrently portraying himself as rightful heir of both the Christian Constantius and the philosopher-king Julian.

Procopius not only understood how to capitalize on visual propaganda, he also had an acute sense of location. He probably knew that his best hopes for easy support lay in Constantinople. The eastern capital had, of course, been refounded by Constantine and owed its name and prestige to the Constantinian family.[197] Constantine and Constantius had filled the city with art and monuments such as the baths of Anastasia, named after the emperor's sister, where Procopius had himself proclaimed.[198] The Senate of Constantinople was also a creation of Constantine, and its membership had been

194. AM 26.7.11; cf. p. 96.
195. On Procopius's issues, see *RIC* 9.192–93 (Heraclea 6–8); 215 (Constantinople 17–19); 240 (Cyzicus 4–7); 251 (4–8). On Constantius's issues, see Mattingly 1933; Kent 1967. See also Austin 1972b, 193; Matthews 1989, 200–201; Wiebe 1995, 73–81.
196. Elmer 1937, 41–42.
197. See esp. Dagron 1974, 29–42, 319.
198. AM 26.6.14. On Constantinian building and benefaction, see Dagron 1974, 88–90, 300–305.

Figure 13. Aes of Constantius proclaiming FEL(icium)
TEMP(orum) REPARATIO. *RIC* 8.523.135. Courtesy
American Numismatic Society.

greatly increased by Constantius, who further expanded the number of senators and increased the importance of offices available to the city's aristocrats.[199] Moreover, Julian had been born in the capital and was initially educated there. During his stay in the city in the winter of 361/62, he made it
eminently clear that he felt great attachment to his *patria,* and the Constantinopolitans returned his affection.[200] It is little wonder, then, that Constantinople provided the springboard for the revolt. Its population consisted
of people like Andronicus, Procopius's vicar of Asia, whose families had come
there to take advantage of the opportunities created by Procopius's "forebears."[201] Themistius indicates that Andronicus was by no means alone
among Constantinopolitan senators who joined the cause.[202]

In response to the revolt, Valens, of course, employed propaganda of his
own. We have already seen that his official rhetoric downplayed the supposed
connections of Procopius, the lowly secretary, to Constantine's family and
labeled him a brigand and criminal. Once Valens had secured support from
the general Arbitio, he could also provide a foil to counter the usurper's family connections. Although Arbitio was not a Constantinian dynast, he had
been Constantius's trusted commander, and his claims to authority with the

199. Petit 1957, 347–82; A. H. M. Jones 1964, 545–62; Dagron 1974, 119–90; Chastagnol
1976, 341–56; 1982, 180–84; Vanderspoel 1995, 62–70, 105–8.

200. AM 22.9.2, 25.3.23; Zos. 3.11.2; *Pan. Lat.* 3 [11].2.3, 14.6; Them. *Or.* 4.58d–59a; Jul.
Ep. 59 (Bidez): εἰς τὴν ἐμὴν πατρίδα Κνωσταντίνου πόλιν... ἐγὼ δὲ ὡς μητέρα φιλῶ. καὶ
γὰρ ἐγενόμην παρ' αὐτῇ καὶ ἐτράφην ἐκεῖσε, καὶ οὐ δύναμαι περὶ αὐτὴν ἀγνώμων εἶναι. See
Dagron 1974, 193–94.

201. *PLRE* I, Andronicus 3, esp. Lib. *Or.* 62.58–60. See Seeck, *Briefe,* 74 (Andronicus II), on
the entry of Andronicus's family into the Senate of Constantinople from Italy. On the repopu-
lation of the city and Senate by Constantine and his successors, see Dagron 1974, 120–35, 519–20.

202. *Or.* 7.97d. For more on connections between Procopius and those with links to the
house of Constantine, see pp. 99 and 109.

army were assured by his seniority among living generals. Before the show-down at Thyateira, he was able to persuade Procopius's forces to desert by begging them "to obey him as a parent who was known for his successful campaigns" rather than following the "public brigand."[203]

Later, Themistius would flatter Valens with favorable comparisons to the Constantinian dynasts, no doubt a reflection of Valens's official stance toward his predecessors.[204] Nevertheless, while Valens took delight in his purported superiority to the Constantinians, he also recognized their importance for his own legitimacy and made efforts to connect himself with their glory. Sensing this, Themistius also told Valens that he had taken over rule from the Constantinian dynasts "without letting anyone perceive a change of dynasty."[205] To prove the connection, Valens took responsibility for completing Constantine's Church of the Holy Apostles and apparently played a role in connecting it with the adjacent imperial mausoleum, where both Constantine and Constantius had been buried.[206] When Valentinian died in 375, his body was interred there among the remains of his predecessors. Valens, whose body was lost, seems to have prepared a sarcophagus there for himself as well.[207] Valens also completed the cistern and aqueduct begun by Constantius at Constantinople and affixed his own name to the latter. And he finished both the Thermae Constantinianae[208] and the Anastasian baths, where Procopius was proclaimed, which he rechristened "Anastasianae," this time after his own daughter.[209]

The attempts to rival the Constantinians or, better yet, to join their family to the Valentinians, went even deeper. The moment she reached marriageable age in 374, Constantia, who had served as Procopius's dynastic talisman in her infancy, was sent west to marry Valentinian's son Gratian.[210] Themistius

203. AM 26.9.4–5; Zos. 4.7.4. For Arbitio's career, see *PLRE* I, Flavius Arbitio 2. Procopius himself had courted Arbitio (AM 26.8.13) as a potential link in his chain of Constantinian generals.

204. Them. *Or.* 6.76a, 83b, 8.113c, 115c–d, 11.151a–b; cf. 9.128c. Themistius's criticism of Constantine's betrayal of Licinius is echoed at Eutr. 10.5; cf. 10.6. Themistius *Or.* 5.70d had used such rhetoric before Jovian.

205. Them. *Or.* 7.92b: οὐκ εἴασας αἰσθέσθαι τῆς τοῦ γένους μεταβολῆς.

206. Jer. *Chron.* s.a. 370; *Cons. Const.* s.a. 370 and *Chron. pasch.*, p. 559, with Mango 1990a; cf. Dagron 1974, 401–5 on the complications of dating the phases of construction for the monument.

207. On Valentinian, see *Cons. Const.* s.a. 376; AM 30.10.1; cf. Marcellinus Comes *Chron.* s.a. 382. See also Grierson 1962, 23–26, 42; Johnson 1991, 501–2, who notes that Valentinian's wives were also buried there.

208. On the cistern, aqueduct, and Thermae Constantinianae, see app. D, catalog nos. Co 2, 4, 5.

209. See app. D, catalog no. Co 8.

210. AM 29.6.7; cf. Aus. XXI *Grat. act.* 11 [53]; Them. *Or.* 13.168a and Fortina 1953, 26–27. The dating to 374 seems to be confirmed by the dedication of a bath complex in Calabria on

later assured Gratian that Constantinople was rendered secure by his min-
gling of blood with that of the Constantines. By 378, a Roman church council referred to Constantine as "your ancestor" in a missive to Gratian, and in
the same year Gratian himself sent Ausonius a consular robe embroidered
with an image of Constantius, whom the young emperor called *parens noster*.[211] Valentinian apparently sought a similar connection for himself. At some
point, perhaps in 369, he divorced his first wife, Severa (or Mari[a]na?) and
married an Italian named Justina.[212] Some sources report that he had
turned on Severa after she unjustly used her influence to buy an estate fraudulently; be that as it may, his underlying reason for the divorce was no doubt
dynastic.[213] By the time Valentinian remarried, Severa had not born Valentinian any children since Gratian, ten years earlier. Justina bore him four over
the next six years, one of them another son, Valentinian II.[214] More important,
these children could claim a royal pedigree on their mother's side. Justina's
father, Justus—probably from the aristocratic family of the Neratii[215]—was
apparently the nephew of the princess Galla, former wife of Julius Constantius
and the mother of Gallus Caesar.[216] As a child, Justina had already been
drafted for a similar dynastic marriage to the usurper Magnentius, who was
seeking recognition from Constantius.[217] With the Constantinian dynasty all

June 27, 374 [*AE* 1913, 227], by the emperors to their queens (REGINIS SUIS), apparently in
honor of the recent marriage. Gratian was fifteen and Constantia was twelve at their marriage
(cf. Seeck, *Untergang*, 38–40). After the marriage, Gratian was left in charge at Trier while Valentinian moved east to Pannonia, implying that Gratian was now acting with greater independence
from his father (cf. AM 30.10.1; Zos. 4.19.1). His first law at Trier fell in 376 (*CTh* 15.7.3).

211. Them. *Or.* 13.167c: οἷς σὺ καὶ τῷ αἵματι ἀνεμίχθης; *Epistula romani concilii sub Damaso
habiti* 11 (*PL* 13.583): "apud parentem vestrum Constantinum"; Aus. XXI *Grat. act.* 11 [53]:
"palmatam tibi misi in qua divus Constantius parens noster intextus est." See also *CTh* 16.6.2
(a. 377): "lege divali parentum nostrum Constantini, Constanti, Valentiniani decreta sunt."

212. *PLRE* I, Iustina.

213. *Chron. pasch.*, p. 559 (a. 369); Malalas 13.31 (p. 341); John of Nikiu, p. 82 all of which
report the name of Valentinian's first wife as Mari[a]na. These same sources report that Gratian
recalled his mother after the death of his father; cf. AM 28.1.57. Soc. 4.31.13 calls her Severa.
D. Woods has a paper in progress on the question. More on Valentinian's divorce on p. 267.

214. *PLRE* I, Flavius Valentinianus 8; Iusta; Grata; Galla 2. Within a month of Valentinian
II's birth, Justina had acquired the title Augusta, *CJ* 4.22.7 (Aug. 7, 371). Cf. Tomlin 1973, 90–91.

215. *PLRE* I, Iustus 1.

216. First argued at Rougé 1958; accepted at *PLRE* I, Galla 1; cf. Sabbah 1992, 99–100. The
connection is deduced from the names of Justina's brothers, Constantius and Cerealis, and one
of her daughters, Galla. All were names characteristic of the Neratii. Galla's brother, *PLRE* I, Vulcacius Rufinus 25, served as Valentinian's praetorian prefect of Italy from 365 to 368. Barnes
1982, 44, 103, argues that Justina was a great-granddaughter of Crispus Caesar. Justina had considerable family estates which she left to her daughters. Ownership of these was contested by an
orphanus, who eventually won his claim in a trial before Valentinian II (Amb. *De obit. Val.* 37).
This was perhaps a son of one of Justina's brothers, Constantianus (d. 369) or Cerealis (d. ?).

217. Zos. 4.43.1; cf. 4.19.1; Joh. Ant. fr. 187, which indicates that Justina was so young when
she married Magnentius that she could not bear children. Rougé 1974 argues that Soc. 4.31.11–

but extinct, Justina must have seemed once again an attractive mate to an emperor hoping to bolster his dynastic connections.

Valentinian and Valens thus eventually compensated for the disparities between their own family and their predecessors' by competing with, but also absorbing the earlier dynasty. Unfortunately for Valens, the contrasts between the two families still stood out much more starkly than the connections in the second year of his reign. Procopius capitalized on these contrasts to cobble together a revolt with remarkable ingenuity. In what follows, however, we shall see how Valentinian and Valens had already sowed the seeds for revolt by initially drawing the contrasts with their predecessors far too sharply and thus alienating some of the most powerful citizens of the eastern empire.

A CHANGING OF THE GUARD:
PUNISHMENT AND CONCESSIONS BEFORE AND AFTER THE REVOLT

Any change in emperors necessarily brought with it a shift in imperial personnel. At times this was carried out with a minimum of reprisals, at others not. After taking over Constantius's court in 362, Julian, for example, had employed the familiar tool of a formal judicial inquest to facilitate the cashiering of those whom he regarded as threatening. When all was said and done, at least six of Constantius's top officials had been exiled and four more executed, two by burning alive.[218] Despite the attempts of sources favorable to Julian to absolve him of culpability,[219] his actions did not go unnoticed. The year after his death, Themistius contrasted Julian's ruthlessness with the mildness of his successor: "But receiving the empire under compulsion and in its entirety, you [Jovian] kept it more bloodless than those who received it by inheritance, since you did not suspect anyone as ill-willed or fear anyone as more worthy."[220] Themistius was, of course, right. By comparison with his predecessor, Jovian had been a model of tolerance. Aside from dismissing a few generals, including Procopius himself,[221] Jovian kept most of Julian's commanders and bureaucrats in place.[222] Of course this soft touch won praise

---

13 should be construed to mean that Justus was put to death for consenting to his daughter's marriage to Magnentius.

218. AM 22.3.1–12; Lib. *Or.* 18.152; Jul. *Ep.* 33 (Bidez). Executed were *PLRE* I, Ursulus 1 *(comes sacrarum largitionum),* Apodemius 1 *(agens in rebus),* Paulus "Catena" 4 *(notarius),* Eusebius 11 *(praepositus sacri cubiculi).* Exiled were Palladius 4 *(ex magister officiorum),* Flavius Taurus 3 (praetorian prefect), Florentius 3 *(magister officiorum),* Evagrius 5 *(comes rei privatae),* Flavius Saturninus 10 *(cura palatii),* Cyrinus *(ex notarius).* Cf. also *PLRE* I, Thalassius 2 *(ex proximus libellorum).*

219. E.g., AM 22.3.8–9; Lib. *Or.* 18.152–53.

220. Them. *Or.* 5.66d; cf. Vanderspoel 1995, 147–48. See also Eunap. *VS* 7.4.11.

221. *PLRE* I, Flavius Nevitta; Hormisdas 2; Procopius 4.

222. On military officials, see *PLRE* I, Flavius Arinthaeus; Sebastianus 2; Victor 4; Dagalaifus; and Flavius Iovinus 6 (on whom, see AM 25.10.7–9). On civilian ministers, see *PLRE* I, Sat-

from the panegyrist, but it was as much a function of Jovian's desperate situation as of any commitment to appease the friends of his predecessor. Only after the army had been extracted from Persia and marched back to the center of the empire could an emperor have hoped to shed himself of undesirables. Jovian never even made it to Constantinople and was thus never in a position to initiate a purge.

Valentinian, by contrast, was. Having reached the eastern capital, appointed his brother co-Augustus, and cemented his administration with fellow Pannonians, Valentinian had amassed sufficient political capital to undertake the dirty business of weeding out Julian's cronies. We have already noted that he used the fever that afflicted him and his brother in the first months of their reign as an excuse to launch witchcraft investigations with the hidden purpose of "rousing hatred against the memory of the emperor Julian and his friends."[223] Julian's old confidant Sallustius was able to stave off a full-scale witch-hunt, but at least one minister, the *praepositus sacri cubiculi* Rhodanus, was immolated in the hippodrome, and the message got round that Julian's friends were now personae non gratae. Julian's admirer and panegyrist Libanius, for example, learned quickly that "none of our old friends has any influence at court"[224] for these had lost ground to "men who had been of no account in time past but who gained influence as a result of Julian's murder."[225]

Because the narratives for this early purge are thin on specifics, we cannot say precisely how many were investigated and how many punished. From other sources, however, we can document several instances of people who held offices under Julian but seem not to have continued under Valentinian and Valens, or at least not past their first year.[226] To take just one example, the historian and littérateur Sextus Aurelius Victor, who served as Julian's governor of Pannonia II, was apparently dismissed by Valentinian and, although he eventually regained office under Theodosius, was not accorded a post during the remainder of Valentinian's rule. Valentinian might have known Victor personally, because the latter had been serving in Sirmium

urninius Secundus Salutius 3, Flavius Mamertinus 2, Domitius Modestus 2, Aradius Rufinus 10, Helpidius 6, and Caesarius 1.

223. AM 26.4.4; Zos. 4.1.1, 2.1–4; see p. 25.

224. Lib. *Ep.* 1459; cf. 1148, 1154, 1193, 1209.

225. Lib. *Or.* 1.167; cf. *Ep.* 1220, 1264: οὐ γὰρ αὐτοὶ καὶ βλασφημοῦσι ['Ιουλιανὸν] καὶ δύνανται.

226. *PLRE* I, Dulcitius 5, Priscianus 1, Aristophanes, Ambrosius 2, Leontius 9, and Ulpianus 3. Of course, some may have been uninterested in further advancement. Then, too, many of the gaps in our knowledge of eastern careers are attributable to the gap in Libanius's correspondence between the years 366 and 388. Even this, however, reflects Libanius's discomfort with Valens—and later Theodosius—under whom he believed it was dangerous to send and preserve letters, as Lib. *Ep.* 1264.

when the future emperor apparently resided there. Given that Victor's career saw a hiatus that neatly spans the years of Valentinian's reign, and that it resumed under Theodosius, indicating an ongoing interest in office-holding, it is almost certain that the favor shown by Julian provoked disfavor from Valentinian.[227]

More pointedly, several men who had been close to Julian are known to have been forced out of their posts shortly after his death. Already under Jovian, Alexander of Heliopolis was prosecuted for excesses he had committed as Julian's governor of Syria. Although he was eventually acquitted, he is not known to have held office again.[228] Vindaonius Magnus, who had burned a Christian church in Beirut to show solidarity with the Apostate, only escaped with his life after agreeing to pay for its reconstruction; and Libanius, who had been nauseatingly unctuous toward Julian, was physically attacked and later prosecuted while Jovian was in Antioch in October 363.[229] Later, Entrechius, twice governor under Julian, was forced to abandon his post because of the "envy" of opponents.[230] Even Saturninius Secundus Sallustius, Julian's praetorian prefect, who had played a key role in the election of Valentinian, lost his post in 365 because of intrigues by Valens's father-in-law.[231] Although he was later drafted back to help Valens with the Procopius crisis,[232] Sallustius was again forced into retirement in 366, this time permanently.[233] Two letters of Libanius's reveal that Julian's prefect of Constantinople, Domitius Modestus, who would eventually return to service under Valens, was also forced out under tense circumstances in 364.[234] The first

227. *PLRE* I, Sextus Aurelius Victor 13; cf. Bird 1984, 5–15; 1994, vii–xi; 1996. For other such instances, see *PLRE* I, Aradius Rufinus 11 and Philagrius 2 (probably identical with Philagrius 4). Barnes 1987, 220–25, indicates that the orator Himerius probably also compromised his career by excessive attachment to Julian. Barnes 1998, 63, even speculates that Ammianus's career may have been halted because of his enthusiasm for Julian.

228. *PLRE* I, Alexander 5, esp. Lib. *Ep.* 1456, to Clearchus, who helped procure his acquittal.

229. *PLRE* I, Vindaonius Magnus 12, esp. Theod. *HE* 4.22.10. For Libanius, see his *Or.* 1.136–38, with Norman 1965, 188–89; cf. *Ep.* 1220.6.

230. *PLRE* I, Entrechius 1, esp. Lib. *Ep.* 1252. Cf. Lib. *Ep.* 901, which traces Entrechius's career up to 388 and makes it clear that there was a cessation of office after Julian.

231. AM 26.7.4. The last recorded law Sallustius received was *CTh* 12.6.5, July 4, 365, with Pergami 1993, 237; cf. 301.

232. *CTh* 7.4.14, issued to Sallustius as *PPO* on Dec. 1, 365, indicates that he was already back in office by this date.

233. Eunap. *VS* 7.5.9; Zos. 4.10.4. The dismissal probably fell in winter 366/67. The last recorded law he received was *CTh* 4.12.2 (Apr. 4, 366), but the first recorded law received by his successor was *CTh* 10.16.1 (Sept. 1, 367). Sallustius ultimately retired with honor, receiving a gilded statue in the Roman Forum (*CIL* 6.1764 = *ILS* 1255) and possibly the title *patricius* (*Chron. pasch.*, p. 555). He was already old and was apparently suffering from ill-health, Lib. *Ep.* 1428.

234. Lib. *Ep.* 1216. The letter describes Modestus's retirement to an estate furnished by Valentinian and Valens and implies that the retirement followed some sort of acquittal on an

year of the new administration thus witnessed a housecleaning. This does not mean that all of Julian's and Constantius's men were sacked. Indeed, some came to number among Valens's most trusted officials.[235] Nevertheless, all who had benefited under the Apostate, even those who continued to serve the new regime, were made anxious by a palpable air of hostility.

Their fears would have been piqued by the awareness that there was more to fear than simple dismissal. Many were also severely punished. In these cases we hear not about charges of sorcery, as Ammianus and Zosimus would lead us to expect, but peculation. Valentinian seems to have been digging for peculation charges when he called for accusers of the public conduct of Sallustius Secundus.[236] Sallustius proved squeaky clean, but to prove his loyalty to the peculation craze, he lodged his own charges against Julian's *cubicularius* Rhodanus. We also know that Julian's ex-consul and panegyrist Mamertinus was dismissed from his post as praetorian prefect of Italy, Africa, and Illyricum and charged with peculation.[237] Seleucus, a close friend of Julian's since his student days, was dismissed from his post, prosecuted, fined, and exiled to Pontus.[238] Evagrius, who had held a governorship and then perhaps a vicariate under Julian, was dismissed, flogged, and fined the value of his estates.[239] Clematius, a learned polytheist whom Julian had appointed high priest of his native province, was stripped of his property and imprisoned.[240] Julian's former teacher Nicocles, a sophist in Constantinople, was similarly harassed by Valens's officials.[241] Clodius Octavianus, the Roman pagan who had visited Julian in Antioch and won from him the proconsulship of Africa, was forced into hiding.[242] Oribasius, Julian's court doctor, who had helped his friend win proclamation, had his property confiscated and was exiled to

---

unspecified charge. Similar insinuations of mischance and forced retirement are found at *Ep.* 1483.

235. In addition to Modestus, see *PLRE* I, Vindaonius Magnus 12, Clearchus 1, and Fl. Eutolmius Tatianus 5, to which add Roueché 1989, nos. 25–27, 37. Cf., in the west, *PLRE* I, Vulcacius Rufinus 25. Tritle 1994 even argues that Constantius's former court ran affairs under Valens. This ignores the influence of men with little or no connection to Constantius, e.g., Festus, Sophronius, Fortunatianus, Aburgius, Serenianus, etc. If Brauch 1993 is right to assert that Themistius was urban prefect of Constantinople under Julian, he too could be numbered among the officials of Julian who remained in favor. I remain skeptical, however, that Themistius held such a post.

236. Suid. Σ 64; Malalas 13.29 (p. 338); cf. Zos. 4.2.4.

237. AM 27.7.1–2; cf. *PLRE* I, Claudius Mamertinus 2; Nixon and Rodgers 1994, 386–88; Wirbelauer and Fleer 1995.

238. *PLRE* I, Seleucus 1, esp. Lib. *Ep.* 1473, 1508.

239. *PLRE* I, Evagrius 6, esp. Lib. *Ep.* 1287, 1290, 1310–12, 1314, 1317, 1319–22. Evagrius was eventually released and joined the clergy at Antioch.

240. Seeck, *Briefe*, Clematius III, esp. Lib. *Ep.* 1458, 1503, 1504, 1526. Clematius was later released.

241. *PLRE* I, Nicocles, esp. Lib. *Ep.* 1266, 1487, 1533.

242. *PLRE* I, Clodius Octavianus 2, esp. Jer. *Chron.* s.a. 371; cf. AM 29.3.4.

the barbarians.[243] Finally, Maximus and Priscus, the flamboyant philosophical attendants of the apostate, were arrested and investigated. Priscus was acquitted, but Maximus, whom the crowds had hoped to dismember, was initially fined a tremendous sum and later tortured to the brink of death.[244] What we have, then, is evidence for a period of political terrorism directed against Julian's friends and former officials. Those who had enjoyed his benefactions, particularly those who shared his cultural and intellectual interests, were made to pay for the rewards they had received with flight, flesh, and above all fines.

Our sources note that Julian had been particularly liberal to his friends.[245] This liberality, coupled with his generous tax measures and his monumentally expensive Persian expedition, had cost the empire dear. When Valentinian and Valens took over the government, they were thus in desperate need of capital. The law codes and coinage of the period give ample evidence of a scramble to make good on Julian's debt.[246] Ammianus tells us that, in 365, Valens's father-in-law, Petronius, was in the process of carrying out a sweeping campaign to collect money from those who owed the emperor when Procopius revolted.[247] Petronius's methods were apparently ruthless, an indication not only of the desperate state of imperial finances but also, perhaps, of an ulterior, political motive. Given that many of the victims of this early purge were brought up on peculation charges and fined great sums, the evidence hints at an effort to couple administrative reshuffling with a money-making scheme. By prosecuting the men whom Julian had remunerated, Valens and his brother could simultaneously assemble capital and drive Julian's confidants into a squalid impotence.

Ultimately, of course, the scheme backfired. Among Procopius's considerations when he chose to revolt was his awareness that the public was outraged at Valens's ruthlessness in the collection of debts.[248] In these circumstances, he could rely on general support from the broader populace, which was unhappy with its moneygrubbing new emperor. Given his connections with Ju-

243. *PLRE* I, Oribasius, esp. Eunap. *VS* 21.1.5. See also Baldwin 1975, 85–97. Tension against Oribasius seems to be alluded to at Them. *Or.* 6.72a.

244. *PLRE* I, Priscus 5 and Maximus 20, esp. Eunap. *VS* 7.4.11–6.1; Them. *Or.* 7.100a; cf. Zos. 4.2.2. *PLRE*'s entry on Maximus is especially weak. See the much fuller details in Seeck, *Briefe*, 208–10, Maximus X, and the narrative at Penella 1990, 72–73. Vanderspoel 1995, 166 n. 40, argues briefly that Them. *Or.* 7.100a refers not to Maximus but to Sallustius. The case remains open.

245. On Julian's liberality with his friends, see Jul. *Ep.* 4 and 114 (Bidez); Lib. *Or.* 1.125; *Ep.* 1154; Eunap. *VS* 7.3.9; Greg. Naz. *Or.* 4; Philostorg. 9.4. On his liberal economic policies more broadly, see pp. 288–90.

246. See pp. 290–92.

247. AM 26.6.6–9, 17, 8.14.

248. Cf. Elbern 1984, 46–49, on other revolts motivated by economic pressures. Add Zos. 1.20.2.

lian, he could expect even firmer backing from those whom Valens had been terrorizing as former friends of Julian's. Thus, for example, Helpidius, who had apostatized under Julian and had been rewarded with the post of *comes rei privatae,* was easily persuaded to ally himself with Procopius.[249] So was Araxius, whom Julian had called "my comrade" in his *Letter to Themistius.*[250] Also in this circle was Eunomius, a first-rate logician and radical theologian with connections to Julian's family stretching back for years.[251] When Procopius was preparing his revolt, Eunomius helped hide him on his estates outside Chalcedon. Similar aid was offered by another propertied easterner and former palatine official named Strategius.[252] So, too, the Persian Hormisdas, whose father and namesake had marched with Julian to Ctesiphon, gladly joined the new "Constantinian dynast" as governor of Asia.[253] Procopius expected similar support from Julian's associate the philosopher Maximus, who had, however, already suffered enough and prudently chose to stay clear of the contest.[254]

Even Libanius, a thousand miles from any territory controlled by Procopius, was accused of composing a panegyric in favor of the usurper. Although the charge never stuck, it serves to highlight the kind of person contemporaries associated with the rebels.[255] Those who joined Procopius tended to be former adherents of Julian's, whose cultural attainments had forged strong bonds with the pagan emperor. Such men were apparently abundant in 365. Indeed, some were even westerners. We know of several adherents of Procopius from Gaul who fit a similar profile.[256] Euphrasius and Phronemius, who win praise from Ammianus as "most outstanding for their learning in the liberal arts," were among those—like Sallustius—who followed Julian's court to the east and remained there after his death. Procopius made one his *magister officiorum* and the other prefect of Constantinople.[257] Also in their number was the Gallic poet and rhetorician Attius

---

249. *PLRE* I, Helpidius 6, esp. Philostorg. 7.10; cf. Malcus 1967, 109. For more on adherents of Procopius, see Delmaire 1997, 118–20; Wiebe 1995, 36–56.

250. *PLRE* I, Araxius, esp. Jul. *Ep. ad Them.* 259c–d: ἑταῖρον ἡμῖν.

251. Greg. Nys. *Eun.* 35 claims that Eunomius bragged of his connections to the emperors.

252. AM 26.6.5 reports that Procopius stayed at the estate of Strategius, and Philostorg. 9.5, 8 that Eunomius was exiled on a charge of harboring Procopius on his own estate in Chalcedon. Philostorgius 9.6 denies this charge against his hero, but it seems plausible, since Eunomius knew Procopius well enough to exercise considerable influence with him during the revolt. Cf. Zos. 4.5.3.

253. *PLRE* I, Hormisdas 3; Malcus 1967, 110.

254. Them. *Or.* 7.99c, 100b–c.

255. Lib. *Or.* 1.163–65, with Norman 1965, 196–98.

256. See Sivan 1993, 20–22.

257. AM 26.7.4, 10.8. On Julian's intellectual circle in Gaul, see Lib. *Or.* 12.55; cf. Sivan 1993, 98–99.

Delphidius Tiro, who had caught Julian's eye while debating a law case in 359 and apparently also followed him east.[258] All three fit the same mould as their eastern counterparts: educated members of the elite whose careers had blossomed under Julian, and, we may assume, wilted again under Valens. When Procopius offered himself to them as a leader, they happily joined the cause.

All of these connections between the supporters of Procopius and Julian's former confidants have led some to speculate that Procopius headed up a pagan reaction against the new Christian emperors.[259] This seems unlikely for several reasons. First and foremost, all indications are that Procopius was himself a Christian.[260] He had been born and raised in the town of Korykos, on the coast of Cilicia.[261] There he would have lived amid a thriving Christian community, which is well attested in inscriptions and the remains of churches.[262] Like Julian's mother, his parents were probably Christian, and like his cousins Gallus and Julian, Procopius was probably raised Christian as well.[263] During his usurpation, Procopius continued to advertise his Christianity on his coinage by portraying himself holding a labarum and standing in front of a field emblazoned with the "Chi-Rho" (fig. 12),[264] symbols unthinkable on Julian's coinage after 361. Although the same coins portray Procopius with what might be regarded as a pagan attribute—his philosopher's beard—we have already seen that this ambiguous amalgam of signs was designed to promote Procopius to all supporters of the Constantinian family, whether pagan or Christian.[265] Indeed, Procopius's appeals for support always portrayed him as a representative of the broader Constantinian dynasty rather than a reincarnation of the pagan Julian.[266]

We must also be careful of identifying Procopius's revolt as a pagan reac-

---

258. Booth 1978, 237–39, with bibliography at n. 10; accepted at Sivan 1993, 91–93, 98–99. Both argue against *PLRE* I, Attius Tiro Delphidius, which holds that he joined Magnentius's revolt. The case is built around Aus. XI *Prof.* 5.19–24, 29–31, which speaks of an unnamed *tyrranus.*

259. Solari 1932d; Wiebe 1995, 3–86; cf. Blockley 1975, 56.

260. Cf. pp. 96 and 100.

261. Them. *Or.* 7.86c; cf. AM 26.6.1; Philostorg. 9.5.

262. Hill 1996, 115–47; *MAMA* 3: 118–219.

263. On Gallus's and the young Julian's Christian piety, see Greg. Naz. *Or.* 4.24–5; Soz. 5.2.12, 19.12–14; cf. 3.15.8; Philosotorg. 3.27. More on Julian's early adherence to Christianity at R. B. E. Smith 1995, 180–85.

264. *RIC* 9.193 (Heraclea 7–8); 215 (Constantinople 17–18); 240 (Cyzicus (6–7, 9); 252 (Nicomedia 10); cf. Brennecke 1988, 214. Wiebe 1995, 8, 40, 48, 291 n. 22, must strain to argue away this evidence.

265. See pp. 91–101. Magnentius also cast himself with an ambiguous combination of pagan and Christian propaganda (Salzman 1990, 210–11, with bibliography).

266. As such, Procopius distinguished himself from Julian's propaganda, which largely disavowed his dynastic past; cf. Béranger 1972; MacCormack 1981, 192–96.

tion, because, while we know that many of Procopius's supporters were pagans, we know that some were Christian and lack explicit testimony about the religious beliefs of most.[267] On the opposing side, many of Valens's men, both during and after the revolt, were themselves pagans.[268] Given the hybrid nature of both sides, it is difficult to see any clear demarcations along religious lines. Finally, and most important, none of our sources, pagan or Christian, portray the revolt as a religious conflict. If Procopius had wished to parade himself as the paladin of paganism, our pro-pagan sources, such as Ammianus and Zosimus would certainly report this, much as they do for Julian. In light of their silence, it is certainly preferable to regard the factions, if such they should be called, as aligning themselves along different poles: supporters of Constantine's dynasty against the upstart house of Valentinian.[269] Better still, we might regard the revolt as a reaction to a variety of tensions—economic, cultural, dynastic, and political—with only a weak focus of positive support in Procopius and a very firm target for negative reaction in Valens. The east was uncomfortable with its new emperor for a variety of reasons, which united a varied group of people behind a man who seemed very much his opposite. In this sense, the revolt was as much a reaction against Valens as a push for Procopius.

Valens must have understood this brutal reality. Indeed, it was probably for this reason that the reprisals he took in the aftermath of the revolt were surprisingly mild compared to his iron-fisted policies leading up to it. As we would expect, the sources are divided on the question of Valens's harshness or clemency. Neither would be surprising. An emperor's primary concern was to guarantee security; if he felt this could be done through severity, he would have been severe, but more often clemency prevailed.[270] There are a number of reasons for this. Given the technologies of communication and bureaucracy in the ancient world, investigating and punishing everyone implicated in a revolt would have been tremendously expensive. Then, too, because participation was often a matter of geography—with those inside a usurper's sphere of control generally following that usurper—it would have been ridiculous to punish all "supporters." All of this meant that rulers and ruled shared the expectation of leniency.[271] Valens certainly knew the etiquette, if for no other reason than that Themistius reminded him of it in an

---

267. Wiebe 1995, 36–56, argues to the contrary, but his case had been anticipated at Grattarola 1986, 90–94. Procopius's supporter Eunomius was certainly Christian and his general Gomoarius may have been as well, given that he was cashiered by Julian and later opposed his usurpation (AM 21.8.1, 13.16).

268. *PLRE* I, Serenianus 2, Saturninius Secundus Salutius 3, and Clearchus 1; cf. Haehling 1977. See p. 216 on other pagans in Valens's administration later in the reign.

269. Grattarola 1986, 90–94.

270. MacMullen 1985, 75–76; Elton 1996b, 197–98.

271. E.g., Aur. Vict. *Caes.* 39.13–16; cf. 22.11–13.

address delivered the winter after the revolt had ended.[272] By this time, reprisals had begun to abate, and Themistius could still claim that Valens alone had truly won glory from his victory, since he alone had shown *philanthropia*.[273] He had, according to Themistius, proven himself the true philosopher by placing reason above passion and distinguishing those who plotted the revolt from those who were dragged along by force.[274] Now all would be more loyal, for all owed to Valens the debt of their misdeeds, which he had forgiven.[275]

Such was the language of panegyric.[276] For all its rhetoric, however, Themistius's account probably had some basis in reality. Valens had every reason to promote concord, which, after such a rocky start, was possible only with a considerable measure of clemency. This does not deny that he fined, proscribed, exiled, tortured and executed a fair number. Zosimus, for example, claims that "he kept raving furiously against one and all for no just cause, with the result that there were destroyed both those who participated in the insurrection and those who, wholly innocent themselves, were relatives or friends of the guilty."[277] This portrayal is, however, no less rhetorical than that of Themistius, and what evidence we have indicates that Themistius's panegyric is as close to the truth as Zosimus's history. Writing safely after Valens's death, Libanius, for example, praised his clemency, even despite his general animosity toward the Pannonian.[278] Indeed, Libanius himself may have benefited from this period of détente, for a passage in Eunapius hints that in ca. 368, Valens offered him an honorary praetorian prefecture, which he declined.[279] What we know of the fate of the participants in the revolt tells the same story. We have already seen that Procopius and his fellow

272. On the date, see Dagron 1968, 21; Vanderspoel 1995, 162; cf. 161–67 and Errington 2000, 881–83, on this speech.

273. *Or.* 7.87c–88a.

274. Them. *Or.* 7.93b. As we would expect, in the aftermath of the revolt, the participants often offered compulsion as their excuse, and Valens generally accepted this in order to perpetuate the notion that his subjects had only turned on him out of necessity (Them. *Or.* 11.148b–c; AM 26.7.1, 6, 9.8; Lib. *Or.* 20.26, 62.58–59).

275. Them. *Or.* 7.95c–d. On Valens's clemency after the revolt, see also Them. *Or.* 8.110d–111a, 9.122c, 11.148b–c; cf. Symm. *Or.* 1.21.

276. Similar language recurs at *Pan. Lat.* 2 [12].45.5–7, 12 [9].13.1–5; Jul. *Or.* 1.48c–d, 3.99a–100c; cf. Aur. Vict. *Caes.* 22.11–13, 39.13–16.

277. Zos. 4.8.4–5; cf. 10.1. Eunap. *Hist.* fr. 34.9 (Blockley) is probably from Eunapius's account of Valens's reprisals. Ammianus paints an equally terrible tableau at 26.10.6–14; cf. 26.8.10, which is, like Zosimus, too light on specifics and too heavy in rhetoric to be of great probative value. See also AM 26.6.5; Joh. Ant. fr. 184; Jer. *Chron.* s.a. 366, followed by Prosper *Chron.* 1131; Jord. *Rom.* 308; Oros. 7.32.4. On the aftermath of the revolt, see Grattarola 1986, 101–5; Wiebe 1995, 56–61.

278. Lib. *Or.* 1.171, 19.15, 20.25–26, 46.30; but cf. *Or.* 24.13.

279. Eunap. *VS* 16.2.8 with Banchich 1985. Lib. *Or.* 1.171 also indicates a period of reprieve in the middle years of Valens's rule.

usurper Marcellus were executed.[280] This was only natural. Also executed were Procopius's betrayers, Barchalba and Florentius—the latter quite justly for his ruthless conduct—and Andronicus, a victim of court intrigues.[281] No doubt many others also lost their lives, but many who could easily have been killed were not. Procopius's wife, for example, seems to have lived on, as did enough of his family that a descendant later came to occupy the western throne.[282] The tribune Aliso and the commanders Gomoarius and Agilo were spared, as was Agilo's father-in-law, the prefect Araxius, who was merely exiled. The Gallic participants Euphrasius and Phronimius were sent for judgment to Valentinian, who punished only the latter, as a close confidant of Julian's, and then only with exile. Close ties with Julian also resulted in the imprisonment of Helpidius, but other men with such connections, like Hormisdas, were let free. If we can believe Themistius, Valens was quite moderate with soldiers and commanders more broadly: he at least seems to have avoided disbanding any of the units that had sided with the usurper, because even the Divitenses et Tungrecani, with whom the revolt had begun, remained intact.[283]

In addition, Valens's eased his intransigence against the supporters of Julian whom he had attacked before the revolt. Thanks to the pleading of Clearchus, Maximus of Ephesus saw his property restored in recompense for his loyalty. Similarly, Oribasius, then in exile, was allowed to return.[284] Eunomius was likewise, for the time being, acquitted of harboring Procopius. These middle years in Valens's reign even saw the return of some of Julian's key officials to power, particularly Domitius Modestus and Vindaonius Magnus. Moreover, it witnessed a relaxation of the policies that had helped provoke unrest in the first place. The unrelenting exactions were brought to an end, taxes were cut, and efforts were made to take account of the financial concerns of wealthy aristocrats.[285] The revolt thus effected a change in the way Valens conducted affairs, making him milder in the middle years of his reign than he had been initially.

280. All information on the punishment of Procopius's officials can be found in the *PLRE* I references already given for each personality.

281. On schemes against Andronicus, see Lib. *Or.* 1.171. On Florentius's cruelty, see Philostorg. 9.5.

282. Procopius's wife is probably referred to at Joh. Chrys. *Ad vid. iun.* 4; cf. *PLRE* I, Artemisia. On his descendants, see *PLRE* II, Anthemius 3; Procopius 2.

283. Hoffmann 1969–70, 1: 398; cf. Tomlin 1972, 258. More broadly, see Them. *Or.* 7.97c–d, 8.110d–111a.

284. On the return of Maximus's estates, see Eunap. *VS* 7.6.1. On Oribasius's return, see Eunap. *VS* 21.1.5. The exact date is unknown. Oribasius was probably recalled under the influence of his son, Eustathius, who became an *archiatros* under Valens. Cf. Basil *Epp.* 151 (a. 373), 189 (a. 374/75, probably by Gregory of Nyssa), which confirm that Eustathius, unlike his father, had converted to Christianity.

285. See pp. 292–95.

Even despite this reprieve, the event left a bitter taste in Valens's mouth. This is especially evident in the ongoing resentment he harbored against the cities of Constantinople and Chalcedon. The Senate of Constantinople waited for about nine months after Procopius's death before sending Themistius to congratulate Valens on his success. The orator naturally felt compelled to apologize for taking so long to offer thanks for the suppression of a revolt begun within his own city.[286] At some point around this time, the citizens of Constantinople also saw their tax privileges *(ius italicum)* revoked. Although Valens eventually forgave most Constantinopolitans and restored this perquisite,[287] he never forgot what they had done and the insults they had heaped on him. In the coming years, he studiously avoided the eastern capital, choosing to reside instead at Marcianople (367–70) and then Antioch (370–78). From the time of the revolt until his death, he spent only a total of about one year in Constantinople, and never more than six months at a time.[288] When he made his final visit in 378, en route to deal with the Gothic uprising, he was greeted with riots in the Hippodrome, and within two weeks, he stormed out swearing that he would return to level the city for its insolence and support of Procopius.[289] Who knows what would have happened had he survived, especially given that he was inclined to keep such promises. He certainly did in the case of Chalcedon. When the Chalcedonians had flagrantly mocked Valens from their walls, he took an oath that he would one day dismantle those walls and transport the stones to Constantinople for his construction projects. This he actually did, although Socrates reports that legations from Constantinople, Nicaea, and Nicomedia, pleading on behalf of their neighbor, persuaded him to relax his wrath by rebuilding the dismantled ramparts in smaller fill after carting off the ashlars.[290] His anger clearly ran deep, even if the necessities of imperial decorum dictated moderation.

---

286. Them. *Or.* 7.84b–c, 85d–86a. See also Lib. *Or.* 19.15, which seems to allude directly to Themistius's speech; cf. *Or.* 20.25–26.

287. *CTh* 14.13.1 (ca. 373); cf. Them. *Or.* 14.183c–d, 15.196c. On the date of the law, see Pergami 1993, 257.

288. Seeck, *Regesten*, 239, 241, 251; Dagron 1974, 84; Barnes 1998, 250–54. It is unclear how much time Valens spent in Constantinople in the winter after the revolt (a. 366/67). Pace Barnes 1998, 250, no source mentions his stay there and Zos. 4.10.3 indicates that he moved to Marcianople fairly quickly, where he is attested from May 10, 367 (*CTh* 12.18.1). However, Them. *Or.* 7 seems to have been delivered while Valens presided over the Senate of Constantinople (Dagron 1968, 21). It would be logical to assume that Valens prosecuted the participants in the revolt in the capital, and Soc. 4.8.11 seems to confirm this.

289. Soc. 4.38.5; Soz. 6.39.2–4; with Vanderspoel 1995, 191–92. Cf. p. 335.

290. Soc. 4.8.1–14; Zon. 13.16; Cedrenus, pp. 542–43; Joh. Ant. fr. 184. Chalcedon's walls had been built by Constantine, providing all the more reason for Valens to have punished the city (Cedrenus, pp. 496–97). Valens must have confiscated a good deal of the prime property in the area, at least some of which—an entire village—wound up in the hands of his *prae-*

These feelings also affected broader policies in the course of Valens's reign. In what follows, we shall see how the revolt provided the proximate cause for Valens's war against the Goths, who had sent Procopius auxiliaries. Over the long term, it also awakened in Valens a nagging fear of usurpers.[291] Following the revolt, he issued a series of particularly harsh laws against the distribution of *famosi* like those spread in Constantinople during the revolt, and he took measures to restrict the production of gold coinage and the manufacture of imperial gold brocade.[292] This fear eventually resurfaced in the magic trials of 372, during which, as we shall see, persecutions were renewed against those who had enjoyed favor under Julian.[293] The early experience of revolt thus had profound and lasting effects. In many ways, it had been less dangerous than other usurpations in the fourth century: because it was not a military revolt, it did not cost tremendous manpower resources or tie up the army for long periods. On the other hand, precisely because it was peculiar, it must have been doubly disorienting. Unlike military revolts, which were dangerous but somewhat predictable, this civilian uprising was eerily insidious. Valens's clash with it at the beginning of his reign must have left him with a feeling that he was not safe on any front.

---

positus sacri cubiculi Mardonius (Soz. 7.21.2–3). Valens was also harsh with Philippopolis (AM 26.10.6).

291. AM 29.1.11.

292. On gold brocade, see *CTh* 10.21.1 (a. 369). On the coinage reform, see pp. 299–302.

293. For Julian's men killed in 372, see AM 29.1.5–2.28, esp. 29.1.42, 44; cf. 29.3.7; Eunap. *VS* 7.6.3–6; Lib. *Or.* 1.158, 24.13; Zos. 4.15.1.

Chapter 3

Valens's First Gothic War

THE GOTHS IN THE FOURTH CENTURY

Shortly after Valens left Constantinople in the summer of 365, he received reports that the Goths were conspiring to invade the territory of Thrace. He sent the auxiliary units of the Divitenses et Tungrecani to forestall their attack and then continued eastward. As these units marched through Constantinople on their way to the Danube, Procopius suborned them and used them to initiate his revolt.[1] Next the usurper sent a letter to the Goths themselves, calling on them to provide him with auxiliary troops: since at least 332, the Goths had been treaty-bound to supply men to fight in Roman military expeditions, and Procopius was once again ordering them to uphold their obligation. Thinking the usurper to be a legitimate heir to the Constantinian dynasty, the Goths complied and sent 3,000 warriors. Unfortunately for Procopius, these never reached him before he was captured and killed.[2]

Valens was naturally offended by this affront to his imperial legitimacy, and once he had regained control of the east, he had the Gothic auxiliaries arrested as they tried to escape back to their homeland and sent an embassy to the Goths demanding an explanation. The Gothic leader Athanaric then produced Procopius's original letter demanding the *auxilia*: with this as his proof, Athanaric argued that he had only acted in accord with his sworn obligations to the empire and insisted that Valens return his men.[3] For his part, Valens gave little regard to this "vapid excuse" and maintained that these

---

1. AM 26.6.11–12, 7.5, 9.

2. AM 26.10.3, 27.4.1, 5.1, 31.3.4; Eunap. *Hist.* fr. 37 (Blockley); Zos. 4.7.2, 10.1–2. Zosimus claims 10,000 men were sent, but Ammianus's report of 3,000 has generally been taken as more plausible.

3. AM 27.5.1; Eunap. *Hist.* fr. 37 (Blockley); Zos. 4.10.2.

Gothic soldiers had been legitimately apprehended as enemies.[4] Rather than return them, he distributed them as garrisons in border cities in Thrace.[5] Meanwhile, after consulting with his brother, Valens prepared to attack the Goths in a full-scale expeditionary campaign. Between 367 and 369, he undertook two invasions into Gothic territory, which, although well organized, had disappointing results. The consequences of this discomfiture would have repercussions that affected foreign policy for the remainder of Valens's reign.

Relations between Goths and Romans were not always so tense in the fourth century. Like other barbarian peoples surrounding the empire, the Goths maintained a decided ambivalence toward their Roman neighbors, at times attacking them, at others offering military support; at times persecuting the Romans within their territory, at others welcoming these and the trade goods they brought. For their part, the Romans built forts and walls opposite Gothic territory with the nominal intent of protecting their lands from raids and larger invasions. Yet in times of peace, these same forts often doubled as centers of trade and cultural contact between the two peoples.[6] The Romans also often drafted into their ranks the very Goths against whom they had fought in previous engagements. The Gothic frontier, like other border regions, was thus hardly impermeable to social and economic interchange. Rather, it constituted a coarsely woven net through which individuals and small groups easily passed.[7] When Valens brought war to the Goths in 367, he was thus interrupting a state of relatively peaceful interaction that had prevailed on the Danube frontier for over thirty years.

Gothic dwellings and gravesites have been identified with the remains of the Iron Age culture first discovered at the archaeological sites of Sîntana de Mureş in Romania and Tcherniakov in the Ukraine (see map 3).[8] Sîntana de Mureş–Tcherniakov remains show that the Goths migrated south from modern Poland and into the territory of modern Ukraine, Moldova, and Romania beginning in the late second century and continuing into the third century.[9] There they took up permanent settlements as a sedentary people engaged in agriculture and animal husbandry.[10] The archaeology indicates

4. AM 27.5.2: "excusationem vanissimam."

5. Eunap. *Hist.* fr. 37 (Blockley); Zos 4.10.1–3; cf. Paschoud 2.2: 350 n. 124; Wanke 1990, 75–77.

6. See, e.g., the Danube fortlet called *Commercium*, *CIL* 3.3653 = *ILS* 775. On Roman trade with Germans, see Todd 1992, 88–103; Whittaker 1994, 98–131; cf. Elton 1996a, 83–90.

7. Recent work on frontiers has emphasized the importance of interaction between Romans and non-Romans, Headeager 1987; Whittaker 1994; Elton 1996a; Wells 1999, 224–58.

8. On the archaeology, see the helpful surveys at Häusler 1979; Heather and Matthews 1991, 51–101; Kazanski 1991b, 29–61; Harhoiu 1997.

9. Kazanski 1991b, 20, 28; Mitrea 1957.

10. Ioniţă 1975, 78; 1966, 254; Heather and Matthews 1991, 56–9, 87–93; Kazanski 1991b, 47–55. Contrast Elton 1996b, 22–26, 278–81. Many literary sources confirm that the Goths

a culturally homogeneous group that lived cheek by jowl with the older ethnic elements in the Dacian and steppe territory, either assimilating, or more
likely, dominating them militarily and economically.[11] Sîntana de Mureş–
Tcherniakov remains also make clear that this culture reached its peak of
economic and social development in the fourth century. In this period, mass-
produced, wheel-made pottery becomes commonplace, a testament to widespread high-level production techniques;[12] specialized manufacturing centers for articles like combs and metal wares crop up, pointing to a developed
distribution of labor;[13] and random coin finds are abundant, indicating the
diffusion of monetized trade.[14] A marked, although far from striking, range
of differentiation between the size of Sîntana de Mureş–Tcherniakov settlements and dwellings and the number and quality of their burial goods
further confirms some degree of social distinction by wealth.[15] Even so, there
is no archaeological evidence for wide gaps between mass and elite and no
real evidence of latent class tensions, as some have asserted.[16] The fourth-
century Goths were thus a sedentary people with surprisingly developed production capacities and a growing, although far from pronounced, degree of
social stratification.

Both archaeological and literary sources indicate that contacts between
the Goths and the Roman Empire were quite common. Trade activity is attested by the regular occurrence of Roman glass, ceramics, tools, metal wares,
jewelry, and amphorae at Sîntana de Mureş–Tcherniakov sites. Naturally,
these finds tend to be concentrated in border regions and along trade routes,
but Roman goods can be found throughout Sîntana de Mureş–Tcherniakov
territory.[17] Roman coins, which are common in the region, help pinpoint
the period of heaviest trade across the Danube to the decades between ca.
320 and 360.[18] Literary sources from the period further support the assumption that trade with Rome was widespread. The fourth-century translation of the Bible into Gothic, for example, often employs Latin vocabulary

---

were agricultural rather than nomadic, *Pan. Lat.* 2 [12].22.3; SHA *Clod.* 9.4; Them. *Or.*
16.211b, 212b, 34.22; AM 31.3.8, 4.5–8; Claudian *VI Cons. Hon.* ll. 183–84.

11. On the thorny question of ethnic identities, see Palade 1980; Kazanski 1991b, 39–45;
Heather and Matthews 1991, 94–8; Heather 1991, 91–97; 1996, 84–93; Ellis 1996.

12. Ioniţă 1966, 253; Häusler 1979, 37–42; Heather and Matthews 1991, 69–77; Ellis 1996,
106–12.

13. On production centers, especially the bone comb factories at Bîrlad-Valea Seacă, see
Häusler 1979, 29–36; Palade 1980, 237; Heather and Matthews 1991, 77–86.

14. Mihăilescu-Bîrliba 1980, 207–18, 224–27, 246–50; cf. Bursche 1996.

15. Diaconu 1975, 73–4; Kropotkin 1984, 47; Magomedov 1995; Heather 1996, 65–75.

16. As Thompson 1966, esp. at 43–63; cf. Ioniţă 1975, 84–6; Häusler 1979, 56–58.

17. Ioniţă 1972, 99; 1994, 110–12; Häusler 1979, 52–56; Palade 1980, 229; Kazanski 1991b,
52–55, 58; Harhoiu 1997, 134–35.

18. Preda 1975; Duncan 1983; 1993, 112–14.

to render trade-related words.[19] Even architecture in the Sîntana de Mureş–
Tcherniakov territory near the Danube seems to have been influenced by
contact with Rome.[20]

More important, cultural contacts went beyond economic interests. Because of the privileged survival of Christian sources, this is nowhere better
evinced than in the relations we can trace between the Christian communities in Gothic territory and their Roman counterparts. Since the late third
century, there had been Christians among the Goths, and these provided a
ready avenue of exchange with Roman Christians, which has left an easily
traceable record.[21] Ulfilas, for example, the grandson of Cappadocian Christians captured by the Goths in the third century, was appointed bishop to
the Goths under imperial auspices in 336 (or perhaps 340/41). Although
he was expelled from Gothic territory within seven years of his appointment,
he retained control of a community of Gothic Christians in Moesia and probably continued to exercise pastoral influence over Christians inside Gothic
territory until his death in 383.[22] The continued strength of Christianity
north of the Danube after Ulfilas's expulsion is well attested in the martyrologies produced in the wake of the Christian persecutions stirred up after
Valens's Gothic war in 369. In the *Passio S. Sabae*, the Gothic priest Sansalas
is said to have traveled easily back and forth between "Gothia" and "Romania" to avoid persecution, and the Roman *dux Scythiae* Junius Soranus used
agents operating in Gothic territory to recover relics of the Gothic martyr
Saba.[23] Letters of Basil's related to these same events indicate that clergymen
of Roman descent were also traveling in and out of Gothic territory as missionaries,[24] and a decade after the death of Saba, the Gothic "queen" Gaatha
and her daughter made similar treks back and forth across the Danube transporting relics from Gothic to Roman territory.[25] Goths and Romans were
thus far from isolated from one another. The relationship between these

19. For an excellent introduction to this specialist topic, see Heather and Matthews 1991,
155–97; cf. Wolfram 1988, 112–14.

20. Ioniţă 1994, 112–13.

21. For Christianity among the Goths, see Mansion 1914; Schäferdiek 1992; Lenski 1995a,
75–86.

22. Auxentius 35 [56]–37 [59]; Philostorg. 2.5; cf. Soc. 4.37.6–12. On Ulfilas, see Shäfer-
diek 1979; 1992, 36–50; Barnes 1990a; Heather and Matthews 1991, 133–53. The date of his
consecration and expulsion are a matter of dispute; cf. p. 125.

23. On Sansalas, see *Pass. S. Sabae* 4. On Junius Soranus, see *Pass. S. Sabae* 8; Basil *Ep.* 155.
On the persecution of 369–72, see pp. 320–21.

24. On Roman missionaries, see Basil *Ep.* 164–65, with Lenski 1995a, 78; cf. Zuckerman
1991a, 473–79.

25. Delehaye 1912, 279. Pace Ioniţă 1975, 79–80, inhumation burials should not be taken
as archaeological evidence for Christianity; see Heather and Matthews 1991, 59–69; Niculescu
1993.

neighboring peoples was complex and involved as much exchange and interaction as it did hostility.

The people whom we call generically "Goths" were, of course, not a unified political entity in antiquity. Indeed, we know from Ammianus that the larger *ethnos* of Goths (Gothic, *Gutthiuda*; Latin, *Gothi*; Greek, Γότθοι) was in fact divided into at least two tribal confederations with which the Romans had contact in the fourth century, the Tervingi and the Greuthungi. The former inhabited the eastern half of the old Roman province of Dacia, from Oltenia in the west to Bessarabia along the Dniester in the east.[26] The latter lived largely beyond the Dniester eastward up to the Don, and northward as far as Kiev in the Ukraine.[27] We know little about society and politics among the more distant Greuthungi in the fourth century. They appear to have been fragmented into several autonomous groups, at least some of which were ruled under a hereditary kingship.[28] More than this we cannot say. Evidence for social and political structures among the Tervingi, however, is more readily available. Their confederation was made up of locally powerful lords referred to as *reges* in our sources, a Latinized version of their Germanic—originally Celtic—title *reiks*.[29] Each *reiks* controlled a fairly circumscribed territory and its associated peoples—called a *kuni*—more or less independently.[30] Even so, the *reges* did cooperate under the overlordship of a single hereditary chieftain whose unknown Gothic title was translated by Roman and Greek authors as "judge"—*iudex*, or δικαστής.[31] The Tervingi were thus a segmented society, which nevertheless achieved some degree of vertical hierarchization under the leadership of their *iudex*.

Throughout Valens's reign, it would seem, the *iudex* of the Tervingi re-

---

26. The approximate border is deduced from AM 31.3.5, although AM 27.5.6 may imply that some Greuthungi lived southwest of the Dniester. The Tervingi are first mentioned at *Pan. Lat.* 11 [3].17.1 (a. 291) and last mentioned at *Not. dign. or.* 6.61 (ca. 395). On the names Tervingi and Greuthungi and the later—and unrelated—names Visigoth and Ostrogoth, see Wolfram 1988, 24–29; Heather 1991, 331–33.

27. AM 31.2.13 reports that the Alans lived from the Don eastward and AM 31.3.1 that they bordered on the Greuthungi; cf. AM 22.8.29. Archaeological finds confirm that Gothic culture stretched up to the Don. On the history of the Greuthungi prior to the Hunnic invasions, see Wolfram 1988, 85–89.

28. Heather 1991, 88–89; 1996, 52–57.

29. Such leaders are attested at AM 26.10.3: *regibus*; Delehaye 1912, 279: 'Ιγγουρίχου βασιλέως; cf. *Pass. S. Sabae* 6 for the *reiks* Atharid and his father Rothesteos.

30. On the Gothic title *reiks* and the *kunja*, see Wolfram 1975, 303–10; 1988, 96–97; 1997, 15–20; Heather 1991, 97–98; Ulrich 1995, 65–74, 80–88; Geary 1999, 110–17. For Gothic social structures more generally, see Wolfram 1988, 89–116; 1997, 69–73; Ulrich 1995; cf. Elton 1996b, 32–37.

31. AM 27.5.6, 9, 31.3.4; Auxentius 36 [58]; Ambrose *De spiritu sancto praef.* 17 (*CSEL* 79.23): *iudex regum*. See also the pun at Them. *Or.* 10.134d: (δικαστής), with Heather 1991, 102 n. 57 and Heather and Matthews 1991, 42 n. 91.

mained a powerful figure named Athanaric. The degree of control he exerted over his confederation is not entirely clear, but it was probably greater than earlier scholarship has often assumed.[32] Athanaric's treaty with Valens at the conclusion of the Gothic war in 369 was binding on all Tervingi. Moreover, his coordination of defenses during that war and later against the invasion of the Huns bespeaks a good deal of centralization. The scope of the persecution Athanaric was able to organize against Christians between 369 and 372 likewise provides good evidence that the Tervingi were unified to a considerable extent under the central control of their *iudex*.

When Valens ranged his army against the Goths, the Tervingi were bound by treaty to the Romans. Indeed, as in the realm of trade and social contacts, political relations between Goth and Roman were characterized by a liberal admixture of aggression and cooperation. The Romans had first encountered the Goths in the mid third century, when the latter regularly invaded Thrace and Moesia and even killed the Roman emperor Decius in battle.[33] By the late 270s, the empire had recovered from the initial shock of this Gothic inundation, and by the 290s, Romano-Gothic relations had stabilized to the point where the Goths were willing to offer aid to Galerius in his famous Persian expedition of 298.[34] Although tensions remained and conflicts continued to arise, cooperation had been established. Thus, in 324, the Goths once again chose to supply troops to help the eastern emperor Licinius in his efforts to fend off his aggressive co-emperor Constantine in a bloody civil war.[35] Unfortunately for the Goths, Constantine defeated his rival and shortly thereafter turned his forces against the Tervingi. In 328, he spanned the Danube with a tremendous stone bridge between Roman Oescus (Gigen) and Sucidava (Celeiu) in Gothic territory.[36] He also inaugurated a fortified bridgehead further downstream at Daphne (Spantov), again in Gothic territory.[37] By exerting this pressure on Oltenia and lower Wallachia, Constantine provoked a migration of Tervingi and neighboring

32. Heather 1991, 97–107 (contrast Thompson 1965, 43–55); Wolfram 1975, 30–24; 1988, 94–96; Ulrich 1995, 113–28.

33. On Romano-Gothic relations in the third century, see Wolfram 1988, 43–57; cf. Heather and Matthews 1991, 1–11.

34. Jord. *Get.* 110; cf. Schmidt 1934, 223–24; Wolfram 1988, 57–59.

35. *Exc. Val.* 5 [27]. Constantine had already attacked the Goths in 323, see *Exc. Val.* 5 [21]. Joh. Lyd. *De Mag.* 2.10, 3.31, and 3.40 refers to a Gothic attack on Scythia and Moesia that must be related to one of these incidents, but it is unclear which. On the earlier war, see Chrysos 1972, 48; Wolfram 1988, 60.

36. Aur. Vict. *Caes.* 41.18; *Epit.* 41.14; *Chron. pasch.* p. 527; cf. Alföldi 1926; Chrysos 1972, 51–52; Tudor 1974, 135–66. Seeck, *Regesten,* 178, places Constantine in Oescus in July of 328. On the fortification of Sucidava, see Proc. *Aed.* 4.6.34.

37. Proc. *Aed* 4.7.7; cf. *RIC* 7.73, 563, 574–75 (Constantinople 36–38). The fort across the river at Transmarisca was Diocletianic, see *CIL* 3.6151 = *ILS* 641. See Wanke 1990, 92–94, for recent debate on the location of Daphne.

Taifali westward into the Sarmatian Banat,[38] thus providing himself with an excuse to send his son Constantine II against the Goths. In 332, the Caesar trapped these in Sarmatian territory and forced their surrender after starving to death as many as 100,000 men, women and children.[39]

Constantine celebrated his son's victory with an elaborate propaganda campaign designed to convey the message that "Gothia" had been conquered and "Dacia" restored to Rome.[40] Following this lead, a number of modern historians have argued that Constantine may have temporarily retaken a significant part of the old Trajanic province of Dacia.[41] More likely, he established only a toehold across the Danube, but the stereotyped propaganda of expansion and reconquest typical of the fourth century has misled modern scholars into assuming more for his achievement than they should.[42] The same scholars who accept a Constantinian reconquest of Dacia also hold that Constantine established a new and unique kind of hegemony over the Goths. Specifically, they argue that Constantine was the first to use the Goths as *foederati*, autonomous subjects of the empire legally obliged to offer service to Rome as part of their ongoing transformation into full-blown imperial subjects.[43] Since the late 1960s, this scheme has been challenged. *Foederati* the Goths certainly were, since they were bound to Rome by the formal treaty (*foedus*) struck in 332, but their relations were apparently no different than those of any of the many other barbarian peoples bound to Rome by treaty at this period. They were certainly nothing like the autonomous "federate" allies who became such a common feature of Romano-barbarian politics in the fifth and sixth centuries.[44] Grander claims for special allied relations and Roman hegemony over part of "Gothia" cannot be supported by contemporary evidence.

38. *Exc. Val.* 6 [31]; Eus. *Vit. Const.* 4.6.1; cf. Soproni 1969.

39. *Exc. Val.* 6 [31], 6 [34]; Eus. *Vit. Const.* 1.8.2, 4.5.1–6.1; Aur. Vict. *Caes.* 41.13; Eutr. 10.7; Jer. *Chron.* s.a. 332; *Cons. Const.* s.a. 332. See also Oros. 7.28.29; Soz. 1.8.8–9; Optatianus Porfyrius 18.11–12. Cf. Wolfram 1988, 61–62; Heather 1991, 107–9. Barnes 1976b, 151–52; 1981, 250; 1982, 80, holds that Constantine campaigned north of the Danube again in 336.

40. This is implied by the coins with the legend GOTHIA (*RIC* 7.215), by Constantine's assumption of the title *Dacicus maximus* reported at *AE* 1934, 158, and by the boast attributed to Constantine by Julian. *Caes.* 329c that he had retaken territory conquered by Trajan; cf. Eus. *Vit. Const.* 1.8. In celebration of this victory, Constantine also erected a porphyry column in Constantinople (*CIL* 3.733 = *ILS* 820; cf. Fowden 1991), and initiated *ludi Gothici* there (Fiebiger and Schmidt 1917, 1: 164; Wolfram 1988, 62).

41. Tudor 1937–40; 1974, 160–65; Thompson 1966, 11–13; Chrysos 1972, 52–63; 1997; Barnes 1976b, 152; 1981, 250.

42. Brockmeier 1987, 88–93; Heather 1991, 113; 1997, 63; Lippold 1992b.

43. Schenk von Stauffenberg 1947, 107–21, and Chrysos 1972, 55–76; 1973; 1996; cf. Schmidt 1934, 227–28; Demougeot 1979, 327–28.

44. Stallknecht 1969, 16–31; Barceló 1981, 54–56; Brockmeier 1987; Heather 1991, 107–115; 1997; Lippold 1992b. Wheeler 1998, 85–86, goes so far as to question that there was a formal treaty. Elton 1996b, 91–94, makes some effort to pinpoint the meaning of *foederatus* in the fourth century.

Even despite its rejection of more elaborate arguments for Constantine's 332 treaty, much modern scholarship has continued to read too much into our scanty evidence for the agreement. If we reject the material offered by Jordanes—which is certainly exaggerated and anachronistic[45]—we have only two sources that specifically mention the treaty, the quirky biographies of Constantine offered by Eusebius and the Anonymous Valesianus.[46] Eusebius, whose report is the fullest, claims that Constantine forced the Goths to regard the Romans as their leaders, that he was unwilling to pay them annual tribute, and that he reformed them from their previous beastly state into a reasoned one. Later, Eusebius seems to imply that the Goths were also adopted as allies and thus required to render military service to the Romans.[47] The Anonymous Valesianus tells us only that Constantine received hostages, among whom was the son of the Gothic king Ariaric.[48] This boy was probably the father of Valens's rival Athanaric and would thus have been the same man whom, Themistius tells us, Constantine honored with a portrait statue placed behind the Senate House of Constantinople.[49] Such an honor indicates that Constantine held the Gothic leadership in high esteem. The sources confirm that the feeling was mutual: Constantine came to be regarded by the Goths with great respect as well.[50] In this sense, it is fair to say that the 332 treaty did create a special bond between the Tervingi and the house of Constantine, although more a personal than a legal one.[51] Procopius's success in assembling Gothic aid to support his own dynastic bid as a "Constantinian" gives certain proof that this bond was strong enough to last through several generations.[52] The 332 treaty thus demanded hostages,

45. Jord. *Get.* 112, with Heather 1991, 34–67.

46. The sources related to Constantine's Gothic treaty are laid out most schematically in Lippold 1992b and Brockmeier 1987.

47. Eus. *Vit. Const.* 4.5. Nowhere does Eusebius state directly that the Goths were required to offer military service, but the implication that they delivered symbols of ὑπηρεσία καὶ συμμαχία at *Vit. Const.* 4.7 seems to imply this; cf. Brockmeier 1987, 82; Lippold 1992b, 375; Heather 1991, 110; 1997, 60.

48. *Exc. Val.* 6 [31].

49. Them. *Or.* 15.191a. On the statue and the identification between Athanaric's father and the son of Ariaric, see Schmidt 1934, 228; Thompson 1966, 45; Wolfram 1975, 3–4 n. 11; 1988, 62; Heather 1991, 99.

50. Eutr. 10.7: "ingentemque apud barbaros gentes memoriae gratiam conlocavit"; Joh. Ant. fr. 170: μεγίστας παρὰ τοῖς βαρβάροις ἔθνεσι δικαιοσύνης τε καὶ ἰσχύος μνήμας ἀπέλιπεν; Philostorg. 2.5: τὰ τῇδε βάρβαρα ἔθνη ὑπεκέκλιτο τῷ βασιλεῖ; cf. Eus. *Vit. Const.* 1.8.4.

51. See Lib. *Or.* 59.89: βασιλέα τὸν ἡμέτερον ἐν ἴσῳ τοῖς οἰκείοις ἄγειν (of Constantius) and the listing of Constantius's death as an annual feast in the Gothic liturgical calendar reproduced at Schäferdiek 1988, 119; cf. 129–30. On the special relationship between the house of Constantine and the Goths, see Barcelò 1981, 59; Brockmeier 1987, 95–96. Compare the bond between the Frankish *rex* Silvanus and Constantius, which was strengthened by the close ties of Silvanus's father, Bonitus, with Constantine (AM 15.5.33).

52. See p. 151.

cut annual tribute and required auxiliary military support for Roman armies. Further provisions there may have been, but these cannot be reconstructed from the sources.

Unfortunately, the paucity of direct information on the 332 treaty has not prevented historians from attempting to glean more about the agreement from sources describing Romano-Gothic relations in the decades that followed it. Ammianus, for example, indicates that Procopius received 3,000 Gothic auxiliaries in 365, a number that many have taken as the standard established in 332. Constantine may have demanded a much higher quota, but we have no reliable evidence by which to judge.[53] With respect to tribute, although Eusebius states clearly that Constantine regarded annual payments as unacceptable, we know from Themistius that tribute was being paid annually before 369.[54] Because Julian reports generically that Constantine did offer subventions to "barbarians," some have argued that perhaps Constantine continued to pay the Goths, but only when they supplied the Romans with auxiliary troops.[55] Here again, we have no hard evidence, especially since Julian's reference is polemical and by no means specific to the Goths. So, too, Themistius makes clear that trade between Goths and Romans on the Danube was unrestricted before 369. This has led some to assume that this, too, was a provision of the 332 treaty, yet we have no confirmation in the sources.[56]

To add to our problems, given the lack of reliable sources for the period between 332 and the beginning of Ammianus's narrative in 353, we have little idea how many of the Gothic policies attested in later sources represented implementations of the 332 treaty and how many were actually adaptations, alterations, or even abrogations of the terms of that treaty. Tensions certainly arose after 332, and these could easily have led to emendations in the treaty, whether de jure or merely de facto. Small-scale Gothic raiding into Roman territory continued, which could easily have led to policy shifts.[57] Moreover,

---

53. AM 26.10.3. Zos. 4.7.2 claims Procopius was sent 10,000 men (μυρίους συμμάχους) and Jord. *Get.* 112; cf. 145 that Constantine arranged for 40,000. Although the last figure is certainly exaggerated, there is no reason to assume that the lone attestation in Ammianus of 3,000 was necessarily normative in Constantine's treaty.

54. Them. *Or.* 10.135a–b; cf. 8.119c. The Goths may have been receiving tribute as early as 238, Petrus Patricius fr. 8 (*FHG* 4.186).

55. Julian. *Caes.* 329a. See also Eus. *Vit. Const.* 4.7, which speaks generically of all barbarians and Joh. Ant. fr. 171, which is specific to the Goths but probably apocryphal. AM 20.8.1, cf. 26.10.3, does imply that the Goths were at times paid for service in Rome's armies but indicates that this was negotiated according to circumstances rather than prescribed by treaty. Those who argue that Constantine continued to pay some form of tribute to the Goths include Brockmeier 1987, 84–85; Heather 1991, 109, 114; 1996, 59; 1997, 70–71; cf. Chrysos 1972, 55.

56. Them. *Or.* 10.135c–d. Those who argue that Constantine allowed free trade include Brockmeier 1987, 98–9; Heather 1991, 109 n. 79, 113; 1996, 59.

57. Them. *Or.* 10.136c–137a makes it quite clear that some Goths raided Roman territory regularly. AM 22.7.7, 26.4.5; Zos. 4.10.1 provide further proof that the Goths practiced such

there is at least one piece of evidence for larger-scale problems in the 340s. In this decade, Ulfilas, who had been appointed bishop to the Goths by Constantine or Constantius, was forcibly expelled from Gothia, together with a sizeable number of fellow confessors. All were settled by Constantius only fifty kilometers from Gothic territory, just south of Nicopolis ad Istrum in Moesia.[58] The incident betrays both the extent to which the barbarian leadership felt threatened by its people's assimilation of Roman culture, and the degree to which the Romans fed those fears by aiding Goths with religious ties to Rome.[59] Tensions thus existed that could have led to alterations in the 332 treaty.[60] We must therefore draw a distinction between what we can know of the treaty terms of 332—hostages, a cessation or reduction of tribute, and a demand for military support—and what we know of Romano-Gothic relations later in the fourth century—annual payments of tribute and free trade.

Nor would alterations necessarily have sprung from tension. An absence of conflict could also have led to a relaxation of harsher treaty terms—as perhaps on trade—which once again escapes notice in the spotty sources. Indeed, although there is some evidence of tension, there are even stronger indications of a general peace. It is all but certain that Romans and Goths never engaged in open warfare between 332 and 367. Neither Constantius nor Julian ever felt compelled to cross the Danube against the Goths, and it seems that neither engaged the Goths in any large-scale military conflict on Roman soil.[61] Archaeological evidence confirms that the Goths themselves

---

raids prior to crossing the Danube in 376 and the references on pp. 333–34 that they continued to do so after their crossing. Indeed, plundering raids were an integral part of Germanic culture, especially in as far as they strengthened the position of a *reiks* over his *Gefolgschaft* by providing him with military glory and wealth for redistribution (cf. Elton 1996b, 48–54). To alleviate this problem, limitanean forts and fortlets were regularly constructed along the Danube with the express intent of limiting small-scale raiding (*CIL* 3.12484 = *ILS* 724: "gentilium Goth[oru]m [t]emeritati . . . latrunculorumque impetum"; cf. *CIL* 3.12376; *CIL* 3.3385 = *ILS* 395; *ILS* 8913). One lower Danube fort was actually named Latro (thief) (Anon. Rav. 4.7; *Not. dign. or.* 40.8; Proc. *Aed.* 4.7).

58. Auxentius 36[58]-37 [59]; Philostorg. 2.5; Jord. *Get.* 267; cf. Isidore *Hist. Goth.* 10 (*MGH.AA* 11.271–72). The chronology of this incident remains in question. Schäferdiek 1979 and Barnes 1990a would date it to 343, while Heather and Matthews 1991, 142–43, date it to 347/48. On Nicopolis, see Poulter 1995, esp. 15 and 32. On this settlement, cf. Velkov 1989.

59. Many Gothic refugees were offered asylum across Roman territory; see Oros. 7.32.9; August. *De civ. Dei* 18.52; *Pass. S. Sabae* 4; Delehaye 1912, 279.

60. Further conflict may be indicated by the apparent disappearance of Constantine's stone bridge at Oescus-Sucidava. When Valens attacked the Goths in 367, he went to the trouble to build a boat bridge just downstream at Daphne, an unlikely maneuver had the stone bridge still stood (AM 27.5.2; cf. 27.5.6; Tudor 1974, 167–70). Even so, Thompson 1956, 375; 1966, 13–24, has made too much of its disappearance, which could just as easily have been occasioned by natural causes.

61. The sources for Julian's reign, which are abundant, explicitly deny military engagements with the Goths (see p. 150). Ammianus also says nothing of engagements between Constantius

did not invade Roman territory between the late third century and the late 370s.[62] Certainly from the beginning of Ammianus's narrative in 353, we would expect to hear of Gothic problems had there been any; the fact that we do not confirms that peace prevailed. Ammianus does mention two squabbles between the Goths and Romans in the 360s, but these were grounded in misunderstandings and never resulted in open war.[63] Indeed, Ammianus states flatly that up to 365, the Goths had remained "a people friendly to the Romans and bound by the treaties of a long-continued peace," and Themistius, a contemporary and eyewitness of Gothic affairs, actually reminded Valens in 368 that the Goths, although haughty, had remained at peace up to the eve of battle in 367.[64]

There is also a more subtle piece of evidence for peace in the mid fourth century. According to Ammianus, the Gothic *iudex* Athanaric had sworn an oath to his father never to cross into Roman territory. When Valens concluded a treaty with Athanaric at the end of his Gothic war in 369, the *iudex* defiantly refused to cross the Danube to conduct negotiations lest he violate this oath. Some have read into this incident scorn for the empire that had held Athanaric's father as a hostage, but royal hostages were quite well treated by the Romans and often developed intense loyalty to the empire; the statue Constantine dedicated to Athanaric's father indicates that he was no exception. With this oath, then, Athanaric's father may have aimed to secure his son's loyalty to an empire with which the Goths had long been at peace by demanding that he promise never to invade. On this reading, only after Valens dared to disturb the delicate equilibrium between Roman and Goth did Athanaric exploit the oath ironically to niggle the emperor.[65]

All the indications are, then, that the Goths were hardly serious aggressors in the years between 332 and 367. Trade and commerce between Goths

---

and the Goths after 353, and for earlier periods the extensive catalogs of Constantius's military activities in Julian. *Or.* 1 (a. 355) and *Or.* 3[2] (a. 357) mention nothing either. Only Lib. *Or.* 59.89–93 (a. 348) gives any hint of Gothic problems, although here too open conflict is explicitly denied (cf. p. 148). Constantius did bear the title *Gothicus Maximus* (*CIL* 3.3705 = *ILS* 732), but this was clearly won through association with Constantine's 332 victory rather than a later victory of his own (cf. Kneissl 1969, 178–79, 241, 244).

62. Scorpan 1980, 121–22; cf. 71, has found no levels of destruction between 332 and 378 in his comprehensive survey of Danube fortifications; cf. Tomovic 1996, 79.

63. See pp. 149–51.

64. AM 27.5.1: "gens amica Romanis foederibusque longae pacis obstricta"; Them. *Or.* 8.119c. AM 26.6.11 notes that in 365, the Gothic *gens* was dangerous because it had long remained *intacta*.

65. AM 27.5.9, 31.4.13. On the treatment of hostages, see Braund 1984, 9–21. This oath admits of other interpretations as well: it is commonly taken to indicate that Gothic *iudices* were only allowed to fight within Gothic territory, as Wolfram 1988, 94–95, indicates, expanding on 1975, 18–19, 323. This assertion is extrapolated solely from this passage, which actually says nothing about such a generic restriction.

and Romans flourished in these decades. Cultural and religious contacts were common. The archaeological and historical records offer no traces of large-scale Gothic invasions of Roman territory and very little evidence of tension whatsoever. We must therefore ask whether Valens was necessarily motivated by strategic necessity when he undertook his war against the Goths. In what follows, we shall see that this seems unlikely. Rather, Valens used a diplomatic infraction as an excuse for a foreign war designed to boost his position as emperor and to satisfy the policy demands of his aggressive brother.

THE GOTHIC WAR OF 367–69

In the winter of 366/67, within half a year of defeating Procopius, Valens began preparing his trans-Danubian expedition against the Goths.[66] He replaced the aging praetorian prefect Sallustius with the vigorous Auxonius and sent the new prefect ahead to Marcianople (Devnja) in Moesia Inferior in order to arrange for supplies to be shipped up the Danube.[67] A number of laws survive that confirm Auxonius's role in coordinating manpower, money, and materials from this city over the next three years.[68] Valens arrived with his army the following spring, when he is attested at Marcianople from May 10.[69] There, he supplemented his rather deficient strategic knowledge with the new manual *De rebus bellicis*, written for him in the period following the Procopius revolt. The manual not only recommended the sort of border fortifications that he soon built and the manufacture of the *ballistae* with which he equipped these forts, it also had advice on shirts to protect his men from cool and damp weather, and portable bridges, which would have been ideal for the marshy territory in which he was about to campaign.[70]

After outfitting his units, Valens had a pontoon bridge built at the bridge-head established by Constantine between Transmarisca (Tutrakan) and

66. For substantive treatments of the first Gothic war, see Nagl, "Val.," 2106–11; Thompson 1966, 17–24; Chrysos 1972, 94–108; Zahariade 1983; Wolfram 1988, 65–69; Wanke 1990, 73–110; Heather 1991, 115–21; Gutmann 1991, 112–32; Chauvot 1998, 190–99; Seager 1999, 599–601.

67. Zos. 4.10.3–4; cf. Eunap. *VS* 7.5.9. *PLRE* I's Auxonius 1 was still serving as *vicarius Asiae* on Oct. 6, 366 and is not attested as praetorian prefect until Sept. 1, 367, but must have assumed office earlier that spring. Auxonius apparently worked himself to death, for he died in office (Zos. 4.11.4) some time after Dec. 29, 369 (cf. *CTh* 5.1.2, with Pergami 1993, 476).

68. *CTh* 7.4.15 (a. 369), 6.2, 10.20.4 (a. 368), 11.17.1 (a. 367); cf. Velkov 1980, 175–76, 189. On outfitting expeditionary armies, see Elton 1996a, 65–69; 1996b, 237; Lee 1998, 221.

69. *CTh* 12.18.1, with Seeck, *Regesten*, 231.

70. For fortifications, see *DRB* 20.1; cf. *praef.* 10, 1.4. On the *ballista fulminalis*, see 18.1–5. Valens's forts are cataloged in app. A. His manufacture of *ballistae* is attested at Them *Or.* 10.136a. On the *thoracomachus*, see 15.1–3, 19.2. On the *ascogephyrus*, see *praef.* 14, 16.1–5, 19.3.

Daphne (Spatnov). From there, he crossed into Tervingi territory sometime after May 30 and began an earnest search for an opponent with whom to fight. The Tervingi had fled north into what Ammianus calls the *montes Serrorum*, probably the southeastern Carpathians.[71] Flight before Roman forces was a tactic barbarians had often used before and that could only be countered when scouts were available who knew roads and passes well enough to avoid ambushes and circumvent barbarian roadblocks.[72] Gothia certainly had roads, whether of Gothic construction or dating to the Roman occupation of Dacia, but Valens's scouts were apparently unable to lead his army along them and into the mountains to ferret out the enemy.[73] So as not to return without any claim to success for the season, Valens sent his *magister peditum* Arinthaeus with raiding bands to round up those barbarians who had not yet escaped into the defiles. This foray, reported in Ammianus, is probably to be connected with the notice in Zosimus that Valens offered a fixed sum of gold for each barbarian head that his men brought back to him.[74] The Roman raiders no doubt worked widespread destruction on farmsteads, burning houses and crops and capturing or killing stragglers. Such random violence was de rigueur in translimitanean campaigns.[75] Sometime in September, Valens crossed back into Moesia, perhaps at Durostorum, downstream from where he had traversed the river in May.[76] After a disappoint-

71. AM 27.5.2–3; cf. Them. *Or.* 10.139a–c. Both AM 27.5.2: *crescente vere* and Zos. 4.11.1: ἔαρος ἀρχομένου are in accord that Valens attacked the Goths in early spring, a problem given our knowledge that he remained in Marcianople until at least May 30; cf. *CTh* 11.17.1, with Seeck, *Regesten*, 231. Zahariade 1983, 59–60 offers possible explanations for the discrepancy. On the location of the *montes Serrorum*, see Cazaru 1972: "im Gebirgsbogen, der die Ost- mit den Südkarpaten verbindet," perhaps to be associated with the range now called Siriul, which divides Wallachia from Siebenbürgen (cf. Wanke 1990, 96–97).

72. AM 27.10.7, 30.5.13, 31.8.12; cf. Elton 1996b, 80–81. Athanaric also took refuge from the Huns in 375–76 by fleeing to the mountains (cf. AM 31.3.7). The stereotype of the Scythian who wins his victory in flight was alive and well in the mid fourth century (e.g., Lib. *Ep.* 192; *Pan. Lat.* 6 [7].12.2).

73. On Gothic roads, see *Pass. S. Sabae* 4.1. On scouts in barbarian territory, see AM 17.10.2, 5, 27.10.7, 29.4.5; Veg. *Mil.* 3.6; cf. Austin and Rankov 1995, 39–54. On barbarian roadblocks, see AM 16.11.8, 12.15, 17.1.9, 10.6; Gregory of Tours *Historia Francorum* 2.9; cf. Lee 1993, 87.

74. AM 27.5.4; Zos. 4.11.2–3. Paschoud 2.2: 352 n. 125 follows Schmidt 1934, 231–32, 237, in dating this passage to 369, but the short season and constant marching that year probably precluded such guerrilla raids. It is interesting that the *magister equitum* Victor rather than Arinthaeus was awarded the consulship in 369.

75. E.g., AM 16.11.11, 17.1.7, 12.6, 13.13, 24.1.14–15, 2.22, 4.25, 4.30, 29.5.10–11; *Pan. Lat.* 6 [7].12.3, 12 [9].22.6; cf. Elton 1996b, 221–23. For images of Roman abuse of barbarians, see Calò-Levi 1952; Krierer 1995.

76. Valens is attested at Durostorum from Sept. 25, 367, at *CTh* 10.1.11 + 12.6.14, with Seeck, *Regesten*, 231.

ing summer, he returned to Marcianople, "without having inflicted or suffered serious harm."[77]

Several months later, in early 368, Themistius arrived on embassy from Constantinople. He reviewed Valens's troops and delivered an address in honor of the emperor's quinquennalian celebration on March 28.[78] The address, oration 8, provides us with a window into the official assessment of the campaign after a year of less than signal performance. Themistius came bringing the *aurum coronarium* tax from Constantinople, which made his oration the perfect forum for discussing Valens's enlightened taxation policies.[79] The Procopian revolt had led Valens to curb the harsh exactions initiated in the first years of his reign in order to placate the widespread discontent that had set the stage for the usurper's uprising. Themistius's praise for Valens's tax cuts now made a virtue of necessity. The orator laid particular emphasis on the cost of military operations relative to the limited number of people they profited: whereas low taxation was of universal benefit, barbarian campaigns aided only those who lived on the borders.[80] High taxes and harsh collection procedures were thus more dangerous to the empire than the "Scythians": "It is of no importance to one who is ill-treated whether it is a Scythian or a Roman who wrongs him; whosoever causes him to suffer wrong, that man he considers his enemy."[81] Themistius's embassy thus offered a chance to warn the new emperor that the expenses of continued campaigning could force the renewal of the exactions that had nearly cost Valens his throne. By undertaking this campaign, Valens had raised the expectation that he would gain a victory; Themistius was notifying him that it would have to come soon.[82]

The following summer, Valens was once again disappointed when flooding on the Danube prevented him from crossing. He had set up a base camp near Vicus Carporum—probably ancient Carsium—downstream from where

77. AM 27.5.4: "nec illato gravi vulnere, nec accepto." Valens is first attested back at Marcianople on Mar. 9, 368, at *CTh* 10.17.2, with Seeck, *Regesten*, 34, 233. Cf. Theoph. a.m. 5859–60 on Valens's stay in Marcianople during his Gothic war.

78. Them. *Or.* 8.116a–b. On the date, see Vanderspoel 1995, 168, 251; Chastagnol 1987.

79. On *aurum coronarium*, see *Or.* 8.115b. On taxation policies, see *Or.* 8.113a–114b, 116d; cf. 10.129c and 292–95.

80. *Or.* 8.114c–115a, 118c. Themistius's praise of Valens's choice to cut taxes in precisely the period when military expenditure demanded vast monetary outlays (*Or.* 8.113b) is echoed in a passage of Zosimus (4.10.3–4) that praises the praetorian prefect Auxonius for providing resources for the campaign without raising taxes. *CTh* 7.4.15 (May 3, 369) to Auxonius confirms Valens's concern that provincials not be overburdened with demands for provisioning. Cf. Heather and Matthews 1991, 27 n. 39.

81. *Or.* 8.115c; cf. 115a.

82. Heather 1991, 117–18; cf. Heather and Matthews 1991, 25; contra Vanderspoel 1995, 169–71.

he had crossed the previous year. Ammianus gives us the impression that he remained inactive there all summer,[83] but other sources prove this wrong. He is attested at Tomi (Constantia) in a passage from the ecclesiastical historians that can plausibly be assigned to this year. A milestone along the road between Durostorum and Tomi marks the route Valens would have taken there, and an inscription from near Tomi further confirms the emperor's presence in the area.[84]

Nor was Valens simply making the rounds. Valentinian had initiated a massive fortification program in the west that year, and Valens was following his brother's lead, putting the enforced hiatus in his campaigning to good use.[85] Indeed, Valentinian's fortification program in the western empire is notorious and has been well documented with epigraphical and archaeological finds on the Rhine and upper Danube.[86] Fewer have recognized, however, that Valens himself expended enormous amounts of capital and effort fortifying the east. Unfortunately, the slower pace of archaeology on the lower Danube has uncovered less material to fill in our picture of Valens's efforts.[87] Even so, enough remains to reconstruct something of what he accomplished.

Our documentary sources offer the names of three forts built or rebuilt along the Danube by Valens: the Codex Theodosianus contains three constitutions issued by Theodosius from "Valentia," and Valentinian and Gratian were also honored with eponymous forts—Gratiana and Valentiniana—attested in Procopius and the *Notitia dignitatum*.[88] Valentiniana was apparently garrisoned with a new unit instituted under Valens, the Milites Primi Gratianenses. Numismatic evidence can also be used to buttress the argu-

83. AM 27.5.5: "impeditus mansit immobilis prope Carporum vicum, stativis castris ad usque autumnum locatis emensum." Wanke 1990, 61, 100–101, argues that Valens's base camp was in fact at Cius (Girliciu) and that the fort described is that which remains at Carsium (Hiršova).

84. On the visit to Tomi, see Soz. 6.21.3–6; cf. Theod. *HE* 4.35.1–2, with Velkov 1980, 179, 192–93. See also *AE* 1978, 716 (Valuls lui Traian, near Tomi). The milestone of Miristea (*CIL* 3.12518b) can be dated after Gratian's elevation in late summer 367; cf. *CIL* 3.13755b from Axiopolis (Rasovo). In contrast to their normally jejune entries, both Eutropius and Festus include catalogs of Thracian cities that may be some of the places Valens visited during his Gothic campaigns: Eutr. 6.10: Uscudama/Adrianople, Cabyle, Apollonia, Callatis, Parthenopolis, Tomi, Histrum, and Burziaonis; Festus 9: the same list, plus Eumolpiada/Philippopolis; cf. Bird 1993, 103 n. 14.

85. On Valentinian's and Valens's fortifications, see app. A; cf. Lander 1984, 263–93.

86. See esp. Soproni 1985; Petrikovits 1971.

87. See esp. Scorpan 1980; Aricescu 1980, 72–103.

88. For Valentia, see *CTh* 8.5.49, 11.1.22, 12.1.113. For Gratiana and Valentiniana, see Proc. *Aed.* 4.11.20; *Not. dign. or.* 39.27. Wanke 1990, n. 17, argues that Gratiana was located at the northeastern extreme of the province. Aricescu 1980, 95, puts it rather on the Danube riparian road between Carsium and Troesmis.

ment. Coin finds indicate that Valens constructed a fortlet that has been excavated near Lake Topraichioi in the Dobrugea. This installation was a *burgus*, a small, rectangular watchtower of a sort Valentinian and Valens favored. Here in Scythia and in other riparian hot spots, they placed these at close intervals—as little as one mile apart—so that limitanean troops could survey the frontier and monitor interactions between barbarians and Romans.[89] To advertise their favoring of *burgi*, Valentinian and Valens also at this time began minting medallic bronzes featuring these fortlets on their reverse (fig. 14).[90] Above all, a prominent if fragmentary inscription from a fort at Cius (Girliciu)—near the Vicus Carporum mentioned by Ammianus—confirms Valens's completion of this structure *temporibus quinquennalibus*, that is, in 368.[91] Two years later, Themistius included a long section in his address *On the Peace* lauding the same project. He was particularly keen on Valens's work repairing, restocking, and regarrisoning existing forts.[92] As noted above, the archaeology indicates that the frontier had suffered little disturbance since its last reconstruction under Constantine. To implement the currently mandated program on the lower Danube, then, Valens needed mostly to undertake routine maintenance and add only a few new forts. Even so, forts did not spell a victory, and victory there had to be. The following winter, he returned to Marcianople to prepare for another chance.[93]

On January 1, 369, Themistius once again came on embassy to Valens to celebrate the first consulship of his infant son, Valentinian Galates. The address he delivered (*Or.* 9) is less revealing about the Gothic war than its predecessor, although it does bring to life something of the mentality of triumphal rulership as it was foisted onto the two-year-old prince.[94] Themistius lauded the auspicious infancy of the child, noting that he had been born in the same year as the victory (νίκη) against Procopius and that he now shared the consulate with the *magister equitum* Victor, "a man whose name means victory."[95] He had already watched the boy amid the troops and seen him

89. Zahariade and Opait 1986. On *burgi*, see p. 375. Valentinian's and Valens's favor for *burgi* can be seen in the fact that four of the five occurrences of the word in *CIL* 3 are from their forts (cf. Lander 1984, 264–70, 289–93).

90. *RIC* 9.19–20 (Trier 29a–c); 9.219 (Constantinople 40); Bastien 1988, 201 n. 69. The type clearly postdates Aug. 24, 367, since it was minted for Gratian as well. The "S" shown above the fortlet may stand for *speculum*, another common name for a *burgus*, as at *CTh* 1.6.6.

91. *CIL* 3.7494 = *ILS* 770; cf. Mommsen 1882.

92. *Or.* 10.136a–b. See also Mackensen 1999, 234–38, on the systematic construction of *horrea* at Valentinianic forts to facilitate grain storage.

93. AM 27.5.5; Valens is attested at Marcianople from Nov. 9, 368, at *CTh* 9.1.10–11, 9.34.8, with Seeck, *Regesten*, 34, 36, 235.

94. On the speech and its date, see Vanderspoel 1995, 171–72, 251. *Pace* Vanderspoel 1995 and Downey 1965–74, 1: 182, Them. *Or.* 9.123c implies that the author was present at Marcianople to deliver this speech; cf. Errington 2000, 885 n. 128.

95. *Or.* 9.120c–121a: νίκης ἐπώνυμος ἀνήρ.

Figure 14. Valens advertises one of his fortification towers. Aes of Constantinople. *RIC* 9.219.40. Glendening sale catalog, July 17, 1929, no. 1023.

testing a bow and engaging in a mock contest with barbarians. Young Galates was being raised to standards that would please his father and teach the boy to follow in his footsteps.[96]

In early July 369, Valens once again moved downstream and crossed the Danube on a boat bridge he built at Noviodunum (Isaccea).[97] He first headed north, deep into the territory of the Gothic Greuthungi in Bessarabia. After further minor engagements, he finally met fixed resistance when Athanaric chose to confront him in battle. Valens routed the Tervingi leader but did not pursue him. Rather, he returned south of the Danube again to Marcianople, where he planned to pass the winter with his troops.[98] The Goths, unable to confront the Romans effectively and reeling under the weight of starvation and economic collapse after three years of conflict, sent a number of embassies begging for peace.[99] Since he had not succeeded in achieving a decisive victory in three years and was confronted with growing problems elsewhere, Valens consented. He sent his *magistri militum* Victor and Arinthaeus, along with the omnipresent Themistius, to propose conditions. Athanaric consented, although he insisted that he not be forced to cross the Danube so as not to violate his oath to his father never to set foot on Roman soil. On a hot summer day, Valens and Athanaric were rowed out in boats to the middle of the Danube, where they concluded the treaty of Noviodunum.[100] Valens then returned to Marcianople, where he remained until

96. *Or.* 9.121a–c. On the martial education of fourth-century princes, see Straub 1939, 32–35; cf. Campbell 1984, 49–50.

97. AM 27.5.6; cf. Them. *Or.* 10.133b. Valens is last attested at Noviodunum on July 5, 369, at *CTh* 10.16.2, with Seeck, *Regesten*, 237.

98. AM 27.5.6. Them *Or.* 10.132c confirms Ammianus's testimony that the expedition penetrated deep into barbarian territory. The date of Valens's return to Marcianople is not certain, pace Seeck, *Regesten*, 237. One can assume late summer.

99. AM 27.5.7. Them. *Or.* 10.133a confirms that the Goths sent multiple embassies.

100. AM 27.5.8–9; Zos. 4.11.4; Them. *Or.* 10.134a; cf. 132d, 133b. See also *Or.* 11.146a–b, 148d, and Köhler 1925, 40. It is not certain that Themistius was a member of the embassy to the Goths, although his use of the first person at *Or.* 10.132d–133a and 11.144a point in this direction; cf. Dagron 1968, 22, 102; Vanderspoel 1995, 173.

at least January 31, 370, before returning to Constantinople en route to the eastern frontier.[101]

The three-year war had hardly been an unequivocal success. The Romans did not suffer any significant losses, but they also did not inflict any grave defeat on the Tervingi.[102] Valens engaged Athanaric in only one set battle and, although he routed the *iudex*, he was never able to pursue his advantage. By late summer 369, he had other preoccupations. He had been moving to the eastern frontier in 365 when Procopius's revolt triggered the series of incidents that brought him to campaign against the Goths. While he remained on the Danube, the situation in the east continued to grow worse. The Persians invaded Armenia and expelled its young king Pap. Already by his quinquennial address in early 368, Themistius could report of Pap's arrival at Valens's court in Marcianople.[103] By the summer of 369, affairs in the east had reached a critical state, forcing Valens to send his *magister peditum* Arinthaeus to the Persian frontier immediately after he returned from negotiations with Athanaric.[104] Ammianus confirms the threat in a passage that is often misunderstood. Valens, he reports, had to come to terms "because the fear of the enemy *[metus hostilis]* was increasing through the emperor's ongoing stay." Taken in its proper sense, this *metus hostilis* must refer to the *Roman* fear of the (eastern) enemy rather than the Goths' fear of

---

101. AM 27.5.6–10 says that after routing Athanaric, Valens returned to Marcianople, with the intention of wintering there, arranged the treaty there, and then returned to Constantinople. Seeck, *Untergang*, 448 n. 18, takes Them. *Or.* 10.134a (ἐφ'ἡλίῳ στὰς ἐπὶ τῆς νεώς, ἡνίκα μάλιστα ἑαυτοῦ φλογωδέστερος ἦν) to imply that the Noviodunum agreement was reached in late summer 369; cf. Schmidt 1934, 232; Stein 1959, 186. At *Regesten* 34, 239, however, he argues for a date in early 370, a date recently defended at Errington 2000, 902–4. Valens definitely remained at Marcianople until at least Dec 11, 369 (*CTh* 10.10.11), and probably as late as Jan. 31, 370 (*CTh* 7.13.2, with Seeck, *Regesten*, 34), and he could plausibly have struck his treaty any time into the winter of 369/70. Although AM 27.5.10 and Zos. 4.11.4 place Valens's return to Constantinople immediately after concluding the treaty of Noviodunum (which would imply that he struck it in early 370), a summer date seems more likely given Themistius's eyewitness testimony about the heat. Indeed, as Errington himself agrees, Valens had already visited Constantinople in December 369, as per *CTh* 5.1.2. The issue is important because a winter date for the treaty would imply that Valens may have hoped for further Gothic campaigns in 370 but eventually abandoned his intentions. In fact, however, he seems to have concluded the treaty in late summer or early autumn 369, while his troops were in winter quarters, to have passed the rest of the winter at Marcianople, and to have returned to Constantiniple with his army only in early 370. Cf. AM 30.3.7, where Valentinian chose to winter at Trier in 374 despite the fact that he had learned of the Sarmatian invasion of Pannonia in June of that year and fully intended to march east the following spring.

102. AM 27.5.4, 6; Them. *Or.* 10.139a–c; cf. Köhler 1925, 41–42; Schmidt 1934, 232; Nagl, "Val.," 2108; Hoffmann 1969–70, 1: 440; Heather 1991, 117–8.

103. Them. *Or.* 8.116c; cf. p. 171.

104. AM 27.12.13.

Valens.[105] Whether or not he had achieved what he set out to do, Valens had no choice but to come to terms.

Themistius was, as mentioned, at the Danube in 369 as a negotiator, and he later witnessed the treaty ceremony. In early 370, he reported his experience to the Constantinopolitan Senate in a dramatic speech (*Or.* 10) that glorified what was in fact an uncomfortable agreement for both sides.[106] As we might expect, Themistius's veil of triumphal imagery is not difficult to see through: he argues that Valens had so unquestionably proven his superiority that he did not need, or rather did not want, a full-scale barbarian slaughter. This idea emerges most clearly in his peroration, where he compares Valens to the prudent hunter who spares some of the quarry for future outings.[107] Such a measured use of victory entitled Valens to claim rule over not just the Romans, but all races, doubly justifying his right to the title *Gothicus Maximus:* "Whom, then, is it most fitting to call *Gothicus:* him through whom the Goths exist and are preserved or him at whose hands they would have ceased to exist, if he were given his choice?"[108] Themistius's portrayal of the treaty ceremony is equally revealing. He evokes the hackneyed image of barbarians, normally boisterous and unruly, cowering in obeisance in countless numbers on the left bank of the Danube. Across from them glisten Roman legions, ranged in perfect order, in a ceremony encapsulating the world order that all Romans hoped to project.[109] Between the two groups, Valens and Athanaric engage in negotiations, which are depicted as an agonistic rivalry, a single combat between the leaders, with a single, undisputed winner, Valens.[110]

In reality, of course, the situation was much more ambiguous.[111] Atha-

---

105. AM 27.5.7: "quod ex principis diuturna permansione metus augebatur hostilis"; cf., e.g., Rolfe 1935–39, 3: 33, "because the long stay of the emperor was increasing the enemy's fears." See Ammianus's similar use of *metus* at 30.2.8. Blockley's reading (1981–83, 2: 138 n. 81), of Eunap. *Hist.* fr. 37 as ironic would add Eunapius to the list of sources who understood that the treaty was a compromise. Zosimus's litotes at 4.11.4 is also revealingly unenthusiastic, σπονδαὶ μὴ καταισχύνουσαι τὴν Ῥωμαίων ἀξίωσιν.

106. For the date and circumstances, see Vanderspoel 1995, 173–76, 251.

107. *Or.* 10.139d–140a.

108. Them. *Or.* 10.140c–d; cf. the same themes at 130d–131b, 131d–132a, 133b, 139a–c, and *Or.* 19.229c.

109. Them. *Or.* 10.133c–d. For similar scenes, see AM 17.12.9; *Pan. Lat.* 3 [11].7.2.

110. Them. *Or.* 10.134a–135a, 139b–c.

111. The case is put most succinctly at Heather 1991, 117–118: "It was clear to all that Valens's policy had changed from one of confrontation to negotiation; Themistius was attempting to hide the fact that Valens compromised because he had been unable to win on the battlefield." Cf. Köhler 1925, 46–48. However, as Gutmann 1991, 127–30, points out, we must be careful not to read Themistius's rhetoric of φιλανθρωπία with too much skepticism. Φιλανθρωπία was a standard theme in all of Themistius's orations, including an earlier speech to Valens that had no bearing on Goths: *Or.* 6.69d–80a, 94b, 95a–b; cf. *Or.* 13.176a–c and Downey 1955;

naric was not admitting defeat, as indicated by his bold demand that the treaty be concluded in midstream on the Danube, and he would later refrain from requesting asylum from the Huns because "he recalled that he had treated Valens with some contempt at the time of the treaty, when he declared that he was bound by a solemn vow not to set foot on Roman soil."[112] Normally, barbarian leaders driven into submission were forced to come to Roman territory or to submit ceremonially before Roman standards in their own land. A treaty arrived at in midstream thus represented an outward sign of compromise.[113]

Compromise is also evident from what we can know about the terms of the treaty itself.[114] Ammianus, unfortunately, reports only that it was secured by the exchange of hostages, nothing more.[115] Our understanding of the Noviodunum agreement is, however, considerably enhanced by the reports in Zosimus and Themistius. Zosimus says: "The Romans kept whatever they had before with complete security, and the barbarians were forbidden to make crossings and ever to set foot on Roman territory at all." This would seem to imply a considerable tightening up of the frontier in favor of the Romans, but Themistius implies with his description of the treaty ceremony that the barbarians also kept whatever was theirs before: there were no net gains for Rome.[116] The passage in Zosimus also implies, and Themistius openly asserts, that trading along the Danube, which had previously been unrestricted, was to be limited to two cities.[117]

Themistius explained that this last measure was designed to curb barbarian attacks and frivolous profiteering by Roman troops,[118] but one wonders if

---

Dagron 1968, 95–118; Daly 1972; Vanderspoel 1995, 28–29, 174 n. 70. Indeed, it was a standard theme in ancient rhetoric more generally: Men. Rhet. 2.374–75 recommends precisely the trope used by Themistius (ἐνταῦθα στήσας φιλανθρωπίᾳ τὰς πράξεις ἀνῆκα συγχωρήσας τὸ λείψανον τοῦ γένους σώζεσθαι); cf. Symm. *Or.* 2.10–12: "tibi incola vivit Alamanniae; quos ferro subtrahis, addis imperio".

112. AM 31.4.13; cf. Them. *Or.* 15.191a: ὁ πάλαι σεμνὸς καὶ ὑψηλογνώμων.

113. Valentinian negotiated a treaty with the undefeated Alamannic *rex* Macrianus in similar circumstances (AM 30.3.4–5, with Wanke 1990, 105 n. 95; Heather and Matthews 1991, 25–26; Heather 1991, 119–20). Here, too, the argument should not be pushed too far, since a similar treaty of Julian's with the Chamavi was negotiated after their complete submission (Eunap. *Hist.* fr. 18.6 [Blockley]; cf. AM 17.8.5).

114. This is generally agreed, as Schmidt 1934, 232–33; Klein 1952; Dagron 1968, 102–3; Stallknecht 1969, 62–63; Wanke 1990, 107–9, esp. n. 100; Heather 1991, 117–21; Heather and Matthews 1991, 22–23; Chauvot 1998, 197–99. On barbarian treaties more broadly, see Elton 1996b, 183–90.

115. AM 27.5.10: "acceptis obsidibus."

116. Zos. 4.11.4. Them. *Or.* 10.133c describes barbarians lined up along the left bank of the Danube, implying that the Romans made no claim to their territory.

117. Them. *Or.* 10.135c–d. Velkov 1980, 184–85, and Barnea 1968, 2: 395, both argue independently that the two trade sites were Noviodunum and Daphne.

118. Them. *Or.* 10.135d, 136b. For the profitability of Gothic trade, see SHA *Max.* 4.4.

there were not deeper, ideological issues at play. Although earlier centuries had generally seen minimal limitations on barbarian trade,[119] according to Themistius, Valens was quite insistent on the importance of these restrictions in 369.[120] Indeed, Valens's intentions here may have been rooted in a larger Valentinianic policy of opposition to foreign trade. A Valentinianic law of 370/75 forbade the sale of wine, oil, and *garum* to barbarians, and a related law—this one datable to 370 or 373 and probably originally part of the same constitution—imposed capital penalties on those who married barbarians.[121] It is thus no surprise that Valens himself threatened corporal punishment for anyone who exported gold into eastern *barbaricum* in a law of 374.[122] His interest in restricting trade on the Danube is entirely in keeping with a broader closed-door policy toward non-Romans promulgated by both emperors. Nor did the embargo go unimplemented. Valens's strong new system of fortifications,[123] his fleet of patrol boats *(lusoriae)* on the Danube,[124] and the personnel at the disposal of his *comes commerciorum*[125] would certainly have been capable of choking off trans-Danubian commerce. The fact that they succeeded is well attested by the coin finds from Gothic territory, which are only one-fifth as abundant per annum under Valens as they had been under Constantius and Julian.[126] Valens thus effected a reversal in the more normal situation between Goths and Romans discussed above. He apparently felt strongly that the divide between Roman and barbarian should be drawn as firmly as possible.

Themistius also says that Valens cut off the previous payments of annual tribute to the Goths, once again in keeping with his and his brother's hard-

119. This is not to say that trade limitations were unknown in earlier treaties, as Dio Cass. 71.11, 15–16, 18–19, 72.2, 15; cf. Priscus fr. 46 (Blockley). On the question, see Thompson 1966, 14–15; Pitts 1989; Potter 1992; Lee 1993, 71–74.

120. Them. *Or.* 10.135c–d.

121. *CJ* 4.41.1; *CTh* 3.14.1. Both constitutions were addressed to Count Theodosius during his wars against Firmus, as noted in Seeck, *Regesten*, 124; cf. Pabst 1989, 347–48. The contention of Rugullis 1992, 68–73, that we should see these orders as specific to North Africa is vitiated by Ambrose's allusions to the laws as if they were general, *Ep.* 62 [19].7, 34; *De off.* 3.13.84.

122. *CJ* 4.63.2. For trade restrictions on the eastern frontier, see Rugullis 1992, 105–15; Lee 1993, 61–64.

123. Themistius *Or.* 10.136a explicitly links Valens's forts and his trade restrictions.

124. AM 31.5.3 implies there were regular boat patrols on the Danube up to 376, and *Not. dign. or.* 39.35 and 40.36 indicate that units continued to be assigned to this duty up to ca. 394. Indeed *CTh* 7.17 indicates that 225 patrol boats were still in operation as late as 412. On river patrols and patrol boats, see Höckmann 1986, 410–12; 1993; Bounegru and Zahariade 1996, 91–109.

125. *Not. dign. or.* 13.8; cf. A. H. M. Jones 1964, 429, 826.

126. Preda 1975. These numbers are extrapolated from the table at p. 444. See also Harhoiu 1997, 140–47.

line stance against interaction and economic exchange with barbarians.[127] While we may doubt the feasibility of this measure over the long term, there is no reason to deny that Valens was willing and able to call a halt to tribute after 369, and the 374 law forbidding gold exports surely indicates that it remained in force for at least five years. More important, however, Themistius admits that the cessation of tribute was arranged while granting a single, unnamed concession to the Goths.[128] Although we have no specific evidence for what this was, it is often assumed to have been the cessation of the requirement that the Tervingi provide *auxilia* for Roman expeditionary forces.[129] It had probably been the case that previous participation by Gothic auxiliaries in Roman expeditions had come to be contingent on payment, and it is thus reasonable to assume that the cessation of payment went hand in hand with the cessation of military support. Given the role the Goths had played in previous campaigns, this concession would have been massive.

In the end, then, Valens's Gothic war had been anything but a rousing success. He had defeated but hardly overwhelmed the Goths in three years of frustrating conflict. He had then struck a treaty that, while not wholly unfavorable to Roman interests, had clearly been the result of a compromise. In this Noviodunum agreement, Valens neither gained nor lost territory; he sharply curbed trade along the Danube; he halted the annual payment of tribute; and he apparently surrendered Roman claims to Gothic auxiliary forces. In comparison with the situation that had obtained before— the situation established by Constantine in 332 and then gradually modified over the next thirty years—the end result of Valens's war was a sclerosis of Romano-Gothic relations. The coarse net that had formerly encouraged interaction while guaranteeing a remarkable degree of peaceful cooperation had been pulled tighter, creating a situation that ultimately benefited neither side.

SOME PRINCIPLES OF LATE ROMAN FOREIGN POLICY

When we last left Menander Rhetor's panegyrically perfect emperor, we had covered only his qualities of character (*ēthē*), not yet his actions (*praxeis*). This, of course, is only half the picture, for every emperor's identity was constructed as much around what he did as around who he was. Indis-

127. Them. *Or.* 10.135b–c. On Valentinian's and Valens's hostility to tribute, see pp. 150–51.
128. *Or.* 10.135a–c: οἷς δὲ ἔτυχε τῶν σπονδῶν ἀπαυθαδιαζόμενος (of Athanaric).
129. Schmidt 1934, 232; Nagl, "Val.," 2109–10; Klein 1952, 191; Heather 1986, 290; Ulrich 1995, 129, 139–40. This would seem to be confirmed by the fact that the detailed testimony for Valens's campaigns against Shapur in the 370s says nothing of Gothic auxiliaries.

pensable among the ideal emperor's virtues was, of course, ἀνδρεία, in Latin, *virtus*, martial valor. Although this had been true since Augustus, it was doubly so for fourth-century rulers, whose basis for power was always grounded in the ideology of triumph.[130] The emperor was heralded on the coinage, in inscriptions, and in official correspondence as *Victor terra marique, Triumfator gentium barbararum,* and *Domitor gentium et regum.*[131] The troops acclaimed these titles before entering battle, and civilians echoed imperial victory slogans in triumphal celebrations.[132] The central element in a fourth-century emperor's curriculum vitae was thus success in military campaigns and especially campaigns against barbarians.

For this reason, fourth-century panegyrics often concentrate on the military exploits of their addressee, and even when they focus on other subjects, they invariably pay some homage to military issues.[133] Valens himself heard his Scythian feats publicly lauded more than once. In the late winter of 370, Themistius delivered his celebratory oration *On the Peace* in Constantinople, perhaps in conjunction with a triumphal festival that Valens held, hinted at in passages in Eutropius.[134] Later, Libanius delivered a similar panegyric on the Gothic war when the emperor took up residence in Antioch.[135] And in the years that followed, Valens continued to win praise for his Gothic victory in panegyrics, praise that was apparently effective in generating a public perception of him as "a man valiant in war."[136] The pursuit of this image no doubt played into his decision to attack the Goths in the first place.

Panegyrics were, of course, more than just an occasion for fawning adulation. They advertised imperial achievements to an audience hungry for

130. On triumphal rulership in Late Antiquity, see Gagé 1933; McCormick 1986; cf. Lendon 1997, 116. Contrast the relative unimportance of *virtus* over against *aequitas* and *pietas* in the second and early third centuries, Noreña 2001, 156–60.

131. Kneissl 1969, 174–75; Barbieri 1980.

132. E.g., AM 19.2.11, 21.5.9; Veg. *Mil.* 3.5; Lactant. *De mort. pers.* 44.7; cf. Roueché 1984.

133. Men. Rhet. 2.372–75. Military exploits are treated throughout the *Panegyrici Latini*. L'Huillier 1992, 213–34, 275–86, 325–45, estimates that 37 percent of the corpus is devoted to *militaria* and offers extensive statistics on military vocabulary. For *militaria* in Greek panegyric, see, e.g., Julian. *Or.* 1.17cff.; 3.55dff.; Lib. *Or.* 12.48ff; 17.16ff.; 18.53ff.; 59.56ff. For triumphal ideology in imperial panegyric, see also Asche 1983.

134. On Themistius, see p. 134. Eutropius's obsession with triumphs may indicate that Valens celebrated one in 370; see p. 191. Festus 30 actually praises Valens *de Gothis palma.* Kondić 1973, 48–49, holds that a medallion now in the Belgrade museum (fig. 16) may be connected with a triumph as well, but the reverse legend (VIRTUS DD NN AUGUSTORUM) would seem to date before Gratian's accession in 367.

135. Lib. *Or.* 1.144. The oration is not preserved. Greg. Nys. *Eun.* 1.127 indicates that Valens was especially proud of his Gothic victory. Basil *Ep.* 269 may imply a panegyric or history on the feats of Valens's general Arinthaeus, although no time frame can be established.

136. Malalas 13.34: ὁ γενναῖος ἐν πολέμοις; cf. MX 3.29. On continued praise for the Gothic war, see Them. *Or.* 11.146a–b, 148d–149a, 13.166a–c, 179c–d.

such fare. In Valens's case, the need for advertisement was particularly acute. The new emperor had gotten off to a rocky start with the Procopius revolt. During that revolt, he had witnessed the mass desertion of his troops to a man whose dynastic claims commanded far too much support for Valens to remain comfortable with his position as it stood. Following the revolt, Valens badly needed to shore up his emperorship with a military success against a foreign enemy. The fact that the Goths had supported Procopius offered him the justification he needed to break the peace on the Danube against a people whom he might have regarded as an easier target than the Persians. Themistius was thus setting the stage as early as late 366 for Valens to open hostilities in this direction.[137]

That Valens's war was rooted as much in triumphalist expectations as in strategic necessity is clear from his readiness to be content with less than decisive results. When, in the first year of the campaign, Valens failed to force a conflict, he chose instead to keep the army content with plundering raids and headhunting.[138] The following winter, he was already—somewhat prematurely—claiming that "the Goths had been conquered and overcome."[139] In 369, when the Tervingi again proved elusive targets, he turned the army against the Greuthungi, who had not threatened Roman territory and had no connection with the revolt of Procopius.[140] And after three years of such bullying, Valens felt comfortable advertising his victory by assuming the title *Gothicus Maximus.*[141] The fourth-century military machine was thus operating on its own inertia. Because it demanded active campaigning and defined imperial success in military terms, Valens felt compelled to live up to these demands in his struggle to retain power.

Nor is it folly to assume that the blurring of boundaries between the demands of military necessity and the construction of triumphalist rhetoric filtered into the actual formation of policy.[142] The development of Roman foreign policy was hardly based on a scientific conception of what would ensure stability on the frontier. Rather, it has been argued with some success

137. Them. *Or.* 7.94c: γνοὺς ... ὅτι βαρβάρων μὲν Ῥωμαίους ἄχρι παντὸς ἐπεξιέναι προσήκει.

138. AM 27.5.4. Zos. 4.11.2–3. On the importance of plundering and headhunting for morale, see Lib. *Or.* 18.45, 73; Zos. 3.7.2–3, 4.22.2; SHA *Prob.* 14.2; cf. Krierer 1995, 126–28; Goldsworthy 1996, 271–76. For similar views on the campaign's importance in establishing Valens's imperial authority, see Wanke 1990, 110.

139. *CIL* 3.7494 = *ILS* 770: "victis superatisque Gothis."

140. AM 27.5.6. Wolfram 1988, 68, offers no evidence for his speculation that the Greuthungi had aided the Tervingi.

141. *CIL* 6.1175 = *ILS* 771; Eutr. *praef.*: "Domino Valenti Gothico Maximo"; Them. *Or.* 10.140a–c: Γοτθικόν; cf. Arnaldi 1980. On the title *Gothicus Maximus* more broadly, see Wolfram 1988, 55–56. Valentinian I and Gratian were the last emperors to assume official victory titles in the west, and Valens was the last to do so in the east before Justinian (Kneissl 1969, 179–80).

142. See Heather 1999a; Mattern 1999, esp. 162–94.

that Roman policy was only ever created in response to specific situations, and not according to broader theories of "political science."[143] This being said, however, a common set of assumptions did affect the way that emperors chose to respond when situations arose. These included the belief that all barbarians necessarily posed a threat, that barbarian problems were best dealt with through direct invasion, that barbarian territory was at least nominally subject to Roman dominion, and that barbarian leaders could be effectively managed by elimination. Each of these notions can be traced in the policy of both Valentinian and Valens. In what follows, we shall see how they might have affected the choices these made in their treatment of foreign affairs.

As we examine these questions, it is also important to keep in mind that no firm distinctions should be drawn between the foreign policy of Valens and that of his brother. The two worked so closely together that, even if tactical decisions were surely left to each emperor individually, the fundamental strategic program was largely the same for both. Ammianus is quite explicit that "Valens, in accordance with the desire of his brother, whom he consulted and by whose will he was guided, took up arms against the Goths."[144] In some sense, then, Valens's Gothic war was conceived as much by his brother as by himself, and it is thus necessary to examine the policy assumptions of both emperors before drawing any conclusions about the structural causes of Valens's first Gothic war.[145]

Nowhere is it clearer that Valens and his contemporaries regarded barbarians as a uniform and constant threat than in the anonymous treatise *De rebus bellicis*, written for him at precisely the time of his Gothic war.[146] Its author states baldly:

> Above all, it must be recognized that wild nations are pressing upon the Roman empire and howling round about it everywhere, and treacherous barbarians covered by natural positions are assailing every frontier. . . . These mu-

143. Millar 1982; 1988.

144. AM 27.4.1: "ut consulto placuerat fratri, cuius regebatur arbitrio, arma concussit in Gothos." See the similar language at Malalas 13.30 (p. 338) regarding Persian affairs.

145. For a similar interpretation of the effects of Valentinian's aggressive barbarian policies on Valens, see Seeck, *Untergang*, 24, with 433; Chrysos 1972, 99–101, 171–72. We need not assume that Valentinian's foreign policy was in principle identical with that of other fourth-century rulers. Frézouls 1983, for example, demonstrates that Julian's and Constantius's barbarian policies differed markedly, with Julian favoring domination and repulse, while Constantius relied on compromise and accommodation; cf. Stallknecht 1969, 46–48, 56–8. Pabst 1989, 329–55, offers a portrait of Valentinian's foreign policy that appears much more rationalized than what follows here. I prefer the tack taken at Drinkwater 1999.

146. For attitudes toward barbarians in the *DRB*, see Chauvot 1998, 219–33. For more on Roman attitudes to barbarians, see Ladner 1976; Dauge 1981; Shaw 1982–83; Cunliffe 1988.

tilate our peace and quiet by unexpected forays. Nations of this kind, then, that are protected by such defenses or by city and fortress walls must be attacked by means of a variety of new military machines.[147]

Valens, like his adviser, never needed to question the justifications behind actions against barbarians. Even when the Romans broke with treaty terms, scorned barbarian ambassadors, and slaughtered barbarian families in guerrilla raids that mirrored those they decried when perpetrated by barbarians,[148] this was considered a legitimate response to an omnipresent and intractable menace.

Moreover, Valentinian and Valens apparently believed that their reigns in particular were afflicted with an unusual danger from beyond the frontiers. This is certainly the impression left by Ammianus:

> At this time [i.e., the beginning of Valentinian's and Valens's rule], as if trumpets were sounding the war-note throughout the whole Roman world, the most savage peoples roused themselves and poured across the nearest frontiers. At the same time as the Alamanni were devastating Gaul and Raetia, and the Sarmatae and Quadi Pannonia, the Picts, Saxons, Scots, and Attacotti were harassing the Britons with constant disasters. The Austoriani and other Moorish tribes raided Africa more fiercely than ever, and predatory bands of Goths were plundering Thrace and Pannonia. The king of the Persians was laying hands on Armenia, hastening with mighty efforts to bring that country under his sway again.[149]

Zosimus reports similar mayhem at the start of Valentinian's and Valens's reigns, making one wonder if there were indeed particularly acute problems beginning precisely in 364.[150] Both he and Ammianus place their notices immediately after the death of Julian, and both thus seem to attribute the simultaneous collapse of all borders to the cosmic consequences of Julian's death.[151] In fact, impressive as Ammianus's catalog seems, it lumps together in the series of border disputes some that had already erupted before Valentinian was appointed Augustus and others that only arose in the penultimate year of his reign.[152]

The similarity between Ammianus and Zosimus has led to reasonable spec-

147. *DRB* 6.1–4; cf. similar rhetoric at Eus. *Tric.* 8.1–2; Lib. *Or.* 59.135–36.

148. E.g., AM 16.11.9–11, 17.1.3–7, 13.17–18, 18.2.12, 27.2.9.

149. AM 26.4.5–6; cf. AM 27.1.1.

150. Zos. 4.3.4; cf. 4.9.1.

151. AM 30.7.5 confirms that Ammianus associated the collapse of the frontiers with Julian's death. For similar notions, see Lib. *Or.* 17.30, 18.290, 306 and *Or.* 24 passim; cf. Paschoud 1992, 75.

152. Tomlin 1979 rightly demonstrates that the passage conflates incidents that stretched across the years 363–75; cf. Heering 1927, 26.

ulation that the two shared a common source for the passage in the lost *Annales* of Nicomachus Flavianus.[153] Even if this be the case, the *Urquelle* for their idea can be traced to the contemporary propaganda of Valentinian and Valens themselves. Thus we find in Themistius's eighth oration:

> What I shall say will in the first instance concern both emperors. They assumed command of the empire when it was like a ship assailed from all sides; events in the east had hewn it at the edges, and what the enemy did not expect to gain by arms, they bought with treaties. The Germans were disturbing the west and, checking its course slightly, did not so much alarm as irritate; the Scythians loomed threateningly over the middle territories and exacted tribute for staying their hand. Taking on such a circle of war and peace, all vying with each other in wrongdoing, you suffered the opposite of what one might have surmised.[154]

In some sense, then, Valens and his brother themselves—through the agency of their panegyrist—projected the image that their times were especially troubled by barbarian threats. While we should not deny the reality of the problems they faced, in many ways the same could be said of the reign of almost any fourth-century emperor. In a very real sense, then, the intention on the part of the emperors seems to have been to offer the justification for regular military campaigns through the magnification of threats posed by the barbarians of their time.

In Valentinian's case, we have even further evidence that he was obsessed with the suppression of the barbarian menace. Indeed, his fear was so overweening that contemporaries could play off of it for personal advantage: when the *magister officiorum* Remigius wanted to placate Valentinian during one of his notorious outbursts, he insinuated that a barbarian invasion was imminent, reducing the emperor to silence.[155] Nor could his anxieties always be turned to good effect. After Valentinian learned that his comitatensian unit of Batavi had fled the Alamanni in an engagement, he threatened to sell them all into slavery if they did not redeem themselves quickly with a military success.[156] Indeed, Valentinian ultimately suffered a fatal stroke when a group of ambassadors from the Quadi provoked him to apoplexy by trying to excuse their invasion of Pannonia. The ecclesiastical historians reproduce his infuriated response: "The Roman empire is in a sorry state if it has come to the point where such a worthless race of barbarians is not content to remain protected by their own land but takes up

153. Paschoud 2.2: 338 n. 112; 1975, 151–52.
154. Them. *Or.* 8.119c. See similar rhetoric at *Pan. Lat.* 2 [12].3.3–4, 4 [10].18.1–6; Them. *Or.* 15.195a–b; SHA *Hadr.* 5.1–2; *M. Ant.* 22.1.
155. AM 30.8.12.
156. Zos. 4.9.2–4. This episode, confused though it is, should be linked with the events of early 366 described at AM 27.1.1–5. See the similar incident at AM 28.2.9.

arms and treads on Roman territory and plucks up courage for war."[157] So saying, he collapsed and died.

Little wonder, then, that Valentinian's army was engaged in major military operations against barbarians every year from the time he arrived in Gaul in 366 until his death in 375. Valentinian's generals crossed the Rhine or Danube borders in 368, 369, 370, 371, 374, and 375, and he accompanied them personally on all but one of these missions.[158] He was not alone among Roman emperors, particularly post-tetrarchic emperors, in regarding regular campaigns beyond the frontier as essential for the maintenance of border security and the acquisition of military glory.[159] The two Latin panegyrics to Maximian draw particular attention to his *transrhenana victoria*.[160] So too, in his two panegyrics to Constantius II, Julian praises his cousin for crossing the Rhine once and the Tigris many times.[161] Not surprisingly, after rebelling, Julian changed his tone and contrasted Constantius's indolence with his own boldness in crossing the Rhine no fewer than three times.[162] In his *Caesares,* Julian's caricatures of bygone rulers square off with boasts comparing the number of times they had crossed the major river frontiers.[163] And Julian's uncle Constantine shared this preoccupation as well, claiming in an inscription to have carried war into the lands of the barbarians and to have brought back victories thence from the beginning of his reign.[164]

Valens no doubt also believed that translimitanean campaigning and attempts to extend the Roman frontiers were essential tools of foreign policy and essential obligations incumbent on him as emperor. This was certainly the message he received in a verse communiqué written by Ausonius to announce his brother's trans-Rhenan success in 368 and to solicit news of his

157. Soc. 4.31.4; cf. Soz. 6.36.3; Cedrenus, p. 547; Theoph. a.m. 5867. We must, of course, keep in mind that this passage reflects the rhetoric of its authorship, but this was no doubt grounded in a widely held consensus about Valentinian's mentality. On the incident, see also AM 30.6.1–3; Zos. 4.17.1–2; Jer. *Chron.* s.a. 375; Prosper *Chron.* 1155; *Cons. Const.* s.a. 375; *Chron. pasch.,* p. 560.

158. On Valentinian's Rhine campaigns, see Heering 1927, 26–43; Nagl, "Vt.," 2178–80; Tomlin 1973, 99–174; Gutmann 1991, 3–50; Seager 1999, 594–97. For his Sarmatian campaigns, see Heering 1927, 53–57; Nagl, "Vt.," 2182–85; Tomlin 1973, 175–208; Gutmann 1991, 86–95; Seager 1999, 597–99.

159. On the importance of personal participation by emperors in military operations, see Straub 1939, 28–29; Millar 1983, 11–15, 22; Campbell 1984, 17–156.

160. *Pan. Lat.* 11 [3].5.3, 7.2, 16.1, 10 [2].2.6, 7.1–7, 9.1; cf. 7 [6].8.4.

161. Julian. *Or.* 1.17 (22a–c); 3 [2].19 (74b).

162. *Ep. ad Ath.* 279d–280c. Julian's Rhine crossings took place in 358 (AM 17.10.1–10), 359 (18.2.7–19), and 360 (20.10.1–2). Cf. Matthews 1989, 81–84.

163. *Caes.* 320d, 327d.

164. *CIL* 5.8269: "hos[tium] sedibus bellis in[latis r]eportatisque sua [vir]tute et divina [direc]tione victoriis"; cf. *Pan. Lat.* 6 [7].12.2, 12 [9].22.6.

own Gothic victory and the conquest of the northern bank of the Danube.[165] A widely accepted emendation of an inscription on his fort at Cius indicates that Valens boasted his successes *[in solo barb]arico* already after his first, lackluster year against the Goths.[166] His decision to fight in Gothia was thus, at least in part, conditioned by an assumption, common among fourth-century emperors, that campaigns *in barbarico* were an indispensable tool of foreign policy.

The desire to extend Roman might beyond the frontiers also led Valentinian to undertake the construction of forts, bridgeheads, and fortified landing places in barbarian territory.[167] Using these to secure crossings, Valentinian built temporary bridges across both Rhine and Danube, winning accolades from the orator Symmachus.[168] A recently excavated bridge in the Rhine delta has also been dated to Valentinian's reign using dendrochronology.[169] Following earlier panegyrists, Symmachus lauded such operations as evidence that Valentinian was indeed reclaiming what he regarded as Roman territory in "Alamannia."[170] Although there was never any intention of reintroducing provincial control over the formerly Roman Agri Decumates, the empire demanded the assertion of boundless rule, and Valentinian, like other emperors, attempted to oblige with these toeholds across the river.[171] The

165. Aus. XIII *Epig.* 3.8–10 (a. 368): "nec Rhenum Gallis limitis esse loco. / quod si lege maris refluus mihi curreret amnis / huc possem victos inde referre Gothos." Cf. Aus. XIII *Epig.* 4.6–8; XVI *Mos.* ll. 423–24: "hostibus exactis Nicrum super et Lupodunum / et fontem Latiis ignotum annalibus Histri."

166. Alfred von Domaszewski's emendation of *CIL* 3.6159 = 7494, correcting Mommsen's "in fidem recepto rege Athan]arico." The emendation is printed at *ILS* 770 *(addenda)*; Fiebiger and Schmidt 1917, 167; Nagl, "Val.," 2110; Chastagnol 1987, 261. The epitomators writing for Valens also portrayed translimitanean successes as crucial achievements of good leaders, Festus 6 ("ultra Rhenum"); 8 ("in solo barbariae"); 14 ("supra ripas Tigridis"); 17 ("trans Euphraten"); Eutr. 6.17 ("trans Rhenum"); 24 ("supra Tigridem"); 7.9 ("longe ultra Rhenum"); 8.2 ("trans Rhenum . . . trans Danubium").

167. The remains of three fortified landing places on or near the Rhine (Breisach, Mannheim-Nekarau, and Engers) and one on the Danube (Szob) have been firmly connected with Valentinian and many others are thought to be Valentinianic, Soproni 1978, 185–87; Höckmann 1986, 399–406; Sangmeister 1993, 150–51. The bridgehead at "Nemetes" attested at Symm. *Or.* 2.28 has not been identified.

168. AM 20.10.2; Symm. *Or.* 2.4, 23, 26, 3.9, with Pabst 1989, 158 n. 44. The passage at *Or.* 3.9 seems to imply a more permanent structure, but no other evidence, literary or archaeological, exists for a stone or wood bridge built by Valentinian on the Rhine.

169. Goudswaard 1995.

170. Symm. *Or.* 2.4, 12–16: "turpiter amissa revocastis, neclegenter facta corrigitis. In eam condicionem venit Alamannia, ut quae sua conpellebatur amittere, fateretur se nostra tenuisse"; 28, 30; cf. Aus. XVI *Mos.* ll. 420–27 and Chauvot 1998, 177–89. This rhetoric of expansion was typical of the late empire and especially the fourth century; cf. Asche 1983, 96–111; Straub 1986; Pabst 1989, 338–55; Mann 1979, 176–79.

171. Asche 1983, 29–47. On translimitanean installations, see Brennan 1980; Austin and Rankov 1995, 26–27, 33.

barbarians, of course, perceived things differently. On both the Rhine and Danube frontiers, barbarian ambassadors were sent to protest Valentinian's violation of earlier treaty terms with his new installations in their territory. On the Rhine, Valentinian's *dux* Arator disregarded Alamannic complaints in 369 and was eventually slaughtered with his men in a raid, provoking a Roman invasion the following year.[172] On the Danube, early concessions made by the *magister militum* Aequitius were contravened after Valentinian sent the hard-line *dux* Marcellinus to continue the construction of forts across the river. When Gabinius, king of the Quadi, came to protest, Marcellianus had him murdered and thus provoked a barbarian invasion of Illyricum.[173]

Here again, Valentinian's policies were typical of post-tetrarchic rulership. Constantine constructed Rhine and Danube bridges to allow the "opportunity of crossing into enemy territory *[in hosticum]* as often as you wish."[174] His son Constantius II openly boasted of his "close-jointed bridge" over the Danube, which allowed him to invade Sarmatia successfully.[175] Julian built a Rhine bridge at Moguntiacum (Mainz) following his victory at Strasbourg, not to forestall an invasion of the Alamanni—who had already been subdued—but to pursue his advantage.[176] Similarly, the tetrarchs Diocletian and Maximian had gained great prestige through their heralded "extensions" of the Roman *limes*.[177] Valens, too, may have hoped to regain the trans-Danubian foothold that Constantine had established at Sucidava and Daphne and thus to carry through his brother's policy of securing access into *barbaricum* with trans-Danubian bridgeheads and landing sites.[178] Then, too, during the course of his Gothic war, he twice spanned the Danube with temporary bridges like those that won praise for Valentinian from Symmachus.

Finally, Valentinian was extremely interested in capturing barbarian leaders and manipulating the power structure in barbarian tribes. He had a burning passion to capture the Alamannic king Macrianus. When a Rhine cross-

172. AM 28.2.5–9.

173. AM 29.6.1–16; cf. 30.6.2; Zos. 4.16.4–5, with Paschoud 2.2: 364 n. 135. Valentinian did not investigate the murder of Gabinius, indicating that he regarded it as justified or at least beneficial, AM 30.5.3; cf. Pitts 1989, 52–53.

174. *Pan. Lat.* 6 [7].13.1–5 at 1, "facultatem, quotiens velis, in hosticum transeundi"; cf. Asche 1983, 37–39. For the bridge between Colonia (Cologne) and Divitia (Deutz), built ca. 312/15, see Petrikovits 1972, 182–83; Nixon and Rodgers 1994, 235 n. 56; cf. Carroll-Spillecke 1993. For the Danube bridge, see p. 121.

175. AM 17.13.28.

176. AM 17.1.2. See SHA *Prob.* 13.5–15.7 for praise of similar policies under Probus.

177. *Pan. Lat.* 10 [2].7.5–7, 9.1–2, 11 [3].5.3.

178. Festus and Eutropius certainly touted territorial expansion as a key element in imperial *felicitas;* see Festus 16, 21, 28, 30; Eutr. 7.9–11, 8.3, 5, 15, 18, 9.1–2, 17, 10.7; cf. Ratti 1996, 108. See Asche 1983, 29–47, for more on the late Roman policy of installing toeholds across the borders.

ing for this purpose failed to achieve its aim, he contented himself with substituting Fraomarius for Macrianus as king of the Bucinobantes.[179] Similar efforts to capture the king Vithicabius were also thwarted, so Valentinian had
the prince killed by a retainer.[180] Here, too, Valentinian was following his imperial predecessors. Maximian touted his installation of Gennobaudes over
the Franks, and Constantius I could boast the capture of an Alamannic *rex*.[181]
Early in his reign, Constantine made much of his capture of the *reges* Ascar-
ius and Merogaisus,[182] and his son Constantius II was extremely proud of his
role in manipulating the Sarmatian kingship.[183] Julian achieved a double coup
by capturing the Alamannic *rex* Chnodomarius in battle and later taking Vadomarius alive at a banquet arranged for the purpose.[184] Ammianus argues that
Valentinian's own obsession with the capture of Macrianus was prompted by
his desire to emulate Julian's achievement. Valens probably harbored similar
designs against Athanaric, and these were no doubt involved in his ongoing
pursuit of the leader for three long years of less than stellar campaigning.[185]

Ultimately, these policies were natural reactions to the border tensions that
had been mounting since the late second century.[186] Yet we need not pre-
sume, as did most Romans, that they were always effective or even necessary
responses to strategically threatening events. On the contrary, the aggressive
frontier policies of fourth-century rulers were sometimes deliberately an-
tagonistic and often—as with Valentinian's fortification policy—escalated the
tensions they were supposed to extinguish. Where more evidence exists for
the dynamics of sustained military operations against tribal peoples, it indicates that the effects are the creation or strengthening of powerful tribal confederations and the increase in the capacity and desire for war among the

179. AM 29.4.2–7; cf. 30.7.11. Symm. *Or.* 2.1 praises Valentinian's control of foreign kings.
180. AM 27.10.3–4; cf. 30.7.7.
181. *Pan. Lat.* 10 [2].10.3–5, with Nixon and Rodgers 1994, 68 n. 35; 8 [5].2.1. Klose 1934,
143–45, indicates that this concern with the manipulation of barbarian kings was not as common in the early empire; Todd 1992, 86–87, argues the opposite; cf. Elton 1996b, 38, 192.
182. *Pan. Lat.* 4 [10].16.5–6, 6 [7].10.2, 11.5–6, esp., "compendium est devincendorum
hostium duces sustulisse"; cf. 6 [7].4.27, 7 [6].12.1, with Nixon and Rodgers 1994, 233–35.
183. AM 17.12.20, 13.30; Aur. Vict. *Caes.* 42.21, with Nixon 1991, 122–23.
184. On Chnodomarius, see *Ep. ad Ath.* 279c–d; AM 16.12.60–61; *Epit.* 42.14; Eutr. 10.14.
On Vadomarius, see AM 21.4.1–6; Zos. 3.4.2, 7.6; Aur. Vict. *Caes.* 42.17; cf. Nixon 1991, 120–21.
Late Roman historians regularly emphasize the importance of domination over foreign kings
as an achievement of leadership; see Aur. Vict. *Caes.* 2.3–4, 39.35, 42.21–22; SHA *Hadr.* 12.7;
Ant. Pius 9.6–8; *Aurel.* 22.2, 33.3; *Epit.* 2.8, 9.13, 14.10, 42.14.
185. The capture or imposition of barbarian kings was certainly emphasized by Valens's
epitomators; see Festus 14, 16, 18, 20, 24, 25; Eutr. 3.13, 23; 4.1, 2, 3, 8, 14, 22, 27, 6.16, 8.3,
9.27, 14.
186. Indeed, barbarian society was every bit as aggressive as Roman society, although far
less organized. See Elton 1996b, 45–57. On the role of aggression and terror in the strategy of
the principate, see Mattern 1999, 109–22.

tribal peoples.[187] Thus, while the initial shock value of Roman war efforts must have brought temporary relief from barbarian counterattacks, the overall impact was an escalation of the problem.

Valens's motivations for undertaking his first Gothic war were thus complex and probably involved elements that had very little to do with military necessity or strategic advantage. Both he and his brother, who had, after all, ordered the campaign in the first place, were interested in the acquisition of military glory as a way to satisfy the expectations of their subjects and to shore up their newly established claim to the throne. Both were also quite convinced that all barbarians posed an omnipresent threat that had to be regularly beaten back in open combat. Both assumed that such combat was most effective when undertaken inside barbarian territory, that barbarian cooperation could best be ensured through permanent encroachment on barbarian soil, and that barbarian leaders could be effectively controlled through capture or annihilation. Whether these assumptions were correct and these measures effective is difficult to say. That they affected the foreign policy decisions of both Valentinian and Valens is certain.

DYNASTIC SHIFTS AND ROMAN PROVOCATION

As noted, Constantine's 332 treaty apparently required the Goths to supply auxiliary forces to fight for the Romans. We have good evidence that these were indeed employed in numerous expeditions down to 365. Even so, each use of the Gothic auxiliaries may have involved negotiating individual agreements,[188] and each could thus occasion the assertion that the Romans were coercing their otherwise rebellious neighbors into redirecting their martial passions for Rome's benefit. Thus, when Constantius II drew on the Goths for reinforcements against the Persians in 348, Libanius pleaded astonishment that the emperor had been able to recruit Gothic manpower in light of earlier Gothic intransigence.[189] So, too, in the winter of 359/60, when Constantius again called up Gothic auxiliaries, Libanius claimed in a letter to the incoming governor of Euphratensis—who had recently been with Constantius on the Danube—that "the emperor leveled the impudence of the Goths by brandishing his weapons."[190]

187. Whitehead 1992; Abler 1992. For evidence of an increase in militarization among peoples along Roman borders, see Headeager 1987, 132–33, 138–39; Kazanski 1991a.

188. E.g., AM 20.8.1: in the winter of 359/60, Constantius requested Gothic auxiliaries *mercede vel gratia;* cf. 26.10.3, where Marcellus thought he could win over the Gothic auxiliaries sent to Procopius *parva mercede.* See Heather 1991, 110.

189. Lib. *Or.* 59.89–93.

190. Lib. *Ep.* 125 (359/60): οὗ (the Danube) βασιλεὺς τὰ ὅπλα δείξας ἐστόρεσε τὸ φρόνημα τῶν Σκυθῶν. I take Libanius to refer to the Goths rather than the Sarmatians, contra Seeck, *Briefe,* 244.

Much has been made of the first incident by those who wish to see in Libanius's reference an allusion to a Gothic upheaval in 347. After all, Libanius does mention "earlier raids" (προτέρας καταδρομάς) by the Goths, and this could be taken as a reference to recent troubles.[191] Ultimately, however, Libanius's language is quite vague and hardly seems applicable to a specific incident in a specific year. Indeed, Libanius states openly in the same passage that Constantius's skill in negotiation compelled the Goths to follow him as allies without open resistance. The implication that Constantius somehow worsted the Goths thus betrays more about triumphal rhetoric than about any real Gothic threat: the orator could only admit that an emperor turned to the Goths for military aid if he could somehow portray Gothic cooperation as a response to Roman coercion.[192] This assumption is confirmed by the second incident Libanius mentions, that of 359/60, which has not been mentioned in previous scholarship. Ammianus, who informs us that Constantius drew on the Goths at precisely this time, says nothing of the need to quell a Gothic upheaval.[193] Libanius's reference here, like that in 348, is rather a rhetorical flourish. Once this is understood, we must admit that there is almost no evidence of Gothic resistance to Constantine's 332 treaty before the 360s.

On the contrary, we have numerous indications that the Goths were remarkably consistent in their compliance with Roman requests for auxiliaries after 332. Because all sources are sparse before the beginning of Ammianus's narrative in 353, the only confirmation that Gothic troops were used prior to this year is Libanius's speech of late 348. This makes clear that the Goths sent a force to fight on the Persian frontier in this year.[194] With the beginning of Ammianus, however, we learn of several more Gothic auxiliary forces under Roman command. In 358, Constantius used a force of Taifali, a people of Wallachia allied to the Goths, in his attacks against the Quado-Sarmatian Amicenses and Picenses.[195] Again in the winter of 359/60, as noted, Constantius called up *auxilia Scytharum* as he prepared to move east to confront Sha-

191. Thompson 1956, 379–81; 1966, 13–24; Wolfram 1975, 7–8; 1988, 63; Wheeler 1998, 91; cf. Heather 1991, 115; Heather and Matthews 1991, 19.

192. *Or.* 59.90. The passage also claims that this was the first time that Gothic allies had joined the Romans against the Persians (§ 91). We know, however, at least that the Goths fought with Galerius in 298 (Jord. *Get.* 110) and can assume that they probably joined Roman armies between 332 and 348, when Persian conflicts were rife. We must thus accept that, throughout the passage, Libanius is exaggerating this specific incident to magnify its significance; cf. Brockmeier 1987, 98–99; Lippold 1992b, 389.

193. AM 20.8.1.

194. Lib. *Or.* 59.92: στρατόπεδον Σκυθικὸν τῇ μὲν ʿΡωμαίων χειρὶ συμβαλούμενον; 93: ἀντὶ δὲ πολεμίων συμμάχους. Diaconu et al. 1977, 208, 220, have found possible evidence for the inhumation of Gothic auxiliaries at Pietroasa.

195. AM 17.13.19–20. Gothic links with the Taifali have been built around *Pan. Lat.* 11 [3].17.1 (a. 291); cf. Wolfram 1988, 57–58.

pur.[196] When Julian assumed sole rule and marched east to conquer Persia in 363, he, too, brought Gothic auxiliaries, as both Zosimus and Ammianus attest.[197] Far from chaffing under the terms of their treaty, then, the Goths seem willingly to have complied with it.

Strangely enough, only a few lines before reporting that Julian brought Gothic auxiliaries into Persia, Ammianus says that the emperor turned down the barbarian embassies that offered him reinforcements. Libanius seconds this with specific reference to the Goths: "our emperor did not think it proper to call upon the Goths for assistance."[198] The discrepancy is disturbing, but might be resolved if we assume that the Goths who accompanied Julian in 363 were already considered part of the eastern army when Julian turned down barbarian offers of aid. Constantius's final mobilization of the Goths had come in 361, when he solicited auxiliaries to help him confront the rebel Julian on his eastward march.[199] Once Constantius had died, the Goths sent an embassy to Julian "quibbling over their sworn obligations."[200] Peter Heather has taken this sentence as evidence of a more general and ongoing Gothic discomfort with the 332 treaty. More likely, however, the reference is quite specific to the incident just mentioned: the Goths had been caught in a double bind, wherein compliance with the treaty in support of one rival led to condemnation by another.[201] The same situation arose in the 320s when Gothic support for Licinius eventually brought on attacks by his rival Constantine.[202] Although they could argue in 361 that they had fulfilled their sworn obligations, Julian took their support of Constantius as an act of war. As such, he may have felt justified in retaining the *auxilia* they sent as captured enemies in his forces, precisely as Valens would do after the death of Procopius. This would explain the contradiction between Julian's stated re-

---

196. AM 20.8.1.

197. AM 23.2.7: "cum exercitu et Scytharum auxiliis"; Zos. 3.25.6, with Paschoud 2.1: 178 n. 71. Shahid 1984a, 116 n. 38, suggests that the "Khazars" mentioned by Tabari 840 (p. 59 Bosworth) as being among Julian's auxiliaries were in fact these Goths.

198. AM 23.2.1–2; Lib. *Or.* 18.169.

199. Lib. *Or.* 12.62: παρεκαλεῖτο δὲ τὸ Κελτικόν, ἐκινεῖτο δὲ τὸ Σκυθικόν. As the passage reveals, Constantius also demanded that the German tribes along the Rhine join the resistance against Julian; cf. Julian. *Ep. ad Ath.* 286a–c, 287c; AM 21.3.4–5, 4.6; Lib. *Or.* 13.35, 18.107; *Pan. Lat.* 3 [11].6.1; cf. Nixon and Rodgers 1994, 401–2 n. 38.

200. Lib. *Or.* 12.78: ἐν τοῖς ὅρκοις ἀκριβολογουμένους.

201. Heather 1991, 115–17. Heather's reading results in part from an overinterpretation of Libanius's Greek. "[A] Gothic embassy came to Julian asking for alterations to the terms of their treaty," he contends (ibid., 116; cf. Heather and Matthews 1991, 20–21), but this is not what Libanius says: the Goths were not asking for changes in their treaty more generally but arguing that they had only done what they were bound by oath to do. Norman 1969–77, 1: 74 n. b, recognizes in *Or.* 12.78 the reference back to *Or.* 12.62, which Heather overlooks.

202. See p. 121. Elton 1996b, 228–29, and Shaw 1999, 150, show that emperors and usurpers regularly called up barbarian auxiliaries in civil wars.

fusal to draft Goths and his obvious use of them in Persia. The Goths had upheld their treaty obligations, but they had been stung for it.

As noted, Julian did not take the Gothic aid sent to Constantius lightly.[203] Before he departed from Constantinople for the Persian frontier, his troops called on him to attack the Goths as enemies both near to hand and "often deceptive and treacherous." Julian declined, saying that he sought better foes and was willing to leave the Goths to Galatian slave traders.[204] Even so, he dismissed the Gothic ambassadors with threats of a coming assault, and Libanius later confirms that he anticipated a Gothic campaign at some point in the future.[205] The fact that he did not feel obliged to undertake such a maneuver while still in Thrace, however, indicates that he felt the Goths posed no real threat in 362. Thus, when Eunapius writes that in a letter Julian predicted a major Gothic uprising—surely a reference to Adrianople—this no doubt represents Eunapius's own *prophetia ex eventu*.[206] Had Julian felt the Goths constituted an immediate problem, he would have dealt with them before heading east.

After Julian's death, when the Goths encountered the new and highly confrontational Valentinianic dynasty, Romano-Gothic relations continued to deteriorate. Valentinian was, as we have seen, not inclined to favor non-Roman peoples, and his *magister officiorum* Ursacius, with whom the Goths would have dealt in 364, was apparently cut from the same cloth. Within months of his arrival in the west, Ursacius provoked the Alamanni to invade Gaul by insulting their ambassadors and sending them away with drastically reduced tribute.[207] For his part, Valentinian prided himself on his intransigence toward barbarian requests for such payments. Symmachus raved that his emperor was at once iron-fisted and tight-fisted:

> Kingdoms bow down to you rather than being bought off, and the fates of your cities are not weighed out for sale. Thus you enter all regions as if you were returning to your own. We are not driven out by the force of iron nor cheated for the price of gold or bronze. The same fear checks the enemy's greed and restrains their impudence; once their trust in confrontation is removed, there is no room left for them to bargain.[208]

---

203. He certainly used Constantius's missives requesting barbarian aid for their propaganda value, Lib. *Or.* 18.113; Julian. *Ep. ad Ath.* 286a–c.

204. AM 22.7.8. On Galatian slave traders, cf. Aug. *Ep.* 10*.7.2.

205. Lib. *Or.* 12.78, 17.30.

206. Eunap. *Hist.* fr. 27.1 (Blockley); cf. Wolfram 1988, 64.

207. AM 26.5.7; cf. 27.1.1. Valentinian arrived at Milan in October 364 (Seeck, *Regesten*, 218). AM 27.1.1 implies that the Alamanni had already revolted by Jan. 1, 365; cf. Tomlin 1973, 149–51. On the *MOff.* as the primary liaison with foreign ambassadors, see Lee 1993, 40–48.

208. *Or.* 2.17 (a. 370).

This same attitude was apparently also ingrained in Valens. We must never forget that he, too, insisted that tribute to the Goths be cut off entirely after 369.

Despite the fact that tribute was a highly cost-effective and indeed sociologically sound means of maintaining peace with barbarians,[209] it did not square with the mentality of fourth-century military rulers. These boasted when they avoided paying and only ever paid in silent discomfort. Their blanket abnegation of such subventions as a legitimate policy tool makes the fourth-century rhetoric on the subject extremely difficult to evaluate, but it is quite clear that in times of strength, the imperial leadership preferred not to buy peace.[210] If Valentinian and Ursacius applied this policy in their first encounters with the Goths in 364—as they would with the Alamanni in 365—they would have compromised an already delicate relationship.

The trouble provoked by such intransigence and by the affront already offered under Julian in 362 would have gone a long way toward inciting the rumblings among the Goths that commenced in 365. We have already seen that in the summer of that year, Valens's learned that the Goths were conspiring to attack Thrace. Given that the emperor sent only a limited force of comitatensian units to respond to this threat, he cannot have expected a major incursion, but the notice gives certain proof that the Goths were agitated.[211] It is thus little wonder that they chose to support Procopius in his bid to unseat Valens when the chance arose. Even here, however, this was not necessarily an aggressive move. In his letter to the Goths, Procopius emphasized the same claim to the Constantinian legacy that had proved so effective in mustering support in years past. Constantine, it must be remembered, had established firm ties with the Goths in 332. By dint of his relationship to the Constantinian house, Procopius had a legitimate right to Gothic troops under Constantine's treaty.[212] Convinced by this rhetoric and still piqued by the harsh new order, the Goths sent 3,000 men.

Here again, Peter Heather has questioned the motivations behind this support of Procopius. He argues that in fact the Goths' action betrays their

209. Iluk 1985; cf. Headeager 1987, 129–31; Elton 1996b, 189–90. Jordanes predicates much of his narrative around Roman refusals to pay tribute as a cause for Gothic disputes (*Get.* 76, 89, 146, 270–72). Although many of his instances are certainly bogus, they give some idea about the importance of tribute as a diplomatic tool. An excellent example of the way Germans used gift exchange to lubricate social relations is found at Cass. *Var.* 5.1. On the sociological importance of gift-exchange more broadly, see Mauss 1921; 1990.

210. Julian, for example, made a show of resisting tribute payments; see *Ep. ad Ath.* 280a–b (Franks); AM 24.3.4, 25.6.10 (Saracens). Cf. Klose 1934, 138–39; Gordon 1949.

211. AM 26.6.11–12, 7.5, 9.

212. AM 26.10.3: "Constantianam praetendenti necessitudinem"; 27.5.1; Eunap. *Hist.* fr. 37 (Blockley); Zos. 4.7.1, 10.1–2.

ongoing desire to improve the terms of the 332 treaty, in particular their obligation to send *auxilia*.[213] Not only is this nowhere stated in the sources, but it speaks against the abundant evidence we have just seen for Gothic cooperation with the 332 treaty on precisely the question of *auxilia*. In light of this cooperation, it is safer to accept the account offered in both Eunapius/ Zosimus and Ammianus: the Goths could justly argue that they were doing their duty, but they simply chose the wrong side.[214] This was not naïveté; it was simply a bad bet. Likewise, as both source traditions confirm, Valens's stated rationale for undertaking the war was not to battle down a people who presently posed a major threat to the empire but rather to avenge this Gothic affront to his imperial majesty.[215]

Here we must remember that communication between Goths and Romans in the period was extremely difficult, making whatever the Goths decided a gamble.[216] We have already seen that Procopius was a masterful manipulator of information. There is every reason to think that he could have convinced Athanaric that his claims to the throne were both well founded and easily vindicated.[217] Moreover, while Heather may be right that the Goths' readiness to help Procopius was partly rooted in a desire to improve their situation vis-à-vis the empire, their dissatisfaction did not apparently stretch back before 362. It was above all the intransigent new house of Valentinian that Athanaric and his Tervingi resented, not the 332 treaty. The fact that he and his Goths responded to the crisis of 365–66 by once again upholding their treaty obligation rather than carrying through with their planned attack on Thrace confirms this. Once Procopius's bid for power collapsed, this decision naturally seemed unwise. The Goths had wagered on the house of Constantine and lost.

213. Heather 1991, 116, 119–21.

214. See esp. Eunap. *Hist.* fr. 37 (Blockley): ὁ μὲν γὰρ ἔφασκε βασιλεῖ δεδωκέναι κατὰ συμμαχίαν καὶ ὅρκους, language remarkably similar to that used at Lib. *Or.* 12.78 (n. 200) to excuse the same affront to Julian in 362.

215. AM 27.4.1: "ratione iusta permotus, quod auxilia misere Procopio civilia bella coeptanti"; cf. AM 31.3.4; Zos. 4.10.2; Eunap. *Hist.* fr. 37 (Blockley). Them. *Or.* 11.146a–b also implies that Athanaric was at fault.

216. AM 31.4.3 says that Romans rarely learned of wars within barbarian territory until they were over; *CTh* 12.12.5 (a. 364) proves that Valens was himself aware of the deceptions and falsifications that trans-border communication involved. On communication problems across the northern frontier, see Millar 1982, 15–20; Lee 1993, 128–39.

217. See pp. 97–101, esp. AM 26.7.5.

Chapter 4

Valens and the Eastern Frontier

ROMANO-PERSIAN RELATIONS, A.D. 298–363

Valens faced an eastern frontier that offered a confusing tangle of problems. Unlike the lower Danube, where Gothic hegemony confronted him with a single, albeit very dangerous, enemy, the eastern limits of the empire were home to a frustratingly complicated web of interrelated peoples, whose threats and demands had to be balanced one against the next. At no point in his reign was Valens free to let down his guard in the east, for as soon as problems with one group ceased, those with another arose. By investigating all of the conflicts that Valens faced in Persia, Armenia, Iberia, Syria, Isauria and Arabia, we shall see how the eastern emperor struggled to keep pace with unceasing demands on his military and financial resources. Before we begin the investigation, however, it is necessary to look briefly at the social and historical background of the peoples and lands on whom Valens concentrated so many of his resources.

Older textbooks would term much of the terrain with which this chapter deals "the fertile crescent" (see map 5).[1] That is to say, much of Valens's activity on the eastern frontier was concentrated around the territory that stretches in a broad arc from Palestine in the west up through Syria and northern Mesopotamia south of the Taurus Mountains and down again along the base of the Zagros Mountains in the east. The concave side of this "crescent" was roughly outlined by the 200 mm p.a. isohyet, which provided enough precipitation for the dry farming of cereal crops. Beyond this, to the east and south of the isohyet from a Roman perspective, lay desert. Rome had controlled the western end of this crescent since the first century B.C., while

---

1. For the topography and historical geography of the region, see Oates 1968, 1–18; Frye 1984, 1–20; Kennedy and Riley 1990, 24–46.

Persia remained master of the east throughout the Roman period. At the top of the crescent, in northern Mesopotamia, the territories of the two empires met along the natural avenue of communication between west and east. This bottleneck of cultivable territory at the edge of both empires became a bone of bloody contention from Rome's first arrival in the region until its departure in the wake of the Arab conquests. In this struggle for control of northern Mesopotamia, Rome had since the end of the third century enjoyed the upper hand. When Valens was born in the 330s, it controlled all of northern Mesopotamia up to the Greater Zab. In the year before Valens came to power, however, much of this territory had been ceded, and with it Rome's position of dominance on its eastern frontier.

Among the major subjects of conflict between Rome and Persia were the territories of Armenia and Iberia, in the rugged sub-Caucasus, just north of the Fertile Crescent. Valens's own efforts to maintain hegemony over these kingdoms continued a drama that had been unfolding since the first century B.C.[2] Pompey had first asserted Rome's right to crown the Armenian and Iberian kings in 66 B.C., and Rome continued to claim suzerainty in these regions into the fourth century. Even so, its claims had not gone uninterrupted, for they had always been disputed, first by the Parthians and then by the Sassanians, and these had been successful at various periods in imposing their own sovereigns over the kingdoms of the sub-Caucasus. Fuel was added to the fires of discord by the fact that both Armenia and Iberia were inhabited by staunchly independent peoples whose loyalty either side could maintain only with great effort.

Armenia had been ruled since the first century A.D.—with some interruptions—by a monarchical dynasty of Parthian descent called the Arsacids. Arsacid domination was, however, hardly monolithic. Rather, the Armenian throne was locked in a constant struggle to impose its sovereignty on a series of over one hundred powerful territorial princes with origins predating the imposition of central rule. These princes, designated *nakharars* in Armenian, claimed autonomy in their own regions, which they ruled as the hereditary heads of nobiliar households.[3] Because they regarded themselves as virtual equals to the Arsacid kings, their loyalty to the throne was always contingent and always depended heavily on the furtherance of their own interests. Thus, in exchange for cooperation, the Arsacids ceded to the most powerful *nakharars* control of a wide array of political and military fiefs: the Mamikonean family, for example, dominated the position of commander in

2. On Romano-Armenian relations in the first three centuries, see Chaumont 1969; 1976; Redgate 1998, 65–113. On Romano-Iberian relations, see Braund 1994.

3. On *nakharars*, see Toumanoff 1963, 112–41, 192–252; Adontz 1970, passim, esp. 183–371; cf. Hewsen 1996; Redgate 1998, 97–102.

chief *(sparapet)*,[4] the Bagratuni the positions of royal coronant and commander of the cavalry *(t'agakap* and *aspet)*, and the Arkruni that of grand chamberlain *(mardpet)*. Even despite these concessions, indeed, partly because of them, the *nakharars* guarded their independence fiercely and often broke into open rebellion against their Arsacid rulers.[5] The Arsacids were thus under constant compulsion to renegotiate—through force and diplomacy—dominion over their feudal princes.

Because of the inherent weakness of their authority, the Arsacids often turned to the Roman state to help realign *nakharar* loyalties. Yet the Arsacid kings were themselves willing to grant the empire only limited influence, making their own loyalty to Rome yet another variable in the complex equation of Romano-Armenian relations. Arsacid kings refused to travel in Roman territory without military escorts and reserved the right to decide whether or not to support Roman military endeavors.[6] Politically, Arsacid cooperation was contingent upon enticements and sometimes even threats: the retention of royal hostages, the concession of privileges, the payment of tribute, and even the diplomatic exchange of women. In 358, for example, Constantius II offered Olympias, the daughter of a former praetorian prefect, to Arshak II of Armenia in marriage; two years later, still hoping to retain Arshak's friendship, Constantius summoned the king to Edessa to offer him generous gifts and an exemption from tribute in exchange for a promise of loyalty during Constantius's planned expedition in Mesopotamia that year.[7] Only with such cozening could the Arsacids be won over, for their loyalty was contingent and needed always to be maintained at a price.

Such precautions were essential in a world where the Persian shahanshah constantly lobbied the Armenian kings and *nakharars* with threats and enticements of his own.[8] The Persians regarded Armenia as part of their ancestral territories; indeed, they considered the Armenian throne, which was after all held by a Median dynasty, second in importance only to that of Iran.[9]

4. On the *Sparaptetut'iwn*, see Bedrosian 1983.

5. E.g., *BP* 3.8–9, 4.23, 5.8–19; MX 3.4–6.

6. Tac. *Ann.* 2.56: "Ambigua gens ea antiquitus hominum ingeniis et situ terrarum . . . maximisque imperiis interiecti et saepius discordes sunt, adversus Romanos odio et in Parthum invidia." For escorts, see AM 20.11.3, 27.12.9, 30.1.5; Proc. *Bella* 1.5.16. On military support, see AM 23.2.2; Zos. 2.51.4; Lib. *Or.* 18.215; Soz. 6.1.2–3.

7. On gifts and exemption from tribute, see AM 20.11.1–2; *CTh* 11.1.1; Proc. *Bella* 2.3.35. On marriage, see AM 20.11.3; *BP* 4.15; MX 3.21; *Vita Nerses* 8 p. 29; cf. Garsoïan 1969; 1989, 285–86 n. 40. Similar enticements were offered to both the Armenian and Iberian kings in 361, AM 21.6.8. On hostages, see *BP* 4.5, 11, 15, 55. For more on the client king's position and role at the frontier, see Braund 1984, 91–107.

8. AM 20.11.2, 27.12.3, 14, 16, 30.2.1; *BP* 4.16, 19, 21, 5.37–38; Proc. *Bella* 1.5.14–16.

9. Garsoïan 1976, 6–8 esp. n. 17 and ead. 1980.

This comes as no surprise, given that, in terms of culture, politics, and so-cial structures, Armenia had much more in common with Persia than with Rome.[10] It is, therefore, also natural that Armenia often shifted its allegiance to its southern neighbor. In the thirty years prior to Valens's reign, Armen-ian kings are known to have allied themselves with the Sassanians temporarily in 312, 337, and again in the late 350s.[11] And rebellious *nakharars* shifted their allegiance to Persia with equal regularity. Armenia was thus constantly in flux from the Roman perspective—indeed, from the Sassanian as well. Its allegiance could never be taken for granted.

Even despite these interruptions, it is fair to say that Rome largely suc-ceeded in commanding Armenian loyalty against the Sassanians through the first two-thirds of the fourth century. As we shall see, much of this stemmed from a reassertion of Roman military supremacy in the region in the last years of the third century. Rome's success in retaining Armenian loyalty also stemmed at least in part from its greater willingness to grant the Arsacids a freer rein than the Sassanians had allowed when they controlled Armenia in the second half of the third century. Precisely because Armenia was so close to Iranian society culturally and to the Iranian heartland geographi-cally, the Sassanians always expected greater power inside Armenia when they gained the upper hand there. For this reason, Armenia and its kings knew well that they needed to maintain political distance from Iran by cultivating their alliance with Rome. After the conversion of Rome's empire to Chris-tianity, this meant the conversion of the Armenian monarchy as well. In 314, the Armenian king Trdat (probably IV) the Great (ca. 298–ca. 330) con-verted from Armenian Zoroastrianism to Christianity and began the slow and painful process of converting his kingdom.[12] This he did in alliance with Ar-menia's first patriarch, Grigor Lusaworic' (Gregory the Illuminator), who had been raised as an exile in Cappadocian Caesarea and baptized a Christian. As with all offices in Armenia, that of patriarch promptly became hereditary, and their hold on religious authority, and the wealth and territory that went with it, gave Grigor's family, the Gregorids, a great deal of influence. It also brought them into frequent conflict with the throne and the *nakharars* over both social and political issues.[13] Christianity thus introduced yet another

10. Asdourian 1911, 86–87; Garsoïan 1976; Redgate 1998, 81–83, 104–12.

11. For 312, see Malalas 12.46–47; cf. Eus. *HE* 9.8.2–4. For 337, see Jul. *Or.* 1.18d–19a, 20a–21a; cf. *BP* 4.20. For the 350s, see *BP* 4.11, 16, 20; MX 3.25; Vita Nerses 8 p. 31; cf. Gar-soïan 1969. None of these sources is undisputed. For recent bibliography, see Garsoïan 1989, 290 n. 8; Dodgeon and Lieu 1991, 380 n. 22, 383 n. 2.

12. On Trdat's conversion, see Kettenhofen 1995, 92–104, 163; cf. Redgate 1998, 113–19. On Armenian Zoroastrianism, see Russell 1987, 173–211. Early Armenian Christianity retained many Zoroastrian elements, and fourth-century *nakharars* often apostasized; cf. Russell 1987, 126–30.

13. Redgate 1998, 119–38.

complication into the formula of Romano-Armenian relations. In all, however, Rome managed to take advantage of this religious common ground to strengthen its grip on this proud kingdom.[14]

Iberia sat directly north of Armenia and was thus frequently at loggerheads with its neighbor over the border territory between the two kingdoms along the river Cyrus (Kur). Iberia was perhaps closer to Rome culturally than Armenia, although there was also much about it that was Persian.[15] Even so, Iberia differed from Armenia in that its monarchs succeeded in establishing firmer control over the nobles within their more circumscribed domains.[16] As in Armenia, the Persians vied with Rome for authority over the Iberian throne, and in the late third century, they successfully asserted their claim by crowning a Persian dynast named Mirian III.[17] Mirian, founder of the Mihranid dynasty, which ruled Iberia into the sixth century, maintained a tight hold on his kingdom down to his death in 361. Nevertheless, although he had been a Persian appointee, after 299, Rome established suzerainty over his kingdom, which would last through Valens's reign.[18] It was during this period of Roman control that Mirian also converted himself and his kingdom to Christianity. Indeed, the strongest cultural bond cementing Romano-Iberian relations in the fourth century was, as with Armenia, Christianity.[19]

Thus Iberia and especially Armenia were not faithfully obedient subjects but powerfully independent friends. They were not fixed points in the geometry of Rome's eastern frontier but variables in the calculus of Roman foreign policy. As we shall see, this complicated Valens's relations with both kingdoms, and particularly Armenia, even in periods when Persia had backed away from conflict.

While Iberia and Armenia posed problems for Rome, Persia posed a definite threat. Much of the tension between Persia and Rome in Valens's day stemmed from disputes over the control of northern Mesopotamia. In two wars between 195 and 199, Septimius Severus had extended Roman authority deep into the Parthian-controlled territories of northern Mesopotamia, which he formed into the Roman provinces of Osrhoene and Mesopotamia.[20] Within two decades of Severus's death, however, the Parthians had succumbed to a new south Persian dynasty, the Sassanians, and these quickly set about retaking Severus's gains. Unlike the Parthians, the Sassani-

---

14. Garsoïan 1967 and ead. 1969.

15. Braund 1994, 253–59.

16. Toumanoff 1963, 84–103, 141–44.

17. *RGDS* ll. 2–3; Braund 1994, 239, 245.

18. Petrus Patricius fr. 14 (*FHG* 4.189). For the survival of Roman suzerainty through 361, see AM 21.6.7–8, and see n. 65 for the period of Valens's reign.

19. Thelamon 1981, 85–91; Braund 1994, 239, 246–61.

20. Oates 1968, 73–92; Birley 1972, 115–7, 129–35; Millar 1993, 121–41.

ans succeeded in breaking the power of Persia's own formidable landed aristocracy to form a centralized and highly organized political machine.[21] Much of the newfound vigor they injected into the Persian state was channeled into conquest, particularly the recapture of northern Mesopotamia. Major victories over the Romans enabled Shapur I (r. 240–72), the second Sassanian dynast, to reconquer most of northern Mesopotamia and, after 244, to regain suzerainty over the kingdoms of Armenia and Iberia.[22]

Third-century Rome faltered in the face of this formidable enemy and only began to regain its balance in the 270s. This process culminated in 298, when Diocletian's Caesar, Galerius, crushed the forces of the shahanshah Narses (r. 293–303) and captured his royal harem.[23] Narses was forced to settle an agreement in 299 under which he turned over control of the remaining territories that Shapur had wrested from Rome.[24] Thus the treaty of 299 reextended Rome's territorial claims on its eastern frontier up to the Tigris, reasserted Roman suzerainty over Armenia and Iberia,[25] and limited commercial exchange between Rome and Persia to the city of Nisibis (Nusaybin).[26] New to the 299 agreement was the provision that Rome would also gain direct suzerainty over five Armenian satrapies that lay north and east of the Tigris—Ingilene, Sophene, Arzanene, Corduene, and Zabdicene (see map 4).[27]

These south Armenian principalities, separated from the Armenian midlands by the Taurus,[28] had always enjoyed even greater independence vis-à-vis the Armenian throne than the *nakharar* territories to their north. They were inhabited by a multi-ethnic agglomeration of Syrian and Armenian peoples and were ruled by hereditary satraps, who had frequently claimed total

21. For the growing consensus on the early development of strong centralized state structures, see Adams 1981, 200–214, 246–47; Gnoli 1989, 129–74; Gyselen 1989; Lee 1993, 15–20. The classic study on Sassanian Persia remains Christensen 1944, to which Frye 1984, 287–339, adds useful new material. On Romano-Sassanian relations, see now Dodgeon and Lieu 1991 and Blockley 1992.

22. On Shapur's campaigns, see Kettenhofen 1982; Millar 1993, 159–73. Sources at Lieu and Dodgeon 1991, 49–67. On Armenia, see n. 85. On Iberia, see Braund 1994, 240–44.

23. Winter 1988, 130–45; Millar 1993, 177–79. Sources at Dodgeon and Lieu 1991, 125–31.

24. The treaty terms are reported at Petrus Patricius fr. 14 (*FHG* 4.189). On the date, see Barnes 1976a, 182–86. For the extensive bibliography on the treaty, see Winter 1988, 152–215, and id. 1989, to which add Blockley 1992, 5–7.

25. Rome had already restored an Armenian king, whose son, Trdat III (r. 287–98), regained much of Armenia from the Sassanians; see Agathangelos 1.46–47; MX 2.82, with Redgate 1998, 94–95; cf. Chaumont 1969, 93–111.

26. Lieu 1986, 491–95; Rugullis 1992, 105–15; and Lee 1993, 62–64 argue that this last measure may have been designed to limit cross-border espionage.

27. For the locations and history of these territories, see Dillemann 1962, 110–12, 116–26; Winter 1989, 563 nn. 4–7; Dodgeon and Lieu 1991, 377 n. 48, and above all *ASX* v.22.ii–iii, v–vi, with Hewsen 1992, 153–62, 168–76.

28. AM 18.9.2.

independence from the Arsacids in preceding centuries.[29] Indeed, the Arsacids had granted two of the satraps in question—those of Arzanene and Corduene—the further distinction of recognition as viceroys (Latin *vitaxa;* Armenian *bdeashkh*) of the Arabian and Syrian marches.[30] These two marches controlled access over the Taurus into the Armenian heartland and as such constituted the most strategically important territories in the region. By claiming direct suzerainty over these and the three remaining trans-Tigritane satrapies in 299, Rome gained a footing beyond the Tigris in what were now a whole series of tiny client kingdoms.[31] Indeed, from 299 on, the satrapies were, like client kingdoms, free from taxes but expected—if not legally obliged—to supply troops for Roman armies, fortifications to protect Roman frontiers,[32] and crown gold for Roman coffers.[33] The 299 treaty was thus a major coup for Rome, not just reclaiming the Severan frontier up to the Tigris but also extending Roman control over client territories situated beyond it.

Just as Rome's gains were great, Persia's loss was devastating, so much so that the Sassanians never accepted the treaty. Not until the 330s, however, was Narses's grandson, Shapur II, in a position to reassert Persian power in the region. Between 337 and 350, Shapur agitated for control of the Armenian throne, thrice laid siege to Nisibis, defeated a massive Roman army near Singara and captured that stronghold. In the seven years that followed, tensions subsided, because both Shapur and Constantius II were occupied with wars elsewhere in their empires, but in 357, Shapur was again demanding the return of the territories lost by Narses. Having failed to achieve his aim through diplomacy, the shahanshah once again undertook strikes into upper Mesopotamia in 359–60, during which he destroyed the Roman

29. Roman and Greek sources refer to these territories as *gentes* or ἔθνη, and to their leaders as *satrapae;* cf. Festus 14; Eutr. 8.3; Zos. 3.31.1; AM 18.9.2; *CTh* 12.13.6; *CJ* 1.29.5; *Nov. Just.* 31; Proc. *Aed.* 3.1.17. On the status of these satrapies, see Güterbock 1900; Toumanoff 1963, 131–37, 170–75; Adontz 1970, 25–37; cf. Matthews 1989, 51–57.

30. There were a total of four of these viceroys, who controlled the Arabian, Syrian, Median, and Iberian marches (Asorestan, Aruastan, Nor Sirakan and Moskhia). R.H. Hewsen (1988–89; 1990–91) overturns the widely held theory, first introduced by Markwart 1901, 165–79, that Petrus Patricius's groupings of "Ingilene along with Sophene" and "Arzanene with the Corduenes and Zabdicene" (fr. 14 = *FHG* 4.189) correspond to the Syrian and Arabian Marches.

31. AM 21.6.7 speaks of "Transtigritani reges et satrapae"; cf. Proc. *Aed.* 3.1.18–23. See Güterbock 1900, 34–39, and Toumanoff 1963, 133–35, 154–92 (but cf. also 170–71, 176), on the legal and political status of the satraps of these regions, who continued to cooperate with the Arsacids even while under Roman dominion between 298 and 363.

32. On troops, see Güterbock 1900, 36–37. *Pace* Dillemann 1962, 218–20, Rome still claimed fifteen fortresses beyond the Tigris in 363 (cf. AM 25.7.9; Zos. 3.31.1). Archeological remains of at least two—at Tilli and Hiksan—have been discovered (cf. Mitford 1986; Lightfoot 1986; Algaze 1989, 244 with figs. 12, 14, 33). These were probably garrisoned by native, not Roman forces.

33. *CTh* 12.1.6 (a. 387). See more on crown gold at p. 289.

fort of Amida, again overcame Singara—since regained by the Romans—and captured and regarrisoned Bezabde as a Persian stronghold.[34]

A full-scale Roman response to these aggressions came only in 363, when Julian invaded Persia in a lightning strike down the Euphrates.[35] He reached the capital of Ctesiphon in less than a month and laid siege to it with spectacular pomp. After his efforts failed, though, Julian's plans quickly went awry, and his army eventually found itself marching out of Persia along the Tigris under constant attack from the Sassanians. On June 26[36]—as we saw in the first chapter—the emperor fell back to help fend off an enemy raid, and was struck and killed in the melee. For the fifth time in Roman history, the empire had lost its ruler in the midst of eastern hostilities.[37] With no time for ceremony, the army quickly proclaimed Jovian emperor and continued its retreat up the Tigris.

Jovian's situation grew worse as the Persians pressed his army and supplies dwindled to desperate levels.[38] Under these circumstances, Shapur sent an embassy led by his chief commander, Suren to offer peace.[39] Jovian had little choice but to accept. He sent his praetorian prefect Sallustius and the general Arinthaeus to Shapur's camp, where they negotiated for four days before finally reaching an accord. The length of their negotiations in the midst of such trying circumstances indicates that terms were not simply dictated by Shapur but were actually debated.[40] In fact, Shapur's bargaining position

34. Sources in Dodgeon and Lieu 1991, 164–230. Analysis at Warmington 1977; Frye 1984, 308–16; Blockley 1988; 1989; 1992, 12–24; Matthews 1989, 41–66; Portmann 1989; Seager 1997, 253–62.

35. Sources on Julian's Persian campaign in Dodgeon and Lieu 1991, 231–74. Analysis at Bowersock 1978, 106–16; Matthews 1989, 130–79; Blockley 1991, 24–30; Barnes 1998, 162–65. The Sassanians were said by Libanius (*Or.* 18.305; 24.18–19) to have depicted Julian as a lightning bolt.

36. On the date, see p. 14.

37. Rome also lost Caracalla, Gordian III, Valerian, and Carus.

38. On the dearth of supplies, see AM 25.7.7, 8.1, 15; Zos. 3.30.5, 33.1; Lib. *Or.* 18.278, 280; Festus 29; Eutr. 10.17; Greg. Naz. *Or.* 5.12; Philostorg. 8.1; August. *De civ. Dei* 4.29; *Pass. Artemii* 70; Soc. 3.22.5–9; Soz. 6.3.2; Ruf. *HE* 11.1; Zon. 13.4; Joh. Chrys. *De S. Babyla* 22 (*PG* 50.569). The supply problems continued when Jovian reached Antioch; cf. Theod. *HE* 4.4.1–2. On the effects of Shapur's attacks, see Eutr. 10.17; cf. Lib. *Or.* 18.264–67.

39. The sources agree that Shapur initiated negotiations; cf. Festus 29; AM 25.7.5; Zos. 3.31.1; Lib. *Or.* 18.277; Malalas 13.27 (p. 336); *Chron. pasch.*, p. 553; Theod. *HE* 4.2.2; Ruf. *HE* 11.1; Tabari 842–3 (p. 62 Bosworth).

40. AM 25.7.7–8; cf. Malalas 13.27 (p. 336); *Chron. pasch.*, p. 553; Lib. *Or.* 18.277–79. Blockley 1984, 30, 34, 37, argues that Jovian's legates were inexperienced negotiators and that the negotiations were rushed, leaving the treaty ambiguous. Lee 1993, 40–48, however, demonstrates that professional negotiators did not exist in the ancient world: Sallustius and Arinthaeus, both experienced officers, were typical and quite appropriate diplomatic liaisons. Moreover, as Ammianus and Libanius indicate, four days was actually quite a long time, given that Jovian and Shapur were camped in close proximity, eliminating the need for lengthy

was not ironclad: his own supplies must have been limited, since both he and the Romans had destroyed Persian crops and supply depots,[41] and he had learned that a Roman reserve force of nearly 15,000 men was poised in Mesopotamia, putting his own men in ever greater danger as Jovian continued north.[42]

Because there were reasons for concessions on both sides, the treaty that emerged was a compromise: Persia came off the clear winner, but Rome did not lose all that it might have.[43] Shapur's aim in the negotiations was the same it had been since he initiated his attacks on the Roman frontier: he hoped to recover control over Mesopotamia, Armenia, and the trans-Tigritane satrapies ceded by his grandfather in 299.[44] Not surprisingly, the terms of the treaty—best preserved in Ammianus and Zosimus[45]—indicate that he achieved his aim only in part. As in 299, five satrapies were ceded, but not the same five Narses had lost. Galerius had gained Ingilene, Sophene, Arzanene, Corduene, and Zabdicene, but Shapur regained only the last three, that is, only those east of the river Nymphius.[46] Together with these, Shapur

---

embassies. The treaty was indeed ambiguous, but more because it was a compromise than because it was poorly constructed.

41. Lib. *Or.* 18.222–23, 232, 250; Tabari 843 (p. 62 Bosworth).

42. AM 25.7.2. Cf. Lib. *Or.* 18.214; AM 23.3.5, 25.8.7, 16; Zos. 3.12.5, 4.4.2; Malalas 13.21, 27; Soz. 6.1.2. For debate on the exact numbers of men involved, see Hoffmann 1969–70, 1: 304–8.

43. For the treaty as a successful compromise, see Honigmann 1935, 5; Dillemann 1962, 223–24; Wirth 1984, 364–69; Blockley 1984, 28; Isaac 1998, 442. Even so, the contemporary Themistius (*Or.* 5.66a–c [a. 364]) certainly overstates the mutual goodwill of Persians and Romans in 363, as a later oration proves (cf. *Or.* 5.65a with 9.124a). For a similarly rosy picture, see Greg. Naz. *Or.* 5.15; Theod. *HE* 4.2.2; Malalas 13.27 (p. 336); Ruf. *HE* 11.1.

44. AM 17.5.6, 25.7.9; cf. 26.4.6; Lib. *Ep.* 331; Zon. 13.9. Note the legal language Ammianus uses to describe Shapur's recapture of Armenia, AM 27.12.1: "iniectabat Armeniae manum ut eam . . . dicioni iungeret suae"; cf. 26.4.6. *Manus iniectio* was the civil law term for the personal execution of a properly adjudicated debt.

45. AM 25.7.9–14; Zos. 3.31.1–2. Various pieces of the agreement are also reported at Them. *Or.* 5.66a–c; Philostorg. 8.1; *Pass. Artemii* 70; August. *De civ. Dei* 4.29; *Chronicon miscellaneum*, p. 134; Eutr. 10.17; Festus 29; Lib. *Or.* 1.134, 18.278, 24.9; Eunap. *Hist.* fr. 29.1 (Blockley) = Suid. *I* 401; Greg. Naz. *Or.* 5.15; Joh. Chrys. *De S. Babyla* 22 (*PG* 50.569–70); Soc. 3.22.6–7; Soz. 6.3.2; Theod. *HE* 4.2.2–3; Ruf. *HE* 11.1; Oros. 7.31.1; Malalas 13.27 (p. 336); Theoph. a.m 5856; Zon. 13.14.4–6; Jer. *Chron.* s.a. 363; *Chron. pasch.*, p. 554; Tabari 843 (p. 62 Bosworth); *BP* 4.21; Agathias 4.25.7; Joh. Ant. fr. 181; Jord. *Rom.* 306; Josh. Styl. *Chron.* vii–viii. Julian's death and the 363 treaty may be represented in a rock relief at Taq-i Bustan; see Azarpay 1982. Previous bibliography on the treaty is summarized at Blockley 1984, to which add Blockley 1987 and Seager 1996.

46. Ammianus makes it clear that Shapur's rhetoric of reconquest did not jibe with reality; cf. AM 25.7.9: "Petebat autem rex obstinatius, *ut ipse aiebat,* sua dudum a Maximiano erepta, *ut docebat autem negotium,* pro redemptione nostra quinque regiones Transtigritanas." Cf. Blockley 1984, 29; Dillemann 1962, 219–20. Dillemann 1962, 217–20, rightly argues that much of what Shapur gained de iure in 363 he had already retaken de facto; cf. Winter 1988, 176–78;

also obtained Moxoene and Rehimene. The latter, it seems, had been subsumed under the larger unit of Corduene in the 299 treaty.[47] Although it has been argued that the former was similarly considered a part of the larger satrapy of Arzanene, it is just as likely that this territory had simply not been under discussion at all in the first treaty.[48] There was thus a discrepancy between the satrapies ceded in 299 and those retroceded in 363, but it did not, however, matter as much as the fact that the numbers matched: Narses had lost five trans-Tigritane satrapies in 299, and Shapur had won five back in 363.[49]

Rome also surrendered eastern Mesopotamia, together with its key fortresses of Nisibis, Singara, and Castra Maurorum.[50] Nevertheless, it retained control of western Mesopotamia and did not even surrender the inhab-

---

1989, 558–59. In the case of these satrapies, this was as much due to the shifting loy-alties of their princes as to military or political successes on Shapur's part. Thus, for example, the satrap of Corduene Jovinianus is said to have been under Persian suzerainty in 359 (AM 18.6.20), but his father must have been a Roman client, because he had sent Jovinianus as a hostage to Syria. By 363, Ammianus (25.7.8; cf. 24.8.5) indicates that Corduene had turned back to Rome, and the "Passion of Mar Sabha" (Hoffmann 1880, 23) confirms this. Corduene was thus favorable to Rome in the 330s, to Persia in 359, and to Rome again in 363. The satrapy of Sophanene was equally quick to shift allegiance in 502 (cf. Proc. *Aed.* 3.2.1–10). Under such circumstances of constant flux, it is difficult to say that either Rome or Persia had firm control; it is at least true, however, that Rome made every effort to keep alive its claims up to 363, as indicated at AM 19.9.2, 21.6.7, 22.7.10, 25.9.3, 12; cf. Festus 14, 25; Ephrem *CJ* 2.19–20, 4.15.

47. Blockley 1984, 41 n. 19; Winter 1988, 174 n. 2; 1989, 556 n. 10. On the complex divisions of the territory of Corduene (Arm., Korduk'), see Hewsen 1992, 170–76. See also ibid., 344 for, the suggestion that the elusive territory of Rehimene should be localized in the Zarva River valley.

48. Zos. 3.31.1, who explicitly names only the regions that Rome relinquished—as opposed to those which Persia gained—omits Moxoene. This may indicate that Moxoene was never claimed by Rome in 299. It was, after all, some distance north and east of the Tigris (Hewsen 1992, 168–69) and thus quite remote from Roman territory. Contrast Winter 1988, 174 n. 1; 1989, 556 with n. 9, summarizing earlier opinions, and yet another reconstruction at Hewsen 1990–91, 161–63.

49. Festus 14, writing seven years after the 363 treaty, confirms that contemporary rhetoric emphasized the exchange of "quinque gentes trans Tigridem constitutas" as central to the treaties; cf. AM 25.7.9 "quinque regiones Transtigritanas." On this point, see Adontz 1970, 36; Blockley 1984, 31–32. Hübschmann 1904, 220 n. 3; Chaumont 1969, 123, and Winter 1988, 174–76; 1989, 557, argue that nine territories were ceded in 299 and only the five retroceded. This assumes too strict a correlation between the 299 and 363 treaties and disregards the fact that the territorial units ceded in 299 subsumed smaller territories. This was true not only of Corduene (see n. 47) but of "Sophene," which technically included Greater Sophene (or Sophanene), Ingilene, Anzitene, and Lesser Sophene, all of which were later treated by Rome as independent satrapies; see *ASX* v.22.ii, with Hewsen 1992, 154–55; cf. Adontz 1970, 27–35.

50. Shapur had already made significant strides in regaining the fortresses of Upper Mesopotamia; see AM 20.7.1–16, with Dodgeon and Lieu 1991, 214 (Bezabde); AM 18.10.1–2 (Busan and Reman); AM 19.6.1–2 (Ziata); cf. AM 18.6.3–5 (Amudis).

itants of Nisibis[51] and Singara.[52] Based on the placement of Rome's eastern frontier forts in the years that followed, it seems that an effective border was established, which ran north from the Euphrates along the Chabur, then just west of the Mygdonis over the Mons Massius (Tur Abdin) to the Tigris, and finally along the Nymphius (Bohtan Su) into the Taurus Mountains.[53] By this reckoning, Rome lost only half of its claims in Mesopotamia.[54]

The treaty thus created a situation wherein both powers had an equal footing in this strategic region. Although it represented a clear gain for Persia and a devastating loss for Rome, relative to the 299 treaty, it remained a compromise: Rome and Persia each controlled half of upper Mesopotamia and half of the trans-Tigritane satrapies. As such, the treaty created a parity that neither side could easily transgress, and perhaps for this very reason, it proved extremely durable. Aside from its provision on Armenia, which was modified in the two decades following and completely rearranged in 386, the treaty, which had originally been brokered for only thirty years, determined the shape of the Romano-Persian frontier down to 502.[55]

Regarding Armenia, however, the situation was, as indicated, somewhat different. In listing the terms of the 363 agreement, Ammianus reports very specifically:

51. On the preservation of the Nisibenes, see AM 25.7.11; Ephrem *CJ* 2.26; Theoph. a.m. 5865; Zon. 13.14; Malalas 13.27 (p. 336); *Chron. pasch.*, p. 554. Most were transferred to Amida, which Valens rebuilt; see Zos. 3.34.1; *BP* 3.10; *Historia S. Ephraemi* 10 col. 26; cf. Chrysos 1976, 27 n.1. Under other circumstances, Shapur would have been happy to transfer the inhabitants of Nisibis to Persian territory, a fate that befell the inhabitants of the fifteen fortresses in the trans-Tigritane satrapies (Zos. 3.31.1; cf. Lieu 1986, 476–87, 495).

52. Singara had been captured in 360 (AM 20.6.1–8) and its inhabitants led off into slavery. Thus, Ammianus's notice (25.7.11; cf. Zon. 13.14) that Jovian was able to rescue the inhabitants of Singara from Persian captivity seems puzzling. Given this explicit testimony, it is likely that the force Julian sent to Mesopotamia in 363 had regarrisoned the city. Ephrem *CJ* 2.15 says that Julian planned to rebuild Singara (cf. AM 23.5.18), and evidence that he did so may be found in the *Notitia dignitatum*. AM 20.6.7–8 tells us that Singara was defended by the *legio* I Flavia and *legio* I Parthica in 360 when Shapur overcame the fortress and captured these. The *Not. dign. or.* 36.29 registers a *legio* I Parthica Nisibena at Constantina (Tella). Julian's Mesopotamian force may have reconstituted the *legio* I Parthica at Singara from inhabitants of Nisibis. Lightfoot 1988, 108–9, offers a different solution to this conundrum. On Singara, see Kennedy and Riley 1990, 125–31.

53. Honigmann 1935, 3–16; Sinclair 1987–89, 3: 367; Blockley 1984, 35; 1992, 27. Cf. Dillemann 1962, 223–40, with fig. 31.

54. Festus 29: "ut Nisibis et *pars Mesopotamiae* traderetur"; Jer. *Chron.* s.a. 363: "Nisibin et *magnam Mesopotamiae partem* Sapori regi tradidit"; cf. Oros. 7.31.2; Jord. *Rom.* 306; August. *De civ. Dei* 4.29; Proc. *Bella* 1.17.25.

55. On the thirty-year term, see Lib. *Or.* 24.20; AM 25.7.14; Zos. 3.31.1; Philostorg. 8.1; Cedrenus, p. 539. Them. *Or.* 5.66a–c, 69b, seems to have had some sense of the value of this compromise already in early 364. For the Romano-Persian wars of the fifth and sixth century, see Greatrex 1998.

To these conditions there was added another, which was destructive and impious, that after the completion of these agreements, Arsaces, our steadfast and useful ally, should never, if he asked for it, be given help against the Persians. This was contrived with the double purpose that a man who at the emperor's order had devastated Chiliocomum might be punished and the opportunity might be left of presently invading Armenia without opposition.[56]

Ammianus's phrasing implies that Rome surrendered only the right to defend Armenia's current king, Arshak II.[57] Later in his narrative, though, Ammianus implies that Rome was also forbidden to defend Arshak's son Pap and to impose him as Arshak's successor.[58] Other sources also point to a broader abandonment of the Armenian throne. Zosimus indicates that the treaty surrendered "most of Armenia"; the Armenian *Epic Histories* confirm that Rome allowed Persia a free hand in the "Armenian Midlands"; Libanius claims that "all of Armenia" was abandoned; and the Syriac *Chronicon miscellaneum* speaks of the surrender of "the whole of Armenia together with the regions subject to Armenia itself."[59] Ammianus's initial testimony thus seems to be contradicted by his later statements and by our remaining sources.

This ambiguity may not, however, be entirely Ammianus's fault. Indeed, it may reflect a more general ambiguity in the treaty itself and a willingness on the part of both Persia and Rome to reinterpret this vagueness to their own advantage. As Robin Seager has shown, it is difficult to reconstruct the provisions on Armenia and Iberia from what we learn about the manner in which the treaty was implemented in the years that immediately followed it. In this period, both sides were only too willing to bend the agreement to their advantage, rendering their behavior a poor gauge of the specifics agreed upon. The ability of both sides to manipulate the treaty terms must, however, reflect a certain vagueness on the question of Armenia and Iberia to begin with.[60]

Ammianus seems right to argue first that Rome was debarred from defending the Armenian king, and later that it was forbidden to crown a successor. For this reason Valens was initially very hesitant to do either, expressly because it might violate the 363 agreement.[61] Yet the treaty may only have

---

56. AM 25.7.12.

57. It has been taken thus by Chrysos 1976, 33–35; cf. Blockley 1987, 225.

58. AM 27.12.10, 29.1.3; cf. 27.12.15, 18.

59. Zos. 2.31.2: Ἀρμενίας τὸ πολὺ μέρος; Lib. *Or.* 24.9: Ἀρμενία πᾶσα; cf. 1.134; *Chronicon miscellaneum*, p. 134; *BP* 4.21: "I give you Mcbin [Nisibis] and I am withdrawing from the Armenian Midlands. If you are able to attack and subject them, I shall not support them." "Armenian Midlands" (Mijnasxarh Hayoc') refers to the central region of Greater Armenia, the core of Arsacid power (cf. Garsoïan 1989, 481). Following the German translation of M. Lauer, Blockley 1987, 224, and Chrysos 1976, 33, have mistranslated the phrase as "half of Armenia," with serious consequences for their arguments.

60. Seager 1996, clarifying Blockley 1984, 36–38; 1987; Chrysos 1976 .

61. AM 27.12.10, 29.1.3.

forbidden Roman interference without expressly sanctioning a Persian invasion. This would explain why Ammianus twice refers to Shapur's attacks on Armenia as violations of the treaty.[62] More important, though, once he was militarily able to do so, Valens did occupy Armenia and impose his own nominee there, Arshak's son Pap.[63] Indeed, by 377, Valens was protesting that his new arrangement should stand, since Rome and Persia had agreed that Armenia was to be free of external interference. As we shall see, this new specificity represented a temporary reshaping of the 363 agreement that Valens had coerced out of Persia in 371.[64]

On Iberia, the surviving sources mention nothing of what was agreed in 363. Themistius, however, states that Iberia sent an embassy to Constantinople in 365/66, apparently with crown gold for Procopius. This would seem to imply that Rome never lost its claim to suzerainty over Iberia.[65] Here, it would seem, Shapur was the first to violate the treaty by invading Iberia and replacing its king. Once again, a separate agreement had to be reached to fill the silence of the 363 treaty after Valens had reasserted Rome's claim to at least the western portion of this kingdom.[66]

The situation in Armenia and Iberia was thus ambiguous. It is certainly so to us and was apparently ambiguous to Valens and Shapur as well.[67] Both exploited this ambiguity to gain as much influence over these kingdoms as possible, even when this meant distorting or contravening specific treaty terms.[68] The maneuverings of Valens and Shapur make it difficult to reconstruct the treaty's terms with respect to Armenia and Iberia, but they gain interest from what they reveal about mutual dissatisfactions with this compromise peace.

Indeed, to contemporary Romans, far from representing an acceptable entente, the 363 treaty was regarded as a shameful disaster. It had denied Rome military superiority in upper Mesopotamia, cost it an extremely pro-

62. AM 26.4.6, 27.12.1, 11

63. AM 27.12.13, 29.1.2–3. Blockley 1987, 225, argues that the Roman advance up to Bagawan by 371 proves that the Romans were allowed to garrison Armenia up to Bagawan, obvious *petitio principii*. The Romans occupied the territory by force, not necessarily by right.

64. AM 30.2.4. On the rearrangement of treaty terms in 371, see pp. 175–76.

65. *Or.* 7.92a. It matters little whether the ambassadors were genuine or imposters; Themistius's intention is clearly to demonstrate support from the provinces and client states known to have been under Roman jurisdiction. Christensen 1944, 238, and Toumanoff 1963, 150 n. 5, 360, 460–61, argue that Shapur did gain claims to Iberia in 363. Contrast Chrysos 1976, 45–8. None noticed the reference in Themistius.

66. On Shapur's invasion, see AM 27.12.4. On Valens's restoration, see AM 27.12.16–17. Cf. Braund 1994, 260.

67. This seems to be at the heart of Shapur's statement (AM 30.2.3) that the disputes over the treaty could not be resolved in the absence of those who had actually struck it in 363.

68. On the exploitation of ambiguities, see Köhler 1925, 76–77; Blockley 1984, 36; 1987; 1992, 34–36.

ductive chunk of land,[69] and belied Rome's core political ideology of limitless power. Particularly significant was the loss of Nisibis, the "strongest bulwark of the east," which had stood up to no fewer than three major Persian sieges in the thirty years preceding the treaty.[70] When Jovian arrived there in 363 to surrender the city, his shame was patent: he refused to go within the walls personally, preferring to order the evacuation from a camp he established outside.[71] The citizens, who protested that they would gladly defend their city alone, were threatened with death if they did not depart within three days.[72] Ammianus and the deacon Ephrem—a citizen of Nisibis himself—both vividly recalled watching Shapur's legate Bineses flying the Persian flag from the citadel, "so that this standard bearer would declare to the onlookers that the city was slave to the lords of that standard."[73] Shapur would soon transfer 12,000 Persians to Rome's *urbs inexpugnabilis* in order to repopulate it as a bulwark of Persian defense.[74] The abandonment of Nisibis provoked the violent protests against Jovian in Antioch mentioned in chapter 1 and quickly came to be regarded as the symbolic manifestation of a shameful peace.[75]

The sentiment was undoubtedly shared by Valens, who must have felt tremendous pressure to overturn the treaty when he occupied the eastern throne in 364. We shall see in what follows that this is precisely what his propagandists advocated, and precisely what Valens attempted to do: by 370, his ministers were directly lobbying for a violation of the treaty; by 371, he had reoccupied Armenia and half of Iberia and garrisoned both with Roman troops; shortly thereafter, he and the Armenians recaptured the satrapies of Arzanene and Corduene; and by 377, he was preparing for a larger invasion of Persia. At every step, then, Valens exploited the *pax* of 363 as a shelter behind which to hatch his plans. For his part, Shapur had also manipulated the treaty as he struggled to regain those territories that his grandfather had surrendered in 299 that remained in Roman hands. Later,

---

69. Matthews 1989, 48–51.

70. AM 25.8.14: "orientis firmissimum claustrum." On the importance of Nisibis in the eastern command structure, see AM 14.9.1, 18.6.8, 20.6.1. Cf. Ephrem *CJ* 2.18, 25–26, 3.3; Joh. Chrys. *De S. Babyla* 22 (*PG* 50.569–70). See also Dilleman 1962, 221–23; Lightfoot 1988; Pollard 2000, 71-81, 286–87.

71. AM 25.8.17; Zos. 3.33.2; Malalas 13.27 (p. 336); *Chron. pasch.*, p. 554.

72. AM 25.8.13–9.6; cf. Malalas 13.27 (p. 336); *Historia S. Ephraemi* 8 col. 23.

73. *CJ* 3.1; cf. AM 25.9.1. Malalas 13.27 (p. 336) and *Chron. pasch.*, p. 554, name the Persian legate Junius. Bineses may be the Persian commander Vin who, according to *BP* 4.26, invaded Armenia in the mid 360s.

74. Tabari 843 (pp. 62–63 Bosworth). Jul. *Or.* 1.27a–b suggests that Shapur planned to repopulate recaptured Roman cities as early as 350.

75. For the protests in Antioch, see p. 18. For the subsequent reaction to the loss of Nisibis, see Turcan 1966.

he also accused Valens of having infringed its terms. For both Valens and Shapur, the ink of the 363 treaty was thus never truly dry.

Despite the ultimate longevity of this agreement, then, it was hardly regarded as satisfactory in its immediate aftermath. It lasted so long not because it satisfied both sides, but because, as a mutual compromise, it had granted both sides a strong enough position that neither could gain the upper hand needed to overturn it. Only with time did the fragile balance of power it created solidify into lasting peace, and this only after the deaths of both Shapur and Valens. In the years of Valens's reign, as we shall see, this compromise seemed neither viable nor acceptable. Rather, it left Persia and Rome locked in a border war for almost two decades.

VALENS'S RELATIONS WITH PERSIA, ARMENIA, AND IBERIA

On taking the throne, Valens's first military ambition was to prevent a Persian attack on the eastern frontier.[76] In the summer of 365, he headed east from Constantinople toward Antioch, whence he could have moved quickly to check any threat from Shapur.[77] Valens's resolve was apparently quite firm, given that, even when he learned that the Gothic Tervingi were planning a raid across the Danube that summer, he stopped only long enough to dispatch a pair of mobile units and then continued east.[78] Ultimately, he never reached Antioch that summer, nor indeed for the next five years. Only in 370 did Valens finally make good on his initial plans and devote his undivided attention to the eastern frontier. This long delay in what first seemed like urgent plans may reflect the fact that, at least in these first few years of Valens's reign, the eastern frontier remained more stable than some of our sources indicate.[79]

Indeed, Valens's initial move toward the east was probably directed more at a potential than an actual threat.[80] After Valens and Valentinian had divided the administrative and military machinery at Naissus and Sirmium in

76. For secondary studies of Valens's relations with Persia, Armenia, and Iberia, see Baynes 1910, 636–42; Asdourian 1911, 155–62; Seeck, *Untergang*, 58–69; Köhler 1925, 70–94; Solari 1932c; Nagl, "Val.," 2113–17; Stein 1959, 186–87, 205–6; Piganiol 1972, 175–77; Blockley 1975, 62–72; 1987; 1992, 30–39; Demandt 1989, 118–19; Redgate 1998, 132–39; Greatrex 2000, 35–41.

77. AM 26.6.11; Zos. 4.4.1, 13.1–2; Soc. 4.2.4; Philostorg. 9.5. For the chronology of all that follows, see Lenski 1995b, 499–522.

78. AM 26.6.11–12; see p. 116.

79. Zos. 4.4.1 indicates that the Persians had initiated attacks on τὰς τῆς ἑῴας ... πόλεις in the first year of Valens's reign. Ammianus (26.4.6) also implies that the Persians invaded in the year after Julian's death, although this rhetorical passage is not to be trusted for purposes of chronology (see pp. 141–42). See Blockley 1992, 189 n. 25; cf. Blockley 1987, 224–25.

80. Soc. 4.2.4–5 and Soz. 6.7.10 indicate that Valens suspected the Persians but that they remained quiet.

midsummer 364, Valens returned to Constantinople, where he remained until the end of July 365.[81] He probably had only vague information about Shapur's activities on the Tigris, nevertheless had he known of urgent trouble, he would not have remained in Constantinople so late into the summer.[82] Moreover, even after he undertook his journey eastward, Valens halted once again in Cappadocia to wait out the late summer heat.[83] He did not yet know, therefore, of problems demanding immediate attention in 365. With the revolt of Procopius and the Gothic war, Valens continued to be detained west of the Bosporus for the next five years.[84] The fact that he undertook the latter extended and arguably unnecessary war in late summer 366 indicates that he had not yet heard of a serious catastrophe in the east by this time either.

In these early years, it seems, Shapur implemented the 363 agreement by simply aligning his newly won territories under his rule, without necessarily invading them.[85] He seems to have divided the new acquisitions in upper Mesopotamia between two governors *(mobed)* directly related to him—Adurad and Zamasp.[86] This we know from hagiographic sources, which report that his governors began persecuting Christians inside these former Roman holdings in an effort to force conformity to Persian religious customs.[87] Ammianus indicates that he also initiated efforts to win political allegiance by offering enticements or employing force to garner support from Armenian *optimates et satrapas.*[88] The historian's terminology here is precise, designating the Armenian *nakharars* more generally *(optimates)* and specifically the satraps of south Armenia, whose territories had just been ceded to him. The Armenian *Epic Histories* confirm that power was not simply transferred in these regions but that Shapur had to win them over through guile, threat, and eventually violence against the resistance of their local rulers.[89] The same source also reports, however, that the Armenian forces initially held the shahanshah at bay. This would seem to confirm our intimations that major problems had not yet been reported to Valens by 366. In the years im-

---

81. Seeck, *Regesten,* 225, with 33, 37. Cf. AM 26.6.11: "consumpta hieme."

82. Lib. *Or.* 12.73 indicates that Valens would have been seventy days' journey from the eastern frontier in Constantinople. On the problem of intelligence at the eastern frontier, see Lee 1993, 109–28, who demonstrates that large invasions were generally learned of in advance even if tactical movements were difficult to determine.

83. See p. 77.

84. Zos. 4.10.1: ἀνεκόπτετο τῆς ἐπὶ Πέρσας ἐλάσεως.

85. Similarly, it took Shapur I eight years after winning suzerainty over Armenia at the battle of Misik to invade the region and depose its Arsacid ruler; cf. Chaumont 1969, 49–66; 1976, 167–76; Kettenhofen 1982, 38–43.

86. Hoffmann 1880, 23–24 ("Passion of Mar Sabha").

87. *BHO* 174–76, 1031, with Fiey 1977, 166–70; cf. *Historia S. Ephraemi* 10 col. 26.

88. AM 27.12.2; cf. 27.12.12.

89. *BP* 4.21–43, 45–49. Garsoïan rightly cautions against assigning too much credence to *BP* on these Armenian resisters (1989, 295 n. 1).

mediately following the treaty of 363, then, Shapur was preoccupied with the implementation of its provisions in Mesopotamia and the south Armenian principalities. He was not yet able to make serious attacks on Roman territory or even to overrun the Armenian Midlands.

The account of events following 363 given in the *Epic Histories* is perhaps generally acceptable, but their exaggerated portrayal of Armenian victories over the Persians in these early years masks the more gradual progress Shapur made in gaining control of individual *nakharars* and satraps. Some of these even included princes beyond the territories to which he had legal claims. Thus he was especially fortunate to win the early defection of Meruzan Arkruni, the lord of Sophene, which technically remained under Roman suzerainty by the terms of the 363 treaty.[90] With this defection, it seems, Shapur obtained the toehold he needed to begin laying waste to Rome's remaining client satrapies. Probably in 367, while Valens was busy with his first Gothic war and King Arshak stood guard against a Persian assault on Armenia's southeastern border, Shapur launched a devastating attack on the western flank of Armenia. He penetrated as far north as Ani (Kemah) in Akilisene, opposite Roman Satala (Kelkit) along the Euphrates. This fortress he plundered, capturing among other treasures the bones of the Arshakuni kings, which had traditionally been entombed there. His desecration seems to have been a gesture symbolic of what he planned for Arshak and his house.[91] In this bold drive, Shapur had further overstepped the 363 agreement with his invasion of the Roman-controlled satrapies of Ingilene and the two Sophenes.

Shapur's drive through Rome's client principalities was probably meant less to provoke Rome than to surprise the Armenian forces under Arshak, who had been prepared for attacks at the opposite end of his kingdom. Indeed, only after they had already heard of Shapur's raid in the west did Arshak and his *sparapet* Vasak Mamikonean hasten to move their forces from the Median border to the Armenian Midlands to forestall further encroachment. Although they successfully prevented an invasion of the central territory of Ayrarat, Shapur's successes had been undeniable. In their wake, Arshak could no longer prevent most of his *nakharars*—who had grown disgusted with what had in effect been a state of active hostility with Persia since 337—from defecting to Shapur.[92] By deserting their king, the *nakharars*, who constituted the backbone of the Armenian cavalry, deprived Arshak of

90. *BP* 4.23; cf. MX 3.29, 35–37. On Meruzan as satrap of Sophene, see Garsoïan 1989, 391–92.

91. *BP* 4.24; cf. MX 3.26, 28; cf. Garsoïan 1980, 43–45. *BP* 17–18 confirms that Shapur continued to retain the loyalty of Ingilene, Greater Sophene, and Anzitene until after 371.

92. *BP* 4.50–51. *BP* speaks of a 34-year war with Persia at 4.50, but of a 30-year war at 4.20, 54. Proc. *Bella* 1.5.10, whose source was *BP,* speaks of a 32-year war. The *terminus post quem* is clearly the rise of hostilities at the end of Constantine's reign (see Garsoïan 1989, 291 n. 19).

any hope of further resistance. In the face of impossible odds, Arshak was himself persuaded to go over to Shapur in 367.

The *Epic Histories* tell the tale of what ensued with characteristically legendary coloring. After fêting Arshak in traditional Sassanian fashion, Shapur is said to have set a test to prove the king's newfound loyalty. He prepared a tent half of whose floor was covered with Persian soil and half with Armenian. When Arshak was led to the Persian soil, he protested his loyalty to Shapur, but once he returned to the Armenian, he slandered Shapur and promised to attack him. Apocryphal though the story may be, it demonstrates marvelously the underlying principles of Perso-Armenian relations. Indeed, the test constitutes a literary crystallization of what past experience had already shown to Shapur: Arshak's promises of alliance were not to be trusted. In light of this knowledge, Shapur had Arshak blinded and thrown into his Prison of Oblivion, where he kept him into the 370s.[93]

After suppressing the Armenian monarchy, Shapur sent a Persian invasion force into Armenia and ordered it to besiege the fortress of Artogerassa. There Arshak's wife, Paranjem, and son, Pap, were holed up with the Armenian treasure, defended by a troop of *azats*—nobles of a lower grade than the *nakharars*.[94] Ammianus tells us that Shapur's invasion force was led by the Armenian defectors Cylaces and Artabanes, and that Shapur had entrusted Armenia to these two.[95] Based on this testimony, R. C. Blockley has argued that Shapur intended to replace the traditional Arsacid monarchy with a non-Arsacid but still Armenian *nakharar* dyarchy.[96] The *Epic Histories* indicate that the situation was considerably more complex.[97] These say that Shapur commanded two officials with Persian noble titles, Zik and Karen, to besiege Artogerassa and rule Armenia. They also speak of two Armenian *nakharars*, Meruzan Arkruni and Vahan Mamikonean, in leadership positions under Shapur's suzerainty.[98] A careful comparison reveals that the *Epic Histories* and Ammianus have intersections, but that any attempts to recover Shapur's administrative scheme in Armenia based on the two is futile. The sources name up

---

93. *BP* 4.52–54; cf. AM 27.12.3; Proc. *Bella* 1.5.13–29; *Vita Nerses* 10 p. 33. MX 3.34–35 locates Arshak's capture after Valens's death in his narrative. AM 27.12.3 implies that Arshak was murdered shortly after his capture, but *BP* 5.7 (cf. MX 3.35; *Vita Nerses* 10, p. 33; Proc. *Bella* 1.5.30–40) relates that Arshak committed suicide with the help of Drastamat after the K'usan war of ca. 372/75. The latter version, although embellished in the *Epic Histories*, seems preferable; one can imagine the value of keeping Arshak alive, especially if the treaty of 363 specifically granted Shapur control over him (see p. 164).

94. AM 27.12.5 with *BP* 4.55, which gives the figure of 11,000 men; cf. MX 3.36. On the status of the *azat*, see Christensen 1944, 111–13; Toumanoff 1963, 124–27; Adontz 1970, 213. Arshak may have rebuilt Artogerassa during his reign; cf. *BP* 4.19, with Garsoïan 1989, 289 n. 6.

95. AM 27.12.5.

96. Blockley 1987; cf. Baynes 1910, 638 n. 71.

97. See app. B.

98. *BP* 4.55, 58–59, 5.1.

to five figures with leadership roles: Zik and Karen, Meruzan Arkruni, Cylaces (who is probably to be identified with a figure the *Epic Histories* name Glak), and Artabanes (who may be identifiable with the *Epic Histories'* Vahan Mamikonean). Given these confusions, we can say only that Shapur combined Persian administrators *(marzban)* with traditional Armenian aristocrats *(nakharars)* in a system that completely suppressed the Arsacid house. This system never had time to solidify, because the *nakharars* whom Shapur set up in positions of power—Cylaces/Glak and Artabanes/Vahan—did not remain faithful to him but played all sides against one another to their own advantage. Armenia was in flux, and Shapur was only beginning to experiment with administrative structures he thought he could control.

In the same year in which Shapur ordered the siege of Artogerassa, 367, he also seized Iberia, once again in contravention of the 363 treaty. He deposed its king, Sauromaces, the son of Rome's ally Mirian III, and installed Sauromaces' cousin Aspacures in his place.[99] Meanwhile, the siege of Armenian Artogerassa continued through the winter of 367/68. In midwinter, Cylaces was able to initiate negotiations for the surrender of the fortress, during the course of which Paranjem, Arshak's wife, appealed to Cylaces and Artabanes in the name of her husband. In typical fashion, the two Armenian defectors defected back to the Armenian throne and engineered a treacherous foray against the Persian forces they had been leading. In the event, the Persians were badly beaten, and Pap escaped to make his way to Valens, who was then wintering at Marcianople. Pap's arrival was noted by Themistius, who mentioned the young prince in an oration delivered to Valens on March 28, 368.[100] Valens eventually sent Pap back to Neocaesarea (Niksar) in Pontus Polemoniacus, three hundred kilometers from the Armenian border. There the young king seems to have spent the rest of 368 enjoying "liberal support and education" while Valens prepared for a final year of campaigning against the Goths.[101] Meanwhile, the siege of Artogerassa continued, and the *Epic Histories* inform us that Pap, in "the land of the Greeks," was in communication with his mother inside the fortress, whom he encouraged to await his rescue.[102]

Unfortunately for Paranjem, Valens was willing to intervene and reimpose

---

99. AM 27.12.4: "eiusdem . . . gentis"; cf. 27.12.16: "consobrinus."

100. *Or.* 8.116c. Seeck, *Untergang,* 448 n. 26, associates this reference with Pap. Hoffmann 1978, 314–16 (cf. Heather and Matthews 1991, 23, 31. n. 5) believes rather that it refers to the Iberian prince Bacurius. I favor Seeck's reading, but either interpretation supports an attack on the sub-Caucasus in this year and the flight of the Armenian and Iberian dynasts.

101. AM 27.12.5–9. *BP* 4.15 claims that when Pap reached puberty, he was sent to the "land of the Greeks"; 4.55 says that Pap was with the "king of the Greeks" when Artogerassa was first besieged (cf. MX 3.29). *BP* clearly preserves the memory of Pap's presence at Valens's court, but he seems to have elevated his status there by converting him from a refugee to a hostage. On the status of royal hostages and refugees, see Braund 1984, 9–21, 165–80.

102. *BP* 4.55; cf. MX 3.25.

Pap only in 369. The emperor had received legates from Cylaces and Arta-banes requesting that Pap be returned as their king, along with a military force.[103] Ammianus's wording implies that Cylaces and Artabanes were not with Pap when they made their request, but inside Armenia. If their identi-fication with the *Epic Histories*' Glak and Vahan is correct, they did indeed re-main in Armenia, acting nominally under Shapur's direction during the siege of Artogerassa. Their communications with Valens show, however, that they were also working clandestinely for an Arsacid restoration.[104] In the summer of 369, Valens responded timidly to their request ordering a Roman general, the *comes* Terentius, to escort Pap back into Armenia, but forbidding him to confer royal honors on the prince, lest this be judged a violation of the 363 treaty.[105] When Shapur learned of Pap's restoration, he became so incensed that he invaded Armenia personally, apparently in the autumn of 369. In the wake of this invasion, Pap was again forced into hiding somewhere in the southwestern Caucasus at the Roman frontier with Lazica. There he remained for the next five months, that is, until the spring of 370.[106] Rather than hunt down Pap, Shapur laid waste to Armenia and concentrated his forces against the long-besieged Artogerassa. The fortress finally fell, after more than two years, in the winter of 369/70. The Persian forces captured the royal treasure and Arshak's wife, Paranjem, whom they brutally raped until she was dead.[107] They also captured and destroyed the Arsacid capital of Artaxata and a num-ber of other urban foundations, former strongholds of Arsacid influence.[108] When Shapur returned to Persia after these victories, he left behind *ostikans*—overseers—charged with holding the fortresses he had built or captured.[109] He also began systematically persecuting Christians, forcing apostasy to Maz-daism, closing churches, and consecrating fire temples.[110] He thus tightened

---

103. AM 27.12.9. *BP* 4.55, 5.1, says that the sparapet Mushel Mamikonean negotiated di-rectly with Valens on behalf of Pap. More likely Ammianus is correct to say that legates were used.

104. AM 27.12.8 implies that Pap escaped without Cylaces and Artabanes, with whom he is next associated only after returning to Armenia at AM 27.12.14. Vahan clearly remained in Armenia until his death at *BP* 4.59. Glak and his anonymous alter ego in the *Epic Histories* ap-parently did as well (cf. *BP* 4.55, 5.3).

105. AM 27.12.10. Here MX 3.36–37 is to be preferred to *BP* 5.1, who fuses the restora-tion of Pap by Terentius (Terent) with that of Arinthaeus (Ade/Adde); cf. Markwart 1896, 215; Blockley 1975, 187–88; Garsoïan 1989, 307 n. 4.

106. AM 27.12.11.

107. AM 27.12.12; *BP* 4.55–58. *BP* indicates that Shapur was not present for the capture of Artogerassa but only invaded Armenia personally after its fall. *BP* also mentions a plague that devastated the garrison of Artogerassa. MX 3.35 says that the garrison surrendered.

108. AM 27.12.12; *BP* 4.55, 58.

109. *BP* 4.58.

110. *BP* 4.55–57, 59, 5.1. MX 3.36 says that Meruzan destroyed all written texts in an ef-fort to wipe out Christianity. On Shapur's Christian persecutions more broadly, see Decret 1979, 135–48. On fire temples, see Christensen 1944, 160–62.

his grip on Armenia after his attempts to combine Persian and Armenian administrative structures had failed. Both politically and culturally, Armenia was to become Persian.

By late summer 369, Valens had finally brought his protracted Gothic War to a close, not least because of the desperate state of affairs in the east.[111] He sent his *magister peditum* Arinthaeus to negotiate peace with the Goths in the late summer of 369 and then ordered him straight to the eastern frontier with a full military command.[112] It probably was not until the following spring that Arinthaeus entered Armenia with his army and restored Pap for the second time.[113]

Arinthaeus's arrival came none too soon, given that Shapur had contacted Pap, apparently still in hiding, and persuaded him to come over to the Persians. Under Shapur's influence, Pap had murdered the duplicitous Cylaces and Artabanes and sent their heads to the shahanshah as a sign of loyalty.[114] When Arinthaeus reached Armenia, he halted this rapprochement, and his presence in Armenia through the summer headed off a second Persian invasion. Shapur had to content himself with an embassy to Valens protesting this obvious violation of the 363 treaty.[115] After this first Persian embassy, Valens also sent his general Terentius with twelve legions— about 12,000 men—to restore Sauromaces in Iberia. When this force reached the river Cyrus, Terentius and Sauromaces worked out an agreement with Sauromaces' cousin Aspacures to divide the kingdom in two, with the river as the boundary. Aspacures indicated that he had considered defecting to Rome, but feared for the life of his son, who was by then a Persian hostage. The agreement was later approved by Valens, although not by Shapur, who regarded it as grounds for war. Even so, Valens did not hesitate to refer to this settlement later as the legal basis for his occupation of western Iberia.[116] It was probably at this point that Valens also put two garrison forts on the Georgian coast and fortified the major passes of the Caucasus. This action may be at the heart of a confused passage in John Lydus to the effect that the Persians and Romans settled a quarrel over the terms of the 363 treaty by mutually agreeing to fortify the Caucasus pass(es) against the Huns.[117]

111. AM 27.5.7; Zos. 4.11.4; cf. p. 133.

112. AM 27.5.9.

113. AM 27.12.13; MX 3.37. Arinthaeus probably took the road between Amaseia and Satala, a stretch over which three milestones of Valens have been found, indicating that repair work was done to facilitate the transport of troops and supplies; cf. *RRMAM* nos. 59, 63, 933.

114. AM 27.12.14. Cf. p. 382.

115. AM 27.12.15.

116. AM 27.12.16–17, 30.2.4. Cf. Braund 1994, 260–61.

117. On Valens's Georgian garrisons and fortification of the Caucasus, see app. A. Joh. Lyd. *De mag.* 3.52 clearly has some chronological confusions, which led Blockley 1985, 63–67,

Valens had thus finally met Shapur's earlier violations of the 363 treaty with violations of his own. He had regained part of Iberia—to which Rome probably still had claims—and all of Armenia—to which it did not. He did so, not in the belief that he was still operating within the provisions of the Dura agreement, but because he now had the military might to enforce his occupation. His Gothic war had ended, he had already been able to send advance comitatensian forces eastward, and, as we shall see, his propagandists Festus and Eutropius had already begun openly advertising Valens's intention of breaking the treaty. In the spring of 370, after a brief stay in Constantinople, he raced east himself and reached Antioch with his army by late April.[118] Soon afterward, he moved out to Hierapolis, from where he could coordinate frontier operations, and for most of the following eight years, he operated on a similar pattern, wintering in Antioch and traveling east for the summer to coordinate the army from Hierapolis, Edessa, and even Caesarea.[119] As long as he remained near the eastern frontier with his massive army, Rome retained control of the Armenian kingdom. However, although Valens continued to take measures to avoid open warfare, he stood in clear violation of the 363 accord.

Naturally, Valens's recapture of Armenia and his dispositions in Iberia did not sit well with Shapur , who declared the peace void in the winter of 370 and promised an invasion the following year.[120] The shahanshah began collecting an army and assembling support from his allies,[121] and, as he had promised, in the spring of 371, he sent an invasion force into Armenia. Valens had dispatched his generals Traianus and Vadomarius to meet

---

and Chrysos 1976, 30 n. 3 to reject it as anachronistic. This is unnecessary. The passage clearly refers to an agreement reached shortly after 363 because of ongoing disputes over the construction of a fort (φρούριον) to guard the pass (εἰσφόρος) through the Caucasus. There were in fact two main Caucasus passes, the Dariel in the west and the Derbend in the east. A division of Iberia at the Kur would have left Rome in command of one and Persia of the other. Once Persia assumed control of all defenses in the region, it began demanding tribute from Constantinople to fulfill the Roman half of the agreement.

118. Soc. 4.14.1; Soz. 6.13.1; Zos. 4.11.4.

119. This is clearly the meaning of Zos. 4.13.2; cf. Barnes 1998, 248 n. 4. Valens is attested at Hierapolis in the summers of 370, 373 and 377; see Seeck, *Regesten*, 241, 245, 249; Barnes 1998, 252–53; Greatrex 2000, 37–38. To these add *P Lips.* 34, 35. This is also how Constantius operated in the 340s; see Lib. *Or.* 18.207; cf. *Or.* 15.17; AM 22.23.2, 7: "Hierapolim solitis itineraribus venit" (of Julian). For Valens at Edessa, see Soc. 4.18.2–10; Soz. 6.18.2–7; Theod. *HE* 4.17.1–4; Ruf. *HE* 11.5. Valens's visit to Edessa may be dated to 373 at *Chron. Edes.* no. 31 (a. 684 = A.D. 373). For Valens in Caesarea, see pp. 252–54. Here again, Constantius had used Caesarea as a base for conducting affairs with Armenia; cf. AM 20.9.1, 11.1–4. For Valens's winter camp in Antioch, see Theod. *HE* 4.26.1; Theod. *HR* 8.5.

120. AM 27.12.18: "velut obseratis amicitiae foribus."

121. AM 27.12.18, 29.1.1. *BP* 5.4 and *Vita Nerses* 11 p. 34–35 confirm that Shapur's army included numerous allies, not least the Hun king Urnayr; cf. Baynes 1910, 640. On the use of auxiliaries by the Sassanians, see Christensen 1944, 209–10.

the Persians, although he ordered them to defend rather than attack, apparently in hopes of breaking the treaty without breaking the peace. The Persians met Traianus and Vadomarius at Bagawan, a valley at the foot of Mount Npat, near the source of the Arsanias River.[122] The Roman troops at first resisted combat, but they were eventually forced to respond to the Persian cavalry attacks and came off victorious.[123] The *Epic Histories* paint a picture that gives considerable credit for the victory to Pap's *sparapet*, Mushel Mamikonean, although they admit that Pap personally played no role but watched the battle from Mount Npat. It is impossible to determine the relative contributions of Armenians and Romans, although it is certain that the Armenians would have been hard-pressed to repel the Persians without Roman help. In the aftermath of the battle, several other engagements were fought, which initiated the process of reclaiming additional Armenian territories.[124] According to the *Epic Histories*, these included the satrapies of Arzanene and Corduene, which had been ceded to Persia in 363.[125] With these acquisitions and the capture of Armenia, Valens had broken the treaty on several counts.

At the end of the summer, a truce was settled, leaving Shapur to return to Ctesiphon and Valens to Antioch. It is by no means clear that Valens or Shapur regarded this agreement as a long-term accord in 371: it was hardly a treaty, and Ammianus states explicitly that both sides remained at odds even in its aftermath.[126] As it turned out, though, this temporary settlement had the effect of sanctioning Roman control of Armenia for the rest of Valens's reign. The sixth-century Greek historian John Malalas confirms this:

> Valens did not fight himself, but marched out and made a peace treaty [εἰρήνης πάκτα]. . . . The Persians had come and sued for peace. Thus, having arrived in Antioch in Syria with the greater part of the military forces on November 10 in the fourteenth indiction, Valens lingered there to conclude the peace treaty [τὰ πάκτα τῆς εἰρήνης] with the Persians. He negotiated a treaty for seven years, with the Persians suing for peace and ceding half of Nisibis [τὸ ἥμισυ τοῦ Νιτζίβιος].[127]

---

122. On the location, see *ASX* v.22.xiv with Hewsen 1992, 215–16 n. 287; cf. Kettenhofen 1989, 69. Bagawan was just across the Arsanias River from the former Persian camp at Zarehawan; cf. *BP* 4.55, 58.

123. AM 29.1.2–3; cf. *BP* 5.4, which continues to name "Terent" as the "Greek" commander rather than Traianus; cf. 5.5–6. MX 3.37 and *Vita Nerses* 11, p. 34, confuse the battle of Bagawan with the later battle of Jirov.

124. AM 29.1.4; *BP* 5.5, 8–19; MX 3.37. In the early part of 371, Valens had been in Constantinople. He only moved to the eastern frontier late in the summer; cf. p. 280.

125. *BP* 5.10, 16. Cf. Adontz-Garsoian 1970, 176; Toumanoff 1963, 181; Hewsen 1992, 158.

126. AM 29.1.4: "pactis indutiis ex consensu, aestateque consumpta, partium discessere ductores etiam tum discordes."

127. Malalas 13.30 (p. 338).

Some of the details had become hazy by Malalas's day, but much of this information corresponds with what we know from other sources. Malalas's notice that the Persians asked for terms seems logical, since it was they who had suffered setbacks. What Malalas means by the Persian return of "half of Nisibis" is vague but interpretable. It would have been difficult to relinquish half of a city, but Malalas may be implying that the Persians had given up half of the Nisibis accord, which, in effect, they had. The notice that the "peace agreement" lasted seven years corresponds precisely with Ammianus's account, which portrays no open conflict on the frontier for the seven years between 371 and 378. In fact, Ammianus's notice on events from early 372 directly confirms that peace with Persia had begun that winter.[128]

Other sources tell the same story. Socrates indicates that peace prevailed in 375, when Valens instituted severe measures against recalcitrant Nicenes, and Themistius confirms peace with Persia in the same year.[129] This "peace" is best attested in Themistius's eleventh oration (March 373): "[Valens is] sated with victory and even willing to put aside [war], but he is insatiable for the logos of philosophy. He more gladly concedes leisure to the soldier than silence to the philosopher."[130] In the same speech, Themistius notes that Valens had armies in the Caucasus, Iberia, Albania, and Armenia.[131] The emperor had thus regained much of what the empire had lost in 363 and now held it with Roman troops under the sanction of a truce. Only the Armenian tradition informs us as to why Shapur allowed this. The *Epic Histories* report that the Kushans—a people on the northeastern edge of the Sassanian empire—occupied the shahanshah with war after his loss at Bagawan.[132] The notice is credible, given that Ammianus himself reports how these same people had kept Shapur from attacking the Roman frontier in the early 350s.[133] Whether Shapur was already aware that the Kushans had revolted when he sanctioned the truce of 371 is unclear. Ultimately, however, this conflict enforced a "peace" that allowed Valens to hold Armenia for seven years, in direct contravention of the 363 agreement.

128. AM 29.2.21: "parthico fragore cessante"; cf. 29.1.4: "securus interim hostium externorum"; 30.4.1: "in eois partibus alto externorum silentio."

129. Soc. 4.32.1; Them. *Or.* 13.166c, delivered in 376 but referring to 375; cf. Vanderspoel 1995, 179–84, 251.

130. *Or.* 11.144a; cf. 148d–149a; on the date, see Vanderspoel 1995, 177, 251.

131. *Or.* 11.149b.

132. *BP* 5.7. At *BP* 5.37, Shapur was still fighting the Kushan war after Pap had been murdered. Proc. *Bella* 1.5.30–40 and MX 3.29, both of which drew on the *Epic Histories*, report the same war. On this Kushan war, see Markwart 1901, 50–52; Seeck, *Regesten*, 65; Garsoïan 1989, 313 n. 3. On the Kushans more broadly, see Frye 1984, 249–69.

133. AM 16.9.3–4, 17.5.1; cf. 14.3.1, 15.13.4, 18.4.1, 6.22, 19.1.7, 10. See also Matthews 1989, 62, with 488 n. 26, on the Chionitae, a Hunnic people, who also occupied Shapur at this time.

While peace prevailed with Persia, the situation inside Armenia began to crumble. As we have seen, in the period after the victory at Bagawan, Pap's *sparapet* Mushel Mamikonean regained control over many of the *nakharars* who had defected to Shapur in the 360s.[134] This was probably largely an Armenian concern. Themistius says that a Roman army remained stationed in Armenia, but the *Epic Histories* are probably right in saying that it was left to the Arsacid king and his *sparapet* to realign the *nakharars* under their authority. This is apparently what Themistius was referring to in 373 when he said of Valens:

> For, without touching his sword, but using only the clemency of his spirit, he won back no small section of the neighboring barbarians who are normally hard to persuade and control, and he bound peoples more untrustworthy than the ancient Thessalians. So that, although they still quarrel with one another, they cooperate with and are in spirit with the Romans. Toward each other they follow their usual nature, but toward the emperor, they follow necessity. They have been defeated neither by spears nor by bows and slings but by the open patience in which they exist—a fact surprising to the listener.[135]

If we are to believe Themistius, Valens's clemency had achieved a realignment of the *nakharars* and thus benefited Rome. The Armenian sources, by contrast, reveal that the *nakharars* had in fact been won back by the Arsacid sword, but with only limited success.

It seems safest to assume that the situation inside Armenia was far from settled. The young Pap was probably struggling to hold together a kingdom that Shapur had only just dismantled. His tenuous grip on power led him to measures that were less than judicious. Unfortunately, we have no firm chronological indicators for the dates of most of Pap's activities. Pap had the powerful Armenian patriarch—and close Roman contact—Nerses poisoned at some point, perhaps late in 371.[136] After doing so, the young king nominated a certain Yusik as a replacement and sent him for consecration to Caesarea, as was the custom for Armenian patriarchs. The *Epic Histories* tell us that the bishop of Caesarea—who would have been Basil—refused the nominee. In the meantime, Pap began systematically dismantling the religious

---

134. See n. 125. *BP* 5.8–19. Not at MX 3.8, probably reflecting MX's anti-Mamikonean bias. On the extent of the territories regained, see Hewsen 1965, 336–37; Toumanoff 1963, 458–60 n. 98; Adontz 1970, 178–80.

135. *Or.* 11.149d–150a; cf. 13.166c.

136. *BP* 5.23–24; *Vita Nerses* 12–14, pp. 36–42; MX 3.38. Inasmuch as he was present at the battle of Bagawan (*BP* 5.4), Nerses's murder must have occurred after summer 371; most have assumed he was poisoned shortly before Valens's visit to Caesarea on Jan. 6, 372 (Giet 1943, 363–65; Hauschild 1973–93, 1, at *Ep.* 99 n. 15 and *Ep.* 120 n. 74). May 1973, 54, 58, dates the murder to 373 (cf. Seeck, *Untergang*, 59–63). Pap was not the first Arsacid king to murder a Gregorid patriarch; see *BP* 3.12, 14.

foundations that Nerses had established.[137] Valens responded by having his general Terentius invest Basil with the authority to resolve the dispute over the ecclesiastical succession. A number of Basil's letters regarding the incident survive.[138] Apparently, Basil never succeeded in appointing an acceptable successor, in part because of Pap, in part because of the intrigues of Basil's rivals Theodotus and Anthimus. This failure meant that, from the death of Nerses on, the Roman see of Caesarea ceased to claim its traditional authority over the consecration of Armenia's patriarch.[139] This loss of ecclesiastical control from inside the empire would certainly have disturbed both Terentius and Valens.

Insofar as Terentius was charged with the resolution of the episcopal problem, we might assume that he was the commander of the Roman army stationed in Armenia at this time. This would explain why he is one of only two Roman generals whose names survive in the Armenian sources for the period.[140] It would also explain why it was Terentius who first began writing to Valens to complain of Pap's activities. Terentius had allied himself with a number of the *nakharar* lords *(gentilibus)* whom, as Themistius indicates, Pap had disaffected through his heavy-handed tactics.[141] Terentius complained of this to Valens and reminded the emperor that, in 370, Pap had murdered Cylaces and Artabanes and nearly defected to Shapur.[142] Terentius was rigorously Nicene and probably did not take kindly to Pap's murder of the Nicene patriarch Nerses or to Pap's refusal to cooperate with Terentius's personal friend Basil. Because Terentius was a staunch Christian, it is natural that Ammianus chose to play up his morose carping, but some weight must be given to the credibility of his complaints. According to the *Epic Histories*, Pap's behavior was even more outrageous than Ammianus indicates: he began openly courting Persia and sent to Valens demanding control of Caesarea and ten other Roman cities, including Edessa, which he claimed were Arsacid foundations.[143]

---

137. *BP* 5.29–31. MX 3.39 names Pap's nominee for successor as Shahak of Manazkert; cf. Garsoïan 1989, 322 n. 1, 432.

138. Basil *Ep.* 99, 102, 120–122. Basil names Pap's replacement "Faustus," perhaps a Latinizing version of the Armenian "Yusik" (Hopeful One). Garsoïan 1983, followed by Rousseau 1994, 281–82, argues that Basil was assigned to appoint a metropolitan for the province of Armenia Minor rather than a patriarch for the kingdom of Armenia, but her argument must be rejected on several counts; see Lenski 1996, 441–42.

139. On Caesarea's role in consecrating Armenian patriarchs, see *BP* 3.12, 16, 17, 4.4, 5.29; *Vita Nerses* 3, p. 24; Basil *Ep.* 122.

140. *BP* 5.1, 4–6, 32; MX 3.36, 37, 39; cf. Seeck, *Untergang*, 63, with 450 n. 25. Theod. *HE* 4.32.1 also implies that Terentius was commander in Armenia.

141. *Or.* 11.149d–150a.

142. AM 30.1.2–3.

143. *BP* 5.32; cf. MX 3.39. AM 30.2.1 confirms that Shapur had been negotiating with Pap. C. F. Lehmann-Haupt argued that a very fragmentary inscription he discovered at Martyropolis

In response to this insubordination, Valens decided to arrest and execute the brash young Armenian king. He invited Pap to a meeting in Tarsus. Pap came with a 300-man mounted escort but, after arriving, became anxious when Valens would not receive him in audience. According to Ammianus, Pap learned that Terentius had secretly recommended that he be replaced, so as not to disaffect other *nakharars* or run the risk of Pap defecting to Persia. On learning of Terentius's plan, Pap made a break for Armenia. In his race to escape, he threatened the local governor in Tarsus with death and attacked a legion that was sent to pursue him, thus making himself an open enemy of Rome.[144] The young king continued east to the Euphrates, which he reached within two days. While he and his men struggled across, Count Danielus and the tribune Barzimeres, sent by Valens in pursuit with a force of Scutarii, outflanked Pap and crossed the river first.[145] They set up roadblocks on the two routes Pap might take east, but did not manage to capture the fugitive king. A traveler who had seen the roadblocks helped Pap escape along an intermediary path between them. Valens's assassination attempt had thus failed, and he knew well that he stood in grave danger of losing Pap's loyalty and with it the control of Armenia.

Under considerable pressure to explain the debacle, Danielus and Barzimeres claimed that Pap had used magical powers to disguise his party and mask them in a cloud of darkness, under which they had escaped. The charge fits well with claims in the *Epic Histories* that Pap was reputed since birth to have been possessed of demons *(dews)*, who dictated his erratic behavior. Daniel and Barzimeres seem merely to have capitalized on this reputation to save themselves from charges of incompetence. Given that at least Barzimeres kept his office, the story was apparently accepted.[146] More important,

---

(Farkin) confirmed Pap's demands for former Arsacid territory (Lehmann-Haupt 1908; 1910, 408–18). Markwart 1930, 134–59, expressed reservations, and Mango 1985, 95–104, has since demonstrated that the text is best placed in a late sixth-century context. Garsoïan doubts *BP*'s veracity with regard to Pap's demand for the Roman cities because of a lack of outside corroboration (1989, 324–25 n. 3). Nevertheless, other sources attest Armenian claims to Edessa/Urha (Markwart 1901, 160), and Pap's execution by Valens implies that his transgressions were serious. For the charges against Pap, see Baynes 1910, 640; Nagl, "Val.," 2116; Blockley 1992, 35.

144. AM 30.1.1–7.

145. AM 30.1.8–12. To judge by their names, Danielus and Barzimeres were of Ibero-Armenian origin, and Ammianus makes it clear that their familiarity with the terrain helped them outmaneuver Pap. On Danielus's (south Armenian?) and Barzimeres's (Iberian?) origins, see Markwart 1930, 139–40 nn. 2–3. Hoffmann 1969–70, 1: 240–41, makes a strong case that Danielus and Barzimeres led the Tertii Sagitarii Valentis and Sagitarii Domnici, auxiliary archery units newly formed under Valens.

146. AM 31.1.16. On Pap's possession by demons, see *BP* 4.44, 5.22; *Vita Nerses* 12, p. 36. See also Markwart 1930, 135–48; Russell 1987, 341–42. Garsoïan 1967, 311–13, believes that Pap's supposed "possession" is code for his Arian heresy, but the fact that his demonic powers

however, its significance stretches beyond this single incident. The stories of Pap's demonic possession and magical powers bespeak a strong undercurrent of pagan sentiment in the young king. Taken with his murder of Nerses and his resistance to Roman intervention in the appointment of a patriarchal successor, these stories help confirm that Armenia's peculiar version of Zoroastrianism was alive and well in the later fourth century, despite its nominal conversion to Christianity two generations earlier.[147] As noted at the beginning of this chapter, religion was only one of many battlegrounds on which Persia and Rome competed for Armenian loyalty.

Pap's escape probably occurred in 373 or 374. Upon his return to Armenia, he was received, according to Ammianus, "with the greatest joy by his subjects."[148] Ammianus also tells us that, despite the offenses he had endured, Pap remained loyal to Valens. Whether we can trust Ammianus, who favored Pap just as much as he hated Valens and his generals, remains in doubt. The *Epic Histories* make Pap's position in Armenia look much less stable and his loyalty to Valens much less firm. At any rate, Valens was aware that amends had to be made and new plans laid to avert the loss of Armenia. He thus dismissed Count Terentius, who had engineered the bungled assassination plot, and turned over the army in Armenia to Traianus, with instructions that he should win his way back into Pap's confidence.[149] At the same time, Valens sent a secret missive instructing Traianus to have Pap killed as soon as he could.

Traianus convinced Pap that he had nothing to fear from Valens by showing him letters that indicated Valens's favor. With this ploy, he won his way into the king's feasts, important occasions for the social cohesion of the Armenian aristocracy. When Traianus invited Pap to a banquet of his own, Pap came with little reluctance, indicating that the general had indeed succeeded in gaining Pap's confidence. This was no doubt because Traianus played his role well, as the circumstances of the feast would seem to confirm: the general organized the meal according to Armenian principles, at midday, with musical entertainment on strings and winds, and with the honored seat being reserved for the king himself.[150] These amenities lured Pap into com-

---

are noted in both Armenian and Roman traditions points to a more straightforward interpretation. Barzimeres remained a tribune of the *scutarii* in 378 (AM 31.9.9).

147. Russell 1987, passim, esp. 437–80.

148. AM 30.1.15.

149. As noted on p. 178 above, Terentius seems to have been commander-in-chief in Armenia after the battle of Bagawan; cf. AM 30.1.2–4; Basil *Ep.* 99. A letter of Basil's (*Ep.* 214) plausibly dated to 375 (Loofs 1898, 21) indicates that Terentius had retired or been relieved from his command and was residing in Antioch. After Pap's return to Armenia, Traianus is attested as commander; see AM 30.1.18; cf. 31.7.1–2.

150. On feasting in Armenian society, see Garsoïan 1976, 27–30; 1980, 46–63; cf. *BP* 4.2, 16, 54.

placency, making it easier for a barbarian guard to go in at a signal and murder him.[151] The Quadic king Gabinius had been lured to his death in this way by Valentinian's general Marcellianus, and Valens's general Lupicinus would attempt similar tactics against the Gothic leaders Alavivus and Fritigern in 377. Ammianus draws an explicit parallel between the treacherous murders of Gabinius and Pap. To Valens, as to most of his contemporaries, such acts no doubt seemed as justified as they were expedient.[152]

Even so, the *Epic Histories* tell us, the Armenians were furious. However, as Valens had probably calculated, their rage would have been tempered by resignation to the reality of the current situation. The presence of a Roman army in Armenian territory probably left the Armenian nobility with little option but to accept Pap's murder without resistance. They also accepted the Roman imposition of a replacement for Pap, an Arsacid prince named Varazdat.[153] According to the *Epic Histories*, Varazdat, still a boy, ruled under the regency of the sparapet Mushel Mamikonean.[154] The regency of a Mamikonean, a notoriously pro-Roman family, helps explain Armenia's continued loyalty to Valens in this trying period. Moreover, the *nakharars* accepted what had happened because they still believed that they were best served by remaining Rome's ally. In the *Epic Histories,* they are reported as saying: "We cannot become servants of the heathen Persians or be hostile to the king of the Greeks. Neither can we carry on hostilities with both of them. We cannot maintain ourselves without the support of one of them."[155] The Armenians knew they had to play one side against the other. Fortunately for Valens, despite his oppressive manipulations, Christianity proved a strong enough bond to decide the *nakharars* in his favor. Here again, religion constituted a key element in mediating the struggle for Armenian loyalty.

Pap's murder occurred in 375. Naturally, it triggered a reaction from Shapur, who had been courting the king in hopes that he would defect to Persia. With Pap's death and replacement by a Roman nominee under a pro-Roman regent, the shahanshah had to find other avenues back into Armenia. In the autumn of 375, Shapur reopened negotiations with Valens. He sent a legate demanding that Valens either evacuate Armenia, the "perpetual

---

151. AM 30.1.18–21; *BP* 5.32. MX 3.39 offers a completely different account; cf. *Vita Nerses* 15, p. 42. The *Epic Histories* are remarkably close to Ammianus. Although they do mistakenly attribute the murder to Terent rather than Traianus, they alone give us the name of the place where Pap was killed, "Xu in the district of Bagrawand," the same place where the Roman army retained its camp; cf. *BP* 5.1, 4.

152. On Gabinius, see AM 29.6.5. On the Goths, see p. 328. For Ammianus's parallel between the two murders, see AM 30.1.22–23. At 31.1.3, Ammianus contends that the murder of Pap haunted Valens before the disaster at Adrianople.

153. *BP* 5.32–34, 37. Cf. MX 3.40. AM mentions nothing of Pap's successor.

154. *BP* 5.34–35.

155. *BP* 5.33.

source of troubles," or withdraw from the part of Iberia where Roman troops now supported Sauromaces.[156] Shapur, who had apparently ended his war with the Kushans, was thus demanding the return of half of what Valens had gained in 370 and 371. Valens responded that he could not renege on agreements made with the consent of both sides.[157] A brief lacuna in Ammianus's text mars an exact understanding of what followed, but it is clear that Shapur responded with a second embassy, this time in midwinter 375/76. Here, the shahanshah claimed that the discord could not be rooted out unless the original negotiators of the 363 treaty were present, an impossibility, given that some of them were already dead. This statement seems to add weight to the assumption that the spirit of the treaty and perhaps even its text were not entirely clear.[158] Shapur was attempting to exploit the chinks in the treaty through which Valens had wormed his way back into Armenia to root him out again.

The following summer, 376, Valens sent an embassy of his own under Victor, the *magister equitum,* and Urbicius, the *dux* of Mesopotamia. These told Shapur that his demands for Armenia were unjust, given that its inhabitants had been granted the right to live according to their own decisions.[159] They also informed Shapur that unless the Roman troops assigned to protect Sauromaces in western Iberia were allowed to return to Iberia unhindered, as had been agreed *(ut dispositum est),* Shapur would be compelled to do what he had refrained from doing on his own. This last clause was a threat to force Shapur into the war he had hoped to avoid through diplomacy. Valens thus raised the stakes by promising to reopen hostilities after five years of peace. As Ammianus notes, Valens's confidence was boosted because he could now chose from an array of options rather than being compelled to diplomatic

---

156. AM 30.2.2: "Arrace legato ad principem misso, perpetuam aerumnarum causam deseri penitus suadebat Armeniam: si id displicuisset, aliud poscens, ut Hiberiae divisione cessante, remotisque inde partis Romanae praesidiis, Aspacures solus regnare permitteretur, quem ipse praefecerat genti." *Deseri* is a conjecture for *deleri.* Chrysos 1976, 37–38, and Blockley 1987, 226, make the case for the MS reading. Both attach great significance to the proposal to "destroy Armenia," which they take to mean that Shapur intended to eliminate the Arsacid crown and divide Armenia (cf. Blockley 1992, 35–36; Seager 1996, 281–82). This reading is unsatisfactory, first because it fails to recognize the parallel nature of Shapur's proposals—either withdraw from Armenia or from Iberia—and second because it incorrectly assumes that Ammianus understood "Armenia" to mean the "Armenian crown" or "Armenian government." Ammianus invariably uses "Armenia" to refer only to the territory or people of Armenia (cf. Viansino 1985, 133). Shapur did hope to destroy the Arsacid monarchy, and had already attempted to do so, but *deseri* must be read, since "deleri penitus . . . Armeniam" makes no sense, at least in a pre-atomic age.

157. AM 30.2.3: "placitis ex consensu firmatis"; cf. 27.12.17–18, 29.1.4.

158. AM 30.2.3. Blockley 1987, believes this dispute indicates that some of the terms were agreed to orally, a possible, although not necessary, interpretation of the passage. On foreign policy records, see Lee 1993, 33–40.

159. AM 30.2.4: "ad arbitrium suum vivere cultoribus eius permissis."

tergiversation.[160] He had apparently learned that he would soon be able to fill the ranks of his army with auxiliary recruits from the Goths, whom he now permitted to settle in Thrace.[161]

Ammianus tells us that Valens based his firm stance in both Armenia and Iberia on previous agreements.[162] Since Valens was plainly not referring to the 363 treaty, under which Rome had relinquished Armenia—although not Iberia—he must have issued his ultimatum on the strength of later accords: that reached about Iberia at the river Cyrus in 370, which, as Ammianus indicates, allowed the Romans to send troops to protect Sauromaces each year, and the truce reached at Bagawan in 371, which must have granted the *nakharars* the right to choose their own form of rule.[163] This latter agreement would clearly have favored Rome, since the *nakharars* were generally inclined to maintain the Arsacid monarchy, which had for so long leaned—however tenuously—in Rome's favor. Victor and Urbicius had thus presented Shapur with a hard-line stance based on what they could claim were Rome's sanctioned rights. Shapur either had to accept the "previously agreed" Roman presence in Iberia and Armenia or go to war.

Fortunately for Shapur, the two legates had committed a blunder. During their diplomatic journey, they had improperly accepted offers from two *regiones exiguae* to be accepted under Roman suzerainty.[164] This diplomatic infraction offered Shapur a new bargaining chip with which to revive negotiations. Later in 376, he sent a third embassy under the Suren offering the two territories illegally accepted by Victor and Urbicius in exchange for con-

160. AM 30.2.4: "ingravescente post haec altius cura, imperator eligere consilia quam invenire sufficiens. . . ." Given the boldness of the demands that follow this phrase, it only makes sense when translated as "though concerns grew worse after this, the emperor, being in a position to make a choice of plans rather than invent them. . . ."

161. See pp. 318–19.

162. AM 30.2.3–4, cited in n. 157.

163. For Iberia, see AM 27.12.17–18: "dividi placuit Hiberiae regnum"; cf. 30.2.4: "ni Sauromaci praesidia militum impertita principio sequentis anni (ut dispositum est) inpraepedita reverterint." For Armenia, see AM 29.1.4: "pactis indutiis ex consensu." See p. 176 for further evidence that the truce after Bagawan was treated as a separate agreement. Seager 1996, 282, is thus wrong to argue that at AM 30.2.3 "there is no good ground for supposing that a reference to anything other than the peace of 363 is intended."

164. AM 30.2.5 (cf. Theod. *HR* 8.4, with Greatrex 2000, 40 n. 27). Chrysos 1976 is surely wrong to regard this as the occasion for the division of Armenia commonly dated to 386 (cf. Greatrex 2000, 39). Adontz 1970, 36–37, argues more plausibly that the two territories were rather the satrapies of Asthianene and Belabitene, which later show up among the satrapies under Roman suzerainty (cf. *CJ* 1.29.5; *Nov. Just.* 31.1.3). These, together with the principalities of Sophene, Sophanene, and Ingilene-Anzitene were later referred to collectively as the "five satrapies" (see Proc. *Aed.* 3.1.17: σατράπαι... πέντε; cf. Toumanoff 1963, 131–33; Hewsen 1992, 18). If Valens was indeed the first to gain suzerainty over Asthianene and Belabitene, he may have been looking for the rhetorical kudos to be gained by having reestablished "five trans-Tigritane principalities", the same number won in the treaty of 299.

cessions. Valens received the Suren graciously but sent him back with the same message: the Romans were unwilling to negotiate and would launch a tripartite invasion of Persia the following spring, 377. For this purpose, Valens was already mustering a huge army and assembling auxiliaries from the Goths who had entered Thrace that autumn.[165] Given that this was the first time that Valens had had the strategic potential to seize back the Mesopotamian territory lost in 363, and given that he jumped at the opportunity, we can assume that he had been intent on invading Persia and restoring Roman territory for some time. He now had both the excuse and the military means to do so.

Shapur responded to Valens's rebuff by ordering the Suren to seize back the two territories offered to Victor and Urbicius and to harass the troops who would be sent into Iberia in the spring of 377. As Ammianus indicates, Valens never had the chance to respond.[166] News of the Gothic revolt in early 377 reached Valens sometime that spring, and he was forced to send a second embassy to Shapur, this time asking for a settlement rather than war.[167] Once again, Victor conducted the negotiations, whose outcome is not reported. While he did so, Valens withdrew the units he had stationed in Armenia and sent them west to face the Goths in early 377. Later that summer, they were defeated in two engagements in Scythia Minor.[168] The defeat of this army would necessitate Valens's own journey to Thrace the following spring. He arrived at Constantinople on May 30, 378,[169] and was killed in battle at Adrianople that August.

As we might imagine, the situation in Armenia collapsed after the withdrawal of the Roman forces in 377. The Roman nominee Varazdat, who was young and inexperienced, had been governing under the regency of Mushel Mamikonean, who had fought with the Romans at Bagawan and maintained strong Roman connections. So strong were Mushel's ties that Varazdat came to suspect that he himself stood in danger of suffering the same fate as his predecessor. He thus eventually had Mushel killed, probably some time after the withdrawal of Roman forces.[170] The power vacuum created by the

---

165. AM 30.2.5–6; cf. AM 31.6.1–2. Septimius Severus's invasion of Mesopotamia in 195 had been in three divisions, as was Severus Alexander's Parthian expedition in 232 (Dio Cass. 75.2.3; Herodian 6.5.1–2).

166. AM 30.2.7–8.

167. AM 31.7.1. Cf. Eunap. *Hist.* fr. 42 (Blockley): Βασιλεὺς δὲ ἐπειδὴ τούτων ἐπύθετο τῶν ἀδιηγήτων κακῶν, πρὸς μὲν τοὺς Πέρσας ἀναγκαίαν εἰρήνην συνθέμενος; Oros. 7.34.6: "Persae qui . . . nunc etiam Valente in fugam acto recentissimae victoriae satietatem cruda insultatione ructabant."

168. AM 31.7.1–2, 5–16, 8.9–10. The date of the Gothic revolt is confirmed at *Cons. Const.* s.a. 377; Jer. *Chron.* s.a. 377; Prosper *Chron.* 1160. *Cons. Const.* s.a. 377 also confirms the date of the first dispatch of Roman troops against the Goths in this year.

169. *Cons. Const.* s.a. 378; Soc. 4.38.1.

170. *BP* 5.35–36.

death of this *sparapet* was quickly filled by another Mamikonean, Manuel. Manuel had served under Shapur in the recent Kushan war, and his loyalty to Persia proved strong after he assumed the *sparapetut'iwn*. He eventually quarreled with Varazdat and expelled him from Armenia. While Varazdat sought refuge with Rome, Manuel began courting Persia. Together with Varazdat's wife, Zarmandukht, and his son, Arshak III, Manuel established regency over what remained of the Arsacid dynasty and allied that dynasty to Persia.[171] Shapur then sent the Suren with a 10,000-man army to garrison Armenia, much as Valens had been doing up to 377. Eventually, however, Manuel revolted even against Persia and defended Armenian independence from both powers down through the early 380s.[172]

Armenian independence was possible in a political climate where Rome was preoccupied with the Goths and the death of Shapur II in 379 and his heir Ardashir II four years later left the Sassanian house weak. Only after Manuel's death was a settlement reached between Shapur III and Theodosius in 386 by which "Armenia was divided and split into two parts like a worn-out garment."[173] Rome retained only the western fifth of the country, while Persia controlled the eastern four-fifths. After the death of Arshak III (387), Rome abolished the Arsacid monarchy and established the province of Armenia.[174] Forty years later, the Sassanids followed suit, abolishing their branch of the Arsacid monarchy in "Persarmenia" by A.D. 428. Valens was thus the last Roman emperor to regain suzerainty over an independent Armenian kingdom. Although his settlement was always tenuous and crumbled immediately after he withdrew his troops, he had restored Armenia as a Roman client state for the last time in history.

FESTUS AND EUTROPIUS: HISTORICAL PROPAGANDA AND THE EASTERN FRONTIER

As his first Gothic war dragged on into 369, Valens must have grown increasingly agitated at the state of affairs on the eastern frontier. Shapur had occupied most of the former Roman territories and fortresses in Mesopotamia; he had deposed the pro-Roman kings of Armenia and Iberia; he had imposed a new king in Iberia, dismantled the Arsacid kingship in Armenia,

---

171. *BP* 5.37. As we would expect, MX 3.41 does not mention the regency of Manuel Mamikonean; cf. Thomson 1978, 303 n. 1. Oros. 7.34.8 implies that Valens suffered a defeat at the hands of Persia, but his passage is too rhetorical to be taken seriously.

172. *BP* 5.38–39. *BP* 5.42 says that Armenian independence lasted for seven years, perhaps from Shapur II's death in 379 until the division of Armenia in 386; cf. MX 3.42.

173. Lazar P'arpec'i 1 [1]–8 [11] with reference to Matt. 9.16. Cf. *BP* 6.1. See also Seeck, *Untergang,* 69; Blockley 1987, 229–32; 1992, 42–45; Greatrex 2000; contrast Chrysos 1976, 37–40, who dates the division to 378.

174. Proc. *Bella* 2.3.25; *Aed.* 3.1.14–15; MX 3.46.

and begun eradicating Armenian Christianity. Shapur could do most of this under the authority of Jovian's 363 treaty, and even what the treaty did not officially sanction, it tacitly allowed through its ambiguities. No Roman was under any illusion but that the 363 agreement had seriously compromised Roman power in the east and weakened Roman claims to world dominion. Once Valens brought his Gothic war to a close in late summer 369, he began making preparations for a strategic response to this new shift. Along with mustering troops and arranging supplies, Valens took care to establish the ideological framework for his challenge to Shapur's new claims. This he did with the help of two successive *magistri memoriae,* Eutropius and Festus, whom he set to the task of composing separate abbreviated accounts of Roman history. A close examination of their *breviaria* gives some idea of how Valens hoped to use the power of historical discourse to his advantage as he undertook his attack on Shapur's position.

Fortunately, we are able to date both *breviaria* with great precision. Since Eutropius accords Valens the epithet *Gothicus Maximus* in his preface, he must have finished his work after Valens claimed that title in late summer 369.[175] In the same preface, Eutropius refers to himself as *magister memoriae,* a post that he ceased to hold in early 370. He must then have written shortly after the close of the first Gothic war.[176] Festus succeeded Eutropius as *magister memoriae* in the period after Valens's arrival in Antioch in spring 370.[177] One of the oldest and best manuscripts of his *breviarium* indicates that he too was serving in this office when he dedicated his work. Since he held the post down to 372, he cannot have written later than this date,[178] and Mommsen noticed that it is possible to offer even greater precision. The provincial lists cataloged in Festus omit the British province of Valentia, newly created and named after Valens himself in late 369. Festus must then have written before news of this had reached the east.[179] If so, both *breviaria* can be dated around the period when Valens was preparing to confront Shapur directly in early 370.

175. Eutr. *praef.* To judge from his detailed knowledge of Thrace and the Gothic confederation (*Brev.* 8.2, 9.15), Eutropius was with Valens during the Gothic war; cf. Bird 1986, 12; 1993, xiii. On the career of Eutropius, see *PLRE* I, Eutropius 2; cf. Herzog-Schmidt 1989, 202–3, with recent bibliography, esp. Bonamente 1977, on the authenticity of the dedicatory preface, and Bird 1993, vii–xviii.

176. Bird 1993, xiii–xiv, suggests that the *Breviarium* was composed for Valens in celebration of a triumph over the Goths in Constantinople in winter 369/70. This seems likely given Eutropius's obsession with triumphs (see p. 000).

177. On Festus's identity and career, see *PLRE* I, Festus 2; cf. Eadie 1967, 1–9; Herzog-Schmidt 1989, 207–8, with bibliography, esp. the caveats at Boer 1972, 178–83.

178. MS B: "Incipit breviarium Festi vc magistri memoriae." Baldwin's 1978, 197–99, caveat that only this MS refers to Festus as *magister memoriae* was already sufficiently anticipated at Eadie 1967, 6. On the dedication to Valens rather than Valentinian, see Eadie 1967, 3, 22–23.

179. Mommsen 1862, 587, accepted at Eadie 1967, 1. Contrast Boer 1972, 198, who (oddly) believes Festus omitted Valentia because he was assembling his provincial list from memory. Tom-

Abbreviated histories were very much a fourth-century vogue. They appeared sometimes as epitomes of earlier histories, sometimes as abbreviated accounts of a given period, sometimes as short biographies or lists of exempla.[180] At least two other epitomes dedicated to fourth-century emperors survive, and one of these bears striking resemblances to the *breviaria* of Eutropius and Festus. The concise biography of Alexander and Trajan known to us under the misleading title *Itinerarium Alexandri* was dedicated to Constantius II. It was written for the eastern Augustus in the early part of his reign, probably in 340, by the well-connected courtier Flavius Polemius.[181] Constantius was preparing a Persian invasion for that year, and Polemius openly states that his *Itinerarium* was designed to serve as an incitement to Constantius as he set out.[182] It survives in a single manuscript, which breaks off before the narrative on Trajan has begun,[183] but the extant text, with its hortatory introduction, its information on strategy and battle sites, and its choice of Alexander and Trajan as exempla of successful invaders of Persia, leaves no doubt about the intentions of its author. He was using history and historicizing rhetoric to influence the events of his own day.

Festus and Eutropius did much the same, although they differ from one another in the degree of emphasis they place on the east. Eutropius devotes great attention to the importance of military activity and territorial expansion throughout Roman history. He is especially careful to catalog affairs on the eastern frontier, but his decision to treat periods even before Roman expansion eastward makes it more difficult to identify a geographical center of gravity for his work. Perhaps for this reason, within months after Eutropius had completed his *breviarium*, Valens set Festus to compose a *breviarium de breviario*, which kept a much narrower focus on the east.[184] Festus organized his history geographically rather than chronologically. Unlike Eutropius, he did not begin "from the foundation of the city" and was thus able to gloss over most republican history before Rome's first encounters with Parthia.

---

lin 1974 tried to redate Theodosius's renaming of Valentia to 368, but Salway 1981, 382, still accepts 369.

180. Momigliano 1963; Eadie 1967, 10–20; Herzog-Schmidt 1989, 173–75; Chauvot 1998, 207–19.

181. *It. Alex.* 1, 4. On the date, see Barnes 1985a, 135. On the authorship, see Lane Fox 1997, 240–47. I use the critical edition of Tabacco 1992, 112–51, for sections 1–23 and the *editio princeps* of Mai 1817 for the remainder. For bibliography, see Herzog-Schmidt 1989, 214–15 and Lane Fox 1997, 239 n. 1.

182. *It. Alex.* 3: "scilicet ut incentivum virtutibus tuis."

183. Milan, Ambros. P 49 sup., fols. 54v–64v.

184. The incipit: "Breviarium Festi de breviario rerum gestarum populi romani" is found in MSS E B P. Momigliano 1963, 85–86, had suggested—perhaps half in jest—that Valens felt Eutropius's brief history remained too long and commissioned Festus to abbreviate it further. To the similar conclusion of Eadie 1967, 14–16, see the review of Cameron 1969. On this question, see also Boer 1972, 173–6; Bird 1986, 18–20; 1993, xxiv.

He divided his narrative into three parts, set off by programmatic lemmata. These begin with a survey of Rome's acquisition of provincial territories west of the Hellespont (4–9) and then move, with much greater emphasis, to the acquisition of eastern territories (10–14). This second part is introduced: "In obedience to your command, I shall now explicate the eastern territories and the entire Orient and the provinces placed under the neighboring sun in order that the zeal displayed by your clemency for the propagation of those same may be incited all the more" (10). A similarly revealing programmatic passage introduces the third and longest part (15–29), which enumerates the conflicts between Rome and Persia down to Festus's own day.[185] Thus more than two-thirds of Festus's *breviarium* is devoted to the eastern empire, most of it to Romano-Persian military history. Lest there be any doubt as to his purpose in assembling this information, Festus closes with a valedictory wishing Valens a Persian victory to match his recent Gothic success.[186] In both *breviaria*, then, and particularly in that of Festus, the purpose is beyond doubt: to employ historical discourse as a practical instrument to prepare for and justify a war against Persia.[187]

On the simplest level, this implied cataloging the essentials of warfare. Thus, Festus and Eutropius, like Polemius before them, offer statistics on troop strength and casualty figures in previous engagements.[188] Much more important than practical concerns, however, were ideological issues. Late Romans were obsessed with the growth of their empire, both as a historical fact and as a contemporary desideratum. Imperial panegyrics gush with the rhetoric of conquest, forever encouraging emperors to extend the *limites* or praising them for doing so.[189] Festus and Eutropius were also active participants in this discourse. With Festus, this is obvious in the schematic outline he offers of the growth of the empire. He prefaces this with an overview of "how much Rome expanded *[quantum Roma profecerit]*" under each of three "types of rule": kings, consuls, and emperors (3). He then proceeds to offer

185. Festus 15: "Scio nunc, inclyte princeps, quo tua pergat intentio. Requiris profecto, quotiens Babyloniae ac Romanorum arma conlata sint et quibus vicibus sagittis pila contenderint."
186. Festus 30: "ut ad hanc ingentem de Gothis etiam Babyloniae tibi palma pacis accedat."
187. Both Festus and Eutropius openly state that they were writing at Valens's request (Eutr. *praef.*: "ex voluntate manseutudinis tuae." Festus 1: "clementia tua praecepit; parebo libens praecepto"; cf. 10, 15, 30). Previous scholars have placed too much emphasis on the personal role of these authors in actively directing Valens's eastern policy (see, e.g., Peachin 1985, 159; Bird 1986; 1993, xx). In fact, Valens must have known what his stance toward Persia would be before he ever set his *magistri memoriae* to work. Their *breviaria* are not reflections of their personal opinions, but rather historical justifications for Valens's intended eastern campaigns.
188. Festus 6, 12, 16, 25. Eutr. 2.5, 6, 9, 13, 14, 20, 21, 24, 27, 28, 3.8, 13, 16, 20, 4.4, 6, 5.1, 6, 6.8, 12, 20, 9.22. *It. Alex.* 17, 56, 59, 80–81, 95–96. Cf. Boer 1972, 142–45.
189. See pp. 143–45. On the rhetoric of expansion earlier in the empire, see Campbell 1984, 394–401.

region-by-region summaries describing, "in what order the Roman state acquired its individual provinces."[190] These summaries culminate in precisely the territories in Armenia and Mesopotamia whose control Valens wished to dispute.

In the second half of his narrative, Festus follows a similarly schematic pattern, in which Roman territorial compromises are always followed by new conquests. Nero loses Armenia to the Persians, but Trajan regains it and forms new provinces (20). Hadrian abandons Trajan's eastern provinces, but Severus creates them anew (20–21). Gallienus allows Mesopotamia to lapse, but Galerius and Diocletian regain it (23, 25). This cycle of loss and reconquest concludes with Jovian's loss of Nisibis and Mesopotamia (29). By the pattern of history established in Festus, it fell to Valens to restore these territories.[191] Themistius confirms that the emperor intended to do so in an oration of 368, where he names the reacquisition of Mesopotamia at the head of a wish list that includes the Gothic and Alamannic victories also anticipated by Valens and his brother.[192]

Eutropius, although less schematic, was equally concerned with Rome's expansion. His early chapters chart Rome's slow early growth as it conquered peoples twelve, then sixteen, then eighteen miles from the city.[193] With the advent of republican magistrates, Eutropius notes an increase in the pace of expansion, which continued down through Augustus (2.1). This phenomenon was particularly remarkable under Julius Caesar, who added a region that extended "in circumference up to thirty-two hundred miles" (6.17), and Augustus, who gained control of a previously unprecedented number of territories and peoples (7.9–10). Augustus's acquisitions were matched only by those of Trajan, whom Eutropius ranks above all emperors: "He extended far and wide the boundaries of the Roman Empire, which, after Augustus, had been defended rather than honorably enlarged."[194] With his Dacian

190. Festus 4: "quo ordine autem singulas provincias Romana res publica adsecuta sit." Sicily and Africa (4), Spain (5), Gaul and Britain (6), Illyria and Greece (7–8), Thrace (9), Asia Minor (10), Anatolia (11), Syria and Palestine (12), Egypt and Cyrenaica (13), Armenia and Mesopotamia (14). On the provincial lists that conclude each section, see Eadie 1967, 154–71; Boer 1972, 197–99; Peachin 1985, 159–60.

191. Eadie 1967, 153, offers the odd interpretation that Festus concluded his narrative with the 363 treaty because "there simply was nothing further to report." Bird 1986, 19, is surely right that Festus's aim was to encourage Valens to follow the examples of Trajan, Diocletian, and Julian by re-conquering this land.

192. Them. *Or.* 8.114c; cf. 11.148d–149a.

193. Eutr. 1.4, 5, 8. For further examples of Eutropius's concern with the distance of battles and conquests from Rome, see 1.15, 17, 19, 20, 2.5, 8, 12, 3.14. See also Boer 1972, 120–24.

194. Eutr. 8.2. Cf. Festus 20: "Traianus, qui post Augustum Romanae rei publicae movit lacertos, Armeniam recepit a Parthis." This metaphor is taken from Florus *praef.* 8: "[populus Romanus] sub Traiano principe movit lacertos," where it fits into a larger analogy between the human body and the empire.

province alone, Trajan added a region whose circumference was a thousand miles (8.2). Little wonder that he and Augustus were, for Eutropius, the touchstones of imperial *felicitas*.[195] They better than anyone fulfilled the most important requisite of imperial rule, expansionism.

By contrast, those rulers who failed to acquire territories, or, worse yet, those who actually lost them, were judged harshly. Tiberius was criticized for failing to campaign personally, Nero for nearly losing Britain and suffering setbacks in Armenia, and Gallienus for allowing Dacia to lapse.[196] Worst of all, Hadrian actually chose to abandon Trajan's new provinces of Assyria, Mesopotamia, and Armenia and wanted to desert Dacia as well, out of envy for Trajan (8.6). This shameful retreat was matched only by that engineered under Valens's predecessor: "[Jovian] made what was, in fact, a necessary but shameful peace *[pax ignobilis]* with Shapur, for he was punished territorially and surrendered a certain portion of the Roman Empire. Before his time, this had never happened in practically one thousand and eighteen years since the Roman Empire had been founded."[197] The claim that Jovian's withdrawal was unique in Roman history is contradictory, given that Eutropius has just described Hadrian's abandonment of the same territories and Aurelian's official renunciation of Dacia.[198] Precisely because of its tenuousness, however, Eutropius's claim draws attention to itself as a crucial element in the rhetoric of his *breviarium*. In fact, the claim probably represented the official position of Valens's administration, which is also why Festus repeated it in his own *breviarium*, and Ammianus and Eunapius later took it up as well.[199] Eutropius's "official" version thus became normative for viewing the abandonment of Nisibis and the five trans-Tigritane territories. Placed under his spotlight, the event glared back as an egre-

---

195. As Eutropius 8.5 notes, later emperors were praised as "Felicior Augusto, melior Traiano!" Cf. Aurelius Victor's relative lack of interest in territorial expansion, which he mentions only five times in *De Caesaribus* (1.2, 2.3, 13.3, 20.15–16, 39.37) and the same relative lack of interest at *Epit.* 1.7, 2.9, 5.4, 9.13, 11.2, 48.5. See Bird 1984, 41–59, on Aurelius Victor's general lack of interest in *militaria*.

196. On Tiberius, see Eutr. 7.11. On Nero, see Eutr. 7.14; cf. Festus 20: "amisit Armeniam." On Gallienus, see Eutr. 9.8; Festus 23. On the shamefulness of abandoning territory, see AM 25.9.3; cf. Potter 1990, 12–13.

197. Eutr. 10.17.

198. Eutr. 8.6, 9.15. On Hadrian, see Festus 20. On Dacia, see Festus 8, with Boer 1972, 201–3. Eutropius certainly accompanied Julian's expedition and must have been with the army when Nisibis was evacuated (Eutr. 10.16; cf. Bird 1993, x–xi; xxii). This helps explain his dismay at the treaty, but not his mendacity about its uniqueness.

199. Festus 29: "condicionibus (quod numquam antea accidit) dispendiosis Romanae rei publicae inpositis." AM 25.9.9–11. Cf. Bird 1993, 163 n. 36–7; Matthews 1989, 187. Zosimus (3.32.1–6) must derive from Eunapius, *pace* Paschoud 2.1: 221–23 n. 93 and 1975, 184–206. Similar rhetoric on the unjust loss of territory in 363 can be found at Them. *Or.* 8.119c.

giously disgraceful blemish in Roman history: the treaty was unique and therefore unacceptable.

Hand in hand with the ideology of expansionism goes the ideal of triumphal rulership. Both Festus and particularly Eutropius were obsessed with this as well.[200] Given that military victories constitute high points in history, they feature in all *breviaria*, but Eutropius lists no fewer than sixty-one. Nor was he content simply to relate victories in battle. Rather, he carefully catalogs actual triumphal processions,[201] making special note of years with multiple triumphs, triumphs over new peoples, or significant features in triumphal processions.[202] This obsession partly reflects the fact that Valens had just celebrated a Gothic triumph of his own, but it also betrays an assumption that successful rule can be equated with success in battle.

Nor was military success anywhere more glorious than in the east. Eutropius noted this when he called attention to the simultaneous triumphs of Marcus and Lucius Lucullus over Thrace and Pontus/Armenia respectively. The latter, he says, won greater glory for having conquered such powerful kingdoms (6.10). Indeed, all emperors must have regarded an eastern victory as the apex of success; Alexander the Great had paved a path to glory that every emperor yearned to follow. Some actually did so in a self-conscious, at times even maniacal, fashion. Caracalla was fortunately murdered before he could finish acting out his Alexander fantasy, and Julian's more sober, although equally dangerous, Persian invasion was similarly tinged with *imitatio Alexandri*.[203] Even more temperate sorts found the example of Alexander a powerful stimulus. With his *Itinerarium Alexandri*, Polemius kindled Constantius's ambitions with direct comparisons between Alexander and his dedicatee and directly encouraged the emperor to subjugate all of Persia.[204] So too, Festus and Eutropius used the examples of

200. Boer 1972, 147, 159, 164–66, 203–4. For triumphs in Festus, see 21, 22, 25. On triumphal rulership in late antiquity, see McCormick 1986; Straub 1939, 7–75.

201. Eutr. 1.6, 11, 20, 2.1 (three), 2, 5, 9, 14 (two), 16, 17, 18, 19, 20, 24, 3.2, 3, 4, 5, 6, 23, 4.2, 4, 5, 8, 14 (three), 19 (two), 22, 23, 25 (two), 27 (two), 5.9 (two), 6.2, 3, 5 (four), 10 (two), 15 (three), 7.5, 13, 20, 23 (three), 8.9, 13, 9.27. Cf. Florus, whose much fuller narrative uses *triumphus* and its cognates much more sparingly and much more loosely as an equivalent to "victory in battle." He uses the word to refer to triumphal processions only nine times (1.13.26, 18.9–10, 28.12, 30.5, 34.17, 36.17, 38.10, 2.10.9, 13.88–89); cf. Fele 1975, 685–86.

202. For multiple triumphs, see Eutr. 2.1, 4.14, 19, 25, 27, 5.9, 6.5, 10, 15. For triumphal firsts, see 1.6, 2.9, 14, 3.4, 7.5. For special features, see 3.23, 4.4, 8. He also catalogs generals who won important triumphal titles; see 3.23, 4.4, 6.3, 8.18.

203. On Julian's *imitatio Alexandri*, see Lane Fox 1997, 247–52, with bibliography. On *imitatio Alexandri* more broadly, see Heuss 1954, esp. 99–101; Wirth 1975, 200–209; Meyer 1980, 414–17; Campbell 1984, 391–93; Potter 1990, 372.

204. *It. Alex.* 1, 5, 8–11. Julian also claimed to desire the total conquest of Persia; see Ephrem *CJ* 2.15; Lib. *Ep.* 1402; *Or.* 12.100, 15.2, 18.1, 282.

those successful in the east to incite Valens. Festus offers a catalog of the campaigns of succeeding commanders and emperors in which he judges leaders based almost exclusively on their performance in the Orient.[205] Similarly, Eutropius carefully lists all of the major figures who fought on the eastern frontier,[206] laying particular emphasis on Trajan's successes, to which he devotes an unparalleled number of chapters.[207] Here, Eutropius, like the author of the *Itinerarium Alexandri,* makes a conscious effort to draw attention to the similarity between his patron and his great imperial predecessor. By setting Trajan's Dacian campaigns "in those territories which the Taifali, Victoali and Tervingi now hold," Eutropius emphasizes how Valens's recent victory in the former Dacia mirrored Trajan's own successes there.[208] By extension, it implies the expectation of similar successes in the east to follow those of Trajan.

Most important, Festus and Eutropius provided Valens with practical guides to Rome's historical claims to the territories of the east. With the rise of the Sassanians in the early third century, the Romans came to face an empire that based its aggressive stance toward Rome at least partly on the privileges of the past. From the beginning, Ardashir I seems to have claimed links with the Achaemenid Persians, whose empire had once stretched as far west

205. Lucullus 15; Pompey 16; Crassus 17; Ventidius Bassus and Marcus Antonius 18; Augustus 19; Nero and Trajan 20; Lucius Verus, Septimius Severus, and Caracalla 21; Severus Alexander, Gordian III 22; Valerian, Gallienus 23; Aurelian, Carus 24; Diocletian, Galerius 25; Constantine 26 (planned); Constantius 27; Julian 28; Jovian 29.

206. Lucullus 6.9–10; Pompey 6.12–14; Crassus 6.18; Ventidius Bassus 7.5; Mark Antony 7.6; Augustus 7.9; Trajan 8.3; Lucius Verus 8.9; Septimius Severus 8.18; Caracalla 8.20; Severus Alexander 8.23; Gordian III 9.2; Valerian 9.7; Aurelian 9.13; Carus 9.18; Diocletian, Galerius 9.25; Constantine 10.8 (planned); Constantius 10.10; Julian 10.16; Jovian 10.17. Ammianus (23.5.16–18) portrays Julian as offering a similar catalog of eastern commanders in his harangue to the troops before the Persian invasion of 363 (Lucullus, Pompey, Ventidius / Mark Antony, Trajan, Lucius Verus, Septimius Severus, Gordian III); cf. Jul. *Or.* 1.17d–18a.

207. Eutr. 8.2–5. See also Boer 1972, 149; cf. 199 and 205 on Festus and Trajan. Lightfoot 1990, 121–25, offers interesting insights on the glorification of Trajan's Persian achievements during the fourth century; cf. Syme 1971, 91–112. Eutropius also devotes considerable attention to Aurelian (9.13–15), the restorer of Roman prestige in the east, whose accomplishments (Gothic victory, monetary reform, fortification) also mirror Valens's own.

208. Eutr. 8.2; cf. Bird 1986, 13–14, and 1993, xxi. A comparison is perhaps also implied at Festus 26 between Valens and Constantine, who set out for the east: "recenti de Gothis victoria gloriosior." Eutropius also notes instances where brothers campaigned simultaneously and triumphed in unison (4.4, 4.25, 6.10). The parallel he draws to Marcus Aurelius and Lucius Verus is picked up by Festus 21, who further develops the theme: "Antonini duo . . . *pariter Augusti, imperium orbis aequata primum potestate tenuerunt. Sed ex his* Antonius *iunior* ad expeditionem Parthicam profectus est; . . . ingenti gloria de Persis cum socero triumphavit." See also Eutr. 8.10: "cum fratre eodem socero triumphavit." The clear reference to the equality of the brother Augusti and to the necessity for the *iunior* colleague to campaign in the east were probably meant to reflect Valens's own situation. For the theme of return to the days of Trajan, Marcus, and Antoninus under the Valentiniani, see Them. *Or.* 13.166b.

as the Aegean and even up to the river Strymon in Macedonia.[209] Either he or his son, Shapur I, also began to argue that their Achaemenid background justified claims to these "ancestral" territories.[210] A letter from Shapur II to Constantius that Ammianus preserves confirms that the claim remained very much a bone of diplomatic contention in Valens's own day.[211] Indeed, it probably colored the demands of Shapur II when he oversaw the rearrangement of the eastern frontier in 363. In the face of this historically determined justification for Sassanian aggression, Valens must certainly have understood the importance of historical discourse for his own ambitions.

Here Festus in particular would have been useful in helping Valens make his case. We have seen that his account offers a schematic outline of Rome's eastern acquisitions. This overview (10–14) emphasizes the legal rights Rome had obtained through inheritance, conquest or the requests of indigenous peoples for Roman annexation.[212] Armed with this information, Valens could promote the empire's legal rights to territories that Shapur argued should be his. Of course, the ideal and the reality of Shapur's claims were far from compatible. Although his letter to Constantius promotes an ancestral right to all of Asia, he had little practical expectation of actually winning this land. Thus, despite its rhetoric, Shapur's letter, in fact, demands only the return of the territories on the Sassanian border surrendered by Persia under his grandfather in 299.[213]

These territories, upper Mesopotamia and Armenia, are treated in particular detail in Festus's fourteenth chapter. To summarize his summary: Lucullus first conquered Armenia and the city of Nisibis,[214] although he soon lost both; Armenia was later won back by Pompey, along with the territories of Syria and Phoenice. Trajan won Armenia, Mesopotamia, and Assyria and first extended the "eastern frontier beyond the banks of the Tigris [*limes orientalis supra ripas Tigridis*]"; although these were ceded by Hadrian, Mesopotamia at least remained an object of dispute; it was won and lost again four times until Diocletian (read Galerius) defeated the Persians, established suze-

209. Tabari 814 (p. 3 Bosworth); cf. Christensen 1944, 59–62, and Jul. *Epistulae, leges, poemata, fragmenta varia* 205 (Shapur II as a descendant of Darius).

210. Dio Cass. 80.4.1; Herodian 6.2.1–2, 4.4–5. The origins of the Sassanian demand for the return of Achaemenid lands are much debated. Winter 1988, 26–44; Frendo 1992; and Lee 1993, 21–22, argue for an early origin for the Sassanian claims to Achaemenid ancestry and territory. *Contra* Kettenhofen 1984; Potter 1990, 370–80.

211. AM 17.5.3–8. Ammianus tells us that he does not reproduce the letter verbatim but follows its sense. There is every reason to believe he had at his disposal a copy of the actual missive; cf. Christensen 1944, 237–8; Jonge 1977, 133–34; Matthews 1989, 39–40 n. 2.

212. Inheritance: 10 Asia; 11 Bithynia; 13 Libya. Conquest: 10 Syria, Lydia, Caria, Hellespont, Phrygia; 11 Pamphylia, Lycia, Pisidia, Pontus; 12 Syria, Cilicia, Isauria; 13 Egypt; 14 Syria, Phoenice, Arabes et Iudaei. Request: 10 Rhodes; 11 Galatia; 13 Cyprus.

213. AM 17.5.6; cf. 5.11, 14.1; Lib. *Ep.* 331; *Or.* 59.71.

214. Eutr. 6.9 also notes Lucullus's capture of Nisibis.

rainty over the five trans-Tigritane territories, and restored the "frontier beyond the banks of the Tigris *[limes supra ripas Tigridis]*"; this peace had lasted
down to the time of Constantius II.[215] To drive home the point, Festus develops this synopsis even more fully in the second half of his history. Such
an overview must have been invaluable to an emperor facing a Persian dynasty that pressed its own territorial ambitions under the guise of historical
right. By providing Valens with a blueprint of Rome's historical claims to upper Mesopotamia, Festus was justifying and reinforcing those claims.

Both Eutropius and Festus also note the origin of Rome's right to crown
the client kings of Armenia, Iberia, Panticapaeum, and the Albani and Arabs.
The knowledge that Rome's suzerainty over these client kingdoms stretched
back to Pompey must also have been useful to Valens, who eventually chose
to transgress the 363 treaty in these kingdoms of the sub-Caucasus.[216] By the
same token, Festus and Eutropius make no mention of Philip the Arab's treaty
of 244, which had ceded the right to crown the Armenian king to Persia.
Other sources confirm Rome's loss of Armenian suzerainty in the years after 244, but Festus and Eutropius omit the treaty altogether.[217] If their omission was deliberate, it must have represented an attempt to present Valens
with a stronger "historical" claim than history actually allowed.[218]

Eutropius goes even further in shaping history to meet the exigencies of
Valens's frontier policy. Not only was he obsessed with triumphs, but he offers a good deal of information on treaties as well. He mentions a total of
fourteen treaty negotiations, often with explicit details of terms and obligations.[219] Once again, this was certainly conditioned in part by Valens's recent treaty with the Goths, for which comparanda might have been useful.
Nevertheless, in his presentation, Eutropius gave special emphasis to Rome's
stubborn insistence on obtaining favorable terms and its staunch refusal to

215. Festus 14; cf. 25.
216. Festus 16; cf. 14. Eutr. 6.13–14; cf. 8.3. At Festus 19, Pompey's settlement of the east
after the Mithridatic war is again cited as the basis of Rome's eastern claim in the context of
Gaius Caesar's diplomatic exchange with the Parthians in A.D. 1 ("ex instituto Pompei"). On
the importance of Pompey in Festus's narrative, see Boer 1972, 206–7. Similar historical arguments were already at play in the late first century A.D. (Tac. *Ann.* 13.34, 15.13–14).
217. Rome seems to have reached a nonintervention pact respecting Armenia in 244, but
it was not until 252–53 that Shapur I actually invaded and imposed his son as king of Armenia.
See most recently Winter 1988, 80–123, with full bibliography, and Potter 1990, 221–25. Most
of the literary and epigraphical sources are collected at Dodgeon and Lieu 1991, 45–47.
218. Rather than focus on the empire's losses under the treaty terms of 244, Festus 23 and
Eutr. 9.10–11 shift the emphasis to Shapur's successful invasions of the Roman frontier under
Gallienus, which Festus asserts represented Persia's *first* effort to lay claim to Mesopotamia. Even
here, both historians are quick to point out that Shapur I's efforts in the 250s and 260s were
forestalled by the counterstrikes of the Palmyrenes.
219. Eutr. 2.9, 12–13, 27, 3.21–22, 4.2, 4, 7, 17, 5.7, 6.13, 7.9, 10.7, 17. Eutropius does
not mention the terms of the 299 treaty with Persia.

ratify treaties that were unacceptable. Thus the Romans had refused Pyrrhus's first peace offer in 280 B.C. because he would not evacuate Italy, and Scipio went to war with Hannibal in 202 B.C. when the latter balked at the peace terms offered by Rome.[220] After the disaster at the Caudine Forks in 321 B.C., the Senate had refused to ratify the treaty terms agreed to by T. Veturius and Sp. Postumius, choosing instead to take the war back to the Samnites.[221] When Calpurnius Bestia made an outrageous treaty *(pax flagitiosissima)* with the Numidians in 111 B.C., the Senate had rejected it outright and waged war on Jugurtha. So, too, after the Numantines had defeated Q. Pompeius and forced a shameful treaty on him *(pax ignobilis)* and later worsted C. Hostilius Mancinus and imposed the same on him *(pax infamis)*, the Senate had once again refused to ratify their agreements and made war on Numantia in 133 B.C.[222] It is precisely these exempla that Eutropius later cites when he condemns the latest *pax ignobilis*, Jovian's 363 treaty.[223] He thus sets up a scenario in which it is acceptable to refuse obedience to treaty terms when these are reprehensible. By his logic, not only would Valens be justified in refusing to abide by Jovian's treaty; in keeping with the precedents of Roman history, he was obliged to break it.

Eutropius and Festus were thus engaging in a historical discourse with very real political and military implications. Writing for Valens in precisely the period when his policy was shifting from passivity to aggression, both helped to promote that policy with the rhetoric of aggression, expansion, and realpolitik. Both concentrated heavily on the eastern frontier, whose history they schematized as an ongoing struggle by Rome to retain its just claims to territorial control established in 66 B.C. Both vaunted the glories of imperial expansion and derided past rulers who had allowed subject territories to lapse. And both—but especially Eutropius—emphasized that integral to Rome's history was a stubborn refusal to accept any treaty that—because of its concessions—was a priori unacceptable. When Valens undertook his war against Shapur in 370, then, he had in his arsenal a powerful weapon in the

220. Eutr. 2.12–13, 3.22; cf. 5.7.

221. Eutr. 2.9: "pax tamen a senatu et populo soluta est quae cum ipsis *propter necessitatem* facta fuerat." Cf. Eutr. 10.17: "pacem . . . *necessariam* quidem."

222. Eutr. 4.17, 26.

223. Eutr. 10.17: "nam et Samnitibus et Numantinis et Numidis confestim bella inlata sunt neque pax rata fuit." AM 25.9.11 cites exactly the same examples in making the same argument. Matthews 1989, 187, points out that the constitutional situations were totally different between these republican treaties—which were negotiated by a field commander and could later be ratified or rejected by the Senate—and Jovian's treaty—for which the emperor was solely responsible. This misses the point: Eutropius's and Ammianus's case for dissolution is all the more pointed because of the weakness of the comparison. For the rhetoric of the *pax ignobilis*, see AM 25.7.13: "quo ignobili decreto firmato"; 27.12.1: "pudendae pacis icta foedera"; cf. Zos. 3.32.4: αἰσχίστη εἰρήνη on 244.

ongoing ideological struggle between Rome and Persia over the rights to Armenia and upper Mesopotamia.

BANDITS AND BARBARIANS OF THE EAST: VALENS AND THE MARATOCUPRENI, ISAURIANS, AND SARACENS

While he was defending what remained of Roman Mesopotamia, while he was upholding Roman interests in Armenia and Iberia, while he was keeping an eye on the Danube frontier and guarding against the omnipresent threat of usurpation, Valens was faced with a number of separate and equally dangerous security issues in the east. Some of these involved peoples residing well within what we conceive of as the established "boundaries" of Roman rule; others, peoples intertwined with its fringes, neither firmly within Roman control nor completely outside it. If we are fully to understand Valens's policies on the eastern frontier, we must examine the history and causes of these conflicts between the imperial authorities and the various groups that inhabited Syria, Isauria, and Arabia.

In Roman Syria, Valens faced a security problem with a group of people who called themselves Maratocupreni and dwelt in a homonymous village near Apamea. The name Maratocupreni, from the Syriac *m'arta* (cave), implies that the bandits used the cavernous hillsides north of Apamea to shelter themselves from reprisals by civic and imperial authorities.[224] Ammianus, our best source for their activities, describes just one of their schemes: they formed a band, disguised themselves as an imperial official *(rationalis)* and his retinue, and plundered the house of a wealthy Syrian under the pretense that he had been proscribed. With this and other such plots, the Maratocupreni amassed considerable wealth, which, Ammianus says, they used to establish luxurious homes and settle their families.[225]

Ammianus's placement of the notice in his narrative indicates that these raids became particularly acute around the time of the revolt in Britain between 367 and 369. Although scholars have been reluctant to assign a firmer date to the apex of their banditry, a reference in Themistius may confirm that news of an increase in troubles reached Valens in early 368.[226] In light of this news, Valens apparently felt that the Maratocupreni had become threatening enough to require imperial intervention. Ammianus reports that they were exterminated by an *imperialis motus,* probably the movement of

---

224. For the name, see Shahid 1984a, 172 n. 127. Ibid. 172–74 offers a religious rationale for the Maratocupreni uprising, a suggestion with no basis in the sources.

225. AM 28.2.11–14. For the *rationalis [rei privatae],* see A. H. M. Jones 1964, 412–13.

226. Them. *Or.* 8.117a: σὺ δὲ ἐκ Μυσῶν Φοίνικας ἐφορᾷς καὶ ὑπεραγανακτεῖς ἀδικουμένων. Heather and Matthews 1991, 32 n. 59, suggest a reference to the Mavia revolt, but this was much later; cf. pp. 208–9. Instead, the Maratocupreni seem to be at issue (Lenski 1999a, 311 n. 19). For the raids in Britain, see P. Salway 1981, 374–93.

Valens's army into Syria in early 370. Libanius later described the executions in graphic terms: mothers with babes in arms thrust into the flames.[227] Valens apparently wanted to eliminate the problem root and branch.

Such tares are not, however, so easily extirpated. Prior to this incident, the urban centers of Syria had been unable to check the bandits on their own. Indeed, banditry had regularly presented problems in the region, even long before the arrival of Roman power in the first century B.C.[228] The rocky terrain of the limestone massif north of Apamea was ideally suited to sheltering bandits, and locals regarded raiding as an acceptable occupation. Not surprisingly, then, such raids crop up again in the fifth-century sources. They could no more be ignored than the problems with Persia, since, although smaller in scale, they were often more immediate in their impact on provincials.

A more profound security threat came from a bandit people who were much better organized and far more destructive, the Isaurians.[229] The territory of Isauria, on the southern coast of Anatolia, was home to an indigenous culture dating to Hittite times that remained remarkably resistant to assimilation by larger empires.[230] Here, as in Syria, the presence of mountains, in this case the precipitous peaks of the Taurus, provided refuge from central authorities. Indeed, the terrain of the Isaurian hinterland was so rugged that it afforded its inhabitants refuge equivalent to a giant natural fortress.[231] Even so, literary and archaeological evidence indicates that the problem of Isaurian banditry had been brought under heel in the first two centuries A.D.[232] During this period, the Isaurian elite appears to have become largely sedentarized and to have assimilated itself to the provincial elites in neighboring regions. Unfortunately for Rome, this calm was uncommon for the region and ultimately short-lived. Following Shapur I's invasion of the eastern empire in 260, an invasion that carried a Persian division into the Isaurian Taurus, the problem seems to have flared up with renewed vigor.[233] The wealth and social organization afforded by Roman rule in the region had transformed Isauria's elite into a much more powerful force.

---

227. Lib. *Or.* 48.36; cf. *Ep.* 1385.

228. Isaac 1992, 64–65; cf. 1984. On brigandage in the ancient world more generally, see Shaw 1984 and 1993.

229. Recent secondary work on Isaurian banditry can be found at Minor 1979; Shaw 1990; Lewin 1991; Lenski 1999b.

230. Houwink ten Cate 1965, 190–201; Shaw 1990. See also Er 1991 on the continuity of culture reflected in Isaurian art.

231. See SHA *Tyr. Trig.* 26.6. On topography, see Mutafian 1988, 14–20; Hild and Hellenkemper 1990, 22–29.

232. Lenski 1999b, 431–39.

233. On Shapur I's invasion of Isauria, see *RGDS* ll. 27–31, with Kettenhofen 1982, 111–20. On Isauria as a breakaway territory from the third century onward, see Rougé 1966; Lewin 1991, 172–80. Shaw 1990 contends that the Isaurian hinterland never broke away, because it was never truly controlled by the Roman state in the first place, but see Lenski 1999b; cf. Mitchell 1999.

Thus, by the fourth century, Isaurian troubles had grown to such an extent that the Romans no longer faced isolated, small-scale raids, but an organized, perhaps confederated enemy in what amounted to open warfare.[234]

Thanks again to Ammianus, we have particularly good evidence for Isaurian activities in the mid fourth century.[235] Already in the second chapter of his extant narrative, Ammianus reports a major uprising in 353 that affected territory stretching into Lycia and Pamphylia in the east and Lycaonia in the north.[236] In this revolt, the Isaurian raiders were eventually able to lay siege to the provincial capital of Seleucia, which, like other urban centers surrounding the hinterland, remained in Roman control.[237] Despite resistance from civic and limitanean garrisons stationed in the region, the highland rebels were only forced back into the mountains with the arrival of imperial field troops.[238] In 359, they broke into revolt once again and were only placated after a settlement was brokered by the inhabitants of Germanicopolis, a small city in the hinterland that apparently served as a nerve center for bandit coordination.[239]

Finally, Ammianus tells us that in the first years of Valens's reign, a third large-scale revolt broke out, which was able to gain momentum because Valens failed to send imperial troops to quash it in its early stages.[240] Eunapius reports that the situation was bad enough that Musonius, the *vicarius Asiae*, felt compelled to lead a band of lightly armed civic police (*diogmitae*) against the raiders.[241] These were, however, hardly prepared to contend with fighters as experienced as the Isaurians and were easily overwhelmed and slaughtered. Only later, when Valens sent comitatensian units into the region, were the bandits once again driven back into the highlands and forced to negotiate a peace. Shortly after this, the Isaurian governor constructed a fortified harbor at Corasium, about ten kilometers north of the mouth of the Calycadnus, apparently in anticipation of future troubles.[242] At the same time, Cilicia's governor dedicated three statues to Valentinian, Valens, and Gratian in Tarsus; similar dedicatory bases are found in Iconium and Pisidian

234. Lenski 1999b, 439–46.

235. For Isaurian revolts in Ammianus, see esp. Santos Yanguas 1977; Matthews 1989, 355–67; Hopwood 1999.

236. AM 14.2.1–20.

237. On the cities surrounding the hinterland, see Hellenkemper 1980; A. H. M. Jones 1971, 207–14; Lenski 1999a, 320–22.

238. Even imperial troops seem to have been reluctant to venture into the Taurus (AM 14.2.5–7, 19.3.1–2, 27.9.7; cf. Joh. Ant. fr. 214b5).

239. AM 19.13.1–2. The commander sent by Constantius, Bassidius Lauricius, and his subordinate? Aur. Ious[tus] built secured structures along the route through the hinterland in the wake of this uprising; cf. *ILS* 740 = *CIL* 3.6733; Bean and Mitford 1970, no. 231.

240. AM 27.9.6–7.

241. Eunap. *Hist.* fr. 43 (Blockley). On *diogmitae*, see the bibliography at Robert 1994, 91.

242. *CIG* 4430 = *OGI* 580 = *MAMA* 3: 102 n. 1, with pp. 102–7.

Antioch.[243] All were apparently offered in thanksgiving for the emperors' aid in suppressing the Isaurians, a good measure of how wide an area was affected. A number of indications date this last revolt to 367–68, which would explain Valens's tardiness in sending forces, because he was engaged with the Goths north of the Danube in 367 and would have been better able to spare troops when floods prevented his planned Danube crossing in 368.[244]

The eastern emperor could thus not ignore this major security issue festering in the southern reaches of Roman Anatolia. When the Isaurians attacked, local limitanean units—of which there were at least three—and civic police forces were unable to squelch their raids.[245] The provincials surrounding the Isaurian hinterland were thus forced to rely on imperial intervention to put down these uprisings. Moreover, once the Isaurians had been driven back into the highlands, even the imperial authorities were unable to eliminate these raiders but were forced to settle peace accords with them as if they were a foreign people.[246] Banditry had turned to war on such a scale that it transformed a part of southern Anatolia into a militarized zone that regularly diverted imperial troops and attention.

Ammianus mentions no more Isaurian uprisings after this 367–68 revolt. Zosimus, however, describes an uprising around 375, and Eunapius's fragments seem to confirm problems at this time.[247] While some have questioned the validity of these notices, independent testimony for a revolt in the second half of this year survives in some previously unnoticed passages from the letters of Basil of Caesarea.[248] Taken together, this evidence confirms that the 375 event was again more like war than simple raiding. The Isaurians apparently reached as far east as Lycia and as far north as central Anatolia; there they actually cut off communication routes between east and west during the winter of early 375.[249] Valens was once again compelled to send imperial mobile units, apparently under the direction of the general Saturninus, to combat the Isaurians from both the northern and southern approaches to the Taurus.[250]

243. Tarsus: *CIL* 3.13619–21; cf. *CIG* 4437. Iconium: *CIG* 3992. Pisidian Antioch: Levick 1965, 59–62 = *AE* 1965, 15.

244. Lenski 1999a, 319–20.

245. On limitanean legions, see *Not. dign. or.* 29.7–8; cf. 7.56. See also AM 14.2.14; *VM Thecla* Mir. 28. Other passages indicate the presence of other imperial units as well (AM 14.2.5, 8, 12–14, 19.13.1). On civic police forces, see Hopwood 1989; Lenski 1999a.

246. AM 27.9.7: "per indutias pacem sibi tribui poposcerunt"; cf. *VM Thecla* Mir. 19: σύνθηκαι.

247. Zos. 4.20.1–2; cf. Eunap. *Hist.* fr. 43.4 (Blockley), with Blockley 1981–83, 2: 141 n. 97.

248. *Ep.* 200, 215, 217 canons 55–57, 84, with Lenski 1999a.

249. Lycia: Zos. 4.20.1. Central Anatolia: Basil *Ep.* 215. Later Isaurian raids also closed communication routes in central Anatolia, Joh. Chrys. *Ep.* 69, 70, 135, 136 (*PG* 52.616, 647, 693–94); *VM Thecla* Mir. 16.

250. Basil *Ep.* 200 confirms that troops were sent through Iconium, north of the Taurus. *VM Thecla* Mir. 13 with Dagron 1978, 117, shows that Saturninus led comitatensian units from

As in the earlier cases, the arrival of these imperial forces seems to have settled the 375 uprising quickly, but Valens's men apparently felt compelled to remain in the region to maintain the peace and oversee the rebuilding of the road into Iconium, the northern base of operations against the Taurus.[251] The presence of these units in Isauria in precisely the year when the Persian frontier was beginning to become volatile makes Ammianus's silence about this uprising all the more puzzling. Valens was confronted with a problem that forced him to commit *comitatenses* who might otherwise have been used profitably on the Persian frontier. Since they were retained in the region down to 377, the Isaurian problem also affected troop availability when the time came to resettle the Goths in Thrace in 376.[252] This obviously sheds new light on Ammianus's testimony about the shortage of manpower to oversee the Gothic immigration. The internal security threat posed by Isauria had grown so great that it could distract Valens from his efforts against foreign powers, first Persia and then the Goths.

Similar difficulties faced Valens in yet another marginal region, the Arabian Desert.[253] Desert territory abutted the Roman provinces of Syria, Arabia, and Palestine on the east and south. Even so, eastern Syria and much of Rome's province of Arabia lay within the 200 mm p.a. isohyet, which allows for dry farming and thus settled agriculture. This permitted the Romans to continue the process of sedentarizing and urbanizing the Arab peoples, which was already well advanced when they arrived. Even just beyond the isohyet, Arab peoples regularly settled in oasis communities, the most famous of which was Palmyra, a powerful ally of Rome by the second century A.D. Because of its strategic location in the eastern desert of Syria, Palmyra was able to control not just trade routes and military operations against Persia but nomadic Arab groups as well.[254]

Indeed, despite the remarkable degree of sedentarization around the edges of the desert, pastoral transhumance remained a common way of life in the region. For centuries, pastoral nomads, the Bedouin, had been moving their herds of sheep, goats, and camels between the cultivable edges of Syria and Arabia and the deserts east and south of these. Not surprisingly, after the Romans arrived, the nomads continued to migrate in and out of provincial territory and to maintain contact with the sedentarized commu-

---

the south as well. Two funerary inscriptions from Seleucia (*CIG* 9207, 9230) may record the deaths of soldiers involved in this conflict; cf. Lenski 1999a, 316 n. 33.

251. Milestones make it clear that Valens rebuilt the road between between Colonia Archelais and Iconium after November 375 (*RRMAM* nos. 637, 639, 648–51, 655, 660).

252. Isauria's exemption from the military clothing tax in 377 (*CTh* 7.6.3) confirms that the wounds opened up in 375 were still festering two years later.

253. Recent work on the Arabian frontier has been abundant. See esp. Bowersock 1976; 1983; Isaac 1992; Millar 1993, 387–436; MacDonald 1993.

254. Matthews 1984; Millar 1993, 319–36.

nities whose territory they passed through.[255] Some degree of symbiosis between nomads and sedentarists is documented in the Roman period, but tensions always remained a feature of Romano-Arab relations.[256] After the sedentary stronghold of Palmyra was suppressed in 273, these tensions intensified as new concentrations of power coalesced around the Bedouin. Not surprisingly, at precisely this time, a new word for these nomads first comes into common usage in the Greek and Latin sources, Saracen.[257] A recent and credible hypothesis locates the root of this word in the Arabic *sirkat,* meaning precisely "confederation."[258] It would seem that, with the power vacuum created by the reduction of Palmyra, the Bedouin began to unite in broader associations that came to challenge Roman authority on the desert fringe.[259]

At the same time that the name "Saracen" comes into common currency, we also begin to see more powerful leadership structures emerge among the nomads. Bedouin tribes were ruled by sheikhs, some with thousands of followers.[260] From the late third century, however, we find evidence that these sheikhs began to unite under more powerful rulers who styled themselves kings—Arabic *malik*—and claimed hegemony over broader swaths of territory and broader groupings of tribes. Although fiercely guarding their own independence, these kings often maintained treaty relations with Rome or Persia. Our best evidence for such chiefs comes from an inscription found at Namara that records the burial in 328 of Imru al Qays, son of Amr ibn Adi.[261] We know from the Arab writer al-Tabari (838?–923) that Amr ibn Adi headed a confederation called Lakhm, which was centered around Hira in southern Persia and had been allied with the Sassanians in the third century.[262] The Namara inscription indicates, however, that by the early fourth century, the Lakhmids had moved into Roman territory and shifted their allegiance to the empire. In the inscription, Imru al-Qays boasts of being "the

255. Peters 1978; D. Graf 1989, 366–80; Villeneuve 1989, with modifications by MacDonald 1993, 311–52.

256. The nature of the nomadic menace in Arabia has been hotly debated. Cf. the views of Parker 1986; 1987; 1997; D. Graf 1989; 1997; MacDonald 1993; Millar 1993, 428–36; Isaac 1998, 444–52.

257. Bowersock 1987, 72–75.

258. D. Graf and O'Connor 1977; cf. D. Graf 1978, 10–15. Shahid 1984b, 123–41, has argued against this etymology, but see the defense offered at Bowersock 1986, 113. Further arguments at Sahas 1998.

259. Peters 1978, 324–26; Bowersock 1983, 131–37; Matthews 1989, 348–53. On Palmyra after the 270s see Pollard 2001, 298–300.

260. On sheikhs, see MacDonald 1993, 368–77. On tribes, see D. Graf 1989, 359–66.

261. The inscription was originally published by Dussaud 1902, 409–21; cf. id. 1903, 314–22. I follow here the reading at Bellamy 1985. Debate about this and other readings is ongoing. For interpretation, see esp. Sartre 1982, 136–39; Bowersock 1983, 138–42; Shahid 1984a, 31–53.

262. Tabari 822, 834 (pp. 22, 44 Bosworth).

king of the Arabs," a claim he substantiates with reports of military successes stretching from Syria deep into the Hejaz. He also reports that he "dealt gently with the nobles of the tribes, and appointed them viceroys and they became phylarchs for the Romans." The inscription thus provides evidence of central authority established under a dynasty that initiated allied relations with the Roman Empire and conducted wide-ranging military operations.

Nor were Imru al-Qays and his Lakmids unique. Ammianus refers to a *malik* whom he calls Podosacis *phylarchus* Assanitarum. The Assanitae are almost certainly the Ghassanids, the Saracen group most closely allied to Byzantium in the sixth century. In the fourth century, by contrast, Podosacis and his Ghassanids were friends of Persia. Indeed, Ammianus tells how they had earlier made many raids into Roman territory and how they harassed Julian's army during its retreat from Persia in 363.[263] In addition to Lakhm and Ghassan, confederations of Tanukh and Salih, both allied to the Romans, are reported in other sources for the period. Considerable efforts have been made to pinpoint the geographical locus of these groups and something of their political history, yet only the barest outlines have emerged.[264] What is clear, is that the Saracen nomads had coalesced into powerful confederations under strong leaders, some allied with Rome and others with Persia. Even despite their alliances with the major powers, these groups always maintained sufficient independence to pose a threat to either empire when they chose.

The threat posed by the Saracens is clear from a number of sources. Already in the late third century, a Latin panegyrist briefly alludes to a Saracen uprising around Syria that occurred in 290 and was large enough to demand the intervention of the emperor Diocletian.[265] In the years that followed, Diocletian restructured the old Arabian province by shrinking it to a more manageable size and reassigning much of its southern territory—Sinai and the Negev—to the province of Palestina III.[266] He also began construction of the massive defensive system referred to in contemporary sources as the Strata Diocletiana.[267] This fortified highway stretched from around Callinicum on the Euphrates to Azraq in the south, that is, it followed the 200 mm p.a. isohyet that marked the eastern limit of Roman territorial control along the desert. Considerable recent debate has been focused on the nature and purpose of this defensive system, but it remains reasonable to assume that it was

263. AM 24.2.4; cf. AM 25.1.3; Zos. 3.27.1. See esp. Bowersock 1980, 485; Shahid 1984a, 119–23; *contra* Sartre 1982, 139–40.

264. See Shahid 1984a, esp. 353–417, and the more digestible summaries at D. Graf 1978, 15–19; Sartre 1982, 134–53; Isaac 1992, 235–49; Millar 1993, 431–35.

265. *Pan. Lat.* 3 [11].5.4: "oppressumque captivitatis vinculis Sarracenum"; cf. 7.1. For the date and Diocletian's participation, see Barnes 1982, 51.

266. Sartre 1982, 64–75; Bowersock 1983, 144–47.

267. Parker 1986, 135–45; 1989; Millar 1993, 180–89; Konrad 1999; cf. Speidel 1977, 717–27.

aimed at hampering Saracen attacks. The construction of defensive structures across the desert frontier throughout the early fourth century indicates that further conflicts continued to occur.[268] Even where slight textual evidence of large-scale warfare can be found, then, other literary and epigraphic sources confirm a constant threat from smaller-scale raiding.[269]

Nor is direct testimony of broader conflict in the early fourth century entirely lacking, although the same evidence often indicates cooperation as well. Julian's First Oration, for example, reports serious problems around Syria ca. 337.[270] Later in the same speech, however, Julian indicates that Constantius had engaged the same Saracens in diplomacy and eventually employed them against the Persians, probably in 338.[271] By 354, the Arabs were once again attacking Roman territory, as Ammianus reports.[272] Yet in 363, Julian was met near Callinicum by a group of Saracens who offered him crown gold and joined his expeditionary forces as auxiliaries during his Persian campaign.[273] When, in the course of that campaign, Julian refused their demands for tribute, these Arab allies broke away from his army and hampered its retreat up the Tigris. Indeed, it is likely that these angry Saracens were actually responsible for killing Julian.[274] The Saracen tribes neighboring Roman territory thus acted alternately as friend and foe. They were neither entirely outside nor entirely inside Roman territory and were thus neither entirely outside nor inside the sphere of Roman authority. Instead, they constituted a powerful autonomous group allied to Rome in a tenuous relationship that at times benefited the empire and at others hurt it gravely.[275]

Most have assumed that in the immediate aftermath of Julian's failed Persian expedition, Romano-Saracen relations quickly simmered down. These have failed to take account of two letters from Libanius to Ulpianus, gover-

---

268. E.g., *AE* 1974, 661 (a. 333) with Zuckerman 1994; *AE* 1933, 171 (a. 349) and *AE* 1933, 170 (a. 351); cf. Parker 1986, 145.

269. *AE* 1948, 136 (a. 334); AM 14.4.1–3 (a. 354); cf. AM 14.8.13; *Exp. tot. mun.* 20 (a. 359); Jer. *Vita Malchi* 4 (*PL* 23.57); Nilus *Narrationes* (*PG* 79.589–693), passim, with Mayerson 1963.

270. Jul. *Or.* 1.19a; cf. 20b and Shahid 1984a, 74–100.

271. Jul. *Or.* 1.21b. The *Notitia dignitatum* indicates that by the late fourth century, several Saracen groups had also been organized into regular limitanean units; cf. *Not. dign. or.* 28.17, 32.27–28; cf. 34.22.

272. AM 14.4.1–7.

273. AM 23.3.8, 5.1; cf. AM 24.1.10; Jul. *Epistulae, leges, poemata, fragmenta varia* 98 (401d); Tabari 840–2 (pp. 59–61 Bosworth). Bowersock 1983, 142, suggests that the Lakhmids also played a role in Diocletian's and Galerius's Persian invasion of 298.

274. AM 25.6.9–10. For sources and debate on the role of the Saracen federates in Julian's death, see Bowersock 1978, 116–18; Shahid 1984a, 124–32. Persia's Saracen allies also attacked Julian's army in 363; cf. AM 24.2.4, 25.1.3, 8.1.

275. See Ammianus's assessment, 14.4.1: "Saraceni tamen nec amici nobis umquam nec hostes optandi"; cf. Josh. Styl. 79.

nor of Arabia in 364. In one of these, Libanius expresses surprise that Ulpianus has time to write on top of dealing with provincials and battling against barbarians.[276] Although the reference is vague, it probably alludes to continued tension with the Saracens in the year after they had been snubbed by and perhaps murdered Julian. Even so, at some point early in his reign, Valens must have reestablished concord. By 375, Themistius could visit the eastern frontier and report that the Scenitae—Themistius preserved the older name for the Bedouin—were at peace.[277]

Peace, of course, never meant a cessation of tensions. Many building inscriptions record the construction of forts in the region under Valens: one marks a tower at Khirbet es Samra (ca. 367/75), a second, the rebuilding of the *castellum* on the Strata Diocletiana at Deir el Keif (ca. 368/71), a third, an unspecified military installation at Dibin east of the Dead Sea (ca. 368), and a fourth, fifth, and sixth (ca. 368 and 371), the erection of *burgi* in the area around Umm el Jimal.[278] This intensive activity indicates that Valens felt the need to continue fortifying Rome's desert fringe against Saracen attacks. The *Notitia dignitatum* records the establishment of two units in the province of Palestina under Valens and two more in Arabia, further confirming Valens's defensive efforts.[279] Given that the new structures and garrisons were part of Valens's and Valentinian's larger program of frontier defense, they need not imply a response to specific conflicts.[280] Rather, they were representative of the ongoing effort to control smaller nomadic raids and protect settled populations that abutted on and even shared Saracen territory.

At some point toward the end of Valens's reign, ecclesiastical sources tell us, the king[281] of Rome's Arab allies[282] died, leaving only his wife, Mavia, to rule as queen.[283] In the aftermath of this succession crisis, a major conflict arose, which led Mavia into open war with the Romans.[284] Unfortunately, as

---

276. Lib. *Ep.* 1236: πολεμῶν δὲ τοῖς βαρβάροις; cf. *Ep.* 1127. On Ulpianus, see Sartre 1982, 104, no. 71.

277. Them. *Or.* 13.166c, not noted in previous scholarship.

278. For the inscriptions, see app. A. On the forts, see Parker 1986, 145–46; De Vries 1986; 1993; 1998, 131–47, 229–31; Kennedy and Riley 1990, 179, 183–84.

279. *Not. dign. or.* 34.35: "Ala secunda felix Valentiana, apud Praesidium"; 34.42: "Cohors secunda Gratiana, Iehibo"; 37.29: "Ala prima Valentiana, Thainatha"; 37.30: "Cohors secunda felix Valentiana, apud Adittha". Thainatha is probably not to be identified with Umm el Jimal (De Vries 1998, 36–37; *contra* Shahid 1984a, 415–16).

280. As assumed at Bowersock 1976, 223–26; Speidel 1977, 726.

281. Soz. 6.38.1: τοῦ Σαρακηνῶν βασιλέως.

282. Soc. 4.36.1: οἱ πρώην ὑπόσπονδοι; cf. Soz. 6.38.1: αἱ πρὸς τοὺς Ῥωμαίους σπονδαὶ ἐλύθησαν.

283. Soc. 4.36.1: ἡ τῶν Σαρακηνῶν βασίλισσα; Ruf. *HE* 11.6: "Saracenorum gentis regina"; cf. Theoph. a.m. 5869; Theod. Lect. *Epit.* 185.

284. The most reliable sources on Mavia's revolt are Ruf. *HE* 11.6, Soc. 4.36, and Soz. 6.38. See also Theod. *HE* 4.23; Theoph. a.m. 5869; Nicephorus Callistos *HE* 11.47 (*PG* 146.32–33);

with the Isaurian revolt of 375, Ammianus reports nothing on Mavia. Our sources for the event are entirely Christian and are consequently preoccupied with affairs related to Christianity.[285] Although we cannot deny the religious implications of this uprising, we must also be careful to look beyond them for nonreligious elements that our sources were less interested in treating.

The extent of Mavia's revolt is reported in Rufinus: "Mavia began to disturb the towns and cities of the Palestinian and Arabian frontier and at the same time to lay waste to neighboring provinces."[286] Sozomen further clarifies: "[T]hey plundered the cities of the Phoenicians and Palestinians as far as the regions of Egypt lying left of those who sail toward the source of the Nile, which are generally named Arabia."[287] The raids thus reached a vast territory stretching from the province of Phoenice in the north, through Arabia and Palestine all the way deep into the Sinai. What appears to be a contemporary account of the events, the *Relatio Ammonii*, confirms that the attacks reached as far south as Mount Sinai itself.[288] The *Relatio* records the martyrdom of forty monks who were killed there by the Saracens at some point during the exile of Bishop Peter of Alexandria,[289] that is, between 373 and 378. The Saracens had risen up, reports the *Relatio*, after the death of their phylarch,[290] almost certainly the husband of Mavia. These Saracens beset the anchorite communities around the holy mountain and killed all but a handful of monks, who held out in a tower until a firestorm scared away the raiders. The uprising was thus massive and affected a broad swath of the southeastern frontier from Phoenicia deep into the Sinai.

Mavia's uprising was also apparently quite well organized and dangerous.

Theod. Lect. *epit.* 185. For secondary work, see Bowersock 1980; Mayerson 1980b; Thelamon 1981, 123–47; Sartre 1982, 140–44; Shahid 1984a, 138–202; Rubin 1990, 182–89.

285. The agglomeration of fanciful details in later versions has led Mayerson 1980b to extreme skepticism, but Bowersock 1980, 478–83, has clarified most of the problems by establishing the source tradition.

286. Ruf. *HE* 11.6: "Mavia . . . Palaestini et Arabici limitis oppida atque urbes quatere vicinasque simul vastare provincias coepit."

287. Soz. 6.38.1. This finds confirmation in the notice at Theod. *HE* 4.23.1 and Ruf. *HE* 11.6 that the monk Moses lived on the border between Palestine and Egypt. Since Soz. 6.38.5 tells us that Moses lived in the desert near Mavia, one must assume that her activity skirted Egyptian territory.

288. The text of the *Relatio Ammonii* survives in both Greek (ed. Combefis, 1660) and Syriac (ed. and trans. Lewis, 1912). The Greek purports to be a translation from the Coptic original of Ammonius (Greek, 132; cf. Syriac, 14). The authenticity of this narrative had been questioned by Devreesse 1940, 216–20, but Mayerson 1980a and Shahid 1984a, 308–15, have both defended it. The *Relatio* also reports a simultaneous raid by a group of bandit Blemmyes on the monastic community at Raïthou, discussion of which is omitted here (cf. Mayerson 1980a, 141–48).

289. *Relatio Ammonii*, Greek, 88; Syriac, 1, 14.

290. *Relatio Ammonii*, Greek, 91: ἀποθανόντος τοῦ κρατοῦντος τὴν φυλαρχίαν; Syriac, 2: "[T]he king of the Saracens had died, he who was the guardian of the desert."

Sozomen, who offers the most detail on the events, reports that the limitanean troops stationed in the region could not handle it by themselves. The *comes* (?) of Palestine and Arabia thus had to call in the *magister equitum et peditum per Orientem* for assistance.[291] Given that Julius is attested in this latter office in 371 and again in late 378, it is likely that he is the officer to whom Sozomen refers.[292] According to Sozomen, the *magister equitum et peditum* attempted to meet the Saracens in open battle but was nearly overwhelmed. Indeed, he escaped the fray only with the aid of the commander of Palestine and Arabia, whom he had earlier ridiculed for his inability to suppress this female adversary. The defeat was so noteworthy that, according to Sozomen, the locals continued to talk of it and the Saracens to memorialize it in song into the mid fifth century.[293] Mavia's revolt was thus a major military event. It must have involved a broad Arab confederation and certainly occupied a large number of imperial units.

Indeed, if we are to believe our Christian sources, it was ultimately the Romans who felt compelled to call for peace when their efforts to defeat the Saracens by force had failed. Mavia granted this only on the condition that the Saracens receive as bishop a local holy man named Moses, who was to be consecrated by Roman authorities.[294] When Moses himself refused appointment at the hands of the Arian patriarch Lucius of Alexandria, he was taken into the desert to receive his office from bishops whom Valens had exiled. To further cement the treaty, the general Victor, himself a barbarian, took in marriage the daughter of Mavia.[295] The success of this arrangement is evident from the events that followed. In the aftermath of the peace, the Saracens willingly sent auxiliary troops with Valens to Thrace to fight against the Goths in 378.

Saracen participation in Valens's forces in 378 is confirmed not just by our ecclesiastical sources, but also by Eunapius, Zosimus, and even Ammianus, who, as noted, mentions nothing of the revolt itself.[296] Themistius too mentions Arab participation in the imperial army in Thrace as late as 382.[297] This would seem to indicate that peace prevailed among the Saracens in

291. The latter officer is clearly spelled out at Soz. 6.38.2, although the first (τὸν ἡγεμόνα τῶν ἐν Φοινίκῃ καὶ Παλαιστίνῃ στρατιωτῶν) is nowhere else attested. For speculation about his title and identity, see Shahid 1984a, 150, and Woods 1998, 328–34.

292. Demandt 1970, 704; Shahid 1984a, 151, based on *CIL* 3.88 = *ILS* 773 and AM 31.16.8; cf. Zos. 4.26.1–9.

293. Soz. 6.38.4.

294. Ruf. *HE* 11.6; Soc. 4.34.4; Soz. 6.38.5; Theod. *HE* 4.23.1.

295. Soc. 4.34.12 alone reports this. Details at Shahid 1984a, 158–69. The temptation to see this daughter in the Mavia of *AE* 1947, 193, should be resisted. Shahid 1984a, 222–27, actually identifies the dedicant as Mavia the rebel queen herself, also unlikely given the date (a. 425).

296. Soc. 5.1.4–5; Soz. 7.1.1; AM 31.16.5–6; Eunap. *Hist.* fr. 42 (Blockley); Zos. 4.22.1–3; cf. Shahid 1984a, 175–83. Woods 1996 offers an idiosyncratic reading of the incident, on which see p. 335 n. 94.

297. Them. *Or.* 34.20 (a. 384/85). This reference has not previously been noted.

the early 380s. That the Saracens of the Sinai were quiescent in this period is also confirmed by the testimony of the pilgrim Egeria, who was able to travel along the Sinai desert coastal road unmolested in 382, albeit with military escorts.[298] By 389, however, we learn from Pacatus's panegyric that Saracen resistance had once again erupted in Arabia in the recent past. Based on some references in Libanius, Irfan Shahid has dated this revolt to 383—the year after the Gothic war in Thrace ended.[299] One cannot help but wonder if the continued retention of the Saracen auxiliaries in Thrace between 378 and 382 played a role in provoking problems once these auxiliaries were returned.

Indeed, the issue of supplying auxiliary manpower to the Roman armies may have been at the root of Mavia's uprising as well. Given the absence of explicit testimony, most have avoided attempts to pinpoint a cause for Mavia's revolt. Following the ecclesiastical sources, however, Shahid argues at length that Mavia's Saracens had long been Christian, and that these broke into revolt because Valens attempted to force Arianism on them by having their choice for bishop, Moses, consecrated by the Arian patriarch Lucius.[300] This analysis has several flaws. First, there is no evidence for widespread conversion among the Saracens by this date.[301] Indeed, the ecclesiastical historians trumpet Mavia's tribesmen precisely because they were supposedly the first Saracens to become Christian. Although we do know of earlier instances of conversion by smaller groups of nomadic Arabs, we also know of many more examples from considerably later.[302] Moreover, the same sources on which Shahid bases his case make it quite clear that Mavia's Saracens converted *after* Moses' consecration, at the *end* of the revolt.[303] It is highly unlikely, then, that Nicene Christian piety led Mavia to rise up in the first place. Indeed, the treaty with Mavia that worked out the terms of conversion seems to have stipulated that Moses be consecrated under Roman authority; in the circumstances, this meant by an Arian bishop. It was Moses' own choice, not Mavia's, to refuse consecration by Lucius, and, according to the ecclesiastical sources, Moses was disturbed not by Lucius's Christological stance but by the violence the Alexandrian bishop had perpetrated against fellow Chris-

---

298. *Itin. Eg.* 1–10 (*CCSL* 175.37–51) with Rubin 1990, 177–82; cf. Hunt 1982, 58–60.

299. *Pan. Lat.* 2 [12].22.3: "Dicam a rebellibus Sarracenis poenas polluti foederis expetitas?" Cf. Shahid 1984a, 210–14.

300. Shahid 1984a, 152–8, 185–90.

301. Shahid 1984a, 143, 155, 330–45, collects the evidence for Arab bishops from episcopal lists, but he cannot prove that these were Saracen nomads (as opposed to sedentarists), let alone the Tanukhid Saracens whom he argues Mavia led. He also falls well short of proving his Arab bishops were staunchly Nicene—two were certainly Homoian. See further remarks at Bowersock 1986, 114–16.

302. The evidence is collected at Trombley 1993, 143–73.

303. Soz. 6.38.9; Theod. *HE* 4.23.5; Theod. Lect. *Epit.* 185; Theoph. a.m. 5869.

tians.[304] Mavia herself was probably even more indifferent to questions of doctrine. Rather, she favored Moses because he was himself of Saracen birth and because he had had earlier associations with her tribesmen, near whom he lived.[305] Religion was thus not so much a cause for Mavia's revolt as an element in its settlement.

I would contend, rather, that the major factor in provoking the revolt was Valens's own insistence that the Saracens send military auxiliaries with him to fight the Goths in Thrace. Here the date of Mavia's revolt is crucial. Although there has been much speculation, Glen Bowersock has rightly noted that the most reliable chronological indicator for the revolt can be found in Socrates and Sozomen, who agree that it occurred when Valens attempted to leave Antioch for Thrace to fight the Goths.[306] Bowersock assumes this means the spring of 378, since Valens's is known to have journeyed from Antioch to the west beginning around April of that year. It seems more likely, however, that the revolt began the previous winter. The conflict outlined in Sozomen must have occupied considerably more time than Bowersock allots: it began with widespread Saracen attacks all across the southeastern frontier,[307] led to two separate campaigns, one by local and the second by imperial troops, eventually demanded a diplomatic settlement, which entailed a journey to the desert to arrest Moses,[308] a second journey with Moses to Alexandria, and a third journey back into the desert for Moses' consecration, and was crowned by the marriage of Victor to Mavia's daughter. The beginnings of this sequence must have stretched back into 377, which is precisely the year when Theophanes dates the event.[309] Moreover, the *Relatio*

304. Ruf. *HE* 11.6; Soc. 4.34.6–7; Soz. 6.38.6–8.

305. Soc. 4.34.3 tells us that Moses was Σαρακηνὸς τὸ γένος and Soz. 6.38.5 that he lived in the desert near Mavia's people. He would thus have established trust with Mavia and her Saracens; cf. Theod. *HE* 4.23.1. Similar conversions of Saracen groups by local holy men are reported at Jer. *Vita Hilarionis* 25 (*PL* 23.42) and Soz. 6.38.14–16. Rubin 1990, 182–91, makes a strong case that the Moses who converted Mavia's Saracens was the same Moses who converted the sedentarized Pharanites near Raïthou in the southern Sinai (*Relatio Ammonii*, Greek, 99–101; Syriac, 4–5). Though Shahid 1984a, 186, entertains the possibility that the two Moses were identical, he refuses to see the fatal consequences of this for his argument at 142–50 that Mavia's home was in the north, in the Syrian Hauran. In fact, if Theod. *HE* 4.23.1 is correct that Moses lived near the border between Palestine and Egypt, his neighbor Mavia and her Saracens cannot have been based in Syria; cf. Sartre 1982, 142.

306. Soc. 4.36.1; Soz. 6.37.15–38.1; cf. Bowersock 1980, 485–87. Sartre 1982, 143–44 (followed by Greatrex 2000, 38 n. 20) dates the revolt to 376; Shahid 1984a, 183–84, who offers further bibliography on the question, dates it to ca. 375–78.

307. See p. 205. See also Theod. *HE* 4.23.2: μετὰ παμπόλλας συμπλοκάς; Ruf. *HE* 11.6: "cumque frequentibus bellis Romanum attrivisset exercitum."

308. The sources directly mention arrest; cf. Ruf. *HE* 11.6: "captus Moyses"; Soc. 4.36.5: συλληφθεὶς ὁ Μωυσῆς; Soz. 6.38.6: συλλαμβάνουσι τὸν Μωσῆν.

309. Theoph. a.m. 5869.

Ammonii dates the massacre of the monks of Sinai to December 28.[310] The revolt, which was probably already in full swing by the time the monasteries of the Sinai were attacked, must then have begun sometime in the winter of late 377.[311]

A date in the winter of 377/78 would be entirely in keeping with the theory that Valens provoked the uprising with demands for Saracen auxiliaries to fight in his Gothic war. Already in the summer of 377, the emperor had learned of the defeat of his advance forces in Scythia and had sent Victor to strike a peace with Persia so that he could mobilize his own army. After Victor's return, Valens probably made his first effort to move west, late in 377. As he prepared to leave, he no doubt attempted to draw on the Saracen federates, much as Constantius had done in 338 and Julian in 363. This latter long-range expedition had been extremely unsatisfactory for both sides. The anxiety of a new expedition, this time to the unfamiliar territory of Thrace, apparently provoked an uprising among a people already in turmoil after their king had died without an heir. It would be logical that Valens made his first efforts to mobilize in late 377, since he probably hoped to deal with the Goths as quickly as possible. But because of this Saracen revolt, his efforts were delayed. Indeed, as we shall see, he had probably intended a strike against the Goths much sooner than he was eventually able to muster one. Had he been able to arrive earlier, he might have hit the Goths—battered in their first major engagement in summer 377—with a blow hard enough to force an end to their uprising. Instead, he was tied down with the Saracens until the following spring.[312] The net result was the reconstitution of an expanded Gothic force and the consequent disaster at Adrianople.

We have thus seen that Valens was forced to deal with three peoples who shared environmental and cultural similarities: the Maratocupreni, Isaurians, and Saracens. All lived in marginal terrain that afforded them protection and isolation from Roman authority; all had inhabited that terrain since the arrival of Roman power in their territory; and all operated both inside and outside spheres of Roman influence. The tensions stirred up by the clash between Roman and indigenous elements in these marginal areas created an ongoing cycle of violence. Romans met indigenous violence with violence

310. There is some confusion over the date caused by the author's attempts to make the massacre in Sinai and Raïthou fall on the same day, January 14. The Sinai massacre seems, however, to have occurred "in Tybi on the second," i.e., December 28 (*Relatio Ammonii*, Greek, 95; Syriac, 14; cf. Greek, 129). Mayerson 1976; 1980a, 141–42, is led to mistaken assumptions because he notes only the last reference.

311. A fortlet erected at private expense at Moujedil in the Hauran in 377 may provide further confirmation of trouble in this year (Clermont-Ganneau 1888, 8–10).

312. Valens's false start may be reflected in the fact that Socrates mentions his departure from Antioch in three separate contexts (4.35.2–3, 36.1, 37.1).

of their own in a deadlock where neither side was capable of gaining absolute dominance. When these bandit groups were small enough and weak enough to be crushed by imperial forces, every effort was made to crush them, as with the Maratocupreni. Yet, although this response eliminated one of the organized groups disturbing Syria, it hardly ended the problem permanently, since the Syrian massif quickly sprouted new bandits where the old had been pruned back. In the case of Isauria, the fourth century witnessed the "frontierization" of an entire region. There, Valens confronted an indigenous population that was already so powerful that it could hardly be crushed, although it could be driven back into the highlands by imperial forces. By the fifth century, the Isaurians had gained enough independence to supply the empire with auxiliaries like other foreign peoples.[313] Yet even in the fourth century, they were already threatening enough to derail military operations in other regions by draining off troop strength when they chose to rise. In Valens's reign, this menace affected both his ability to deal with Persia and his efforts to resettle the Goths in Thrace. The Saracens, too, posed a threat that occupied Roman military authorities on an ongoing basis. Already in the early fourth century, they had formed fully articulated confederations, which Rome treated as autonomous federate groups. As such they were often tapped for Rome's military operations, which allowed them to increase their power and thus to grow increasingly independent of Roman authority. The force they could unleash was great enough to cripple Valens's army in the face of the Gothic revolt and help delay his arrival in Thrace until the Gothic problem had spiraled beyond his control.

313. Lenski 1999b, 437–38.

Chapter 5

Religion under the Valentiniani

VALENTINIAN, VALENS, AND THE PAGANS

It was, as we have seen, imperative that a fourth-century emperor be fierce with the enemy. It was equally imperative that he be clement with his subjects. This message reached him loud and clear in the regular rituals of panegyric, which forever shaped an emperor's understanding of the ideals created for him by his culture. In the fourth century, Libanius, Themistius, and the Latin panegyrists all stressed the importance of forgiveness and compromise, of humanity and justice.[1] As they intoned the refrain of clemency, panegyrists could not help but be aware that they were addressing the most powerful men on earth. Should an emperor have chosen to ignore their pleas and slaughter his subjects with abandon, such were the prerogatives of his power. Rarely, however, did he do so. A code of civility dictated that wanton tyranny was, in the main, avoided, in large part because the ideals the panegyrists presented were shared by the emperors themselves: panegyrical word and imperial deed could generally be made to resonate in a chorus of clemency, which ensured that most subjects were free from open persecution.[2] Nor was an emperor incapable of seeing his own advantage in adopting a lighter touch. The emperor, absolute dictator though he was, ruled by consensus, and consensus could only be maintained at the price of compromise. Thus, rulers who failed to understand the principle of clemency

---

1. See esp. Lib. *Or.* 12.85 and *Orr.* 19–23 passim; *Or.* 59.122; Them. *Or.* 1.14d–17b, 5.66d–67a, 19 passim, 34.17; cf. Menander Rhetor 2.375. For the same theme in the Latin Panegyrics, see L'Huillier 1992, 345–47. Clemency also comes through as a crucial virtue in the fourth-century epitomes, Aur. Vict. *Caes.* 10.1, 39.13–16, 41.4–5; *Epit.* 1.21, 10.3, 11.2, 13.3, 15.6, 17.3, 48.9; cf. Ratti 1996, 75–88, 99–101.

2. Nowhere is this better expressed than in Brown 1992, 3–34, 41–47.

not only violated the common code of proper conduct, they also threatened the foundations of their rule.[3]

Valens himself heard the mantra of clemency regularly, and nowhere more than from Themistius. Indeed, throughout the corpus of Themistius's political orations, the message of *philanthropia* is so common as to become a sort of platitude.[4] Already in his second speech before Valens, the Constantinopolitan orator had praised in lofty terms the emperor's clemency toward those implicated in the Procopius revolt.[5] Similar citations of Valens's compassion reverberate throughout Themistius's remaining speeches to the emperor, where they act simultaneously as laudations of and admonitions to proper conduct.[6] Valens was thus well aware of the expectation that he behave with mildness. Despite this abundance of the discourse of clemency, we can only regret the disappearance of a Themistian speech from around 375/76 that apparently took as its theme the subject of toleration toward religious dissenters. The historian Socrates had read the speech and reports something of its content, but unfortunately it has failed to reach us in the extant corpus. In the speech, Themistius urged Valens to abandon his attacks on Christians who differed with him over doctrine, arguing that "[h]e ought not to be surprised at the difference of judgment on religious questions existing among Christians. . . . God wishes to be glorified in a variety of ways in order that each person should honor his greatness more, because knowledge of him is not easily had."[7] Although the speech focused on tolerance of dissenting Christians, one can imagine that, as a pagan, Themistius hoped to encourage a tolerance of paganism as well. Indeed, he had used much the same argument eleven years earlier when he coaxed Jovian toward an edict granting freedom of worship in the aftermath of Julian's reign.[8] The same subject was no doubt on Themistius's mind when he delivered the lost address to Valens.

There was good reason for the reminder. Valens had become increasingly

---

3. Brown 1995, 27–54; cf. id. 1998.

4. See esp. Downey 1955.

5. Them. *Or.* 7.93c–d, 97c–98a, 98d–101a; see p. 112.

6. Them. *Or.* 8.106d, 11.147b–148d.

7. Soc. 4.32.1–5; cf. Soz. 6.36.6–37.1. See Downey 1957; Dagron 1968, 186–88; Vanderspoel 1995, 178–79; Ando 1996, 176–82.

8. Them. *Or.* 5.67b–70c, esp. 68c–69c. See Vanderspoel 1995, 148–52; cf. Daly 1971. For lack of a better word, I have adopted Valentinian's and Valens's terminology (*CTh* 16.2.18) in referring generically to non-Christians as "pagans." Most scholars would agree that ancient non-Christians were only beginning to develop any sense of unity in the late fourth century. Some would thus prefer to avoid the blanket designation, and thus the classification, of the varied religions and practices of the ancient world as "pagan." To be sure, the term is a Christian coinage that is both loaded and inaccurate. Yet it is no less inaccurate than the common modern coinages for the same groups—"polytheists," "traditionalists," "non-Christians." And, loaded though it is, it has the advantage of conveying at least the contemporary Christian perspective of the religious picture, precisely the perspective I hope to elucidate. For previous surveys of Valentin-

intransigent on the question of religious tolerance as his years in office passed. It was precisely in the period of Themistius's oration that he unleashed his wrath on Christians whom he perceived as heretical, and he had similarly attacked certain pagans only three or four years earlier. None of this was acceptable to those who measured Valens against the ideal of imperturbable mildness: Valens was, without question, a religious persecutor and thus earned the reputation that still plagues him to the present. He was not, however, nearly so wicked as some sources would have us believe. Because he lost the battle of Adrianople catastrophically, he became an easy target for attack by the victims of his violence. Yet, certainly in the case of the pagans, and, to a lesser extent, that of the Christians, his behavior was at least understandable in its context. Many fourth-century emperors attacked religious dissenters, but very few suffered a catastrophic fate like Valens's to prove, in the eyes of contemporaries, that they had provoked the wrath of the divine.

Ultimately, Valens's attacks on pagans were limited to a brief window in his reign when he violently suppressed an attempt on his throne by a group of theurgists who had tried to predict and even hasten the rise of his successor. A conspiracy had been formed in 371 with the object of using magic to choose or, rather, to reveal whom the gods had chosen to succeed the emperor; when the conspiracy was divulged, a massive investigation was undertaken, which resulted in a major purge of those implicated, whether directly or even circumstantially; these magic trials, conducted in Antioch and later in Asia Minor in 372 (see map 2), eventually claimed the lives of numerous eastern aristocrats, most of them pagans. Pagan contemporaries like Ammianus, however, saw an offense against clemency, rather than an attack on their own religious beliefs and practices, in Valens's ruthless suppression of the conspiracy. Although some contemporaries and many moderns have argued the opposite, I hope to demonstrate that Ammianus's viewpoint is essentially correct: while Valens may have been ruthless, he was hardly bent on the destruction of a religion.

Modern historians, and particularly F. J. Wiebe, who has treated the subject in a full-length monograph, have wanted to see in the conspiracy a putsch directed by a pro-Julianic "pagan opposition" to the Pannonian emperor.[9] Wiebe has put together an elaborate argument for the existence of a pro-Julianic faction in the east, which he believes first surfaced in the usurpa-

---

ian's and Valens's religious policies, see Heering 1927, 60–63; Nagl, "Vt.," 2198–2201; id., "Val." 2111–13, 2132–35; Stein 1959, 173–78; Soraci 1971, 123–29, 170–97; Fasolino 1976, 19–25; Demandt 1989, 114–18. For surveys devoted specifically to paganism under these emperors, see Funke 1967, 165–75; Hamblenne 1980; Rougé 1987; Matthews 1989, 204–28; Trombley 1993, 49–59; Wiebe 1995, 86–168, 224–23. For surveys devoted specifically to Christianity, see Gwatkin 1900, 228–56; Seeck, *Untergang*, 69–83; Brennecke 1988, 181–242.

9. Wiebe 1995, 86–168; cf. Haehling 1978, 68–69, 566–67.

tion of Procopius and again resurfaced in the coterie that attempted to predict Valens's successor in 371. We have already seen that the Procopius revolt can hardly be viewed as a pagan uprising, especially since Procopius was himself probably a Christian. Here I shall argue just as emphatically that the conspiracy leading to the magic trials, although more overtly pagan in character, was by no means the work of an organized, pro-Julianic pagan opposition. Rather, it was an ill-advised effort on the part of educated pagans to predict the fate of a not particularly successful emperor whom they thought unsavory. Valens's harshness in suppressing the conspiracy is in no way defensible, but from the contemporary point of view, its reprehensibility lay less in Valens's religious intolerance than in his failure to demonstrate the proper measure of moderation expected of an emperor.

To begin, it is worthwhile inquiring whether Valens and indeed Valentinian displayed any general hostility toward paganism outside of the context of the magic trials, as Wiebe has argued in order to prove that both aroused the wrath of pagan aristocrats. Such hostility would certainly have been natural in the years following the reign of Julian. For the first time since Constantine obtained sole power over the empire in 324, Christianity had been put on the defensive in the last two years of Julian's reign. While the Apostate claimed to refrain from open persecution, he happily turned a blind eye to the violence wreaked by his co-religionists on Christians, and himself succumbed to torturing and even executing several Christians under the guise of suppressing treason.[10] Dozens of martyrs and confessors have been identified from Julian's reign, including the Homoian bishop George of Alexandria and a handful of soldiers in Julian's army.[11] In the aftermath of Julian's death, we might expect the pendulum to have swung in the other direction, with Christians openly attacking pagans under imperial sanction. Instead, Jovian seems to have taken only halting steps toward punishing the more flagrant acts of anti-Christian violence perpetrated by Julian's functionaries.[12] Indeed, he retained most of those functionaries in office.[13]

We have already seen that Valentinian and Valens embarked on a more thoroughgoing purge of Julian's personnel and prosecuted numerous people with connections to Julian.[14] Even so, we have very little evidence of systematic religious attacks in the early reign of the Pannonian brothers.

10. On Julian's paganism, see Athanasiadi 1982; R. B. E. Smith 1995.

11. See Brennecke 1984, 114–57, for a full catalog; cf. Woods 1995a. Them. *Or.* 5.69b–c was himself aware of the scale of the problem: χείρους Περσῶν ἀλλήλοις ἦμεν.

12. See p. 104.

13. Eunap. *VS* 7.4.11 and Haehling 1978, 548–55. On Jovian's policies toward pagan practice, see Them. *Or.* 5.70b: καὶ ἱερὰ ἀνοίγων ἀποκλείει μαγγανευτήρια, καὶ θυσίας ἐννόμους ἀφιεὶς οὐ δίδωσιν ἄδειαν τοῖς γοητεύουσιν; cf. Lib. *Or.* 30.7; Greg. Naz. *Or.* 4.98.

14. See pp. 105–8.

On the contrary, in a constitution of 371 that permitted the ongoing practice of certain forms of divination, Valentinian openly boasted that at the beginning of his reign, he had issued general laws (*leges*) "in which the free opportunity was granted to everyone to worship that which he had conceived in his soul."[15] Ammianus, an ardent defender of pagan practice, even praised Valentinian for "remaining neutral amidst differences over religion, neither troubling anyone nor ordering him to reverence this or that. He did not bend the necks of his subjects to his own desire by threatening edicts, but left such matters undisturbed as he found them."[16] Whereas his son Gratian would renounce the pagan office of *pontifex maximus* (chief priest; literally, "chief bridge builder") in the early 380s, Valentinian ostentatiously applied that title to himself, Valens, and Gratian on the bridges he rebuilt in Rome.[17] Indeed, when the pagan senators of Rome tried to persuade Valentinian's second son, Valentinian II, to restore their altar to the goddess Victory to the Senate House in 384, they pointed out that the boy's father had left this pagan symbol untouched. The pagans of Rome wanted only "the same religious conditions that secured the empire for your deified father," the pagan senator Symmachus pointed out.[18] Valentinian had thus become an emblem of tolerance to be waved before his wavering son. [19]

It is not unreasonable to assume a similar posture from Valens. We have already seen numerous instances where the two emperors acted in lockstep on domestic and foreign policies,[20] and it would seem that similar unity prevailed in their attitudes toward pagan religion. Valens, like his brother, paid little mind to the activities of pagans in his half of the empire. Pagan temples continued to be constructed or restored under both of the Pannonian emperors,[21] pagan priests continued to be initiated into mystery cults,[22] and

15. *CTh* 9.16.9: "Testes sunt leges a me in exordio imperii mei datae, quibus unicuique, quod animo inbibisset, colendi libera facultas tributa est."

16. AM 30.9.5.

17. *ILS* 771 = *CIL* 6.1175, 31251. On Gratian's renunciation of the title *pontifex maximus*, see Cameron 1968. Note that Aus. XXI. *Gratiarum actio* 9 [42] still felt comfortable using the title of Gratian in 379.

18. Symm. *Rel.* 3.19: "eum religionum statum petimus, qui divo parenti numinis vestri servavit imperium." Note also Symmachus's comparison of Valentinian's rule to the cult of pagan deities at *Or.* 2.32.

19. Ambrose of Milan, who struggled to counter Symmachus's arguments, was reduced to offering the lame suggestion that Valentinian I might not have known of the altar's existence, *De cons. Val.* 20, 55; *Ep.* 72 [17].4.

20. See pp. 28–35 and 140–46, cf. ch. 6 passim.

21. *ILS* 4003 = *CIL* 6.102, with AM 27.9.10; *CIL* 6.754; *AE* 1933, 33.

22. *ICUR* 129 (a. 370); *CIL* 6.499 = *ILS* 4147 (a. 374); cf. Zos. 4.18.2–3. On Rome, see esp. Matthews 1973. Penella 1985 would also date the attempt at divinatory sacrifice described at Eunap. *VS* 23.4.1–9 to the 370s or 380s.

pagan ministers continued to be used by both eastern and western courts in almost equal numbers with Christians.[23] This insouciance came in for harsh criticism from Theodoret, who claimed that Valens allowed pagans free rein to perform their rites in public at Antioch.[24] Although earlier and especially later emperors allowed and even sanctioned the destruction of pagan temples in the east, we know of no temple destructions under Valens.[25] Indeed, when the pagans of Alexandria rioted and burned the much disputed basilica, or "Caesarion," there, Valens went only so far as to prosecute the leaders of the uprising without attacking the pagan community more broadly.[26] Throughout his reign, Valens also felt quite comfortable employing pagans for his most influential administrative positions: Flavius Eutolmius Tatianus, Aelius Palladius, Vindaonius Magnus, and Fortunatianus were all trusted advisors and committed pagans down to the last years of Valens's reign.[27] Indeed, such pagans proved helpful to Valens in suppressing his Nicene opponents precisely because they had few scruples about using force against Christian holy men. Like his brother, then, Valens was perfectly able to coexist with pagans and felt no need to persecute them, even when opportunity offered.

This is not to say that pagans enjoyed religious freedom in the 360s and 370s. Julian's reign aside, traditional pagan religious practices had been severely curtailed for over four decades when Valentinian and Valens came to power, and these two did little to change that. Laws against sacrifice had first been enacted under Constantine, and they continued to be upheld and even expanded under his sons Constans and Constantius II.[28] Julian had naturally rolled back anti-pagan legislation, and Jovian seems to have done little to replace it.[29] Libanius reveals, however, that Valentinian and Valens, again acting in consort, revived the ban on sacrifice, although relaxing Constantius's strictures by exempting simple offerings of incense.[30] Julian had also

23. Haehling 1978, 556–68. See Beard et al. 1998, 382–87, for the situation in Rome.

24. Theod. *HE* 4.24.2–4, 5.21.3–4; cf. Cedrenus, p. 544; Zon. 13.16; Jacob of Edessa *Chron.*, p. 300; Michael Syrus *Chron.* I, p. 294 (Chabot).

25. See Fowden 1978, esp. 62; Trombley 1993, 108–47.

26. On the burning of the Caesarion, see *Fest. ind.* 38 (July 21, 366); cf. Epiph. *Adv. haeres.* 69.2.2. See also Martin 1996, 597. Note that this was the first anniversary of the great tsunami which had devastated Alexandria; perhaps the pagans were angry with what they perceived as the cosmic consequences of the Christian possession of this much disputed structure. On pagans in Alexandria, see Haas 1997, 128–72.

27. See Haehling 1978, 73, 118–20, 144, 204–5. On Fortunatianus as a pagan, see Delmaire 1989, 57. See also Haehling 1978, 118–9, 144, on the pagan Clearchus, who was tremendously influential earlier in the reign.

28. Barnes 1981, 210–12, 246–48; Bradbury 1994; Beard et al. 1998, 1: 372–74.

29. For Julian's removal of the ban on sacrifice, see Lib. *Or.* 1.119–21. For Jovian's tolerance toward paganism, see pp. 104–5.

30. Lib. *Or.* 30.7.

reversed the laws of Constantine that confiscated temple properties on be-half of the imperial *res privata;* Valentinian and Valens reversed his reversal and reappropriated temple lands to their estates.[31] In so doing, they com-promised pagan practice no more than it had been compromised under their Christian predecessors. Rather, in keeping with their broader favoring of the status quo, they simply returned religious policies to the *status quo ante Iu-lianum.* As good Christians, both found many pagan practices distasteful, yet both had grown up in a world where pagan and Christian had generally co-existed with only low levels of tension.[32] They had little interest in disturb-ing this equilibrium and little motivation to do so.

Indeed, although the Pannonian brothers limited the practice of pagan ritual, they were never intransigent in their restrictions. Zosimus informs us that Valentinian issued a law in the first part of his reign that banned nocturnal sacrifices. In the same passage, however, Zosimus confesses that Valentinian relaxed the order when the pagan governor of Achaea, Vettius Agorius Praetextatus, insisted that it would make life unbearable for his co-religionists by inhibiting the performance of the nocturnal mystery rites that had become so important for late pagans.[33] Wiebe, however, has attempted to deny the concession to Praetextatus altogether. Using elaborate historio-graphical arguments to undermine Zosimus's testimony, he claims that Valen-tinian would never have relaxed his law on nocturnal rites.[34] Had he looked at the epigraphy of Achaea, he might have concluded otherwise. An in-scription of 364/67 on the sacred way between Athens and Eleusis—the road traversed by initiands of the nocturnal Eleusinian mysteries—offers honors to Valentinian and Valens, and a contemporary inscription from the pagan divinatory center of Delphi marks the erection of statues of the imperial pair as "benefactors."[35] Both of these cult centers lay in Praetextatus's jurisdic-tion, and both must have been expressing their gratitude for the new em-peror's decision to relax a decidedly uncomfortable rule. Valentinian was thus anything but unwilling to accommodate religious difference.

The same can be said of Valens. Indeed, here as elsewhere, Valens seems to have followed his brother both by enacting the initial law and then by re-tracting it. The only extant copy of the law survives not from Valentinian's but from Valens's court. It was issued on September 9, 364, shortly after the

31. *CTh* 5.13.3, 10.1.8.

32. On Valentinian's and Valens's distaste for paganism, see the rhetoric at *CTh* 16.1.1, 2.18. On the general air of accommodation between pagan and Christian through much of the fourth century, see Salzman 1990, passim, esp. 205–31; cf. Trombley 1993, 1–35.

33. Zos. 4.3.2–3. Constantius had already enacted such a law: *CTh* 16.10.5 (a. 353).

34. Wiebe 1995, 241–46. Similarly, Rougé 1987, 287–88.

35. For Eleusis, see *CIL* 3.572 = *IG*² II–III.5204. For Delphi, see *AE* 1949, 87: ἡ πόλις Δελφῶν τοὺς ἑαυτῆς εὐεργέτας ἀνέστησεν, with Vatin 1962, 238–41.

two emperors had parted company for their respective realms.[36] The intersection of these two pieces of evidence—Zosimus and the law—provides compelling proof that both emperors enacted the original ban. Given that both issued the same law, it would seem reasonable to assume that both also retracted it, and here again, compelling evidence is available, although Wiebe missed it too. Zosimus's testimony about Valentinian's retraction finds perfect correlation in Theodoret's claim that Valens later openly allowed the worship of Demeter and Dionysus—both mystery deities with nocturnal rites—and in Epiphanius's notice, written under Valens, that nocturnal rites for Kore continued to be celebrated in Alexandria and at Petra.[37] Valens, like his brother, was thus by no means intransigent in his restrictions on pagan practice.

Turning to the magic trials that both emperors conducted, it is thus useful to keep in mind that there is no evidence that either emperor intended to attack pagans. Both are widely reputed to have been tolerant toward non-Christians, and both employed these in their administrations. While they did reenact laws against sacrifice instituted by their Constantinian predecessors, neither launched campaigns to destroy pagan temples or initiated sweeping persecutions of pagan worshippers. Indeed, pagans and Christians seem to have coexisted quite comfortably through both of their reigns. Even when both banned nocturnal rituals, they quickly revised the order so as to accommodate traditional mystery religions. Finally, both seem to have acted in unison in this as in other areas of their administrations. We must thus be extremely cautious about seeing in their magic trials an attempt to stamp out pagan religious practices or even to eliminate a specific group of pagans.

THE MAGIC TRIALS OF ROME AND ANTIOCH

The initial ban on nocturnal sacrifice was, as the wording of Valens's 364 law reveals, primarily aimed not at mystery cults but at suppressing magic; it was designed to prevent "wicked prayers or magic preparations or funereal sacrifices."[38] What bothered the emperors was thus the specter of the occult. Indeed, the fear of magic more broadly, and of its near relative astrology, haunted both

36. *CTh* 9.16.7: "Ne quis deinceps nocturnis temporibus aut nefarias preces aut magicos apparatus aut sacrificia funesta celebrare conetur," with Pergami 1993, 76, on the intersection of this law with Zos. 4.3.2; cf. Wiebe 1995, 224–40.

37. Theod. *HE* 4.24.3; Epiph. *Adv. haer.* 51.22.9–11; cf. Haas 1997, 137–38. Recently published archaeological work has shown that the nocturnal mysteries to Demeter and Kore at Corinth also continued to be practiced throughout the reign of Valens (Bookidis and Stroud 1997, 438–39). Libanius (*Ep.* 1480) also describes his participation in Dionysiac celebrations—although not certainly mysteries—in 365.

38. See n. 36. For the connection between magic and mystery religion, see F. Graf 1997, 96–117.

emperors in the extreme.[39] We have already seen that both initiated a minor witch-hunt in 364 after falling ill when they reached Constantinople. Zosimus and Ammianus claim they feared that the followers of Julian had brought on their infirmities with magic.[40] Although they quickly relented, this initial magic scare set the tone for what was to come. Under Valentinian, a wide variety of people were executed for practicing various forms of magic. Faustinus the nephew of Valentinian's own prefect Viventius, was beheaded, for example, for killing an ass in order to mix a potion to remedy his alopecia.[41] And in the east, Valens was equally uneasy about the power of the dark arts. In 370, he issued a law threatening death to anyone caught teaching astrology, long an art associated with the occult.[42] It was sorcery and astrology, then, the mysterious and private side of ancient religion, that troubled the emperors.

Unfortunately for those whom Valens and Valentinian prosecuted, the boundaries between magic and religion were then, as they are now, far from apparent. Even the very words for magic in the ancient world—*maleficium, veneficium, goeteia, manganeia*—were only vaguely definable and crossed a semantic range that included categories moderns might distinguish as shamanism, sympathetic religion, astrology, charms, foul play, and even poisoning.[43] As understood in the fourth century, magic had connections with both science and religion and had pagan as well as Christian practitioners.[44] In distinction to traditional civic religion, though, it was very much a private form of devotion and generally involved not just entreating divine powers but actually seeking to manipulate them to achieve a desired end: love, victory, and health—but also sex, defeat, and murder. The ancients would have been equally hard-pressed to supply a strict definition of "magic," yet all agreed that its power over the divine—particularly over the lesser divinities called *daimones*—was real. Indeed, everyone, even the practitioners of magic, feared it. Ancient pagans accused others of magic as much as ancient Christians did, because it was equivalent not so much to pagan as to subversive religious activity.[45] For pagans and Christians alike, magic was any form of ritual that could usefully be denounced as illicit.[46]

39. For the connection between magic and astrology in the ancient imagination, see, e.g., Eus. *Vit. Const.* 2.4, 11; cf. F. Graf 1997, 50–57, 205–6.

40. Zos. 4.1.1–2; AM 26.4.4; cf. Them. *Or.* 6.72a–c and pp. 25 and 105.

41. AM 30.5.11; cf. Funke 1967, 172–74.

42. *CTh* 9.16.8 = *CJ* 9.18.8 (a. 370). Wiebe 1995, 247–48, misdates this law to 373. Here again, Julian had rolled back laws against astrology; see *Pan. Lat.* 3 [11].23.5; cf. Lib. *Or.* 1.119 with *CTh* 9.16.4, 6.

43. On ancient magic, see Barb 1963; Gager 1992; F. Graf 1997.

44. On Christian magic, see Meyer and Smith 1999.

45. See, e.g., Lib. *Or.* 1.98–99, 239–41, 264–65, 273, 18.132; Eunap. *VS* 7.2.1–3.

46. For the prosecution of magic, see Funke 1967; Trombley 1993, 59–72; Beard et al. 1998, 1: 232–36.

Problems first arose in Rome late in 369 when a former *vicarius* named Chilo and his wife accused three men—an organ builder, a wrestler, and a haruspex—of attempting to poison them.[47] Poison, the effects of which were not understood scientifically, had been associated with the power of magic since the introduction of Sulla's law against assassins and poisoners in 81 B.C.[48] After these charges had wafted the suspicion of magic under the nose of an emperor whose fears of the occult had been demonstrated from the earliest days of his reign, a veritable feast of accusations was soon cooked up. Valentinian's Pannonian henchman Maximinus, who had been charged with investigating the initial crime while still *praefectus annonae*, issued a report asserting that magic was rampant in Rome and was particularly entrenched among the Roman elite. Valentinian responded by establishing a commission headed by Maximinus and another Pannonian, Leo, to investigate all potentially nefarious activities, all *maleficium*, under the laws of treason.[49] Only the summer before, Valentinian had sent a law reminding the urban prefect that, in cases of treason, senatorials did not enjoy their normal exemption from torture.[50] Thus, when Ammianus implies that Valentinian was violating some sacrosanct privilege by allowing the torture of senators in the trials that followed, he is misleading: magic had often been regarded as treason, and trials for treason had always permitted the torture of aristocrats.[51] Maximinus was soon made *vicarius* of Rome in 370—a promotion that added even greater authority to his inquisition. Even after he was summoned to Gaul in 372 to serve as praetorian prefect, his successors as vicar of Rome, Ursicinus, Simplicius, and Doryphorianus, continued the investigations down to 375.[52] All citizens of Rome, particularly the senatorial elite and even

47. The only extended narrative of the Rome trials can be found at AM 28.1.1–57. The beginning of the investigation is datable by its connection with the prefecture of Olybrius (AM 28.1.6), which is attested from early autumn 368 until summer 370; cf. Chastagnol 1962, 178–84. *Chron. pasch.*, pp. 557–58, dates the beginning of the trials to 369. This is probably correct, for AM 28.1.9 reports that at the start of the incident, Olybrius was suffering from a serious illness, a fact that had registered at the imperial court in Trier by March 19, 370 (*CTh* 11.31.3). Barnes 1998, 233–34, 241–46, has essentially put to rest previous difficulties with Ammianus's chronology, although the conjecture of Thompson 1947, 138–40, on the curious note at 28.1.1 remains enticing.

48. F. Graf 1997, 46–49.

49. AM 28.1.11–12.

50. *CTh* 9.35.1 = *CJ* 9.8.4 (July 8, 369). *CTh* 9.16.6 (a. 358) offers the same proviso; cf. *CTh* 9.5.1 (a. 320) and Coşkun 2000, 86–88. See Funke 1967, 149–50, for the equation of magic and divination with *maiestas* in earlier instances.

51. AM 28.1.11. Ammianus himself knew that torture was allowed in cases of *maiestas* and *veneficium* (AM 19.12.17). Even so, Valentinian seems to have been confused over the issue (AM 28.1.25 with Coşkun 2000, 66–70). See Garnsey 1970, 29–49, 109–11, 143–45.

52. On the chronology, see Barnes 1998, 242–45, which is preferable to Coşkun 2000, 77–80, 88–90. For Maximinus's continued influence over the trials while in Gaul, see *CTh* 9.19.4,

more particularly the pagans among them, lived in fear of prosecution down to the end of Valentinian's life.

Much scholarship up to the present has seen the magic trials of Rome as motivated by Valentinian's disdain for the senatorial elite, from which he felt alienated and by which he felt threatened.[53] This is certainly how the senators perceived things.[54] The rhetoric of reprieve that survives from the immediate aftermath of Valentinian's death makes it clear that they regarded the latter years of his rule as a reign of terror, and modern scholarship has been inclined to follow their lead largely because theirs is the only description of the witch-hunt to survive from the period. Ammianus, who offers our only detailed account of the trials, lists charges against seventeen senatorials—including women and youths.[55] This was no small group, to be sure, yet it hardly constituted a significant fraction of all senators in Rome. Moreover, because Ammianus was concerned with the aristocrats, it is reasonable to assume that those listed constituted most if not all members of this elite who were charged. What is often overlooked, however, is that at least as many commoners met a similar fate; Ammianus—by his own admission—declined to list most of these.[56] Nonetheless, despite his prejudice, ten of the accused he catalogs were not senators, and he freely confesses that many more *humiles* whom he does not name were publicly executed.[57] The trials were thus hardly aimed exclusively at the Roman Senate.

Nor did they accomplish anything like a full-scale purge of that august body. We know of only nine senators and senatorial women who were actu-

---

with Harries 1988, 166–69; contrast Coşkun 2000, passim. Matthews 1989, 212, rightly emphasizes how odd it is that Ammianus avoids discussion of the role of the urban prefects in these trials. Barnes 1998, 205, attempts to solve the question by positing a lacuna at a point in bk. 29 that would have discussed the prefects of the 370s who are omitted in Ammianus's lists of these officers.

53. Schuurmans 1949; Alföldi 1952, 65–84; Piganiol 1972, 206; Fasolino 1976, 22–24. Thompson 1947, 87–107, actually posits that Maximinus unearthed a real senatorial conspiracy, which Ammianus is at pains to cover up. This is not at all what Ammianus says. For assessments more like that offered here, see Matthews 1975, 56–63; Hamblenne 1980; Coşkun 2000.

54. See pp. 232–33. Cf. Lib. *Or.* 24.17: οἱ πλείους οἰκιῶν ὀνομαστῶν; Jer. *Chron.* s.a. 371: "plurimos Romae nobilium occidit"; *Chron. pasch.*, pp. 557–58: πολλοὺς συγκλητικοὺς καὶ ἄρχοντας ἐπαρχιῶν ἐφόνευσεν.

55. *PLRE* I, Aginatius, Faltonius Probus Alypius 13, Anepsia, Avienus, Tarracius Bassus 21, Camenius 1, Cethegus, Claritas, Cornelius, Eumenius 3, Eusafius, Flaviana 1, Frontinus 3, Iulius Festus Hymetius, Lollianus 1, Marcianus 10, Paphius.

56. AM 28.1.15: "non omnia narratu sunt digna, quae per squalidas tansiere personas."

57. AM 28.1.16: "aliique humiles publica morte oppetiverunt." For non-senators, see *PLRE* I, Amantius 2, Frontinus 3, Marcellus 6, and Marinus 3, as well as Sericus, Asbolius, and Campensis (AM 28.1.8), the anonymous *Procurator Monetae* (AM 28.1.29), Auchenius the charioteer (AM 28.1.27), and Athanasius the charioteer (AM 29.3.5). Blockley 1975, 188–89, schematizes similar results in a table that, for Valens's trials, is distorted by the failure to use sources other than Ammianus; cf. Hamblenne 1980, 203–6.

ally put to death.[58] Three others were only exiled, and four were actually acquitted.[59] When the Senate lodged complaints against Valentinian's refusal to acknowledge their exemption from torture, the emperor even backed down on this point.[60] And even despite their protests of procedural irregularity, both the laws of the period and the report of Ammianus indicate that Valentinian exercised considerable care in the handling of senatorial trials.[61] What angered the senators more than anything else was the intrusion of non-Romans, particularly members of Valentinian's Pannonian entourage, into the matter.[62] In using his countrymen to carry out the investigations, Valentinian violated protocol. These things rankled the Senate, but there is no evidence that they were designed to. Rather, their aim was to put trusted confidants in charge of a sensitive assignment. Thus, indignant though the Roman senators were at Valentinian's hijacking of their traditional system of justice, they could hardly claim to be the exclusive victims of a witch-hunt.

The Rome trials were also not, as has been asserted, a purge directed specifically at pagans. Several of those accused were probably Christians, indicating that there was no effort to single out polytheists.[63] Moreover, at the height of the trial Valentinian issued an order specifically exempting traditional pagan divination *(haruspicina)* from criminal association with *maleficium*.[64] It was this vague concept, *maleficium* (criminal mischief), and not the broader range of pagan practices, that was the target.[65] Chief among the offenses prosecuted was, of course, magic, a category slippery enough for what some regarded as valid religious activities to be branded illegal. Even so, most of those convicted seem actually to have engaged in what they themselves knew to be outlawed rites.[66] We have no instances from Ammianus of

58. *PLRE* I, Aginatius, Anepsia, Avienus, Cethegus, Claritas, Cornelius, Flaviana, Lollianus 1, Paphius; cf. Hamblenne 1980, 209–10.

59. Exiled were *PLRE* I's Faltonius Probus Alypius 13, Frontinus 3, Iulius Festus Hymetius. Acquitted were *PLRE* I's Tarracius Bassus 21, Camenius 1, Eusafius, Marcianus 10. Cf. AM 28.1.40.

60. AM 28.1.24–25, with Harries 1999, 40–41.

61. *CTh* 1.6.2 (a. 364), 9.40.10 (a. 367), 9.16.10 (a. 371), 9.38.5 = *CJ* 9.43.3 (a. 371); AM 28.1.22, 26; cf. Alföldi 1952, 71–72; Hamblenne 1980, 217–22; Matthews 1989, 212; Vincenti 1991. For complaints, see Symm. *Or.* 4.5–6, 9, 13.

62. See, e.g., Symmachus's disdainful remark after Valentinian's death, *Or.* 4.13: "abrogata est externis moribus vis nocendi"; cf. 4.9: "iudicio . . . alieno."

63. Christians probably include *PLRE*'s Faltonius Probus Alypius 13 and perhaps Claritas, if we follow Clark's conjecture "Charitas." Esaias, mentioned at AM 28.1.43–45, must also have been either a Christian or a Jew.

64. *CTh* 9.16.9 (May 29, 371); cf. 9.38.5, probably part of the same original law.

65. On *maleficium* as Valentinian's chief concern, see *CTh* 9.16.9: "cum maleficiorum causis"; 9.16.10: "maleficiorum insimulatione adque invidia"; 9.38.4: "maleficiorum scelus"; cf. Jer. *Chron.* s.a. 371: "maleficos."

66. Cf. Coşkun 2000, 73–77; Thompson 1947, 102; Matthews 1989, 214.

people convicted of treason for the practice of pagan civic or even mystery religion. Rather, most of those whose activities Ammianus reports were involved in private rituals for casting charms, spells, and incantations, practices long since banned, even under pagan emperors. And several other defendants were charged with adultery and *stuprum* (sexual perversion), often related crimes because of their association with love charms.[67] Here again, they were not attacked for their religion but for their morals. Sexual morality, like magic, was apparently of serious concern to Valentinian, for we hear of two cases in other parts of the west where he also bitterly prosecuted adultery.[68] The Rome trials were thus an attack on *maleficium* in its various guises and manifestations: they were aimed against magic, poisoning, adultery, and perversion, and they affected not just aristocrats, but also administrators, entertainers, and commoners.[69]

Less than one year after the Rome trials reached their apex, in the early part of 372, Valens and his ministers undertook a series of magic and treason trials of their own.[70] Few scholars have pursued the connection between the two events, even though their relationship is noted in the ancient sources.[71] Two treasury officials, Anatolius and Spudasius, had been charged with embezzlement. Probably not by chance, their accuser, a certain Procopius, and their superior, the *comes rei privatae* Fortunatianus, also found reason to accuse the two of having hired a poisoner named Palladius and an astrologer named Heliodorus in an attempt to murder Fortunatianus. The interest in extending the charges from embezzlement to *veneficium* more than likely arose from Fortunatianus's and Procopius's awareness of the related investigations going on in the west. Magic was in the air, and eastern officials must have had a heightened sense of its importance at the time. Because magic and poisoning were treated as treason, once the ques-

67. As at AM 28.1.50. For love charms, see Gager 1992, 78–115.

68. For Valentinian's concern with sexual morality, see *CTh* 3.7.1 = *CJ* 5.4.18 (July 16, 371); cf. AM 30.9.2. Jer. *Ep.* 1 (written ca. 374 about events ca. 372) reports the draconian prosecution of an adultery charge in Vercellae, and Aus. XI *Prof.* 23 describes a teacher chased out of Bordeaux for adultery. Basil *Ep.* 46.4, 199.34, confirms that adultery was punished as a capital crime in the east at the same time. For the criminal prosecution of adultery in the late empire, see Grubbs 1995, 205–25; Arjava 1996, 193–202.

69. Rome was apparently notorious in its taste for magic and astrology, making it fertile ground for the trials under Valentinian; cf. AM 26.3.1–4, 28.4.24–25.

70. On the Antioch treason trials, see AM 29.1.4–2.28, 31.14.8–9; Eunap. *VS* 7.6.3–7; Zos. 4.14.1–15.3; Lib. *Or.* 1.171–73; *Epit.* 48.3–4; Philostorg. 9.15; Soc. 4.19.1–7; Soz. 6.35.1–11; Joh. Ant. fr. 184.2; Theoph. a.m. 5865, 5867; Zon. 13.16; Cedrenus, p. 548. For secondary work, see Funke 1967, 165–75; Paschoud 2.2: 356–62 n. 129–32; Matthews 1989, 204–28; Wiebe 1995, 86–168.

71. AM 29.2.23–4; Lib. *Or.* 24.14. On the date of the Antioch trials, see Seeck 1906b, 523–24; cf. id., *Regesten*, 243. The Rome trials, which began in late 369, lasted until the end of Valentinian's reign, but reached their high point in 371 (Jer. *Chron.* s.a. 371; cf. p. 220).

tion of *veneficium* had been raised, the case instantly fell under the jurisdiction of the praetorian prefect, Modestus.[72] What started out as embezzlement had thus blossomed into high crimes. Unlike the trials in the west,
though, in this instance the lines of investigation led to a much more nefarious and dangerous plot.

Under questioning, Palladius revealed knowledge of an elaborate conspiracy, again involving magic and divination, that threatened Valens's
throne.[73] The poisoner claimed, and it was later revealed, that a group of di-
viners and imperial courtiers had conspired to learn the name of Valens's
successor and had begun taking steps to put their candidate on the throne.
A fairly small initial coterie, including the governor Fidustius, the *praepositus cubiculariorum* Heliodorus, and the *notarius* Hilarius, had constructed a
tripod from laurel twigs and placed over it a tray cast from various metals.[74]
The tray was engraved with the twenty-four letters of the Greek alphabet and
over it a consecrated ring was suspended from a linen thread. A priest, wearing linen and pronouncing incantations, set the ring swinging and then posed
various questions, which were answered in the manner of a ouija board as
the ring passed over each letter. The inquirers first asked the nature of
Valens's successor and soon his name. When the first four letters were revealed to be ΘΕΟΔ (THEOD-), the inquiry ceased and all thoughts raced to
a fashionable *notarius* named Theodorus, a well-educated Gaul, who had perhaps followed Julian east in 361.[75] Theodorus, who had not been present at
the initial consultation, was soon informed of the pronouncement through
Euserius, who had served as the vicar of Asia. A letter from Theodorus that
was produced during the ensuing trial revealed that he was both willing and
anxious to assume his prophesied role,[76] and soon he had assembled a much

---

72. AM 29.1.5–6; Zos. 4.14.1, with Paschoud 2.2: 359 n. 130.

73. On the fact that the threat was real, see AM 29.1.4, 15; Lib. *Or.* 1.171.

74. The story comes in three versions. The one I follow is reported at AM 29.1.29–33; cf.
Soz. 6.35.3; Zos. 4.13.3–4. The second, involving a chicken pecking grains from a table delin-
eated by the letters of the alphabet, is reported at Zon. 13.16; Cedrenus, p. 548. A third version involves pebbles marked with letters; see Philostorg. 9.15. The first version gains most credence, both because it is reported in the earliest, most reliable sources and because a parallel
ceremony is described in the *Papyri Graecae magicae* 1.3: 290–315 (no. 11). An apparatus like
that described in Ammianus was found in excavations at Pergamum (Agrell 1936; Beard et al.
1998, 2: 188). Wiebe 1995, 98–106, questions the reliability of testimony on this oracle, but I
would incline to follow the sources.

75. *PLRE* I, Theodorus 13; cf. Teitler 1985, 169–70. Theodorus was brash enough to have
already made his displeasure with Valens known to the emperor himself; see Joh. Chrys. *Ad vid.
iun.* 4: παρρησία τῇ πρὸς τὸν βασιλέα πάντων κρατῶν; cf. AM 29.1.8: "solusque paene omnium
erat cuius linguam non infrenem sed dispicientem quae loqueretur nullius claudebat periculi
metus." This would have made him seem like a natural ally to the disgruntled conspirators.
Wiebe 1995, 111–16, sees in Theodorus an *alter Iulianus*.

76. AM 29.1.35.

larger circle of philosophers and court officials, most of them with some connections to the territory of Asia Minor, to support him.[77]

Valens is reported to have exploded with rage at the news of the conspiracy.[78] A tribunal was soon assembled in Antioch under the leadership of Modestus.[79] Suspects were brought in from across the eastern empire in numbers so great that both Ammianus and Zosimus report serious dangers of riots in the bulging gaols and even private houses where prisoners were kept.[80] As in the Rome trials, no one seems to have been exempted from torture. Here, however, few were acquitted, leaving Ammianus, who witnessed the events personally, to lament "everywhere the scene was like a slaughtering of cattle."[81] As in Rome, the charges spread to implicate people with only tenuous connections to the initial conspiracy or those who could be charged with magic or treason in unrelated incidents. During this second phase, books were assembled and burned publicly before the tribunal in Antioch.[82] Many claimed to have sacrificed their entire libraries rather than run the risk of being caught with an illegal text. John Chrysostom, who was a youth living in the city at the time, reports that the streets were filled with soldiers looking for banned books. Walking along the Orontes, he and a friend spied a book floating in the water and fished it out, thinking it a valuable find, only to discover that it contained a magical text. When a soldier approached, they were hard-pressed to dispose of their trove and avoid being caught, which would have been tantamount to death.[83] "[W]e all crept about at that time as if in Cimmerian darkness," Ammianus says.[84]

Ultimately, in a third and final stage of the trials, Valens's proconsul of Asia, Festus, is said to have continued investigations into illicit magic in his

---

77. *PLRE* I's Hilarius 6 was from Phrygia, Patricius 3 from Lydia, Euserius was *vicarius Asiae,* Eutropius—later acquitted—*proconsul Asiae,* Maximus 21—also acquitted—from Ephesus, and Diogenes 5 governor of Bithynia. For Asia as a center of philosophical paganism, see Fowden 1982, 40–43.

78. AM 29.1.10; Zos. 4.14.2; Soz. 6.35.5–7; cf. Lib. *Or.* 1.177. For Valens's anger and cruelty, see p. 231.

79. Modestus was well suited to such investigations given his previous experience (AM 19.12.6).

80. AM 29.1.13; Zos. 4.14.3.

81. AM 29.1.40: "ut pecudum ubique trucidatio cernebatur." Cf. Eunap. *VS* 7.6.5.

82. AM 29.1.41–2.17. This second stage is also distinguished at Lib. *Or.* 1.171; cf. Wiebe 1995, 131–42. The burning of prophetic and magical books had a pedigree stretching back to Augustus (Suet. *Aug.* 31.1; cf. Paulus *Sent.* 5.23.17–18). See Wiebe 1995, 119–30.

83. Joh. Chrys. *In Act. Apost. hom.* XXXVIII.5 (*PG* 60.274–76); cf. AM 29.1.41, 2.4 and Kelly 1995, 25. On book burning, see Blockley 1975, 110 n. 46. Joh. Chrys. *De inc. dei nat.* 3.17 (*PG* 48.726) also gives a vivid and personal sense of the spectacle of terror; cf. *Ad vid. iun.* 4; *In Act. Apost. hom.* XLI.3 (*PG* 60.291–92). See also Basil *Ep.* 178 with a plea for one of the accused.

84. AM 29.2.4; cf. 29.1.24. See Matthews 1989, 513 n. 34, for Ammianus's possible presence at the trials and Barnes 1998, 122, for his friendship with one of the victims, Hypatius.

province, which was after all the seedbed of the initial conspiracy.[85] In Asia, Festus chased down leads on even the most innocuous dabbling in charms and the most tenuous claims of treason. This installment as much as any has won for the whole process its reputation for ruthlessness. Many paid the price for having involved themselves in traditional private rituals that could be branded as "magic" and thus prosecuted under the laws of the state. An old woman who used charms as a healer was executed, as was a boy caught whispering an incantation for his health in the baths.[86] Ammianus claims that Festus conducted his investigations in emulation of his friend Maximinus, who had won the praetorian prefecture on the heels of his magic trials in Rome.[87] The parallels between the western and eastern empires are patent: courtiers in both sought to gain from implementing the policies of their superstitious leaders.

Although the situations in west and east were similar, they were, of course, not identical: both began with specific allegations of poisoning and both devolved into witch-hunts against practitioners of what could be termed "magic," but where Valentinian's trials never actually uncovered any real threat to the empire, Valens's overturned a seamy rock of conspiracy under which were crawling some truly threatening creatures. Even after Procopius's revolt, Valens seems to have agitated the easterners over whom he ruled, and particularly the people of the province of Asia, from whose intellectual and cultural world he was entirely excluded. He no doubt exacerbated the problem by his heavy reliance on professional bureaucrats, like the main instigators behind the trials, Modestus and Festus. We have already seen Valens's unwillingness to cast his patronage net broadly enough to employ eastern aristocrats in the kinds of numbers necessary to keep them satisfied.[88] For this reason, eastern grandees no doubt resented the emperor and were anxious to learn more about the prospects for a more beneficent successor.

Wiebe has attempted to find in this a larger conspiracy of pagans hoping to revive the polytheist empire of Julian.[89] It is certainly true that the vast majority of those involved were pagan, and that the procedures they used to divine Valens's successor were overtly pagan, even "theurgical." Even so, there is very little evidence for firm connections to Julian. None of the original

---

85. AM 29.2.21–8; Eunap. VS 7.6.6–7; Hist. fr. 39.8 (Blockley) = Suid. Φ 279; cf. Wiebe 1995, 143–48.

86. AM 29.2.26–28.

87. AM 29.2.22–24: "ad aemulationem eorum commissa, quae facta sunt Romae." Festus certainly succeeded in using charges of magic to win the proconsulship of Asia from Eutropius; see Lib. Or. 1.158–9 with Norman 1965, 195 on dating.

88. See pp. 58–66.

89. Wiebe 1995, 106–11, 116–19; cf. Blockley 1975, 120–22. For a treatment similar to my own, see Funke 1967, 166–72.

consultants is known to have had connections with the Apostate.[90] Of those who became involved after the consultation, only two seem to have been followers of Julian, Theodorus and Maximus of Ephesus, and of these, only Theodorus willingly participated. Maximus, Julian's flamboyant philosophical advisor, had been tortured and fined early in Valens's reign but had subsequently obtained a reprieve. By the later 360s, he had been allowed to regain considerable influence in Asia and Constantinople but was a natural target for suspicion when the treason trials broke out. He had indeed been consulted by the conspirators on the meaning of the oracle but chose not to participate in their cabal any further than predicting their demise. For this, Valens initially acquitted him at Antioch, but Festus eventually did him in during the final stage of prosecution in his native Asia Minor.[91] Thus, only two followers of Julian even knew of the oracle, and only one participated in the conspiracy.

This is not to say that followers of Julian did not come in for suspicion in the trials that followed. Charges were brought against Eutropius, who before joining Valens as *magister memoriae* and *proconsul Asiae* had served in Julian's court; Libanius, whose oratory had gushed with praise for Julian; and Alypius, who had been charged by Julian with the reconstruction of the temple in Jerusalem. In the end, though, the first two were entirely acquitted and the third, having been fined and exiled, was later reprieved.[92] To be sure, Valens feared a conspiracy of "Julianites," but ultimately there proved to be no such thing. Indeed, these three were not even representative of the treatment received by the broader circle of Julian's followers during the period of the Antioch magic trials. We have already seen that these came in for extremely rough treatment in the early years of Valens's reign. Yet in 372, they were largely left alone. We can count nine of Julian's friends and confidants, most of them pagan philosophers, whom we know to have lived on under Valens without ever becoming enmeshed in the conspiracy and without ever suffering in these trials.[93]

The fulcrum of the conspiracy was not, then, to be found in supporters of Julian or even in the pagan community more broadly. The fact is that not

90. These included *PLRE* I, Fidustius, Hilarius 6, Patricius 3, and two persons not in *PLRE* I, Irenaeus and Pergamius, on whom see AM 29.1.6, 25; cf. Lib. *Or.* 1.172, 176.

91. Eunap. *VS* 7.6.1–7; *Hist.* fr. 39.8 (Blockley) = Suid. Φ 279; cf. AM 29.1.42; Zos. 4.15.1; Lib. *Or.* 1.158. More at Penella 1990, 71–75; cf. R. B. E. Smith 1995, 186–87.

92. See the sources listed at *PLRE* I, Alypius 4, Eutropius 2, Libanius 1. Cf. Zos. 4.14.2.

93. *PLRE* I, Chrysanthius, Eustochius 5, Eutherius 1, Himerius, Nestorius 2, Nymphidianus, Oribasius, Priscus, Theodorus 16 = 17 = 18. The sons of *PLRE* I's Sopater 2, Julian's pagan friend, actually made their way into the senate under Valens. *PLRE* I's Aristoxenus, Eucleides, Eustathius 1, and Pythiodorus, who were philosophical confidants of Julian's, also escape mention in connection with the conspiracy, although we cannot confirm that they were still alive by 371–72.

all those implicated in Valens's trials were even pagan. Several Christians numbered among those charged with treason and even magic.[94] And even if the vast majority of those charged were pagans, many of them termed "philosophers" by our sources,[95] they can hardly be said to have led a crusade for "the pagan opposition" as posited by Wiebe.[96] There is very little evidence that a unified pagan front ever really existed at all, in either east or west. Most pagan philosophers, including those implicated in the conspiracy, were well aware of the treacherous line they walked in practicing the theurgical form of Neoplatonism so popular in the late Greek east. Their reaction to official restrictions on their cultic activities was not one of revolution but of withdrawal.[97] Even in the brief period of freedom they enjoyed under Julian's rule, several philosophers chose to keep their distance from the pagan emperor, and in the years following his death, most avoided the practice of rites that could be deemed magical and therefore prosecuted.[98] We have no evidence that these pagans ever attempted to unite as a political group against the hegemony of the new Christian empire. Their numbers were too small, their ranks too divided, and their interests too otherworldly for them to have posed any serious threat.

In as far as the philosophers involved were a unified front, they were, as with the Procopius revolt, more unified by their opposition to Valens than by any conscious decision to champion the cause of paganism. Many were, as noted, from the area of Asia Minor and its immediate surroundings. As such, they probably despised Valens after his rough treatment of this region during the revolt of Procopius. It is certainly the case that some pagans of Chalcedon (Kadiköy), the city that suffered most in the aftermath of the revolt, put an elaborate curse tablet against the emperor in the walls of their city, where it was discovered when Valens had those walls dismantled for reuse in building projects at Constantinople.[99] This, however, was more typical of the "pagan reaction" to Valens than any sort of political uprising. These were

94. *PLRE* I, Bassianus 2, Fl. Eusebius 40, Flavius Hypatius. It is also likely, given their names, that *PLRE* I, Iacobus 2 and Martyrius, attested at Lib. *Or.* 1.158–59, were Christian. Indeed. Martyrius may even have offered the Christian dedication at *CIG* 8872; cf. Malcus 1967, 112.

95. *PLRE* I, Andronicus 6, Coeranius, Hilarius 6, Maximus of Ephesus 21, Pasiphilus 1, Patricius 3, Simonides.

96. Many ancients also understood this as a conspiracy of philosophers (Zos. 4.14.2; Soz. 6.35.2, 7). Cf. Paschoud 2.2: 362 n. 132: "Que les procès d'Antioche aient fini par se transformer en une chasse aux intellectuals est évident; qu'ils aient été une persécution des païens semble fort douteux."

97. Cf. Ephrem's image of the reaction of Julian's philosophical advisors to his death (*CJ* 1.3): "They fled back into their caverns, dark and primeval. The fear they had stripped off they put on again in their dens." See also Joh. Chrys. *Ad pop. Ant. hom.* XVII (*PG* 49.173–74) and Fowden 1981; 1998; cf. Drinkwater 1983; Cameron 1999.

98. E.g., Eunap. *VS* 6.9.15–11.5, 7.4.4–9, 23.2.1–7, with Penella 1990, 68–71.

99. AM 31.1.4–5, 14.8–9; Soc. 4.8.1–6; Cedrenus, pp. 542–43; Zon. 13.16; Joh. Ant. fr. 184.1.

men from the educated elite,[100] men who probably did disdain Valens's rough-hewn demeanor and his inability to understand the nature of their religious practice. As "philosophers," though, they had few weapons with which to fight the emperor aside from their religion. Thus, even in the aftermath of the magic trials, a theurgical magic text lamented "those men like beasts, ignorant and unlearned, who through want of godly knowledge, know neither the help of divine refuge from man-destroying evil, nor the magical work that brings special wonder."[101] The text goes on to list the theurgical properties of various stones, precisely the sorts of charms that terrified Valens, but also precisely the sorts of amulets that philosophers regarded as sympathetic links to divine power. Far from calling for revolution, though, the author of this text—who hid behind the pseudonym "Orpheus"—was comfortable concealing the marvels of his Hermetic religion from such ungodly authorities. Neither he nor the philosophers of 371 were in any position to make an attempt on the throne, let alone to restore the pagan empire of Julian. Their armies were mustered among the *daimones,* and their battles were fought with prayers, curses, and incantations.

If anything, the "philosophers" involved in the conspiracy were pawns in a broader plot orchestrated by imperial courtiers. We have seen in several instances that Valens—a less than ideal emperor—was not well liked. Ammianus recounts a story that one of his own bodyguards tried to slay the Pannonian as he slept under a tree, and this, he claims, was only one of many threats to the emperor's life.[102] It is thus no surprise that Valens's ministers spearheaded this plot to steal his throne in 371. Of those charged in the first two phases of the trials, one had served as *vicarius Asiae* under Valens, another had worked for him in the office of the *sacrae largitiones,* a third was his tribune, two others were governors, and no fewer than three worked on the staff of the *notarii,* one of them being Theodorus himself.[103] Both Eunapius and Libanius agree that this was a palace conspiracy, perhaps a conspiracy centered among the *notarii.*[104] We must not forget that this was the corps whence Procopius had launched his career, and that it constituted a springboard for other talented intellectuals to attain positions

---

100. Considerable education is known for *PLRE* I, Bassianus 2, Coeranius, Diogenes 5, Euserius, Maximus of Ephesus 21, Simonides, Theodorus 13.

101. *Orphei lithica* ll. 75–79, with Abel 1885, 103, on the date.

102. AM 29.1.16. See Campbell 1984, 113–14, for other guardsmen who murdered emperors.

103. *Vicarius Asiae: PLRE* I, Euserius. *Largitionalis:* Salia 1. Tribune: Numerius 2. Governors: Diogenes 5, Fidustius; cf. Eutropius 2. *Notarii:* Bassianus 2, Hilarius 6 = Hilarius 2, Theodorus 13.

104. Eunap. *VS* 7.6.3: οἱ γὰρ περὶ τὰ βασίλεια τοῖς βασιλεῦσι ἐπιβουλὴν τινὰ συστησάμενοι; Lib. *Or.* 24.13; AM 29.1.12, 34. The usurper Ioannes 6 in *PLRE* II had also vaulted into power from the *notarii.*

of power.[105] Anger within this group and within Valens's bureaucracy more broadly may then have run high, both at the treatment of Procopius and at the generally crabbed tenor of Valens's administration. It is thus entirely conceivable that a group of imperial officials, dissatisfied with their rough and bumbling emperor, began seeking divine input about his successor.

Nor was Valens unjustified in seeking to put a stop to their plans. Magic and astrology, particularly when used to undermine the authority of the emperor, had always been a target for persecution. Magic and treason trials pocked the bloody surface of imperial politics throughout the fourth century, leaving all subjects aware of the consequences of prognosticating the fate of an emperor.[106] Firmicus Maternus, still a convinced pagan when he composed his monumental astrological treatise the *Mathesis* in the 330s, resolutely inserted a disclaimer into the closing of his second book that warned against inquiring into the fate of the emperor using either astrology or sacrifice. Indeed, he was so cautious about treading on this deadly ground that he felt compelled to deny explicitly that an emperor's *numen* could be subject to divine prediction at all.[107] The ideology of empire thus proscribed all inquiries like that pursued by the conspirators of 371, and no ancient author sympathized with them. Rather, all agree that Valens had every right to prosecute their crimes to the fullest extent of the law.[108] Valens had been faced with an open revolt little more than a year after he came to the throne, making him perpetually anxious, especially about threats coming from Asia, where Procopius's uprising had been based.[109] It is thus no surprise that he clamped down hard when the Theodorus affair came to light.

Where Valens, and indeed Valentinian, went wrong was in allowing their treason trials to mushroom out of control. Justice was one thing, persecution quite another. By allowing anger to cloud their judgment and permitting their ministers too much leeway in prosecuting claims of magic and treason, both stepped well beyond the acceptable bounds of clemency demanded of an emperor.[110] Both Valens and Valentinian were notoriously hot-tempered.

105. See Teitler 1985, 162–63; cf. Vogler 1979, 192–97. Valentinian's—and Valens's?—efforts to curb the privileges of the *notarii* at *CTh* 6.35.7 (a. 367) may in part explain the discontent.

106. The standard account remains Cramer 1954, 232–81; cf. Potter 1994, 174–82. See the magic and treason charges in AM 14.1.2–9, 7.7–8, 20, 15.3.7–11, 16.6.1–3, 8.2–11, 19.12.1–14; cf. Funke 1967; Blockley 1975, 104–22; Matthews 1989, 217–18; Wiebe 1995, 169–93.

107. Firm. Mat. *Math.* 2.30.4–7; cf. Syn. *De insomm.* 12. For similar prohibitions against divination and astrological prediction regarding the emperor, see Beard et al. 1998, 1: 231–33.

108. AM 29.1.18; Lib. *Or.* 24.14; Soz. 6.35.8. See similar sentiments at AM 19.12.17.

109. AM 31.14.8–9 shows that Valens always harbored anxiety about the region of Asia Minor.

110. See Brown 1992, 48–61.

Ammianus devotes two entire sections of his narrative to a catalog of Valentinian's anger and cruelty, and that same rage features in numerous independent pagan and Christian sources.[111] He once had a young attendant beaten to death for accidentally letting a dog loose during a hunt and is even reputed to have kept two man-eating bears whom he fatted on the victims of his rage—probably an apocryphal story, but one indicative of contemporary perceptions of the emperor's temperament.[112] So, too, the sources on Valens regularly attribute his often vicious actions to his unbridled temper.[113] Even in the course of these magic trials, Valens is reported to have seethed with rage on learning of the conspiracy and to have allowed that rage to affect both his presumption of guilt and his thirst for cruel punishments like strangulation, burning alive, and whipping to death.[114]

Indeed, Valens probably outdid his brother on this score, because he was present at many of the magic trials in his domain, whereas Valentinian presided only from a distance. Valentinian was also at least willing to make some concessions to the elite in order to remain within the bounds of the law, whereas Valens is reported to have maintained only the façade of legality, regularly stepping outside the law to satisfy his rage.[115] And the problem was only compounded by Valens's less than stellar intellect, which left him easy prey for the self-serving manipulations of his ministers. Both Modestus, his praetorian prefect, and Festus, his *proconsul Asiae*, are said to have capitalized on Valens's hazy sense of justice and his overinflated air of imperial dignity to achieve their own ends.[116] By winning free rein to prosecute even tenuous charges, these ministers were able to collect handsomely from the

111. AM 27.7.4–8, 29.3.1–9. That Valentinian was regarded by contemporaries as cruel is clear from the letter reported at AM 28.1.20. Other instances of Valentinian's cruelty at AM 28.1.19, 23, 2.9, 6.12, 22, 28, 30.5.10, 19, 6.3, 8.1–6, 10; cf. Zos. 4.1.1, 16.3. Many sources refer to Valentinian euphemistically as "severus": Jer. *Chron.* s.a. 365; s.a. 371; *Narratio* 1 (*MGH.AA* 9.629); *Epit.* 45.5; Jord. *Rom.* 307; cf. Malalas 13.28, 31, 34 (ἀπότομος). Ammianus seems to respond to this sobriquet critically at 28.1.11: "acer magis quam severus." See also Blockley 1975, 41–45.

112. AM 29.3.2–3, 9. On the bears, see Sabbah 1978, 501 n. 140; 1992, 101–2.

113. Epiph. *Adv. haeres.* 69.34.1–4 proves that Valens's anger (τὸ τοῦ βασιλέως Οὐάλεντος θυμὸς) was already notorious during the emperor's lifetime. For other instances of Valens's anger and cruelty, see Greg. Nys. *Eun.* 1.140; AM 26.6.7, 10.12, 14, 29.1.18–21, 27, 38, 42, 29.2.10, 12, 17–18, 31.14.5–6; Eunap. *Hist.* fr. 42 (Blockley); fr. 44.5 = Suid. *E* 374; *Epit.* 46.3; Zos. 4.8.4–5, 14.2; Zon. 13.16; Cedrenus, p. 550; *Narratio* 2 (*MGH.AA* 9.629); Ruf. *HE* 11.5; Soc. 4.8.12, 16.1, 18.2, 9, 19.1, 32.5; Soz. 6.8.4–5, 14.2, 18.2–3, 21.6; Theod. *HE* 4.32.2, 34.3. See also Blockley 1975, 45–48.

114. AM 29.1.18–22, 38, 29.2.10; Lib. *Or.* 46.8.

115. AM 29.1.27, 31.14.6; cf. Zos. 4.15.2.

116. AM 29.1.10–11, 19–20; Eunap. *VS* 7.6.7; Zos. 4.15.2–3. For the influence of Valens's ministers on his actions more broadly, see AM 27.5.8, 30.4.1–2, 31.4.4, 12.7; Lib. *Or.* 1.144; ctr. Them. *Or.* 8.106b, 109a, 10.129d. Valentinian is also blamed for allowing his ministers' influence to affect his judgment (*Epit.* 45.6).

confiscated estates of those convicted. Meanwhile, Valens, who cared more about the danger posed to his life and his throne than the danger of ruining his reputation, turned a blind eye to the spectacle of slaughter unfolding before him.[117]

The denunciation of Valentinian's and Valens's handling of the magic trials began immediately after the death of each emperor. In Valentinian's case, this meant that his own son Gratian was complicit in the denigration of his father's reputation, although he shifted most of the blame onto Valentinian's ministers, particularly Maximinus.[118] On January 1, 376, forty-four days after Valentinian died, Gratian sent a reconciliatory speech to the Senate of Rome, which Symmachus called the harbinger of a "new age."[119] Parts of it survive in two laws that tightened the investigation and punishment of criminal charges involving senatorials.[120] A series of laws soon followed limiting denunciations by slaves, relaxing the prosecution of forgery, and forbidding the torture of senatorials.[121] In his fourth oration, later that year, Symmachus bubbled with praise: "How great a thing that good morals no longer know fear, that he who relies on his own judgment is not terrified by that of an outsider, that the whole Senate is not numbered among the guilty, that suspicion alone does not make one a culprit."[122] Before the summer was out, Gratian had executed Maximinus and his successors as vicar of Rome Simplicius and Doryphorianus.[123] Senators, and particularly the pagans among them, could breath easier. From the summer of 376, we know of no fewer than four inscriptions recording mystery initiations by pagan senatorials[124]; a fifth marks the emperor's reconstruction of a temple of Isis at Ostia in 376, and a sixth, from the following year, yet another mystery dedication.[125] Also

117. Many sources claim that Valens attacked guilty and innocent alike, including Lib. *Or.* 1.171; AM 29.1.20; Eunap. *VS* 7.6.7; Zos. 4.14.3–4, 15.2; Philostorg. 9.15.

118. Symm. *Ep.* 10.3: "ferox ille Maximinus"; *Or.* 4.10–13, esp.: "Alienorum simulatione criminum Maximinus fidem fecit suorum."

119. Symm. *Ep.* 1.13: "luminibus accensis novi saeculi fata recitantur"; cf. *Ep.* 10.2 and Bruggisser 1987.

120. *CTh* 9.1.13 and *CJ* 3.24.2 (Jan. 1, 376); cf. Seeck, *Regesten,* 105, on the date and circumstances; contrast Mathews 2000, 230.

121. *CTh* 9.6.1–2 (Mar. 15, 376); *CTh* 9.19.4 = *CJ* 9.22.23 (Apr. 16, 376); *CTh* 9.35.3 = *CJ* 12.1.10 (Jan. 4, 377). Hymetius, exiled by Valentinian in 371, was also recalled in 376 and a gold statue of him erected in the forum (*CIL* 6.1736 = *ILS* 1256). See Alföldi 1952, 84–95; Fortina 1953, 39–45; Matthews 1975, 65–76, on this period.

122. Symm. *Or.* 4.9; cf. *Or.* 4.5–6, 10–13.

123. AM 28.1.57; Symm. *Ep.* 10.2; *Or.* 4.11–12. Barnes 1998, 246, argues that Maximinus died in the spring of 376. See Errington 1996a, 446–47, for recent conjectures on the elimination of these three in the power struggles of early 376.

124. *CIL* 6.751 = *ILS* 4268 (Apr. 8, 376); *CIL* 6.504 = *ILS* 4153 (Aug. 13, 376); *CIL* 6.510 = *ILS* 4152 (Aug. 13, 376); *CIL* 6.31118.

125. *AE* 1968, 86, with Chastagnol 1969 and Salzman 1990, 174–76; *CIL* 6.500 = *ILS* 4148 (May 13, 377); cf. Them. *Or.* 13.178a–179b.

in the summer of 376, Themistius echoed Symmachus's rhetoric of reprieve on his visit to Rome, and the same sense of relief fills the *Gratiarum actio* of Ausonius, still in 379.[126] It was indeed a new age in the west, albeit a short-lived one before Gratian himself clamped down on paganism in the aftermath of Adrianople.

Feelings were no different on the death of Valens. Festus was removed from office and died soon thereafter, having slipped on the steps of a temple of Nemesis where he had gone to consult regarding nightmares of the philosopher Maximus dragging him to hell with a noose.[127] Valens, whose own death by burning alive (according to one report) recompensed his cruel punishments, had himself been haunted with dreams of his victims from Antioch, if we can believe Ammianus.[128] By spring 379, Valens's court orator Themistius was already diverting the emperor Theodosius with veiled digs at the cruelty of his predecessor.[129] These became bolder by 381, when Themistius very clearly referred to Valens's cruelty and death, warning: "There is no refuge for the emperor who cares not for justice, not in the cowardice of his soldiers, nor in the indifference of his generals."[130] Similar allusions in Themistius's remaining speeches to Theodosius make it clear that he despised the behavior of Valens in this regard.[131] It was, after all, he who had warned Valens of the consequences of intolerance. By the time Ammianus was writing in the early 390s, these consequences were clear:

> O noble idea of wisdom . . . how much would you have corrected in those dark days if it had been permitted Valens to know through you that power—as the wise declare—is nothing else than the care for others' welfare; that it is the duty of a good ruler to restrain his power, to resist unbounded desire and implacable anger, and to know—as the dictator Caesar used to say—that the recollection of cruelty is a wretched support for old age![132]

Valentinian and Valens had thus carried things too far. They both initiated magic and treason trials at approximately the same time. Valentinian's trials never turned up any serious threat to his throne, but Valens's, of course, did. The threat was not, however, posed by a group of pagan revivalists or by a conspiracy of Julian's supporters. Rather, it seems to have centered around

---

126. Them. *Or.* 13.169a–c, 171c, 175a–c; Aus. XXI *Gratiarum actio* 1 [3–4].

127. Eunap. *VS* 7.6.9–12. Perhaps the temple of the Nemeseis at Smyrna, on which see Robert 1994, 65–66.

128. AM 31.1.3; cf. 29.2.20.

129. Them *Or.* 14.183b: προπάτορας δὲ σοὺς ὀνομάζω οὐχ ἅπαντας ἁπλῶς τοὺς πρότερον αὐτοκράτορας, ἀλλὰ τοὺς εὐδοκίμους ἐπὶ πραότητι καὶ φιλανθρωπίᾳ.

130. Them. *Or.* 15.189d. See Vanderspoel 1995, 191–92; cf. 198–99.

131. Them. *Or.* 15.190a–c, 192d, 17.213c–d, 34.17; cf. Lib. *Or.* 46.30.

132. AM 29.2.18. Ammianus expresses the same sentiments of Valentinian, 30.8.2–6; cf. 21.16.11–14.

a coterie of imperial officials who were using magic and divination as a means to achieve their ends. The reality of the threat these posed is acknowledged by contemporary sources, which are therefore slow to criticize Valens for prosecuting lèse-majesté. More reprehensible—to ancients as also to moderns—was the zeal with which Valens and his brother attacked those whom they feared.

CHAOS AND TOLERATION:
THE ARIAN CRISIS AND VALENTINIAN'S RESPONSE

No one would envy Valens the woes he faced with the Christian church. The bickering, the posturing, the pressuring, the manipulation and violence of mid-fourth-century Christians were indeed appalling. From the perspective of a pagan like Ammianus, "no wild beasts are such enemies to mankind as are most of the Christians in their deadly hatred of one another."[133] Valens came to power at perhaps the worst possible moment in the history of the fourth-century church. Strife and discord over the nature of Christ had grown steadily since the early 320s and had reached a peak by 360, particularly in Valens's half of the empire. For while the west was generally comfortable with its mildly monarchian presumptions about the trinity and—with the exception of Illyricum—had little stomach for stirring Arianism into its doctrinal pot, the east was a seething cauldron of controversy between so many competing and mutually contradictory positions that there would have been no way to satisfy all parties. Even so, Valens did himself no favors by allowing himself to become embroiled in the issue. While his brother maintained a detached indifference to ecclesiastical controversy, Valens did not or could not succeed in doing the same.

The Arian controversy was ignited over the person of Christ. An Alexandrian priest named Arius had posited that, for Christ to be distinct from the one God (God the Father), he must have been generated by the Father and thus inferior to his divinity. With this Christology, Arius certainly overcame the problem of monarchianism, by which the distinction between the persons of the trinity collapses to the point of nonexistence. On the other hand, he created an entirely new problem by making of Christ something less than God. The controversy this new theory raised in Alexandria soon spread broadly enough to require imperial attention. At the Council of Nicaea (Iznik; see map 2) organized by Constantine in 325, over two hundred bishops met and endorsed an imperially sanctioned formula wherein Christ was mandated to be "of the same nature" as the Father (*homoousios*).[134] But within three years, the unity achieved at Nicaea had broken down, par-

---

133. AM 22.5.4; cf. Greg. Naz. *Or.* 33.2.
134. See Drake 2000, 235–352, with earlier bibliography.

ticularly under the influence of the powerful Arian bishop Eusebius of Nicomedia, who had won his way into the good graces of Constantine and soon began deposing and often exiling his opponents.

When Constantine died in 337, after an Arian baptism at the hands of Eusebius, his sons soon found themselves at odds over Christology: the west—under the sole rule of Constans after 340—cleaved to Nicaea, while the east—under Constantius since 337—invented various revised creeds, which granted at least some of the tenets of Arianism. Among Eusebius's targets for exile had been Athanasius of Alexandria, the canonical paladin of Nicene "Orthodoxy" and one of its only die-hard supporters in the east. In the aftermath of Constantine's death, Athanasius beguiled the bishop of Rome and the emperor Constans into taking up the defense of Nicaea on his behalf. But with Constans's death in 350, this support for Nicaea disappeared, and Constantius, now master of the entire empire, began applying steady pressure to unite east and west under a semi-Arian creed. The 350s saw council after council, synod after synod in a mind-numbing blur of bickering, all aimed at achieving ecclesiastical and imperial concord. Instead, the creation of so many venues for debate only allowed the various rival groups to articulate increasingly firm and mutually exclusive positions.[135]

By 360, there were four well-defined parties, each with considerable followings. In addition to the Homoousians, there were Anomoeans, Homoiousians, and Homoians. Where the Homoousians still held to the sameness of nature formula propounded at Nicaea, the Anomoeans, led by the master logicians Aetius and Eunomius, began preaching a radical Arianism in which Christ was distinctly subordinate to and unlike (anomoios) the father. The Homoiousians, the true compromise party, under their leaders Macedonius of Constantinople and Basil of Ancyra, wished to walk a line between monarchianism and Arianism by declaring that Christ was neither a creature nor the same as the Father but was like the father according to his nature (homoiousios). The Homoians, led by Eudoxius of Antioch and Acacius of Caesarea, carried this one step further. They too denied that Christ was created but refused to employ the word "nature" (ousia) at all, agreeing only that Christ was "like [homoios] unto the Father according to the scriptures." There were thus two radical groups, the Homoousians and Anomoeans, and, in the middle, two more moderate semi-Arian groups, the Homoiousians and the Homoians. Even so, none would have willingly labeled themselves "Arian," for this tag had become anathema after the Council of Nicaea.

The Homoian position was the one ultimately supported toward the end of his life by Constantius II, who assembled grandiose councils in hopes of

---

135. For this period, see Barnes 1993, 34–120, 229–32, who demonstrates that the councils of the 350s, although numerous, were not as unrelenting as has been assumed.

settling the matter once and for all.[136] In the second half of 359, he tried to impose a Homoian formula at dual ecumenical councils held at Ariminium (Rimini) in the west and Isaurian Seleucia (Silifke) in the east. Most of the western bishops at Rimini eventually signed on, although most later revoked their endorsement, claiming they had been forced into it. By contrast, the eastern council in Seleucia bifurcated into separate Homoian and Homoiousian enclaves. Constantius, however, had made up his mind, and as early as January 360, he gave the Homoians another chance to assert their dominance at a council in Constantinople. Here, under the leadership of Eudoxius and Acacius, they succeeded in ratifying their formula of faith and deposing and exiling their opponents, especially the Homoiousian leaders Basil of Ancyra and Macedonius of Constantinople—Constantius had already exiled the Anomoean chief Aetius.[137] In place of Macedonius, Eudoxius was now transferred to the eastern capital to serve as bishop there. His place in Antioch was soon taken by a young protégé of Acacius's named Meletius. And the Homoian bishop George was reimposed in Alexandria, Athanasius being already in exile. Thus, when Constantius died in November 361, Homoianism had been made the Christology of the "imperial church" and much of the east came to follow its formula. Aside from sizeable Homoiousian enclaves in western Anatolia and the Nicene stronghold of Alexandria, the east was essentially Homoian.[138]

The fire of controversy had only begun to die down when Julian threw new fuel onto it. Knowing full well that, left to their own devices, the Christians would begin savaging one another, Julian recalled all the bishops exiled under Constantius, especially those exiled at the council of Constantinople.[139] As predicted, the ecclesiastics quickly began fighting among themselves and organizing synods to restate their positions and bolster their claims to authority. Meanwhile, the pagan jubilee that followed Julian's arrival in the east started producing a number of Christian martyrs and confessors, mostly Homoians.[140] This garnered the seal of legitimacy for the Homoian cause and further strengthened its claim to authority even as its rivals struggled to achieve the same. By the time Julian died, the eastern church was in a state of total chaos, a state best witnessed by the officious parade of pleaders that soon confronted Jovian on his return from Persia in 363.

136. On the doctrinal battles in the last period of Constantius's rule, see Brennecke 1988, 5–86; Barnes 1993, 140–51.

137. *Hist. aceph.* 4.5; Soc. 2.41.5–43.16; Soz. 4.24.1–25.6.

138. See Jer. *Chron.* s.a. 359: "omnes paene toto orbe ecclesiae sub nomine pacis et regis Arrianorum consortio polluuntur"; cf. Basil *Ep.* 92. Brennecke 1988, 186–201, offers a diocese-by-diocese catalog of bishops and their Christological leanings.

139. Jul. *Ep.* 46, 114 (Bidez); AM 22.5.3–4; Ruf. *HE* 10.28; Soc. 3.1.48; Theod. *HE* 3.4.1; Philostorg. 6.7; cf. Barnes 1993, 154, on the date (360?).

140. Brennecke 1988, 114–57; cf. Woods 1995a.

As Jovian and his army hobbled back toward Antioch (see map 5) in the autumn of that year, he was met first by a letter from the Homoiousians, which reached him even as he crossed into imperial territory. Naturally, these wanted to regain the upper hand and sought this by attacking the Anomoeans and requesting their own reinstatement. Jovian is reported to have dismissed their claim, saying that he hated controversy but loved and honored concord.[141] For their part, the Anomoeans sent representatives who met Jovian in Edessa (Urfa) to plead for their cause, but they too were turned away with a call to reconciliation.[142] In his turn, the Nicene Athanasius hastened to Hierapolis (Membij) to meet the emperor's train and represent the Homoousian position, which essentially meant himself.[143] Although Julian had recalled all banished bishops from exile—including Athanasius—the belligerent Alexandrian had succeeded in getting himself chased away again in October 362.[144] After Julian's death was announced in Egypt on August 19, 363, Athanasius came out of hiding in Alexandria but knew he had to obtain imperial support again for the legitimation of his claim to the see.[145] He therefore hastened to meet Jovian's entourage and win his approval.[146] He was especially anxious to catch Jovian before he reached Antioch, where resistance to Athanasius awaited from the fourth party, the Homoians, who soon made their own case to Jovian in an effort to promote their chosen bishop of Alexandria, Lucius.[147]

141. Soc. 3.24.1, 25.1–5, esp. φιλονεικίαν μισῶ, τοὺς δὲ τῇ ὁμονοίᾳ προστρέχοντας ἀγαπῶ καὶ τιμῶ; cf. Soz. 6.4.3–5. See Löhr 1993 for the elimination of the Anomoeans as the Homoiousians' raison d'être. For these embassies, see Brennecke 1988, 168–73.

142. Philostorg. 8.6.

143. Hist. aceph. 4.4; Fest. ind. 36; Athanasius Ep. fest. 36 (Coptic: CSCO-SC 151.27).

144. Jul. Ep. 110, 112 (Bidez); Hist. aceph. 3.3–4; Ruf. HE 10.34–35; cf. Martin 1996, 565–73.

145. Hist. aceph. 4.1 reports the announcement of Julian's death and of an edict granting freedom of worship to Christians but says nothing of Athanasius's reinstallation prior to his visit to Jovian. Cf. Greg. Naz. Or. 21.33; Ruf. HE 10.28; Soc. 3.24.1–2; Soz. 6.3.3–5; Theod. HE 4.2.3–5; Philostorg. 8.5; Theoph. a.m. 5856; Cedrenus, p. 540; John of Nikiu 81.2–16. For analysis, see Martin 1996, 573–83.

146. Most sources report that Jovian initiated the exchange by asking Athanasius for a letter on doctrine, among them Epiph. Adv. haeres. 68.11.3; Greg. Naz. Or. 21.33; Ruf. HE 11.1; Soc. 3.24.3; Theod. HE 4.2.4–5; Theoph. a.m. 5856; Zon. 13.14; Suid. I 401; John of Nikiu 81.10–18; and Synodikon vetus 63. The letter of Athanasius to Jovian survives as Ad Iovianum (PG 26.813–19) = Theod. HE 4.3.1–14. Sozomen (6.5.1) confesses that some said that Athanasius had actually initiated contact with Jovian of his own accord. Regardless, Jovian's request need not imply that the emperor wished to use Athanasius's theology as normative. It is likely that he requested doctrinal statements from all bishops, and that Athanasius liberally interpreted the request as an invitation to visit the new emperor and set him straight on the faith, Martin 1996, 575–76; cf. Brennecke 1988, 171.

147. Hist. aceph. 4.7, which indicates that the effort to install Lucius came after Athanasius's return to Alexandria; cf. Epiph. Adv. haer. 68.11.4; Soc. 3.4.2, 4.1.14. Soz. 6.5.2–4 reports that the Homoians wanted rather the eunuch Probatianus as bishop. The Homoian attacks on Ath-

Of course, Jovian was well aware that Athanasius's support in Alexandria was by this time overwhelming and that the bishop had become an icon of orthodoxy in the west. The emperor would surely have been undermining his self-proclaimed pursuit of concord had he not approved Athanasius's control of the Egyptian metropolis. This, rather than his love of Nicene orthodoxy, explains why he did so. Yet this single act has led to the universal claim in our Nicene sources that Jovian was himself a stalwart Homoousian. Of this we must be skeptical, for there is little substantive proof that the new emperor held any fixed doctrinal position.[148] Even so, sensing that Jovian favored Athanasius, Antioch's formerly Homoian bishop Meletius—who had already been leaning toward Nicaea since his election in 360—called a council at precisely the time Jovian was passing through the city and, together with a number of former semi-Arians, publicly subscribed to Nicaea.[149] Everyone, it seems, was hoping to win the approval of the new emperor and use it to strengthen his position vis-à-vis his opponents. They met instead with Jovian's studied impartiality and call for peace.

Jovian died before his true skills as a manager of ecclesiastical controversy could be tested. His rhetoric of concord was, however, kept alive by his successor, Valentinian. All of our sources claim that Valentinian was a Nicene, and he did indeed support Nicene bishops in the west, where these vastly outnumbered their semi-Arian counterparts. The same sources make it clear, though, that Valentinian did not favor Nicenes any more than any other Christian faction.[150] As with pagan religion, Valentinian seems to have been largely indifferent, an attribute that paid off in the half of the empire where doctrinal controversy was already more the exception than the rule. He was also indifferent toward Jews and passed laws in their favor—as indeed did Valens.[151] The only religious groups he attacked, Manichaeans and Donatists, had long been regarded as part of the fringe and were widely held to be subversive.[152] Otherwise, his attitude toward Christian controversy was well

---

anasius before Jovian reported at *PG* 26.820–4 are of questionable authenticity; cf. Martin 1996, 588–89.

148. Brennecke 1988, 164–9, 178–81.

149. Jer. *Chron.* s.a. 364; Prosper *Chron.* 1124; Soc. 3.25.6–21; Soz. 6.4.6–10; Ruf. *HE* 10.31; Theoph. a.m. 5356. Note especially the synod's awareness of Jovian's mantra of harmony revealed in the opening line of their letter to him reported in Socrates. For various theories on Meletius's change of theology, see Brennecke 1988, 173–78; Spoerl 1993; Zachhuber 2000.

150. Joh. Ant. fr. 182 = Suid. *O* 762: Χριστιανὸς καὶ τὰ τοῦ ὁμοουσίου φρονῶν οὐδὲν τοὺς ἐναντίους ἠδίκει; Soc. 4.1.12, 29.1; Soz. 6.6.10; 21.7; cf. AM 30.9.5 and the passages cited at p. 215.

151. *CTh* 7.8.2; cf. 16.8.13. On Valens's favoritism toward Jews, see Theod. *HE* 4.24.2–3; Cedrenus, p. 544; Jacob of Edessa *Chron.*, p. 300.

152. On Donatists, see *CTh* 16.6.1; Ambrose *Ep. extra coll.* 7.7. On Manichaeans, see *CTh* 16.5.3; cf. *CTh* 16.7.3 and Lieu 1985, 95–111. Valentinian and Valens both employed *PLRE* I's

summed up in the response he gave to a group of Homoiousian bishops who met him in Thrace in 364 and requested permission to hold a council at Lampsacus (Lapseki; see map 3) in support of their position: "I am but one of the laity and have therefore no right to interfere in these transactions; let the priests, to whom such matters appertain, assemble where they please."[153] This impartiality eventually served as the basis for Ambrose's plea that Valentinian's son Valentinian II steer clear of doctrinal partisanship and later won great praise for Valentinian in all our sources.[154]

Even so, the Homoousians soon came to learn that Valentinian's impartiality could cut both ways. When the Nicene crusader Hilary of Poitiers tried to oust Auxentius, the Homoian bishop of Milan, from his see for "Arianism" in 364/65, Valentinian—who was in Milan—set up an inquest under his own *quaestor* and *magister officiorum*. In the event, though, Auxentius discomfited Hilary and won the approval of the emperor, who was clearly more interested in maintaining the peace in Milan than in asserting any one doctrinal position.[155] Once again, in 371, Pope Damasus convened a council in Rome to approve the condemnation of Auxentius. Although he had imperial approval for his meeting, he did not win any imperial aid for deposing Auxentius, who remained in place down to his death in 374.[156] Naturally, controversy cropped up in this year over the question of Auxentius's successor, but here again Valentinian refused to get involved. When his own governor Ambrose—a Nicene—obtruded himself into the position, Valentinian gladly acquiesced.[157] To him it mattered little whether Milan was Nicene or Arian, so long as it remained at peace.

Perhaps the best example of Valentinian's tolerance of religious difference comes in the schism that developed over the election of a successor to the bishop of Rome in 366. On the death of Pope Liberius on September 24 of that year, the two rival factions in the Roman church each elected their own

---

general Sebastianus 2, who was reputed to be a Manichaean. If the tag is not a slander, his case shows that even here religious tolerance was the norm.

153. Soz. 6.7.2; Theod. *HE* 4.6; *Pass. Artemii* 70; Theoph. a.m. 5857; cf. Basil *Ep.* 223, 244. Soc. 4.2.2–4 wrongly reports that it was Valens who granted permission for the council; cf. Urbainczyk 1997a, 359–62.

154. Ambrose *Ep.* 75 [21].2, 5.

155. Hilar. Pict. *Con. Aux.* 7–15 (*PL* 10.613–18). See McLynn 1994, 25–31; cf. Meslin 1967, 41–44. See also Athanasius's indignation that Auxentius retained his see in Italy (*Ep. ad Afros* [*PG* 26.1029, 1048]).

156. Soz. 6.23.5–15; cf. Theod. *HE* 2.22.1–12, and the Latin of the decretal *Confidimus quidem* at Mansi 3.459–60 = *PL* 13.347–9. Imperial approval for the synod is clear in the heading, *ex rescripto imperiali*. See Richard 1949; cf. McLynn 1994, 40–42.

157. Soc. 4.30.1–8, esp. 7: ὁ δὲ βασιλεὺς θαυμάσας τὴν τοῦ λαοῦ ὁμόνοιαν; Soz. 6.24.2–5; Theod. *HE* 4.7.1–6; Paulinus of Milan *V Ambrosii* 3 [6–11]; Ruf. *HE* 11.11; Jer. *Chron.* s.a. 374; Cedrenus, p. 546; Theoph. a.m. 5866. For analysis, see McLynn 1994, 1–52; cf. Williams 1995, 104–27.

candidate: Damasus was chosen by the majority faction and Ursinus by the minority. Within days, conflicts erupted, which led to two or even three bloody melees in the churches of Rome.[158] In response to this rioting, Valentinian showed a moderation uncharacteristic of his personality. He first expelled Ursinus but quickly recalled him and his cohorts saying: "[W]e pity them all both because of the mildness of our nature and in consideration of the law and religion."[159] When riots broke out again, claiming 137 more victims, the emperor again banned the Ursinians—still with misgivings. His orders are preserved in the so-called *Collectio Avellana*, which contains a total of eight of Valentinian's letters on the issue, in each of which he stresses the importance of concord and the need to strive for peace.[160] Valentinian was thus even willing to relax his customary severity in order to achieve peace within the church. He was both savvy enough to avoid attacking believers and pragmatic enough to understand that such violence compromised his own security.

As much as anything, Valentinian distanced himself from the politics of the church, because he knew well that he was not a holy man but a soldier emperor. Thus his laws on Christian religion were generally favorable but hardly lavished the sorts of rewards on the church that his predecessors or successors did. He did not, for example, fully restore Constantine's grants of public revenues to churches, which Julian had eliminated.[161] On the contrary, he severely restricted the rights of churches and churchmen to inherit property, mostly as a way to keep it on the tax rolls.[162] Where money was involved, then, he always held economy above religion. He did, of course, take simple, cost-free measures to promote Christianity, like banning the condemnation of Christians to the games and granting blanket amnesties to convicted criminals at Easter.[163] This record shows an emperor who, while certainly a believer, was hardly concerned with going down as a saint.

Indeed, Valentinian was apparently so indifferent to religious distinctions that he probably altered his initial doctrinal leanings in order to conform with

---

158. *Coll. Avell.* 1; AM 27.3.12–13, 9.9; Jer. *Chron.* s.a. 366; Prosper *Chron.* 1132; Ruf. *HE* 11.10; Soc. 4.29.1–6; Soz. 6.23.1; cf. Ambrose *Ep. extra coll.* 7.2. On these riots, see Seeck, *Untergang*, 70–4; Pietri 1976, 408–23; Kahlos 1996.

159. *Coll. Avell.* 5: "nos omnes . . . et propriae lentitate naturae et ipsius religionis ac legis contemplatione miseremur."

160. *Coll. Avell.* 6: "pro publica securitate metuendum est"; 7: "firma sit rursus in plebe concordia"; 8: "ut nulla in urbe Roma possit esse discordia"; 9, 10, 11: "faventes concordiae populi Christiani"; 12: "propter quietem populi Christiani."

161. Theod. *HE* 4.4.1 reports that Jovian had restored only one-third of the subsidy amounts granted by Constantine, and Valentinian and Valens apparently maintained this reduced level (A. H. M. Jones 1964, 898–99).

162. *CTh* 16.2.20; Ambrose *Ep.* 73 [18].13–14; Jer. *Ep.* 52.6. See also *CTh* 12.1.59 with Ambrose *Ep.* 73 [18].13; *CTh* 13.1.5 with Basil *Ep.* 104; *CTh* 16.2.17, 19, 21; cf. Rougé 1987, 295–96; Grubbs 1995, 138–39; Nathan 2000, 126–27.

163. *CTh* 8.8.1 + 11.7.10, 9.38.3–4, 40.8, 13.10.4, 6.

the norms of the west where he ruled. As noted, all of our sources claim that Valentinian was a Nicene, and Theodoret would have it that Valens was also originally.[164] Theodoret even manipulated a strange synodical decree he had found to make it seem that both emperors remained unsullied supporters of the Homoousion into the middle years of their reigns.[165] In a characteristically misogynistic twist, Theodoret holds that, like Adam, Valens was only later tempted down the path of sin by his wife Domnica.[166] Domnica certainly was an "Arian" of some flavor,[167] but her corruption of a previously orthodox husband sounds prima facie tendentious. The fact is that Valens, and probably Valentinian as well, had probably been "Arians" since they were boys.

Both grew up surrounded by Arians in their native province of Pannonia. Shortly before Valens was born, Arius himself had been banished to Illyricum,[168] and there he is said to have established a loyal group of followers, chief among them another Valens, bishop of Mursa, a day's walk from their native Cibalae, and Ursacius, bishop of Jovian's home town of Singidunum (see map 1).[169] Both Valens and Ursacius became extremely influential in ecclesiastical politics when the semi-Arian emperor Constantius moved into their area in 351. In that year, they imposed a like-minded easterner named Germinius as bishop in Sirmium and, working together with him, eventually designed the official imperial creed—the Homoian creed—which Constantius endorsed at the Councils of Ariminium and Seleucia in 359.[170] Pannonia was thus, in a very real sense, the home of the Homoian church, for which Valens later crusaded.

Moreover, we have some fairly good evidence of what spiritual life in Pannonia must have been like in the early years of the two future emperors. From A.D. 366, we possess a fascinating document recording proceedings against an obstinate Nicene layman named Heraclianus by none other than Germinius of Sirmium.[171] The *Altercatio Heracliani* describes how the Nicene was prosecuted for his belief in the Homoousion, which roused the Arian population of Sirmium to a frenzy. Eventually, Germinius ordered his deacon to knock Heraclianus's teeth out and forbade contact with the dissident as a heretic. St. Martin, whom we met as a son of Pannonia in the first chapter,

---

164. Soc. 4.1.5–7; Soz. 6.6.10, 21.7; Theod. *HE* 4.6.3, 12.4, 13.1; Joh. Ant. fr. 182 = Suid. O 762; John of Nikiu *Chron.* 82.17.

165. Theod. *HE* 4.7.6–9.9 from which Theoph. a.m. 5866; *Synodikon vetus* 71; Jacob of Edessa *Chron.*, p. 297. For one theory on Theodoret's text, see McLynn 1994, 92–94.

166. Theod. *HE* 4.12.3–4; cf. Theoph. a.m. 5860; Zon. 13.16.

167. See Soc. 4.26.21; Soz. 6.16.2; Cedrenus, p. 550.

168. Philostorg. 1.9c.

169. Athanasius *Ep. ad episc. Aeg. et Lib.* 7 (*PG* 25.553). On Ursacius and Valens, see Meslin 1967, 71–84; Barnes 1993, 109, 138–9, 144.

170. On Germinius, see Williams 1996.

171. *Altercatio Heracliani* (*PL* Suppl. 9.345–50).

had been similarly beaten and thrown out of his home town of Savaria for his Nicene beliefs a decade earlier.[172]

Coming out of this world, Valens is unlikely to have held anything but Homoian beliefs. For his part, Valentinian received "Arian" doctrine in equal measure from the bishops of his homeland and the religion of the military camps where he grew up, for these surely followed the mandate of the emperor. It is thus likely that he too started out an Arian and would probably have remained such during his years of retirement in Sirmium—home of the pious hooligan Germinius—after 357.[173] He was at any rate, as we have seen, indifferent to Arians and eventually took one for his second wife.[174].

Whether Valentinian actually converted to Nicene Christianity or simply masked his Homoianism we can no longer say. His indifference to doctrinal issues renders his true position all but opaque. The fact is that he favored Christianity, but not excessively. While granting simple and inexpensive privileges to Christians, he refrained from lavishing his favor on the church or any one group within it. He remained largely indifferent on questions of heresy and schism and thus avoided becoming the focal point for bishops hoping to promote themselves through doctrinal manipulations. Under his influence, Valens attempted to do the same. As we shall see, with the passing of time the eastern emperor found this increasingly difficult and eventually became completely ensnared in religious persecutions. Such was not his brother's wish; indeed, such was probably not Valens's wish. Such was, however, the nature of eastern Christendom in the fourth century.

AUTOCRACY AND PERSECUTION: VALENS'S RESPONSE TO THE ARIAN CRISIS

Valens was not entirely unlike his brother in his treatment of Christian religion. Indeed, even where Valens used strong-arm tactics, he always did so in an effort to coerce "concord" out of the unwilling. Thus when he heard about disturbances over the successor to the see of Constantinople, Valens sent in the troops, but mainly with the object of ending the uprising.[175] So, too, when Valens's praetorian prefect Modestus exiled the Anomoean leader Eunomius, it was in order to prevent him from fomenting further discord in the churches and cities.[176] After ordering Athanasius's exile in 365, Valens granted an appeal from the rowdy populace of Alexandria for the bishop's

---

172. Sulp. Sev. *V Mart.* 6.4.

173. See McLynn 1997, 172–74, who argues for an even slipperier credal position.

174. *PLRE* I, Justina. Sulp. Sev. *Dial.* 1.5.5–10 reports that Justina influenced Valentinian's choice to avoid contact with the Nicene ascetic Martin.

175. Soz. 6.13.3: δείσας δὲ περὶ τῆς πόλεως, μή τι πάθοι ὑπὸ στάσεως. See pp. 250–51 for further sources.

176. Philostorg. 9.11: ὡς τὰς ἐκκλησίας καὶ τὰς πόλεις ἐκταράσσοντος.

reinstatement, again to avoid violence.[177] And even when Valens sent an army to impose the Homoian bishop Lucius in Alexandria after Athanasius's death, he initially hoped to ensure peace with these forces, who only did violence to resisters after offering them the option of an accord on the emperor's terms.[178] When he set on Basil of Caesarea, Valens again made it clear that simple compliance with Homoian doctrine would lead to peace and prosperity.[179] Like his brother, then, Valens desired harmony in the church. Unlike his brother, though, he had not learned from the Christian persecutions of his third and early fourth-century Illyrian predecessors that belief cannot be dictated by force.

In what follows, I begin by discussing Valens's baptism by the Homoians at the beginning of his reign and the influence this had on his subsequent religious position. I then treat Valens's handling of the Arian crisis, which can be broken into three phases. Initially, Valens took a fairly strong position in favor of the leading party in the east, the Homoians. In so doing, he certainly used might to enforce the decisions of the council of Constantinople against those deposed there, the Homoiousians and Anomoeans. Even so, he does not appear to have attacked Christians other than those condemned at Constantinople. In the years between 366 and 373, Valens turned to a more moderate position and brought only mild pressure to bear on non-Homoians in an effort to encourage—not coerce—conformity. In this period, he came much closer to the ideal achieved by Valentinian. Finally, Valens eventually went back onto the offensive against an increasingly intransigent Nicene party toward the end of his reign. After the death of Athanasius in 373, he began to exert considerable force in order to achieve the illusory end of unifying the church around the Homoian creed. His obstinate insistence on a Homoian state church and his consequent attempts to struggle against Nicene opponents turned him into the ferocious persecutor our sources love to hate.

In the same section of his ecclesiastical history where Theodoret claims that Valens was initially orthodox, the author also describes Valens's "Arian" baptism at the hands of Eudoxius of Constantinople. This, he says, was prompted by Valens's wife and by the emperor's fear of death before his upcoming Gothic campaign.[180] Theodoret's date is certainly correct, for Jerome's *Chronicle* reports that Valens was baptized by Eudoxius in 366, the year before the beginning of the Gothic war.[181] But the charge that Domnica made him do

177. See p. 247.
178. Theod. *HE* 4.22.13–15; cf. pp. 255–57.
179. Greg. Nys. *Eun.* 1.132; cf. p. 253.
180. Theod. *HE* 4.12.1–4; cf. Leppin 1996, 96–97.
181. Jer. *Chron.* s.a. 366; cf. Prosper *Chron.* 1133; Jord. *Rom.* 308. In light of the arguments that follow, there is no reason to doubt the testimony of Jerome on this date, as do Seeck, *Untergang*, 456–57, and Woods 1994.

it is, as noted earlier, misleading. From his first arrival in Constantinople, Valens's religious leanings were heavily influenced by Eudoxius.[182] Indeed, most sources claim that it was Eudoxius rather than Domnica who persuaded Valens to undergo baptism in the first place.[183] Moreover, again and again the sources claim that Eudoxius and his Homoian counterpart in Antioch, Euzoius, were behind Valens's religious policies: Eudoxius persuaded Valens to annul the Homoiousian council at Lampsacus in 365;[184] he encouraged Valens to uphold the expulsion of Homoiousians ordered by the council of Constantinople;[185] he prevented Valens from meeting with Eunomius in 366;[186] he instigated Valens to forbid a Nicene council at Tarsus in 366;[187] he traveled to Marcianople with Valens during his first Gothic war and there advised him on religious affairs.[188] Meanwhile, Euzoius encouraged Valens to impose a Homoian bishop in Alexandria in 373;[189] and Valens expelled all those who did not follow Euzoius from Antioch.[190] We have already seen that Valens's lack of education and lack of Greek led him to rely on a small coterie of professional bureaucrats for advice on administrative matters.[191] It seems that Valens was also willing to entrust ecclesiastical affairs to a small though powerful group of Homoian clerics.

Though such claims of unholy influence are stereotyped in our source traditions, we should not assume that they are wrong. They are at least contemporary, for they were reported by Epiphanius in Valens's own lifetime:

> Their gang of snakes won out yet a second time through Eudoxius, who wormed his way into the confidence of the devout emperor Valens, a very pious man and a lover of God, and once again corrupted his sense of hearing. The reason the Arians could maintain their position was Valens's baptism by Eudoxius. . . . By the emperor's patronage, that is, his protection, they won out so as to get to work on all the wrongs that have been done and are still being done by them at Alexandria, Nicomedia, Mesopotamia, and Palestine under the patronage of the same current emperor.[192]

---

182. Philostorg. 9.3: Οὐάλης ... ἐκ τῶν Ἰλλυριῶν ἐπὶ τὴν Κωνσταντινούπολιν ἀφικόμενος, διὰ τιμῆς εἶχεν Εὐδόξιον. Cf. Soz. 6.7.9.

183. Soc. 4.1.6; Soz. 6.6.10; Theoph. a.m. 5857, 5860; Oros. 7.32.6; cf. Theod. HE 4.12.4–13.1, 19.10; Greg. Nys. Eun. 1.122.

184. Soz. 6.7.9.

185. Soc. 4.13.3–4; Soz. 6.10.2–3; Pass. Artemii 70; Theoph. a.m. 5861.

186. Philostorg. 9.8.

187. Soc. 4.12.40; Soz. 6.12.5.

188. Philostorg. 9.7.

189. Soc. 4.21.1–4; Soz. 6.19.2; Theod. HE 4.21.3, 22.10.

190. Soz. 6.7.10.

191. See pp. 65–66.

192. Epiph. Adv. haeres. 69.13.1–3 (trans. Williams); cf. 64.34.1–4 and Basil Ep. 129. See also Griffith 1986, 33–35, for similar sentiments in Ephrem.

Gregory of Nazianzus's *Encomium of Basil,* delivered shortly after Valens's death, says much the same, that Valens was "debased by those who led him," and indicates that the emperor traveled with an entourage of Homoian advisers.[193] Indeed, there may even have been links between this group and the Homoians back home in Pannonia, for Gregory of Nyssa indicates that Valens's second attack on Basil was led by "one of the God-haters from Illyricum."[194] Then, too, after Valens exiled Eunomius for involvement in the Procopius revolt, he recalled him because Valens, the bishop of Pannonian Mursa, convinced the emperor of Eunomius's innocence.[195] If, as seems reasonable, Valens the emperor knew and trusted this homonymous bishop from a city just a day's walk from his home town, we can begin to explain his readiness to relax his order against a cleric who had aided and abetted the usurper. Moreover, Valens of Mursa certainly knew Valens's chief religious advisor, the like-minded Eudoxius of Constantinople: both had attended councils together in the 340s and 350s and both championed the Homoian creed at the respective councils of Rimini and Constantinople. It is quite possible, then, that Valens of Mursa recommended his compatriot Valens of Cibalae to Eudoxius of Constantinople when the new emperor returned from Sirmium to Thrace in late 364.[196]

This would certainly explain why Valens (the emperor) took up the cause of Homoianism immediately after his return to the east in this year. Although he was not baptized until 366, Valens had already begun supporting Eudoxius as early as September 364, when he defended him against Homoiousian detractors who hoped to win the emperor to their cause.[197] We have already seen that Valentinian happily granted the Homoiousians the right to assemble a council at Lampsacus in summer 364.[198] Naturally, these restated support for their position at Seleucia, rejected the Homoian council of Constantinople, and ordered the expulsion of its leaders, especially Eudoxius of Constantinople. They then made a special effort to catch Valens on his return from Illyricum in the fall of 364 before he reached Eudoxius in the eastern capital. But, as Sozomen tells us, Valens had already made an accord with Eudoxius and thus simply ordered the Homoiousians not to be at variance with his favorite. When the Homoiousians persisted and angered the emperor, he banished them and ordered their replacement by partisans of

---

193. Greg. Naz. *Or.* 43.30, 44, 54.
194. Greg. Nys. *Eun.* 1.140: τινος τῶν ἐκ τοῦ Ἰλλυρικοῦ θεομάχων; cf. Soz. 6.15.4.
195. Philostorg. 9.8.
196. Valens of Mursa was still alive and active until at least 370, when Athanasius lamented his continued hold on Illyricum (*Ep. ad Afr.* 10 [*PG* 26.1045–48]).
197. On the date, see Seeck, *Regesten,* 217; Barnes 1998, 248.
198. See p. 239.

Eudoxius.[199] This was only the beginning of a more systematic attack on Homoiousians, which will be discussed in a moment. For now, it must be noted that, in taking this position, Valens was both adhering to his own Homoian Christological assumptions and, more important, upholding the status quo. The Homoians were, as we have seen, the dominant church in the east when Valens attained the throne, and they had gained their dominance at the expense of the Homoiousians. In upholding the council of Constantinople by suppressing the Homoiousians, Valens was carrying on the task initiated by Constantius II of defending the official state church.[200]

In the summer of 365, Valens and his army set out from Constantinople toward the Persian frontier and along the way stopped in Cappadocian Caesarea (Kayseri). Here again we can see the outlines of his efforts to uphold the decrees of Constantinople, not so much in what happened as in what did not. We know from two contemporary letters of Gregory of Nazianzus that the approach of "these wild beasts that are rushing on the Church" was anticipated with some trepidation.[201] It is entirely natural that the arrival of the court struck fear into many a heart in Caesarea, for the bishop there, Eusebius, and his wealthy and influential new priest Basil had both been supporters of the Homoiousians. Fortunately, however, Eusebius had steered clear of the council of Constantinople and, although Basil had gone with the Homoiousians Basil of Ancyra and Eustathius of Sebaste (Sivasli), he left early under mysterious circumstances.[202] In anticipation of the contest with Valens, Basil—who had earlier retreated from Caesarea after bickering with Eusebius—returned to his native city. Gregory would have it that he was eager to defend the local church against the emperor, but the troubles he anticipated seem never to have materialized. This is because Basil and Eusebius of Caesarea were never Valens's targets, for they had not been condemned at Constantinople in 360.

Basil's and Eusebius's anxieties will have been piqued by a decree issued by Valens in the spring of 365 ordering that "bishops who had been deposed and expelled from their churches under Constantius but who had reclaimed

---

199. Soz. 6.7.3–9; cf. 6.8.4; Theoph. a.m. 5857; Cedrenus, p. 541; Jacob of Edessa *Chron.*, p. 296; *Synodikon vetus* 69. Around the same time he banished the homoiousian bishop of Jerusalem Cyril; see Drijvers 1999, 80–81.

200. At precisely the same period (ca. 364/65) Constantius's "orthodoxy" was being defended even by those who later became rabid Nicenes, Greg. Naz. *Or.* 4.3, 33–42, 48, 5.16, 17; Ephrem *CJ* 2.19, 25, 3.8, 10, 4.15; cf. Theod. *HE* 4.1.5–6, with Brennecke 1988, 165 n. 48. See also Valentinian's use of Constantius's religious policies as normative, *CTh* 16.2.18—the first legal text to use the word *paganus* for "pagans." Tritle 1994 has even argued—not entirely successfully—that Constantius's former ministers dictated Valens's religious policies.

201. Greg. Naz. *Ep.* 18–19; cf. *Or.* 43.30–33 and Soz. 6.15.1–5. See also *BP* 4.8 and Zon. 13.16 for more fanciful versions. On the date, see May 1973, 49.

202. See Rousseau 1994, 97–106, and Basil *Ep.* 243.

and retaken their bishoprics in the time of Julian's reign should once again be expelled from their churches."[203] This, too, was aimed at the Homoiousians condemned at Constantinople. Even so, the order naturally raised the question of Athanasius, who certainly fit its specifications. Athanasius was not a Homoiousian and thus not Valens's main concern, but he was a troublemaker, and Valens would have gladly countenanced his disappearance. Naturally, the city council of Alexandria was in a quandary, for they could neither disobey the order nor expel Athanasius without grave consequences. Athanasius was hugely popular among the masses,[204] and these had already begun to raise disturbances on his behalf as the council debated its options. Ultimately, the councilors cleverly threw the question back to the emperor: true, Athanasius was exiled by Constantius and recalled by Julian; but he had been reexiled by Julian and recalled by Jovian, so did the order apply? The question was sent to Valens on June 8, 365. A reply granting Athanasius leave to remain came back only on January 31, 366. We need not assume that Valens granted the reprieve because of any great sympathy for Athanasius. Between the forwarding of the question and the arrival of the response, the Procopius revolt had broken out, and Valens was in no need of riots in Alexandria over the deposition of the local hero.[205] Athanasius's reprieve was a simple question of maintaining the peace.

The Procopius revolt seems also to have affected the Homoiousian question in ways previous scholars have failed to recognize because of mistakes in chronology. Once Procopius gained control of Bithynia and Asia, former Homoiousian strongholds, these partisans were given a new lease on life. Frustrated with their inability to make headway with Valens after the council at Lampsacus, the Homoiousians had held synods in Smyrna (Izmir), Pisidia, Isauria, Pamphylia, and Lycia in the fall of 364. From these, they decided to organize an embassy to proceed to Rome and eventually to the court of Valentinian for redress.[206] Valentinian had, after all, granted them permission to assemble in the first place and may thus have been regarded as a softer target than his brother. The embassy traveled by boat and so is unlikely to have departed until the sea-lanes reopened the following spring. Over the summer of 365, the ambassadors negotiated with Pope Liberius in Rome and gradually came to an accord, but only after having agreed to subscribe to the creed of Nicaea. They did not, however, proceed to Milan to find

---

203. *Hist. aceph.* 5.1–7 reports that the decree was published on May 5, 365, in Alexandria. Cf. *Fest. ind.* 37; Epiph. *Adv. haeres.* 68.11.3–5; Soz. 6.12.5–15; Soc. 4.13.3–6; Theoph. a.m. 5861.

204. E.g., Greg. Naz. *Or.* 21.20, 27; cf. Barnes 1993, 92, 96–97, 152, 164, 167–68. See also, however, Haas 1993 on the significant Arian population in Alexandria.

205. Epiph. *Adv. haeres.* 68.11.4; Soz. 6.12.15; cf. Haas 1993, 240; Martin 1996, 590–96.

206. Soc. 4.12.2–40, 5.4.1, 5.8.7–8; Soz. 6.10.3–12.5, 7.2.2; Basil *Ep.* 263; Epiph. *Adv. haeres.* 75.2.7; Theoph. a.m. 5860; cf. Barnes 1993, 161–62.

Valentinian, for he had already left Italy for Gaul by the time they were free to consult him. This means that they had to have remained in Italy until the fall of 365, when the western emperor is known to have departed from Milan for Paris.[207]

After abandoning the plan to contact Valentinian, the group sailed via Sicily back to the east and there presented western letters of support from Rome and Sicily to a council at Tyana. That group agreed to assemble a much larger council in Tarsus in order to ratify the western decrees—in other words, in order to ratify Nicaea. Under the influence of Eudoxius, Valens forbade the Tarsus council to convene. This cannot have been until early June 366, for up to that time Eudoxius had been in territory controlled by Procopius and would have been incommunicado to Valens. Indeed, Sozomen reports that the Tarsus council was to have taken place "while it was still spring," by which he must mean the spring of 366, the same spring when Valens first reestablished contact with his Constantinopolitan advisor.[208] Once we understand this, we can better see why thirty Homoiousians who were dissatisfied with the proposed shift to Nicaea were able to assemble in Caria shortly before the planned council in Tarsus and reaffirm the creed of Seleucia.[209] That group would also have been in territory controlled by Procopius at the time. It seems, then, that even though Valens had nearly snuffed them out in the summer of 365, Procopius had given the Homoiousians a new lease on life in early 366.

This chronological revelation also explains why, for a short time after the end of the Procopius revolt, Valens needed to continue his efforts to uphold the depositions issued against the Homoiousians at Constantinople. Immediately after the fighting with Procopius had ceased—while Valens was relaxing in Nicaea—he had the Homoiousian bishop of Cyzicus, Eleusius, summoned to a Homoian synod on the fate of his episcopacy.[210] Eleusius had

---

207. Soc. 4.12.4; Soz. 6.10.5. Seeck, *Regesten*, 226 shows that Valentinian departed Italy in September of 365.

208. Soz. 6.12.3: ἔτι ἦρος ὄντος. Barnes 1993, 161–62, dates the entire sequence of events from the rebuff at Lampsacus to the failed synod in Tarsus to late 364 and 365. This cannot, however, be reconciled with our knowledge that Valentinian only departed from Italy in the fall of 365. We must therefore understand a chronological break in Sozomen's version beginning at 6.12.5 (ἐν μέρει), which begins a new section taking us back to spring 365. Brennecke 1988, 216–22, extends the planned synod of Tarsus into the spring of 367, a year too late.

209. Soz. 6.12.4. One must assume that Soz. 7.2.3 reports a separate council, but the two look suspiciously alike.

210. Soc. 4.6.1–7.3; Soz. 6.8.5–8; Theoph. a.m. 5859. Brennecke 1988, 216–17, misdates this incident to 365, with obvious consequences for his interpretation. Socrates wrongly reports that Eudoxius sent Eunomius to fill the see of Cyzicus, clearly a confusion for Eunomius's earlier control over Cyzicus reported at Soz. 4.25.6; Philostorg. 5.3; Theod. *HE* 2.27.21.

also been deposed at Constantinople but—according to Socrates—had regained his footing at Cyzicus during the Procopius revolt. Valens no doubt intended to carry through the deposition if Eleusius did not relent.[211] In the face of threatened expulsion and confiscations, the bishop quailed and agreed to subscribe to Homoianism. His case drives home the point that Valens was aiming to uphold the Homoian state church and the decrees of its council against Homoiousians. It also confirms that Procopius created something of a bump on the road to carrying out this plan.

One final loser at the at the end of Constantius's life had been the Anomoean leader Aetius. He had been exiled in 359 and condemned at the council of Constantinople the following year, but was recalled under Julian, who had been particularly gracious to him as a former friend of his half-brother Gallus.[212] Aetius thus fell under the order of Valens reposing and exiling bishops who had been recalled by Julian. Apparently to escape detection, Aetius went to Lesbos, where Julian had given him estates. At the same time, his protégé Eunomius also withdrew from his failed appointment to the bishopric of Cyzicus and retired to his own property in Chalcedon. There, Eunomius soon offered refuge to Procopius in the months before his rebellion.[213] Naturally, this did not sit well with Valens, who, as we have already seen, ordered Eunomius's exile for aiding and abetting the usurper—Aetius had meanwhile expired. We have also seen that, on the advice of Valens of Mursa, the emperor again recalled Eunomius. Nevertheless, Valens refused him an imperial audience and later upheld his banishment from Constantinople, where Eunomius had been raising trouble.[214] Once Modestus became praetorian prefect late in 370, he again exiled Eunomius one last time.[215] In finally having done with Eunomius, Valens was simultaneously ridding himself of a traitor and upholding the council of Constantinople's ban on Anomoeans.

In the years following the Procopius revolt, Valens seems to have relaxed his religious posture considerably. Some expulsions were effected, but by and large Valens applied only minor pressures to bring bishops in line with his Homoian beliefs. It is not clear whether the revolt, which he had in some ways provoked with his harshness, was a deciding factor in Valens's choice to exercise more restraint. While it may be true that the Procopius incident was the biggest reason for Valens's reprieve of Athanasius, it seems that in most other instances, Valens abated his use of force primarily because he

211. On the advantage gained during the Procopius revolt, see Soc. 4.4.4–6.
212. On the friendship with Gallus, see Brennecke 1988, 89, and esp. Jul. *Ep.* 46 (Bidez).
213. Philostorg. 9.4–6, 8.
214. Philostorg. 9.7–8, which must be presented in reverse chronological order.
215. Philostorg. 9.11.

had accomplished his initial goal. For this reason, Valens left Athanasius almost entirely alone after January 366.[216] A number of Athanasius's letters from the period between 366 and his death in 373 survive, and none of them give any indication of troubles.[217] Indeed, the narrative sources are a bit embarrassed to admit that the arch-persecutor Valens did nothing to their reverend confessor and attribute this clemency to the emperor's fear of insurrection.[218] This was certainly the case, for much as Valens would have loved to see a Homoian bishop in Alexandria, he was wise enough to avoid a fight over the issue while Athanasius was alive. So, too, the Nicene Vetranio of Tomi had a minor run in with Valens but suffered little for it because of the emperor's overriding concern with stability and concord. It seems that when Valens visited Tomi during his first Gothic war in 368, Vetranio upbraided the Pannonian for his Homoianism and then staged a mass walkout from his city to insult the emperor. Valens was so infuriated that he ordered Vetranio's banishment, but he quickly rescinded the order to avoid local unrest.[219] At this stage, it seems, no Nicene bishop was regarded as a particular threat. The Nicene party probably seemed too small and fragmented to bother the emperor in a period when the Homoiousians had been brought to heel and concord had once again become the watchword.

In Constantinople, the situation was a bit more complicated. After Valens set off from there for the eastern frontier in the late spring of 370, his trusted bishop Eudoxius expired, and the Homoians of Constantinople moved quickly to replace him with Demophilus, long the bishop of Beroea in Thrace.[220] At the same time, however, the Nicene party in Constantinople— which must have been tiny at the time—appointed a bishop of its own named Evagrius, otherwise unknown in our sources.[221] Scuffles broke out, and when news of them reached Valens, who had already arrived at Nicomedia (Izmit) with his army, he sent troops back to Constantinople to restore the peace. Meanwhile, a delegation of Homoousian priests had come to Nicomedia to

216. This is certain from *Hist. aceph.* 5.8–10.

217. Athanasius *Ep. ad Epictetum; Ep. ad Adelphium; Ep. Ad Maximum* (*PG* 26.1049–89). See also the fragments of Athanasius's festal letters for the period: Cureton 1854, 137–40, for the Syriac versions of letters 39 and 44; Lefort 1955, 26–54, for the Coptic versions of 36–43. For analysis, see Martin 1996, 597–604, 626–35.

218. Ruf. *HE* 11.2; Soc. 4.13.6, 20.1; Soz. 6.12.16.

219. Soz. 6.21.3–6; cf. Theod. *HE* 4.35.1. Valens's presence in Tomi is attested by the inscription *AE* 1978, 716.

220. Soc. 4.14.1–15.5, who dates the incident for us at 4.14.2; Soz. 6.13.1–4; Theoph. a.m. 5861; Zon. 13.15; *Chronicon ad annum 846* p. 201; Jacob of Edessa *Chron.*, p. 297; cf. Philostorg. 9.8, 10.

221. Soc. 4.14.3, 15.3, and Soz. 6.13.2–4 report that Evagrius was consecrated by Eustathius of Antioch. This is an error, for Eustathius was dead by this time. On the insignificance of the Nicene party in Constantinople prior to 381, see Greg. Naz. *De vit. sua* ll. 652–62; Soc. 4.1.16; Soz. 6.9.1, 7.5.1.

plead their cause before Valens and had been angrily dismissed and ordered into exile.[222] The group, which may have numbered as many as eighty,[223] was put onto a ship that headed out onto the gulf of Astacus, but it caught fire and was gutted before it touched ground. Later rumor had it that Valens had actually ordered the execution of these confessors and that the praetorian prefect Modestus had secretly arranged with the ship's crew to start the blaze. Although we shall never know whether there really was such a plot, we have good reason to doubt it. No matter how fierce his temper, Valens would have known that it would do him no good to immolate a bunch of low-level ecclesiastics. The incident was certainly a tragedy, and one that haunts Valens's reputation, but it is unlikely that it was his fault. He had simply been trying to eliminate discord, and although he had succeeded in Constantinople, he was plagued by bad fortune in the case of the ill-fated priests.[224]

More complicated still was the situation in Antioch. Long wracked by schism, this city could claim no fewer than three bishops in late 370 when Valens arrived there for his first visit as emperor:[225] Paulinus, a Homoousian consecrated by western Nicenes in 362; Meletius, who had replaced the Homoian Eudoxius on the latter's transfer to Constantinople in 360, but had quickly shifted toward the Homoousion; and Euzoius, a Homoian and friend of Eudoxius, who had been substituted for Meletius in 361 after the latter changed his doctrinal stance.[226] The creation of rival Homoian and Homoousian bishops in a single city was common across the east, but the presence of two Nicenes in the same city created an embarrassment and a potential danger. The followers of both Meletius and Paulinus were intransigent in their claims to exclusive legitimacy, and they are known to have later clashed openly in the streets.[227] It was thus unsurprising that Valens chose

222. Soc. 4.16.1–6; Soz. 6.14.1–4; Theod. *HE* 4.24.1; Suid. *Ω* 764; Theoph. a.m. 5862; Zon. 13.16; Cedrenus, p. 544; Jacob of Edessa *Chron.*, p. 300. The incident is already alluded to in Valens's lifetime (Epiph. *Adv. haeres.* 69.13.3) and became a topos in the Cappadocian fathers (Greg. Naz. *Or.* 25.10, 33.4, 42.23, 43.46; Greg. Nys. *Eun.* 1.131).

223. Most sources report eighty, but Greg. Naz. *Or.* 25.10 speaks of only one. The fact that his remaining allusions to the incident mention "priests" (πρεσβύτεροι) should probably be taken to mean that even he knew many were killed. For the opposite view, see Gwatkin 1900, 276–77; cf. Barnes 1993, 291 n. 60.

224. The peace achieved in Constantinople is reflected in Basil *Ep.* 48 (a. 371). For later religious violence in Constantinople, see Greg. Naz. *Ep.* 77–78. Valens also expelled Novatians from Constantinople but later recalled them (Soc. 4.9.1–7; Soz. 6.9.1–3).

225. Soc. 4.2.4—which wrongly posits a visit by Valens to Antioch in 365—is a doublet for 4.17.1–3; cf. Soz. 6.7.10 and 6.18.1.

226. On the schism of Antioch, see Devreesse 1945, 14–38; Barnes 1993, 156–58; Spoerl 1993. For brevity, I omit Apollinaris and his partisans, yet these further complicated the see by adding a fourth bishop toward the end of Valens's reign.

227. For the discord over the Antiochene schism, see Basil *Ep.* 48, 66; Epiph. *Adv. haeres.* 77.20.3–7; Ruf. *HE* 10.28; Soz. 7.3.1–5; Theod. *HE* 5.3.1–16.

to expel Meletius shortly after his arrival at Antioch in late 370.[228] Like Athanasius, Meletius was charismatic and therefore dangerous;[229] he was also, in the eyes of Homoians and many Nicenes alike, an interloper and schismatic.[230] Valens did not exile Meletius, however, but allowed him to return to his home of Getasa in Armenia Minor.[231] He also allowed Paulinus and his followers to remain in Antioch, a sign that his concern was more with eliminating the discord of schism than eliminating Nicenes.[232] Indeed, although Valens forbade Homoousians to meet in the city, they continued to congregate on its outskirts. Half-hearted efforts to scatter them with troops eventually led the group to hold services near Valens's military training ground, a point of contact that, as we will see, proved useful in winning support from Valens's generals.[233] Here again, we see Valens treating Nicenes with relative moderation, and even a certain nonchalance, in the middle years of his reign.[234]

Indeed, at this stage, the Homoousian church in the east hardly presented a consolidated front. The eastern Nicenes were not united in their battle against "Arianism," and neither could they expect support either from their western counterparts or the western emperor.[235] Basil of Caesarea, for example, struggled mightily to win broader Nicene support for Meletius, his favorite in Antioch, yet never even managed to gain the endorsement of Athanasius,[236] let alone of the pope of Rome, Damasus, both of whom favored Paulinus.[237] In light of this infighting and seeming impotence among the Nicenes, it is little wonder that Valens paid little attention to this group at the time.

Basil's "struggles" for Nicene orthodoxy provide the last and perhaps the

---

228. Basil *Ep.* 40, 48, 99; Epiph. *Adv. haeres.* 73.28.2, 34.2; Joh. Chrys. *In Mel.* (*PG* 50.517); Soc. 4.2.5–6, 5.5.2; Soz. 6.7.10; Theod. *HE* 4.13.2–3, 25.1. On the date of Meletius's exile, see Brennecke 1988, 233 n. 64; contrast Martin 1996, 595–96.

229. Joh. Chrys. *In Mel.* (*PG* 50.515–16); Greg. Nys. *In Mel.* (*GNO* 9.444 = *PG* 46.853).

230. See, e.g., Ruf. *HE* 10.25; Athanasius *Tom. ad Ant.* (*PG* 26.796–809), esp. at 3 (*PG* 26.797–800).

231. Where Basil met him in 372 (*Ep.* 99).

232. Soc. 4.2.5, 5.5.1; Soz. 6.7.10, 21.2, 7.3.1.

233. Theod. *HE* 4.24.4–25.5, 32.1–2 and *HR* 2.15, 8.5, 8 refer to the τὸ πολεμικὸν γυμνάσιον as the meeting place; cf. Liebeschuetz 1972, 117 n. 1. Basil *Ep.* 92 and 242–43 seem to describe the plight of the Antiochene Homoousians.

234. See, e.g., Theod. *HE* 4.26.1–27.4; *HR* 8.8 for the open and unpunished criticism of Valens by Nicene monks. Stories of drownings in the Orontes are surely fabrications, Soc. 4.2.7, 17.3; Soz. 6.18.1.

235. This despite Basil's call (*Ep.* 243) for a direct appeal to Gratian.

236. For Basil's attempts to court Athanasius, see *Ep.* 61, 66, 67, 69, 80, 82; cf. 89, 90. For Athanasius's rupture with Meletius, see Zachhuber 2000, 92–100.

237. For Basil's attempts to seek aid from Rome, see Rousseau 1994, 288–317; Martin 1996, 604–19; cf. Richard 1949. Rome quickly changed its stance on Meletius after Adrianople: it began to support Meletius following his 379 synod in Antioch.

best example of Valens's impartiality in the middle years of his reign.[238] We have already seen that Valens avoided persecuting the Caesarean bishop Eusebius in 365 when he came to Cappadocia for the first time. Again in 370, shortly after defeating the Goths, the emperor passed through Cappadocia with his army on his way to the eastern frontier.[239] As was normal for such marches, the praetorian prefect Modestus preceded Valens's soldiers in order to arrange provisions and quartering in advance of their arrival. Among Modestus's charges was to pressure the new Nicene bishop Basil to come over to the Homoian state church. Threats were issued and promises made, but Basil is said to have shrugged these off with otherworldly indifference. Although Modestus grew outraged at Basil's obstinacy, in the end he left the bishop alone and, once Valens had arrived, persuaded the emperor to do the same.[240] It seems odd that Basil could have enjoyed such power so early in his episcopate, for he had been consecrated only late that summer, after a heavily disputed election.[241] His local support was, however, quite secure: the dry winter and spring of 369/70 left Cappadocia with no harvest, and Basil had organized food relief to alleviate the ensuing famine.[242] This well-timed act of charity no doubt won him the support of the masses, securing him the episcopal throne and a certain degree of immunity to imperial attack.

After this initial encounter, Valens and his advisors seem to have dropped the subject of Basil's doctrine until the winter of 371/72, when Valens again visited Caesarea. On the festival of Epiphany (January 6, 372), Valens entered Basil's church in an incident that has been glorified in the annals of church politics as an example of pious ecclesiastical courage in the face of raw state power. This is largely thanks to Gregory of Nazianzus, who has sacralized Basil's scrappiness during the standoff in his "Encomium of Basil."[243] Nevertheless, reading between the lines of his account, we quickly see that, once it is deflated of hot air, little courageous defiance remains on show. Valens apparently entered Basil's church after the start of the Epiphany service and was surprised when Basil refused to stop the proceedings to acknowledge his entry, hardly a grievous affront. During the offertory, Valens

238. On Basil's encounters with Valens, see Greg. Naz. *Or.* 43.44–57; Greg. Nys. *Eun.* 1.120–43; *In laud. Bas.* 10, 14; Ruf. *HE* 11.9; Soc. 4.26.16–24; Soz. 6.16.1–10; Theod. *HE* 4.19.1–16; Cedrenus, pp. 547–48; Theoph. a.m. 5868. Cf. Brennecke 1988, 226–31; Rousseau 1994, 173–75.

239. For the chronology, see Hauser Meury 1960, 41–42; May 1973, 49–54.

240. Greg. Naz. *Or.* 43.44–51; Greg. Nys. *Eun.* 1.126–37; *In laud. Bas.* 10; Soz. 6.16.4–7; Theod. *HE* 4.19.1–7. Basil himself expected potential exile (*Ep.* 71).

241. On the date, see Pouchet 1992. For the disputes over the Caesarean episcopal election in 370, see Greg. Naz. *Or.* 18.35–36, 43.37; *Ep.* 40–44; Basil *Ep.* 47; cf. Rousseau 1994, 145–51.

242. See app. C. On Basil's power over the masses, see Gain 1985, 304–6.

243. Greg. Naz. 43.52–3; Soz. 6.16.7; Theod. *HE* 4.19.11–12; [Amphilochius] *Hom. in vit. Bas.* 325 (Zetterstéen 1934, 90).

himself brought the gifts to the altar but was supposedly so overcome with anxiety that he nearly tripped and fell, again no surprise for a bandy-legged emperor. Gregory then declines to say whether Basil received the gifts from the Arian emperor, probably implying that he did.[244] For Gregory goes on to admit that Basil even received Valens in his sanctuary and conversed with him. Indeed, Gregory also confesses that the Epiphany encounter turned out to be "the beginning and first establishment of the emperor's kindly feeling towards us." Ultimately, then, the incident seems less like a bold defense of the faith than a courtship dance.

Finally, in one more brief interlude, Valens came even closer to attacking the bishop but again stopped short. Apparently, during the same winter of early 372, Valens's ministers—and particularly his *castrensis,* Demosthenes, whom Basil had insulted—convinced him that he had succumbed to Basil too easily and that he should indeed banish the haughty bishop.[245] Valens issued an order of exile but revoked it when his son fell deathly ill, perhaps, thought Valens, because of God's wrath. Basil was brought to the bedside of Galates and prayed for him earnestly, but unfortunately in vain.[246]

The virulence of Valens's persecution of Basil thus fades considerably on closer inspection. Indeed, as Gregory himself admits, Valens actually lavished considerable benefits and responsibilities on Basil. He granted the bishop tax exemptions and perhaps even some imperial lands for his popular new Basileias, a combination hospital and hotel for the downtrodden and road-weary.[247] He entrusted Basil with the appointment of a new bishop for the cities of Armenia Minor and even the kingdom of Armenia.[248] And Basil himself maintained a friendly and beneficial correspondence with Valens's ministers, including some of those accused of attacking the bishop, like Modestus and Demosthenes.[249] Perhaps his greatest coup on this score was to win over the support of Valens's generals. Basil was in regular contact with Saturninus, Ter-

244. Had he refused Valens's gifts, Gregory would surely have reported this; see Bernardi 1992a, 236 n. 3.

245. Valens's ministers were not alone in finding Basil's ego insufferable; see Jer. *Chron.* s.a. 376: "qui multa continentiae et ingenii bona uno superbiae malo perdidit."

246. Greg. Naz. *Or.* 43.54–55, 68; Greg. Nys. *Eun.* 1.139–41; *In laud. Bas.* 14; Soz. 6.16.1–3, 8–10; Theod. *HE* 4.19.7–11. Basil *Ep.* 79 mentions the incident. [Amphilochius] *Hom. in vit. Bas.* 325–27 (Zetterstéen 1934, 90–92) holds that Valens's rescinded the exile order because of a popular protest and that Galates only fell ill later.

247. Theod. *HE* 4.19.13; Theoph. a.m. 5868; cf. Basil *Ep.* 142–43. More on the *Basileias* at Teja 1974, 119–24; Gain 1985, 277–89, esp. n. 60; Rousseau 1994, 140–44. More on tax exemptions or reductions gained by the Cappadocians at Basil *Ep.* 32–33, 83, 104, 303, 308–9; Greg. Naz. *Ep.* 67–69; *Or.* 17, 19; cf. Treuker 1961, 64–97; Mitchell 1993, 73–74, 80.

248. See p. 178.

249. Basil is even said to have saved Modestus from an illness (Greg. Naz. *Or.* 43.55). For letters to Valens's officials, see *PLRE* I, Aburgius, Andronicus 4, Antipater 2, Flavius Arinthaeus, Demosthenes 2, Helias, Eustathius 4, Helladius 3, Magninianus, Martinianus 5, Maximus 23,

entius, Traianus, and Victor, all of whom were committed Nicenes.[250] After Valens's persecution of Nicenes began heating up in the latter years of his reign, these generals came to form something of a wall of opposition to their emperor's religious policies.[251] In Caesarea, then, as in Alexandria, Constantinople, and even Antioch, Valens was more interested in maintaining concord than in promoting his favored Homoian church.[252] For his part, Basil—who was genuinely concerned to promote the Nicene cause—seems to have been wise enough to avoid provoking the emperor and even to garner imperial support while working to undermine the Homoians from behind the scenes.

Unfortunately for all involved, Valens's détente did not last until the end of his reign. Serious troubles began with the death of Athanasius on May 3, 373.[253] The wizened bishop had, of course, been clever enough to groom and duly promote a successor a few days before his death, the Alexandrian priest Peter. Waiting in the wings, though, was the Homoian candidate Lucius, already consecrated bishop of Alexandria in early 362 by the Homoians, who had promoted his cause with Jovian at Antioch in October 363.[254] Even after Athanasius secured the see from Jovian, Lucius continued to harbor designs on it, and he actually entered Alexandria in September 367, perhaps in hopes of regaining control.[255] Six years later, in 373, reports of Athanasius's decease were quickly conveyed to Antioch, and once again the Homoians there set the wheels in motion to maneuver Lucius onto the episcopal throne.

We learn of what followed from a remarkably detailed letter written by Peter of Alexandria himself and preserved in Theodoret.[256] The prefect of Egypt, Aelius Palladius, came to the episcopal palace and arrested Peter, but the Nicene bishop was able to escape, sneak out of the city, and head for Rome.

Domitius Modestus 2, Sophronius 3, Therasius. See also Gregory of Nazianzus's letters to *PLRE* I, Caesarius 2, Hellenius 2, and Sophronius 3. Analysis at Treucker 1961; Van Dam 1986; Bernardi 1992b; Rousseau 1994, 158–69.

250. See Basil *Ep.* 99, 105, 132, 148–49, 152–3, 179, 214–16; cf. Treuker 1961, 48–52; Tomlin 1998, 36–39.

251. See p. 364.

252. Several sources admit that Cappadocia remained free of persecution under Basil, including Greg. Nys. *Eun.* 1.143; Ruf. *HE* 11.9; Soc. 4.11.8–9; Soz. 6.21.1; [Amphilochius] *Hom. in vit. Bas.* 328 (Zetterstéen 1934, 93).

253. Dated at *Hist. aceph.* 5.10. Basil had heard of Athanasius's death but not yet the ensuing persecutions when he composed *Ep.* 133. There must then have been some time lag between the two. Up to this point, I have largely agreed with the interpretation of Brennecke 1988. From here on, I depart from his viewpoint markedly.

254. See p. 237.

255. *Hist. aceph.* 5.11–13; cf. Martin 1996, 593–94. Given that Lucius was offered protection by the prefect and the *dux Aegypti* during this visit, he may have come under Valens's sanction. Epiph. *Adv. haeres.* 68.11.4 confirms that he had more than once consulted with Valens about effecting his return.

256. Theod. *HE* 4.21.1–22.36; cf. Epiph. *Adv. haeres.* 68.11.4–8, 69.13.3, 73.38.1; Greg. Naz. *Or.* 25.12–14, 33.3–4, 43.46; Ruf. *HE* 11.3; Soc. 4.20.1–22.6; Soz. 6.19.1–20.5; Suid. *O* 764;

In the mayhem that followed, the crowds desecrated the Arian church of Theonas and publicly attacked Christian virgins.[257] Meanwhile, to restore order and impose his chosen successor in Egypt, Valens assembled a military force under the *comes sacrarum largitionum* Vindaonius Magnus, a committed pagan and former supporter of Julian. Magnus marched into Egypt with Euzoius of Antioch in train, occupied Alexandria, and imposed Lucius. Nineteen priests and deacons were rounded up and put on trial. After tortures and imprisonment, these confessors were sent into exile to the pagan city of Heliopolis (Baalbek). Supporters who protested were also arrested and sent to the mines, including a group of twenty-three monks.[258] Whether Valens intended this police action to get quite so messy is doubtful. He probably hoped only to use troops to keep the peace while he seized the opportunity afforded by Athanasius's death to change the color of Christianity in Alexandria.

Some time after Euzoius left Alexandria, Lucius was given an order allowing him to range widely in Egypt rounding up Nicene supporters. According to Peter's letter, this raid netted at least eleven bishops, and Rufinus claims a total of 3,000 clerics and monks were arrested.[259] The carnage and suffering were thus great, so great that some have downplayed them as rhetorical exaggeration. Peter's use of a specific number—and a believable number—seems, however, to indicate otherwise, and contemporary sources confirm the scale of the violence.[260] We also have a number of sources that claim more specifically that Valens persecuted monks in Egypt and throughout the empire more broadly. Jerome dates these attacks to 375, when, he claims, Valens issued a law ordering all ascetics into imperial service on pain of death.[261] Here again contemporary sources confirm the story.[262] Valens had been an opponent of ascetics since 365, when his general Lupicinus beat several Messalian extremists to death, probably while trying to draft them into service against the usurper Procopius.[263] In 373, as his persecutions be-

Cedrenus, p. 545; Jacob of Edessa *Chron.*, p. 298; *Synodikon vetus* 72; Theoph. a.m. 5865–66. For analysis, see Barnes 1993, 180–82; Martin 1996, 789–97.

257. Confirmed at Epiph. *Adv. haeres.* 68.11.6; Greg. Naz. *Or.* 25.12, 43.46.

258. Confirmed at Ruf. *HE* 11.6; Greg. Naz. *Or.* 33.4. See also Haas 1997, 258–77.

259. Theod. *HE* 4.22.35; Ruf. *HE* 11.3; cf. Suid. *O* 764.

260. Epiph. *Adv. haeres.* 68.11.6 (a. 377); Ruf. *Apol. ad Anast.* 2 (*CCSL* 20.25); Basil *Ep.* 139; Facundus *Pro def.* 4.2 (*CCSL* 90A.116.7). Cf. Greg. Naz. *Or.* 25.3, 12, 14, Palladius *Dial.* 17 (*SC* 341.332). The supposed martyrdom of Dorotheus in the arena of Alexandria (Theoph. a.m. 5870; *Barbarus Scaligeri* 286) is probably a doublet for the Dorotheus martyred there under Julian; see Mango and Scott 1997, 101 n. f.

261. Jer. *Chron.* s.a. 375; cf. Oros. 7.33.1–4; Jord. *Rom.* 312. Further confirmation of a date for these events after 373 comes at Ruf. *HE* 11.2, which states that Tatianus was a ringleader, presumably as *CSL*, a post he held from early 374 until 380; cf. Barnes 1993, 297–98 n. 7.

262. Ruf. *HE* 11.4; Basil *Ep.* 257 (a. 376); Joh. Chrys. *Adv. opp. vit. mon.* (*PG* 47.319–86), passim. Cf. Soc. 4.24.1–17

263. Epiph. *Adv. haeres.* 80.2.3–4.

gan to heat up, Valens ordered all curials who had turned to monasticism—he called them "seekers of idleness"—to be rounded up and forced back into service.[264] When a military recruitment crisis hit in 375, Valens turned to the same tactics and ordered the enlistment of these same "idle" monks to fill his rolls.[265] A number of sources confirm that monks were pressed into hard labor in the mines, and several others say that ascetics were forced into hiding.[266] Valens was thus quite willing to attack ascetics and above all to put them to work in the mines and the military.[267]

The violence Valens wreaked in Egypt constituted something of a turning point in his relationship with the church. A bridge had been crossed into the realm of open force, which offered a convenient if not entirely effective means to ensure "consensus." Thus, in September of this same year, 373, Valens exiled Barses, the Nicene bishop of Edessa, and expelled his followers from the churches of that city.[268] Edessa had long suffered internecine strife between its doctrinal communities, and with this move, Valens seems to have hoped to alleviate the problem by ridding the city of its Homoousians.[269] His efforts were far from successful. In a visit to the city, which may date to 375, the emperor was apparently outraged to see the continued presence of Nicenes meeting outside the walls at the Martyrion of St. Thomas; he is even reported to have angrily struck his prefect Modestus for failing to clear the area of religious dissenters. Modestus returned the next day to carry out his orders but was met by an intransigent throng of Homoousians, including a woman who openly confessed her eagerness to undergo martyrdom at the hands of Valens.[270] Theodoret, whose sources for the confrontation are good, reports that a group of priests and deacons led by Eulogius and Protogenes also confessed before Modestus and found themselves exiled to various locations in Thrace, Arabia, and the Thebaid.[271] Fortunately, we have other indications to confirm this report. In 383, the pilgrim Egeria

---

264. CTh 12.1.63 = CJ 10.32.26 (Jan. 26, 373): "quidam ignaviae sectatores." See Pergami 1993, 133–34, on the date, and Barone Adesi 1990, 195–203; cf. 125–26 for analysis.

265. On the recruitment crisis of 375, see pp. 312–19.

266. Rufinus (HE 11.6), Cassian (Coll. 18.7.8) and Melania (Pall. Hist. Laus. 46.2–4; Paulinus of Nola Ep. 29.11; cf. Booth 1981, 247–51) had close contact with monks who were persecuted. Cf. Theod. HE 4.22.26–27.

267. Fuller arguments on the circumstances and dating at Lenski "Isaac and Valens' Recruitment of Monks for Military Service" (forthcoming).

268. Chron. Edes. no. 31 (a. 684 = A.D. 373); Theod. HE 4.16.1–3; Chronicon ad annum 846, p. 201; Jacob of Edessa Chron., p. 298; Theoph. a.m. 5866; cf. Basil Ep. 264, 267.

269. For doctrinal feuds, see Jul. Ep. 115 (Bidez); Ephrem CN 26–30; De fide 53.2, 87 passim; Historia S. Ephraemi 59–63; cf. Griffith 1986, 37–47.

270. Theod. HE 4.17.1–18.4; Ephrem De fide 87.21–23; Historia S Ephraemi 76–77; Ruf. HE 11.5; Soc. 4.18.1–10; Soz. 6.18.2–7; Cedrenus, p. 545; Theoph. a.m. 5864.

271. Theod. HE 4.18.1–13, 5.4.6; cf. Chronicon ad annum 846, p. 203 and Wilkinson 1999, 133 n. 1, 137 n. 3, 169.

wrote that she met two clerics—who must be Eulogius and Protogenes—at Edessa and Carrhae (Harran), where they were now bishops after their return from exile as proud confessors.[272] Egeria also claims that the bishop of neighboring Batnae was a confessor as well, probably Abramius, to whom Basil wrote in 373.[273] The Syrian persecution was thus not limited to Edessa. Indeed, Theodoret says that Pelagius the Meletian bishop of Syrian Laodicea (Latakia) was exiled to Arabia, probably in the same wave of expulsions.[274] And in 375, Basil wrote to the citizens of Beroea (Aleppo) and Chalcis (Quinnesrin)—also in the region—about their recent confession in the face of persecutions.[275] These letters provide the date for what must have been a massive wave of expulsions all along the Syrian frontier. Little wonder, then, that in 377 Epiphanius could lament generically "the wrongs that have been done in Mesopotamia" under the patronage of Valens.[276]

Valens also expelled other Nicenes in the period after 373 with somewhat less violent force. In 374, he sent an order to Samosata (Samsat) commanding Eusebius, the bishop there, to surrender himself immediately for exile to Thrace. Eusebius left at night so that the urban mob would not slay the imperial officer charged with the order, a good indication that troops were not present.[277] Subsequently, when a Homoian named Lucius was assigned to the see of Samosata, he saw to the exile of several other supporters of Eusebius, including Euolcius and Eusebius's nephew Antiochus, again at the hands of imperial officers but not large armed retinues.[278] In the winter of 375/76, the vicar of Pontica, Demosthenes—probably the same Demosthenes whom Basil had insulted in 372—also undertook to depose and exile Nicenes at a synod he organized at Ancyra. Hypsinus of Parnassus was banished,[279] and Basil's brother Gregory of Nyssa was charged with financial chicanery and deposed.[280] After consulting at the imperial court, the vicar then returned to Caesarea and Armenian Sebaste in 376 and ordered Nicene priests of curial descent to be defrocked and returned to their *curiae*.[281] At the same time, he seems to have made an attack on the disputed churches of Doara and espe-

---

272. *Itin. Eg.* 19.2–5; cf. Theod. *HE* 4.18.13–14, 5.4.6; *Chron. Edes.* no. 35 (a. 689 = A.D. 378); *Chronicon ad annum 846*, p. 203.

273. *Itin. Eg.* 19.1; cf. Basil *Ep.* 132.

274. Theod. *HE* 4.13.2–3; Theoph. a.m. 5866.

275. Basil *Ep.* 221–22; cf. 220 (a. 375), 256 (a. 376).

276. Epiph. *Adv. haeres.* 69.13.3, quoted at p. 244.

277. Theod. *HE* 4.14.1–7; cf. 4.13.2; Greg. Naz. *Or.* 33.5; Basil *Ep.* 243; Theoph. a.m. 5864. See the flood of letters calling for Eusebius's return that followed; Basil *Ep.* 177–79 (a. 374). Cf. Basil *Ep.* 181, 237, 239, 268; Greg. Naz. *Ep.* 64–66, and Rousseau 1994, 256–58.

278. Theod. *HE* 4.15.8; cf. Basil *Ep.* 168.

279. Basil *Ep.* 237 (spring 376); cf. *Ep.* 239. I equate *PLRE*'s Demosthenes 1 and 2.

280. Basil *Ep.* 225, 231, 232, 237, 239; Greg. Naz. *Ep.* 72, 74; Greg. Nys. *V Macrinae* 2.192 (*GNO* 81.1: 394); *Ep.* 18, 22. On the date, see Hauser-Meury 1960, 92; May 1973, 62–63.

281. Basil *Ep.* 237.

cially Nicopolis (Susheri), where he beat and expelled some priests.[282] Perhaps it was also at this time that the bishop of Amaseia (Amasya)—also in the diocese of Pontica—was exiled and replaced with an "Arian."[283]

In these instances, Demosthenes—and by implication Valens—always used civil laws for religious purposes. Above all, he selectively enforced laws ordering clerics of curial descent to be defrocked and forbidding clerics from holding taxable property to thin the ranks of the Nicenes in the cities of his diocese.[284] A similar instance arose in spring 376, when Basil found himself attacked on state charges, no doubt in part because of his opposition to the emperor's theology: he had been arrested by the vicar of Pontica—by now a relative of Valens's named Eusebius—for offering asylum to a woman who had been pressured to marry by the governor and his assessor.[285] Unfortunately for Basil, the vicar seems to have found incriminating evidence in Basil's bedchamber, provoking him to strip the bishop in preparation for a whipping, for here again Valentinianic laws allowed torture of senatorials like Basil in cases of adultery. In the event, the angry crowds of Caesareans—incited by local imperial factory workers—prepared to take justice into their own hands. The vicar backed down, and Basil narrowly escaped a beating and perhaps exile. Valens was thus pressuring, needling, and muscling Nicenes into either abandoning their views or abandoning their churches. To accomplish his ends, he called the law into service as a way to trip up bishops whose credal stances he could not abide.

What Valens failed to understand was that ecclesiastical loyalties were a local matter and could not be controlled from on high. Local patronage networks were rooted far too deeply to be eradicated by the imperial "arm of flesh" that Epiphanius claims the Arians applied.[286] This fact is only too obvious in the stories of rabid partisanship characterizing some of the popular reactions to Valens's tactics. We have already seen the ground swell of riots in Alexandria when Valens attempted to expel Athanasius in 365. So, too, the threat of local riots prevented the vicar of Pontica from beating Basil in 376. And even in instances where Valens successfully expelled Homoiousian or Nicene bishops, he could not compel local citizens to welcome the outsiders he imposed in their stead. In Samosata, Valens had appointed a Homoian named Eunomius to replace the popular local bishop Eusebius, whom

282. Basil *Ep.* 231, 238, 247; cf. 243; Greg. Naz. *Or.* 13 with Gallay 1943, 123. See also Rousseau 1994, 243–45.

283. Soz. 7.2.5–6. Basil had mentioned exiles earlier (*Ep.* 68, 70; cf. 92) but seems likely to have been referring only to the Homoiousians and Meletius of Antioch

284. On these laws, see p. 276.

285. Greg. Naz. *Or.* 43.55–57; cf. 68 and Greg. Nys. *In laud. Bas.* 10; [Amphilochius] *Hom. in vit. Bas.* 329 (Zetterstéen 1934, 94). See also the tension at Basil *Ep.* 129, 213, from the previous winter. On Eusebius, see Bernardi 1992a, 242 n. 1 and p. 60.

286. Epiph. *Adv. haeres.* 73.23.2: διὰ τὴν τῆς σαρκὸς δεξιάν.

he exiled to Thrace. When Eunomius visited the city baths, none of the Samosatans would enter the complex, and they later emptied all its water, which they regarded as defiled.[287] Feelings were thus so visceral that an emperor had little hope of changing them even with the application of armed force.[288]

Initially, Valens seems to have understood this, particularly in the period when his brother was still alive. We have seen that, until 373, Valens used little force and this only to maintain the peace as he upheld the decrees of the council of Constantinople. Basil himself understood Valens's hesitation at this stage and even took advantage of it. In a letter of 371 encouraging Athanasius to stir up Nicene support in the west he argued that "our rulers [οἱ κράτουντες] are timid about the fidelity of the masses, and the peoples everywhere follow their bishops unquestionably."[289] It was probably this conviction that spurred Basil to face down Modestus and Valens in 370 and 371/72. The fact that he suffered no consequences proves that his assumptions were correct. Thus, before 373, Valens seems to have been operating with the primary intention of maintaining the peace by leaving local bishops alone. Beginning in 373 that picture changed. Valens became increasingly belligerent toward non-Homoians, with his violent treatment of them peaking in 375 and 376. It should not be forgotten that in precisely this period, Themistius is reported to have delivered the speech to Valens mentioned at the beginning of this chapter wherein he begged the emperor to relax his wrath against dissenting Christians.[290] Thus even pagans recognized and regretted the policy shift at this time. It must also be noted that in November of 375, Valentinian died, leaving Valens free of the restraint he had felt from his older brother. Orosius actually saw a connection between the increase in Valens's persecutions and the end of Valentinian's life, but Valens's serious attacks began two years earlier and must therefore have been motivated at least initially by some other factor.[291] Athanasius's death certainly set the ball in motion, and the military crisis that arose in 375 provided the impetus for Valens's prosecution of monks. Above all, though, one suspects that Valens had simply reached the end of his rope. He could no longer see any way to guarantee unity under a Homoian church than by force. After his efforts to impose a bishop on Alexandria dissolved into mayhem,

287. Theod. *HE* 4.15.1–11. Cf. the unbending loyalty of the Cyzicenes to their bishop Eleusius (Philostorg. 9.1; Soc. 4.7.1–3; Soz. 6.8.4–8, 26.1–6).

288. Nor was such partisan behavior peculiar to Nicenes; see Theod. *HE* 5.4.7–8; Greg. Naz. *Or.* 33.5. Cf. the Homoian riots against Gregory of Nazianzus in Constantinople (Greg. Naz. *Ep.* 77–78; Gallay 1943, 137–39).

289. Basil *Ep.* 66; cf. *Ep.* 30 (a. 368), 65 (a. 371/72). For the power of bishops on the local scene, see Brown 1992, 146–58; Mitchell 1993, 2: 77–84.

290. See p. 212.

291. Oros. 7.33.1; cf. Theoph. a.m. 5866.

he lost his compunction about the use of violence and began openly enforcing his religious program.

Only the crises that plagued the last years of his reign prevented Valens from carrying his attacks further. These same crises eventually put a stop to the persecutions and, more important, guaranteed that the Nicenes would win the war for orthodoxy. As we have seen in chapter 4, in 375, Valens faced simultaneous military threats from the Persians and the Isaurians. When in turn he learned that his forces in Thrace had been defeated by the Goths at the battle of Ad Salices in the summer of 377, Valens seems to have issued a law allowing the return of the ecclesiastics he had exiled. This we know from Jerome and Rufinus, both of whom were in the east at the time and both of whom indicate that Valens recalled the Nicene exiles before departing to fight against the Goths.[292] Their assertion is confirmed by a precise notice in the Syriac *Chronicon Edessenum*, which records that the Nicenes expelled from Edessa returned by December 27, 377.[293] We know for certain that Peter returned to Alexandria and expelled Lucius before Valens left Antioch for Thrace in the spring of 378,[294] and we also hear of the rapid return of Meletius to Antioch, Eusebius to Samosata, and Eulogius to Edessa.[295] In light of this policy reversal, we can see that Valens himself understood the deleterious effects of his attacks. The fact that he felt compelled to recall his victims in the face of military crisis meant he believed that a continuation of his intransigence would have been destabilizing to his own empire.

Unfortunately for Valens's reputation, though, his brutal attacks on clergymen were followed quickly by his own death at the battle of Adrianople. His vicious persecution of them had already created a major stir during his lifetime. Once it appeared that God had claimed him in a shameful death without a burial, there was no hope he could escape his reputation as a persecutor of Christians.[296] Already in the first days after his death, the Nicene monk Isaac, whom Valens had persecuted, started claiming prophetic foreknowledge of the emperor's fate and its roots in Valens's heresy and perse-

292. Jer. *Chron.* s.a. 378: "Valens de Antiochiae exire conpulsus sera paenitentia nostros de exiliis revocat"; Ruf. *HE* 11.13; cf. Prosper *Chron.* 1164; Oros. 7.33.12; Soc. 4.35.2–3; Soz. 6.37.17.

293. *Chron. Edes.* no. 33 (a. 689 = A.D. 377/78); cf. *Chronicon ad annum 846*, p. 203; *Chronicon ad annum 724*, p. 105. See Snee 1985; cf. Booth 1981, 253–54 and, against the objections of Martin 1996, 797–801, and Barnes 1997, see Lenski 1995b, app. 2..

294. Cf. Soc. 4.37.1–3; Soz. 6.39.1–2, with Martin 1996, 797–98.

295. On Eulogius, see *Chron. Edes.* no. 35 (a. 689 = A.D. 378); *Chronicon ad annum 846*, p. 203.

296. For Valens's reputation, see Greg. Naz. *Or.* 43.30, 46; Greg. Nys. *Eun.* 1.123; Aug. *CD* 5.26, 18.52; Ruf. *HE* 11.2; Soc. 4.1.13; Soz. 6.6.10; Theod. *HE* 5.7.2; *BP* 4.8; Suid. *O* 764; *Chronicon ad annum 724*, p. 105; John of Nikiu *Chron.* 82.17; *Narratio* 2 (*MGH-AA* 9.629). See also Lenski 1997, 150–52; Urbainczyk 1997b, 152–56.

cutions.[297] This is our first evidence for what became the universally accepted explanation of Valens's death: he had brought disaster on himself through his attacks on the religious.[298] In fact, however, the reputation of being a persecutor already haunted Valens during his own lifetime. In the early 370s, both Basil and Ephrem Syrus began dating the "war of heresy" from the first year of Valens's reign.[299] And by 376, Valens's name became synonymous with heresy and religious violence when John Chrysostom alluded to him while describing attacks by "some wicked demon, like some rustic tyrant who has seized the entire world."[300] Nowhere is the pervasiveness of this reputation better revealed than in a graffito in fractured Greek inscribed in a south Anatolian church shortly after the emperor's death: "Emperor Valens you did wrong, for you surrendered the church to the heretical Arians."[301]

Valens's disaster also guaranteed the victory of the Homoousian party in the long-standing battle over the person of Christ. Very soon after Valens's death, Gratian issued an edict reiterating the recall of those exiled under his uncle.[302] After returning to their native sees, these naturally vaulted to prominence as the victims of one so obviously hated by God. At precisely the same time, Gratian's own religious views crystallized in favor of the Homoousians and led him to take more positive steps to enforce the victory of that sect. This was in part due to the encouragements of Ambrose of Milan, who in his *De Fide*—written for Gratian—directly linked the disaster of Adrianople and the consequent devastation of the central empire to Arianism and Valens's support for it.[303] It is thus little surprise that Gratian soon appointed the Nicene general Theodosius to take control of the eastern empire in early 379.[304] That same year, a synod was called in Antioch at which Meletius was able to take control of that see and steer it toward the Homoousion.[305] Meletius also supported Gregory of Nazianzus, who had set himself up as the Nicene bishop at Constantinople. And he eventually suc-

297. *Vita Isaaci* 7–8 (*Acta sanctorum,* Maii 7: 603–4); Halkin 1948, 77; cf. Soz. 6.40.1; Theod. *HE* 4.34.1–3. See more at Snee 1985, 405–10.

298. For a full list of sources, see Lenski 1997, 153–54.

299. Ephrem *CN* 27.5, 28.7; Basil *Ep.* 242 (a. 376); cf. *Ep.* 164, 243, 248; *De spir. sanct.* 30 [76–77].

300. Joh. Chrys. *Adv. opp. vit. mon.* 1.7 (*PG* 47.328–9); cf. Epiph. *Adv. haeres.* 73.37.6.

301. Rott 1908, 375, no. 1: βασιλεὺς Οὐαλέντι κακῶς ἐπύισας ὅτη ἀπέδοκας τὴν ἐκ[η]σίαν τῦς κακοδόξυς Ἀριανός. Rott argues that the graffito was part of a fresco cycle depicting scenes from [Amphilocius] *Hom. in vit. Bas.*

302. Soc. 5.2.1; Soz. 7.1.3; Theod. *HE* 5.2.1–2; Theoph. a.m. 5871; John of Nikiu 83.2.

303. Ambrose *De fide* 2.136–43, with Williams 1995, 130–84. Against McLynn 1994, 104–5 n. 94, who believes Ambrose was not referring to Valens, see Lenski 1997, 151–52.

304. Although some have recently argued that Gratian had little say in the matter (Sivan 1996; cf. Errington 1996a).

305. Staats 1990 makes clear the connection between the Antioch synod and the council of Constantinople.

ceeded in leading the second "ecumenical" council at Constantinople in 381.[306] There, one hundred and fifty bishops came down decisively in favor of Nicaea and ordered the expulsion of any Homoian bishops who refused to subscribe. To back up the order, Theodosius issued a law establishing the faith of Nicaea as normative and dictating the names of Nicene bishops—many of them Valens's victims—who were to control the major sees of the east.[307] Thus, just three years after Valens's death, the Homoian state church came crashing down and Nicenes clambered onto its ruins to claim the high ground.

This sudden victory of Homoousianism is unlikely to have occurred had Valens not undertaken his persecutions and above all had he not been dishonored in the manner of his death. The combination of the two resulted in the solidification of a formerly divided church around the creed of Nicaea. Even so, it is difficult to blame Valens entirely for losing control of an impossible situation. It is unlikely that any solution to the heresies and schisms plaguing the eastern church could have been devised before God showed his will—in contemporary eyes at least—with Valens's death. Only his inglorious end and the political and military chaos that it provoked guaranteed that support would coalesce around the party of the Nicenes. In some perverse way, then, Valens helped the church become what it is.

306. Sources and discussion at Ritter 1966.

307. *CTh* 16.1.3 (July 30, 381); cf. Soz. 7.9.5–7 and *CTh* 16.1.2, 4.2, 5.5–6. See Errington 1997 and Lizzi 1996 for recent—revisionist—treatments.

Chapter 6

Administration and Finance under Valentinian and Valens

Administering the empire was a thankless job.[1] Few emperors became famous as great administrators whether among contemporaries or moderns. Yet much of their time, probably most of it, was spent on just this.[2] Wars were an occasional high point, but an emperor's subjects were always present to nag with their concerns and rankle with their infractions. Thus, while an emperor could not win a reputation without winning wars, he could not help but lose his reputation if he ignored administration. This reality is reflected in the four cardinal virtues praised in an emperor by panegyrists and historians—temperance, wisdom, justice, and courage—the first three pertained to administration and only last to glory.[3] This was something of a problem for Valens, for if there was any area in which he shone, it was administration. Ammianus tells us that "under no other emperor does the Orient recall meeting a better treatment in matters of this kind."[4] In his first speech to the Senate of Constantinople, Valens argued that he was exceptionally well qualified to oversee an empire because of his previous career

1. For previous surveys of Valentinian's and Valens's administrations, see Heering 1927, 58–60; Andreotti 1931; Nagl, "Vt.," 2188–98; id., "Val.," 2126–30; Stein 1959, 180–81; Soraci 1971, 77–122; Fasolino 1976, 27–36.

2. Constantius claimed that he spent all his time either warring or trying to help his subjects through legal enactments (*Demegoria Constantii* 18c). For the emperor as administrator, see Millar 1977, passim, esp. 203–72.

3. Men. Rhet. 2.373, 375, recommends that all imperial panegyrics be structured around these four Platonic virtues. They were absorbed into the Latin tradition via Cicero *De off.* 1.5.15 and appear as such, for example, at AM 25.4.1; cf. Blockley 1975, 73–103; Barnes 1998, 84 n. 26.

4. AM 31.14.2: "nec sub alio principe in huius modi negotiis melius secum actum esse meminit oriens."

managing an estate.[5] Based on his agricultural background, he could claim both common experience with and sympathy for the majority of his subjects (although he had probably never toiled in the fields as a laborer).

Valentinian was also regarded as a wise and careful administrator.[6] Nor were his life experiences useless in this regard, for his early upbringing in Pannonia and his time as a soldier also gave him a sense of the needs of the common man. Contemporaries were well aware that the two emperors mirrored each other in their emphasis on efficient management.[7] Indeed, Valentinian's and Valens's administrative outlooks were so closely intertwined that it is impossible to discuss them separately. We saw in chapter 1 that they operated in unison or, more precisely, that Valentinian essentially set the tone for his brother's activities.[8] In early 365, in his sixth oration , for example, Themistius described Valens as a sort of doppelgänger created by his brother to facilitate worldwide rule: "The soldiers made him [Valentinian] emperor, but you [Valens] made him a great emperor. By taking the purple, you have given him in return another soul, you have given him another body and the ability to see and hear more, and to speak publicly to those living far apart at one and the same time and to offer justice in the same instant for Syrians and Britons."[9] This parallelism between the administrations of Valens and Valentinian has certainly been recognized in previous scholarship but it has yet to be fully explored.[10] In what follows, I shall examine this problem as it applies to four general areas of legislative concern: combating official corruption; streamlining civic administration; protecting the welfare of the masses; and improving the efficiency of agriculture.

Most of what we know about imperial administration in the fourth century comes from the Theodosian Code, promulgated in 438, which assembles excerpts and fragments from copies of imperial laws gathered from all across the late Roman empire.[11] This is not, however, a comprehensive collection of all the laws issued during the period it covers (306–438), in part

5. Them. *Or.* 6.81b, quoted on p. 54.

6. AM 30.9.1; Zos. 4.3.2; Zon. 13.15; Cedrenus, p. 541; cf. *Exc. Val.* 12 [60].

7. Soc. 4.1.11: περὶ μὲν τὴν τῶν δημοσίων πρόνοιαν ἐν ἀρχῇ παραπλήσιοι ἀλλήλοις ὄντες ἐτύγχανον.

8. See pp. 28–35.

9. Them. *Or.* 6.75c; cf. *Or.* 6.76b, 82a–b, 9.127a–b; Symm. *Or.* 1.22.

10. See DeDominicis 1953, esp. 342–401; Pergami 1993, xxiv–xxxii; cf. Gaudemet 1956. See also Corcoran 1996, 266–92, for the unity of legislation in the tetrarchic period. Throughout the fourth century, laws were issued in the names of every current member of the imperial college and were theoretically valid empirewide (Pabst 1986, 144; Honoré 1998, 129–30). Even so, I hope to show even closer correspondences in the laws of the Valentiniani—i.e., I hope to show that they developed a coordinated program of administrative measures.

11. On the Theodosian Code, see the wonderfully distinct but complementary studies of Honoré 1986; 1998; Harries 1999; and Matthews 2000. On how its construction effects our understanding of Valentinian's and Valens's laws, see Pergami 1993, xi–liv.

because it never managed to assemble all these laws, but also because many of the laws it originally contained have been lost in the transmission of the text.[12] Thus, we learn from various sources of many important laws of Valens and Valentinian that do not survive in the Theodosian Code.[13] There must have been many others, omitted by its compilers or lost in transmission, which will never be recovered. Moreover, because of the way the laws were originally assembled by the editors of the Theodosian Code, we have many more laws for Valentinian than for Valens.[14] Although we might be tempted to assume that this means that Valentinian issued more laws, that assumption would be incorrect. The fact is that, at least for the period down to 379, most of the laws from the Theodosian Code survive from the west, and most of these are from Italy and Africa. In as far as this is true, the relative numbers of laws for the two halves of the empire tell us much more about the production of the Theodosian Code than they do about the legislative activities of the eastern and western courts.[15] Finally, problems arise because any one entry in the Theodosian Code may represent only a piece of a law or only one of several variants of that law that were originally distributed. Modern interpreters of late Roman laws have too quickly assumed that the authority of a law was limited to the sphere of control exercised by the official to whom it was addressed: a law to the praetorian prefect of Gaul is thus regarded as valid only for Gaul. John Matthews has recently emphasized, however, that this assumption is often flawed. The same law may have been issued to many other officials—both eastern and western—in many different versions—tailored to specific addressees—but only survive in the copy to the prefect of Gaul.[16] Below we shall see that many laws attested in the Theodosian Code for Valentinian only are attested in other sources for Valens as well. We shall

12. For the problems created by the manner in which the Theodosian Code was compiled and transmitted, see Honoré 1986, 156–68; 1998, 136–41; Matthews 2000, 57–70, 85–167; Garnsey and Humfress 2001, 52–70.

13. To offer only prime examples, see the laws reported at *AE* 1906, 30 = *IK* 11.1.42; Giardina and Grelle 1983 = *AE* 1984, 250; Them. *Or.* 8.112d–113c; Soc. 4.24.1 = Soz. 6.19.6; Jerome *Contra Iovinianum* 2.7 (*PL* 23.308); *Hist. aceph.* 5.1 = Soz. 6.12.5.

14. From the period after the two emperors separated in August 364 until Valentinian's death in November 375, we have 277 laws of Valentinian compared with only 62 of Valens. For these figures, see the catalog in the preface to Mommsen's edition. After Valentinian's death, we have 46 laws of Gratian and 15 of Valens.

15. Seeck, *Regesten*, 12. Contrast Andreotti 1931, 458–59; Pergami 1993, xxiv–xlv.

16. Matthews 2000, 159–64. See, e.g., *CTh* 6.31.1 = *CJ* 12.24.1, which states that it is an *edictum generale*, although it survives only from a copy "ad Zosimum praesidem Novae Epiri"; cf. *CTh* 10.10.9, with Pergami 1993, 78–79. See also *CTh* 9.42.7 = *CJ* 9.49.7 and *CTh* 10.9.1 = *CJ* 10.10.3, both part of the same original pronouncement, although one was addressed to the praetorian prefect on Mar. 5, 369, and the second to the *comes rei privatae* on Mar. 29, 369. For more on this problem, see Pergami 1993, xxxv–xxxvii; Honoré 1998, 135; cf. Corcoran 1996, 170–98.

also see that many more laws in the Theodosian Code that appear to have been addressed to a fairly circumscribed audience were, in fact, intended to be valid for a much broader cross-section of the populace.[17] As a source, then, the Theodosian Code is bountiful but deceptive, because of the illusion of comprehensiveness it projects. We must lean on this weighty tome heavily, as our best source, but also cautiously.

In light of these caveats, before we turn to our four main areas of focus, it is worthwhile to lay the ground for the single biggest proposition advanced here by examining several instances of laws attested for both Valentinian's and Valens's spheres of power. I shall concentrate on four smaller subjects for which the evidence is good: family law, weights and measures, education, and entertainments. In all instances, we shall see that Valentinian's and Valens's laws mirror each other remarkably closely.

In the area of family law, every fourth-century emperor regarded the protection of chastity and virtue as essential to both Christian and Roman ideals.[18] Unfortunately, however, traditional Roman and Christian conceptions of marital virtue did not necessarily coincide, particularly on the question of divorce. Although the Romans had always frowned on divorce as a social phenomenon, they had made legal provision for it throughout their history. Constantine put a stop to this in order to uphold the higher standards of the church.[19] Julian, however, had removed Constantine's prohibition on unilateral divorce,[20] and Valentinian either upheld or reenacted his law. This relaxation of the Christian standard is apparently at the root of a story proffered by our Christian sources that Valentinian, when he chose to divorce his first wife, Severa, and marry a second, Justina, actually passed a law allowing bigamy: divorce being strictly forbidden, in the eyes of the church, he had indeed taken a second wife.[21] Antti Arjava has collected a number of passages from patristic sources indicating that a law allowing unilateral divorce remained in place for about sixty years after Valentinian's death.[22] He has, however, missed two passages that prove that Valens, like his brother, also upheld the legalization of divorce: Epiphanius, who wrote under Valens, took a remarkably lax stance on the question in a passage that seems to indicate that he was defending the law of the state; and John Chrysostom, in a tirade

---

17. See, e.g. *CTh* 7.4.10 (a. 364), which seems to apply only to *protectores*. If, however, we look at *CTh* 7.4.22 (a. 396), which mentions the original law from which 7.4.10 was extracted, we see that it actually applied to all members of the army.

18. See, e.g., AM 21.16.6; Lib. *Or.* 59.158; cf. Men. Rhet. 2.376.

19. *CTh* 3.16.1. See Arjava 1988; 1996, 177–89; Grubbs 1995, 203–60.

20. Ambrosiaster *Quaest de utr. test.* 115.12 (*CSEL* 50.322); cf. Greg. Naz. *Or.* 4.75: καὶ συζυγίαι σχιζόμεναι.

21. Soc. 4.31.10–18; Joh. Ant. fr. 187; Jord. *Rom.* 310; Theoph. a.m. 5860; Zon. 13.15. See Barnes 1998, 123–26.

22. Arjava 1988; cf. id. 1996, 179–80, and Nathan 2000, 109–16.

clearly alluding to Valens, directly scorns the eastern emperor's approval of divorce.[23] Thus both emperors followed one another in permitting divorce.

Both also altered Constantine's laws forbidding the transfer of property to illegitimate children and concubines in a will. A law of Valentinian's from 371 survives to confirm that he allowed concubines and *illegitimi* to receive up to one-twelfth of a man's estate if he had legitimate children, and one-quarter if he did not.[24] Libanius, who was forever preoccupied with the maintenance of his own illegitimate son Cimon, confirms that Valens enacted, or rather was forced to enact the same law:

> Fate also helped to enact a law in favor of illegitimate offspring. Granted that it may be attributed to the fortune shared by all who stood in need of the law that the senior emperor devised it and made it valid by his decree, but that his junior colleague, who thoroughly disapproved of it, should yet be seen to approve it and ratify it, this must rightly be judged as proper to my own Fortune.[25]

Nothing could make it more clear that Valentinian was calling the shots. For all that Valens disagreed with his brother's law allowing bastards and mistresses to inherit, he was made to approve it so as to guarantee legislative harmony between west and east.[26]

Yet another instance of overlap between west and east stands out precisely because it might otherwise seem a matter of only local concern. Ammianus informs us that Praetextatus standardized weights and measures in the various districts of Rome during his urban prefecture in 367–68.[27] A law of Valentinian to Praetextatus from October of 367 seems to be related: it insists that hogs brought to Rome for the food doles be weighed in scales rather than assigned an estimated weight.[28] If we are right to connect this law to a broader interest in the strict regulation of weights and measures, it indicates that this issue was of concern not just to the urban prefect but to the emperor himself. We shall not, then, be surprised to learn that Valens was doing much the same in the east, where his urban prefect of Constantinople, Domitius

23. Epiph. *Adv. haeres.* 59.4.8–10; Joh. Chrys. *Adv. opp. vit. monas.* 1.7 (*PG* 47.328–9): γάμους διασπῶν.

24. *CTh* 4.6.4 (a. 371); cf. the related law of Valens on the inheritance rights of adopted children, *CTh* 5.1.2 (a. 369). See also Grubbs 1995, 300–21; Arjava 1996, 210–17.

25. Lib. *Or.* 1.145; cf. Norman 1965, 191.

26. *CTh* 4.12.6 (Apr. 4, 366) on the enforcement of the *SC Claudianum* (enslaving women who maintain relationships with slaves) also indicates western influence. If the subscription is correct, it represents a law issued by Valentinian at Trier but directed to Valens's praetorian prefect Sallustius Secundus (Pergami 1993, xlii, 321). Even if not, as asserted by Seeck, *Regesten,* 109, it still represents the eastern enactment of a series of western laws issued in 365, e.g., *CTh* 10.20.3 = *CJ* 11.8.3; *Consult.* 9.7; *CJ* 10.32.29; cf. *CJ* 6.4.2 + 9.68.4 (a. 367).

27. AM 27.9.10.

28. *CTh* 14.4.4. On this law, see Barnish 1987; Durliat 1990, 94–99; LoCascio 1999, 174–77. See *CIL* 6.1770, similar measures for sheep a bit earlier.

Modestus, also standardized weights and measures. This we know from a passage of Heron of Alexandria that describes how Modestus fixed standard weights and volumes for wheat and barley across the east.[29] The same passage indicates that Modestus also set standard weights per cubic foot for wine and bacon, apparently a confirmation that Valentinian's law requiring that hogs be weighed was part of this broader scheme of standardization. Finally, a story first reported in Codinus indicates that "Valentinian" first established in Constantinople the bronze Modion—a publicly displayed measuring standard—shortly after defeating the Goths. If we can assume confusion between Valens and his brother here,[30] this would further confirm and help date Valens's enactment of Valentinian's law. Because Codinus indicates that the emperor himself was in Constantinople to set up the Modion, we can assume he is speaking of Valens's stay in the capital in late 369 or early 370, shortly after the end of the Gothic war and at the period when Modestus was upgrading from the urban to the praetorian prefecture.[31] Valens thus waited a few years before enacting the laws of Valentinian on weights and measures in Constantinople, perhaps because he had been detained from the eastern capital by his first Gothic war until this time.

Valentinian and Valens also enacted interrelated laws on education. Already at the beginning of their reigns, while they were still traveling together in the area of Naissus, they issued a law to Mamertinus, then praetorian prefect of Italy, Africa, and Illyricum, ordering qualified teachers to establish or reestablish schools.[32] Praise soon started pouring in from Themistius for Valens's creation of schools where they were lacking and for his encouragement of students and teachers alike.[33] From 372, we have a law of Valens's creating Greek and Latin copyists for the library of Constantinople and granting them grain rations; from 373, a law granting various immunities to teachers and doctors in Rome; and from 374, a law granting similar immunities to teachers of painting in North Africa.[34] We have already seen that Valens's was cursed by his lack of education and that Valentinian's own schooling was

29. Heron Alexandrinus *Stereometrica* 2.54, with Corcoran 1995.

30. Much as Theoph. a.m. 6258 mistakenly attributes Valens's aqueduct to Valentinian, and Malalas 13.29 (p. 338) attributes Valens's buildings in Antioch to Valentinian.

31. [Codinus] *Patria Constantinopoleos* 97; cf. *Parastaseis suntomoi chronikai* 12; Suid. *M* 131. On the beginning of Modestus's urban and praetorian prefectures, see p. 62, cf. p. 288 n. 153. For Valens's presence in Constantinople at this date, see *CTh* 5.1.2 (Dec. 29, 369).

32. *CTh* 13.3.6 (June 11, 364), with the note of Pergami 1993, 5–12, on the date. The law was aimed above all at repealing Julian's edict against Christian teachers (Rougé 1987, 289–90).

33. Them. *Or.* 9.123b, 11.146b. Themistius seems to have been the impresario of higher education in Constantinople; cf. *Demegoria Constantii* 20d; Greg. Naz. *Ep.* 38.

34. *CTh* 14.9.2 (a. 372), 13.3.10 (a. 373), 13.4.4 (a. 374). Zos. 3.11.3 indicates that Julian had just established the collection at the Constantinopolitan library, which explains the need for major upgrading still in 372; cf. Janin 1964, 161; Vanderspoel 1995, 99–100.

at best moderate. We have also seen that both demonstrated the stock they put in education by the teachers they chose for their children and the emphasis they placed on employing technically educated bureaucrats.[35] Nevertheless, here, as elsewhere, it was not simply a mutual interest that dictated their legal activity with respect to education but a strong nexus of administrative overlap. The most complicated education law from Valentinian's realm set strict standards regulating the registration, behavior, and length of study for students at Rome in 370.[36] We have no direct proof that Valens enacted a similar law in the east, but another passage from Libanius indicates that he probably did. Libanius, discussing a governor of Syria, whom he does not name, but whose administration can be dated to about 370, says that he charged some students with misbehavior and had them stripped and hoisted up for a public flogging as part of a larger effort to crack down on educational abuses in Antioch.[37] Valentinian's 370 law also allowed the public flogging of students who were found to be wastrels. The measure would naturally have been controversial, given that most who had the money to study were of a high enough status to be immune from flogging. In the Syrian incident, an otherwise unknown Olympius convinced the governor of this and got the students off, but the characteristic harshness of the governor's initial resolve has the distinct imprint of the Pannonian brothers: both seem to have been interested in improving education but also in tightening their control over it, even to the point of treading on questionable legal ground.

Finally, both cooperated on the question of public spectacles. Although these were a hallmark of ancient culture in the Mediterranean, they were extremely expensive and had thus become unwelcome to the wealthier classes, who were legally obliged to pay for them. Each region, sometimes each city, had its own traditions regulating these displays of "public munificence." It was thus impossible to issue a blanket law controlling the performance of public spectacles in all parts of the empire. Even so, Valentinian's and Valens's activities in this regard are measurably interrelated. Cooperation is clear already in 365, when we have a copy of a law requiring the presence of *editores* at their own games issued by Valentinian from Milan but received and posted in Constantinople.[38] The quirky heading of this law seems to indicate that Valentinian's law was issued for both halves of the empire and was not even vetted before reissue under Valens in the east. More evidence of cooperation

35. See pp. 64–66 and 95.
36. *CTh* 14.9.1 (Mar. 12, 370).
37. Lib. *Or.* 1.169–70; cf. *PLRE* I, "Protasius" 2.
38. *CTh* 6.4.18 (June 28, 365), with Pergami 1993, xliii, 234–35; cf. DeDominicis 1954, 398, on the accuracy and significance of the heading and subscription. *CTh* 12.1.67 = *CJ* 10.32.28 was probably part of this same law. See also *CTh* 6.4.17 further tightening obligations to give *munera*.

on this question comes in April 372, when we have parts of eastern and western laws regulating the production of games to be given in the provinces.[39] The western law, addressed to the praetorian prefect of Italy, Africa, and Illyricum, was designed to prevent governors from arbitrarily shifting the venue for games from the city that had paid for them to a more popular location. Exactly the same provision was laid down by Valens in another law—also probably from 372—preserved only in an inscription from Ephesus. There the emperor orders the four metropoleis of Asia to take turns hosting their provincial games every fourth year, following "the example of Illyricum and the Italian cities," a clear indication that east was again following west.[40] Some of the concern with games in 372 must have stemmed from the expensive decennalian celebrations anticipated for the emperors the following year. Thus in May of 372, Valens issued a law requiring all four Constantinopolitan praetors charged with giving games to live up to their obligations or face fines.[41] In August of the same year, a long western law shows that Valentinian was also insistent that the praetors of Rome not dodge their responsibility.[42] A law of Valentinian from the summer of 373 allowed Roman praetors ten years' notice to prepare for the expenses of their games and insisted that they be reminded five months before those games in case they wished to protest.[43] Although we have no similar decree from Valens, a law of Arcadius's from 408 confirms the previous existence of "a law of the divine Valens" requiring exactly the same five months' notice in Constantinople.[44] On games, then, as on so much else, Valens acted in unison with his brother.

We have thus seen direct evidence of cooperation between Valentinian and Valens in four unrelated areas of administration. Both emperors enacted similar laws on divorce and inheritance. Both standardized weights and measures at approximately the same time. Both took related measures to benefit education but also to tighten their control over it. And both enacted the same

---

39. *CTh* 6.4.19 (Apr. 13, 372) and *CTh* 15.5.1 (Apr. 25, 372).

40. *AE* 1906, 30 = *IK* 11.1.43, esp.: "[exe]mplo Illyri[ci] a[d]que Italarum urbium recte perspexi[mus] esse firmatum" = ἐξ ὑποδίγματος *[sic]* τοῦ Ἰλλυρικοῦ καὶ τῶν [τ]ῆς Ἰταλίας πόλεων ὀρθῶς λείαν κατενοήσαμεν διακεκρίσθαι. For analysis, see Schulten 1906, 63–70. Foss 1979, 19 n. 22, misunderstands the decree.

41. *CTh* 6.4.20. Constantine first put the games in Constantinople under the charge of praetors from his new Senate (Zos. 2.38.3–5; cf. Dagron 1974, 150–52). Valens reinstated gladiatorial games in the city in 369 after a seventeen-year hiatus (Jer. *Chron.* s.a. 369; *Cons. Const.* s.a. 369); Gratian gave the green light to gladiatorial games in North Africa in 376 (*CJ* 11.41.1). Valens's interest in maintaining the games can also be seen in his restoration of amphitheaters and hippodromes across the east; see app. D.

42. *CTh* 6.4.21.

43. *CTh* 6.4.22 + 6.4.23.

44. *CTh* 6.4.34 (a. 408). See also *CTh* 6.4.24 (a. 376) for further attempts to limit expenditure and corruption. *CTh* 6.4.13 (May 3, 361) already provides for the designation of Constantinopolitan praetors ten years in advance, but says nothing of the five months' notice.

measures about spectacles in the period of their decennalia. In most of these instances, both timing and the testimony of our sources indicate that Valentinian was the initiator of each measure. This implies a sophisticated system of communication between the two courts and a willingness on the part of Valens to bend to his brother's will in order to ensure the smooth running of the empire. In the section that follows, we shall see that these principles also applied in the four main areas of administration on which the two emperors concentrated.

PARAMOUNT CONCERNS: CORRUPTION, CIVIC ADMINISTRATION, THE MASSES, AND AGRICULTURE

Valentinian and Valens were adamant about combating corruption, a common problem in late antiquity.[45] The energy and passion they both devoted to the issue reflect something of a personal crusade. Much of this concern must have stemmed from their background. The diligence and pragmatism they had learned as farmers and soldiers mingled with their innate irascibility to make them highly attuned to the problems of official fraud and relatively effective at eradicating them. Indeed, if we can believe Themistius, the two had personally experienced the bilking by late Roman tax collectors that was so common and the forced impressment of goods and services by the soldiery.[46] It is no surprise, then, that both had a reputation for harshly punishing officials caught out in fraudulent schemes.[47] Ammianus calls Valens "a severe corrector of military and civil discipline" and "a harsh and bitter enemy of thievish officials and of those detected in peculation."[48] John of Antioch regarded Valentinian as "exacting and honorable in his choice of officials [and] unforgiving toward the disobedient."[49]

Nor are we lacking in specific instances to confirm these generalities. Gregory of Nyssa remarks on how bitterly Valens punished corrupt officials, and several letters of Basil's bring home the point with pleas for an ex-governor undergoing severe punishments for peculation.[50] The Antioch magic trials

---

45. See esp. MacMullen 1988, 122–70. See also Alföldi 1952, 28–47, on Valentinian's and Valens's battle with corruption.

46. Them. *Or.* 8.114a.

47. Zos. 4.2.4; Malalas 13.31 (pp. 339–40); John of Nikiu 82.6, 9. AM 30.5.3, 9.1 is more circumspect; while Ammianus agrees that Valentinian harshly punished minor officials, he rebukes his laxity toward those in higher offices.

48. AM 31.14.2: "severus militaris et civilis disciplinae corrector . . . furibus et in peculatu deprehensis iudicibus inimicus asper et vehemens."

49. Joh. Ant. fr. 182: πρὸς δὲ ταῖς τῶν ἀρχόντων αἱρέσεσιν ἀκριβὴς καὶ τιμωρός, τῶν ἀπειθούντων ἀπαραίτητος . . .

50. Greg. Nys. *Adv. eos qui bap. diff.* (*GNO* 10.2: 360 = *PG* 46.420); Basil *Ep.* 147–49; cf. 96 and Teja 1974, 194–95.

began when two officials of the *res privata* were brought up on charges of fraud.[51] Valentinian banished his first wife, Severa, for forcing the sale of an estate at a fraudulent price, had the former *comes largitionum per Illyricum* Diocles burned alive for peculation, and also had the *cubicularius* Rhodanus torched in the hippodrome of Constantinople for defrauding a widow in the purchase of her estate.[52] Both emperors were thus ruthless in their pursuit of official corruption. Not unjustifiably so, however, at least not in the eyes of contemporaries. Both Symmachus and Themistius laud the brother emperors on precisely this point, and the passages just quoted from Ammianus and John of Antioch indicate that their admiration was shared by others.[53]

Although most of their extant laws on fraud and corruption come from the west, this does not necessarily indicate greater efforts by Valentinian in this respect. Rather, both no doubt imposed related measures, but fewer of Valens's laws survive. Thus Valentinian issued several laws forbidding the collection of bogus surcharges on state services by his officers;[54] strictly forbade provincial governors from conducting official business in private homes;[55] and, above all, took numerous measures to minimize fraud and bilking on the part of imperial tax collectors.[56] Although little survives to attest similar laws in the east, we can assume they were issued with equal vigor. Indeed, a constant refrain against corruption recurs in the imperial legislation from both east and west.[57] Nor are Valens's laws in this regard entirely lacking. Like his brother, Valens was well aware that corruption could cut both ways: Libanius's oration 47 describes how small farmers often bribed local garrison troops into defending their interests against curial tax collectors.[58] In a

---

51. AM 29.1.5.

52. On Severa, see Malalas 13.33–34 (p. 341); *Chron. Pasch.*, p. 559; John of Nikiu 82.10–14; cf. p. 103. On Diocles, see AM 27.7.5. On Rhodanus, see Malalas 13.31–3 (pp. 339–40); Joh. Ant. fr. 183; *Chron. Pasch.*, pp. 558–59; Zon. 13.15; Cedrenus, p. 544; John of Nikiu 82.7–8. Rhodanus was probably executed for violating the provisions spelled out in *CTh* 8.15.3 (Apr. 11, 364); cf. *CTh* 8.15.4–5.

53. Symm. *Or.* 1.23; Them. *Or.* 8.114a–117b; cf. *Or.* 13.174b. Men. Rhet. 2.375 recommends similar panegyrical schemes.

54. See p. 293.

55. *CTh* 1.16.9, 12; cf. 1.16.13, and see Russi 1991, 320–22. This did not stop the governor Julianus from inviting Gregory of Nazianzus to his residence to help him prepare tax roles favorable to Gregory's clergy; see Greg. Naz. *Ep.* 67–69; *Or.* 19.11–12; cf. Bernardi 1968, 131–39.

56. See pp. 297–98.

57. *CTh* 11.1.11 = *CJ* 10.16.6: "consuetis fraudibus"; *CTh* 8.1.11 = *CJ* 12.49.3: "fraudium scelere"; *CTh* 12.6.12: "largitionalium et prosecutorum allectorumque fraudibus"; *CTh* 11.17.1: "fraude procuratorum"; *CTh* 9.42.7 = *CJ* 9.49.7: "conludium furto"; *CTh* 1.29.5 = *CJ* 1.55.3: "forensis iurgii fraudibus"; *CTh* 1.15.6: "fraude obnoxius"; *AE* 1984, 250: "remedio illarum fraudium"; *AE* 1906, 30 = *IK* 11.1.42: "actorum fraudibus"; Mazzarino 1974, ll. 3: "[f]raus admissa"; cf. *DRB* 4.3, 6.

58. Lib. *Or.* 47.4–11; cf. *CTh* 11.24.1 (a. 360), 12.1.128 (a. 392), 1.21.1 (a. 393); cf. Bagnall 1993, 219–25.

law of 368, Valens forbade this corrupt practice under penalty of a fine of twenty-five pounds of gold, and a contemporary papyrus from Oxyrhynchus shows that Valens's prefect was enforcing the measure in Egypt.[59]

One subset of administrative belt-tightening in which Valens is certain to have taken an interest is the regulation of state factories. Diocletian had instituted a state monopoly on the control of arms factories, military wool-cloth workshops, and imperial purple-cloth and linen producers.[60] In the summer of 372, Valens issued a series of laws tightening regulations against private individuals who fraudulently employed imperial weavers from these factories and stiffened other laws compelling makers of purple dye to pay taxes.[61] From the year before, we have fragments of a law of Valentinian's requiring anyone who married or cohabited with a worker from the cloth workshops to take the quasi-servile status of that factory worker.[62] These last may have been part of a larger original document that set the tone for Valens's actions in the east. More certainly of Valens's devising is a law of 374 regulating the rate of production at arms factories. The eastern emperor had learned through investigation that, while the *fabrica* in Constantinople was keeping up with that at Antioch in its production of bronze-embossed helmets, it was operating well behind in helmets decorated with silver and gold. His order to the Constantinopolitan *fabrica* to pick up the pace is typical of the micromanagement Valens practiced in his effort to improve efficiency.[63] Valentinian actually executed a *praepositus fabricae* for producing a breastplate that, while beautifully crafted, weighed marginally less than the materials consigned to him, a possible sign of embezzlement.[64] Here, as elsewhere, the emperors used iron-fisted measures to ensure that fraud was snuffed out.

Civic administration is the next area to which the emperors devoted a considerable amount of energy. Within this broad category, their primary concerns were three: maintaining the curial orders, encouraging the repair and construction of practical structures, and provisioning the major urban centers.

Valentinian's and Valens's efforts to maintain the curial orders were far from atypical of their age. Since the third century, Roman emperors had struggled to keep alive the traditions of local civic responsibility that had allowed the cities of the high empire to flourish. The economic elites of every town and city—their curial order—had long been charged with a vast array of responsibilities, including securing a city's food supply, maintaining its

59. *CTh* 11.24.2 (Nov. 12, 368); *P Oxy* 1101 (a. 367/70).

60. See Bowersock et al. 1999, 443, with relevant bibliography.

61. *CTh* 10.20.6 (June 27, 372), 13.1.9 (June 30, 372), 10.20.7 = *CJ* 11.8.5 (Aug. 21, 372); cf. *CTh* 10.20.8 (a. 374).

62. *CTh* 10.20.3 = *CJ* 11.8.3; *CTh* 10.20.5 (a. 371).

63. *CTh* 10.22.1 (Mar. 11, 374).

64. AM 29.3.4.

public structures, organizing its public festivals, and, above all, collecting its taxes and tribute. The burdens were heavy and grew ever heavier as fellow decurions were attracted into more lucrative careers in the military or imperial administration.[65] To shut off this outflow of decurions, who were treated as a hereditary order in late antiquity, fourth-century emperors issued a wide variety of laws blocking the various exits from curial service and defining quite specifically the duties demanded of curials. In continuing this trend, Valentinian and Valens were hardly original.

The fact is that the *curiae* were in a desperate state. The road to power and prestige now led either to the emperor or to God, with the *curiae* representing a dead end taken by ever fewer ambitious and wealthy citizens. We can see in Valens's laws something of the exasperation he must have felt in attempting to keep the city councils alive. He was forced to issue orders punishing decurions who fled to the countryside, or even the desert, and to fine anyone who harbored fugitive decurions.[66] A law of 375 reveals that the situation in Edessa was so desperate that he extracted children from his provincial governor's staff for transplantation into that city's *curia*.[67] Both Valentinian and Valens also used curial service as a punishment for imperial agents who failed to live up to their obligations.[68] The *curiae* were thus in such a state that they had become a sort of prison camp, a career of necessity and last resort.

Nor is it surprising that men of curial status were so hard to keep in place: not only were the burdens of curial service great, many tempting careers pulled them toward an easier and more lucrative lifestyle as senators, administrators, soldiers, or clergy. Here again, Valentinian and Valens acted in tandem to cut off these lines of flight. In two laws of May 364—while the emperors were still together—they forbade councilors to join the senate without first fulfilling their curial obligations and without leaving behind at least one son to fill their spot on their town council.[69] In a constitution of 370, Valens reaffirmed this law and further specified that a new senator would be obliged to leave much of his wealth to his curial son in his will.[70] Another

65. On the decline in the number of curials, see, e.g., AM 27.7.7; Lib. *Or.* 2, passim, esp. 22–4. On the problems of the *curiae*, see Petit 1955, 321–58; A. H. M. Jones 1964, 712–66; Millar 1983; Ward-Perkins 1998, 373–82; cf. Bagnall 1993, 54–62.

66. *CTh* 12.18.1 (a. 367), 12.1.76 = *CJ* 10.32.31 (a. 371). For Valentinian's stringent punishment of errant curials, see AM 27.7.6–7.

67. *CTh* 12.1.79 = *CJ* 12.57.5; cf. *CTh* 12.1.105 (a. 384). See also Basil *Ep.* 84 (a. 372), which tries to prevent a four-year-old from being put on a council.

68. *CTh* 7.22.7, 8.4.8. See also *CTh* 8.7.10 for a purge of curials from an administrative staff.

69. *CTh* 12.1.57–58; cf. *CTh* 12.1.65 (a. 365), 12.1.71 (a. 370), 12.1.77 (a. 372); *AE* 1906, 30 = *IK* 11.1.43 (a. 372/75).

70. *CTh* 12.1.74. This law was aimed at those who had become senators in Constantinople in the period following Constantius's major augmentation of this group in 359. It was reaffirmed in 383 by *CTh* 12.1.90 (a. 382).

law of Valens's from 365 allowed curials who had attained senatorial status before completing their obligations to retain their new status but still forced them to pay for those obligations back home.[71] The law must have been in place in the west as well, since a contemporary inscription from Numidia reports an African senator's restoration of a basilica in Cuicul "for the completion of his required curial obligation."[72] The military was just as enticing. Libanius reports that, because no man would let his daughter marry a councilor, these often chose to join the army so as to win the tax exemptions that could attract a wealthy wife.[73] To combat this problem, Valentinian and Valens granted *curiae* the right to draft soldiering councilors back into city service unless they had already been in the army for at least five years. Even then, the emperors revoked the offer of tax immunity to a curial deserter's wife and forbade his sons to follow in their father's footsteps as soldiers.[74] Indeed, they even allowed any veteran's son who wished to join a *curia* in order to gain exemption from his normal obligation to join the military.[75] Finally, both forbade curials to become clergymen without offering a relative as a substitute on the council or surrendering their wealth to the council.[76] In the east, where monasticism was burgeoning, Valens also ordered that all monks of curial status be rounded up and returned to council service—a law that, as we have seen, he put to good effect in his persecution of Nicenes.[77]

Valentinian and Valens were certainly strict, but they were far from extreme in their measures. Compared to Julian, for example, the Pannonian brothers were actually quite reasonable with regard to the *curiae*.[78] Although they understood the importance of the city councils, they were also aware that these constituted a talent pool for their administrations, which they were not willing to forgo. They thus kept open some loopholes through which cu-

---

71. *CTh* 12.1.69.

72. *ILS* 5535 = *CIL* 8.8324: PRO EDITIONE MUNERIS DEBITI; cf. *PLRE* I, Rutilius Saturninus 14.

73. Lib. *Or.* 2.36, 45, 72; cf. Basil *Ep.* 116.

74. *CTh* 7.1.6 + 12.1.64 = *CJ* 10.32.27 (a. 368). This actually relaxed a law of Julian's that required ten years of service before immunity was granted (*CTh* 12.1.56 [a. 362]). Valentinian's and Valens's new standard of five years lasted until at least 413 (*CTh* 6.27.16).

75. *CTh* 12.1.78 (a. 372).

76. *CTh* 12.1.59 + 16.2.17 (a. 364); cf. *CTh* 16.2.19 (a. 370), which allowed exemption to those who had been clergymen for ten years. Basil seems to be dealing with the consequences of this law at *Reg. brev. tract.* 94 (*PG* 31.1148).

77. *CTh* 12.1.63 = *CJ* 10.32.26 (a. 373), with Pergami 1993, 133–34, on the date.

78. Julian's zeal for curial restoration is attested—and even criticized—in a number of sources: AM 22.9.12, 25.4.21; Zos. 3.11.5; Lib. *Or.* 18.135–58; *Ep.* 699; Jul. *Mis.* 367d; *CTh* 12.1.50–56. See Pack 1986, 224–59.

rials could still escape to military or civilian service.[79] Indeed, this fact seems to have been at the root of criticisms that Libanius aimed at Valens for failing to do enough to protect the *curiae*.[80] This is unfair, for Valens and his brother seem to have understood better than Libanius that the only way to force labor out of this group of entry-level aristocrats was to tap them for higher administrative dignities. For this reason, as we shall see, the emperors experimented with removing the obligation to collect tribute and oversee local justice from curials, shifting it to low-level imperial administrators, many of them former curials.[81] Although the experiment failed, it shows some vision of a new era in imperial administration where locally placed imperial bureaucrats would replace locally spawned elites.

Not all of Valentinian's and Valens's efforts to bolster civic administration involved the compulsion of curials to service. Both also tried to care for the needs of the cities by encouraging or sponsoring the construction and reconstruction of public monuments. For this reason, both emperors won considerable praise for their building efforts in big and small cities alike. Both were also in some sense forced to rebuild by a series of natural disasters that struck northwestern Anatolia, Greece and Crete, southern Italy and Sicily, and Egypt and Syria in the early part of their reigns. No one put it more aptly than Themistius, who marvels in a speech of 373:

> And you might see the entire empire growing all at once like a tapestry . . . here a city is rebuilt, there a posting station, and there a farm. You see where a harbor is cleared out, where the sea is blocked off, where a river is bridged, where a road changes from rough to smooth, and in each city whatever was there before is either restored or increased. So, too, with the state of the sufferings caused by nature; you will now see cities destroyed by earthquake that have been rebuilt and those that were deluged now freed from the sea, and however many suffered from the famine, you see here even enjoying abundance.[82]

The nature and extent of Valentinian's and Valens's building program is laid out in greater detail in appendix D. Here it suffices to note the major conclusions reached there and to point out how well they correspond to the gen-

---

79. E.g., *CTh* 12.1.66, 73, both of which roll back Julian's order that even imperial officials could be enrolled in the *curiae*; cf. *Mis.* 367d. And see *CTh* 8.3.1 relieving comitatensian office staff from curial obligations; cf. Vogler 1979, 163, 169.

80. Lib. *Or.* 48.19–21, if we assume the emperor in question is Valens, with Norman 1969–77, 2: 436 n. a. Lib. *Or.* 2.72–73 may also refer to the indifference of Valens's *PPO* Modestus to complaints about the state of the councils.

81. On noncurial *susceptores*, see pp. 297–99. On the *defensor civitatis*, see p. 282. See also *P Oxy* 2110 (a. 370), which shows how Valens and his ministers upheld measures to prevent curials from being overburdened.

82. Them. *Or.* 11.150c–d.

eralizations in this quotation. First, and not surprisingly, both emperors seem to have cooperated in determining the kinds of projects on which they would focus. Second, they chose structures of practical value to the masses: aqueducts, baths, bridges, basilicas, and grain storage facilities—as opposed to arches, churches, temples, villas, and palaces. In Constantinople, for example, Valens built a grain warehouse, a nymphaeum, a cistern, three bath complexes, and, above all, an aqueduct to supply what had been a very thirsty city with water from 240 kilometers away—the longest known aqueduct in the Roman world.[83] Moreover, by returning certain funds from imperial estates to the local *curiae,* Valentinian and Valens encouraged all the cities, big and small, to work on similar types of structures, as Themistius implies.[84] Third, as Themistius also indicates, both emperors focused on rebuilding or completing existing structures rather than beginning new ones: thus, to stick with Constantinople, two of Valens's bath complexes, his cistern, his aqueduct, and the Church of the Holy Apostles had been begun under earlier emperors and were merely completed by Valens. Finally, all of these efforts were in part dictated by the natural disasters to which Themistius alludes: in the twenty years between 358 and 378, the eastern Mediterranean saw seven major earthquakes, a devastating tsunami, a prodigious hailstorm in Constantinople, and two major famines.[85] All of these created a serious need for reconstruction, and Valentinian and Valens faced this challenge with remarkable vigor.

The last area of civic administration to which the emperors both devoted considerable attention was also of benefit to the masses, the provisioning of the major urban centers. Cities as large as Rome, Constantinople, and Antioch could never have survived without some interference in the market for foodstuffs by the imperial government. Rome had enjoyed state-subsidized grain doles since the second century B.C., and Byzantium had won these on its promotion to the status of the "New Rome" by the Constantinians. The two capitals had roughly 600,000 citizens apiece by the late fourth century, populations large enough that huge amounts of government resources needed to be diverted into feeding their people.[86] Grain was transported to these two cities by state grain shippers *(naviculari)* from across the west—

83. For Valens's structures in Constantinople, see app. D. For the aqueduct's sources (near modern Bizye), see Them. *Or.* 11.150d–152b with Mango 1990b, 40–41; 1995, 13–14; Çeçen 1996; cf. Crow and Ricci 1997.

84. See pp. 295–96.

85. On disasters in the period of Valentinian's and Valens's reign, see app. C. On reconstruction in their aftermath, see app. D.

86. On Rome's grain supply—25,000,000 *modii* per annum—see Durliat 1990, 37–137. On Constantinople's, see Durliat 1990, 185–278; cf. 1995. Contrast the view of Sirks 1991; cf. Garnsey and Humfress 2001, 110–14; and see LoCascio 1999 for an effort at mediation.

but particularly from North Africa—to feed Rome, and from across the east—but particularly from Egypt—to feed Constantinople.[87] There it was stored in state grain houses *(horrea)*, some of it for immediate use and some as a hedge against times of famine. This grain was never distributed directly to the people but sold at fixed prices to members of the public baking guilds *(pistores)*, who then distributed their loaves to qualified citizens or sold them at a reduced price dictated by the imperial government. Pork, oil, and wine were also supplied, although less is known about these commodities, particularly in Constantinople.[88] The smooth functioning of this system was crucial to the order and security of the two imperial capitals. When grain supplies fell short in the capitals—and in other metropoleis like Antioch—riots ensued, which could destroy a city's infrastructure and claim the lives of imperial and local officials.[89] Naturally, Valentinian and Valens were well aware that the food supply in the metropoleis was important. Both worked hard to ensure its smooth delivery, not simply as a matter of comfort but as an imperative for internal security.

The provisioning of Rome was a major issue in the first year of Valentinian's reign.[90] This we know from twenty-two entries in the Theodosian Code, which represent six major laws covering: (1) the baking guilds and grain storage;[91] (2) bakers who sought asylum;[92] (3) grain shippers and bakers;[93] (4) wine provisions;[94] (5) grain shippers;[95] and (6) authority over the grain supply and the use of old stores.[96] In the years that followed, the number of laws tapered off considerably. It would seem, then, that Valentinian felt that major reforms needed to be undertaken in Rome ab initio. The same was apparently not true of Constantinople. We must remember that Constantinople was just beginning to grow into the metropolis that it would become by

87. Eunap. *VS* 6.2.7–8 claims grain reached Constantinople from Egypt, Asia, Syria, and Phoenicia, and Them. *Or.* 27.336d that it came from Egypt, Thrace, the Bosporus, and the Chersonese; cf. Durliat 1990, 225–31.

88. For Rome, see Barnish 1987; Durliat 1990, 48–51; LoCascio 1999. For Constantinople, see Durliat 1990, 217–23.

89. E.g., AM 14.6.1, 7.1–6, 22.14.1; Lib. *Or.* 1.103, 126, 208, 15.21, 18.195–98; Jul. *Mis.* 368d–370d . Cf. Durliat 1990, 355–78.

90. See Tomlin 1973, 359: "The problem of giving Rome its daily bread dominates Valentinian's legislation"; cf. Alföldi 1952, 61–64.

91. A law of June 8, 364: *CTh* 14.3.3–6 + 14.15.1 + 15.1.12 + 9.40.5 + 14.17.2 + 9.40.6, with Seeck, *Regesten*, 215, and, on the date(s), Pergami 1993, 5–12, 48–9, 117. See LoCascio 1999, 171–72, for analysis.

92. A law of Sept. 27, 364: *CTh* 14.3.11, with Pergami 1993, 279, on problems of dating.

93. A law of Oct. 8, 364: *CTh* 9.40.7 + 14.3.7 + 14.21.1 + *CJ* 11.27.1.

94. A law of Oct. 23, 364: *CTh* 11.2.2.

95. A law of Jan. 11, 365: *CTh* 13.5.11 + *CTh* 13.6.2, with Pergami 1993, 137, on the date.

96. A law of Apr. 4, 365: *CTh* 1.6.5 + 11.14.1 + 14.17.3 + 14.17.4 + *CJ* 1.28.1 + 10.26.1.

the end of the century, and that its distribution system was brand-new and still relatively free of problems: Constantius had only recently reorganized the grain supply and built new *horrea,* and Julian had just added a new harbor.[97] Thus, although Valentinian issued a single law on Constantinopolitan grain rations while resident in the capital,[98] it was not until 370 that the food supply there became a serious concern.

In the summer of that year, a major famine struck central Anatolia. It seems to have hit Phrygia particularly hard, and to have driven many of its inhabitants into Constantinople to seek free grain.[99] Although Valens had traveled east earlier in 370 to shore up the collapsing Persian frontier, he hastened back to Constantinople by the coming winter, apparently to calm any potential unrest.[100] At precisely the same time, he split off the provinces of Egypt from the rest of the diocese of Oriens to form their own new diocese under a *praefectus augustalis.*[101] The aim here was probably to improve supervision of the grain supply from this province by putting it under tighter imperial control. A law from Valens's residence in Constantinople during the crisis further indicates that the emperor also offered incentives to encourage people to join the guild of eastern grain shippers *(navicularii).*[102] Valens thus took swift and sure actions to avert a crisis in Constantinople during the famine of 370.[103]

These measures were of course aimed at an immediate problem, but the last shows that even here Valens was following the lead of his brother: in the 371 law, he states directly that the eastern *navicularii* were to follow their African counterparts in only leaving heritable property to other *navicularii,* a regulation of major concern to Valentinian.[104] Valens's imitation of western provisioning policies is further confirmed by a law of his from 372 that

97. See the helpful summary at Durliat 1995. On Julian's harbor, see Zos. 3.11.3; cf. Janin 1964, 231; Mango 1990b, 37–39. On abundant supplies in the mid fourth century, see Them. *Or.* 4.58d, 61a–b.

98. *CTh* 14.17.1 (Mar. 27, 364).

99. Soc. 4.16.7–17.1 reports that people flocked to Constantinople. See app. C for further sources for and discussion of this famine.

100. Seeck, *Regesten,* 239, 241; Barnes 1998, 251–52.

101. Inferred from *Barbarus Scaligeri* 279 and *CTh* 7.6.3 = *CJ* 12.39.2 at A. H. M. Jones 1954. DeSalvo 1979 has been able to pinpoint the date to 370, i.e., between the issuance of *CTh* 12.1.63 and *CTh* 13.5.14.

102. *CTh* 13.5.14 (Feb. 11, 371). Grain shipping was a business only for the rich; see Bagnall 1993, 36–37.

103. The food crisis may have provided the impetus for a law of 370 (*CTh* 10.23.1 = *CJ* 11.13.1) that ordered the dredging of the Orontes, Antioch's supply line. Constantius II had already rebuilt Antioch's harbor at Seleucia (Lib. *Or.* 11.253; Jul. *Or.* 1.33 [40d]). Petit 1955, 119, even speculates that Valens instituted a regular grain dole, although this may not have occurred until 372, when a famine struck Syria (see app. C); cf. Liebeschuetz 1972, 129.

104. *CTh* 13.6.2, 4–5, 13.6.6, 7. On *navicularii,* see Durliat 1990, 80–90; Sirks 1991, 128–45; DeSalvo 1992.

lays down procedures by which *navicularii* who sustained a shipwreck could prove their claims.[105] Virtually the same law, unfortunately without an exact date, survives from Valentinian's realm as well, and we can assume that he rather than Valens established the protocol it prescribes.[106] Finally, Valens seems also to have built his own new storage facility, the Horrea Valentiaca, in the fifth region of Constantinople, perhaps around the time of the crisis.[107] Yet here again, proper grain storage had been a major concern of Valentinian's from the beginning of his reign.[108] To the credit of both emperors, the careful measures they took for provisioning forestalled any potential troubles in the metropoleis. Despite the famine of 370, the Constantinopolitans seem never to have rioted over food under Valens.[109] And in Rome, even a devastating flood in 374 did not interfere with the efficient distribution of food under Valentinian's new system.[110]

The next major area on which the emperors concentrated considerable administrative energy was protecting the welfare of the masses. In so doing, they were once again acting on their instincts as common men, men of the people. This is not to say that Valentinian and Valens were altruists, but rather that they sympathized with the average citizen, more specifically with the average farmer, and understood the nature of the difficulties he faced. Thus, just as threats against fraud and corruption pervade their legislation, so too a concern for the *rusticanus* (countryman), the *collator* (taxpayer), and the *tenuior* (little guy) reverberates throughout the jargon of their day.[111]

Perhaps the single most marked instance of this concern for the common man comes in their reform of the office of *defensor civitatis*. Much debate surrounds the creation and development of this office, but recent work by Robert Frakes has laid to rest old assumptions that Valentinian was the first

105. *CTh* 13.9.1 = *CJ* 11.6.2 (June 5, 372).

106. *CTh* 13.9.2 with Pergami 1993, 599, who dates the law to 372. More on Valentinian's concern with *navicularii* at AM 27.3.2.

107. *Not. urb. Const.* 6.16; cf. app. D. *CTh* 14.17.7 (May 8, 372)—forbidding the transfer of rations and ordering their storage at the *horrea* in case of absence from the city—may serve as a *terminus ante quem* for its construction. Here again, Valens's law follows those of Valentinian (*CTh* 14.17.1–2).

108. *CTh* 15.1.17 (a. 365). More on Valentinian's interest in grain storage at *CTh* 14.15.1 + 15.1.12; AM 28.1.17–18; *CIL* 8.7975 = 19852 = *ILS* 5910. Them. *Or.* 8.115a indicates that Valens, like Valentinian, was concerned with the construction of storehouses more broadly.

109. Socrates, who hated Valens, would surely have reported riots at 4.16.7–17.1 had they occurred.

110. AM 29.6.17–18; cf. AM 27.3.3; *Coll. Avel.* 10. The incident described at AM 27.3.4 is undatable and, more to the point, need not indicate a provisioning crisis; see bibliography at LoCascio 1999, 170 n. 38.

111. E.g., *CTh* 1.29.5 = *CJ* 1.55.3; *CTh* 7.13.7, 8.11.1, 11.1.14 = *CJ* 11.48.4; *CTh* 11.10.1 = *CJ* 10.24.1; *CTh* 11.10.2, 11.11.1 = *CJ* 11.55.2; *CTh* 11.16.10 = *CJ* 10.48.8; *CTh* 13.2.8 = *CJ* 10.53.9; *CJ* 11.48.5, 11.75.2; *AE* 1984, 250.

to invent it or, at least, to popularize it.[112] Frakes has shown that the title can be traced to the third century, and that Constantine first transformed the post into that of a legal arbiter of petty disputes whose aim was to defend the interests of the lower classes all across the empire. Our best understanding of precisely how the post-Constantinian *defensor* worked, however, comes from a group of laws issued by Valentinian and Valens, who took a particular interest in this office in order to further their program of protecting the common man. According to these laws, the *defensor* had as his mandate judgment over petty cases involving small debts, fugitive slaves, or the payment of excess taxes.[113] These types of cases were often disputed between commoners and local curials or provincial administrators. Because, however, precisely those curials and administrators—or their colleagues—generally sat in judgment over the case, the results were predictably frustrating for the commoner. Even where two parties of low status were involved, judicial fees were often so high that they precluded the satisfaction of small claims.[114] To avoid this conflict of interest, Valentinian and Valens ordered in the first months of their reign that all *defensores* be drawn from ex-officials of the imperial bureaucracy who were otherwise detached from the local interests involved.[115] In laws of 368 and 370 respectively, Valentinian and Valens reaffirmed and clarified these requirements.[116] In these same laws, both state openly that their reform of the *defensor* was part of a larger program intended to protect the common man: "Although we have carefully established many things in behalf of the plebeians, we believe that we have provided nothing for them unless we should give them suitable defenders," said Valentinian, and Valens, "wise provision has been made that innocent and peaceful rustics shall enjoy the benefit of special protection." Although the *curiae* soon hijacked the position of *defensor* to "defend" their own interests, at least under the Pannonian brothers, this office represented a carefully cultivated and concrete means of safeguarding the interests of commoners.[117]

112. Frakes 2001. Pergami 1995 argues that Valentinian instituted the office in 368. Lallemand 1963, 114–18, and Mannino 1984, 13–75, acknowledge connections to earlier officials in Egypt (*syndikoi*) but contend that Valentinian first applied the concept all across the empire.

113. *CTh* 1.29.2 = *CJ* 1.55.1 (June 27, 365); cf. *CTh* 8.15.4. On the date, see Frakes 2001, 105–6.

114. For this concern see *CTh* 1.29.5 = *CJ* 1.55.3 (Aug. 10, 370); cf. *CJ* 2.6.7. On judicial corruption, contrast MacMullen 1988, 137–70, with Corcoran 1996, 238–44; Honoré 1998, 25–29; Harries 1999, 53–55, 153–71.

115. *CTh* 1.29.1 (Apr. 27, 364). On the date, see Frakes 2001, 94–103. Contrast Pergami 1995, 430–31, who argues for 368. This measure must be closely related to Valentinian's and Valens's replacement of curial *susceptores* with ex-*officiales* in the summer of 364; see p. 297.

116. *CTh* 1.29.3 + 4 = *CJ* 1.55.2 and *CTh* 1.29.5 = *CJ* 1.55.3 with Frakes 2001, 108–13.

117. For the *defensor* in action under Valens, see *CTh* 13.10.7 with Mannino 1984, 21–23. Note also the anachronistic description of Republican tribunes provided for Valens by Eutropius (1.13), who compares these officers to *defensores*.

Further evidence of Valentinian's and Valens's mutual interest in legal equity for all can be found in their judicial guidelines. *Iustitia* ranked among
the four cardinal virtues of an emperor,[118] a point that did not escape the
panegyrists who praised Valentinian and Valens and the dedicants who offered them honorary inscriptions.[119] Nor were these exaggerating when they
lauded this quality in the Pannonians. Ammianus, for example, claims that
Valens refused to let any of his ministers seize judicially condemned property without introducing rival claimants to challenge their greed. One suspects this concern stemmed from his own family's loss of its estate to the emperor Constantius.[120] The psychological effects on him of that loss must have
been substantial and seem to have motivated a series of laws regulating the
auction of such properties and guaranteeing the rights of family members
to the possessions of many condemned men.[121] Similarly, both emperors enacted laws expediting the appeal of cases from the courts of *iudices ordinarii*
(governors who acted as judges in the first instance). These forced *iudices* to
forward appeals within thirty days,[122] granted three months for the renewal
of claims that had been postponed,[123] and reaffirmed earlier guidelines for
the transferal of cases to the emperor.[124] Both emperors also issued laws insisting that cases be heard in the province where the defendant resided, a
ruling over which Basil had to admonish Valens's vicar Demosthenes when
he brought actions against Gregory of Nyssa.[125]

The final area to which Valentinian and Valens devoted their energies was
one for which their rural background had perhaps best prepared them, improving the efficiency of agriculture. We have already seen that Valens was
a man of the country: in a passage cited in chapter 1, Themistius states baldly
that he had been a yeoman farmer.[126] Indeed, Valens emphasized the same
in his first speech to the Senate of Constantinople, words echoed by Themistius: "I recognized the very things the divine Plato recommended for
rulership in your words: that it is of benefit to your subjects that you were
simple farmers before becoming emperors, that you were raised on the milk

118. AM 25.4.1; Men. Rhet. 2.373, 375. See Millar 1977, 507–47, on the emperor as judge.

119. E.g., Symm. *Or.* 3.9; *CIL* 6.1180 = *ILS* 765: IVSTITIAE AEQUITATISQUE RECTORI; *IRT*
57–58, 472–73: IVSTITIA PARITER AC PIETATE CAELESTI. Valentinian is also praised for his
justice at Cedrenus, p. 541; Zon. 13.15; John of Nikiu 82.9; cf. Andreotti 1931, 473–82.

120. AM 31.14.3.

121. *CTh* 9.42.6, 10.10.9, 11, 11.20.2.

122. *CTh* 11.30.32 = *CJ* 7.62.24; *CTh* 11.30.33–34; cf. Pergami 1993, lii; Harries 1999,
110–13.

123. *CTh* 11.31.1–6, 11.32.1. These measures may be at the root of Symm. *Or.* 2.29–30.

124. *CTh* 1.19.5, 11.29.3 = *CJ* 7.61.2; *CTh* 11.29.5, 30.35, 12.12.3–4. Cf., however, AM
27.7.5, 30.8.13.

125. *CTh* 2.1.4, 9.1.10; cf. Basil *Ep.* 225. Basil also reminds Demosthenes that—as a civil
official—he should not be judging an ecclesiastical affair.

126. Them. *Or.* 8.113d–114a, quoted on p. 54.

of labor, free of flattery, as yeomen, public servants, out in the open air, soldiers, matured by the toughness of human existence."[127] Valens never lost his concern for farmers. The *Epitome de Caesaribus* calls him "a good caretaker of landowners," and Ammianus confirms that he "was a most just guardian of the provinces, each of which he kept free from harm as if it were his own household."[128] Even when he went to war against the Goths, he made sure that his army was able to secure adequate provisions without unduly burdening the provincial farmers in Thrace.[129] The fact is that both Valens and his brother were extremely knowledgeable about the conduct of agriculture, and they put their knowledge to work once they had gained power.

This concern showed up in three primary areas: encouraging the full exploitation of available land, securing servile and semi-servile labor, and tightening the levy on horses for the cavalry. The problem of abandoned land, *agri deserti*, was common in late antiquity.[130] Whether because of a decrease in population or because of the crushing effects of overtaxation, many fields lay fallow, causing a drop in productivity and a decrease in tax flow. To solve the problem, Valentinian issued several laws offering *agri deserti* at auction to any taker and allowing three years' exemption from taxes on the land as an incentive to farm it.[131] Valentinian also granted retired veterans the right to occupy *agri deserti* free of charge and gave them oxen, seed grain, and tax exemptions to help them get started.[132] Although no parallel law exists for Valens, the anonymous *De rebus bellicis*, written for him ca. 367/69, discusses exactly the same measure for veterans, indicating that Valens was probably implementing this policy as well.[133] On the question of labor, Valentinian issued laws forcing the return of slaves and *coloni* (serfs) who had fled their estates and punishing those who harbored them or used their labor.[134] Valens himself invented a clever measure to attract *coloni* on imperial estates back onto the tax rolls. He allowed them to pay taxes at only 1 percent for the indiction (tax cycle) year 367–68, but insisted that they be enrolled on tax registers when they paid. Once on the rolls, they could be sought for higher payments in subsequent years.[135]

---

127. Them. *Or.* 6.81b.

128. *Epit.* 46.3: "fuit possessoribus consultor bonus"; AM 31.14.2: "provinciarum aequissimus tutor, quarum singulas *ut domum propriam* costodiebat indemnes." Cf. Them. *Or.* 8.114a–b: διὰ τοῦτο οἷός τε εἶ πόρρωθεν προορᾶν ὥσπερ οἰκίας μιᾶς τῆς τοσαύτης αρχῆς.

129. Zos. 4.10.4; cf. Them. *Or.* 10.138b–c; cf. p. 127.

130. See A. H. M. Jones 1964, 812–23; Whittaker 1976; cf. Duncan-Jones 1994, 57–59.

131. *CTh* 5.11.8–9, 5.13.4 = *CJ* 11.66.2; *CTh* 5.15.14 = *CJ* 11.59.3; cf. *CTh* 11.1.10, 11.1.12 = *CJ* 11.48.3.

132. *CTh* 7.20.8, 11.

133. *DRB* 5.6.

134. *CTh* 10.12.2; *CJ* 11.48.8, 11.53.1 + 6.3.13, 11.68.3; cf. *CTh* 5.19.1.

135. *CTh* 10.1.11 (a. 367). See also *CJ* 6.1.7 and 11.63.2 on imperial slaves.

On horse levies, the emperors faced tremendous troubles with collection agents *(stratores)* who abused the levy for their own profit: rather than collecting horses in kind, they would collect exorbitant sums of money for their commuted value *(adaeratio)*, then buy cheaper nags for the cavalry and pocket the difference. In 365, Valentinian issued a law aimed at curbing this practice, but it was a law promulgated by Valens in 367 that really got at the root of the problem. Valens insisted that farmers on imperial estates who offered horses be paid quite handsomely at twenty-three *solidi* per animal.[136] This fixed—and quite fair—price won mention from Themistius, who praises Valens's liberality on the horse levy.[137] In 371, Valens also split the province of Cappadocia in two in order to manage the imperial horse ranches there. This created something of a contretemps in the life of the Cappadocian fathers and particularly Basil, whose bishopric was halved.[138] In fact, however, the emperor's aim was to concentrate the imperial horse ranches of eastern Cappadocia into a province separate from the urban centers in the west.[139] Valens's concern with these ranches is also seen in three letters Libanius wrote the *comes domorum per Cappadociam*, the manager of the Cappadocian ranches under Valens. Libanius reports that this manager, a certain Acacius, was sent out specifically to clean up the shoddy state of things. Unfortunately, the third letter reveals that Acacius found himself in some trouble for attempting to obtain a good horse for Libanius while in office, a practice that obviously violated Valens's rules of good management.[140] Indeed, Valentinian is reported to have ordered a *strator* named Constantianus to be stoned to death for similar misconduct in Sardinia.[141] Both emperors were thus quite serious but also quite effective at farm management. They used what they knew to help improve the efficiency of the most important sector of the ancient economy, agriculture.

The Pannonian emperors thus concentrated the bulk of their administrative energies on four areas: corruption, civic administration, the masses, and agriculture. In the first arena, they sought to eliminate fraud and extortion

136. *CTh* 11.17.1, with Giardina 1989, 66 n. 12–14; cf. *CTh* 6.31.1 = *CJ* 12.24.1. The emperors also ordered the rebuilding of public stables (*CTh* 15.1.16–17 [a. 365]).

137. Them. *Or.* 11.143c.

138. Basil *Ep.* 74–76 (a. 371), 98 (a. 372); Greg. Naz. *Ep.* 48–50; *De vita sua* ll. 386–485; *Or.* 9–11 (a. 372); *Or.* 12 (a. 374); *Or.* 43.58–9, 86. See Gallay 1943, 105–21; Teja 1974, 196–20; Gain 1985, 306–9; Van Dam 1986.

139. See Forlin Patrucco 1972; cf. Teja 1974, 37–40. Around the same time, Valens also created the new province of Lycaonia (Belke and Restle 1984, 55). See also AM 28.3.7 on Valentinian's provincial re-creations; cf. *Not. dign. oc.* 1.77, 3.34, 23.4 = 11; *Laterculus Polemii Silvii* 11.6; Nagl, "Vt.," 2193; Eadie 1967, 165–66.

140. Lib. *Ep.* 1174, 1222, 1514; cf. *PLRE* I, Acacius 8. Basil *Ep.* 303 also demonstrates Valens's efforts to crack down on the horse levy.

141. AM 29.3.5.

by imperial officials and proved more than willing to employ violent punitive measures. In civic administration, they worked hard to retain curials in
place, to build structures of broad public benefit and to secure the grain supply of the empire's major cities. To benefit the masses, they reformed the
office of *defensor civitatis* and tightened judicial procedures to the benefit of
the common man. And in agriculture, they encouraged land use, strengthened the labor pool, and reformed the horse levy. Because of their successes,
both Valentinian and Valens more than deserve the praise they received, in
their own lifetimes and afterward, for their abilities as administrators.

ECONOMICS AND FINANCE UNDER THE VALENTINIANI

Taxes were as despised in antiquity as they are at present. Then as now, they
represented the most common way for a government to interfere in the lives
of its citizens. Fiscal responsibility was thus an important imperial ideal. In
his description of imperial panegyrics, Menander Rhetor advises that, where
appropriate, the orator should "mention the tributes he [the emperor] im-
poses and the supply of his forces, pointing out that he is concerned also for
his subjects' ability to bear those burdens lightly and easily."[142] This advice
was followed by many an orator and historian, who lauded the economy of
emperors as a mark of honor.[143] In so doing, they reinforced the ideal by
praising it in action. A striking example of the phenomenon comes in Julian, who played the roles of both orator and emperor. In his first oration to
Constantius II, he praised his uncle's enlightened taxation policy in terms
as glowing as possible in light of Constantius's general heavy-handedness in
this arena.[144] When Julian himself took the helm, first as Caesar and then as
Augustus, he was able to act on the ideal he had preached by offering a series of measures designed to relieve the burdens of taxes and debt. Unfortunately, Julian's freehandedness *(liberalitas)* was so unbridled as to verge on
irresponsibility. The rhetoric of tax relief was thus more than just window
dressing: all emperors understood the crucial importance of not overburdening their subjects.

When they first came to power, Valentinian and Valens were stuck with
the financial mess created by Julian, which they worked hard to clear up be-

142. Men. Rhet. 2.375. See Lendon 1997, 16 n. 57.
143. Eus. *Vit. Const.* 1.14, 4.2; Lib. *Or.* 59.15; *Pan. Lat.* 2 [12].13.1–14.4, 3 [11].9.1,
10.2–11.4, 5 [8].11.1–12.6; *SHA Prob.* 33.1–3. See also Themistius's praise of Valens's generous tax measures (*Or.* 8.112a–115d, 10.129c, 11.143c–144a). See also Ratti 1996, 72–74, for
Eutropius's advice on *liberalitas*.
144. Jul. *Or.* 1.16 (21d); cf. Lib. *Or.* 59.156–59. For Constantius's heavy taxes, see AM
21.16.17.

fore moving on to relief measures of their own. Unlike Julian's *liberalitas*, theirs was tempered with caution and a measure of economic good sense.[145] Both were extremely conscientious about limiting the financial burdens on their subjects, but nonetheless concerned to cover state expenses. Their admirable performance in this regard comes out in Ammianus' obituaries of the emperors, which say that Valentinian was "very sparing toward the provincials, and lightened the burdens of tribute everywhere" and that Valens "lightened the burdens of tribute with a singular zeal, allowed no growth in taxes, and was quite moderate in assigning money values for other articles owed in kind."[146] Here again, their experience as farmers and common soldiers had rendered the emperors sympathetic to the conditions of their subjects and capable of taking efficacious measures to better them.

In the arena of the economy more than any other, Valens was the veteran. It was he who had managed the Pannonian farmstead and who could, as Themistius put it, "look over this great empire from afar as if it were a single household and see its annual income, its expenditure, its deficiencies, its surpluses, where things run easily, where with effort."[147] It was therefore Valens, rather than his brother, who was often the leader in economic reform. This was Valens's genius and the element that did most to redeem his other failings.

Unfortunately, we have no writings of Valens preserved to inform us of the motivations and assumptions behind his economic program. Even so, we can catch a glimpse from a contemporary document of what these might have been. We have already seen that he was the recipient of an ingenious treatise "On Military Matters" (*De rebus bellicis*), which proffered advice on innovative weapons to be used in his first Gothic war.[148] In the same treatise, the anonymous author spent considerable effort on the question of economics, particularly as this related to military expenses. His awareness of economic principles stretched well beyond the primitive conceptions attributed by some modern historians to the ancients. He understood, for example, that an increase in the money supply precipitated inflation. He was also aware that the military was the single biggest drain on government resources. Fi-

---

145. AM 31.14.3: "liberalis cum moderatione"; Joh. Ant. fr. 182 = Suid. O 762: φροντίζων καὶ τῆς τῶν θησαυρῶν δικαίας ὑποδοχῆς; Zos. 4.3.2. For previous surveys of Valentinian's and Valens's economic policies, see esp. Andreotti 1931, 482–95; Mazzarino 1951, 187–206; Soraci 1971, 139–65.

146. AM 30.9.1: "in provinciales admodum parcus, tributorum ubique molliens sarcinas"; 31.14.2: "tributorum onera studio quodam molliens singulari, nulla vectigalium admittens augmenta, in adaerandis reliquorum debitis non molestus."

147. Them. *Or.* 8.113d–114b; see p. 54.

148. See pp. 6 and 127.

nally, and less surprisingly, he was fully aware that debasing the coinage hampered economic interchange.[149]

To remedy the problems of the ancient economy the author of the *De rebus bellicis* made a number of suggestions, which seem to have affected—or to have been affected by—the policies of Valentinian and Valens. He recommended measures for cutting the tribute by 50 percent,[150] an ambition that Valens himself expressed. The anonymous author also called for tighter control on the collection of tribute by provincial governors and particularly on the horse levy, the appropriation of grain and building supplies, and the drafting of troops—and the Pannonians reformed the levying not only of horses but of grain, building materials, and conscripts as well.[151] Finally, *De rebus bellicis* advised the emperor to eliminate the debasement of the currency by confining all moneyers to an island where they could not be corrupted.[152] Valentinian and Valens did undertake a currency reform designed to reduce debasement, but rather by "isolating" those authorized to coin precious metal in the imperial *comitatus*. Ultimately, then, the *De rebus bellicis* comes out seeming as much like a policy statement promoting measures already foreseen by the imperial college as a how-to manual designed to enlighten the emperors. Indeed, the relationship between author and emperor is almost entirely ambiguous, leaving us to guess how much the author knew of and reported the emperors' intentions and how much he influenced them.[153]

When Valentinian and Valens first came to power, fundamental economic reforms were hardly a pressing issue. Both emperors were faced with a much more urgent concern in the economic crisis left for them by Julian. Even Julian's admirer Ammianus admitted that many compared Valentinian to Aurelian in that both had to implement austere economic programs to overcome the debts left to them by their fiscally irresponsible predecessors,

---

149. For inflation, see *DRB* 2.1–2, with Giardina 1989, 51–52. For military expenditures, see *DRB* 1.1–2, 5.1; cf. AM 20.11.5 for the same notion. For debasements, see *DRB* 3.1, with Giardina 1989, 56–60.

150. *DRB praef.* 10: "referemus enim quemadmodum, remissa tributorum medietate, in robur proprium provinciarum cultor habeatur." For *DRB*'s economic proposals, see Vanags 1979.

151. *DRB* 4.1–6, esp. 5, with Thompson 1952, 37–41; Giardina 1989, 64–67; cf. Brandt 1988, 61–94. On the Valentinianic reform of the horse levy, see p. 285. On grain, see pp. 297–99. On recruits, see pp. 312–13. On building supplies, see *CTh* 15.1.14 (a. 365).

152. *DRB* 3.2–3; cf. Thompson 1952, 34–37.

153. At *DRB praef.* 4, the author calls himself a *privatus*, and at *praef.* 16, he says that his *otium* prompts him to write. He was thus not in office, but seems to have been close to the emperor and hankering for work. I have a suspicion that the author may have been none other than Domitius Modestus, whose career picked up again in 369 after a five-year hiatus. Modestus was a native Greek speaker, which would also account for the numerous Greekisms that vitiate the anonymous author's Latin style. See Giardina 1989, xxxiii–xlvii for more on the author.

Aurelian with Gallienus's debts and Valentinian with Julian's.[154] Valens's epitomator Eutropius, who was a pagan and had supported Julian, also granted that Julian had been "freehanded with his friends but less diligent than was fitting for so great an emperor," and that he had been "only moderately concerned with the public treasury."[155]

Julian had cut tributes drastically empirewide. Ammianus claims that Gaul alone saw a reduction from twenty-five *solidi* per tax unit *(caput)* to only seven, and several other territories also saw serious reductions.[156] In addition, Julian remitted fiscal debts, seemingly to any territory that asked him to.[157] He remitted the obligation to provide crown gold *(aurum coronarium)*, a major revenue source for the extremely expensive donatives that every emperor—including Julian—distributed to his troops.[158] He returned temple properties—confiscated by Constantine—to the temples. These had been administered by the imperial *res privata* (privy purse) and had constituted another source of imperial revenue, a source Julian cut off.[159] In addition, Julian also returned to the cities civic estates that had been appropriated by the *res privata*, again sapping imperial income.[160]

Nor did Julian cut expenditures at a pace commensurate with his cuts in revenues. Although he eliminated many unnecessary members of his palace staff,[161] he made up the difference by giving land, buildings, and money to his friends, especially his philosophical friends, with wild abandon.[162] When his massive army created a grain crisis in Antioch, he bought his way out of trouble with a huge infusion of subsidized grain.[163] He then marched 65,000 men into Persia in one of the most expensive expeditions of the fourth century.[164] There, before he died, leaving behind him a mountain of debt, he added to the problem by promising huge donatives to his troops for their

---

154. AM 30.8.8.

155. Eutr. 10.16: "in amicos liberalis, sed minus diligens quam tantum principem decuit . . . mediocrem habens aerarii curam."

156. AM 16.5.14, 18.1.1; cf. Jul. *Mis.* 365b, 366d–367a; *Ep.* 14 (Bidez); AM 17.3.2–6, 25.4.15; Greg. Naz. *Or.* 4.75; *Pan. Lat.* 3 [11].9.1, 10.2; Ambrose *De obit. Val.* 21.

157. Jul. *Ep.* 73 (Thrace); *Mis.* 367d (Antioch); Lib. *Or.* 18.163 (Syria); AM 25.4.15 (general). See Pack 1986, 118–25.

158. *CTh* 12.13.1; Lib. *Or.* 16.19; AM 25.4.15; Bruns *Font.* 96. On Julian's accession donative, see AM 20.4.18; Bastien 1988, 90–92. On *aurum coronarium*, see Duncan-Jones 1994, 7–8, and on the donative as a major economic force, ibid., 67–94; cf. Harl 1996, 220–23.

159. *CTh* 5.13.3, 10.1.8; Eunap. *VS* 19.8.1–2.

160. *CTh* 10.3.1; *CJ* 11.70.1; AM 25.4.15; Lib. *Or.* 13.45; cf. Jul. *Mis.* 371a. Cf. A. H. M. Jones 1964, 732, 1301 n. 44.

161. *Pan. Lat.* 3 [11].10.3–11.4; AM 22.4.1–10; cf. Nixon and Rodgers 1994, 410 n. 77.

162. See pp. 107–8.

163. Jul. *Mis.* 369a–b.

164. On the expenses of the expedition, see AM 30.8.8; Lib. *Or.* 18.168–70. See also Depeyrot 1987, 50–51.

various successes.[165] The imperial economy was thus in a shambles when Julian died in mid 363.

And the debts continued to mount in the aftermath of Julian's demise. A fragment of Eunapius seems to indicate that Jovian felt compelled to institute a superindiction in Asia to help bolster the sagging imperial finances that dogged the first months of his reign.[166] Meanwhile, there was the question of donatives. As noted, on his accession, each emperor offered a donative of five gold *solidi* and one pound of silver to every soldier—more to officers. Because much of a soldier's normal annual pay came in grain rations, this accession donative—and subsequent quinquennial donatives—represented the biggest cash outlays faced by an emperor.[167] Reckoning an army totaling 600,000 men,[168] it would have eaten up at least 3,000,000 solidi, or 41,667 pounds in gold and 600,000 pounds in silver, worth the same in gold at the 1 : 14.4 gold : silver ratio common in the fourth century.[169] At the beginning of their reign, Valentinian and Valens had to pay this twice! Jovian's sudden death after eight months of rule left them with arrears for their predecessor's accession donative in addition to their own.

It is thus no surprise that one of Valentinian's and Valens's earliest extant laws revoked Julian's remission of crown gold and called on local *curiae* to pay this tax immediately.[170] Nevertheless, there must have been some confusion over the payment of crown gold for two donatives in such quick succession. Indeed, this confusion is clear from a fragment of Eunapius's *Histories* that reports that embassies bearing *aurum coronarium* for Jovian had to consign their money to Valentinian, because Jovian was dead by the time they reached the imperial *comitatus*.[171] There is thus no way that Jovian's donative can have been completely paid off by the time Valentinian came to power in February 364. Moreover, we know from several letters of Libanius that Antioch sent two embassies bearing crown gold, one to Jovian and

---

165. AM 24.3.2; Zos. 3.13.3, 18.6; cf. AM 20.4.18, 22.9.2, 24.4.26.

166. Eunap. *Hist* fr. 29.2 (Blockley) = Suid. *M* 1306, with Blockley 1981–83, 2: 138 n. 69. A shortage of money is also evident in Libanius's difficulty securing an imperial subvention for the games of Antioch from Jovian (*Ep.* 1148, 1399, 1459).

167. See Hendy 1985, 187–92; Bastien 1988; Burgess 1988.

168. For the variety of opinions on the size of the late Roman army, see Treadgold 1995, 44–59; Elton 1996b, 210–13; Lee 1998, 219–20; *contra* MacMullen 1980.

169. On gold : silver ratios, see Hendy 1985, 481, with table 16. The senates of Rome and Constantinople could be expected to yield ca. 3,000 lbs of gold in *aurum oblaticium*—one of the sources for donatives. *Aurum coronarium* could be expected to yield ca. 30 lbs of gold for each large city. The rest came from the tax on business people, the *collatio lustralis*. This explains Valentinian's and Valens's strict legislation on this tax (*CTh* 12.1.72, 13.1.5–6, 8–10; cf. *P Oxy* 4381). More at Hendy 1985, 175–78.

170. *CTh* 12.13.2 (Aug. 28, 364); cf. *CTh* 12.13.3 (a. 368).

171. Eunap. *Hist.* fr. 31 (Blockley).

a second to Valentinian.[172] Valentinian and Valens did not, then, attempt to equate the two donatives or remit one but demanded *aurum coronarium* twice and thus paid donatives twice: one imagines that the troops would have accepted nothing less. Given the scale and expense of this operation, we should not be surprised to learn that it took over two years for the emperors to complete it. Still in 365, an embassy from Tripolis was being sent to consign *aurum coronarium* to Valentinian, and in the latter part of that year, an official of the imperial *largitiones* in the Pontic diocese was still distributing donatives to troops there when the Procopius revolt broke out.[173] This confirms that the office of imperial *largitiones* was committed to a continuous outflow of cash for well over two years between the summer of 363 and the fall of 365.

To cope with the expense of Julian's prodigality and the cost of this double donative, Valentinian and Valens issued a huge number of gold and silver coins under the legend RESTITUTOR REI PUBLICAE (fig. 15) in the first three years of their reign.[174] They must have been hard pressed to obtain the bullion for this. Indeed, as just mentioned, the new emperors felt compelled to reinstitute the crown gold tax immediately after their accession. They also revoked Julian's devolution of temple properties to religious authorities and reappropriated these and their incomes to the *res privata*.[175] And they reappropriated the municipal estates that Julian had returned to the *curiae*.[176] None of these measures would have been popular, but all were eminently necessary in the face of financial crisis. Even more unpopular were the extreme debt collection procedures the new emperors instituted in their efforts to meet expenses. We have already seen that—according to Ammianus—a major impetus behind the Procopius revolt in 365 was the ruthless collection of tax debts "with fourfold indemnities" by Valens's father-in-law, the patrician Petronius.[177] This interest in back taxes is reflected in two laws of 365 ordering the collection of tribute from delinquent landholders.[178] More striking, a contemporary letter of Basil complains that "all the world is teeming with men who demand payment and make accusations" and specifically mentions the

172. On crown gold to Jovian, see Lib. *Ep.* 1436, 1439. On crown gold to Valentinian, see Lib. *Ep.* 1184–86. Cf. Petit 1955, 417, nos. 6–7; Liebescheutz 1972, 267, nos. 7–8.

173. On Tripolis, see AM 28.6.7, with Warmington 1956, 58, on the date. On the Pontic payout, see AM 26.8.6, with A. H. M. Jones 1964, 624.

174. *RIC* 9.13, 42–43, 61–62, 75, 94, 116–18, 158, 173–74, 191, 209–12, 239, 250–51, 272–73. See Depeyrot 1987, 107–8, 113.

175. *CTh* 5.13.3, 10.1.8; cf. *CTh* 10.1.9, all from A.D. 365.

176. See pp. 295–96.

177. AM 26.6.6–9, 17; cf. p. 72.

178. *CTh* 11.1.13 (Oct. 18, 365); *CTh* 12.6.10 = *CJ* 10.72.3 (Oct. 31, 365). Since both dates record receipt of the laws, they probably represent pieces of the same original order.

Figure 15. RESTITVTOR REI PVBLICAE
solidus of Antioch. *RIC* 9.272.2. Courtesy
American Numismatic Society.

"much talked-about fourfold."[179] Ammianus was thus not exaggerating the
frantic demand for revenues. In addition, we have seen that Valentinian and
Valens attacked former members of Julian's entourage—particularly those
who had benefited from the Apostate's largesse—at least in part as a means
to generate revenues.[180] Maximus of Ephesus, for example, was fined "a sum
of money so large that a philosopher could hardly even have heard of such
an amount."[181] These draconian measures, necessary though they were,
helped prepare the ground for the Procopius revolt.

In the aftermath of the revolt, Valens seems to have done an about-face
on taxation and revenue generation. We have already seen that he exercised
considerable restraint in his reprisals against supporters of Procopius.[182] But
he also seems to have understood that there was a need to slash taxes and
debt collection more generally. Indeed, something of the emperor's attitude
at the time may be reflected in a passage from the *De rebus bellicis* that calls
for sweeping protections for the taxpayer. There the author claims that it
was Constantine—a favorite whipping boy in the aftermath of Procopius's
usurpation[183]—who had fomented the revolution by putting too much gold
and silver into the economy and thereby encouraging the rich to cram their
houses full of splendor to the detriment of the poor:

> But the poor driven by their afflictions into various criminal enterprises and
> losing sight of all respect for law, all feelings of loyalty, entrusted their revenge
> to crime. . . . And passing from one crime to another [they] supported usurpers
> [i.e., Procopius and Marcellus], whom they brought forth for the glorification
> of your virtuous majesty. Therefore, Most Excellent Emperor, you will take care
> in your prudence to limit public grants and thereby look to the taxpayer's in-
> terest *[collatori prospicere]* and transmit to posterity the glory of your name.[184]

179. *Ep.* 21: ἡ πολυθρύλλητος αὐτὴ τετραπλῆ; cf. Treucker 1961, 66–67. *P Oxy* 3393–94
(a. 365) reflect the same anxiety about tax debts.
180. See pp. 107–8.
181. Eunap. *VS* 7.4.13.
182. See pp. 111–13.
183. See p. 102.
184. *DRB* 2.1–7, esp. 5–7. Cf. *DRB* 1.1–2. Ammianus (26.7.1, 7, 10.3) and Themistius (*Or.*
7.91c) speak of those who supported Procopius in very similar terms.

Throughout the remainder of his treatise, the anonymous author stresses the necessity of safeguarding the interests of *collatores*.[185]

This concern expressed to Valens is hardly surprising, given that we have already seen similar language permeating his legislation.[186] Indeed, a concern for the average taxpayer was evident even before the revolt of Procopius. In late 364 and early 365—the year of their first consulship—both emperors issued laws forbidding officials to demand *sportulae*—superindictions supposedly appropriated to "celebrate" state occasions but actually used as a front for extortion.[187] In the years during and after the Procopius revolt, the emperors issued even more laws forbidding such shakedowns: in 370, they banned obligatory gifts to officials (*formale*); in summer 365, they outlawed surcharges for issuing receipts (*apochandi*); and in 368, they ordered exile for officers who attempted to demand transport commutations (*xenia* and *munuscula*).[188] They even offered serious relief from the imposts associated with their decennial donative in 373 (*collatio lustralis* and *aurum oblaticium*).[189] These were relatively simple measures but no doubt helped provide welcome relief to taxpayers.

More important, however, Valens in particular understood that such occasional annoyances were minor compared with the more common and far more onerous burden of tribute, *capitatio-iugatio*. Here again it must be remembered that most taxpayers of the late empire surrendered far more in kind than in cash: the grain, wine, and meat used to feed a huge and very hungry army and civil service constituted most of what they paid. Valens's concern with lightening this burden became abundantly evident in the year following the Procopius revolt. In a difficult passage of Themistius's eighth oration (delivered in March 368), we learn that, from late 367 onward, Valens chose to cut tribute in kind by one-quarter. Themistius begins and ends his discussion of the tax cuts with jabs at the Constantinians—much like the *De rebus bellicis*—for having doubled the tribute rates over the past forty years.[190] In between these criticisms, he reports:

> Arresting this pernicious growth, you first held it in place against expectation, and for three successive years [i.e., 364–66] the affliction did not make its usual advance; and in the fourth [beginning in late 367] you eliminated an equitable portion of the burden. Decrees that were beyond belief were published:

185. *DRB* 1.1, 1.7, 4.1, 4.3, 5.6.
186. See p. 281.
187. *CTh* 8.11.1–2; cf. 11.16.11. See Pergami 1993, xxxvii–xxxviii.
188. *CTh* 1.31.2, 11.2.1; *CTh* 11.11.1 = *CJ* 11.55.2; cf. Them *Or.* 8.116d. See also the epigraphic fragments of a law on *apochae* in Mazzarino 1974.
189. Symm. *Rel.* 13: "divis parentibus tuis ob decennium singulis minor summa decreta est"; Them. *Or.* 11.143c, 144a: τὸ χρυσίον μὲν δαπανήσει καὶ τὸ ἀργύριον.
190. Eus. *VC* 4.2 holds that Constantine actually cut tribute by one quarter, an assertion whose value is difficult to assess (Barnes 1981, 255–58).

"the measures of grain and wine you shall pay in taxes shall be reduced by such and such an amount and remaining items shall also fall short of what you used to pay by equal quantities.". . . Because of this, those who made increases measure-by-measure over a forty-year period [i.e., the Constantinians between 324 and 363] got away with doubling the taxes, while the contributions we shall pay to you next year will be halved, if the measures of the return turn out according to expectation.[191]

Valens thus cut tribute rates by one-quarter in the indiction year 367–68 and seems to have expressed the intention that, within the next year, they would fall to one-half the level they had reached by the beginning of his reign. This sentiment is remarkably close to the goal of halving taxes expressed by the *De rebus bellicis* at precisely the same time.[192]

One questions, however, whether this lofty aim was ever achieved.[193] The fact that the year 367–68 was a benchmark in setting indiction rates is clear from two laws of Theodosius II that remitted tax delinquencies "since the eleventh Valentian indiction *[ex indictione undecima Valentiaca].*"[194] The indiction of 367–68 had thus been reified as a base year for setting tax rates. This fact and the wording of the law tell us two things about what Valens actually accomplished: first, Valens is unlikely to have implemented his further anticipated cut in 368–69—otherwise Theodosius would have used Valens's "twelfth indiction" as the base year for his remittance; second, the indiction rate was attributed to Valens rather than his brother and was thus perhaps Valens's invention. Further evidence that Valens was the leader on the question of tribute reductions comes from several passages in the literary sources. To be sure, Ammianus claims that both emperors cut tribute, but he indicates that Valens did so with particular zeal;[195] more tellingly, Zosimus openly laments the fact that in the latter part of his reign, "Valentinian was very oppressive in his demands for taxes, exceeding the usual exactions";[196]

---

191. Them. *Or.* 8.113a–c; cf. *Or.* 10.129c. On this passage, see Vanderspoel 1995, 169–71.

192. *DRB* 5.3 claims that this reduction could be achieved by dismissing soldiers once they had attained a pay rank of five *annonae*. Just as with Valens's cutbacks, tribute rates (i.e., payments in kind of grain) are in question, leaving one to wonder whether Valens actually intended to implement *DRB*'s recommendation on early dismissal.

193. Heather and Matthews 1991, 27 n. 38 believe that Them. *Or.* 8.112d–113c confirms a 50 percent cut. While it is true that that the last sentence quoted above implies this intention, they have mistranslated Themistius's quotation from Valens's law in a way that makes the second—proposed—cut seem more certain than it must have been. καὶ τὰ λοιπὰ ἐξ ἴσης ἀποδέοντα τοῦ συνήθους should be rendered as above rather than "and for the future also shall fall short of what is customary by equal quantities," a translation that implies τὸ λοιπὸν for τὰ λοιπά. For the correct translation, see both Maisano 1995, 391, and Leppin and Portmann 1998, 163 and n. 139; cf. Vanderspoel 1995, 169 n. 52.

194. *CTh* 11.28.9–10.

195. AM 30.9.1, 31.14.2, see n. 146.

196. Zos. 4.16.1.

and Ammianus lends circumstantial credibility to this claim when he says that Valentinian turned a blind eye while his prefect Probus impoverished Pannonia with ever-rising taxation in the 370s.[197] On the question of tribute reductions, then, Valens seems to have been the leader: he apparently initiated the program and kept it in place even when his brother abandoned it at the end of his reign.

Valens also broke his own ground on the question of revenues from civic estates, the lands formerly held by individual cities in endowment. As already mentioned, these had been appropriated to the imperial *res privata* since the days of Constantius II but had been returned to the cities by Julian. Valentinian and Valens reappropriated the civic estates at the beginning of their reigns, but Valens soon partially reversed the policy again. This we know from a wonderful inscription of Ephesus recording a rescript of Valens to Eutropius who was serving as proconsul of Asia in 371.[198] The rescript shows that Valens had undertaken an experiment in which, rather than returning ownership of the estates to the cities, he returned to them revenues from some of those estates, while retaining ownership and administration for the *res privata*. The revenues were to be used for restoring civic *moenia* (public structures), an undertaking that, as we have seen, was dear to Valens's and Valentinian's hearts.[199] Because the experiment had worked, Valens ordered Eutropius to make an assessment of the current state of all imperially held civic estates in Asia and then begin distributing revenues from these to other Asian cities. These estates, Valens's knew, amounted to 6,736½ *iuga* of productive land and 703 *iuga* of nonproductive land, with an annual income of 11,000 solidi.[200] This remarkable decree tells us three important things: first, Valens had an amazing grip on financial administration and an astonishing cache of precise information at his fingertips; second, contrary to common assumptions, emperors did not simply react to demands but actually plotted out policies and tested them in advance;[201] third, it must have been Valens and not Valentinian who invented the system attested in the law codes whereby cities were granted one-third of the revenues from their old estates for the purpose of restoring public structures ("ad reparationem moenium

197. AM 30.5.5–6: "denique tributorum onera vectigaliumque augmenta multiplicata"; cf. Jer. *Chron.* s.a. 372.

198. *AE* 1906, 30 = *IK* 11.1.42. See May 1973, 52, with Zos. 4.13.1 on the date. For analysis, see esp. Heberdey 1906; Chastagnol 1986; cf. Foss 1979, 25. On civic estates more broadly, see A. H. M. Jones 1964, 732–73; Liebeschuetz 1972, 149–61.

199. See app. D.

200. These figures seem somewhat low given that the Syrian city of Cyrrhus alone controlled 10,000 *iuga* of imperial land; cf. A. H. M. Jones 1964, 416.

201. Cf. *CTh* 11.1.9 (a. 365), which describes the same sort of experimentation followed by empire-wide implementation. Corcoran 1996 also argues that a more active approach to legislation was typical of the later empire.

publicorum"). This law is first seen being implemented in two western issues of 374 but is only defined in detail in a law of Honorius from 395, which attributes it to Valentinian.[202] The Ephesus decree makes it clear, however, that already in 371 Valens was perfecting this new system in the east, which he must then have passed on to his brother for implementation in the west.

Another interesting feature of the Ephesus rescript is that it orders Eutropius to produce lists (*breves*) cataloging all civic properties, their holders, the nature of their possession, their annual rents, and the quality of their land.[203] The order is striking given that lists seem more generally to have been a hallmark of the Pannonian emperors. By the time he moved to Asia, Eutropius had already produced a catalog of history (*breviarium*) for Valens, and soon Festus was ordered to do the same.[204] The author of the *De rebus bellicis* also understood that he had to lay out his list of engineering and economic proposals in brief (*brevius*) to please Valens.[205] In a law of 365, Valentinian ordered the vicar of Africa to produce annual lists (*breves*) of those with property in Africa who lived in Rome.[206] In 369, Valentinian laid out procedures for appropriating proscribed property that ordered officials of the governor's office to produce a list of all items on the estates, which could then be checked by an official of the *res privata*.[207] In 371, Valens ordered lists (*breves*) of eastern grain shippers to be drawn up in duplicate.[208] In an inscription from Apulia, Valentinian ordered local civic officials to produce monthly lists (*mestrui{s} breves*) of tribute collected, and another of Valentinian's laws ordered all students in Rome to be enrolled on lists (*breves*) to be sent to the emperor annually.[209] In 374, the urban prefect Tarracius Bassus produced lists of regular cheaters on the grain dole, which still survive in several fragments from inscriptions in Rome.[210] Finally, a passage of John Lydus indicates that it was Valens who first instituted the record archives of the *instrumentarius*—located under the arcades of the Constantinopolitan hippodrome—which kept lists of documents associated with the law courts.[211] Both emperors were thus obsessed with keeping lists of infor-

---

202. *CTh* 4.13.7, 15.1.18 (a. 374), 15.1.33 (a. 395); cf. 15.1.32.
203. *AE* 1906, 30 = *IK* 11.1.42 l. 23.
204. See pp. 185–96.
205. *DRB* 5.2.
206. *CTh* 11.1.13.
207. *CTh* 9.42.7 = *CJ* 9.49.7; *CTh* 10.9.1 = *CJ* 10.10.3.
208. *CTh* 13.5.14.
209. Giardina and Grelle 1983 = *AE* 1984, 250 and *CTh* 14.9.1. See also *CTh* 8.5.18 and 9.21.8 for *breves*. A glance at the Heidelberg index to the Codex Theodosianus reveals that *breves* only became a fashionable administrative tool after the Valentiniani.
210. *CIL* 6.31893–99; cf. *CTh* 14.17.5 (a. 369).
211. Joh. Lyd. *De mag.* 3.19.

mation, a trait they no doubt developed as estate managers. This obsession must have proved extremely useful in mapping financial transactions and extirpating corruption.

Such records would have been necessary in implementing the sophisticated new methods of tribute collection adopted by both emperors. Already in the first two years of their reign, Valentinian and Valens undertook a major overhaul of the entire system for paying tribute. As noted, the vast majority of taxes paid in the later empire were consigned in kind. The system was administered under the office of the praetorian prefect, who controlled the collection of these goods and their distribution as rations *(annonae)* for men and fodder *(capitus)* for horses.[212] Prior to Valentinian's and Valens's reigns, initial collections had been the responsibility of curial appointees called *susceptores.* These consigned their supplies, particularly grain, to local storehouses *(horrea),* which were administered by *praepositi,* again drawn from the curials. This grain could then be requisitioned and distributed to soldiers and officials by officers called *actuarii,* a group notorious for fraud.[213] The system was awkward and something of a holdover from the inflationary period of the third century, when taxes had to be collected in kind because the coinage was too debased to be trusted. Even Valentinian and Valens understood that the system was cumbersome and thus encouraged the gradual process of commuting tributes to money equivalents *(adaeratio).*[214] But the old system could not be changed overnight, and neither did Valens and Valentinian ever seriously consider a complete conversion to *adaeratio.* Here as elsewhere, their focus was narrower and aimed more at the microeconomic than the macroeconomic level.

Even in the first months of their reign, Valentinian and Valens reworked the old tribute system. Although they kept the system in place, they implemented a top-to-bottom overhaul in an effort to make things run more smoothly.[215] In 364, they relieved curials of responsibility for collecting tribute as *susceptores* and turned over that function to members of the office staffs of the governors—apparently because these could more easily be punished for fraud.[216] In the same year, they instituted the practice of allowing provincials to pay their taxes in three yearly installments, a measure of benefit both to the taxpayer—who could spread out payments to coincide with the two-harvest crop cycle in the Mediterranean—and the state—which could avoid

---

212. On the system, see A. H. M. Jones 1964, 456–57, 626–30, 727–28; cf. Bagnall 1993, 153–60.

213. On the fraud of *actuarii,* see Aur. Vict. *Caes.* 33.13; cf. Vogler 1979, 277–80.

214. E.g., *CTh* 7.4.14 (a. 365). Mazzarino 1951, 193–98, has made too much of the problem of *adaeratio* in my estimation.

215. Them. *Or.* 8.115a, 118c–d praises the measures laid out.

216. *CTh* 12.6.7; cf. Giardina and Grelle 1983, 272–76.

overburdening its transport system with huge influxes of grain.[217] This same year also saw the beginnings of efforts to restore the state *horrea* for the storage of grain.[218] Here again, efficiency was improved by limiting spoilage. Finally, 364 saw orders that *actuarii* produce requisition orders *(pittacia)* either daily or every two days before any supplies could be paid to them out of the *horrea.*[219] This prevented them from fraudulently requisitioning more than was necessary and keeping the surplus. The totality of these measures was clearly designed to improve the previous system by eliminating corruption and improving efficiency.

Nevertheless, the new order began to spring leaks almost immediately, and only some parts of it survived for any length of time. The weakest link in the process was the requirement that *susceptores* be drawn from praesidial *officiales.* Tax collection had been the least welcome job of the curials, and it was no easier to persuade *officiales* to take on the burden. Immediately, the emperors began having to clarify that no military officer or palatine official could be forced into tribute collection, but only members of the governors' staffs.[220] Already in 365, Valentinian chose not to try to implement the new system in Africa, and in the same year, Valens had to abandon it in Cilicia for lack of enough qualified *officiales* to do the job.[221] By the 390s, the praesidial *susceptores* had been dropped altogether.[222] The arrangement for payments in quadrimenstrual installments, by contrast, proved more durable, lasting well into the fifth century.[223] The order to restore *horrea* also must have been beneficial over the long term. As to the *pittacia,* we know that Valens was still using them in 377, but beyond this we cannot say.[224] They were certainly a clever idea and very much in keeping with the brother emperors' obsession with recordkeeping, but given the complication of issuing daily requisition orders, they are unlikely to have survived the Pannonians by much.

Some of the intention behind this new system can be seen in a marvelous inscription from Canusium in southeastern Italy. The inscription was apparently one of many put up in provincial capitals on orders from the prae-

---

217. If we can assume that the law from which *CTh* 11.19.3 (Sept. 12, 364) was drawn applied to all *collatores* and not just *emphyteuticarii.* Cf. *CTh* 11.7.11 (a. 365), 5.15.20 (a. 366), 11.1.15 (a. 366), 12.6.15 (a. 369); Gaudemet 1978.

218. *CJ* 10.26.2 (Aug. 25, 364); cf. *CTh* 15.1.17 (a. 365) and *CIL* 8.7975 = *ILS* 5910. To eliminate some of the strain on storage space, Valentinian and Valens also ordered provincials near military *castra* to consign their tribute directly to these; see *CTh* 11.1.11 = *CJ* 10.16.6 (a. 365); *CTh* 7.4.15 = *CJ* 12.37.4 (a. 369); cf. *CTh* 7.4.23 = *CJ* 12.37.8 (a. 396).

219. *CTh* 7.4.11, 13 (late 364); cf. 7.4.16 = *CJ* 12.37.5 (a. 368).

220. *CTh* 12.10.1 = *CJ* 12.52.2 (Nov. 18, 364); *CTh* 8.7.8 = *CJ* 12.52.1 (a. 365); *CTh* 12.6.6 (a. 365). See also *CTh* 1.16.5, with Pergami 1993, 203–4, on the date.

221. *CTh* 12.6.5, 9.

222. See Giardina and Grelle 1983, 300–301.

223. See Giardina and Grelle 1983, 280.

224. *CTh* 7.4.17 = *CJ* 12.37.6.

torian prefect. It recorded a decree requiring curial chiefs (*praepositi pago-rum*) and curial overseers of local storehouses (*curatores horrearum*) to pre-pare monthly lists recording "how much and in what material each person paid on each day and what was taken from each in debts" and to turn these over to the provincial governor.[225] The governor was then to travel through-out the province and consult with individual taxpayers in order to confirm that the reported sums were correct and to ensure that taxpayers were not hiding anything. This was quintessential Valentinian and Valens: a sophisti-cated recordkeeping system with built-in checks and balances designed to protect taxpayers from greedy *susceptores* while simultaneously monitoring their attempts to cheat. Not surprisingly, pieces of the system are also attested elsewhere. A Theodosian Code entry from 369 seems to be part of the same original law ordering governors to make the rounds to all villages and villae in order to ensure that taxes were not collected with force or avarice (*inso-lenter aut cupide*).[226] Another law of 372 orders vicars to police governors in their dioceses and make sure they were restraining the fraud of their tax re-ceivers and accountants.[227] Moreover, the elements necessary for this system show up already in a law of 365 subjecting praesidial fiscal accountants (*tab-ularii*) to torture for failing to report due and delinquent tribute regularly,[228] and another of 375 ordering that receipts (*apochae*) be issued when tribute was consigned to local *horrea*.[229] One such receipt survives in a papyrus from Oxyrhynchus from April of 374.[230] Here again, recordkeeping and strict over-sight were used to eliminate fraud and protect the interests of taxpayers and the state.

Perhaps the most significant economic measure undertaken by Valentin-ian and Valens was a major reform of the coinage implemented between 366 and 371. We have already seen that the anonymous *De rebus bellicis* lamented the debasement of the gold solidus and the ill effects this had on commerce: because the coin was widely known to be debased, it was not accepted at the value of its weight in bullion but was the subject of market speculation. *De re-bus bellicis* recommended that Valens solve the problem by removing all mon-eyers to an island in order that they be "cut off from association with the neighboring land, so that freedom of intercourse, which lends itself to fraud-

225. Giardina and Grelle 1983 = *AE* 1984, no. 250, esp. ll. 9–10: "quantum et in qua specie diebus singulis singuli quiq(ue) dissolverint quidve ab unoquoq(ue) trahatur in reliquis."

226. *CTh* 1.16.11 (Apr. 1, 369); cf. Giardina and Grelle 1983, 286–88. Basil *Ep.* 86–87 may show the system in action in Cappadocia.

227. *CTh* 1.15.6 (Feb. 27, 372).

228. *CTh* 8.1.9 = *CJ* 12.49.2; cf. *CTh* 8.1.11 = *CJ* 12.49.3.

229. *CTh* 12.6.16 = *CJ* 10.72.6 (Apr. 9, 375); cf. *CTh* 5.15.20 = *CJ* 11.65.4 (May 19, 366) ordering *rationales* to give receipts to *empytheuticarii*.

230. *P Turner* 45. See also *CTh* 14.15.2 = *CJ* 11.23.1 ordering *nautici* to use receipts to track their grain shipments, and see *P Oxy* 3395 (a. 371) for such a receipt.

ulent practices, may not mar the integrity of a public service."[231] The author apparently believed that the moneyers colluded with *privati* or fellow officials to mix gold bullion with base metal so that extra solidi (always weighing one-seventy-second of a pound) could be produced from the extra metal.[232] This was precisely the sort of problem that Valentinian and Valens attacked, and in a fashion not unlike that proposed by *De rebus bellicis*.

Their first extant law on the question dates from November 10, 366, although it indicates that it is merely repeating an earlier order. Here Valentinian commanded his praetorian prefect Rufinus to insist that solidi collected in payment of taxes be melted into a mass of pure gold *(in massam obryzae)* so that "every avenue of fraud shall be barred for the representatives of the largesses *[largitionales]*, the official escorts *[prosecutores]* and the tax-gatherers *[allectores]*."[233] The same order also survives in two laws issued in January and August of 367.[234] The object of this measure was to eliminate the possibility of officials substituting debased coins for pure in large caches of tax money. Because, as the January 367 law states, "a pound of gold shall be credited for seventy-two solidi," any dross skimmed off in the process of reducing the gold to bullion would do the peculating tax-gatherer no good: tax payments were now evaluated based on their weight in gold bullion, not the number of coins consigned. Not surprisingly, at precisely this period we begin to get large numbers of gold bars in the archaeological record.[235] Moreover, beginning in 368, we also begin to see the symbol OB for *obryzum* (the word from the laws for "pure gold") appearing with the mint mark on gold solidi.[236] The order to melt down and thereby purify tax payments was thus in no way ignored. This empirewide order met with empirewide results.

This first measure was certainly sufficient to eliminate the introduction of debased coins by tax gatherers, but the problem of fraud on the part of moneyers remained. Here, no laws of Valentinian and Valens survive, but we still have sufficient evidence to prove that major changes were made. A law of Arcadius's issued to the eastern *comes sacrarum largitionum*, who ran the mints, indicates Valens had essentially laid out the infrastructure for that office in a major constitution.[237] A separate law of 384 actually catalogs that

---

231. *DRB* 3.1–3, esp. 2: "a societate videlicet in perpetuum contiguae terrae prohibiti, ne commixtionis licentia fraudibus oportuna integritatem publicae utilitatis obfuscet." For market speculation in coin, see Hendy 1985, 291–94.

232. Lib. *Or.* 18.138 describes the same process; cf. Hendy 1985, 320–24.

233. *CTh* 12.6.12. For this coinage reform, see Harl 1996, 159–61.

234. *CTh* 12.6.13 = *CJ* 10.72.5; *CTh* 12.7.3.

235. See Overbeck and Overbeck 1985, with bibliography.

236. *RIC* 9.15–18, 177, 216–7, 275–79. Perhaps the reform was designed to coincide with the *quinquennalia* of February 25, 368. Papyri also begin insisting on payments in coin marked ὀμβρύζης (*P Lips.* 61 ll. 10–12, 62 ll. I.8, 20, 29, II.6, 12, 22, 27).

237. *CTh* 6.30.13 (a. 395).

infrastructure, apparently as Valens—and Valentinian—had organized it, including the various subdivisions of the comitatensian mint.[238] Imperial moneyers had, since the reign of Diocletian, worked in approximately fourteen mints scattered across the empire, approximately one per diocese. Most of these had minted in all three metals—gold, silver, and bronze—at various times down to the 360s. Under Constantine, though, a separate group of minters came to follow the imperial train, the so-called comitatensian mint. These comitatensian moneyers tended to issue only precious metal coins and seem to have worked out of the mint facilities closest to the imperial *comitatus* at a given time.[239] M. F. Hendy has shown that under Valentinian and Valens, this comitatensian mint was exclusively charged with the production of all gold and silver coinage.[240] The emperors thus "isolated" the moneyers in gold and silver in their immediate train, much as *De rebus bellicis* had recommended confining them to an island.[241]

Not surprisingly, a recent metrological study has demonstrated that these measures were highly effective in improving the purity of the gold coinage: prior to the OB coins of 367, the average solidus contained about 4.0–6.0 percent silver and 0.25 percent copper; beginning with the OB coins, the average solidus contained only 0.5–0.7 percent silver and 0.025 percent copper, a 90 percent reduction in impurities.[242] Although we have no laws concerning silver coinage, Valentinian's silver issues also acquired a new mark around 367, PS or P for *pusullatus* (purified).[243] We thus might assume that similar regimens were applied to the collection, melting, and production of silver coin. Here again, metrology confirms a 75 percent drop in the amount of copper in the silver coinage after 367.[244] The Pannonian emperors thus dealt with the problem of currency debasement identified by the author of *De rebus bellicis* in a fashion not unlike the latter's recommendations. Tax monies were quickly reduced to bullion bars to avoid the surreptitious substitution of bad coins and were then reminted by minters confined to the emperor's train. The net result was a drastic increase in the purity of the precious metal coinage.

Curiously enough, at the same time that Valentinian and Valens were refining the silver and gold coinage, they were also debasing the empire's copper coin. When they came to power, only two copper coins were commonly minted, the heavier Aes 1, which was 2.0 percent silver, and the lighter Aes

238. *CJ* 12.23.7; cf. *CTh* 6.30.7.
239. On mints, see Hendy 1972b; cf. id. 1985, 378–86.
240. Hendy 1972a, 125–30; cf. id. 1985, 386–94.
241. The connection is made clear in Cracco Ruggini 1987.
242. Amandry et al. 1982, 280–81.
243. *RIC* 9.18–19, 45–6, 65, 147–50. Valens's mints did not use this symbol; cf. Amandry et al. 1982, 282 n. 20, for possible reasons.
244. Amandry et al. 1982, 282–84; Reece 1963.

3, which was 0.3 percent silver. After 365, Valentinian and Valens ceased to produce the heavier coin and debased the lighter to 0.2 percent silver.[245] A law of 371 ordered the recall of the heavier billon coin and simultaneously threatened "melters of shaped bronze and counterfeiters of money" with capital punishment.[246] The emperors seem to have been trying to close a loophole for any who still tried to extract silver from the billon coinage or to remelt billon into the gold and silver. Indeed, a related law of 369 ordered punishment for those who brought their money to the public mint for recoining. Once again, the emperors were attacking the sort of collusion between mint workers and private citizens decried in *De rebus bellicis*.[247] The two were thus obsessed with the problem of counterfeiting, whether by fraudulent officials or collusive citizens. Here again, their instincts as former estate managers seem to have been at play, since their actions represented a net benefit to taxpayers. Economic exchange runs smoothest in an environment of monetary stability.

Unfortunately, by focusing on the benefits to taxpayers, the emperors were not necessarily benefiting themselves. What they had done was to create an unusually level playing field for economic exchange: all three coinages were essentially minted as pure bullion, such that their valuation could be fixed to the market rates for gold, silver, and copper. This certainly would have helped the empire's subjects, especially those rich enough to use gold and silver.[248] For imperial finances, though, debasements were not necessarily a bad thing: small debasements actually increased the money supply available to the emperor without creating serious inflation.[249] In closing the gap between the real and the market value of their coinage, Valentinian and Valens cost themselves a measure of revenue. By removing the 4 percent impurity content of their precious metal coins, they removed 4 percent of their precious metal supply, and thus 4 percent of their money supply. This was a huge drop for a painfully slow-growing economy. It was also a drop with repercussions for years to come, because the emperors were forced to mint 4 percent fewer gold and silver coins from any new bullion supplies in all future issues.

---

245. Amandry et al. 1982, 284–88.

246. *CTh* 11.21.1; cf. *CJ* 11.11.1. Hendy 1985, 468–73; cf. Harl 1996, 163–75, on *aes* in the mid-fourth century.

247. *CTh* 9.21.7. *CTh* 9.21.8 (a. 374) relaxes the order somewhat but demands so high a franking charge that it would have still rendered re-coining impossible. Valentinian's fear of fraud among moneyers is confirmed by his execution of a *procurator monetae* in Rome (AM 28.1.29; cf. Eutr. 9.14).

248. The elimination of silver from the bronze coinage did not have a great inflationary effect on bronze, perhaps because the silver content of the AE 3 had been so low to begin with (Bagnall 1985, 43–48, 60–61). Even so, *CJ* 11.11.2 would indicate some inflationary pressure on the bronze coinage.

249. Walker 1978, 106–48.

Their understanding of economics was simply not sophisticated enough to recognize the ultimate effects of their actions. As with the author of the *De rebus bellicis*, they knew that fraud could be eliminated and free exchange facilitated by the purification of the coinage. They did not realize, however, that by curbing the money supply, they would create an overall deflationary effect on state spending power. Their 25 percent cut in tribute likewise certainly benefited the average taxpayer but had a negative impact on imperial finances. For this reason, it was abandoned by Valentinian, although retained by Valens. As a farmer, Valens seems to have stood solidly by the maxim, purveyed in *De rebus bellicis* and Themistius, that "the less the king exacts, the more he bestows"—in other words, that tax revenue could be increased by beneficence to the taxpayer.[250] The end results were wonderful for the empire's subjects but disastrous for the empire.

To overcome this loss in state revenue, the emperors had to resort to other means of assembling money. This they did through three measures, only one of which was sustainable over the long term: intensified mining, confiscations, and the sale of imperial estates. The surest way for an ancient government to increase the money supply was to increase the metal supply.[251] In the late Roman world, this could be effected through any number of mines scattered across the empire but particularly in Spain, Gaul, and the Balkans. Some of the mines were privately owned and others were in the hands of the government. From the private mines, the government collected a fixed quota of minerals per miner per year; from the government mines, a percentage of product.[252] In either case, miners and their children were hereditarily bound to carry on their profession. Valentinian and Valens recognized the importance of this money source already in 365, when they issued a law calling for volunteers to take up mining at a quota of only eight scruples of gold dust per miner per year and offering to buy any other gold the miners produced.[253]

Shortly after the coinage reform, however, such gentle encouragement gave way to downright coercion. A law of 369 issued stiff fines for any ship captain who illegally transported mine workers to Sardinia as refugees. The same law was repeated in 378.[254] In 370, Valens issued a law authorizing posses to seek out fugitive miners, and in 373 Valentinian joined in the hunt for escaped Thracian miners, who had made their way as far west as Illyri-

---

250. Them. *Or.* 8.112d; cf. Eutr. 10.1.2. This antiquated mode of thinking has returned to fashion among contemporary "supply-side" economists.

251. This was already understood in the fourth century B.C. by Xenophon in his *Ways and Means*. See Duncan-Jones 1994, 103–5.

252. A. H. M. Jones 1964, 838–39 and 1351–52; Edmondson 1989; Bowersock et al. 1999, 579–80.

253. *CTh* 10.19.3 = *CJ* 11.7.1; cf. *CTh* 10.19.4 = *CJ* 11.7.2 (a. 367).

254. *CTh* 10.19.6, 9.

cum.[255] Thrace was indeed the treasure-house of the eastern empire, and Themistius implies that Valens's was driving his miners and quarriers there quite hard in 373.[256] Valens's pressures on this province eventually became so great that, when the Goths revolted in the region in 377, they were quickly joined by "numerous gold miners who had been unable to bear the heavy burdens of taxes."[257] Nor did Valens let up on miners in other regions during the latter part of his reign. A letter of Basil's from 372 asks for relief from the exorbitant taxes on iron miners in Cappadocia, and in 373, Valens began regularly condemning dissident Christians to work in the copper mines of Egypt.[258] Valens was thus driving mineral producers to the breaking point. Meanwhile, he not only tried to increase the inflow of bullion into the market but also to staunch its outflow from the empire with a 374 law threatening torture to any who exported gold into *barbaricum*.[259] Indeed, yet another metrological study has shown that Valens was in part motivated to defend Roman interests in Armenia because he had discovered new gold reserves in the region, which he desperately needed to boost his money supply.[260] It seems then that his tribute reduction and coinage reform in the 360s were taking their toll by the 370s. He had become desperate to assemble money without going back on his principles of "good economics," namely, tax cuts and coinage refinements like those recommended in *De rebus bellicis*.

Perhaps the least savory revenue-generation exercise undertaken by the Pannonian emperors was the confiscation of property from condemned "criminals." Surprising as it is to moderns, the confiscation of private property actually constituted a significant, if highly unpopular, source of imperial revenue throughout antiquity.[261] Valentinian and Valens were no doubt well aware of this, having experienced the loss of their father's estate to the *res privata*. Despite this experience, however, they seem not to have shied away from confiscations in their pursuit of cash. For this reason, both are accused of avarice, a fault that the *Epitome de Caesaribus* calls Valentinian's worst vice and that Ammianus attributes to Valens in his obituary.[262] This assessment

255. *CTh* 10.19.5, 7.
256. Them. *Or.* 11.152c; cf. 14.181b. On Thrace as a gold-mining region, see *Pan. Lat.* 2 [12].28.2; Veg. *Mil.* 4.24.
257. AM 31.6.6: "auri venarum periti non pauci, vectigalium perferre posse non sufficientes sarcinas graves"; cf. Them. *Or.* 14.181b.
258. Basil *Ep.* 110. On condemnations to the copper mines of Phaeno, see Theod. *HE* 4.22.26, 28. Cf. *CTh* 7.18.1 (a. 365) condemning those who harbored deserters from the mines.
259. *CJ* 4.63.2. On other laws to halt the eastward flow of gold, see Rugullis 1992, 105–15. Valens had actually lost a source of revenues when Nisibis was surrendered, since this city was a major supplier of *portoria;* see Winter 1988, 186–200.
260. Depeyrot 1995.
261. See Millar 1977, 163–74; Hendy 1985, 231; Duncan-Jones 1994, 5–7.
262. On Valentinian, see *Epit.* 45.5–6: "infectus vitiis maximeque avaritia"; cf. AM 30.5.7: "ex rebus minimis avidus"; 30.8.8: "aviditas plus habendi sine honesti pravique differentia";

of the emperors started to be officially expressed almost immediately after their reigns. Already in 382, Jerome claimed that Valentinian was commonly accused of cruelty and greed, and in the same year, Gregory of Nazianzus called Valens "the most gold-loving and Christ-hating emperor."[263] Given their efforts to relieve taxpayers, it seems odd that the sources should come down so hard on the emperors for avarice. In the eyes of the ancients, though, this assessment was justified by their ruthless appropriation of wealth during their treason and magic trials. Judicial condemnations had certainly helped Valentinian and Valens to fill their coffers during the financial difficulties at the beginning of their reign,[264] and they seem to have kept these gains in mind when they undertook to root out magic in Rome and Antioch beginning in 369.[265] In his account of both sets of magic trials, Ammianus emphasizes again and again that Valentinian, Valens, and their ministers focused on wealthy victims, hoping that their criminal charges would reap rich rewards.[266] Already in 376, Symmachus implied the same motivation behind the Rome trials, and Zosimus as well as his source Eunapius baldly state that Valens's Antioch trials had money as their primary object.[267] To be sure, such charges constituted a stereotyped accusation against any emperor who pursued confiscations, but their pervasiveness in Valens's and Valentinian's cases lends them some credence. It was hardly unthinkable that two cash-strapped emperors would regard revenue generation as at least a secondary benefit of the widespread inquisitions they undertook.

Ultimately, however, even these measures did not suffice to prop up imperial finances when Valens's empire began to fall apart after 375. Because Valens had been struggling to recoup his deficits for years, he had little choice but to begin selling imperial estates when confronted with barbarian problems in Thrace, Isauria, Armenia, and Arabia from 375 to 378. The ancient economy of empire provided no adequate means for the government to meet extraordinary expenses on credit.[268] If crises arose, assets sometimes had to be sold to generate revenues. Valens's epitomator Eutropius had pointed this

30.8.10. On Valens, see AM 31.14.5: "magnarum opum intemperans adpetitor"; cf. AM 26.6.6: "cupiditate aliena rapiendi succensum"; 31.4.4; cf. Ratti 1996, 96.

263. Jer. *Chron.* s.a. 365: "severitatem eius nimiam et parcitatem quidam crudelitatem et avaritiam interpretabantur." Greg. Naz. *Or.* 43.30: βασιλεὺς ὁ φιλοχρυσότατος καὶ μισοχριστότατος. Cf. Them. *Or.* 18.219b (a. 384).

264. See p. 108. Cf. AM 26.10.11–14; Lib. *Or.* 62.159–60.

265. Thus the law of March 369 laying out protocols for the acquisition of proscribed properties, *CTh* 9.42.7 = *CJ* 9.49.7; *CTh* 10.9.1 = *CJ* 10.10.3.

266. On the Rome trials, see pp. 231–32. On the Antioch trials, see AM 29.1.19: "admovente stimulos avaritia et sua et eorum qui tunc in regia versabantur"; 21: "quorum in aerario bona coacta et ipse ad quaestus proprios redigebat"; cf. AM 29.1.43, 44, 2.3, 5, 11, 31.14.5, 15.13.

267. Symm. *Or.* 4.9: "nullius divitis crimen optatur." Zos. 4.14.4; Eunap. *Hist.* fr. 39.9 (Blockley).

268. Hendy 1985, 237–42.

out when he noted that Marcus Aurelius had had to auction off imperial treasures to meet the expenses of his Marcomannic wars. Eutropius was quick
to note that Marcus later recouped the goods by offering their purchase price
to buyers, a happy ending to a sorry affair.[269] Valens might also have hoped
for a similarly felicitous outcome when he decided to begin selling off imperial estates at rock-bottom prices at the end of his reign. This we learn from
a fragment of the sixth-century chronicler Hesychius who reports:

> The emperor Valens sold off nearly all the imperial estates when he was sorely
> strapped for money because of the barbarians. Whoever was able to buy be-
> came the owner of these for a very low price, since they reduced the true in-
> come of these with the favor and release of government administrators. And
> some, where absolutely no tribute would be imposed, bought the estates for
> a slightly higher price, which form of possession the Romans call *relevatum*.
> Others. . . .[270]

Unfortunately, the fragment breaks off, but we can assume it would report
that others paid less for imperial estates with the proviso that their new properties would be subject to tribute. At any rate, the government was liquidat-
ing its own revenue-producing lands in an effort to meet mounting expenses
on what had already been inadequate revenues. The cuts in tribute and in
the money supply, for all that they may have improved efficiency in tax collection, rendered the emperor incapable of generating sufficient money to
keep the ship of state afloat.

We have thus seen that Valentinian and particularly Valens were quite ingenious economic administrators. They were able to reorganize revenues from
civic estates, to overhaul the collection of tribute, and to reengineer the collection of money taxes and the production of coin. These measures certainly
improved the economic situation for many businessmen and taxpayers—
particularly the richest ones—and probably improved government efficiency.
And Valens went further, cutting tribute rates by at least one-quarter, which
also helped taxpayers at every level of the economic scale. In designing and
implementing these measures, Valens had been acting on his instincts as a
former farm manager. He was excellent with the microeconomics of the
household and performed admirably in meeting the needs of householders
throughout his realm. Unfortunately, however, these benefits to the citizenry
proved to be a net loss for the government. The loss in tax revenues brought
on by the reduction in tribute and the reduction in the money supply caused
by the coinage reform cost both emperors—and especially Valens—dearly.

269. Eutr. 8.13. On this method of revenue generation, see Hendy 1985, 229–30; Duncan-
Jones 1994, 10.
270. Hesychius Mil. fr. 6 (*FHG* 4.155). Independent confirmation of this sell-off seems to
come at *CJ* 11.62.5 (Nov. 2, 377); cf. *CTh* 10.2.1 (Sept. 2, 378).

Because of this, both were forced to generate revenues elsewhere, from mining, confiscations, and, in Valens's case, the sale of imperial estates. Valens's microeconomic savvy, although it helped taxpayers, brought his empire to the brink of macroeconomic collapse.

RECRUITING LAWS AND MILITARY MANPOWER

Administrative and military concerns come together in the realm of manpower. An emperor's need to fill the ranks of his army imposed demands on the labor and finances of his subjects in the most fundamental way. Thus before leaving the subject of Valentinian's and Valens's administrative policies for more strictly military concerns in the final chapter, it is important to look at the constraints placed on both emperors, and particularly Valens, by the difficulties of recruiting soldiers. We shall see here that in many ways this concern more than any other set the stage for the series of events that eventually led to Valens's demise at Adrianople.

Ammianus tells us that Valentinian and Valens divided the army between themselves at Naissus in 364.[271] Most of the troops they were working with would have been the survivors of the expeditionary force Julian had led into Persia the previous summer. These constituted the bulk of available mobile units who were not otherwise committed to regional field commanders at the time. Ammianus states explicitly how this division affected the top ranks: those generals who had been in the east before 361 remained with Valens in the east; those who had come from the west with Julian returned there with Valentinian. What happened to the rank and file is less certain, since no surviving source describes explicitly how these infantry and cavalrymen were split. Nevertheless, using clues from Ammianus, epigraphy, and, above all the *Notitia dignitatum*, it is possible to set out in some detail what probably occurred.

The forces Valentinian and Valens divided consisted almost exclusively of the small mobile units that had come to characterize the Roman army in the west since the early years of Constantine's reign. These units (we do not know their generic name) were made up on average of 1,000 men each,[272] often drawn from barbarian recruits. They were given colorful names, distinct from the legions of the high empire, and formed into pairs, which generally operated in unison, as for example the Cornuti et Bracchiati. Ultimately, they represented a full-fledged extension of the emperor's personal bodyguard (*comitatus*), which had developed from a corps of elite soldiers into a mas-

271. AM 26.5.1–4; cf. Zos. 4.2.3–3.1; Philostorg. 8.8; p. 26. Recent studies of the late Roman army have been abundant; see Carrié 1986; Treadgold 1995; Southern and Dixon 1996; Elton 1996b; Nicasie 1998; Lee 1998; and cf. Alston 1995, 143–55.

272. Duncan-Jones 1990, 105–17, 214–17; Nicasie 1998, 67–74.

sive mobile field army *(comitatenses).*[273] Because Constantine had initially built his comitatensian forces while in the west, and because Roman and especially barbarian recruits were always easier to enlist there, the east lagged behind in the development of *comitatenses.* From the 330s until the 360s, Constantius had struggled to remedy this situation by transferring a number of mobile units from the Danube and Rhine to his eastern theater of operations.[274] Indeed, while Julian was Caesar on the Rhine in 360, Constantius made demands that four of his best comitatensian units be transferred east and that a levy of 100 men from each of his remaining units be sent as well.[275]

The demand caused such agitation in the ranks of Julian's army that it helped precipitate his elevation to Augustus and eventual march against Constantius in 361. When Constantius died later that year, Julian was able to unite the western mobile army he had brought with him with the *comitatenses* formerly under Constantius in the east. By joining these two imperial field armies, Julian amassed an expeditionary force of about 65,000 men for his Persian invasion in 363. Of these, he left 15,000 in Mesopotamia and marched the remainder down the Euphrates.[276] After they failed in their bid to overwhelm the army of Shapur and eventually lost their emperor, these expeditionary forces made their way back to Antioch at the end of the summer, having lost about 15,000 men.[277] The remaining 50,000 eventually fell to Valentinian and Valens, and it was these that the emperors divided in 364.

Both Roger Tomlin and Dietrich Hoffmann determined the outlines of this division based on a careful reading of epigraphic material and the *Notitia dignitatum.* They showed that units that appear in the *Notitia* with the epithet *Seniores* tend to cluster in the western empire, and that homonymous units with the corresponding tag *Iuniores* are generally eastern. It seems that at Naissus, Valentinian, and Valens split a number of paired units into eastern and western homonyms, which they then distinguished as *Seniores*—for the units that followed the senior Augustus—and *Iuniores*—for those that followed his junior colleague.[278] Thus Ammianus can report that the Divi-

---

273. On *comitatenses,* see Elton 1996b, 89–99; Southern and Dixon 1996, 9–11, 35–37; and esp. Nicasie 1998, 4–42.

274. Hoffmann 1969–70, 1: 199–202. Gaul and Pannonia were especially fruitful recruiting grounds; cf. Nicasie 1998, 102–5. Even so, recruitment from the eastern provinces has to some extent been underestimated; cf. Speidel 1980; Mitchell 1993, 1: 136–42; id. 1994.

275. AM 26.4.2; Jul. *Ep. ad Ath.* 280d, 282d; cf. Lib. *Or.* 12.58, 18.90–91.

276. Zos. 3.13.1; cf. pp. 70 and 161. The image of east united with west was contemporary; cf. Them. *Or.* 5.66b, 69c–d; Festus 28.

277. Hoffmann 1969–70, 1: 306–8.

278. Hoffmann 1969–70, 1: 117–130, 329–404; Tomlin 1972; cf. Tomlin 1973, 59–61. Drew-Bear 1977 has offered evidence that the reconstruction of Hoffmann and Tomlin cannot be accepted in its entirety: a *Seniores* unit is attested epigraphically already in 356. Taking

tenses et Tungrecani Seniores were on the Rhine under Valentinian in 365, while the Divitenses et Tugrecani Iuniores were in Thrace under Valens that same year.[279] Furthermore, Hoffmann was able to demonstrate that the number of units divided and correspondingly labeled in 364 was indeed about fifty—that is, about equal to the surviving units from the Persian expedition— and that these were primarily barbarian auxiliaries of the sort the east so desperately needed.[280] Thus, the 364 division represented an equalization between the western mobile army and its eastern counterpart.[281]

This is not to say that either Valens or Valentinian enjoyed abundant military manpower during their reigns. Indeed, both faced gaps in their troop strength even before they divided Julian's forces. Already in the spring of 364, when the two emperors were still moving together in tandem, they had issued a general edict reasserting the legal obligation of veterans' sons to enlist for military service, an obligation in place since Diocletian.[282] Their division of forces at Naissus only exacerbated the problem by leaving each emperor fifty units with only half-complements. Thus, in late 364, Valens had to issue another law aimed at bolstering enlistment among veterans' sons.[283] Again in early 365, a recruitment order directed specifically at the sons of veterans was posted in Palestine, near Antioch, where Valens was soon hoping to arrive. It is not unreasonable to assume that both laws were promulgated in anticipation of the military activities that Valens planned for the eastern frontier in the summer of 365.[284]

Similar measures were taken as part of preparations for Valentinian's various campaigns in the west. Valentinian issued an edict in March 365 against those who harbored deserters,[285] and two years later, he initiated a major re-

---

this evidence as their cue, Scharf 1991 and Nicasie 1998, 25–42, offer their own theories about earlier divisions. I still believe Hoffmann's and Tomlin's theory—if modified—remains the best: the *Seniores/Iuniores* distinction in the *Notitia*—even if it already existed before 364—is largely a reflection of the 364 division; cf. Woods 1997, 270 n. 7; Lee 1998, 222.

279. AM 26.6.11, 27.1.2.

280. Hoffmann 1969–70, 1: 382–86; Tomlin 1972, 265, offers slightly different numbers.

281. Hoffmann 1969–70, 1: 169–73.

282. *CTh* 7.1.5 (Apr. 29, 364). On recruiting laws under Valentinian, see Lander 1984, 291–92; Garrido-González 1987. On the enlistment of veterans' sons, see Elton 1996b, 128–29.

283. *CTh* 7.1.8 (Sept. 24, 365). On the date, see Seeck, *Regesten*, 85, 217; Pergami 1993, 274–75. *CJ* 11.68.3 (demanding the discharge of slaves and *coloni* who wrongly enlist) appears to be a fragment of the same law; cf. Seeck, *Regesten*, 134; Pergami 1993, 278.

284. *CTh* 7.22.7 (Apr. 13, 365). The consular dating ("Valentiniano et Valente AA conss.") can only apply to 365, because the heading, "Valentinianus et Valens AA ad Petronium Patricium," falls before the accession of Gratian (a. 367) and before the decline of Petronius's authority (a. 366). Cf. Köhler 1925, 74, who wrongly dates the order to 370. In early 368, Themistius *Or.* 8.116a would praise the results of Valens's efforts to ferret out those who were evading their military obligations.

285. *CTh* 7.18.1.

cruiting program in preparation for his own expedition against the Alamanni, which he planned for 367.[286] What must have been a much longer
law from early April 367 survives in two fragments, one lowering height standards for recruits and a second forbidding exemption for men who had amputated their fingers to avoid service.[287] Another law from February of the
same year ordered those who evaded active service by becoming camp followers to be ferreted out and enrolled in the ranks.[288]

Valens's next big recruitment drive once again coincided with ambitions
to campaign, this time in 370. While he prepared his forces for his trek to the
eastern frontier early that year, he issued a law clarifying the collection of recruitment tax from tenants on imperial estates.[289] After he reached the east
later in the summer, he issued another order that further systematized recruitment procedures and offered generous tax incentives for enlistment: new
recruits were immediately exempted from capitation taxes, and after five years,
their wives were as well.[290] Such expensive measures demonstrate the difficulties Valens faced in filling the ranks of his army. Finally, yet another set of laws
went out in the spring of 372, this time aimed at mustering recruits in Italy,
probably in coordination with the elder Theodosius's planned campaigns
against the African usurper Firmus that summer.[291] The timing of all these
laws demonstrates that Valens and Valentinian always felt compelled to step
up recruitment in anticipation of major military operations.[292]

Given his fervor for recruitment, it is not surprising that Valens enjoyed
some success in filling his ranks. As noted, the division of 364 left both Valens
and Valentinian with fifty units at only half strength. In the years that followed, Valens's recruiting work appears to have successfully filled these units
back up to their full complements. Indeed, by 370, the army he led east was
probably as large as it would ever be in the fourteen years of Valens's rule.
In that year, Valens simultaneously sent twelve units (12,000 men) into Iberia
under the *comes* Terentius, and a division that must have been equally large

286. Zosimus (4.12.1) reports a major recruitment effort in precisely this year; cf. AM
27.10.6. On the date, see Hoffmann 1969–70, 2: 58 n. 355. The campaign was eventually postponed to 368 owing to Valentinian's illness in 367; cf. AM 27.6.19.

287. *CTh* 7.13.3 + 4 (both Apr, 17, 367). The old height standard is attested at Veg. *Mil.*
1.5. *CTh* 7.13.5 from April 368—the year when Valentinian actually undertook his campaign—
was even more stringent on amputators. See p. 314.

288. *CTh* 7.1.10 (Feb. 14, 367).

289. *CTh* 7.13.2 (Jan. 31, 370, at Marcianople); cf. 7.13.12 (a. 397).

290. *CTh* 7.13.6 (Sept. 18, 370, at Hierapolis). Similar exemptions had been granted earlier; cf. *CTh* 7.20.4 (a. 325).

291. *CTh* 7.22.8 (Feb. 16, 372); 12.1.78 (May 16, 372), 6.4.21 (Aug. 22, 372); cf. Giglio
1990, 90–97.

292. Other examples of recruitment in anticipation of campaigns at AM 14.11.4, 20.8.1,
21.6.6, 27.8.3. This was true in earlier periods as well; cf. Brunt 1974; Mann 1983, 49–68; Alston 1995, 46–47.

into Armenia under Arinthaeus.[293] In addition, Valens retained a considerable praesental force and apparently a fourth mobile division as well. This we know from Themistius, who describes the military situation in 373: Valens himself remained in Mesopotamia, with a general in Iberia and Albania, one in Armenia, and one in the Caucasus.[294] A similar situation prevailed in 377, when Ammianus tells us that Valens threatened to invade Persia "with three divisions."[295] Assuming that he intended to leave one division behind to guard his rear—as Julian had in 363—Valens must still have maintained a total of four divisions. If the four divisions reported by Themistius were initially equal in size to that led by Terentius in 370, the eastern comitatensian army would have amounted to about 48,000 men that year. This number coincides remarkably well with Hoffmann's calculation that Valentinian and Valens each received fifty split mobile units in 364.[296]

Even if the number of Valens's divisions was fixed at four, Hoffmann shows that the eastern emperor was at some point forced to return one-third—sixteen—of the mobile units he had received in 364 to the west. Indeed, over one-third of the Iuniores units created in 364 were stationed in the west by 395, and most of these appear to have been transferred while Valentinian was still alive. This probably occurred as part of the larger deescalation of eastern conflicts that followed Valens's truce with Shapur at the end of 371. After it became clear that Shapur's preoccupations with the Kushans rendered Valens's reoccupation of Armenia and Iberia secure, the eastern emperor was able to return a huge number of units to his brother.[297] Here again,

293. AM 27.12.16. If we can trust *BP* 5.38, Shapur sent a similar number of cataphracts to Armenia in 378.

294. Them. *Or.* 11.149b. Valens's divisions were not permanently garrisoned in the territories they protected. AM 30.2.2–4 (cf. 30.2.7) implies that the Armenian and Iberian divisions returned to Roman territory each winter, perhaps to the legionary fortresses of Melitene and Satala. In the summers, the division that guarded Armenia apparently made its base at Bagawan (*BP* 5.32; cf. 5.4), and the Iberian division probably remained close to the river Cyrus. *BP* 5.34–35 does indicate that Valens had plans to garrison Armenia more permanently.

295. AM 30.2.6: "cum trinis agminibus"; see p. 184.

296. On army size, see pp. 308–9.

297. Based on the knowledge that Valentinian transferred a large division out of Illyricum for his major Alamannic assault in 368, Hoffmann 1969–70, 1: 425–36, argues that he ordered Valens to send the units in 369. We know that most of the eastern units Valens sent remained under the control of the *magister militum per Illyricum;* thus the transfer does seem to have been designed to fill the gap left in the Illyrian army by Valentinian's transfer. Two of the units sent by Valens turn up in Africa, and Hoffmann suggests, plausibly, that they were transferred there with the *comes* Theodosius to quell the Firmus revolt in 372 or 373. This would provide a *terminus ante quem* for the transfer, although Hoffmann's *terminus post quem* seems to be in error. Hoffmann assumes that after Valens's Gothic victory in 369, the eastern army was freed from conflict until 373. He bases this assumption on a misdating of the battle of Bagawan to 373 instead of 371. A correct dating reveals that Valens's army was no more free in 369 than in preceding years. A more likely date for the transfer would thus be 372—the first year of Theodo-

we have intimations of coordination and cooperation between the brother emperors. Even so, it was cooperation that cost Valens and the eastern army a sizeable chunk of military manpower.

Valens's surrender of these mobile units to his brother is a further sign that, at least for the first few years after 371, Valens abandoned any plans to regain more of Mesopotamia. His new situation is clear from a passage in Themistius *Or.* 11 of 373. Themistius asks why Valens is waiting to carry out his resolve to ravage the Persians. The only thing holding him back, the orator concludes, is the need for careful preparation: "And because of this, just like a good hunter, he does not set out right away after the beast, but tracks it down here and there and sics the hounds on it and assembles fellow hunters and sets the net stakes and the nets, so that he will not be aggrieved in the hunt itself because of his hunting preparations."[298] Although Valens had not abandoned the half-accomplished plans laid out in Festus and Eutropius to retake all of upper Mesopotamia and its adjacent satrapies, the troop transfer after 371 deprived him of the resources he needed to complete them. Themistius's rhetoric glosses this enforced hesitation as careful preparation, but as time wore on, Valens's lack of adequate military manpower must have grated on the emperor. In 375, this same transfer would leave Valens ill-equipped to deal with the conflicts that began to erupt across the east when Shapur began agitating at the close of his Kushan war and Isauria broke into open revolt. Valens's need for soldiers in the field must then have become acute after 375.

Indeed, this same need can be gauged by the next in the series of recruiting laws to survive from Valens's reign. From the summer of 375, we have the longest constitution on recruitment in the Theodosian Code (7.13.7), a law that claims to revolutionize the previous system. To understand how this was so, we must examine in more detail the procedures for recruitment in place when Valens came to power. Military recruits of Roman origin came from three main sources in the fourth century: the sons of veterans, volunteers, and new conscripts.[299] We have already noted the laws of Valentinian and Valens designed to enforce enlistment by veterans' sons, laws whose very frequency and stringency confirm that, even among military families, pressure had to be brought to bear. So, too, although volunteers enlisted regularly, their numbers were nowhere nearly sufficient to fill the ranks. For this reason, enforced conscription was a necessity and had been em-

sius's campaign against Firmus—since, as we have seen, after the truce of 371, a de facto peace prevailed until 378; see pp. 175–76.

298. Them. *Or.* 11.149a.

299. On fourth-century recruitment, see A. H. M. Jones 1964, 614–19; Southern and Dixon 1996, 67–75; Elton 1996b, 128–34; Nicasie 1998, 83–96.

ployed annually since the reign of Diocletian.[300] The conscription system inherited by Valens required estate holders or *curiales* to provide a fixed number of men or a commutation of their value in gold, *aurum tironicum,* each year. Less wealthy individuals were not required to offer a recruit or his full value by themselves but were grouped into *capitula,* members of which took turns providing the recruit *(protostasia)* or jointly paid his commuted value. At times when the state had sufficient military manpower, it regularly ordered the *capitula* to pay only *aurum tironicum* rather than supplying men. Valens's reform of this system in 375 apparently consisted in eliminating exemptions to this rule and eradicating the tax gatherer's practice of collecting arbitrarily elevated sums from the *capitula* and skimming off the excess.[301] To remedy this, Valens mandated a universal price of thirty solidi per recruit for the *aurum tironicum,* plus six more to pay for the recruit's clothing and supplies, a tax called the *vestis militaris,* which was always pegged to the *aurum tironicum.*[302] Valens also attempted to entice new enlistees by extending an exemption from capitation taxes to their fathers and mothers, provided the recruits enlisted in comitatensian units.[303] The law shows how high a price Valens was willing to pay to solicit enlistment in 375.

We are fortunate to possess a number of sources from the period that further enhance our understanding of the challenge Valens faced. These confirm the expenses of recruiting new soldiers from among Roman citizens. *CTh* 7.13.7 itself indicates that when a recruit was demanded from a *capitulum,* the member who offered the recruit and not the state received from his fellow *capitularii* the remainder of his commuted value in gold. In cases of *protostasia,* then, the state derived no net monetary gain from the *aurum tironicum.* Moreover, a contemporary papyrus records that, when a volunteer enlisted, he was offered a bounty of thirty solidi. Given that six more solidi were awarded him to pay for clothing and supplies, volunteers also ate up their own value in *aurum tironicum* leaving no net gain for the state.[304] In most instances where Romans were drawn on, then, the *aurum tironicum* was a drain on taxpayers that generated no surplus capital for other state ex-

---

300. Early evidence for the system at *CJ* 10.42.8 (a. 293); *P Oxy.* 3261 (a. 324). The best analysis can be found at Carrié 1986, 464–65, 468–69, 478–79; 1989, 30–31, 39–44; 1993, 121–30.

301. *DRB* 4.5 indicates this was a concern under Valens. For fuller analysis of this law, see Giglio 1990, 87–90.

302. On the *vestis militaris,* see Sheridan 1998. Carrié 1989, 30–31; 1993, 117–28, has shown that the *aurum tironicum* was linked with other military taxes (the *vestis militaris, aurum primipili,* and *mularum fiscalium*) as part of a comprehensive unit called the *aurum comparaticium.*

303. See p. 310. For reluctance to join the *comitatenses,* see *P Abinn.* 19.

304. Wilcken *Chr.* 1.466 = *P London* 3.985; cf. *CTh* 7.13.17, which offers an enlistment bonus of 10 solidi in A.D. 406.

penses. Further sources confirm, however, that even this enlistment bounty was not sufficient to eliminate the need for more coercive measures. They attest that recruits had to be tattooed—to inhibit desertion—and, as noted above, that many amputated a thumb in order to dodge service.[305] At one point, Valentinian, who would brook no such evasion, ordered the latter to be burned alive,[306] and a papyrus from Valens's reign shows equal zeal for the strict enforcement of recruiting laws. It records a request for the transport of recruits from Egypt to Antioch and orders that, if any escaped the detail, they had to be recaptured or replaced at the expense of the senders.[307] Recruitment of new manpower from among provincials was thus a burdensome and expensive process.

As with other matters of administration, Valens was concerned about this drain on his subjects, especially since it did him no good in relieving his deficits in other areas.[308] Yet in times of military emergency, even the normal burdens and expenses do not appear to have sufficed for Valens's needs. Thus in the summer of 371, when Valens undertook his showdown with Shapur that ended at the battle of Bagawan, he felt compelled to issue a superindiction on recruits and military clothing. Of this there is no explicit testimony in the sources, but the papyri give strong clues. We have several from the archive of Flavius Isidorus, the official charged with transferring the *aurum tironicum* and the closely related *vestis militaris* from Hermopolis to Valens's court in Syrian Hierapolis at the time. Two of these, both dated after 375, deal with a charge brought against Isidorus for the theft of 177 solidi. The first reveals that he had been sent to Valens's court with 238 solidi in 373 but, upon arriving, learned that his city owed only 61.[309] The remainder was handed back to him for return to Hermopolis, but he claimed

---

305. On tattooing, see Veg. *Mil.* 2.5; *CTh* 10.22.4; cf. C. P. Jones 1987, 149. More on recruitment difficulties in the late empire at Liebescheutz 1990, 13–20; Bagnall 1993, 175–76; Lee 1998, 221–22.

306. *CTh* 7.13.5 (Apr. 26, 368). Valentinian's was far and away the most stringent punishment for amputators; cf. *CTh* 7.13.10 (a. 381), 7.22.1 (a. 312); AM 15.12.3.

307. Wilcken *Chr.* 1.469 = *P Lips.* inv. 281. Wilcken's dating of the papyrus to the 380s is too late. C. Valerius Eusebios, its addressee, is attested as *comes Orientis* under Valentinian; cf. *ILS* 8947 and Rémondon 1955, 27–29. See also Wilcken *Chr.* 1.467 = *P Lips.* 54 (a. 376), where the Hermopolites must pledge security for the man they assign to the στρατολογία, and Greg. Nys. *Encom. in XL martyres* 2 (*PG* 46.784), which indicates that soldiers overseeing the στρατολογία regularly engaged in shakedowns.

308. As is reflected in the suggestions laid out by his adviser at *DRB* 5. Valens's concern with the burden of the *aurum tironicum* and the *vestis militaris* can also be seen in the rules that curial *susceptores* of the *vestis militaris* need serve no more than one year (*CTh* 7.6.1, 12.6.4) and that they could be excused if they had more burdensome duties (*P Oxy.* 2110).

309. *P Lips.* 34, 35. § 35 has a different figure for the original total (138 instead of 238 solidi), probably a scribal error, like the misreporting of the name of the governor of the Thebaid in line 14.

to have been robbed on his journey home. The Hermopolitans would only have entrusted Isidorus with so large a sum if they believed they owed it in recruitment taxes, and it would only have been returned if these taxes had been cut. The second papyrus confirms that they were: Isidorus paid only the 61 solidi because he had just "learned of the divine and humane law that had been promulgated at the time that only ten gold [solidi] needed to be paid for recruits."[310] It seems then, that, contrary to expectations, Valens cut the *aurum tironicum* and *vestis militaris* drastically between 372 and 373.[311]

What precisely happened may be explained by yet another papyrus, which is probably—although not certainly—datable to 372. P. Oxy. 3424 indicates that Valens had issued a superindiction on a number of items—including the *aurum tironicum* and the *vestis militaris*—for the fifteenth and first indiction years, 371/72 and 372/73.[312] This surtax would have been instituted in the summer of 371, when Valens expected to be fighting Shapur for some time to come. It apparently stayed in force into early 372, when two letters of Basil's indicate that Caesarea had taken up a general collection to meet extraordinary demands for *aurum tironicum* and *vestis militaris* and was having trouble keeping its youths from entering the diaconate to avoid military service.[313] In the same year, we have a cluster of papyri from the governor of the Thebaid ordering a roundup of all *cephalaiotai* (that is, *capitularii*), apparently to pressure them for arrears.[314] When instead of ongoing war, a truce was struck in late 371, the need for men and clothing suddenly disappeared, and Valens was thus able to remit the second year's superindiction. This explains Isidorus's pleasant surprise when he learned that the imperial treasury was actually remitting three-fourths of the *aurum tironicum* he was carrying in 373. To seal the case, a passage of Themistius from March 373 states directly that the emperor had indeed recently cut the *aurum tiron-*

---

310. *P Lips.* 35 l. 7–8: τῆς θείας ὑμῶν καὶ φιλανθρώπου νο[μ]οθ[εσ]ίας τ[ῆ]s τηνι[ι]καῦτα καταπεμφθήσης ἐσθόμενος [sic] περὶ τοῦ δεῖν δ[έ]κα μόνους χρυσίνους παρασχεῖν τοῖ[s] νεολ[έ]κ[τ]οις ...; cf. *P Lips.* 34 l. 8: χρείας μὴ ἐπιγούσης.

311. It is not entirely clear whether Isidorus was carrying money for the *aurum tironicum* or *vestis militaris*. Mitteis 1906, 173–75, is convinced it was the latter, but his reading is subjective. In either case, it affects my argument little, since the two taxes rose and fell at the same rates.

312. The editors date the first indiction mentioned at *P Oxy.* 3424 l. 5 to either 357 or 372. The latter seems preferable in light of the other evidence presented here for a shift in tax rates in precisely that year.

313. .Basil *Ep.* 88 shows that in early 372, Caesarea was struggling to meet its obligations to pay the πραγματευτικὸν χρυσίον (*aurum comparaticium*), the collective name for the combination of *aurum tironicum, vestis militaris* and *mularum fiscalium* (see n. 302 above and Treucker 1961, 32–33). *Ep.* 54, undatable, tells *chorepiscopi* to send lists of those who tried to dodge service via the diaconate. It forbids this for any beyond the first indiction, probably because the recruitment drive had been relaxed at that point.

314. *P Lips.* 48–53, with Bagnall 1993, 65.

icum and *vestis militaris.*[315] In the military crisis of summer 371, then, Valens was only able to keep up with his need for military manpower by pressing the taxpayer with a superindiction. Once the crisis passed, he relaxed it.

We have already seen that Valentinian's laws of 367 and 372 and Valens's of 365, 370–71, and 375 all correspond to periods when the emperors were gearing up for military operations. The last of these, *CTh* 7.13.7, issued in a year when Isauria broke into revolt and Persia began threatening, must have found Valens desperate for new blood. After 372, he had relaxed his recruitment efforts and surrendered up to one-third of his mobile units to his brother. Now just three years later, he was back in the emergency market for troops with *CTh* 7.13.7. Here again, papyri are available to confirm a steep increase in recruitment tax payments that year.[316] Jerome's notice that Valens began conscripting monks into the army in 375 drives home the fact that he had to scramble to fill the ranks.[317] Nor, as we have seen, did he have ready money to entice new volunteers with enlistment bounties.[318] He was desperate for gold by this time and must have been sorely vexed that the recruitment of Roman soldiers represented so massive an expense.

Given the way the recruitment system was structured, though, it was possible to make money and enlist recruits at the same time, provided these were not natives. Not surprisingly, the cheapest and indeed fastest mode for filling the ranks in the fourth century was to bypass the recruitment of Roman citizens altogether and turn instead to barbarians. Recent studies have rightly downplayed the formerly exaggerated reliance of the late Roman army on barbarian military manpower.[319] Even so, it cannot be denied that barbarians provided a cheap alternative to their provincial counterparts. For this reason, the majority of the new units constituted since Constantine were assembled, at least originally, from barbarians.[320] When barbarians were enrolled in the army, individual terms of enlistment were apparently negotiated so that enlistment bounties, clothing, and supply provisions could often be done away with or at least reduced. Likewise, because the *capitula* were bypassed, gold collected in *aurum tironicum* did not have to be returned to

---

315. *Or.* 11.143c–144a.

316. *P Flor.* 95 shows a sharp jump in the receipts of *aurum tironicum* from Antinopolis between 375 and 376 and *P Lips.* 61 (Nov. 11, 375) shows Hermpolis paying at what appears to be the new rate, 72 solidi—two recruits' worth. The *aurum tironicum* was certainly not—*pace* Carrié 1986, 468–69, 478–79—permanently fixed at 30 solidi per recruit; *CTh* 7.13.13 (a. 397), for example, demands only 25, and *P Lips.* 62 offers a receipt recording the collection of differing amounts from Hermopolis between 384 and 385.

317. Jer. *Chron.* s.a. 375. See Lenski, "Isaac and Valens' Recruitment of Monks for Military Service" (forthcoming).

318. On the expense of mustering armies in the east, see Jul. *Or.* 1.21c–d.

319. Elton 1996b, 136–52; Nicasie 1998, 97–116.

320. Shaw 1999, 133–4, 146.

citizens who provided a recruit through *protostasia* or to enlistees who volunteered. If favorable recruitment terms were negotiated with a barbarian group, the emperor could go on extracting the *aurum tironicum* from his subjects but could now divert the funds he raised to other expenses.

Unfortunately for Valens, the process of enlisting barbarians had always been more difficult in the east than in the west. Along the Rhine frontier, the Alamanni and particularly the Franks had become quite accustomed to joining the Roman ranks for permanent service.[321] That this disproportionate advantage of west over east continued under Valentinian and Valens is clear from the relative number of new units each was able to create: Valentinian posted between ten and fourteen new units over his eleven-year reign, while Valens created only between two and four over fourteen years of rule.[322] Zosimus openly confirms that many of Valentinian's new troops had been actively recruited from trans-Rhenan barbarians.[323] Ruling the east thus had its disadvantages when it came to recruiting this least expensive source of troops. This was certainly on Valens's mind when a large group of Goths came to the Danube petitioning for entry to Thrace in 376. Thus, when they agreed to supply military *auxilia* in exchange for land, Valens looked on their request with very great interest indeed.[324]

Valens's inability to draft Gothic allied forces since his treaty in 369 was no small matter. With the conclusion of this treaty, Valens had apparently surrendered Rome's right to use native Gothic auxiliary forces in his expeditionary armies. Such forces were not, as with the Alamanni and Frankish recruits on the Rhine, permanent enlistees in Roman units, but were occasional participants in Roman expeditions, bound only by treaty to serve and paid only when they fulfilled the conditions of this occasional service. Since the third century, such Gothic auxiliaries had provided one of the few reliable sources of barbarian military manpower for the eastern frontier. Two inscriptions in the Hauran indicate that, as early as Septimius Severus's eastern campaign of 195–97, a unit of Gothic *gentiles* had been brought to Ara-

---

321. Hoffmann 1969–70, 1:390–93; cf. Burns 1994, 112–47.

322. Hoffmann 1969–70, 1: 142–43, 165–68, 197–98 lists the 10–14 auxiliary units created by Valentinian. At 1: 169–70, 239–41, 502–3, Hoffmann notes that only two auxiliary units were definitely created by Valens: the Tertii Sagitarii Valentis and the Sagitarii Dominici (*Not. dign. or.* 5.56, 6.56). The first bears Valens's name and the second the name of Valens's wife, which Hoffmann did not recognize. Hoffmann tentatively suggests that Valens may also have created the Hiberi, Thraces, and Regii (*Not. dign. or.* 5.60, 6.60; cf. 6.49). The Hiberi were probably the Sagitarii attested under the Iberian prince Bacurius in 378, AM 31.12.16. If so, their paired auxiliary unit of Thraces at *Not. dign.* 6.60 was probably also created by Valens. The *Regii*, however, were initiated under Constantine (Speidel 1996a, 163–67).

323. Zos. 4.12.1; cf. AM 30.7.6 and Paschoud 2.2: 354 n. 126. For similar trans-limitanean recruiting, see AM 20.4.4.

324. AM 31.4.1–4; Eunap. *Hist.* fr. 42 (Blockley); Soc. 4.34.3–4.

bia and charged with garrisoning a fortress.[325] The *Res gestae divi Saporis* proves
that the Goths supplied troops for Gordian III's expedition against Shapur I
in 242,[326] and Goths also served among the forces used by Galerius against
Narses in 298.[327] We have seen already what a crucial role Gothic auxiliaries
played in the eastern expeditions undertaken in the years between 332 and
363, and we know that in the years following Adrianople, the Gothic *regulus*
Munderich came to serve as *dux limitis per Arabiam.*[328] Valens's loss of the right
to employ Gothic auxiliaries after 369 must have seriously aggravated his recruitment problems when military troubles arose in 375.

It is little wonder then that he and his ministers were eager to engineer
a Gothic migration into Thrace in 376. As Ammianus reports:

> The affair caused more joy than fear; and experienced flatterers[329] immoder-
> ately praised the good fortune of the prince, which unexpectedly brought him
> so many young recruits from the ends of the earth that by the union of his own
> and foreign forces, he would have an invincible army; also that instead of the
> levy of soldiers that was contributed annually by each province, there would
> accrue to the treasuries a vast amount of gold.[330]

The Gothic migration offered Valens the perfect solution to his recruiting
problems and helped relieve some of his economic woes into the bargain.
Finally he would have a large body of Germans living within imperial territory whom he could draft into service to fill his ranks, and finally he would
not have to compromise his tax base with expensive recruitment procedures.
On the contrary, he could bypass civilian recruitment altogether and redi-
rect the *aurum tironicum* to other expenses. We have some information that
he did just that. Socrates and Sozomen report that, once he had arranged
the Gothic migration, Valens began universally to commute provincial troop
recruits into *aurum tironicum* in cash as a money-making exercise. If we can
believe Socrates, he even raised the *aurum tironicum* as high as eighty *solidi*

---

325. *AE* 1911, 244; *AE* 1933, 185 = *SEG* 7.1194 with analysis at Speidel 1978, 712–16.

326. *RGDS* ll. 6–7 (p. 12).

327. On Galerius's expedition, see Aur. Vict. *Caes.* 39; Jul. *Or.* 1.18b; Eutr. 9.25.1; Oros.
7.25.10; Festus 25. Only Jord. *Get.* 21 [110] attests to Goths on the expedition, although Hoffmann 1969–70, 1: 223, believes they may appear as the Scythae of *Not. dign. or.* 6.44. Licinius
also used Goths against Constantine; cf. *Exc. Val.* 5 [27].

328. On campaigns between 332 and 363, see pp. 148–49. On Munderich, see AM 31.3.5.

329. Heather 1991, 134, believes that Ammianus alludes here to Themistius. This seems
likely, for Themistius is known to have addressed Valens in 375/76 on the eve of the Gothic
immigration; see Soc. 4.32.1–5; Soz. 6.36.6–37.1. The speech may have supplied Socrates with
his detailed understanding of Gothic politics in the early 370s (Lenski 1995, 60–61). Unfortunately, we cannot confirm this since the speech has dropped out of the corpus. Its absence
may be attributable to the bad advice it proffered.

330. AM 31.4.4; cf. Eunap. *Hist.* fr. 42 (Blockley); Soc. 4.34.3–4; Soz. 6.37.15–16; Jord.
Get. 132.

per man.[331] Further confirmation that Valens was now commuting recruiting taxes comes in a law of 377 that orders that the *vestis militaris*—normally consigned to the government only in kind (i.e., in clothing)—be commuted entirely to gold as well.[332] Ammianus was thus entirely correct in his assessment of Valens's intentions. The emperor saw in the Gothic migration the chance to build a barbarian base for recruitment and at the same time to generate new revenues in gold. For these reasons, he welcomed it as an opportunity.

331. Soc. 4.34.4–5; Soz. 6.37.16. *P Oxy.* 3401 (a. 360/80) shows a run on gold because of a recent rumor about the collection of *aurum tironicum.* Unfortunately, it is not datable precisely but may be related to these events.

332. *CTh* 7.6.3 (Aug. 9, 377). Sheridan 1998, 90–92, shows that the *vestis militaris* was collected in money but then converted to clothing by nome officials for most of the fourth century. *P Lips.* 59 indicates that this was still the case as late as 371.

Chapter 7

The Disaster at Adrianople

In the late 360s, Valens engaged the Goths in a three-year war, which was in some sense compromising for both sides. The Goths had supported the usurper Procopius in his bid for power by supplying him with 3,000 auxiliaries and would later argue that they had merely been upholding the terms of the treaty they had struck with Constantine in 332. Valens did not brook the affront, however, and prepared a major military expedition against them. Between 367 and 369, he launched two invasions north of the Danube, during which he ravaged the territory of the Tervingi—the Gothic confederation closest to Rome—and even attacked the more distant Greuthungi—who were concentrated east of the Dniester (see map 3). Despite a huge expenditure of money and effort, Valens never succeeded in cornering the leader of the Tervingi, Athanaric, and overwhelming him in a decisive battle. Even so, because the Persian frontier was collapsing, Valens was forced to conclude his war in midsummer 369 and come to terms with the Goths. This agreement was typical of his policies in its uncompromising refusal to allow cooperation with the barbarians: it interrupted the normal flow of trade, cut off the payment of tribute and apparently halted the use of Gothic auxiliaries in Roman forces.

Given that Valens concluded his 369 treaty without having achieved a total victory, it was necessarily a compromise. Even so, it was a compromise that hardened relations between Roman and Goth with negative effects for both sides. The Romans, desperate for military manpower, had blocked off one obvious avenue of supply. For their part, the Goths, already devastated by Valens's invasion, were left without Roman contacts or tribute to help them recover. The effects in Gothia quickly became obvious. In response to Valens's aggression, Athanaric initiated a persecution of Christians in 369 that lasted at least until 372.[1] Though his intention was undoubtedly to re-unite the Tervingi under traditional religious structures while eliminating the religious legacy of Roman contact,[2] the end result was not what he might have planned. Partly in response to the persecution, but also as a reaction against the devastation caused by Athanaric's war, the Gothic subchieftan *(reiks)* Fritigern began agitating against Athanaric.[3] With help from Roman forces stationed in Thrace, Fritigern actually defeated the Gothic *iudex* and initiated the fragmentation of the previously unified Tervingi confederation.[4] In the end, then, Valens's first Gothic war began a process that weakened both Romans and Goths and left the latter divided and vulnerable.

Unfortunately for the Tervingi, this vulnerability was soon exploited by a devastating new rival from the steppes of central Asia, the Huns, who swept across the region in the mid 370s and finished the process of fragmentation that Fritigern had begun.[5] Having conquered the Alans east of the Don and absorbed them as allies,[6] these nomadic raiders overran the territory of the Greuthungi and then the Tervingi, fractured what remained of their political unity, and terrorized the Goths into chaos. It was this invasion, the sources are unanimous in reporting, that provoked a mass exodus of the Goths—Tervingi and Greuthungi—from their homelands north of the Danube down to the border of the Roman Empire.[7] The lightning speed with which the

1. Jer. *Chron.* s.a. 369; Prosper *Chron.* 1140; *Pass. S. Sabae* passim, esp. 7, which dates the martyrdom of St. Saba the Goth to Apr. 12, 372; Oros. 7.32.9; Soc. 4.33.7; Soz. 6.37.12–14; Basil *Ep.* 155, 164–65; Ephiph. *Adv. haeres.* 70.15; August. *De civ. Dei* 18.52; [Joh. Chrys.] *Sermo* 1 (*PG* 52.808); Gregory of Tours *Historia Francorum* 2.4; *Passio Innae Rimae et Pinnae* at Delehaye 1912, 215–16. Most of the sources are collected and translated at Heather and Matthews 1991, 103–31.

2. Soc. 4.33.7: ὡς παραχαραττομένης τῆς πατρῴου θρησκείας; cf. Soz. 6.37.12; Ephiph. *Adv. haeres.* 70.15.4.

3. The martyrologies cited above provide good evidence of fissures in the Gothic community after 369; cf. Rubin 1981, 36–41; Lenski 1995a, 83–84. So, too, Basil, who was well informed on Gothic events, spoke of infighting among Gothic chieftains in this period; see *In Psalm.* 7.7.5 (*PG* 29.239); *De invid.* 4 (*PG* 31.380).

4. Soc. 4.33.1–4. Thompson 1956; 1966, 78–93, 103–10, and Heather 1986; 1991, 127–28, have questioned the validity of Socrates' account. On closer examination of the sources, however, their objections can be laid to rest; see Lenski 1995a with 52–54 nn. 1–9 for previous bibliography. Valens's ongoing military activity near Gothic territory is also attested by an inscription datable between 369 and 375 from Cherson in the Tauric Chersonese (*AE* 1984, 804). Zuckermann 1991b, 546–53, has connected the inscription with the story of the seven bishops of Cherson (*BHG* 265–66) to show that Valens established a garrison of 500 *ballistarii* there in the 370s. He believes the garrison was created in response to the Hun invasions. Given, however, that the seven bishops story claims the garrison was sent specifically to protect Christian missionaries, it is more likely that it should be connected with Valens's efforts to aid Christian Goths in the early 370s.

5. On the Huns and their origins, see Maenchen-Helfen 1973; Thompson 1996.

6. On the Alans in the fourth century, see Kazanski 1995.

7. As early as 386, this knock-on effect of Huns into Alans, Alans into Goths, and, ultimately, Goths into Romans is reported at Amb. *Exp. evan. sec. Lucam* 10.10 (*CSEL* 34.458). The same

Huns came onto the scene is clear from the sources that report their invasion. Ammianus and Eunapius both apologize for their lack of accurate details about the Huns, saying that information was simply not to hand for "a people hardly known from ancient records."[8] For Goths and Romans alike, this sudden blitz must have been all the more terrifying because it confronted them with an "unknown race," a group of people who moved faster than the speed of knowledge.[9]

The specifics of the Gothic response to the Huns are spelled out most fully in Ammianus. The Greuthungi, being the farther east of the Gothic confederations, were naturally the first to be hit. Their chief Hermanaric, after being defeated in battle and losing control of his vast estates, committed suicide; his son Vithimer succeeded him, but was quickly killed in battle; Vithimer was in turn succeeded by his own son, Vitheric, still a mere boy and thus under the regency of two Greuthungi subchieftains, Alatheus and Saphrax. These helped Vithimer and his people retreat to the Dnieper and construct defenses there, but they ultimately failed to stave off the Hunnic advance and eventually ended up at the Danube begging for entry into Roman territory.[10]

Meanwhile, Athanaric and his Tervingi, who dwelt south and west of the Greuthungi, had had more time to prepare for the onslaught. They constructed a camp along the Dniester and sent an advance force east to distract the attackers, but to no avail. The Huns simply skirted past these defensive measures, attacked Athanaric's main forces, and compelled his retreat into the eastern Carpathians. Here, Athanaric once again took steps to slow the Huns' advance by building a wall along the Prut extending to its confluence with the Danube, yet once again the Huns fell on his forces and

---

cause for the Gothic migration is reported at AM 31.2.1, 12.8; Zos. 4.20.3–5; Eunap. *Hist.* fr. 42, 59 (Blockley); *Cons. Const.* s.a. 376; Jer. *Chron.* s.a. 377; Prosper *Chron.* 1161; Soc. 4.34.1; Soz. 6.37.2–4; Philostorg. 9.17; Ruf. *HE* 11.13; Jord. *Get.* 121–30; Proc. *Bell.* 8.5.10–12. See esp. Maenchen-Helfen 1973, 18–27.

8. AM 31.2.1: "gens monumentis veteribus leviter nota." Eunap. *Hist.* fr. 41 (Blockley) with Paschoud 2.2: 372 n. 142; Blockley 1981–83, 1: 3–4. The inaccuracies and stereotypes in Ammianus's and Eunapius's ethnographies are not, of course, simply a result of inadequate source material. Classicizing historians deliberately reproduced superannuated information about barbarian *gentes*. Indeed, Eunapius's ethnographic account is followed by Zos. 4.20.3; Soz. 6.37.3–4; Jord. *Get.* 123–25; Proc. *Bell.* 8.5; Agath. 5.11.2–3; Cedrenus, p. 547. For this phenomenon, see Maenchen-Helfen 1973, 9–15; Dauge 1981; Shaw 1982–83.

9. Soz. 6.37.3: ἔθνος ἄγνωστον; cf. Zos. 4.20.3: φῦλον τι βάρβαρον... πρότερον μὲν οὐκ ἐγνωσμένον; AM 31.3.8: "inusitatum antehac hominum genus"; 31.4.2.

10. AM 31.3.2–5, 4.12. Jord. *Get.* 129–30 offers a different account, which is accepted at Maenchen-Helfen 1973, 21–22. On the status of Alatheus and Saphrax, see Wolfram 1977, 232. For archaeological evidence of contact between Huns and Goths in this period, see Erdélyi 1992.

overwhelmed them.[11] Most of his remaining followers, reeling from the economic and social repercussions of the invasion, deserted him and took council as to where they might seek refuge. After some debate, they determined to request permission from the Romans to cross the Danube and settle in Thrace. Under the leadership of the Gothic *reges* Alavivus and Fritigern, the latter of whom had already become Rome's ally in the 370s, these Tervingi put their demands for refuge to the Roman provincial authorities.[12] Meanwhile Athanaric himself seems to have approached the Danube contemplating a similar request. Although he would later return to the Carpathians without contacting Valens—he knew that the emperor would never honor a request from a leader who had shown him such flagrant disrespect in 369—he remained near the river at least until word had arrived from Valens about the fate of the other refugees.[13] Thus at least three Gothic groups, one of Greuthungi and two more of Tervingi, approached the Danube in 376 with hopes of entering the empire.

For their part, the Roman border troops had insisted that the Goths remain north of the river until Valens, then in Antioch, could be consulted.[14] A surviving letter of Basil's seems to record the swift progress of these long-distance negotiations in the tense spring of 376.[15] Not surprisingly, there was some debate in Valens's court over whether to grant entry.[16] Indeed, the very fact that complicated negotiations were carried out over the thousand kilometers between Antioch and the Danube makes it clear that the Roman authorities hardly took the request lightly. This was only natural given the dangers involved in such an operation. In fact, had Valens been able to know the total number of barbarians hoping to cross, he would certainly have been even

11. AM 31.3.4–8. Vulpe 1960, 322, believes he has located the wall in some earthworks that ran northwest to southeast in the zone between the Siret and Prut. Heather 1996, 100 argues instead that Athanaric reused the old Roman fortifications of the Limes Transalutanus. For similar large-scale defensive construction by trans-Danubian peoples, see Soproni 1969; 1985, 13–17.

12. AM 31.3.8–4.1; Eunap. *Hist.* fr. 42 (Blockley); Zos. 4.20.5; Jord. *Get.* 131; Soc. 4.34.1. Soz. 6.37.5–6 actually reports that Ulfilas led the Gothic embassy to Valens.

13. AM 31.4.12–13.

14. AM 31.4.2–5; Eunap. *Hist.* fr. 42 (Blockley); Zos. 4.20.6; Jord. *Get.* 132.

15. Basil *Ep.* 237 (early 376) records that the *vicarius Thraciae* and in turn the *praepositus thesaurorum* of Philippopolis rushed in and out of Caesarea so quickly on their journeys west that they did not have time to carry with them Basil's letter to Eusebius of Samosata, then in exile at Philippopolis. They must have been returning to Thrace with official correspondence on the Goths. The date of the letter, established at Loofs 1898, 11, is challenged by Hauschild 1973–93, 3: 207 n. 226, although his revised chronology has serious problems; cf. Lenski 1999a, 319 n. 50.

16. Eunap. *Hist.* fr. 42 (Blockley): πολλῆς δὲ ἀντιλογίας γενομένης, καὶ πολλῶν ἐφ᾽ἑκάτερα γνωμῶν ἐ τῷ βασιλικῷ συλλόγῳ ῥηθεισῶν...

more cautious about opening the floodgates. Given the information he had, however, he chose to grant permission, but only to Alavivus, Fritigern, and their followers.[17] Valens seems to have believed that he could control the situation by limiting his offer to only one group, the group with which he had already established diplomatic contact in the years immediately preceding.

Our sources indicate that the Goths initiated their request for exile with a promise to provide troops for Roman armies.[18] They were thus well aware of the most valuable asset they had to offer the empire. Barbarian settlements within Roman territory had often been contingent upon similar concessions, particularly as Rome's armies grew more and more reliant on barbarian manpower.[19] We have just seen that Valentinian formed barbarian recruits into as many as fourteen new auxiliary units during the course of his reign.[20] He also dabbled in resettlement, transplanting a group of Alamanni to the Po valley and another of Sarmatians to the Mosel.[21] He even engineered a cooperative military venture by calling up a force of 80,000 Burgundians, with whom he hoped to unite against the Alamanni. Although the plan was eventually abandoned, it shows the degree to which the emperor was willing to employ allied barbarian groups who would cooperate with him militarily.[22]

We have also seen that Valens always struggled to provide sufficient recruits to maintain his own armies and that, after 369, he had been forced to do without even the auxiliary troops formerly supplied by the Goths.[23] Thus, when the Tervingi and Greuthungi refugees arrived in 376 offering a ready source of new manpower, far from resisting their request, Valens welcomed it.[24] His readiness to take full advantage of the situation can be seen already in 376, when he began plucking Gothic youths to be trained for service from among the new settlers.[25] In 377, Ammianus tells us that he was

---

17. AM 31.4.12–5.3; cf. Eunap. *Hist.* fr. 42, 45.3 (Blockley); Zos. 4.20.6, 26.2; Jord. *Get.* 132; Soz. 6.36.6; Soc. 4.39.2.

18. AM 31.4.1: "et daturos (si res flagitasset) auxilia"; cf. 31.4.4; Eunap. *Hist.* fr. 42 (Blockley): προσθήκην τῇ συμμαχίᾳ παρέξειν ἐπαγγελλόμενοι; cf. fr. 45.3 (Blockley) with Cesa 1985; Zos. 4.20.5: ὑπισχνεῖσθαι τε πληρώσειν ἔργον αὐτῷ συμμάχων πιστῶν καὶ βεβαίων; cf. 4.26.1; Soc. 4.34.3–4; Soz. 6.37.16. Eventually, of course, the Goths did provide troops, *Pan. Lat.* 2 [12].32.3–5, 22.3; Them. *Or.* 16.211d, 34.22.

19. See, e.g., AM 28.5.4, 30.6.1, 31.10.17; cf. Hoffmann 1969–70, 1: 131–40; Liebeschuetz 1990, 11–25; Mirković 1993.

20. See p. 317.

21. AM 28.5.15; Aus. XVI *Mos.* l. 9, with Mócsy 1974, 291; cf. AM 29.4.7.

22. AM 28.5.8–13; Jer. *Chron.* s.a. 373; Oros. 7.32.11–13; Symm. *Or.* 2.13; cf. Tomlin 1973, 167–69. For similar active solicitation of barbarian aid, see Zos. 2.53.3; Lib. *Or.* 18.33. Gratian continued to rely on barbarians, perhaps too much; cf. *Epit.* 47.6; Zos. 4.35.2–3; Them. *Or.* 13.176c–d.

23. See p. 137.

24. See pp. 317–19.

25. Eunap. *Hist.* fr. 42 (Blockley).

hiring Goths in preparation for his planned Persian war, and later that he ordered the eastward mobilization of a band of Goths previously received into the empire—perhaps the same Goths whom Athanaric had sent to aid Procopius.[26] In addition, Valens had young Gothic troops placed under the charge of the *magister militum per Orientem*, Julius, who used these to garrison cities along the eastern frontier.[27] Valens was thus cautiously optimistic about the windfall he had received when the Huns drove the Goths out of their homelands and into his hands.

THE COLLAPSE OF THE GOTHIC SETTLEMENT
AND THE DISASTER AT ADRIANOPLE

The Tervingi had put their request for asylum to the Thracian army in the early part of 376.[28] It was not until late spring or early summer that news arrived of Valens's permission to cross. Immediately, the Tervingi were ferried across the Danube, probably at Durostorum (Silistra), where the river is only one kilometer wide and riparian units already stationed there could supervise the crossing.[29] The enormous operation took several days and was complicated by the fact that the river was swollen with spring rains; many Goths were thus swallowed up in its current.[30] Valens had given orders that once the Tervingi had crossed, they should be given food to supply their present needs and land to cultivate for the following year. This order was not carried out with alacrity, in large part no doubt because of the overwhelming number of refugees.[31] Even so, the sources agree that the Roman failure to

26. AM 30.2.6, 31.6.1–2. On the latter, see Vetters 1954–57; Wolfram 1988, 120–121; Wanke 1990, 76–78.

27. AM 31.16.8; Zos. 4.26.1–3. Cf. Blockley 1992, 37, and p. 352.

28. The events surrounding the battle of Adrianople have been treated by numerous researchers, including Judeich 1891; Runkel 1903; Seeck, *Untergang*, 84–134; Köhler 1925, 48–70; Schmidt 1934, 400–413; Straub 1943; Klein 1955; Hoffmann 1969–70, 1: 445–48; Austin 1972a; Chrysos 1972, 129–34; Burns 1973; 1994, 23–42; Wolfram 1977; 1988, 117–30; Demougeot 1979, 140–46; Cesa 1984, 63–77; 1994, 13–30; Wanke 1990, 111–230; Heather 1991, 142–47; Gutmann 1991, 140–59; Williams and Friell 1994, 13–22, 176–81; Nicasie 1998, 233–56; Chauvot 1998, 255–69.

29. AM 31.4.5; Eunap. *Hist.* fr. 42 (Blockley); *Cons. Const.* s.a. 376; Soc. 4.34.2–3; Oros. 7.33.10; Isidore *Hist. Goth.* 9 (*MGH.AA* 11.271). On Durostorum as the probable crossing site, see Wanke 1990, 116–20, with earlier bibliography. For the riparian units stationed there, see *Not. dign. or.* 40.26, 33.

30. AM 31.4.5. Wanke 1990, 120–22, contends that the crossing took place in May or June when the Danube flood is highest. Ammianus's claim that the river was running in spate due to rains is our only indicator for the time of the year. This does, however, leave an uncomfortably long gap between the Tervingi crossing and the transfer of the Goths to Marcianople by early 377. On the chronology of Ammianus bk. 31, see Austin 1972a.

31. AM 31.4.8–11; cf. Eunap. *Hist.* fr. 45.3 (Blockley). On supply shortages, see AM 31.5.1, 5, 7.3, 8, 8.1, 4, 11.5. Following Jord. *Get.* 133–34, Cesa 1994, 22–23, believes that the Goths

supply the Goths adequately could also be traced to the corruption of the commanders charged with the resettlement, Lupicinus, the *comes per Thracias,* and Maximus, probably the *dux Moesiae.* Because adequate supplies for so many refugees were difficult to assemble, the dearth generated a black market in foodstuffs, which the Romans used to exploit the Tervingi beyond the bounds of decency. Ammianus describes the exchange of Gothic slaves for dogs to be eaten as meat, and Eunapius and Zosimus lament the frenzy of Roman commanders racing to acquire sex slaves and agricultural laborers on the cheap.[32]

The moralizing content in these reports is evident, but the ruthless exploitation they describe should not be downplayed as facile exaggeration, especially since this explanation of the collapse of the Gothic settlement had already entered the source tradition by 381.[33] For late Roman easterners, the words *Gothus* and *Σκύθος* were synonymous with slave. Julian, for example, scorned the Goths as a race fit only for Galatian slave traders.[34] Every household had Scythian slaves, Synesius remarked, since these were best adapted to serving Romans.[35] Even Themistius describes the Danube border troops as regularly engaging in ruthless slave trading.[36] In this atmosphere, it would not be surprising if Lupicinus, Maximus, and their troops saw in the vulnerability of the refugees an opportunity for economic gain. Moreover, enforced starvation was a common technique employed by the military to cow barbarians into submission.[37] Lupicinus and Maximus may thus have been acting in a manner they regarded as efficacious in their resettlement when they withheld food and forced the Goths to degrade themselves in their efforts to survive. Finally, a broader disdain for all barbarians prevailed among even the most enlightened fourth-century Romans.[38] The average soldier would have been accustomed to entertaining himself with

---

had already been settled on agricultural land before they began agitating. Ammianus is to be preferred.

32. AM 31.4.11; cf. 31.6.5; Eunap. *Hist.* fr. 42 (Blockley); Zos. 4.20.6.

33. Jer. *Chron.* s.a. 377 followed by Jord. *Get.* 134–35; *Rom.* 313; Oros. 7.33.11; Isid. *Hist. Goth.* 9 (*MGH.AA* 11.271). On the moralism of Ammianus bk. 31, see Barnes 1998, 182–83.

34. AM 22.7.8. Julian himself had a Scythian slave as a tutor (*Mis.* 352a–b).

35. Syn. *De regno* 23d; cf. SHA *Clod.* 9.5. Many of the slaves in Thrace, being Goths, deserted to their fellow tribesmen after 377–82 (AM 31.6.5). On barbarian slaves and slave trade in late antiquity more generally, see Symm. *Ep.* 2.78; AM 29.4.4; Zos. 2.42.1; *CTh* 3.4.1, 5.6.3, 13.4.4; *CJ* 4.63.2; cf. Thompson 1965, 40–43.

36. Them. *Or.* 10.136b.

37. Valens had used starvation to his advantage in the first Gothic war, and his commanders would recommend it in the conflicts leading up to Adrianople; see p. 132; AM 31.5.5, 7.3, 8.1, 4, 10.15; Eunap. *Hist.* fr. 44.1 (Blockley); Zos. 4.23.6. Julian also used this technique against the Franks (AM 17.2.1–3; Lib. *Or.* 18.70), and Veg. *Mil.* 3.3, 9, 26 praises the strategic benefits of starving out an enemy.

38. See Dauge 1981, passim, esp. 307–78, 413–508, 681–715, 742–72.

Figure 16. Emperor dragging a captive barbarian by the hair. Medallion of Constantinople now in Belgrade. *JRS* 63 (1973), pl. viii. Courtesy *Journal of Roman Studies.*

games and stage plays mocking barbarians, would regularly have celebrated festivals in which barbarians were fed to the beasts, and would have daily thumbed coins depicting Romans forcibly pulling barbarians from their houses or running them down on horseback (fig. 16; cf. figs. 12 and 13).[39] Surrounded by such images and spectacles, most Roman soldiers would have felt a sense of moral rectitude about perpetrating what we would today term human-rights abuses. Thus the mistreatment of the Gothic refugees was probably a very real threat.

These affronts, needless to say, angered the Tervingi, and by early 377, they showed signs of rebellion. They had been lingering along the Danube since the middle of 376, and Lupicinus decided it was best to hasten the restless group on its move 100 kilometers southeast to Marcianople (Devnja).[40] This was the capital of Moesia II and had been well outfitted during Valens's three-year residence there between 367 and 370. The transfer had to be implemented with a large force of troops, most of whom were drafted from the riparian garrisons and river patrols along the Danube. Their absence from the river naturally opened the way to a further influx of migratory peoples, this time the Greuthungi who had been denied access by Valens earlier in the summer of 376.[41] Their leaders Alatheus and Saphrax landed the Greu-

39. On games, see McCormick 1986, 34. On stage plays, see Cazzaniga 1958. On barbarians fed to the beasts, see *Pan. Lat.* 12 [9].23.3, 6 [7].12.3; Symm. *Rel.* 9, 47; AM 14.2.1; Eutr. 10.3. On coins, see Constantius's FEL TEMP REPARATIO issues at Mattingly 1933; Kent 1967. See Heather 1999a and Mattern 1999, 66–80, 195, for more on this point.

40. AM 31.5.1–2.

41. AM 31.5.3; cf. 31.4.12–13, 9.3 Taifali.

thungi at a safe distance from the Tervingi, perhaps near Noviodunum (Issacea).[42] Meanwhile, Alavivus and Fritigern advanced only slowly toward Marcianople with their people. Ammianus tells us this was deliberate, in order to allow the Greuthungi to come up and join forces. The Goths were beginning to prepare a full-scale revolt.

Upon reaching Marcianople, Lupicinus invited Alavivus and Fritigern to a banquet. The two were admitted into the city walls with a Gothic escort, while the main body of Tervingi was kept under Roman guard outside. Ammianus tells us that troubles arose when the main group quarreled with their Roman guards over permission to enter the city and supply themselves. Lupicinus, fearing a riot, had Alavivus's and Fritigern's escort murdered inside the city and only let Fritigern escape on the promise that he would quiet his restless people. Ammianus does not reveal what became of Alavivus; indeed, he never mentions him again: one can assume that he was captured or murdered.[43] In fact, it is not unlikely that Lupicinus intended to capture or kill both Tervingi *reges* from the beginning. Roman commanders often used banquets as occasions to isolate foreign leaders and seize or execute them. Both Valens and Valentinian had tried the same thing, with varying results.[44] Jordanes implies that Lupicinus planned a similar trap for Fritigern, and, although his account is often unreliable, he may in this instance be reporting the truth.[45] The annihilation of the Tervingi *reges* would have left the group fragmented and malleable for more direct enlistment into the army and scatter-shot resettlement across the empire. Thus once Lupicinus had isolated Alavivus and Fritigern from their retinues, he may have found the Gothic riot outside Marcianople a convenient excuse to execute a prearranged ambush.[46]

Of course, when Fritigern survived and was sent back to his people, the incident backfired. The Goths openly revolted and began plundering neighboring *villae*.[47] Lupicinus responded by hastily assembling a band of troops

42. Wolfram 1977, 234.

43. AM 31.5.5–7. At 31.5.7: "veritus ne teneretur obsidis vice cum ceteris" may imply that Alavivus was captured rather than killed.

44. Valens attempted to capture and eventually killed Pap; see pp. 179–81. For Valentinian's attempts on foreign kings, see pp. 145–46. See other instances at AM 18.2.12–13, 21.4.1–8. Barbarians, too, were capable of such treachery; see AM 27.4.9, 12.3; *BP* 3.20, 4.54; Eunap. *Hist.* fr. 59 (Blockley).

45. *Get.* 135–36. If the banquet was intended as an ambush, this would help explain the reluctance of the Goths to send high-ranking tribesmen to the Romans in subsequent negotiations (AM 31.12.8–9, 13–14; Them. *Or.* 15.190c).

46. For similar interpretations, see Köhler 1925, 60–63; Burns 1973, 338; Wanke 1990, 137; Heather 1991, 132–33.

47. For damage to *villae* in Thrace and Moesia in the period around 377, see Nikolov 1976, 25, 57, 70; Poulter 1983, 90.

and marching out to meet the rebellious refugees. This he did nine miles from Marcianople, where an engagement ensued in early 377, which annihilated his forces and nearly killed him as well.[48] The Gothic victory effectively eliminated the Roman forces in the area, and the Tervingi were thus allowed to continue their raids unchecked. Their successes led to an increase in their numbers as other tribal peoples and outcasts within the empire came to see an advantage in allying themselves with the Goths.

Among the groups to join Fritigern was a band of Goths under two leaders named Sueridas and Colias. These had been settled near Adrianople (Edirne) some time before 376 and were under orders to move east and reinforce Valens when a conflict broke out between them and the citizens of Adrianople. The local magistrate, who had chaffed under their presence for some time, decided to charge them with pillaging his villa and incited the workers from the city's arms factory to attack them. Sueridas's and Colias's Goths had the better of the engagement but, now being enemies of the state, were forced to turn for support to Fritigern, who was operating nearby. Together with Fritigern, Sueridas and Colias laid siege to Adrianople, but they were eventually forced to retreat.[49] From this it is clear, not only that Fritigern was constantly supplementing his forces with new followers, but also that his raiding groups had broken south of the Haemus mountains (Stara Planina) following their victory at Marcianople and were operating in the province of Thrace into the first half of 377.[50] From there their raids would only spread.

By midsummer, Valens—still in Antioch—had learned of the uprising in Thrace. He clearly understood its gravity and quickly sent his *magister equitum*

---

48. AM 31.5.8–9. Jer. *Chron.* s.a. 377 provides the year for the outbreak of the rebellion. He is to be preferred to both Soc. 4.35.1–4 (who implies that it took place in 376) and Prosper *Chron.* 1163 (who miscopies the notice to 378). Marcianople sits in a small valley surrounded by hills and scrubby terrain. To its west stretches a broad fertile plain well suited to *villae* (Hodinott 1975, 167–68). Thus the Goths probably moved west-northwest from Marcianople.

49. AM 31.6.1–3. On the ineptitude of non-Romans in siege operations, see Elton 1996b, 82–6.

50. Wanke 1990, 134–41, holds that it would have been all but impossible for Fritigern to move all his people with their possessions and wagons from Marcianople across the Haemus to Adrianople ca. 300 km to the south and then back north again to face the Romans at the battle of Ad Salices in Scythia by late summer 377. For this reason, he believes that Ammianus's account of the Sueridas and Colias incident is a doublet of the revolt at Marcianople and proposes to emend Ammianus's "apud Hadrianopolim" to "apud Marcianopolim." This argument must be rejected for three reasons: first, because the circumstantial differences between Ammianus's descriptions of the two incidents are too great to regard them as pertinent to a single event; second, because Wanke's argument wrongly assumes that Fritigern was traveling with all of the Goths (including women and children), but our sources indicate that the Gothic band often split into smaller guerrilla parties (pp. 331–34); and, finally, because the barbarian presence on the Thracian plain in 377 is explicitly attested three more times in Ammianus (31.6.5, 7.1, and, esp., 7.3).

Victor to the Persians to negotiate a truce.[51] While awaiting the outcome of these negotiations, he also sent to Gratian in the west to request reinforcements from the comitatensian troops in Gaul and Illyricum.[52] Finally, he created two new *magistri militum*, Profuturus and Traianus, to lead an advance force of eastern *comitatenses* to Thrace and hold the barbarians at bay.[53] These drove the Goths north of the Haemus and into the desolate *baltas* of the Dobrugea.[54] Here they awaited the arrival of the troops from Gratian, who were approaching under the command of the *comes domesticorum* Richomer. Richomer met Profuturus and Traianus near the town of Ad Salices in the northeastern Dobrugea, where they were blockading the Goths.[55] The combined Roman command now attempted to harry the barbarians in skirmishes, while it starved them out on the steppe. The Gothic leadership realized that it needed to force a battle and recalled its plundering bands to the attack. The ensuing battle, fought in late summer 377, was devastating for both sides, killing the Roman commander Profuturus, crippling the Roman forces, who retreated to Marcianople, and leaving the Goths so shaken that they did not emerge from the security of their wagon circle *(carrago)* for seven days.[56]

After the slaughter, Richomer returned west to solicit more reinforcements from Gratian.[57] Having seen the size and ferocity of the Gothic band, he was well aware that the conflict was far from over. So too was Valens, who created yet another ad hoc *magister equitum*, Saturninus, and sent him west to take over the cavalry and help relieve Traianus.[58] When Saturninus arrived in late 377, the Romans in Thrace had managed to fortify the passes of the Haemus in the continued hope of walling off the barbarians and starving them into submission.[59] Fritigern responded by enlisting the aid of Hun and Alan mercenaries with the promise of booty. When Saturninus recognized that his Roman troops were no match for this reinforced Gothic band, he decided to abandon the Haemus blockade.[60] The Goths quickly spilled over the mountains back into Thrace and attacked territory as far south as the Rhodope Mountains and as far east as the Hellespont. Saturninus's with-

---

51. AM 31.7.1; Eunap. *Hist.* fr. 42 (Blockley); cf. p. 184.

52. AM 31.7.3; cf. p. 356.

53. AM 31.7.1–3; Demandt 1970, 705–6; cf. pp. 362–63.

54. AM 31.7.3: "trusos hostes ultra Haemi montis abscisos scopulos faucibus inpegere praeruptis." On the topography of the Dobrugea, see Wanke 1990, 145–47.

55. On the location, see Wanke 1990, 63, 157–58, with full bibliography. Contrast Heather 1991, 144.

56. AM 31.7.5–8.2. On Profuturus's probable death, see p. 363.

57. AM 31.8.2.

58. AM 31.8.3 reports that Saturninus was given "equestris exercitus ad tempus cura"; cf. Demandt 1970, 705–6.

59. AM 31.8.1, 5, 9.1.

60. AM 31.8.4–6; cf. 31.16.3; cf. Maenchen-Helfen 1973, 27–30.

drawal had given them free run from the Danube to Macedonia and from Moesia to the Black Sea.[61]

Part of the reason the barbarians were able to cover so much territory was that their numbers had swollen tremendously. At some point, Fritigern and his Tervingi had been joined by the Greuthungi of Vitheric, led by Alatheus and Saphrax, perhaps before the engagement at Marcianople.[62] We have also seen how a Gothic band under Sueridas and Colias attached itself to Fritigern's group in early 377. Also in 377, Farnobius, another Greuthungi chieftain who had crossed the Danube with Alatheus and Saphrax, won over a band of Taifali as allies.[63] That same year a combined force of Huns and Alans also joined the growing group as mercenaries.[64] In addition, disgruntled local miners and slaves, some of Gothic descent, joined the band, as did deserters from the Roman army.[65] What had begun as a controlled migration of a limited group of Tervingi had thus snowballed into an avalanche of rebels loosely united around the original Gothic core.

From the time when the Greuthungi linked forces with the Tervingi in early 377, Ammianus ceases to refer to the group led by Fritigern as Tervingi and begins to call them generically *Gothi*, or simply *barbari*.[66] His generalization was probably intentional, designed to convey his awareness that the group had metamorphosed into a heterogeneous agglomeration of ethnicities. These included Goths, Taifals, Huns, Alans, and Romans.[67] The ethnic diversity of this barbarian band has been emphasized by recent historians, who have carefully plotted the tremendous cultural, political, and ethnic transformations that the group underwent in response to their new contacts

---

61. AM 31.8.6: "et vastabundi omnes per latitudines Thraciae pandebantur impune, ab ipsis tractibus quos praetermeat Hister exorsi ad usque Rhodopen et fretum, quod immensa distermnat maria"; cf. 31.11.2; Jer. *Chron.* s.a. 377: "superatis in congressione Romanis Gothi funduntur in Thracia"; Lib. *Or.* 1.179; Eunap. *Hist.* fr. 44.1 (Blockley); Zos. 4.20.7; cf. 4.22.2–4. Eunap. *Hist.* fr. 42 (Blockley), describes Gothic raiding as far south as Thessaly. This certainly occurred, but not until after 378; see Lenski 1997, 133 n. 14, on the extent of the raiding after Adrianople.

62. AM 31.5.4 implies that it was before Marcianople. The Greuthungi are next attested specifically at the battle of Adrianople in 378 (AM 31.12.12, 17, but see also 31.9.3 [a. 377]).

63. AM 31.9.3.

64. See p. 330.

65. On miners and slaves, see p. 304. On deserters, see AM 31.7.7, 15.4, 8–9, 16.1; cf. 31.11.3; Basil *Ep.* 268. On other incidents of Roman desertion to barbarian raiding bands, see Rugullis 1992, 40–66; De Ste. Croix 1981, 474–88.

66. The shift occurs between AM 31.5.8 and 31.5.9; cf. Wolfram 1988, 120; Wanke 1990, 71.

67. AM 31.16.3: "Gothi Hunis Halanisque permixti"; cf. *Epit.* 47.3: "Gothis Taifalisque atque . . . Hunnis et Alanis"; 48.5: "Hunnos et Gothos"; *Pan. Lat.* 2 [12].11.4, 32.4: "Gothus . . . Chunus . . . Halanus"; Them. *Or.* 16.207c: αὐθάδεια Σκυθικὴ καὶ τόλμα Ἀλανῶν καὶ ἀπόνοια Μασσαγετῶν; Veg. *Mil.* 1.20: "Gothorum et Alanorum Hunnorumque"; *Cons. Const.* s.a. 379: "Gothos, Alanos atque Hunos"; Oros. 7.34.5: "Alanos Hunos et Gothos"; cf. Aus. XX *Precatio consulis designati* ll. 37–38.

and allegiances in the years down to their settlement in Gaul in 418.[68] Historians have been less quick, however, to comprehend the significance of this ethnic and political fragmentation in the period when its effects were most pronounced, the years between 377 and 382.[69] This has led to a tendency to examine the "Gothic War" as if "the Goths" constituted a monolithic political and strategic unit with coordinated actions and goals. Our sources make it clear that this was hardly the case. The peoples whom modern scholars call "the Visigoths" were, in these early stages, still a fragmented and fissiparous group.

This fragmentation must have hampered attempts by Fritigern to control the peoples he had assembled under his leadership. Each of the various subgroups he oversaw had its own chief or chiefs, who were only loosely allied under his overlordship. Most of the Greuthungi were led by their king Vitheric and his regents Alatheus and Saphrax,[70] yet some apparently followed the *rex* Farnobius.[71] Sueridas and Colias, although subordinate to Fritigern, also probably retained some personal control over the men whom they had originally commanded.[72] The Alans and Huns in the Gothic band were mercenaries rather than refugees, and the fact that Ammianus generally distinguishes them from the Goths seems to confirm that they too operated under their own leadership.[73] Indeed, Fritigern himself initially had to share leadership over the Tervingi with his fellow chief Alavivus.[74] Fritigern must then have faced a struggle in trying to maintain supreme hegemony.

In fact, there is clear evidence that Fritigern did indeed face difficulties controlling the various groups he led. During later negotiations with Valens,

---

68. Wenskus 1961, 475–77; cf. 75–76, 439–445; Wolfram 1975, 31; 1977, 236–37; 1988, passim. Heather 1991, 12–18, accepts these views but cautions that the migratory group always retained a fundamentally Gothic core; cf. Heather 1999b. Culturally, this is true, but politically it had little effect until years of battle had solidified the group into a more unified entity.

69. See, however, Gutmann 1991, 147–54.

70. AM 31.5.4: "regibus validis"; cf. 31.5.7.

71. AM 31.9.3: "Gothorum optimatem"; cf. 31.4.12.

72. AM 31.6.1: "Gothorum optimates."

73. AM 31.8.4 (late 377), 31.16.3 (late 378). AM 31.2.7–8 reports that the Huns did not at this period have a centralized leadership; cf. Eunap. *Hist.* fr. 60 (Blockley). Thompson 1996, 29–30, and Heather 1995, 10–11, concur, but see Maenchen-Helfen 1973, 12, 191–203. Várady 1969, 20–6, 31–40, and Wolfram 1977, 228–31; 1988, 120–22, argue that the Greuthungi, Huns, and Alans operated in a "Drei-Völkerkonfederation," but the evidence does not support such a view. AM 31.4.12 and 31.12.12 refer to Alatheus and Saphrax without connection to the Huns or Alans; AM 31.3.3 implies that Vitherich hired Hunnic mercenaries to fight against the Alans; and AM 31.12.17 implies that Alatheus and Saphrax went raiding with a band of Alans only in 378. Thus, while the Greuthungi are occasionally associated with Huns or Alans, nowhere are all three mentioned as forming a coordinated unit. See also Maenchen-Helfen 1973, 29–30; Heather 1991, 144–45.

74. When the Goths initially cross, Alavivus is the only leader mentioned at 31.4.1, but 31.4.8 implies that Fritigern was a key figure among the Tervingi from before the crossing.

he was twice compelled to state his own desire for peace in independent missives that contravened the decisions of the body or council representing the collective leadership.[75] Ammianus and other texts refer to this same collective leadership on numerous occasions.[76] When the group faced serious battles at Ad Salices and Adrianople, it was apparently this collective (optimates) and not Fritigern that assembled the scattered barbarian units for battle.[77] Fritigern was unable to dissuade the band from undertaking a dangerous siege of Adrianople in 378, and after besieging Constantinople later that summer, his coalition, which had been bickering over what its course of action should be, seems to have dissolved.[78] By the time peace was made with the "Gothic band" in 382, Fritigern seems to have dropped entirely out of the picture.[79] He was thus never in firm control of the semi-independent units collectively referred to in modern scholarship as "the Visigoths." This fragmentation of leadership makes it difficult to speak of intentions and goals on the barbarian side with total confidence during the years Valens faced them. It would also have made it difficult for Valens to learn the enemy's intentions and goals, or even to feel comfortable negotiating with a group that had only a relatively weak leader.

This same fragmentation made the barbarian band a much trickier and more dangerous enemy for the empire. Their atomization allowed the barbarians to cover a remarkably broad swath of territory with raids that were extremely effective at disturbing Roman communication and supply systems.[80] The group probably always retained a center of gravity where the main concentration of wagons and most of the women and children could be moved and protected together.[81] Nevertheless, after Ad Salices, its subgroups

75. AM 31.12.9, 14. In the first instance, Fritigern is trying to win recognition from Valens as a client king (amicus et socius), a coup that would have bolstered support within his confederation. See Heather 1991, 178–81.

76. E.g., AM 31.7.8: "principibus gentis"; 31.7.9: "ductores"; Them. *Or.* 16.210b: τοὺς ἐξάρχους καὶ κορυφαίους; Joh. Chrys. *Ad vid. iun.* 4: τινα τῶν παρ'ἐκείνοις βασιλέων; Jord. *Get.* 134: "primates eorum et duces qui regum vice illis praeerant." See Thompson 1965, 44.

77. AM 31.7.7: "iussis optimatum acceptis"; 31.15.13: "monitu optimatum . . . agmina praeeuntium ductorum."

78. AM 31.15.2–3, 15, 16.1, 7. Zos. 4.34.2 and Jord. *Get.* 141–42 used in conjunction indicate that the Greuthungi under Alatheus and Saphrax split from Fritigern and went west to Pannonia and Moesia in 380 while the Tervingi remained in Thessaly and Macedonia. For an incisive analysis of these two vexed passages, see Heather 1991, 151–54, 335–40. On Fritigern's weakness and the lack of strong central leadership, see Klein 1956, 67; Burns 1973, 337–40.

79. Heather 1991, 180–81, 188–92, who also emphasizes that the tribulations faced by the Gothic band helped strengthen their unity. Cf. Thompson 1963.

80. Gothic pillaging is attested at AM 31.5.8, 6.3–8, 7.7–8, 8.6–8, 9.3, 11.2, 4, 5, 13.12, 16.3. Them. *Or.* 16.212b and 34.24 indicate that the roads through Thrace were closed between 377 and 382. See also Burns 1994, 39–40; Lenski 1997, 132–34.

81. In 378, before the battle of Adrianople, the band had fixed camps at Beroea (Stara Zagora: AM 31.11.2), and later 80 km east at Cabyle (Jambol: AM 31.11.5). The first notice is

were able to conduct actions independently of one another all over Scythia, Moesia, and Thrace. In late 377, Ammianus describes a band of mounted Gothic raiders who overwhelmed Roman infantry units under the command of Barzimeres at the town of Dibaltum (Develt) near the Black Sea.[82] These raiders were probably Greuthungi, given that, in contrast with the Tervingi, the Greuthungi generally used cavalry.[83] Shortly after this incident, yet another band of Greuthungi, this one led by the *rex* Farnobius, was operating 130 kilometers to the west near Beroea (Stara Zagora) when they were captured by Gratian's general Frigeridus.[84] The two bands were apparently acting independently. So, too, was another group that Ammianus says was raiding in the Rhodope Mountains, while the main body of Goths was stationed 100 kilometers to the north, near Beroea.[85] In the summer of 378, some Alans are attested as far west as Castra Martis (Kula) in Dacia Ripensis, and Goths are known to have reached as far east as the walls of Constantinople.[86] Already in the days before the battle of Ad Salices, the barbarian nobles had been forced to call in their plundering bands for the fight, and Fritigern would have to issue the same call to the "scattered bands" of his alliance before he faced Valens in 378.[87] Even so, on the day of the battle of Adrianople, the main force of Greuthungi cavalry was absent from the central group until late in the afternoon.[88] The fragmented nature of the barbarian group thus made it extremely effective at ravaging a broad swath of territory with devastating guerrilla raids.[89]

The mayhem that prevailed as a result forced Valens to cancel his plans for a Persian invasion, settle a truce with Shapur, and prepare his march west. As we have seen, however, his commitments against Persia represented only one of the obstacles he faced in trying to break free from the eastern frontier. Isauria had only recently flared up, demanding that he commit troops there, when these might have been sent to Thrace, and the Saracens broke

---

marred by its statement that the Goths were based "circa Beroeam et Nicopolim." The Goths may have crossed the Haemus between these two cities, but it is impossible that a single band could have encamped near both at once, contrast Poulter 1995, 115–16.

82. AM 31.8.9–10; cf. 12.15.

83. Wolfram 1988, 98–99.

84. AM 31.9.1–4. No exact location for the incident is given, but Frigeridus was moving west from Beroea when he encountered Farnobius.

85. AM 31.11.2.

86. For Castra Martis, see AM 31.11.6; cf. Zos. 4.24.4. See Maenchen-Helfen 1973, 30–36, for a different account of Zosimus's notice. For Constantinople, see n. 94. For more on the extent of Gothic raiding, see pp. 329–31.

87. AM 31.7.7: "per diversa prope diffusas accivere vastatorias manus"; 11.5: "dispersos licenter suorum globos."

88. AM 31.12.12: "disiectis adhuc per itinera plurimis."

89. To be sure, many of these "raiding bands" were simply foraging for food. The net result, however, was a dissemination of violence across the dioceses of Thrace and Moesia.

into open revolt even as Valens was preparing to depart Antioch in late 377. Because of these conflicts, Valens was only able to head west with his *comitatenses* in early April 378 and thus to reach Constantinople on May 30.[90]

Both Ammianus and the ecclesiastical historians report that he was greeted with rioting. Only the ecclesiastical historians specify that this was provoked by Gothic raiding, which had reached as far as the suburbs of the city. By their account, in the face of this imminent threat, the Constantinopolitans openly mocked Valens in the circus and called for arms to fend off the barbarians themselves.[91] Military problems had thus spawned domestic problems. Rumors of the raiding had also spread well beyond the boundaries of Thrace. Basil had heard of the depredations in the spring of 378 and was reluctant to send a letter to his friend Eusebius of Samosata—exiled in Philippopolis (Plovdiv)—lest he be held responsible for the death of the courier at the hands of raiders.[92] Theodoret read Eusebius's own description of the mayhem, which, had it survived, would be an invaluable source of firsthand information about the terror and devastation.[93] The Goths and their allies had rapidly overrun the entirety of Thrace, provoked chaos in the cities they attacked, and aroused terror throughout the east.

Given that the Goths had already reached the outskirts of Constantinople, Valens and his men would have been wedged into the city when they first arrived in May 378. Before he could begin strategic operations against the barbarians, then, Valens needed to open the routes leading out from the city and clear the roads of Thrace. He began by sending Saracen cavalry—who had come west with him after the end of the Mavia revolt—out from the city to disperse the barbarians.[94] These opened the roads west for his

90. *Cons. Const.* s.a. 378; Soc. 4.38.1. Cf. AM 31.11.1; Eunap. *Hist.* fr. 44.1 (Blockley); Zos. 4.21.1; Soz. 6.37.17, 39.2. On Valens's date of departure from Antioch, see Barnes 1997, 5.

91. AM 31.11.1; Soc. 4.38.2–4; Soz. 6.39.2–4, 40.2; cf. Joh. Ant. fr. 184.2; Theoph. a.m. 5870; Cedrenus, p. 549. Dagron 1974, 108–13, 314, notes that the city was particularly vulnerable because it lacked a garrison. Velkov 1983, 180, also notes that the Constantinopolitans would have been provoked by supply shortages, since Thrace, a major supplier of food and manufactured goods, was inaccessible.

92. Basil *Ep.* 268, with Barnes 1997, 9–12, on the date.

93. Theodoret *HE* 4.15.11. For descriptions of the ravages in Thrace, see also Lib. *Or.* 24.15–16; Them. *Or.* 16.206d, 34.24; Eunap. *Hist.* fr. 47.1 (Blockley); cf. Lenski 1997, 134–37.

94. Eunap. *Hist.* fr. 42 (Blockley) and Zos. 4.22.1–3 both report that the Goths had reached the walls of Constantinople before Valens's arrival, and that Valens sent the Saracen cavalry against them before he moved west. Some have argued that they mistakenly place this notice before rather than after the battle of Adrianople, where Ammianus 31.16.1–7 locates it. The most elaborate case is built by Woods 1996, with earlier bibliography at 261 n. 3. Shahid 1984a, 179–81, has already demonstrated, however, that there were in fact two such incidents, one before and one after the battle, as indicated at Soc. 5.1.1: πάλιν ἕως τῶν τειχῶν τῆς Κωνσταντινουπόλεως ἐλθόντες; cf. Soz. 7.1.1–2; Theoph. a.m. 5870; Joh. Ant. fr. 184.2. Woods believes that the Saracens were part of a guard unit assigned to the empress Domnica and first called into action after Valens's death. This is highly unlikely given that Zosimus and Socrates openly

army to begin its advance. He also replaced the *magister peditum,* Traianus, with the western general Sebastianus, who had just come from Italy to offer support. Sebastianus assembled a levy of picked men from each infantry legion and set out from the city to ambush stray raiders. Both Ammianus and Zosimus describe an encounter where Sebastianus's detachment ambushed some barbarians along the Hebrus river near Adrianople and annihilated them. Although they describe only one such incident, Ammianus implies that it was representative of a broader series of successes.[95]

Once the roads west were reopened, Valens did not linger in the capital. He departed on June 11, only twelve days after his arrival. Disgusted with the uprising there, he promised reprisals against the Constantinopolitans when he returned.[96] He then proceeded west on the road toward Adrianople up to the imperial villa of Melanthias, twenty-seven kilometers from the city.[97] There he mustered and trained troops and began a long wait for the arrival of the supplementary forces that he had requested from Gratian. Gratian had sent only limited aid in the previous year, and in 378, he delayed his march east to make a foray against the Alamannic Lentienses. As we shall see, rivalry between the two emperors surely contributed to their failure to join forces before Valens faced the Goths.[98]

Meanwhile, Fritigern had grown anxious over the arrival of the emperor in the region and especially over the vulnerability of his scattered allies to ambushes like those of Sebastianus. He issued a call to the various barbarian groups to assemble near the town of Cabyle, where the core of the Gothic band had moved from its former base at Beroea.[99] Ancient Cabyle sat on the Tonsus (Tundza) river, which runs south to meet with the Hebrus (Maritza)

---

state that the Saracens remained tribal federates, not fully enlisted soldiers (Zos. 4.22.2: τὸ Σαρακηνικῶν φῦλον; Soc. 5.1.4; cf. 4.36.1: Σαρακηνοὶ ὑπόσπονδοι). Moreover, Ammianus's (31.16.6) report of their comportment—riding naked and cutting the throat of an enemy to suck his blood—hardly seems in keeping with the conduct of imperial guardsmen. While Woods argues that only Ammianus provides accurate reportage on the broader incident, he chooses to dismiss this uncomfortable information as slander. In fact, however, both the throat-cutting and the nakedness are reported of Saracens in independent sources, Nilus *Narrationes* 47 (*PG* 79.628) and Jer. *Vita Malchi* 4 (*PL* 23.57). Finally, Wood's argument is weak because it is predicated on his assumption that Ammianus says nothing of the Goths reaching Constantinople before Adrianople. This contention is untenable in light of 31.8.6, which Woods seems not to have noticed.

95. AM 31.11.1–4; cf. 31.12.1; Zos. 4.22.4–23.6, with Paschoud 2.2: 380 n. 147; Eunap. *Hist.* fr. 44.3–4 (Blockley). Sebastianus had experience in such advance attacks (see AM 30.5.13). On the incident, see Speidel 1996b; cf. Wanke 1990, 187–91.

96. See p. 114.

97. AM 31.11.1. On the date, see *Cons. Const.* s.a. 378; Soc. 4.38.5. On the distance from Constantinople, see Agathias 4.14.5; cf. Wanke 1990, 44–45.

98. See pp. 356–67.

99. AM 31.11.5.

near Adrianople. Its ready access to water and to the croplands of the Thracian plain, coupled with its location at the base of a rock citadel, made it a defensible post.[100] Fritigern could have waited out the Romans from there, but he was fully aware that it was to his advantage to press the issue. Once his forces had assembled, he began the ninety-kilometer trek down the Tonsus toward Adrianople, apparently late in July.

At this point Ammianus's narrative falters. At 31.11.2, he reports that Valens had set out from Melanthias for the *statio* of Nike before he sent Sebastianus on his guerrilla mission. The same departure appears again, however, at 31.12.1, after the news of Sebastianus's successes, and indeed those of Gratian against the Lentienses, had been reported to him. Other than postulating two journeys to Nike, we can only explain this as a doublet. If so, we must assume that the chronology of the second notice is preferable, that is, Valens moved east toward Adrianople *after* Sebastianus had cleared the area of Gothic raiders. He reached Adrianople perhaps at the end of July.[101] It was probably there that he learned that some Goths were attempting to block his supply route from behind and sent archers and cavalry to defend the passes they would take.[102]

Meanwhile, the main body of Goths had moved down the Tonsus valley and began making for Nike, east of Adrianople. Thus Fritigern veered southeast from the Tonsus to bypass Valens at Adrianople and once again attempt to block the army road back to Constantinople.[103] Had Fritigern reached Nike, this brilliant move would have put the main barbarian force between Valens and his supply center. But Valens, who had set up a stockade outside Adrianople to help garrison his massive army, became aware of the delicacy of the situation and agitated for an attack. Despite a letter from Gratian exhorting him to await the western auxiliaries, Valens held an immediate council of war to determine an independent course of action. The sources contradict each other on which generals favored battle and which delay. Given the evidence, it is impossible to determine, but we can say that the forces for

100. Hodinott 1975, 103–4; cf. Wanke 1990, 36.

101. On this *crux*, see Judeich 1891, 9 with n. 2, 12 with n. 1–2, who tries to explain the double mention with an elaborate account but is refuted by Runkel 1903, 22–23. Runkel, in turn, believes that the first notice signals Valens's departure from Melanthias; cf. Nagl, "Val.," 2133; Hoffmann 1969–70, 1: 446; Wolfram 1977, 240; Wanke 1990, 178–84. Austin 1972a, 81, is on firmer ground when he argues that the move from Melanthias was contingent on Valens's decision to engage the Goths independently of Gratian; cf. Speidel 1996b, 435 n. 3.

102. AM 31.12.2.

103. AM 31.12.3. Seeck, *Untergang*, 105, with 472, originally took Nike to be north of Adrianople in the Tonsus valley. He is followed by Hoffmann 1969–70, 2: 186 n. 160; Wolfram 1988, 124. Judeich 1891, 9, had already demonstrated, however, that it was in fact east-southeast of the city, on the road to Constantinople. He is followed by Runkel 1903, 22; cf. Wanke 1990, 41–43, with full argumentation.

action were encouraged by a mistaken report from scouts who claimed to have seen only 10,000 men in the Gothic army assembled nearby.[104] This, too, reflects the perils of dealing with a group fragmented into a variety of semi-independent units: the 10,000 they saw were, as Ammianus implies, only a small part of the total fighting contingent that would later assemble.[105]

On the day before battle, August 8, Fritigern sent a Christian *presbyter* as an envoy to Valens's camp outside Adrianople. He presented a note asking that the Goths should be granted Thrace with its crops and livestock in return for a "perpetual peace." He also bore a secret dispatch from Fritigern to the effect that Valens could frighten the barbarians into submission if only he would range his army against them. The embassy was sent away empty-handed.[106]

On August 9, Valens left the imperial entourage and treasury in the city and marched his army across rough terrain to the Gothic camp, probably near the modern Demirhanlı, about seventeen kilometers east-northeast of Adrianople.[107] In the early afternoon, they caught sight of the wagons of the enemy drawn up in a circle. While the Romans ranged for battle, the barbarians sent another peace embassy to their camp. This was at least partly motivated by Fritigern's awareness that the forces under Alatheus and Saphrax were away from the main barbarian core and had not yet responded to an order to return. There was also an element of strategy involved; Fritigern apparently hoped to wear down the Romans by detaining them in the hot sun while he temporized, and even had brushfires kindled to irritate them with smoke. Once again Valens rejected his embassy, this time because its representatives were of lowly origin.[108] Fritigern responded with a third embassy calling for an exchange of noble hostages and further negotiations. Valens finally agreed, probably sensing that the fatigue of the August sun had exhausted his men. The western general Richomer prepared to be sent to the Gothic camp with proofs of his rank and birth.[109] What happened next is slightly unclear because of a lacuna in Ammianus's account, but where it

104. AM 31.12.3–7; Zos. 4.23.6–24.1. Cf. Solari 1932a.

105. Austin and Rankov 1995, 40–67, 214–43, have demonstrated that Roman tactical intelligence was generally quite good, that intelligence gathering improved in the fourth century, and that intelligence gathering before Adrianople was largely effective. The failure of Valens's *procursatores* to establish the full size of the barbarian forces on August 8 should thus be attributed to the confusing fragmentation of the band rather than the ineptitude of the scouts.

106. AM 31.12.8–9. Cesa 1984, 76; 1994, 28, points out that this agreement would have created an independent Gothic state in Roman territory, something that did eventually happen, but that the Romans were not prepared to accept in 378.

107. Dated at AM 31.12.10; *Cons. Const.* s.a. 378; Soc. 4.38.7. For the location, see Runkel 1903, 33–36, modified by Wanke 1990, 214–17; cf. *Cons. Const.* s.a. 378, twelve miles from Adrianople.

108. AM 31.12.11–13.

109. AM 31.12.14–15. The imperfect *pergebat* must be translated as inchoative (was about to set out) if it is to be reconciled with 31.12.17: "nusquam ire permissi."

picks up again, Valens's *sagittarii* and *scutarii* made an impetuous foray against the barbarians and then beat a hasty retreat. Richomer thus never got far in his embassy before battle erupted. This was probably welcomed by the Goths, whose cavalry forces under Alatheus and Saphrax had just returned and rushed onto the scene with devastating effect.[110]

Ammianus's account of the battle is heavily overlaid with dramatic embellishments, but it preserves an outline that allows some reconstruction of events. Valens's cavalry was quickly put to flight by the unexpected onslaught of the Greuthungi horsemen under Alatheus and Saphrax. His left wing had advanced as far as the Gothic camp, but because of the desertion of his cavalry, it was easily outflanked, surrounded, and crushed. The right wing fought on but eventually collapsed late in the afternoon and was slaughtered.[111] By the end of the day, *two-thirds* of the Roman soldiers had been lost, most of them infantry—and the cavalry had fled. As Themistius would later remark, "an entire army disappeared like a shadow."[112] Dietrich Hoffmann has pinpointed and cataloged sixteen units from the eastern army that were completely obliterated. These included two cavalry vexillations (500 men each), nine mobile legions (1,000 men each), and five auxiliary infantry units (800 men each), for a total of 14,000 casualties. To this figure must be added the 6,000–12,000 lost from units that were only partially destroyed, giving a total of 20,000–26,000 Roman dead out of the 30,000–40,000 men that Valens commanded at the start of battle.[113] These included thirty-five military tribunes, the *tribunus stabuli* and *cura palatii*, Aequitius and Valerianus, and the *magistri militum* Traianus and Sebastianus.[114] The eastern army was thus devastated. Of the fifty mobile units with which Valens had begun his reign in 364, fourteen had been transferred west in 369–71, and sixteen had been lost at Adrianople. Only twenty remained, and those were severely weakened.[115]

Valens was killed with his men, although how exactly he died is a matter of debate. Ammianus reports two versions that were current when he wrote in

110. AM 31.12.16–17.

111. AM 31.12.17–13.11; cf. Jer. *Chron.* s.a. 378: "deserente equitum praesidio Romanae legiones a Gothis cinctae usque ad internecionem caesae sunt"; Prosper *Chron.* 1165; Oros. 7.33.13; Soz. 6.40.3; Soc. 4.38.7; Gregory of Tours *Historia Francorum* 1.41. For analysis of the battle, see Hoffmann 1969–70, 2: 186 n. 160; Burns 1973, 342–43; Crump 1975, 91–96; Wanke 1990, 215–16; Nicasie 1998, 247–53.

112. Them. *Or.* 16.206d: στρατοπέδων δὲ ὁλοκλήρων ἀφανισθέντων ὥσπερ σκιᾶς; cf. *Or.* 14.181a; AM 31.13.18: "constatque vix tertiam evasisse exercitus partem."

113. Hoffmann 1969–70, 1: 449–457. For Valens's troop strength at the start of battle, see Schmidt 1934, 408; Stein 1959, 518–19 n. 189; Wolfram 1988, 124; Williams and Friell 1994, 177; Burns 1994, 31, 33; Nicasie 1998, 246. Contrast Austin 1972a, 82; Heather 1991, 146–47; 1996, 135.

114. AM 31.13.18.

115. Hoffmann 1969–70, 1: 457.

the early 390s. According to the first, in the midst of the melee, Valens took refuge among the Mattiarii et Lanciarii. As these grew weak, Traianus called for auxiliaries to be brought. Victor went in search of the Batavi, but he was unable to find them and fled the battlefield. He was followed by Richomer and Saturninus. Valens, now deserted by most of his commanders, was never seen again. Ammianus says it was conjectured that he was hit by an arrow and fell amid the slaughter where his corpse was never recovered.[116] He also reports a second story, according to which Valens was hit by an arrow but was able to retreat with some bodyguards and attendants to a fortified house nearby. A group of Goths approached to plunder the place without knowing that the emperor was inside. When they were shot at from its upper story, they set the house ablaze, and the emperor died in the fire. A single bodyguard, who jumped out of the burning building, escaped to relate the tale.[117] Ammianus does not inform us which account he believed, although an earlier reference to the portentous cries of "Let Valens be burned alive!" by the Antiochenes before Valens's death may indicate his preference for the latter.[118]

This was certainly the version preferred in the source tradition. The *Epitome de Caesaribus* reports only this version, as does Zosimus.[119] So, too, only this version appears in the ecclesiastical historians Rufinus, Sozomen, Theodoret, and Philostorgius.[120] Ultimately, the conflagration story became canonical because it perfectly suited historians—pagan and Christian—wishing to portray Valens's death as divine punishment for the emperor's religious persecutions.[121] Its aptness for such an interpretation and its gothic morbidity naturally call the story into question. But its confirmation in separate traditions, its circumstantial detail, and its claim to eyewitness testimony render it perfectly plausible. If it is a fabrication of hostile sources, it had found its way into the tradition within five years after Valens's death, because both Jerome and Chrysostom report it before 382.[122]

Nevertheless, Ammianus's first version, which is, as he admits, specula-

116. AM 31.13.12: "ut opinari dabatur (neque enim vidisse se quisquam, vel praesto fuisse adseveravit)." On Valens's death, see Lenski 1997, 150–55.

117. AM 31.13.14–16; cf. 16.2.

118. AM 31.1.2: "vivus ardeat Valens." See Lenski 1997, 153 n. 69, for similar allusions in Themistius.

119. *Epit.* 46.2; Zos. 4.24.2 with Paschoud 2.2: 383 n. 149.

120. Ruf. *HE* 2.13; Soz. 6.40.3–5; Theod. *HE* 4.36.1–2; Philost. 9.17. Cf. Joh. Chrys. *In epist. ad Philip. IV hom.* 15.5 (*PG* 62.295); Theoph. a.m. 5870.

121. Ruf. *HE* 2.13: "impietatis suae poenas igni exustus dedit"; Oros. 7.33.15, 17, 19, 35.9, 17; August. *Con. lit. Petiliani* 2.206 (*PL* 43.327); Jord. *Get.* 138; *Vita Isaaci* 7–8 (*Acta sanctorum Maii* 7: 603–4, 611); Theod. *HE* 4.36.2; MX 3.33; *Narratio de imperatoribus domus Valentinianae et Theodosianae* 2 (*MGH.AA* 9.629); Isidore *Hist. Goth.* 9 (*MGH.AA* 11.271). See also the strange version at Malalas 13.36 (p. 343). For commentary on Valens's death, see Judeich 1891, 18–19; Courcelle 1964, 22.

122. Jer. *Chron.* s.a. 378 (a. 380/81); Joh. Chrys. *Ad vid. iun.* 5 (a. 380/81).

tion based on Valens's total disappearance, also has external confirmation. Indeed, the earliest source for Valens's death, Libanius's oration 24 (a. 379), tells a story like it. Libanius portrays Valens nobly refusing to ride free of the fray when he realized that the day was lost. It seems that Libanius's sources reported only Valens's total disappearance, and Libanius embellished this with conjectural details.[123] Curiously, the ecclesiastical historian Socrates, like Ammianus, reports both the conflagration and the disappearance story. The fact that Socrates, a Nicene with obvious reasons for bias, chose not to privilege either account indicates that he believed there was no good touchstone by which to judge.[124] We would do well to follow his lead. In either case, the fact that Valens remained unburied was a supreme humiliation.[125] His end at Adrianople would be the most significant event of his career. It brought a closure to his reign that would allow him no escape from the sins of his imperial past. It guaranteed that history would view Valens with a jaundiced eye.

THE REASONS FOR THE COLLAPSE OF THE GOTHIC SETTLEMENT

Any attempt to reconstruct the origins of the collapse of the Gothic settlement are necessarily speculative. The agreement between Valens and the Goths fell apart for a variety of complex and interrelated reasons, no one of which can be pinpointed as a single cause. Moreover, the sources on the agreement are fragmentary and often contradictory, and their difficulties are magnified by the fact that the arrangement disintegrated before it was ever fully implemented. Even so, we can at least in outline reconstruct both the agreement and the reasons for its failure with some degree of accuracy.

Much of the modern debate has focused on the nature of the agreement by which the Goths were settled in 376: was it a *deditio* or a *foedus*?[126] Relying on legalistic definitions, researchers have defined the two in contradistinction to each other. Under the former, the subject peoples *(dediticii)* submitted un-

---

123. Lib. *Or.* 24.3–4; cf. *Or.* 1.179 and *Cons. Const.* s.a. 378: "ex ea die Valens Aug. nusquam apparuit." Eunap. *VS* 7.6.9 also seems to imply that Valens simply disappeared, an interesting contrast with Zosimus's version. The discrepancy would imply Zosimus's familiarity with the Christian tradition.

124. Soc. 4.38.8–10; cf. 5.1.

125. AM 31.13.17: "nec Valenti sepulturam (qui supremitatis honor est) contigisse"; Eunap. *VS* 7.6.4: οὐδὲ ταφῆς ἀξιωθείς, οὐδὲ ἐνδόξου τάφου; cf. 7.6.9; Jer. *Chron.* s.a. 378: "sepultura quoque caruit"; cf. *Ep.* 60.15: "eundem locum et mortis habuit et sepulchri"; Oros. 7.33.15; Joh. Chrys. *Ad vid. iun* 5. Evagrius *HE* 3.41 reports that only Basiliscus and Valens have died miserably since the imperial sanction of Christianity.

126. See Wolfram 1977, 233; 1988, 117–19; Cesa 1984, 66–67; 1994, 14–22. Oros. 7.33.10 even reports there was no treaty: "sine ulla foederis pactione suscepti." This is highly improbable in light of the arguments presented.

conditionally, usually after a defeat in battle. They could thus be split off from tribal and family units for redistribution on estates as slaves or semi-servile *coloni*. *Foederati*, in contrast, remained as yet unconquered and were thus treated more honorably. Under *foedera*, barbarians were relocated in ethnically homogeneous groups as freeholders on their own land and perhaps with their own leaders.[127] Because the sources report that the Tervingi were called on to surrender their weapons in 376—the most common sign of a *deditio*—it has generally been assumed that they entered the empire as *dediticii*.[128]

In his provocative study of the Goths, Peter Heather, has demonstrated that such terminology and the typologies associated with it are anachronistic. *Deditio* (surrender) was part—at least ceremonially—of every treaty agreement, even in cases where peoples had not been defeated in battle.[129] The best way to determine the nature of a resettlement treaty is thus not to slot it into modern taxonomies but to examine its specifics. With regard to the 376 agreement, Heather has shown convincingly that the Goths received surprisingly favorable terms from the Romans—indeed, that they played a serious role in determining the nature of their resettlement. Ammianus reports that Alavivus and Fritigern's Tervingi requested and received permission to be relocated to the rich farmlands in *Thracia*—that is, the diocese of Thrace.[130] The fact that they had input into the selection of this location indicates that this provision was not simply dictated by Valens. Similarly, Ammianus hints that the Goths were to retain some measure of control over the troops they would send to serve the Romans as auxiliaries, another sign of less than total submission.[131] And, as was customary in such arrangements, oaths were taken and hostages given, another sign that the Goths remained independent enough to require some surety for good behavior.[132] To this list we might add that the Tervingi were allowed to bring wagons and perhaps household pos-

127. On the distinction, see Stallknecht 1969, 5–31; Mirković 1993.

128. Stallknecht 1969, 24–26; Demougeot 1979, 2.1: 138–39; Cesa 1984, 66–72; 1994, 17–19; Wolfram 1988, 117–19; Guttmann 1991, 137–39. Ulrich 1995, 163–87, recognizes that some concessions were made to the Tervingi but still regards them as *dediticii*.

129. Heather 1991, 122–42; cf. 1996, 131–34; 1997.

130. AM 31.3.8, 4.5, 8. Jord. *Get.* 131–33 locates the resettlement in the provinces of Moesia, Thrace, and even Dacia Ripensis, confirming that the diocese and not just the province of Thrace was in question. Soz. 6.37.5–6 implies that it was Valens who chose Thrace for the Goths, but Ammianus is to be preferred. The Goths continued to request farmland in Thrace even after their revolt against the Romans (AM 31.12.8), and eventually they were in fact settled there, Them. *Or.* 16.209c–213a, 34.22; Zos. 4.34.5; cf. Heather 1991, 158–59; Cesa 1994, 36–45.

131. AM 30.2.6 reports that Valens planned to hire Tervingi soldiers as mercenaries. Cf. AM 31.4.1: "et daturos (si res flagitasset) auxilia," implying that there would be no standing units of Gothic auxiliaries.

132. For oaths, see Eunap. *Hist.* fr. 48.2 (Blockley). For hostages, see Eunap. *Hist.* fr. 42 (Blockley); Zos. 4.26.2. On the Gothic custom of oath-taking, see *Pass. S. Sabae* 3.4; AM 27.5.9, 31.7.10; Priscus fr. 49 (Blockley).

sessions and slaves with them, since these show up in their retinues after 376.[133] This indicates that they were to be settled as independent farmers, not sold off as slaves. Moreover, the agreement allowed the Romans to cross north of the Danube and help transport the Tervingi over on boats.[134] This should have eased the process of transfer, although it did not. At any rate, the settlement was anything but unilaterally dictated: the Goths were clearly given a voice in their future and were—at least by the terms of the agreement— to be treated with more dignity than mere battle captives or slaves.

Although Heather has done much to advance our understanding of the 376 agreement and of resettlement agreements in general, he has perhaps pushed too far in his case for pro-Gothic terms. He has argued, for example, that the Goths were to be resettled as *laeti*, semiautonomous barbarians relocated in large groups on freehold lands.[135] But the sources make it clear that the Goths were to be broken up and scattered across various "parts of Thrace," not relocated en masse.[136] Moreover, Heather has built a case that the Goths were not required to surrender their weapons on rather shaky ground. In the absence of solid evidence that they were allowed to keep their arms, he holds that a priori they would never have agreed to disarm on entering an empire with which they had a "long history of conflict." This is hardly conclusive, especially when Eunapius and Zosimus state explicitly that the Roman commanders *had* been ordered to disarm the Goths.[137] Here, Heather holds, the report is mistaken. After all, in typically moralizing fashion, Eunapius and Zosimus attribute the failure of this disarmament order to the avarice of the commanders Lupicinus and Maximus, who were more interested in acquiring slaves than disarming barbarians as they crossed the Danube. Ammianus, notes Heather, only mentions this sort of abuse in an incident he locates some time *after* the Goths had already crossed, a possible indication that Eunapius's and Zosimus's report is confused on this point and not to be trusted.[138] In the same passage, though, Ammianus insists that this incident was only one of many such occurrences.[139] Heather thus over-

133. AM 31.7.5, 7, 12.11; cf. Zos. 4.27.3. On Gothic wagons and wagon trains, see Wanke 1990, 152–57. Jord. *Get.* 135 mentions slaves and furniture, and Eunap. *Hist.* fr. 42 (Blockley) mentions slaves as well.

134. AM 31.4.5; Zos. 4.20.6; Eunap. *Hist.* fr. 42 (Blockley). Cf. the Roman supervision of the crossing of the Limigates in 359 (AM 19.11.8).

135. On Laeti, see Demougeot 1969.

136. AM 31.4.5: "partes Thraciae"; Soc. 4.34.3: τὰ μέρη τῆς θράκης; cf. Cesa 1994, 19–21, for further problems with Heather's interpretation.

137. Eunap. *Hist.* fr. 42 (Blockley): δεχθῆναι κελεύει τοὺς ἄνδρας τὰ ὅπλα καταθεμένους ... εἰ μὴ τὰ ὅπλα καταθέμενοι γυμνοὶ διαβαίνοιεν; Zos. 4.20.5–6: δέχεσθαι τούτους Οὐάλης ἐπέτρεπε πρότερον ἀποθεμένους τὰ ὅπλα.

138. Heather 1991, 124–25.

139. AM 31.4.10–11; cf. Chauvot 1998, 257–60.

interprets Ammianus's silence on earlier misbehavior. As positive evidence that the Goths were allowed to retain arms, Heather cites Ammianus's lament that they poured over the frontier in "columns of armed men spreading like the sparks of Etna." Here, however, Ammianus alludes to Vergil in a highly rhetorical aside that is clearly not meant to be taken as a comment on the terms of the agreement of 376.[140] In fact, Ammianus says nothing explicit at all on the terms of 376. His reticence is regrettable, but should not be given heuristic weight. Eunapius and Zosimus must be believed when they say that the Goths were required to disarm.

Even if we accept Ammianus's comment on the "columns of armed men" as relevant to the 376 agreement, it does not imply that the Goths were permitted by the agreement to keep their weapons: in fact, if many Tervingi did retain their arms, they did so despite the resettlement terms.[141] This was in part because of the corruption of the Roman command, as Eunapius and Zosimus hold. Above all, however, it would have stemmed from the logistics of searching thousands of refugees in the chaotic circumstances of the 376 crossing. The number of barbarians was so large that all manner of craft were used to transport them over the Danube, including hollowed-out logs, many of which capsized in the swollen river.[142] The disorder that ensued could easily have allowed many to reach Roman soil with their weapons in contravention of their agreement. Moreover, although the Romans could exert some control over the weaponry of the Tervingi, the Greuthungi, Taifali, Alans, and Huns—who crossed without Roman supervision before joining the Gothic band—were obviously able to bring weapons with total impunity. Ammianus's lament is thus appropriate, even though there was an order to disarm. Not surprisingly, later indications make it clear that the order had been at least somewhat effective. In the years after 376, the Goths were so short on arms that they needed to raid arms depots, reuse Roman projec-

---

140. AM 31.4.9; cf. Virg. *Aen.* 3.571–73, with Seyfarth 1968–71, 4: 360 n. 42.

141. Jer. *Chron.* s.a. 377 reports that the Goths crossed "sine armorum depositione." He is followed by Prosper *Chron.* 1161; Oros. 7.33.10; Isidore *Hist. Goth.* 9 (*MGH.AA* 11.271). This notice says nothing about the terms of the crossing agreement, only that the Goths did not in the end lay down their weapons. Even in 376, Alavivus and Fritigern retained bodyguards (AM 31.5.6), although we cannot be certain they were armed. Armed with *hastae* and *gladii*, the Goths overcame the guards posted to them at Marcianople in 376 (AM 31.5.5). In the battle of Ad Salices the following summer, they used traditional Gothic fire-hardened clubs (AM 31.7.12) as weapons, and in 378 they used axes (AM 31.13.3), also a traditional weapon (Wolfram 1988, 99–100; cf. Elton 1996b, 60–72). It is highly unlikely that these could have been manufactured while on the move; they are more likely to have been transported with the Tervingi in 376. On the failed disarmament order and its impact on Adrianople, see Thompson 1965, 119; Chrysos 1972, 129–30; Burns 1973, 336–37; Demougeot 1979, 2.1: 138–39; Cesa 1984, 72; Wolfram 1988, 121; Wanke 1990, 124; Nicasie 1998, 235–36 n. 184.

142. AM 31.4.5.

tiles, and plunder Roman casualties.[143] The disarmament order thus had some impact, although ultimately it did not prevent the assembly of a large band of armed barbarians on Roman soil. Heather is thus right to argue that many provisions of the agreement were favorable to the Goths. The treaty was not, however, as conciliatory as he has claimed: the Tervingi had agreed to the surrender of their arms and the division of their group for resettlement, but were given some say in the location of that resettlement and the terms of their service in the Roman army. Although they would be subject to the empire, they were to be treated with some degree of respect.

Heather's arguments on the terms of the agreement are part of a larger effort to explain the collapse of the Gothic settlement as a result of mutual distrust. Valens accepted the Goths because he was simply unable to prevent them from entering the empire, Heather argues.[144] Nevertheless, the emperor intended—or at least hoped—to force them into submission once they had crossed the Danube by restricting their food supply and depriving them of leaders. The Goths, however, were not as desperate as our sources imply, Heather contends. There was actually some time lag between the Hunnic invasion and the Gothic crossing of the Danube, during which the Goths were able to organize defenses and, when these failed, deliberate about their future course of action.[145] Moreover, Eunapius reports that, while still in their own territory, the Goths had entered into a secret pact to overthrow all Romans, a sign that they harbored plans to resist cooperation all along.[146] This would seem to be born out by Ammianus's notice that Fritigern deliberately slowed the march of his people to Marcianople to allow the Greuthungi time to catch up with them.[147] By Heather's reckoning, then, the Tervingi and Greuthungi were "two organized Gothic groups who had made a careful decision to move into imperial territory."[148]

Here again, Heather has advanced our understanding of the issues but

143. They plundered for arms twice in 376 (AM 31.5.9 and 31.6.3), and they were forced to recycle Roman projectiles at Adrianople (31.15.11). They raided the *fabrica* at Constantinople in 378 (AM 31.16.7) and attempted in 376 to raid Adrianople, where there was also a *fabrica* (AM 31.6.3). On *fabricae* in the Balkans, see Velkov 1983, 179.

144. Heather 1991, 130–35, esp. 132: "The new relationship with the Tervingi was forced upon Valens and there is no reason to assume that he wanted it." Cf. Williams and Friell 1994, 14–15.

145. Heather 1991, 135–42. Heather 1995, 5–10, revises the picture further, allowing "ten to twenty years" for the Hun invasions to work their effects, an exaggeration that cuts entirely against the grain of all our sources (see pp. 321–22). Much of Heather's revisionism is perhaps, I believe, based on a misunderstanding of Ammianus's idiom, particularly his use of the adverb *diu*, on which see Lenski 1999a, 314.

146. Eunap. *Hist.* fr. 59 (Blockley).

147. AM 31.5.4.

148. Heather 1991, 136.

has carried the argument too far. Valens certainly was under strong pressure from circumstances to accept the Tervingi: when the Goths came knocking, he was keeping a lid on Isauria with one hand and fending off Shapur with the other. But, as we have seen, this does not negate the fact that he had strong reasons to believe that he stood to benefit from the Gothic resettlement. Ammianus's note that he hoped to reinforce his army while increasing revenue from recruitment taxes is well supported by a variety of contemporary sources and should not be so lightly dismissed as mere propaganda.[149] So, too, the fact that the Goths were able to organize defenses against the Huns tells us nothing about their condition when they finally decided to beg for entry into the empire. Even granting that they were not as desperate as the sources imply, they hardly remained well organized and defiant. Moreover, Heather himself admits that Eunapius's note on the barbarian vow to destroy Rome is not a solid support for his case. Rather, it is a classic example of the anti-Gothic paranoia that permeates Eunapius's *Histories*, a *post eventum* conspiracy theory that tries to explain a foreign policy debacle as a pre-planned cabal.[150] The only indication to the contrary, Fritigern's coordination of his march to Marcianople with the Greuthungi, is also misapplied in this instance. According to Ammianus, Fritigern only began cooperating with the Greuthungi *after* crossing the Danube and *after* he had begun to experience the exploitation of the Roman commanders who were supposed to be helping his people.[151] This was no organized conspiracy but a natural reaction to a real and present threat.

Above all, Heather's argument falters because it does not take into account the fact that, while the Romans and the Tervingi must have been suspicious of one another, they at least initially had reasons for mutual trust. Here we must remember that Ammianus clearly says that Valens granted permission to cross only to the followers Fritigern and Alavivus. When Vitheric's Greuthungi requested asylum, they were flatly denied; Athanaric took this as a sign that his followers would also be rejected and returned to the Carpathians.[152] During the course of negotiations, Roman troops actually attacked a Gothic group that tried to force an early entry, and in the

---

149. Ibid., 131–35, esp.: "we can deduce in fact that Valens's reacted less positively to the Goths than the sources would have us believe."

150. Ibid., 139–40. Cf. Zos. 4.56.2 on the oath. Reports of such treacherous oaths became a commonplace in imperial propaganda (Claud. *Bell. Goth.* ll. 77–82, 518–31; *VI cons. Hon.* 300–309; Oros. 7.43.3–4). On the cliché of barbarian untrustworthiness more generally, see Wanke 1990, 131–32, with earlier bibliography.

151. *Pace* Heather 1991, 138, neither AM 27.5.6 nor 31.3.4 assert or even imply earlier cooperation between the Tervingi and Greuthungi. On the contrary, the latter says the opposite, that Athanaric kept his distance as his neighbors were being attacked.

152. AM 31.4.12–5.3. Indeed, archaeological evidence makes it clear that the majority of the Goths remained north of the Danube after 376 (Kazanski 1991b, 66–74).

early stages of the settlement, riparian reinforcements were stationed to prevent crossings by unauthorized bands.[153] The immigration was thus, at least in its conception, controlled and limited to a specified group, Alavivus's and Fritigern's Tervingi.

This was not accidental, for, as noted earlier, the Tervingi confederation had split in the years since 369, and Valens had reestablished contact with Fritigern and his followers.[154] He had offered Fritigern asylum when the Gothic *reiks* was first defeated by Athanaric and later supplied him with military aid to help Fritigern return and defeat Athanaric. In thanksgiving for Valens's aid, Fritigern had converted to Christianity and had insisted that his followers do the same.[155] The fact that Fritigern was already Christian probably played a role in Valens's decision to grant him the right to resettlement in 376. It is certainly true that Fritigern used Christian intermediaries in subsequent negotiations, a sign of his awareness of the power of this link.[156]

There may even be evidence that Valens had resumed the payment of tribute to this group of Tervingi. Some of the largest gold medallions extant in the world—the biggest weighing a pound—were minted by Valens between 370 and 378 and shipped into Gothia (fig. 17).[157] Although the originals do not survive, barbarian copies have turned up in what was at the time Tervingi territory at Simleul Silvaniei.[158] If, as Themistius indicates and the coin finds confirm, Valens strictly implemented his no-tribute policy against the Goths after 369, it seems odd that these prize pieces—clearly not simple trade goods—should have found their way across the Danube. Their presence in Gothic territory becomes easier to explain, however, if Valens reestablished diplomatic contact with at least some of the Tervingi after 369. Although it

153. Eunap. *Hist.* fr. 42 (Blockley); AM 31.5.3.

154. See pp. 320–21.

155. Soc. 4.33.1–4; Oros. 7.33.19; cf. Soz. 6.37.7; Joh. Ant. fr. 184.2; Theod. *HE* 4.37.1–2; Jord. *Get.* 131–32. Basil *Ep.* 155 (a. 373) implies that the *dux Scythiae* Junius Soranus was involved in the military operations; cf. Lenski 1995a, 85.

156. See Eunap. *Hist.* fr. 48.2 (Blockley) with Lenski 1995a, 70–71, 81–86; Chrysos 1972, 126. On the use of Christian ambassadors, see AM 31.12.8–9, 15.6, with Lenski 1995a, 85–86.

157. In the period when these medallions were produced, gold and silver was only minted in the presence of the imperial *comitatus* (see pp. 301–302). Because all of the examplars in question bear a mint mark of A-N (Antioch), they can only have been minted between 370 and 378, when Valens's *comitatus* was present in that city. Valens would have had direct control over their production and eventual distribution.

158. The medallions in question, Gnecchi 1.36.9 pl. 17.1 = *RIC* 9.282.38 and Gnecchi 1.36.8 pl. 16.1 = *RIC* 9.282.37, have been republished recently, with the remainder of the Simleul Silvanei (Szílagy Sómlyo) hoard, in Harhoiu 1993; cf. 1997, 73–89. The similar medallic copy of unknown provenance with reverse legend RESIS *[sic]* ROMANORUM and mint mark A-N at Dressel 1973, 265, pl. 29, is commonly taken to have been from the same hoard; cf. Harhoiu 1993, 228–29.

Figure 17. Nimbate emperor approaches turreted female (Antioch?). Medallion of Antioch. *RIC* 9.282.37. Courtesy Kunsthistorisches Museum, Vienna.

can only remain speculation, it is certainly possible that Fritigern or his followers were the original recipients. If so, they were treated quite favorably, indeed, well before they chose to enter the empire.

The 376 agreement was not, then, doomed from its inception by the hidden agendas and concealed animosity of its negotiators. On the contrary, it represented the continuation of an alliance between two parties who had benefited each other in the past and hoped to continue to do so in the future. Why, then, did the agreement so dramatically collapse? The answer, I would contend, lies in the way the resettlement was carried out. As stated unanimously in the sources, the abuses perpetrated on the Gothic settlers by the Roman riparian units charged with their resettlement led to a rebellion, which exploded out of control. To be sure, such brutal techniques were quite commonly used to resettle barbarians and had often proved effective in pacifying smaller groups. In the instance of 376, however, when too few Romans were attempting to coerce far too many barbarians into submission, these same techniques backfired.

Orderly relocations of non-Romans within Roman territory had been engineered since the early empire. Such settlements had been common be-

ginning in the time of Augustus and continued with increasing frequency into the later empire. We know of four along the Danube in the first two centuries A.D. and another eleven between A.D. 250 and 376.[159] We have seen that Valens himself had organized the settlement of a small group of 3,000 Tervingi in Thrace in 365/66, and Gratian's general Frigeridus effected a similar arrangement in the midst of the conflicts in 377 by transferring a group of Greuthungi and Taifali to lands in northern Italy.[160] Ultimately, even the main body of rebellious Goths was "settled" on Roman territory by the terms of the treaty of 382, although their arrangement was up to that time unique in the degree of autonomy granted to the barbarians.[161] Barbarian settlements were thus commonplace. Moreover, most were touted in imperial propaganda for precisely the reasons Valens used to promote his own agreement: they simultaneously provided agricultural laborers, increased tribute, and intro-

159. The most complete list of barbarian settlements can be found at De Ste. Croix 1981, app. 3.509–518. The Danube settlements are listed at 3, 5a, 5b, 8, 10, 11, 12, 13, 14a.iv, b, c?, 15, 16a, c, 19a. For details on the archaeology of barbarian settlements along the Danube, see Mócsy 1974, 53–79.
160. Zos. 4.10.1–2; Eunap. *Hist.* fr. 37 (Blockley); AM 31.9.3–4.
161. Heather 1991, 158–65; cf. Errington 1996b, 15–22.

duced new military manpower.[162] When Constantius II considered whether to allow the Limigantes to relocate in Illyricum in 359, for example, his advisers encouraged the transfer, arguing that "[n]ow that foreign troubles were quieted and peace made everywhere, he would gain more child-producing subjects to be able to muster a strong force of recruits; for the provincials are glad to contribute gold to save their bodies."[163] All of this should caution against assumptions that Valens faced the circumstances of 376 with reluctance or trepidation. He was doing something quite normal for the period— indeed, something he had already done previously, if on a much smaller scale.

It was also normal for troubles to arise during the process of resettlement. Constantius's attempt to resettle the Limigantes, for example, eventually exploded into chaos. The similarities between this incident and the troubles in 376 are marked and thus call for a brief examination. The Limigantes appealed to riparian authorities and were permitted to cross the Danube under the supervision of Roman troops. The Romans established a stockade near Acimincum to receive the barbarians, and Constantius was himself present to deliver an address to the refugees. During his speech, the Limigantes were heard uttering their war cry, and Ammianus reports that they set upon Constantius. Roman troops had been posted at the rear of the stockade in case anything like this happened, and these quickly descended on the Limigantes and slaughtered them indiscriminately.[164] The incident shows both the degree of tension that prevailed in the early stages of resettlements and the readiness of the Romans to annihilate refugees if trouble arose.

Because it is reported by Ammianus with uniquely developed detail, Constantius's run-in with the Limigantes seems striking. The evidence indicates, however, that both in the immediate aftermath of submission and in places and periods at some remove, uprisings were common among peoples undergoing enforced Romanization. In the first century A.D., these occurred regularly when Rome imposed provincial authority on peoples still living within their native territory.[165] As imperial boundaries became more defined, the problems shifted from subduing and reforming native groups on their own land to transferring them within Romanized territories, which was equally prone to difficulties. In A.D. 171, for example, some Quadi settled in Italy by Marcus Aurelius broke into revolt and seized the city of Ra-

---

162. E.g. *CIL* 14.3608 = *ILS* 986; *CIL* 10.6225 = *ILS* 985; *Pan. Lat.* 6 [7].6.2, 8 [5].8.4–9.4, with Nixon and Rodgers 1994, 121–22 nn. 28–9; Eus. *Vit. Const.* 4.6; Lib. *Or.* 59.85; Them. *Or.* 16.211d–212a, 34.22; SHA *Prob.* 15.1–6; AM 28.5.15; Soz. 9.5.4.

163. AM 19.11.7. On the drafting of settlers into the military, see Elton 1996b, 129–34.

164. AM 19.11.1–16; cf. Seager 1999, 583–87.

165. E.g., Strabo 7.1.4 (291–92); Vell. Pat. 2.118–19; Dio Cass. 56.19–22, 62.1–12; cf. Tac. *Ann.* 1.60, 3.40–46, 14.31–37; *Hist.* 4.13–14; *Agr.* 16.1–2. On native revolts in the early empire, see esp. Dyson 1971; 1975; Isaac 1990, 59–60; Elton 1996a, 44–57; Mattern 1999, 101–6; Wells 1999, 187–223.

venna.[166] A group of Franks settled in the empire under Probus revolted, seized some ships, and embarked on a piratical tour of the Mediterranean, which eventually ended beyond the straits of Gibraltar.[167] In the fourth century, aside from the eruptions of 359 and 376, we know of two other instances where non-Roman groups transferred to Roman territory rose in revolt. After one of his Gothic wars, Constantine resettled a group of Taifali in Phrygia, who rebelled, obliging the emperor to dispatch three military units to quash them.[168] In 399, a group of Goths also settled in Phrygia broke into revolt under their leader Tribigild and ravaged much of central Anatolia. Zosimus informs us that all the barbarians in the region flocked to Tribigild's forces rather than defending their new Roman neighbors.[169] Troubles were thus hardly unusual among barbarians undergoing forced resettlement and reorganization in Roman territory.

By Valens's day, however, the Roman authorities were well practiced at these relocations and applied techniques that generally succeeded in diffusing threats: they demanded hostages,[170] directly recruited able-bodied men into military service, separated leaders from their peoples or killed them,[171] transported the peoples a safe distance from their homelands,[172] and split them into smaller groups to effect the disintegration of tribal structures.[173] All of these techniques were used in varying degrees in 376. All of them also required the exertion of force and must have provoked tension and resentment when they were introduced. Indeed, despite their general effectiveness in diffusing the threat of large-scale revolt, these resettlement techniques could easily have provoked the troubles they were designed to prevent.

Given what we know about the harsh treatment of non-Roman groups by the late Roman military, it should come as no surprise that such groups often rebelled. Indeed, it would have been easy for peoples undergoing resettlement to sense that they were only one step away from extermination. The Romans always regarded barbarians as expendable and never hesitated to seize opportunities to eliminate them, as when Constantius's men exterminated

---

166. Dio Cass. 71.11.5.

167. *Pan. Lat.* 8 [5].18.3; Zos. 1.71.2; cf. SHA *Prob.* 18.2–3.

168. Symeon Metaphrastes *Vita S. Nicolai* 17, 20 (*PG* 116.337, 341), with Zos. 2.31.3; cf. Thompson 1965, 11.

169. Zos. 5.13.2–4, 14.5–18.9. Further sources at *PLRE* II, Tribigildus; cf. Liebeschuetz 1990, 100–103; Cameron and Long 1993, 223–33. Priscus fr. 5 (Blockley) may record the collapse of yet another settlement in Thrace in the late 430s; cf. Blockley 1981–83, 1: 380 n. 8.

170. See p. 342.

171. See p. 328.

172. Ca. 170: Dio Cass. 51.11.4–5; ca. 170: SHA *Marc.* 22.2; a. 276: SHA *Prob.* 14.7; Zos. 1.68.3; ca. 293: *Pan. Lat.* 8 [5].9.1, 21.1; a. 334: Eus. *Vit. Const.* 4.6; Anon. Vales. 6 [32]; cf. AM 17.12.19; a. 358: AM 19.11.5–6; Aus. *Mos.* ll. 8–9; a. 370: AM 28.5.15; a. 376: Zos. 4.26.3; a. 377: AM 31.9.3–4; a. 409: Soz. 9.5.6; Zos. 4.26.3; *CTh* 5.6.3.

173. SHA *Prob.* 14.7; *CTh* 5.6.3.

the Limigantes in 359. In 370, Valentinian's *magister peditum*, Severus, violated a safe-passage agreement he had made with a group of Saxons and annihilated them. Ammianus regarded the device as "insidious but useful."[174] In 386, another safe passage agreement was being negotiated with some Greuthungi who wished to cross the Danube as settlers when the *magister equitum* Promotus set a trap for them. He sent spies to encourage the barbarians to attempt a clandestine night crossing and, when the Greuthungi took the bait, he killed them all. Theodosius later celebrated the treacherous plot with a triumph in Constantinople.[175] Roman military authorities thus had no qualms about reneging on diplomatic agreements or shifting into extermination mode in the early stages of relocation. This must have been evident to the settlers and would surely have increased the sort of tensions that could lead to rebellion.

Nor could barbarian groups expect an end to mistreatment once they had begun to be integrated into Roman state structures. In the mid 380s, the local Roman commander at Tomi ambushed a group of Gothic troops garrisoned outside his city and exterminated all but a few who took refuge in a church.[176] Another clash occurred when Theodosius attempted to effect an exchange between a group of trans-Danubians with some Egyptian troops. The Egyptians crossed paths with the barbarians in Lydian Philadelphia, and, when a row broke out, they stabbed or drowned over two hundred of the foreigners in the sewers.[177] Finally, some of the Goths who had been received in 376 and transferred to the eastern frontier as junior troops *(adcrescentes)* attracted attention when they began agitating after learning of the fate of their families back in Thrace. In early 379, the *magister militum per Orientem* Julius cool-headedly ordered these to assemble in certain cities, where he promised to deliver their pay. When the Goths came as called, the Romans waited for a fixed day and then massacred the barbarians to a man.[178] Barbarian groups were thus constantly confronted with hostility and often remained only a hair's breadth from outright annihilation.

Hostility came not only from imperial authorities but from all native Ro-

---

174. AM 28.5.5–7; cf. 17.8.4, 30.7.8.

175. Zos. 4.35.1, 38.1–39.5; *Cons. Const.* s.a. 386; Hyd. *Chron.* s.a. 385; Claud. *IV cons. Hon.* ll. 619–37; possibly referred to at Lib. *Or.* 19.16. On Theodosius's triumph, see McCormick 1986, 42–43.

176. Zos. 4.40.1–8, with Paschoud 2.2: 430 n. 180–181; cf. Schmitt 1997.

177. Zos. 4.30.1–5. Seeck, *Untergang*, 128, with 482–83, suggested that these troop transfers might be the source of the Egyptian units mentioned in Thrace/Illyricum and Thracian/Danubian units in Egypt found in the *Notitia dignitatum;* cf. Remondon 1955, 29–32. Contrast Hoffmann 1969–70, 1: 226–36; Errington 1996b, 6 n. 33.

178. Zos. 4.26.1–27.1; AM 31.16.8. Paschoud's 2.2: 388 n. 154 criticism of Zosimus has been overturned by Zuckerman 1991a, 479–86, who shows that much of Zosimus's information is confirmed at Greg. Nys. *Adversus eos qui baptismum differunt* (*GNO* 10.3: 364–65); *Vita Theodori* (*GNO* 10.1: 70). See also Elbern 1987 and Speidel 1998.

mans who had contact with the foreigners. The assault of the Adrianopolitans on the Gothic auxiliary troops of Sueridas and Colias offers a perfect case in point. It had taken very little provocation from the barbarians to bring on the wrath of the massed local citizenry.[179] Under Theodosius, a Goth was singled out, lynched, and tossed into the sea by the angry citizens of Constantinople.[180] The German general Butheric was killed in Thessalonica during a stadium riot in 390.[181] And in 400, the Goths living in Constantinople were attacked by the citizenry and 7,000 of them were burned alive in a church.[182] Popular violence against barbarians inside Roman territory was thus commonplace.

For this reason, we should hesitate to dismiss the significance of the violence and abuse reported in our sources for the settlement of 376. Even though Valens and Fritigern had reasons to hope for mutual benefits, the coercion so common in resettlement situations and the nervousness of the barbarians in the face of open hostility undermined any chances for success. Part of this was systematic: the Romans regularly mangled barbarian social and family structures to facilitate relocation and, when the slightest problem arose, regularly exterminated the refugee groups they had planned to relocate. Part of the violence was also endemic, rooted in a Roman discomfort about the presence of non-Romans in their territories. Thus tensions remained even after peoples had been relocated, leading to open attacks against barbarian groups and individuals. When the Tervingi suffered repression at the hands of Lupicinus and Maximus in 376, they were experiencing what all barbarian settlers must have encountered in varying degrees. Whether Valens had actually ordered his generals to treat the Tervingi as they did or the generals were acting on their own instincts, we cannot know.[183] Clearly, however, the techniques of repression that both they—and Valens—would have regarded as acceptable played a major role in provoking the Gothic rebellion.

Even so, the troubles need not have mushroomed into the disaster they did had the number of barbarians involved not been so great. Here again, Constantius's extermination of the Limigantes in 359 offers a good case for

179. See p. 329.

180. On Antioch and Constantinople, see Lib. *Or.* 19.22, 20.14; cf. Heather 1991, 181–88, on tension in the years after the settlement of 382.

181. Soz. 7.25.3; Ruf. *HE* 11.18; Theod. *HE* 5.17.1.

182. Syn. *De prov.* 2.1–3; Soc. 6.6.18–29; Soz. 8.4.6–17; Theod. *HE* 5.30.32–3; Zos. 5.18.10–19.5; Philostorg. 11.8; Marcellin. *Chron.* s.a. 399; Joh. Ant. fr. 190; cf. Cameron and Long 1993, 199–223.

183. Eunap. *Hist.* fr. 42 (Blockley) claims that Valens actually prosecuted some of his riparian commanders for attacking a group of overly anxious barbarians during the negotiations of 376. This would imply that Valens would have called a halt to the misbehavior of his troops had he been present. In several instances, we learn of late Roman emperors attempting to dampen their troops' zealousness to kill or despoil barbarians; see AM 18.2.7, 27.2.9, 29.4.5–6; Zos. 4.40.4–6; Eunap. *Hist.* fr. 18.1 (Blockley); Symm. *Or.* 2.10–11.

comparison. As stressed above, Valens believed he could control the Gothic migration by limiting permission to cross to a group with whose leader he had already established ties. When the repression these Tervingi faced provoked revolt, Valens and his men might still have hoped to control or exterminate them had the group they faced been limited only to Fritigern's Tervingi. In the event, they had not taken account of the gravity of the situation provoked by the Huns north of the Danube. Even while his mobile army was tied up on an eastern frontier rife with its own problems, Valens entrusted his limited riparian forces in Thrace with a task they were in no way capable of handling. The flood of barbarians that poured in after the Tervingi broke into rebellion swelled the original group with Greuthungi, Alans, Huns, and Taifali. This was a horde like none the empire had seen since the third century, and Valens's stopgap efforts to combat it in 376 and 377 only exacerbated the situation by robbing him of the men he lost in these unsuccessful preliminary engagements. By the time Valens himself came onto the scene, the problem had grown from a rebellion among a limited group of settlers into a full-scale invasion by a gargantuan, multiethnic horde. The problem was thus above all one of numbers. Valens might have contained Fritigern's Tervingi alone, but he could never hope to control the masses that coalesced around them.

In light of this, it is natural to wonder precisely how many barbarians there were. Ammianus relates that the Tervingi crossing took several days and nights to complete, and that the officials charged with reckoning the numbers gave up in despair. He, too, despairs of precision, saying that to make such an estimate would be like reckoning the sands of Libya.[184] The only historian bold enough to specify a figure, Eunapius, claims that the barbarians who fled to the Danube numbered almost 200,000 a figure that has often been dismissed as artificially inflated.[185] This may, however, be unfair, especially if the number is taken as an indication of the total who eventually crossed, rather than the number of Tervingi alone. Previous Roman settlements tended to be relatively small, generally under 10,000, where figures are given.[186] However, there exist claims for relocations involving 50,000

184. AM 31.4.5–6; cf. 31.7.2, 31.8.9; *Vita Isaaci* 5 (*Acta sanctorum* Maii 7: 602): ἀπείρῳ πλήθει.

185. Eunap. *Hist.* fr. 42 (Blockley). The part of Eunapius's text relating to the number of Goths (Blockley 1981–83, 2: 60, ll. 4–5) is not secure; it may either convey the total number of barbarians or the total number of barbarian warriors. Based on the latter reading, Schmidt 1934, 403, rightly regards Eunapius's estimate as impossible, although his own estimate of 18,000 warriors is surely too low. Similarly low figures are manufactured at Paschoud 2.2: 375 n. 143; Austin 1972a, 83; Heather 1991, 139 n. 44; Nicasie 1998, 244–45. Eunapius's figure is taken to represent the total number of barbarians and thus accepted at Nagl, "Val.," 2119; A. H. M. Jones 1964, 195; Burns 1973, 337.

186. Dio Cass. 71.21 (3,000 Naristae); *AE* 1920, 45 (12,000 Dacians); Herodian 6.4.6 (400 Persians); AM 17.8.3–4; Lib. *Or.* 18.75, 15.32 (1,000 Franks); Zos. 4.10.1 with AM 26.10.3 (3,000 Tervingi).

"Getae," 100,000 "Transdanuviani," the same number of Bastarnae, and as many as 300,000 Sarmatians and the same number of Naristae.[187] It would not be unthinkable that the Tervingi numbered 80,000 men, women, and children, including 15,000–20,000 men of fighting age. If we add to these an equal number of Greuthungi and a smaller mix of Taifali, Alans, and Huns (ca. 20,000–30,000), we could easily arrive at "almost 200,000." Caesar reckoned that 368,000 Helvetii attempted to migrate into Aquitania in 58 B.C.[188] A group totaling 200,000 men, women, and children is thus hardly unthinkable, and would have been able to muster an army of 40,000 to 50,000 warriors, a bit larger than the Roman force they defeated at Adrianople.[189] This "Gothic band" was able to sustain tremendous losses in the seven years of continuous engagements and punishing migrations they endured between 376 and 382 and still retain a sufficient fighting force to win deep concessions from Theodosius. To do so, they must have been very numerous to start with, so the figure of 200,000 is not beyond reason.

THE REASONS FOR THE DISASTER AT ADRIANOPLE

Untangling the roots of a military disaster as complex as Adrianople is no easy task. Its causes could be attributed to a host of factors, including weather conditions, miscalculations of relative strength, improper training, strategic errors preceding the battle, and tactical errors. No account could completely reconstruct a single causal chain that would satisfactorily explain the interplay of all these elements, but any history that hopes to fill out the bare bones of narrative must grapple with causality. It is thus necessary to examine the battle of Adrianople with an eye to the factors that may have contributed to its catastrophic outcome.

The most obvious causes of the Roman defeat are, of course, the tactical and strategic errors made in the days and hours before the battle itself. Valens chose not to await the arrival of eastern reinforcements; he acted on insufficient information about the strength of the Gothic force; he chose to march his troops some seventeen kilometers east of his base on a hot August

187. On the Getae, see Strabo 303 (pre A.D. 4). On Transdanubiani, see *CIL* 14.3608 = *ILS* 986 (A.D. 60/67). On Bastarnae, see SHA *Prob.* 18.1 (A.D. 276/80). On Sarmatians, see *Exc. Val.* 6 [32] (A.D. 334). On Naristae, see Dio Cass. 72.21 (A.D. 180). Cf. 40,000 Suevi and Sugambri at Suet. *Aug.* 21.1; *Tib.* 9.2; Eutr. 7.9; Oros. 6.21.24.

188. Caes. *BG* 1.29.

189. On Valens's forces, see p. 339. Williams and Friell (1994, 178–79) argue at length for 20–25,000 barbarian warriors, but their figures are based on common sense rather than the sources. The Alamannic confederation was able to muster 35,000 warriors at Strasbourg in 357 (AM 16.12.26), Gratian faced 40,000 Lentienses in 378 (AM 31.10.5), and Constantius I is said to have defeated as many as 60,000 Alamanni in 298 (Eutr. 9.23; cf. *Pan. Lat.* 6 [7].6.3 with Nixon and Rodgers 1994, 225 n. 25).

day, but, once in range, delayed the engagement to carry on negotiations while his men languished; his own units seem to have brought on an unwelcome battle when they broke a truce; and, when the Greuthungi horsemen unexpectedly arrived early in the conflict, his cavalry fled, leaving the unprotected infantry to be surrounded. All of these elements combined with deadly effect on August 9.[190]

Nevertheless, the story stretches back much earlier. Valens waited a full year after the outbreak of the initial revolt to come west. Ammianus believed this was too long, and other sources confirm that Valens came late and under compulsion.[191] We have already seen the reasons for this in chapter 4. Valens had faced a crisis in Isauria in 375, another with the Arabs from late 377 on, and a much larger conflict with the Sassanians at the same time. The Goths, whom he had hoped would help him diffuse some of these crises, instead added a fourth complication, which stretched Valens's capacities beyond their limits. Valens's presence, or at least the presence of large numbers of troops, was needed in four places at once. To deal with the new problem, Valens was forced to remove garrisons from Isauria, settle a truce with Persia and the Arabs, withdraw his forces in the east, and petition Gratian to send reinforcements from the west.

This last request was filled only with the greatest reluctance. In 377, Gratian sent men from Gaul under the command of Richomer, and from Illyricum under the *comes* Frigeridus. The number of units—Ammianus calls them *cohortes aliquas*—cannot have been great (perhaps 6,000 men), and the Gallic units Gratian sent were apparently of the worst quality.[192] On the way to Moesia and Scythia, Frigeridus decided not to participate in the operation, feigned an illness, and turned back.[193] Richomer continued on and met with Valens's men at Ad Salices, but his reinforcements were not sufficient to tip the scales in favor of the Romans. Once he had seen the power of the Goths, though, Richomer became aware of the threat they posed and hastened back to Gratian to request further reinforcements immediately.[194] Again Frigeridus was sent east in 378, only to withdraw to Illyricum. Later that year, rather than joining Valens's forces for the conflict at Adrianople, he remained at the Succi pass protecting the road west until he was relieved

190. Wanke 1990, 199–206, summarizes the various arguments on the proximate causes of the disaster. Writing under Theodosius, Vegetius seems to have understood most of these problems and cautioned against them in future engagements; see 3.3, 9, 10, 11, 14, 26, with Lenski 1997, 148.

191. AM 31.11.1: "Valens tandem excitus Antiochia"; Jer. *Chron.* s.a. 378: "Valens de Antiochia exire compulsus"; Prosper *Chron.* 1164; Soc. 4.38.3: μὴ ἀντεπεξῆγεν εὐθύς, ἀλλὰ παρεῖλκεν τὸν πρὸς τοὺς βαρβάρους πόλεμον.

192. AM 31.7.4; cf. Hoffmann 1969–70, 1: 471–76, on the numbers.

193. AM 31.7.5.

194. AM 31.8.2.

of duty—apparently because of his lackluster performance.[195] The aid offered by Gratian was thus far from satisfactory.

Zosimus tells us that both Gratian and Valentinian II were reluctant to send troops because they did not regard the Danube crisis as pertinent to their own realms.[196] This insouciance was marked by at least two western generals. Richomer lobbied vigorously for more support, as did Sebastianus, to whom Valens eventually entrusted the command of his infantry. Sebastianus had arrived in the east in the summer of 378 from the court of Valentinian II, whom he had been forced to petition for leave to aid Valens. Valens received him willingly, not just because of his military abilities, but probably also because he had chosen to stand up to the western emperors.[197]

Indeed, Valens was never comfortable with the dynastic shifts that had taken place on the death of his brother in November 375. The imperial *comitatus* in Brigetio had appointed Valentinian's four-year-old son Valentinian II full co-Augustus and then presented his election to Gratian and Valens as a fait accompli.[198] Socrates and Sozomen report that neither emperor was happy with the election, and Philostorgius even indicates that Gratian punished some of those responsible for engineering it.[199] Valens's annoyance would have been compounded by the fact that Valentinian II quickly became a virtual puppet of his half-brother. Valens had willingly submitted himself to the seniority of his own brother for nearly ten years. In an inscription from the Chersonese, he actually spells out his inferior position explicitly by calling himself "the brother of Valentinian, Greatest in all things."[200] He always remained less comfortable, however, with the equal status accorded to Gratian in 367 and with the introduction of a second nephew as Augustus in 375. In the inscription just mentioned, Valens distinguished Gratian with a title signifying inferiority, "the Nephew of Valens" (NEPOTI VALENTI[S]).

195. AM 31.9.1–4, 10.21–22.
196. Zos. 4.22.4.
197. Zos. 4.22.4; AM 31.11.1, where the subject of *petierat* in the ablative absolute clause, "Sebastiano paulo ante ab Italia (ut petierat) misso," must be Sebastianus. Sebastianus's discomfort with Valentinian II's court stretched back to the young prince's accession; see AM 30.10.2–3. Indeed, Errington 1996a, 441–43, argues that he was promptly cashiered by Valentinian's court in 375.
198. On Valentinian II's accession, see sources at *PLRE* I, Flavius Valentinianus 8; cf. Straub 1939, 18–20, and esp. McLynn 1994, 84–85. On Valentinian's age in 375, see p. 91 n. 144.
199. Soc. 4.31.8; cf. Soz. 6.36.5; Philostorg. 9.16; cf. Zon. 13.17. AM 30.10.6 reports that people expected Gratian to be angry at his brother's election, but he was not. This can probably be explained by the fact that Ammianus wrote when the Valentinianic dynasty was still in existence and thus needed to downplay any infighting; cf. Straub 1939, 19, with 220 n. 122. Errington 1996a, 440–47 paints a much seamier picture of tension and intrigue in the wake of the election.
200. *AE* 1908, 178 Va]LENTEM̄ FRATRE [m̄ Valentiniani omnia] MAXIMI; cf. Alföldy 1984 = *AE* 1984, 804.

This ongoing squabble over Gratian's—and Valentinian II's—position is quite evident in the coinage. J. W. E. Pearce showed that Valens deliberately limited the circulation of bronze types in the eastern empire after the accession of Gratian to protest the appointment of the new Augustus.[201] After Valentinian I's death, Valens became more open with his claims to superiority over his young nephews in the coinage. One medallic reverse features Valens standing between the boys, distinguished from both by his height and by a *nimbus* to indicate elevated status (fig. 18).[202] A number of coins and multiples from the period also bear the obverse legend DN VALENS MAX(imus) AVGVSTVS (figs. 19–20), recalling the title *Maximus Augustus* used earlier by Valentinian.[203] Constantine had also employed *Maximus* to distinguish himself from his sons, a telling analogy for Valens's presumed claim to paternalistic authority over his nephews.[204] A pictorial representation of Valens as *Maximus* can be found in a consular solidus type minted at Antioch in 376 or 378, which shows Valens dwarfing his nephew and consular colleague Valentinian II (fig. 21); another consular solidus actually omits Valentinian II altogether.[205] Valens was thus at pains to represent his claims to rank first in the imperial college.

Gratian was probably less willing to concede them. His reluctance was no doubt conditioned by his awareness that there was more at stake than mere titulary niceties. At issue was control of a significant portion of the empire. Although Valentinian II was appointed co-Augustus with theoretically equal powers to Gratian and Valens, the four-year-old was hardly capable of ruling his share of the empire. For this reason, both he and the territory of Italy, Africa, and Illyricum, which he nominally controlled, actually fell under the regency of Gratian and his court.[206] Thus when Philostorgius tells us that

---

201. *RIC* 9.xviii; 264–65.

202. Gnecchi 1.37.11, pl. 16.3; Gnecchi 1.37.11, pl. 8.2 = *RIC* 9.178 (Thessalonica 28). On the nimbus, see Bastien 1992, 179, who holds that here it distinguished Valens as *primus Augustus*. On the subject of Valens's claims to superiority as represented in the coinage, see Stein 1959, 514 n. 146; Barbieri 1980, 533–34. For similar iconography, cf. Grierson and Mays 1992, nos. 370–73.

203. Gnecchi 1.36.1, pl. 15.1 = *RIC* 9.122.25; Gnecchi 1.36.1; Gnecchi 1.36.6, pl. 16.2; Gnecchi 1.36.6, pl. 17.2 = *RIC* 9.122 (Rome 26). Bastien 1988, 97–98, dates these pieces to Gratian's decennalian donative of 376.

204. On the title *Maximus Augustus*, see Pabst 1986, 74–82. Pabst, 339 n. 553, holds that the Roman exemplars listed do not represent claims to superior authority since Valentinian, Valens, and Gratian had already shared the titles *Victores Maximi* and *Principes Maximi* before 375 (*CIL* 3.7494 = *ILS* 770, *CIL* 3.3653 = *ILS* 775, *CIL* 6.1176 = *ILS* 772). However, these titles do not carry the same implications as *Maximus Augustus*, and, more important, Pabst fails to notice the representations on the medallions cited and the solidus types listed.

205. On Valens dwarfing Valentinian II, see Lacam 1990, 237. For Valens alone in consular dress, see Cohen 1862, 413 n. 25 (not in *RIC* 9); cf. Delbrueck 1933, pl. 13 n. 4.

206. On the territory partitioned to Valentinian II, see Zos. 4.19.2, 42.1–2, with Paschoud 2.2: 370 n. 140; cf. Stein 1959, 183–84; Fortina 1953, 116–18 n. 42. Piganiol 1972, 223–24,

Figure 18. Large Valens between smaller Gratian and Valentinian II. Medallion of Thessalonica. *RIC* 9.178.28. Courtesy Kunsthistorisches Museum, Vienna.

Gratian played the role of a "father" to his half-brother, he speaks not so much of brotherly love as of official control.[207] Gratian, for example, clearly controlled his brother's prefecture of Illyricum, since he offered it to the grandfather and nephew of his tutor Ausonius.[208] Valens appealed to Gratian, not Valentinian II, for military aid in 377, and Gratian responded by dispatching the *comes per Illyricum*—Valentinian II's general. No laws are extant for Valentinian II while he was in Sirmium, and his coins generally bore only the unbroken legend of a junior Augustus and were often distinguished with the title IVN(ior).[209] The same title also appeared in consular datings on official documents and inscriptions.[210] Valentinian II was thus hardly an equal partner.

cf. Grumel 1951, 7–9, believes that Valentinian II was given only Illyricum and not Italy and Africa, but this contradicts our only evidence for the partition in Zosimus. Palanque 1944, 59–60, denies the partition altogether.

207. Philostorg. 9.16; cf. Zon. 13.17; Aus. XXI *Grat. act.* 2 [7]: "instar filii ad imperium frater ascitus." On Gratian's control over Valentinian II, see Seeck, *Untergang*, 39–40; Straub 1939, 68; Ensslin 1948, 2207–8; Grumel 1951, 7–8; Fortina 1953, 38–39; Pabst 1986, 97–99; Errington 1996a, 441–43.

208. *PLRE* I, Julius Ausonius 5; cf. Q.Clodius Hermogenianus Olybrius.

209. *RIC* 9.xxxviii–xxxix. Only the mints of Aquileia and Rome give Valentinian II both unbroken and broken legends, *RIC* 9.96–97, 122–3. On "*Iunior*" status, see pp. 32–33.

210. Full references at Bagnall et al. 1987, 286–87, 290–91.

Figure 19. DN VALENS MAX(imus) AVGVSTVS rides a six-horse chariot. Medallion of Rome. *RIC* 9.122.25. Courtesy Kunsthistorisches Museum, Vienna.

Themistius tacitly confirms that the empire was essentially controlled by two and not three emperors. His oration 13, delivered to Gratian in early 376, assumes that Valens and Gratian were co-rulers without mentioning their third colleague. Themistius refers to Valens and Gratian in the dual, speaks of his love for the *two* emperors, and flatters Gratian with the boast that he ruled all the world in conjunction only with his uncle.[211] On Valens's death, it was Gratian and not Valentinian II who chose Theodosius as

---

211. Them. *Or.* 13.167c, 169b, 177b–c, 179c. On the date of Them. *Or.* 13, see Dagron 1968, 22–23, 197. Errington 2000, 889–93, has advanced an enticing argument that Themistius delivered *Or.* 13 in Trier at the request of Valens, who wished to set up some sort of meeting with Gratian in Rome to settle their division of the empire. Although the evidence is scanty, the argument corresponds well with the scenario I portray here—the frustrated uncle trying to assert authority over his upstart nephew. Once Theodosius was proclaimed, Them. *Or.* 15.194d,

co-Augustus,[212] and it was Gratian who ceded control of the Illyrian dioceses of Dacia and Macedonia—theoretically part of Valentinian's territory—
to Theodosius.[213] At just sixteen years old, then, Gratian was effective master of two-thirds of the empire, just as his father had been. Valens, who was
after all the Senior Augustus, must have found this imbalance irritating.

Gratian's decision to transfer control of the Illyrian dioceses to Theodosius shows quite clearly that Gratian recognized the strategic importance of
a consolidated Danube frontier for defensive and offensive purposes. Valens
would no doubt have loved to control this area himself. Indeed, it probably

196d, 198b still assumes only two Augusti; cf. *Pan. Lat.* 2 [12].45.3. Symmachus also appears
to ignore the authority of Valentinian II, *Ep.* 1.13 (a. 376).

212. For recent debate on Theodosius's election, see Errington 1996a; Sivan 1996.

213. Soz. 7.4.1. Theodosius's authority in Macedonia is confirmed at *CTh* 9.35.4 issued at
Thessalonica (by Theodosius) to the vicar of Macedonia in 380. Cf. Grumel 1951, 8–14; Vera
1983, 392–93.

Figure 20. DN VALENS MAX(imus) AVGVSTVS with Rome on the reverse. Medallion of Rome. *RIC* 9.122.26. Courtesy Kunsthistorisches Museum, Vienna.

annoyed him that many of the troops stationed in Illyricum were from the mobile units he had sent to Valentinian in 371.[214] Despite his recognition of the strategic advantage to a unified Balkan region, Gratian nevertheless maintained a firm hold on this area and its armies while Valens was still alive. Control of Illyricum gave Gratian both a second comitatensian command structure and excellent ground for recruiting domestic troops. These were advantages that Valens did not enjoy. Rather, from the early years of his reign, he was forced to use a single command structure to deal with two fronts. Eastern commanders had always been torn between the lower Danube and the Euphrates/Tigris frontier, since, for the easterner "there are two great barbarian powers, Scyths and Persians."[215] In 365, Valens had faced the conflict between the two frontiers and chose to concentrate on the east, but he could not avoid a simultaneous dispatch of troops to Thrace and Moesia to quell Gothic unrest. After the Procopius revolt, he neglected the Persian frontier to wrangle with the Goths, and Shapur overran Armenia. In 377, it was the Danube he ignored, and the Goths made havoc of Thrace. Later that year, he withdrew troops from Armenia to send west, and Shapur promptly overran Armenia once again.[216] In order to deal with both the Goths and the Persians, then, Valens sorely needed the Illyrian army, which Gratian held fast.

He eventually took some steps to deal with this dilemma in the year and a half leading up to Adrianople. He created a system of five *magistri militum*

214. See pp. 311–12.

215. Lib. *Or.* 59.89. Cf. *CIL* 14.3608 for the strain placed on the Danube by the transfer of units eastward.

216. AM 30.2.8. Cf. similar problems under Licinius at Joh. Lyd. *De Mag.* 2.10, 31, 3.40; cf. *Exc. Val.* 5 [21].

Figure 21. Large Valens beside diminutive Valentinian II. Solidus of Antioch. *NC* 150 (1990), pl. 23A. Courtesy *Numismatic Chronicle.*

in response to the problems of the two eastern fronts. In 376, he had only three, Julius, who was serving on the southeastern frontier as *magister equitum et peditum*, and his two *praesentales*, the *magister peditum* Arinthaeus and the *magister equitum* Victor. When Valens learned of the crisis on the Danube, he appointed both Traianus and Profuturus as additional *magistri militum* and sent them west in 377. He later added to their ranks Saturninus as *magister equitum ad tempus*. In the confrontation with the Goths at Ad Salices, Profuturus was apparently killed, and in 378 Valens replaced Traianus. Later in 378, he reappointed Traianus, probably to replace Arinthaeus who seems to have died this year. This meant that Valens went into the battle with four *magistri militum in praesenti*, and he retained a fifth stationed in the east.[217] When Theodosius took over the eastern army after Valens's death, he established a permanent system much like that created ad hoc by Valens in the face of the Gothic crisis. Indeed, such a system was necessary, for a realm with two major fronts and a number of other active military zones needed as many as three command structures to deal with its various military hot spots.[218]

While Valens still lived, though, the multiplication of so many commanders in so short a space of time created as many problems as it solved. In fact, there is considerable evidence of carping and disputation in Valens's upper ranks. On the eve of Adrianople, the commanders were at odds over whether to give battle or await Gratian. According to Ammianus, Victor favored caution, while Sebastianus pressed for immediate action, but Zosimus reports

217. Demandt 1970, 703–9; cf. Austin and Rankov 1995, 228–29. Demandt indicates that Valens had up to seven *magistri militum* in 378, but this includes Profuturus—about whom nothing is heard after Ad Salices (a. 377)—and Arinthaeus—who probably died before Adrianople in 378; cf. Basil *Ep.* 269; AM 30.2.3; Barnes 1997, 12. Woods 2001 redates Arinthaeus's death to 373, but only at the expense of rejecting Theodoret's story (*HE* 4.33.1–3) that the general was still alive in the spring of 378.

218. Theodosius had two *magistri militum praesentales*, one *per Orientem*, one *per Thracias* and one *per Illyricum* (Zos. 4.27.2; *Not. dign. or.* 1.5–8). Demandt 1970, 720–24, demonstrates that the structure was less systematic than the *Notitia* would indicate; cf. Hoffmann 1969–70, 1: 490–516.

that it was Sebastianus who wanted to wait out the Goths but was overruled by his opponents. We shall never know whose version is accurate, and it does not matter.[219] More important is the inference we can draw about the disputes that arose in Valens's court and the later debate they provoked over which generals were to blame for the decisions leading to the disaster. As early as 379, Libanius confirms that many blamed Valens's commanders for the defeat.[220] This explains why Zosimus, and his source Eunapius, were at pains to defend the character and conduct of Sebastianus against detractors. Ammianus, who ranked among those detractors, engaged in a partisan defense of his own favorite, the *comes* Frigeridus, whose excessive caution was interpreted by "ill-willed disparagers" as cowardly negligence.[221] Even before this, Sebastianus is said to have aroused the emperor's jealousy with his early successes.[222] And Traianus also generated criticism with his failure to stop the Goths at Ad Salices: Theodoret reports that Valens lashed out at him, rebuking his "weakness and cowardice." Traianus shot back with accusations that Valens's religious persecutions were at the root of his defeat, and other Nicene commanders supported this defiance.[223] Tension was thus rife in the top-heavy upper ranks that Valens had so hastily assembled and must have contributed to the disaster that followed.

The disputes were also exacerbated by the desperate straits in which Valens's eastern army found itself. Despite his restructuring of the brass, Valens continued to confront a serious shortage of troops. We have already examined the efforts he needed to exert in order to build and maintain his army on the eastern frontier. By the time he arrived in Constantinople in 378, however, his forces and their quality had only diminished. He had lost any effective control of residual riparian forces in Thrace; those who had not deserted or been killed were cut off from lines of communication.[224] His comitatensian ranks had been greatly thinned by the battle of Ad Salices, a battle for which he had already been forced to bleed off large numbers of troops from the eastern frontier.[225] Most of his remaining *comitatenses* had to follow him to Thrace, and these had to be supplemented by numerous native ethnic units, which Ammianus mentions in Thrace in 377 and 378,

219. AM 31.12.6; Zos. 4.23.6–24.1. Wanke 1990, 199–201, summarizes the debate over whether the account of Ammianus or that of Zosimus is to be credited.

220. Lib. *Or.* 24.3–5; Greg. Naz. *Or.* 22.2; Them. *Or.* 15.189d; Joh. Chrys. *Ad vid. iun.* 4. Valens, too, came in for criticism, Aus. XXI *Grat. act.* 2 [7], 10 [48]; *Epit.* 48.5. See also Lenski 1997, 145–48.

221. Eunap. *Hist.* fr. 44.2–4 (Blockley); AM 31.7.5, 9.1, 10.21.

222. Zos. 4.23.5; Eunap. *Hist.* fr. 44.3 (Blockley); cf. Solari 1932a, 503–5.

223. On Traianus's dismissal, see p. 336. On his dispute with Valens, see Theod. *HE* 4.33.2–3; Theoph. a.m. 5867; cf. Lenski 1997, 150–52; Klein 1956, 56–62.

224. Soc. 4.38.2; Soz. 6.39.2.

225. AM 31.7.1–2. See Hoffmann 1969–70, 1: 444–45, and p. 184.

and which Themistius confirms remained there until at least 382.[226] Eunapius reports that, when Valens arrived at Constantinople, he began scrambling to collect troops, and Ammianus tells us that he had to coddle his men with payments in cash and kind and with frequent exhortations.[227] When Sebastianus was given orders to assemble a guerrilla unit, he selected his men from totally inexperienced recruits, and when Valens set out from Melanthias, he brought with him a number of veterans whom he had called back into service.[228] Included in this ragtag band were even monks, whom Valens had begun drafting into service as early as 375.[229] Valens had been wanting for manpower even before the Goths entered the scene; once they had destroyed his advance armies and taken over Thrace, his needs were only redoubled.

It was thus imperative that Valens gain and maintain troops from any and all quarters. For this reason, it is surprising that he chose not to await the western reinforcements Gratian was supposed to be bringing. His rationale becomes clearer when we consider other circumstances. Valens had reached Constantinople at the end of May. After setting up camp twenty-seven kilometers from the city at the villa of Melanthias, he waited for Gratian for a month and a half before finally moving against the Goths. Given that Valens waited until late July, we must assume that his hopes for the arrival of Gratian were real. We have already seen that he only set out for Adrianople to prevent the Goths from occupying the east-west road there, and that he moved against them on August 9 to prevent them from cutting off that same road back to Constantinople.[230] The situation had thus grown desperate: Valens joined battle without Gratian because Gratian simply took too long to arrive.

Gratian's dilatoriness is clear from Ammianus's account. When he learned that a band of Alamannic Lentienses had crossed the Rhine on a raid in February of 378, Gratian recalled advance troops he had sent eastward to use against the invaders. Although the Lentienses had already been repulsed in Raetia, Gratian sent these advance troops, who might otherwise have helped Valens, on a punitive expedition against this tribe. In a pitched battle at Ar-

226. The Armenian *tribunus* Barzimeres probably led Armenians in 377, and in 378 Valens used Saracens and probably Iberians under the Iberian prince Bacurius. On eastern troops in general, see Zos. 4.22.1. On Saracens, see p. 335. On Barzimeres, see AM 31.8.9–10. On Bacurius, see AM 31.12.16: "sagittarii et scutarii quos Bacurius Hiberus quidam tunc regebat," the former of whom are probably to be associated with the Hiberi at *Not. dign.* 5.60, see p. 317 n. 22. Themistius three times mentions the presence among the Danube armies of easterners (Arabs, Iberians, and Armenians), most of whom must have come west with Valens, *Or.* 15.189d (Iberians and Armenians); 16.207a (Celts, Assyrians, Armenians, Libyans, Iberians); 34.20 (those collected from the Tigris and Arabia).

227. Eunap. *Hist.* fr. 44.1 (Blockley); AM 31.11.1.

228. Zos. 4.23.3–4; AM 31.12.1.

229. Lenski, "Isaac and Valens' Recruitment of Monks for Military Service" (forthcoming).

230. See p. 337.

gentaria and in subsequent conflicts, the Romans destroyed all but about 5,000 of the original 40,000 Lentienses, but Gratian insisted on total annihilation. Sometime after late April, he diverted his own army—then mobilizing to aid Valens—across the Rhine and began the lengthy process of starving out the remaining barbarians, who had taken refuge in the mountains.[231] He eventually failed and was forced to concede a peace in order finally to come to the aid of his uncle. Thus, when Ammianus praises Gratian's "swiftness" *(celeritas)* in dealing with the Lentienses, one cannot but detect a note of irony. Even when Gratian began his attack on the Lentienses, Richomer had long before informed him of the gravity of the Gothic threat, making his obsession with these Alamanni seem at best stubborn, at worst perverse.[232]

After this long delay, Gratian finally did hasten east by taking boats down the Danube, but the benefits of his speed were nullified by the fact that it restricted the size and strength of his forces. Traveling in this fashion, Gratian could not have transported more than a few thousand light-armed men.[233] He had only reached Castra Martis—some 450 kilometers from Adrianople— by the time Valens had to fight. There, Gratian was held up with a fever and by a group of Alan raiders who put a halt to the progress of his light-armed force.[234] Thus, when Richomer arrived at Adrianople bringing not troops but only a letter insisting that Valens await Gratian's arrival, it is little wonder that Valens chose to dismiss the request.

This is even less surprising given the animosity between Valens and Gratian. We have just seen that the question of hegemony over Valentinian II and the territory of Illyricum was eating at Valens. His anger would have been exacerbated, however, by Gratian's own propaganda machine, which seemed determined to demonstrate how the young man was outperforming his feckless uncle. Gratian's flatterers deliberately exaggerated the significance of his victory over the Lentienses, inflating the number of invaders from 40,000 to 70,000 and broadcasting the achievement in propaganda.[235] Even Gratian's

231. Gratian was still in winter quarters at Trier on Apr. 20, 378; cf. *CTh* 8.5.35.

232. AM 31.10.2–18; Jer. *Chron.* s.a. 377; Prosper *Chron.* 1160. For the date, see Seeck, *Regesten,* 250. Seeck, *Untergang,* 112 criticizes Gratian's obsession with the Lentienses as a "törichte Unternehmen"; cf. Wanke 1990, 176–77.

233. Zos. 3.10.2 reports that when Julian did the same in 361, he could bring only 3,000 men.

234. AM 31.11.6; cf. Maenchen-Helfen 1973, 30–36. Ammianus's geography in this passage is a bit confused. He reports that Gratian reached Bononia, proceeded to Sirmium, then followed the Danube to Castra Martis. Bononia (Vidin) is ca. 300 km downstream from Sirmium and Castra Martis (Kula) is ca. 30 km inland from Bononia on the route south to Naissus. Presumably, Gratian reached Sirmium, then Bononia by boat, and from there marched to Castra Martis.

235. AM 31.10.5; cf. *Epit.* 47.2; Jer. *Chron.* s.a. 377. For examples of such flattery, see Aus. XX *Precatio consulis designati* ll. 29–35, XXI *Grat. act.* 2 [7–9]; cf. Green 1991, 535; and see Oros. 7.33.8.

letter insisting that his uncle await his arrival was used to advertise this recent success. In the face of much greater threats, Gratian's boasts must have seemed particularly impudent and must have led to feelings of indignation and jealousy. For this reason, Ammianus is right to assert that it was partly envy that spurred Valens into premature action.[236]

We have seen that Valens had difficulty getting Gratian to send him troops in 377, and that Gratian had recalled the advance forces he sent in 378. Zonaras writes that he deliberately avoided sending troops to his uncle because of his Arianism,[237] and Zosimus even informs us that Gratian was not particularly upset when he learned of Valens's death. "[T]hey harbored a certain suspicion toward each other," Zosmius notes.[238] Valens had always been jealous of his nephew and the privileges he had enjoyed. For his part, Gratian did little to assuage his uncle's envy and never offered recognition of Valens's superior status. The ill will that resulted affected all aspects of relations between the two emperors. According to Eunapius, it even influenced Valens's decision to offer entry to the Goths in 376: "For he was rather chagrined at his fellow emperors, who, being sons of his brother . . . had decided to divide up their empire between themselves without referring the division to their uncle. Because of this and in order that the Roman forces might be greatly increased, he ordered that the men should be received."[239]

If this is true, the same problem led Valens both to accept the Goths in 376 and to march to his death against them in 378. Had he been granted control of Illyricum and Macedonia on his brother's death, Valens might not have been so desperate for military manpower when the Goths came knocking. So, too, had he been aided by his nephew rather than worsted in the next move of their ongoing game for Augustal superiority, he might not have marched against the Goths with less than adequate forces. His poor relations with a western colleague whom he deeply resented helped both set and spring the trap that caught Valens.

---

236. AM 31.11.6–12.1: "aequiperare facinore quodam egregio aduliscentem properans filium fratris, cuius virtutibus urebatur"; 31.12.7: "ne paene iam partae victoriae (ut opinabantur) consors fieret Gratianus."

237. Zon. 13.17. Theod. *HE* 4.31.1 mistakes Valens's ἀδελφός (Valentinian I) for his ἀδελφιδίος (Gratian); cf. Cedrenus, p. 546; Theoph. a.m. 5866. For the effects of religious conflict on the disaster of Adrianople, see Klein 1956.

238. Zos. 4.24.4: ἦν γὰρ τις ὑποψία πρὸς ἀλλήλους αὐτοῖς. On Valens's resentment of Gratian, see Pabst 1986, 99–101.

239. Eunap. *Hist.* fr. 42 (Blockley).

Epilogue

For the past thirty years, the field of late antiquity has received well deserved and long overdue attention. More recently, in the past decade, it has become fashionable to write extended apologies debunking perceived misconceptions about the period and building it up as in every way the equal of the classical world. No one is more convinced of the importance of such efforts than I. Having been trained as a classicist, I am aware of the attraction of classical standards and of the pull to regard them as normative and any deviation from them as inferior. This is surely wrong, for as so many recent studies have shown, the people of late antiquity rivaled the brilliance of their forebears in art, architecture, literature, rhetoric, philosophy, law, warfare, diplomacy, and government. Of course, their ideals were different from those of their predecessors, but to regard these differences as symptomatic of decline says much more about modern tastes than about late antique culture.

The model of decline and fall is thus a modern invention, which we have finally begun to cast off in our postmodern world. Although it traces to the Renaissance, its greatest proponent was, of course, Edward Gibbon, a figure of the Enlightenment. Gibbon brought to his study of the Roman Empire his assumptions about the superiority of rationalism over mysticism, realism over idealism, moralism over relativism, and classical civilization over its medieval successors. All of these tendencies have been rejected in contemporary scholarship, which has begun to engage the late antique world on its own terms. When applied to the fields of culture, society, religion, art, and literature—and here one thinks above all of Peter Brown—this new approach opens remarkable vistas onto the late ancient world. Attempts to cross-apply this same approach to politics and warfare, however, have tended to seem more artificial and strained. One thing Gibbon did have right was that, as a state, Rome did decline and eventually fall. The fact that this process took a millennium to work itself out does not vitiate the claim that, from the late fourth century onward, the Roman empire was in a steady process of retreat.

Just as contemporary historians are no longer afraid to profess that there is interest in the nonrational world of late antique religion and philosophy or that there is beauty in the late antique preference for abstraction in art and literature, I would hope that they will also acknowledge that there is value in studying the struggle of the late Roman empire to cope with this net decline in power. This book represents an effort to describe a specific and very prominent instance of this decline. My goal in writing it has not been to discredit Valens or his empire, but it has also not been to idealize them. I have tried, rather, to show how both Valens and the empire faced an overwhelming range of problems with varying degrees of success, but ultimately failed to overcome them. My title is thus not so much intended to condemn Valens, let alone the empire, but rather to acknowledge an empirically verifiable failure on the part of Valens—and the empire—to meet certain challenges. Both emperor and empire "lacked / were failing in"—and this gets at the etymological wordplay intended in the title—the proper combination of tools to assert their "power / empire" successfully.

As with the changes documented in the fields of late antique religion, philosophy, art and literature, Rome's changed power status resulted from transformations of the classical past and from interactions with nonclassical cultures. The late antique world was a very different place from the classical world whence it derived. It was in most ways more complex, in large part because it followed in the footsteps of a classical civilization that had radically complicated the cultural, social, and political situation of the Mediterranean basin. For historians of culture, society, and politics, this complexity is tremendously exciting and productive of meaning. For the denizens of the late antique world, however, this same complexity must often have seemed jarring and, for its rulers, extremely taxing. The rulers who succeeded in coping—Constantine, for example, and Justinian—did so above all because they were able to stage-manage the new problems without seeming to be overwhelmed. Those who did not—and here I would include Valens—failed not for lack of trying but for want of the proper resources, both internal and external, to make themselves look like winners. In concluding, then, it is worthwhile to catalog these new complexities confronted by a late Roman emperor and to tie together their various strands in order to delineate in brief the web that caught Valens.

In the first chapter of the book, it became clear that late Roman rulership was more complex than its first- and second-century incarnation. First and foremost, power was generally divided between multiple emperors, who were forever renegotiating their share of what in theory remained undivided dominion. Then, too, in contrast with classical Roman rulers, late Roman emperors like Valentinian and Valens tended not to derive from aristocratic or even Italian stock. They—and in turn their ministers—thus found themselves rivals with the traditional elite, which retained considerable power and remained uncomfortable with these arriviste emperors. The center was now ruled by the periphery—geographically and sociologically—and the periphery thus became the center in a way that complicated power structures and imperial rule.

In the second chapter, we saw yet another new problem faced by late Roman rulers, usurpation. The first two and a half centuries of Roman emperorship witnessed only sporadic and often quite harmless challenges from usurpers. Only in the third century did usurpation become a regular threat, and it remained so throughout the rest of late antiquity. This happened for a variety of reasons—structural, military, psychological, and, in Valens's case, ideological. Here again, the late Roman world differed from earlier periods in that it witnessed the solidification of a more complex ideal for emperors, which demanded an all but impossible combination of mutually contradictory virtues. When Valens failed to live up to this ideal, especially because of his background, homeland, and education, he became an easy target for the ambitious dynastic claimant Procopius.

Late Roman rulers like Valens also faced a more active and aggressive threat from non-Roman peoples on the empire's northern frontier, as we saw in the third chapter. Two centuries of contact with Roman power had made northern—largely Germanic—barbarians more culturally and economically sophisticated and more immune to the application of Roman force. Thus the Goths whom Valens faced could not be conquered or absorbed, but had to be handled with cautious respect and careful negotiation. Rather than gain dominion over them, Rome chose instead to harness Gothic power for use in foreign and domestic military conflicts, a situation that further increased Gothic power and prestige. Valens seems not to have fully understood how best to manage this new situation, and he thus undertook a war with the Goths that was at once unnecessary, unsuccessful, and damaging to Roman power.

A similar situation obtained on the eastern frontier, where Rome faced a much more organized and powerful threat from the Sassanians than it had from their predecessors the Parthians. Here again, the mid third century constituted a turning point beyond which Rome was confronted with a new and unprecedented problem of direct and deep invasion from the east. It attempted to counter this problem by fortifying northern Mesopotamia and thus blocking Persian access into the empire. When Valens came to power, Rome had just surrendered much of its bulwark in Mesopotamia, and Valens was forced to rebuild its claims there through negotiation and, eventually, force. Adding to his difficulties was a growing struggle with other cultures in the east, and particularly the Isaurians and Saracens. Both of these peoples revolted late in Valens's reign and occupied his armies when he needed troops in Thrace to manage the outbreak of the Goths.

On the domestic front, the rise of Christianity as a state religion eventually led to a division of religious loyalties into Christian and pagan camps. Although Valentinian and Valens, who were Christian, attempted to steer clear of open persecution of pagans, they both became embroiled in the prosecution of magic in a way that has led subsequent generations to accuse them of religious intolerance. The new strength of Christianity in the fourth century also opened an alternative avenue to power through the bishop, who successfully challenged the authority of the emperor and his officials at the local and even the imperial level. The rise of powerful bishops also helped fractionalize the church and pulled emperors into ecclesiastical power struggles. Here again, both emperors tried to avoid this new pitfall, but Valens eventually failed and went down in history as a persecutor of Christians.

The efforts of Diocletian and his fellow tetrarchs to exercise a firmer control over their subjects, to increase tax revenues, and to control the new barbarian threat led to the creation of a much more complex bureaucracy and more powerful army than the earlier empire had known. The burgeoning of government inevitably created more work for an emperor, both because of the growth of his sphere of control and because of the consequent rise in the problems of corruption. Here, Valens was able to use his experience as a landowner to good effect, yet this same experience led him to undertake costly monetary and tax reforms, which threatened his ability to finance this expanded bureaucracy and army. Above all, the expense of filling the ranks of his army made him particularly favorable toward the idea of importing Goths to solve his military manpower problems.

Finally, for the first time under Valens, Rome was forced to come to grips with the issue of large groups of barbarians living autonomously inside traditionally Roman territory. This problem arose only at the end of Valens's reign, after his attempt to resettle the Goths unraveled and left him struggling to gain control of this hostile group. More than any other problem, this crisis of "barbarians within the gates" would compromise Roman power in the centuries to come. It simultaneously diminished Rome's taxation and recruitment base, by removing territories from its political control, and destabilized political dominion in those territories Rome retained, by opening them to attack.

All of these problems arose in late antiquity, and all of them combined to force a decline in the state's political and military power. To describe them and acknowledge this decline is not, however, to pass a negative value judgment against late antiquity, or even the empire. It is rather to highlight yet another way in which this period stands apart, and to open yet another vista onto productive fields of investigation. I have used Valens as my touchstone for this study largely because his reign illustrates well the range and severity of the problems faced by a late Roman ruler. As something of a failure, Valens's reign can show where the new stresses and strains of managing the late Roman empire were most likely to cause fissures in the imperial superstructure. By focusing narrowly on one emperor, I have been able to examine all of those stresses and strains in their particularity, and all of the ways that they interacted with each other in the aggregate. I hope I have shown that it was not any one of these but rather their combination that led to Valens's demise and the diminution of power precipitated by his fall.

Datable Evidence
for Valentinianic Fortifications

The empire witnessed a flurry of frontier defense activity under Valentinian and Valens. The Pannonian brothers concentrated huge financial and military resources into a centrally organized effort to strengthen the *limites* in all regions.[1] This they did with the construction of new forts,[2] the repair of old ones, the building or rebuilding of city walls, the resupply of outposts, and the creation of new garrisons. Their efforts were aimed especially at sealing off the boundaries of the empire with small *burgi* (watchtowers),[3] which they constructed en masse along the river frontiers, at major crossroads, and at locations vulnerable to raiding. Considerable evidence survives with which to reconstruct this program. The catalog that follows, however, includes only those items that can be assigned more narrowly datable termini than the span of Valentinian's and Valens's reigns. The emperors advertised their campaign in panegyrics, poetry, coins, and inscriptions many of which can be used to date specific projects quite precisely. Excluded here is the abundant evidence of archaeology, which—with the help of tile stamps and coin finds—has been used to attribute over one hundred forts and fortlets securely to Valentinian and Valens, without, how-

---

1. For general accounts, see Johnson 1983, passim; Lander 1989, 270–93. On Valentinian's zeal for frontier fortifications, see AM 28.2.1–4, 29.4.1, 6.2, 30.7.6, 9.1; Zos. 4.3.4–5; cf. Fasolino 1976, 47–51.

2. They were particularly concerned to draw attention to the *new* fortifications they constructed, always marking them epigraphically as forts built *a fundamentis* or ἐκ θεμελίων (*a fundamentis*: AE 1996, 1612–13; CIL 8.23849 = AE 1903, 241; CIL 3.10596 = ILS 762; CIL 3.3670a = ILS 774; CIL 3.3653 = ILS 775; CIL 3.6730; CIL 3.88 = ILS 773; Soproni 1967; ἐκ θεμελίων: CIG 4430 = MAMA 3.102 n. 1; CIG 8610 = OGI 722. Cf. Them. *Or.* 10.137b: ἐπιτείχισε φρούριον ἐκ καινῆς).

3. On *burgi*, see Isaac 1992, 178–86; Elton 1996b, 158–60.

ever, being able to date them more closely than 364/75. For this material, see the studies cited in the notes for each region.

When we confine our examination to more precisely datable material, we cannot help but notice the relatively narrow chronological limits within which the bulk of the program was carried out. Most of the textual evidence for the fortification program is concentrated between the years 369 and 370. Even more striking, the second oration of Symmachus and the tenth of Themistius—which bear remarkable resemblances in the format and language they use to describe the program—were both delivered within a few days of one another in early 370. They were clearly part of a pre-planned propaganda effort to advertise the building campaign in both halves of the empire at precisely the period when it was being pursued most intensely. When we turn to documentary sources, no inscriptions record forts from before 367 and only two mark forts after 375. Of these, only one records a construction (in Numidia) conducted under imperial auspices; the second (from Syria) is from a tower built at private expense. Indeed, where exact dates can be known, even narrower termini are recorded. Most firmly datable inscriptions are concentrated in the years 368–72, with 368 and 371 marking high points in the campaign. Although forts were no doubt built or rebuilt in all periods of Valentinian's and Valens's reigns, the parallel dating of so many forts and the coincidence of these dates with the textual sources shows that these years represented the apex of a pre-planned and coordinated effort. This revelation has two major implications. First, it adds to our pool of evidence confirming that Valentinian and Valens cooperated in jointly orchestrated, prearranged military and administrative ventures. Second, on the broader scale, it shows that fortification programs were at times tightly controlled from the imperial center and that forts were not simply constructed haphazardly to counter immediate and localized threats as some have argued.[4]

GENERAL TEXTUAL EVIDENCE

CTh 15.1.13: encourages the construction of towers in Dacia Ripensis (a. 364)

DRB praef. 10, 1.4, 20.1: encourages the beginning of a fortification campaign (a. 368/69)

AM 28.2.1–6: introduces the Rhine campaign (a. 369)

AM 28.3.7: describes the campaign in Britain (a. 369)[5]

Them. *Or.* 10.136d–138a: describes the lower Danube campaign in progress the previous year (a. 370)

Symm. *Or.* 2.1, 12–16, 18–20: describes the Rhine campaign in progress (a. 370)[6]

Symm. *Or.* 3.9: mentions the Rhine campaign (a. 370)[7]

---

4. Esp. Isaac 1992.

5. For archaeological evidence, see Welsby 1982, 104–24.

6. On the importance of Valentinian's fortification program in this oration, see Pabst 1989, 310–38.

7. On the date, see Del Chicca 1987; Shanzer 1998a, 286–87.

Festus 9: assumes the campaign on the lower Danube is complete (a. 370)

Auson. XVI *Mos.* ll. 2, 435, 456–57: alludes to the Rhine campaign (c. 371)[8]

AM 29.4.1: describes the Rhine campaign (a. 372)

AM 28.5.11 with Jer. *Chron.* s.a. 373: mentions the Rhine campaign (a. 373)

AM 29.6.2–7: describes a translimitanean fortification campaign on the upper Danube (a. 373)

Them. *Or.* 13.166a: assumes the campaign on the eastern frontier is complete (a. 376)

EVIDENCE FOR SPECIFIC FORTS

Rhine

Cuijk: Goudswaard 1995 (a. 368/69)

Alta Ripa (Altrip): *CTh* 11.31.4, with Symm. *Or.* 2.20; AM 28.2.2–4 (a. 369)[9]

Altinum (Alzey): *CTh* 11.31.5, with Oldenstein 1993 (a. 370)

Rote Waag near Etzgen: *CIL* 13.11538 = *ILS* 8949 (a. 371)

Summa Rapida (Kleiner Laufen near Koblenz): *CIL* 13.11537 (a. 371)

Magidunum: *CIL* 13.11543 (a. 371)

Brecantia (Bregenz): Mackensen 1999, 233–34 (a. 372)

Robur (Basel): Amm. 30.3.1, with *CTh* 8.5.33 (a. 374)

Africa

Castellum Biracsaccarensium (Bisica): *CIL* 8.23849 = *AE* 1903, 241 (a. 374)

Cellae (Bou-Taleb): *CIL* 8.20566 (10937) (a. 375/78)

Upper Danube

Solva (Esztergom): *CIL* 3.10596 = *ILS* 762 (a. 367)

Adiuvense? (Ybbs): *CIL* 3.5670a = *ILS* 774 (a. 370)[10]

---

8. On the date, see Shanzer 1998a; 1998b. Roberts 1984 argues that the entire poem is a metaphorical elaboration on the theme "the river as boundary."

9. Symm. *Or.* 2.4, 20 speaks of the fort as complete in 370. Schnurbein and Köhler 1989 date the fort to 369 based on dendrochronology. Archaeological evidence of Valentinian's Rhine fortifications is discussed at Petrikovits 1971; Bogaers and Rüger 1974; Tomlin 1974, 157–78; Johnson 1983, 136–68; Lander 1984, 276–83; Mackensen 1999, 231–36. For Valentinian's new garrison units on the Rhine cataloged in *Not. dign. oc.* 41, see Hoffmann 1969–70, 1: 344–52.

10. See esp. Genser 1986, 220–23. Archaeological evidence for Valentinian's fortifications in Pannonia is discussed at Mócsy 1974, 291–94; Soproni 1978; Johnson 1983, 169–95; Genser 1986; cf. Visy 1995, who identifies 62 of the 125 known *burgi* in Hungary as Valentinianic. On

Burgus near Solva: *CIL* 3.3653 = *ILS* 775 (a. 371)

Visegrád: Soproni 1967 (a. 372)

Carnuntum (Petronell): *CIL* 3.14358 (a. 367/75)

Lower Danube

Cius (Girliciu): *CIL* 3.7494 (6159) = *ILS* 770 (a. 368)

Tomi (Valul lui Traian): *AE* 1978, 716 (a. 368)[11]

Bargala (Goren Kozjak): Aleskova and Mango 1972, 265–76 (a. 370/71)

Western and Central Anatolia

Ephesus (Efes): *IK* 11.1.42 = *AE* 1906, 30 (a. 371)

Aphrodisias: *CIG* 2745 = *MAMA* 8:427 (late 360s)[12]

Corasium (Tchuk Ören): *OGI* 580 = *CIG* 4430 = *MAMA* 3: 102 n. 1 (a. 367/75)

Eastern Anatolia and Upper Mesopotamia

Amida (Diyarbekir): *CIL* 3.6730 (213) (a. 367/75)[13]

Arabia and Palestine

Umm el Jimal: *AE* 1996, 1612 (a. 368)[14]

Umm el Jimal: *AE* 1996, 1613 (a. 368)

Dibin: *AE* 1933, 178 = *SEG* 7.1164 (a. 368)

Umm el Jimal: *CIL* 3.88 = *ILS* 773 (a. 371)

---

the epigraphy, see Soproni 1985, 107–12; cf. 1989. The close epigraphic dating of the forts on the Danube bend has been confirmed in studies on the mint of Siscia, which indicate that coin circulation in Pannonia increased to a highpoint between 367 and 370 and then tapered off markedly, see Lanyi 1969; Soproni 1969; contrast Nixon 1983.

11. This is not certain to be from a fort, but its editor argues as much. Archaeological evidence for Valens's fortifications on the lower Danube is discussed at Barnea 1968, 2: 395–97; Scorpan 1980; Aricescu 1980, 72–103; Biernacka-Lubanska 1982; Ivanov 1996. Valens also built or rebuilt forts named Valentia, Valentiniana, and Gratiana, attested at *CTh* 8.5.49, 11.1.22, 12.1.113; *Not. dign. or.* 39.27; Proc. *Aed.* 4.11.20.

12. Roueché 1989, 42–45, no. 22, republishes the inscription and discusses the date.

13. On these walls see, Gabriel 1940, 85–205; cf. Berchem and Strzygowski 1910, 6–12; Pollard 2000, 288–90. Archaeological evidence for Valens's fortifications in these regions is discussed at Crow 1986; Mitford 1980, 1206–10. On Valens's garrisons in the region, see *Not. dign. or.* 38.33, 37, with Zuckerman 1991b, 527–40.

14. See De Vries 1998 and Atallah 1996. For archaeological evidence, see Parker 1986, 136–43; 1989. For Valens's new garrison units in the region, see *Not. dign. or.* 34.35, 42, 37.29, 30.

Deir el Keif: *CIL* 3.14381–2 (a. 368/71)

Khirbet es Samra: Humbert and Desreumaux 1990, 258 (a. 367/75)

[El Moujeidel: Cleremont-Ganneau 1888, 8–10 (a. 377)][15]

Egypt

Egypt?: John of Nikiu *Chron.* 82.20 (p. 84 Charles) (a. 367/70)[16]

Syene: *AE* 1909, 108 = Bernand 1990 (a. 367/75)[17]

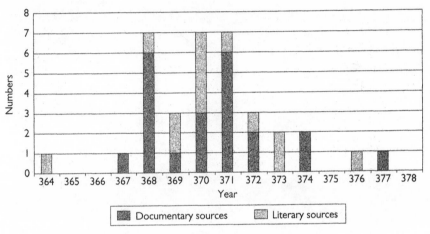

Figure 22. Datable evidence for forts, 364–378.

15. This inscription records the dedication of a πύργον by an otherwise unknown Rufus Magnus at his own expense. It is probably to be connected with local defenses in the wake of the revolt of Mavia and not with the imperial building program (see p. 209 n. 311 above).

16. John of Nikiu reports that Tatianus built Abrakjun (?) and fortified the country of Egypt while he was prefect (i.e., between 367 and 370); cf. *PLRE* I, Fl. Eutolmius Tatianus 5. For Valens's new garrison units in the region, see *Not. dign. or.* 31.36, 39.

17. The related *POxy* 4381 (a. 375) does not, unfortunately, help date this inscription more firmly.

Shapur's Administrative Structures in Armenia

When Shapur first sent troops to take over Armenia, he apparently intended to dispense with the Arsacid monarchy and set up new administrative structures. Modern attempts to describe those structures have oversimplified the matter by tending to rely too heavily on the evidence of Ammianus (AM).

AM reports that Shapur's invasion force was led by the *nakharar* defectors Cylaces and Artabanes and that Shapur had entrusted Armenia to these two.[1] If we follow this evidence, we might agree with R. C. Blockley that Shapur was trying to replace the traditional Arsacid monarchy with a non-Arsacid but exclusively Armenian dyarchy.[2] The *Epic Histories (BP)* indicate, however, that the situation was considerably more complex. *BP* says that Shapur commanded two officials with Persian titles, Zik and Karen, to besiege Artogerassa and to rule Armenia (4.55). A simple equation between Zik and Karen and Cylaces and Artabanes has been proposed, but proven to be incorrect.[3] In fact, *BP* speaks of a total of four leaders: Zik and Karen and the two Armenian *nakharar* defectors, Meruzan Arkruni and Vahan Mamikonean (4.55, 58–59, 5.1).

Here, we propose to identify AM's Cylaces and Artabanes with parallel figures among the leaders mentioned by *BP*:

1. Markwart first suggested that Cylaces be identified with a pair of Armenian *hayr-mardpet* in *BP*.[4] Ammianus says Cylaces was a eunuch and prefect, two

---

1. AM 27.12.5: "Cylaci spadoni et Arrabanni, quos olim susceperat perfugas, commisit Armeniam (horum alter ante gentis praefectus, magister alter fuisse dicebatur armorum)."

2. Blockley 1987; cf. Baynes 1910, 638 n. 71.

3. Langlois 1867–69, 1: 273 n. 2, has been disproven at Markwart 1896, 213–14; cf. Christensen 1944, 105 n. 3; Garsoïan 1989, 303 n. 3.

4. Markwart 1896, 213–15; cf. Adontz 1970, 513 n. 43. Garsoïan (1989, 304 n. 9) questions the identification, although her reasons assume that *BP* was far more consistent than is probably the case. Cf. Toumanoff 1963, 177 n. 118.

qualifications that perfectly describe the hereditary Armenian office of *hayr-mardpet*. AM also tells us that Cylaces defected to Persia, was present at the siege of Artogerassa, conducted negotiations there with the queen Paranjem, and was eventually beheaded by Pap on suspicion of Persian collaboration (AM 27.12.5–6, 14). This *vita* corresponds marvelously with *BP*'s description of two consecutive *hayr-mardpet*s, one anonymous and the second named Glak. The latter name is certain to be identified with Ammianus' "Cylaces." More-over, although *BP* distinguishes between Glak and the anonymous *hayr-mardpet* who preceded him, both had careers remarkably like that of Ammianus's Cy-laces: the anonymous conducted negotiations with Paranjem and was later punished for his insolence to the queen (4.55, 5.3); Glak was entrusted by Pap with a command but later beheaded for going over to Persia (5.3, 6). We can thus propose that *BP* mistakenly creates an anonymous doppelgänger for one and the same person. AM's Cylaces is at once *BP*'s Glak and the anony-mous *hayr-mardpet*.

2a. Markwart also noted similarities between AM's "Artabanes" and *BP*'s "Mushel Mamikonean." Both were military commanders *(magister armorum / sparapet)*, both were credited with conducting negotiations with Valens to en-gineer Pap's return to Armenia, both were eventually suspected of treason, and Mushel is mentioned as collaborating with the *hayr-mardpet*, just as Artabanes did with Cylaces (AM 27.12.5, 10, 14; *BP* 5.1, 4, 33). The identification is ob-viously not so firm as that of Glak with Cylaces, since there is no resonance be-tween the transmitted names, and *BP*'s Mushel was—like AM's Artabanes—executed, but only after Pap's death (*BP* 5.35).

2b. Yet another possible parallel to Artabanes occurs in *BP*'s Vahan Mamiko-nean, a member of the same *sparapet* house of Mamikonean. Like Artabanes, Vahan defected to Persia, was granted dominion in Armenia by Shapur, and was murdered before the battle of Bagawan in 371.[5] Moreover, Artabanes is the common Greco-Latin rendering of Armenian Vahan. This identification also has weaknesses, in that *BP* mentions no contact between Vahan and Pap and says that Vahan was murdered by his own son rather than by Pap (*BP* 5.4, 59). Even so, here again, *BP* may be creating a double. We can tentatively iden-tify Ammianus's Artabanes with aspects of the two *sparapet* whom *BP* names Mushel and Vahan Mamikonean.

None of the identifications made here can be proven. Nevertheless, comparison of *BP*'s account with Ammianus's demonstrates both the importance of *BP* to the question and the caution we should exercise before accepting oversimplified schemes for Shapur's administration in Armenia based solely on AM. The fact that *BP* ap-

5. *BP* 4.50 describes the defection of Vahan and claims that Shapur offered Vahan his sis-ter in marriage and entrusted him with "the cushion and diadem that formerly belonged to his ancestors." All this implies that Shapur intended him to rule with Meruzan (but cf. MX 3.36 on the marriage). Vahan's and Meruzan's joint Armenian rule is confirmed at 4.58–59. Like Ammianus's Artabanes, *BP*'s Vahan played an important military role, *BP* 4.58; MX 3.35. *BP* 4.59 places Vahan's murder before Bagawan (a. 372).

parently refers to the leaders named in Ammianus but also identifies further leaders would indicate that Ammianus has not given us a complete picture. We must therefore speak not of two but of at least five figures with leadership roles, possibly more depending on the credibility of the proposed identifications: (1) Zik, (2) Karen, (3) Meruzan, (4) Cylaces/Glak, (5) Artabanes/Mushel/Vahan. This combination would imply that Shapur intended to combine Sassanian provincial administrators (the Zik and Karen) with Armenian *nakharars* (Meruzan, Cylaces/Glak, and Artabanes/Mushel/Vahan), not to create an independent dyarchy.

Natural Disasters
and the Reign of Valens

Valens's reign and the period immediately preceding it witnessed an extraordinary number of natural disasters. The sources describe as many as seven major earthquakes in the twenty years between 358 and 378, as well as a devastating tsunami, a prodigious hailstorm in Constantinople, and two famines, one in Anatolia and the second in Syria. Not surprisingly, we have contemporary evidence indicating that those who lived under Valens were well aware of the unusually high number of fateful events coincident with his reign.[1] Indeed, even before 378, some writers began to lump these together as evidence of divine displeasure with the state of affairs under Valens. When Valens died his ignoble death at Adrianople—yet further proof of divine anger—it became even more convenient to describe the entire reign as a period of undifferentiated catastrophe.[2] This tendency to package the unrelenting concatenation of disasters under Valens as an indistinguishable blur of cataclysm has filtered into much present scholarship. Until an outstanding article by F. Jacques and B. Bousquet began to sort out the various events in the order they occurred, many scholars simply clustered all of them around the spectacular tsunami of 365.[3] Jacques and Bousquet, whose work focused on this tsunami, have

---

1. See, e.g., Them. *Or.* 11.150d; cf. *Or.* 8.106d.

2. Basil *Homilia IX quod Deus non est auctor malorum* 5 (*PG* 31.337–40); Greg. Naz. *Or.* 16.5 and 19 (*PG* 35.933 and 962); cf. Oros. 7.32.5; Soc. 4.3.3–5, 11.1–2, 16.7–8; Soz. 6.10.2; Anonymous *V Athanasii* 29 (*PG* 25.ccx); Photius *V Athanasii* 14 (*PG* 25.ccxxii); Simeon Metaphrastes *V Athanasii* 17 (*PG* 25.ccxlv); Jacob of Edessa *Chron.*, p. 296; Cedrenus, pp. 543–44. Lib. *Or.* 18.292 attributes the concentration of natural disasters in the 360s to the earth's anguish over Julian's death.

3. Jacques and Bousquet 1984 with earlier references. From a more global perspective, Horden and Purcell 2000, 304–12, downplay the long-term consequences of such disasters; they

shown that there is enough chronologically precise information to make much finer distinctions. This appendix carries their work further by covering events over a broader chronological span and treating nonseismic disasters as well. It should give some idea of the scale and frequency of the problems Valens faced. These troubles affected both the way he was forced to administer his territory and his ability to finance his government.

EARTHQUAKE: AUGUST 24, 358

Ammianus's report, which is filled with circumstantial details, indicates that the earthquake, centered at Nicomedia, occurred at the break of dawn (contrast Theophanes and the *Chronicon paschale,* who report that the quake occurred at the third hour of the night, and Sozomen, who says the second hour of the day).[4] According to Ammianus, much of the city tumbled down the hillside and, as Sozomen confirms, anything that remained standing was consumed in an ensuing conflagration, which lasted for five days. Ammianus also reports that the quake(s) affected Macedonia, Asia, and Pontus, which coincides with the testimony of the *Consularia Constantinopolitana* that 150 other cities were damaged simultaneously with Nicomedia.[5]

EARTHQUAKE: DECEMBER 2, 362

Only Ammianus reports this quake, which apparently further leveled Nicomedia and also damaged parts of Nicaea.[6]

EARTHQUAKE: MAY 19, 363

This quake, in Syria Palaestina, which put a stop to Julian's reconstruction of the Temple in Jerusalem, received considerable attention from Christian authors.[7] Their descriptions of fireballs are probably accurate, for earthquakes often create explosions

---

cannot, however, deny the short-term social and economic impact on both the local and—in cases like the tsunami of 365—regional level.

4. AM 17.7.1–8 (Aug. 24, 358); cf. 22.9.4; *Cons. Const.* s.a. 358 (Aug. 24, 358); Soc. 2.39.2–3 (Aug. 28, 358); Jer. *Chron.* s.a. 358; Aur. Vict. *Caes.* 16.12 (a. 358); *Chron. Edes.* no. 25 (a. 670 = A.D. 358/59); *Chron. Pasch.,* p. 543 (Oct. 359); Theoph. a.m. 5850 (a. 357/58); Cedrenus, p. 530; Philostorg. 4.10; Soz. 4.16.2–11; Lib. *Or.* 61.12–23; *Ep.* 388, 1187.

5. We need not be skeptical of the concentration of seismic events mentioned by the sources in this area. Nicomedia lies on the North Anatolian Fault, one of the most seismically active regions in the world. In the past 2,000 years, the fault has caused 600 documented quakes—40 of magnitude 7 or above—in the area around the Sea of Marmara on which Nicomedia lies. Moreover, earthquakes here as elsewhere tend to occur in clusters as with the recent quakes on August 17 and November 12, 1999, in and around Izmit (Nicomedia) itself. The fault consists of a number of fissures interlocked in such a way that a major quake on one often triggers less powerful quakes all along the fault line.

6. AM 22.13.5 (Dec. 2, 362); cf. Lib. *Or.* 18.292.

7. AM 23.1.3; Ruf. *HE* 10.39; Soc. 3.20.8–15; Soz. 5.22.7–8; Theod. *HE* 3.20.5–6; Lib. *Or.* 1.134, 17.30, 18.292.

through the release of subterranean methane gas. The destruction stretched as far east as the Dead Sea and the valley of the Jordan.[8]

TSUNAMI: JULY 21, 365

The earthquake of July 365, centered on western Crete, and the resulting tidal wave, which ran west-northwest to Sicily and east-southeast to Egypt, was the most devastating natural disaster in the reign of Valens and one of the most devastating in Roman antiquity.[9] Here again Ammianus's account is the most detailed: early in the morning, the coastal waters in affected areas began to recede, exposing marine wildlife and leaving boats stranded on the seafloor; a massive inundation followed, reaching inland as far as two miles in some regions and leaving boats marooned on rooftops. Many thousands were killed (Cedrenus reports 50,000) and the destruction to monuments was widespread, as the inscriptions from as far apart as Nauplion in the Peloponnese and Putorti in Sicily indicate. Sicily, Epirus, Achaea, Boeotia, Crete, and Egypt are mentioned in the sources as having been affected. Some areas were forever destroyed, such as, for example, the prosperous lands of Panephysis east of Alexandria, which, according to Cassian, were transformed into a brackish inland swamp.[10] Many sources also report the earthquake that triggered the tsunami. Jerome actually knew an eyewitness who lived through the quake on Crete, as he reports in his *Commentary on Isaiah*. That the epicenter of the 365 quake was on or near Crete is clear from testimony in the *Lives of Athanasius* reporting the collapse of over 100 cities on the island. Indeed, to this day the coast of western Crete still bears geologically identifiable marks of a sudden nine-meter uplift datable to 365 through radiocarbon tests on fossilized marine life.[11]

HAIL: JULY 4, 367

Socrates reports hand-sized chunks of hail in Constantinople in 367, and Jerome indicates that several people were killed by their impact.[12] It is difficult to gauge the

---

8. See Jacques and Bousquet 1984, 433–34.

9. The event is dated to July 21, 365, at AM 26.10.15–19; *Chron. Pasch.*, p. 556; *Cons. Const.* s.a. 365; *Fest. ind.* 37; and *Consularia Italica* 478 (*MGH.AA* 9.295). See also *CIG* 1166 = *IG* 4.674, at Nauplion (a. 365/67); *AE* 1913, 227, at Putorti; Soc. *HE* 4.3.3–5 (a. 365); Jacob of Edessa *Chron.*, p. 296 (a. 365); Them. *Or.* 11.150d; Jer. *Chron.* s.a. 366; *V Hilarionis* 40 (*PL* 23.51); *Comm. in Esaiam* 15 (*CCSL* 73.176); Soz. 6.2.14–15 (reign of Julian); Theoph. a.m. 5859 (a. 366/67); Cassian *Coll.* 7.26.2, 11.3.1–2; Anonymous *V Athanasii* 29 (*PG* 25.ccx); Photius *V Athanasii* 14 (*PG* 25.ccxxii); Simeon Metaphrastes *V Athansii* 17 (*PG* 25.ccxlv); Cedrenus, pp. 543–44 and 550; Oros. 7.32.5; John of Nikiu *Chron.* 82.21. Jacques and Bousquet 1984 treat both the history and the seismology of this event in superb detail. In their appendix, they list most—although not all—of the sources offered here, as well as a number of derivative accounts that I omit.

10. See A. Martin 1996, 597–98, for details on the psycho-spiritual consequences of the tsunami in Alexandria.

11. Kelletat 1998.

12. *Cons. Const.* s.a. 367 (July 4, 367); *Chron. Pasch.*, p. 557 (June 2, 367); Soc. *HE* 4.11.1–2 (June 2, 367); Jer. *Chron.* s.a. 367; Soz. 6.10.2.

scale of destruction to monuments and crops in the area, but the psychological effect was great for those wishing to see divine displeasure in the current state of ecclesiastical affairs.

EARTHQUAKE: OCTOBER 11, 368

Most sources, especially Gregory of Nazianzus, whose brother narrowly escaped death there, report massive destruction in Nicaea.[13] Socrates and Sozomen indicate that the quake also cut a broader swath across Bithynia.

EARTHQUAKE: CA. 368

Socrates alone reports that shortly after the Nicaea event, Germas, further to the east, was also destroyed by an earthquake.[14]

FAMINE: 370

Jerome, the *Consularia Constantinopolitana*, and Socrates provide good evidence for a major famine *(magna fames)* centered in Phrygia and extending across central Anatolia in 370.[15] The extent of the territory affected by the famine seems to have been much wider than just Phrygia. Socrates confirms that food troubles affected Constantinople when hungry provincials flocked to the city to take advantage of the surplus grain stockpiled there. Indeed, food supply problems probably explain why Valens rushed back to Constantinople in late 370 after having raced to the eastern frontier earlier in the year to halt the collapse of Armenia. He is first attested back in the capital in December 370,[16] and a law of February 371 confirms that one of his major objectives in returning was to restructure grain shipping to the eastern capital. It was perhaps at this time that he constructed the new Horrea Valentiaca, and he may also have worked on the port facilities.[17]

The famine apparently affected territories much further east as well. Valens issued a law in the twelfth indiction year (September 1, 369/August 31, 370), which ordered the clearing of the river Orontes, Antioch's grain-supply line, by marines placed temporarily under the charge of the praetorian prefect.[18] Although it is unlikely that a drought in Anatolia reached south of the Taurus, the shortage of grain empirewide may have affected Valens's decision to take this precautionary measure. Above all, several passages from the Cappadocian fathers describe in some detail the effects of

---

13. The earthquake is dated to Oct. 11, 368, at *Cons. Const.* s.a. 368, *Chron. Pasch.*, p. 557, and Soc. 4.11.4. See also Jer. *Chron.* s.a. 368; Greg. Naz. *Or.* 7.15; *Ep.* 20; Basil *Ep.* 26; John of Nikiu *Chron.* 82.19; Malalas 13.36 (p. 343: Sept. 368); Soz. 6.10.2.

14. Soc. 4.11.5.

15. *Cons. Const.* s.a. 370; Jerome *Chron.* s.a. 370; Soc. 4.16.7–17.1.

16. Seeck, *Regesten*, 241; cf. Barnes 1998, 252.

17. *CTh* 13.5.14 (Feb. 11, 371); *Not. urb. Consp.* 6.16; cf. Them. *Or.* 11.150c on the port.

18. *CTh* 10.23.1 = *CJ* 11.13.1.

"the most severe famine ever recorded."[19] This Cappadocian famine has generally been dated to 368/69, but on closer inspection, there is every reason to redate it to 370.[20] First of all, in his "Encomium of Basil," Gregory of Nazianzus places the famine immediately before his discussion of Basil's election, which occurred in September 370.[21] Secondly, we have four homilies delivered by Basil during the period of the famine in which he treats the divine causes of the disaster and encourages the wealthy of Cappadocia to open their grain stores to the needy.[22] In one of these, Basil mentions earthquakes, which has confused editors familiar with the Cappadocian corpus, who have wanted to see in this a reference to the earthquake of October 11, 368— the quake from which Gregory of Nazianzus's brother narrowly escaped—and thus dated the famine to 368/69. This dating must be rejected. In fact the passages in question refer to multiple disasters: "destructions of cities, earthquakes, [and] tidal waves."[23] Basil was thus not alluding to a single event but to the series of natural disasters that had plagued Anatolia in the previous decade. Even though the previously assumed 368/69 date is not proven by Basil's homilies, the homilies can give us a clue to the chronology. Basil describes the prelude to the famine in his "Homily on Hunger and Drought": the winter had brought no snow and the spring no rain, leaving no grain for a summer harvest.[24] The famine thus began in early summer. But which summer? This we can determine from three letters of Basil, written to Eusebius of Samosata with excuses for Basil's failure to pay a promised visit, which also make reference to the circumstances of this famine. In one, Basil mentions the close of winter and the anticipation of famine, and in the second, the actual manifestation of the famine.[25] The third, although it does not mention the famine, is clearly related by mention of the postponed visit. Fortunately, this last letter can be dated by its reference to the death of Basil's mother, Emmelia, to 370.[26] The famine was thus that summer.

One of the homilies of Basil also makes several mentions of a plague *(nosos).*[27] In a homily datable to 373, Gregory of Nazianzus also describes a recent hailstorm that was only the third in a series of disasters to strike Cappadocia, the first two being a livestock

19. Greg. Naz. *Or.* 43.34–6; Greg. Nys. *In laudem Basilii* 17; Greg. Nys. *V Macrinae* 972 (*GNO* 8.1: 384); Greg. Nys. *Eun.* 1.103 (*GNO* 1: 56–57).

20. For various attempts at dating see Loofs 1898, 50–52; Bernardi 1968, 60–61; Hauschild 1973–93, 2: 20–21.

21. On the date of Basil's election, see Pouchet 1992.

22. Basil *Homilia VI in Illud: Destruam horrea mea* (*PG* 31.261–77); *Homilia VII in divites* (*PG* 31.277–304); *Homilia VIII dicta tempore famis et siccitatis* (*PG* 31.304–28); *Homilia IX quod Deus non est auctor malorum* (*PG* 31.329–54). On these homilies, see now Holman 1999; 2001, 64–98, 182–92; cf. Bernardi 1968, 60–68; Rousseau 1994, 136–40.

23. Basil *Homilia IX quod Deus non est auctor malorum* 5 (*PG* 31.337–40): Πόλεων δὲ ἀφανισμοὶ, σεισμοί τε καὶ ἐπικλύσεις, καὶ στρατοπέδων ἀπώλειαι, καὶ ναυάγια, καὶ πᾶσαι πολυάνθρωποι φθοραί. Cf. ibid. 2, 3 (*PG* 31.331, 334); Greg. Naz. *Or.* 16.5 (*PG* 35.933).

24. *Homilia VII dicta tempore famis et siccitatis* 2 (*PG* 31.308–9).

25. Basil *Ep.* 27, 31.

26. Basil *Ep.* 30. Emmelia's death is datable shortly before Basil's election in 370 at Greg. Nys. *V Macrinae* 973 (*GNO* 8.1: 384–85); cf. Hauser-Meury 1960, 63.

27. Basil *Homilia IX quod Deus non est auctor malorum* 2, 3, 5 (*PG* 31.332, 333, 337).

epidemic and a drought.[28] We might assume that the drought was that of 370 but are left wondering whether the epidemic was somehow connected. This seems entirely plausible. Although the food shortage was most acute for humans in the summer of 370, for animals the dry winter and spring would have been just as bad, leaving them with no fodder. Further confirmation of a livestock plague under Valens comes in a little noticed passage of Jerome where the author notes that Valens had recently issued a law forbidding the consumption of veal in the eastern empire as a measure to benefit agriculture.[29] This would make best sense in the context of a major cattle plague.

FAMINE: SUMMER 372–SPRING 373

In oration eleven, delivered to Valens in Syria in 373, Themistius mentions recent efforts to relieve the victims of a famine.[30] While we might be tempted to associate this with the famine of 370, a more recent and local event would better fit the date of the speech. A hymn of Saint Ephraem's dated to 372 describes a shortage of the "bread of truth" in terms that make it quite clear that an earthly famine was occurring as he wrote in Syrian Edessa.[31] This famine can be dated more securely by a passage from the *Historia Lausiaca*, where Palladius describes how Ephraem undertook relief efforts for a famine at Edessa in the last year of his life. This involved extensive work and would have lasted up to the next year's harvest. Indeed, Palladius tells us that Ephraem only completed his labors and returned to his retreat one month before his death. This occurred on June 9, 373.[32] The famine thus hit in the summer of 372, and its effects were felt into the following year.

EARTHQUAKE: 375

Symmachus reports rebuilding at Beneventum in Campania after a recent quake, and his testimony seems to be confirmed by a series of rebuilding inscriptions from the region.[33]

EARTHQUAKE: WINTER 375/76

Zosimus reports that shortly after Valentinian's death (November 17, 375) earthquakes occurred in Crete, the Peloponnese, and the rest of Greece.[34] An inscription

---

28. Greg. Naz. *Or.* 16.10 (*PG* 35.948).

29. Jer. *Contra Iovinianum* 2.7 (*PL* 23.308): "Unde et imperator Valens nuper legem per Orientem dederat, ne quis vitulorum carnibus vesceretur, utilitatis agriculturae providens." Opelt 1971 offers a different interpretation.

30. Them. *Or.* 11.150d.

31. Ephraem *Carmen Nisibenum* 29.25–37 (*CSCO-SS* 219.84–5). On the date, see Beck 1961, iv.

32. Palladius *Hist. Laus.* 40.1–4 and *Chron. Edes.* no. 30 (a. 684 = A.D. 373); cf. Outtier 1973, 14–15.

33. Symm. *Ep.* 1.3.3–4; Cappelletti 1999.

34. Zos. 4.18.1–4; Lib. *Or.* 2.52; *AE* 1933, 197; *AE* 1929, 23 = *SEG* 11.773 with Robert 1948, 63.

from Gortyn datable to 372/76, which styles the praetorian prefect Petronius Probus εὐεργετὴν καὶ σωτῆρα, may be associated with relief efforts on Crete in the quake's aftermath, and a verse inscription of Sparta from 376 points to rebuilding after a quake there; an oration of Libanius's datable to 380/81 confirms that the quake also affected Cyprus—which lies on the same fault line as Crete and the Peloponnese.[35]

35. Norman 1969–77, 2:39 n. c, associates Libanius's reference with the quake mentioned at Zos. 4.18.1–4.

Civic Structures Built under Imperial Sponsorship, A.D. 364–378

The construction of public works and architectural showpieces had been an important duty of all emperors since the time of Augustus. Indeed, fourth-century emperors as much as their predecessors actively sought the glory associated with public architecture.[1] Thus it is no surprise that the *Panegyrici Latini* resound with praise for imperial building projects, and fourth-century epitomators were always keen to catalog the architectural feats of admirable emperors to serve as exempla for the present generation.[2] Ancient authors agree that Valentinian, Valens, and Gratian gladly lived up to this expectation with extensive building projects of their own.[3] And, like their predecessors, the Valentiniani were themselves regaled with praise for their projects in panegyrics.[4] Perhaps most striking among these is Themistius's eleventh oration, where the rhetor hails Valens as the true founder of Constantinople because of his completion of the aqueduct and imperial baths there.[5] Both of these were structures initiated under the Constantinians, leading Themistius to argue that the baths, which had already been named after Constantine, might more appropriately be renamed for Valens himself. After all, Valens did affix his name to the aqueduct, several of whose imposing arcades still stand in Istanbul.[6] Indeed, Valen-

1. See, e.g., AM 16.10.15–17, 17.4.6–16; cf. Lendon 1997, 116.

2. For the *Panegyrici Latini*, see *Pan. Lat.* 3 [11].9.1, 4 [10].35.4, 38.4, 6 [7].22.4–6, 9 [4].18.1–5; cf. Them. *Or.* 4.58b–d, 18.222c–d. For epitomators, see Aur. Vict. *Caes.* 9.7, 8, 10.5, 11.4, 12.2, 13.3–5, 17.3, 41.18; *Epit.* 1.18, 4.4, 9.8–10, 11.3–4, 14.4–5, 41.13. See also the admonition at *DRB* 1.4.

3. Malalas 13.29–31, 35 (pp. 338–39, 342); AM 30.9.1, 31.14.4.

4. Symm. *Or.* 3.9; Them. *Or.* 6.83a, 13.167b–168b.

5. Them. *Or.* 11.151c–152b; cf. 150a–d.

6. Evidence in the catalog at Co 5. Cyril Mango (1990b, 20; 1995, 10–12) has raised the question whether the remains of "Valens's aqueduct" (Turkish, Bozdogan) in Istanbul were not

tinian, Valens, and Gratian never hesitated to name structures after themselves and members of their families.[7] Architecture, they knew, would long outlast them and serve as a monumental reminder of the glory they hoped to project, especially if it advertised their names.

Even so, there was more to the building program of the Valentiniani than the simple pursuit of renown. Some of this can be gleaned from Themistius's insistence that Valens's completion of half-finished structures counted for more than their initiation. This rhetoric reflects a broader ideology of pragmatism and renewal that underlay the administration of all three emperors. The same ideology comes out already in the first months of their reign when the new emperors issued a law insisting that no new construction should be undertaken until old buildings that had fallen into "disfigured ruins" *(deformes ruinae)* were first repaired.[8] Within the next year and a half, this law was restated in four extant constitutions, making it clear that the rebuilding and completion of monuments was a key priority in these early years.[9] From epigraphy, we can confirm that these laws were carried out. In North Africa, where the epigraphic record is uniquely abundant, 27 of the 40 buildings known to have been built or rebuilt under Valentinian I were completed between 364 and 367.[10] Moreover, the inscriptions marking these reconstructions echo with almost uncanny consistency the language of the laws by heralding the restoration of structures "disfigured by the decay of ruin" *(ruinarum labe deformes).*[11]

Some of this insistence on restoration was a matter of simple necessity. The period leading up to and encompassing Valentinian's and Valens's reigns witnessed an extraordinary number of natural disasters, including seven earthquakes and a devastating tsunami (see appendix C). Our epigraphic material attests directly to the

---

rather those of Hadrian's earlier construction. I retain the traditional identification following Berger 1997, 379–80.

7. See examples in the catalog at Af 26, It 2, 4, Ro 4, 6, Co 5, 7–9, Or 4, and An 7. See also Cularo, which Valentinian renamed Gratianopolis, whence the modern Grenoble in Switzerland (*Notitia Galliarum* 11.3).

8. *CTh* 15.1.11 = *CJ* 8.11.5 (May 25, 364).

9. *CTh* 15.1.14 (Jan. 1, 365), 15.1.15 (Feb. 16, 365), 15.1.16 (Mar. 15, 365), 15.1.17 (Oct. 6, 365). Baldini 1979 demonstrates that these were part of a *lex generalis* that is no longer extant. Cf. Valens's law of 377 ordering curials to repair their old houses (*CJ* 8.10.8).

10. Thus an average of 6.75 buildings were built per year in the first four years of Valentinian's reign compared with 1.5 per year for the last eight years. The statistics are different for Valens's reign primarily because Valens became engrossed in the Procopius revolt precisely when Valentinian was building most vigorously. For a second wave of building clustered around the decennalia of the two emperors, see catalog numbers It 2, 3, Ro 7, Co 4–6, and Or 4. Most of these projects predate Valentinian's and Valens's return to cities of revenues from their civic estates in 372 (see p. 295).

11. See catalog numbers Af 1, 2, 6–8, 11, 12, 14–16, 18, Ro 3, and As 1; cf. *CIL* 10.7017; Them. *Or.* 11.150c–d. Themistius used similar rhetoric in a speech to Gratian from 376 (*Or.* 13.167b), mirrored in Gratian's own speech to the Senate on January 1, 376 (*CTh* 15.1.19; cf. 10.19.8 and Symm. *Ep.* 1.13). Here again the rhetoric shows up on contemporary inscriptions (cf. Af 28–33). Further epigraphic confirmation of central control can be found in the stereotyped use of "golden age" language *(pro magnificentia / splendore felicium saeculorum)* in inscriptions from 364–67, see catalog numbers Af 1, 2, 5–7, 9, 10, 12, 14, and 16–18.

fact that several monuments destroyed by these events were targeted for restoration, and Themistius confirms that rebuilding after these disasters was a high priority.[12] Even so, much of the effort to rebuild old monuments rather than undertaking new ones must have sprung from the inherent pragmatism of these two soldier emperors. Both were aware that abundant architectural resources already existed and that rebuilding decrepit structures or completing unfinished ones offered both a more practical and a more economical means to shore up the architectural infrastructure of the empire.

The pragmatism of Valentinian's and Valens's building program can be seen in the kinds of structures on which they focused: both were concerned with projects of benefit to the masses. For this reason, both were obsessed with the construction of waterworks. Valens's aqueduct in Constantinople is an excellent example: when it opened in 373, it provided water to a city that had formerly been "enfeebled" by lack of water.[13] To store this new supply, Valens also saw to the construction of a new cistern and nymphaeum.[14] Although Rome was already well outfitted with aqueducts, we know from a law of Valentinian's that these were rebuilt at the same time and an inscription records the construction of a water tower in 365.[15] And several other cities also witnessed the construction or reconstruction of aqueducts between 364 and 378.[16] So too, both emperors were obsessed with the construction or reconstruction of baths. In the west, we know of eleven bath complexes rebuilt in the period between 364 and 378; in the east, Valens built or completed three baths in Constantinople and a fourth, named after himself, in Antioch.[17] Waterworks and baths, inherently pragmatic and quintessentially Roman necessities, were thus of major concern to Valentinian and Valens.

Similar pragmatism can be seen in Valentinian's and Valens's interest in bridges. Valentinian rebuilt every bridge along the Tiber between Rome and Ostia—thirteen of them we now know from one of his inscriptions.[18] Although we have no epigraphic testimony for similar efforts by Valens, a reference in Themistius indicates that he too constructed or reconstructed bridges, and a reference in Malalas confirms that he built a vaulted superstructure over the torrent called Parmenios in

12. See catalog numbers Mo 3, It 2, As 1–2; cf. Mo 1–2, with Kent 1966, 165, and Them. *Or.* 11.150d. See also *AE* 1929, 23 = *SEG* 11.773, with Robert 1948, 63; Beschaouch 1975; Cappelletti 1999; cf. Foss 1979, 188–89.

13. Them. *Or.* 11.151a: ὀλιγοδρανέοντι. Cf. *Or.* 14.183c.

14. For the Cistern, Aqueduct, and Nymphaeum, see catalog numbers Co 2, 5, and 6 respectively.

15. *CTh* 14.6.3 (a. 365) and Ro 2. For other waterworks, see catalog numbers Af 8 and Or 1.

16. See catalog numbers Af 24, It 5, As 2, and An 1; cf. *CIL* 10.7017 (ca. 370/79). Aqueduct construction and repair was, of course, not unique to the Valentiniani; see *Pan. Lat.* 3 [11].9.2, 10.1, 5 [8].4.4, 9 [4].4.3; cf. Robert 1948, 64–72.

17. See catalog numbers Af 1, 6, 17–19, 32, 33, It 2, 4, 7, Co 4, 7, 8, and An 7; cf. Af 8. Often these included porticoes, apparently a favorite architectural feature of the two emperors (Af 1, 8, 23, 26, 28, 29, Ro 5, 8, It 6, An 5). Valentinian also remodeled the *Kaiserthermen* of Trier, see Wightman 1971, 113–15.

18. *AE* 1975, 134 = Floriani Squarciapino 1973–74. For some of these bridges, see catalog numbers Ro 3–5. Cf. Them. *Or.* 13.167c and *CTh* 10.10.2. See also Canali de Rossi 1999 on the evidence for extensive road repairs under the Valentiniani.

Antioch.[19] What with their concern for justice, the Pannonian emperors also constructed or reconstructed ten basilicas across the empire, at least one of which was outfitted with the requisite *tribunal* and *secretarium* called for in their law of 364.[20] Fora, markets, and grain storage facilities were also a high priority.[21] And we have evidence for the reconstruction of several racecourses and amphitheaters, again projects designed to serve the needs of the masses.[22]

With the buildings of Valentinian and Valens, we thus have further evidence to confirm a number of hypotheses presented in the main text. First, the imperial brothers concentrated on the completion or reconstruction of existing buildings rather than the inception of new ones. This fits well with the pragmatism we have already witnessed in their laws on the economy, taxation, and justice. Second, both were primarily interested in the same types of structures, particularly aqueducts, bridges, baths, and basilicas. This points up the fact that they worked together closely on their architectural programs, as on so much else. Finally, both focused their building efforts on projects of benefit to the masses. This fits well with the concern for the common man that we have seen in their broader administration of the empire.

CATALOG OF EPIGRAPHIC AND TEXTUAL SOURCES

The evidence in this catalog is broken down by dioceses and is then presented in chronological order. Material from Antioch, Constantinople, and Rome, because it is particularly abundant, is grouped separately.

Africa

Af 1 Baths in Madaura (a. 364): AE 1917–18, 91 = *ILAlg.* 1.2101

Af 2 Amphitheater? In Gelma (a. 364): *CIL* 8.5336 = *ILAlg.* 1.255; *CIL* 8.5337 = *ILAlg.* 1.254

Af 3 Temple in Henchir Mest (a. 364): *AE* 1933, 33

Af 4 Unknown structure in Henchir el Abiadh (a. 364/67): *AE* 1909, 222

---

19. Them. *Or.* 11.150c implies the construction not only of bridges but of other structures with broad public benefit. We cannot specify further the location or identity of these projects. For the Parmenios, see catalog number An 9.

20. See catalog numbers Af 12, 14, 20, 22, It 1, 3, Ro 10, Mo 3, and An 3–4; cf. Af 27. On the *tribunal* and *secretarium* connected to the basilica at Luceria, see Russi 1991, 319–21, with *CTh* 1.16.9; cf. *P Oxy* 4381.

21. For fora and markets, see catalog numbers Af 11, 30, 31, Ro 7, 8, Mo 1–3, An 2, 6. For *horrea*, see Af 10 and Co 9; cf. *CTh* 15.1.17. See also Valentinian's reconstruction of the *horrea* of Trier (Wightman 1971, 118).

22. See catalog numbers Af 2, Or 3, and An 8. Naturally, many of these projects were paid for at civic expense. Even so, the catalog below presents only structures that were at least overseen by imperial officials and were thus clearly mandated from the pragmatically minded emperors on high, thus, e.g., Af 1–4, 6–9, 12–14, 17–23, 26–30, 33, and It 1. Lib. *Ep.* 196, 242, and 617 illustrate well how important a role pressure from imperial officials played in coaxing along civic building projects. Moreover, even civic projects were closely linked to imperial finance under the Valentiniani (see p. 295).

Af 5 Unknown structure in Kenchela (a. 364/67): *CIL* 8.2242[23]

Af 6 Baths in Kenchela (a. 364/67): *AE* 1911, 271

Af 7 Quadroporticus in Timgad (a. 364/67): *CIL* 8.2388 = *ILS* 5554

Af 8 Fountain temple in Aïn-Drinn (a. 364/67): *CIL* 8.2656

Af 9 Arch in Ksur el Ahmar (a. 364/67): *CIL* 8.4767 = 18701 = *ILS* 5571

Af 10 Horrea in Rusicade (a. 364/67): *CIL* 8.7975 = *ILS* 5910

Af 11 *Forum Transitorium* in Lambaesis (a. 364/67): *CIL* 8.2722

Af 12 *Basilica Vestiaria* in Cuicul / Djemila (a. 364/67): *CIL* 8.20156 = *ILS* 5536

Af 13 Unknown structure in Cuicul / Djemila (a. 364/67): *AE* 1911, 110

Af 14 Basilica in Cuicul (a. 364/67): *AE* 1913, 35; *AE* 1946, 107

Af 15 Unknown structure in Madaura (a. 364/67): *AE* 1917–18, 58

Af 16 Unknown structure in Taparura/Sfax (a. 364/67): *CIL* 8.22830 = *AE* 1902, 58

Af 17 Baths in Madaura (a. 366/67): *AE* 1907, 237

Af 18 Piscina in Calama (a. 366/67): *CIL* 8.5335 = *ILS* 5730

Af 19 Baths in Carthage (a. 368/70): *AE* 1975, 873

Af 20 Praetorium in Aradi (a. 368/70): *AE* 1955, 52

Af 21 Triporticum in Henchir Sidi Ahmed el Hocheni (a. 368/70): *CIL* 8.27817 = *ILS* 5557

Af 22 Basilica in Cuicul/Djemila (a. 367/74): *CIL* 8.8324 = *ILS* 5535

Af 23 *Porticus nova* in Aïn Nechma (a. 367/75): *CIL* 8.17517 = *AE* 1892, 34

Af 24 Aqueduct in Kenchela (a. 367/75): *AE* 1899, 216

Af 25 Arch in Henchir el Abiadh (a. 367/75): *AE* 1909, 223

Af 26 Portico in Constantina (a. 367/75): *CIL* 8.7015 = *ILS* 5555

Af 27 Basilica ? in Vicus Maracitanus (a. 373/74): *AE* 1998, 1531

Af 28 Portico in Thuburbo Maius (a. 376/77): *AE* 1915, 59 = *AE* 1919, 32

Af 29 Portico and stairway in Henchir Tut el Kaya (a. 376/77): *CIL* 8.14346 = *ILS* 5556

Af 30 Rostra in Abthungi/Henchir Souar (a. 376/77): *AE* 1991, 1641–4

Af 31 Forum in Abthungi/Henchir Souar (a. 376/77): *AE* 1995, 1655

Af 32 Baths in Sabratha (a. 378): *IRT* 103

Af 33 Licinian Baths in Dougga (a. 375/83): *AE* 1925, 31

---

23. Publilius Caeionius Caecina Albinus, who restored this and many other monuments during his tenure as *consularis Numidiae*, is also recorded in fragmentary inscriptions that probably mark building restorations in Lambaesis (*CIL* 8.2735 = 18229), Constantina (*CIL* 8.19502 = *ILAlg.* 2.618 and *CIL* 8.6975 = *ILAlg.* 2.541), and Tasbent (*AE* 1909, 220).

Italia

It 1 *Secretarium* and *Tribunal* in the Basilica at Luceria (a. 364/67): Russi 1991[24]

It 2 Baths in Putorti (a. 374): *AE* 1913, 227

It 3 Basilica in Putorti (a. 374): *AE* 1913, 227

It 4 *Thermae Gratianae* in Segusio (a. 375/78): *CIL* 5.7250 = *ILS* 5701

It 5 Aqueduct in Segusio (a. 375/78): *CIL* 5.7250 = *ILS* 5701

It 6 Temple and portico of Isis (a. 376): *AE* 1968, 86

It 7 *Thermae Maritimae* in Ostia (a. 377): *CIL* 14.137 = *ILS* 5694

Rome

Ro 1 Doorway in St. Peters (a. 364/67): *CIL* 6.1170 = *AE* 1976, 102

Ro 2 Water Tower on Via Ostiense (a. 365): *CIL* 6.3866

Ro 3 Bridge on Fossa Galeria (a. 365/66): *AE* 1975, 134

Ro 4 *Pons Valentinianus* (Ponte Sisto) (a. 366/67):[25] *CIL* 6.31402–12 = *ILS* 769; AM 27.3.3

Ro 5 *Porticus Deorum Consentium* (a. 367/68): *CIL* 6.102 = *ILS* 4003

Ro 6 *Pons Gratianus* (Ponte Cestio) (a. 369): *CIL* 6.1175 = *ILS* 771; *CIL* 6.1176 = *ILS* 772; *CIL* 6.31251; Sym. *Or.* 3.9; Them. *Or.* 13.167b

Ro 7 *Forum Palatinum* (a. 374): *CIL* 6.1177 = *ILS* 776

Ro 8 *Porticus Eventus Boni* (a. 374): AM 29.6.19

Ro 9 *Macellum Liviae* (a. 375?): *CIL* 6.1178 = *ILS* 5592

Ro 10 *Basilica Iulia* (a. 377): *CIL* 6.11566 = *ILS* 5537

Moesiae

Mo 1 Colonnade of west shops in Corinth (a. 364/67): *AE* 1989, 654

Mo 2 Stoa in Corinth (a. 364/67): Kent 1966, 166–7 no. 505

Mo 3 Basilica in Nauplion (a. 366/67): *CIG* 1166 = *IG* 4.674

---

24. Russi 1991, 312–13, makes the case that these structures were part of a basilica.

25. *CIL* 6.31405–7 indicate that the bridge was dedicated VOTIS DECENNALIBUS DOMINI NOSTRI, i.e., in 373, yet AM 27.3.3 implies that it was dedicated earlier. Floriani Squarciapino 1973–74, 255 n. 14, argues convincingly for 366/67. See also Mommsen 1880; Bertinetti 2000.

Constantinople

Co 1 Tribunal in Hebdomon (a. 364/65):[26] Them. *Or.* 6.83a

Co 2 *Cisterna Modestiaca* (a. 369):[27] *Cons. Const.* s.a. 369; *Not. urb. Const.* 12.12

Co 3 Church of the Holy Apostles (a. 370):[28] *Cons. Const.* s.a. 370; Jer. *Chron.* s.a. 370; Prosper *Chron.* s.a. 370; *Chron. Pasch.* p. 559

Co 4 *Thermae Constantinianae* (ca. 373):[29] Them. *Or.* 11.152a; Soc. *HE* 4.8.2; AM 31.1.4; John of Antioch fr. 184

Co 5 Aqueduct of Valens (a. 373):[30] Jer. *Chron.* s.a. 373; Them. *Or.* 11.150d–152b, 13.168a-c; 14.183c; Greg. Naz. *Or.* 33.6; Soc. 4.8.7; *Parastaseis syntomoi chronicae* 74; Cedrenus, pp. 543, 544; Theoph. a.m. 5860; Zon. 13.16.33–35

Co 6 Nymphaion of Clearchus (a. 373):[31] Them. *Or.* 13.168b; *Not. urb. Const.* 11.14; Soc. 4.8.8–9; Zon. 13.16.33–5; Cedrenus, p. 543

Co 7 *Thermae Carosianae* (a. 375): *Cons. Const.* s.a. 375; *Chron. pasch.*, pp. 556, 560; *Not. urb. Const.* 8.17; Soc. 4.9.5; Soz. 6.9.3; Theoph. a.m. 5860

Co 8 *Thermae Anastasianae* (a. 375?):[32] Soc. 4.9.5; Soz. 6.9.3; *Chron. pasch.*, p. 556; Theoph. a.m. 5860; *Not. urb. Const.* 10.8

Co 9 Horrea Valentiaca (a. ?): *Not. urb. Const.* 6.16

---

26. See Van Millingen 1899, 326–31; Janin 1964, 139. Dagron 1974, 88–92, provides a useful list of imperial building projects in Constantinople during the fourth century.

27. Lib. *Ep.* 827 indicates that the cistern was begun in 363 by an architect named Helpidius under Modestus's direction. See more at Janin 1964, 209; Berger 1997, 371.

28. On the completion of this church see Mango 1990a, 56.

29. Them. *Or.* 11.152a indicates that Valens considered renaming this structure after himself even though it had been begun under Constantius II (cf. *Or.* 4.58b–c; *Chron. pasch.*, p. 534 [a. 345]). The *Notitia urbis Constantinopolitanae* 11.10 makes it clear that the name *Thermae Constantinianae* was in use in the early fifth century. But in 427, the *Constantinianae* were remodeled and rededicated as the *Theodosianae* (*Chron. pasch.*, pp. 580–81). Even so, Evagrius *HE* 1.20 indicates that some also referred to the complex as τὸ Βάλεντος λουτρόν. On the location of these and other baths in Constantinople, see Mango 1990b, 41; Berger 1997, 369–70.

30. Them. *Or.* 11.151a–b makes it clear that, here again, Valens completed construction of the aqueduct begun under Constantine and Constantius. Indeed, *Or.* 4.58b (πηγάς τε μασ-τεύων ἀφθονωτέρων ναμάτων) confirms that the Constantinian aqueduct was not complete as of 357. More on the aqueduct at Çeçen 1996, with earlier bibliography, especially Dalman 1933.

31. Socrates reports that this structure was commonly referred to as the Δαψιλὲς ὕδωρ. See more at Janin 1964, 200–201; Mango 1995, 14–15; Berger 1997, 380.

32. Among extant sources, Socrates first reports that Valens named separate public baths after his daughters, Anastasia and Carosa. His notice is followed closely by Sozomen, the *Chronicon paschale*, and Theophanes. The *Notitia urbis Constantinopolitanae* makes it clear that *Thermae Anastasianae* there were, but Ammianus 26.6.14 (cf. 21.15.6) states explicitly that they were named after Constantine's sister, *PLRE* I's Anastasia 1. Perhaps, as with the baths of Constantine, these were completed by Valens and then rededicated in the name of Valens's own homonymous daughter. Cf. Berger 1997, 369.

Asiana

As 1 *Moenia* in Ephesus (a. 371): *AE* 1906, 30 = *IK* 11.1.42

As 2 Aqueduct of Magnesia (a. 371/72): Robert 1948, 63

Pontica

Po 1 Unknown structure in Nigde (a. 369/77): Rott 1908, 379, no. 102

Oriens

Or 1 *Fluvius Tatianus* in Alexandria (a. 367/70): *Barbarus Scaligeri* 297 (*MGH.AA.* 9.296)[33]

Or 2 *Portae Petrinae* in Alexandria (a. 367/70): *Barbarus Scaligeri* 297 (*MGH.AA.* 9.296); cf. John of Nikiu *Chron.* 82.20; *P. Cair. Masp.* 67168: Πυλῶν Τατιανο (ῦ).

Or 3 Stadium in Tarsus (a. 367/75): *CIG* 4437

Or 4 Tetrapylon in Athribis / Benka el Assel (a. 373): *OGIS* 722 = *CIG* 8610

Or 5 Julian's tomb in Tarsus (a. ?): Lib. *Or.* 24.10

Antioch

An 1 Aqueduct at Daphne (a. 370): *CTh* 15.2.2

An 2 Forum of Antioch rebuilt (a. 370/75):[34] Malalas 13.30–1 (p. 338–39)

An 3 *Caesarion* of Antioch (a. 370/75): Malalas 13.30 (p. 338–39)

An 4 Basilica opposite the Baths of Commodus (a. 370/75): Malalas 13.30 (p. 339)

An 5 Four colonnades (a. 370/75):[35] Malalas 13.30–31 (p. 339)

An 6 Market (a. 370/75): Downey 1961, 406 n. 59

---

33. Placed under the consular year 375 but clearly datable between 367 and 370, when Tatianus was prefect of Egypt. I do not list the rebuilding of the Caesarion in Alexandria, which was apparently funded entirely by the church; see *Fest. ind.* 40; cf. *Fest. ind.* 38; Ephiphan. *Adv. haeres.* 69.2.3. I do not separate Egypt from the diocese of Oriens for this table, although in 370 Valens did split it off from Oriens to create an Egyptian diocese (see p. 280).

34. Malalas 13.30 (p. 338) indicates that Valens's building activities in Antioch only began after he first arrived there in 370. Because he states that they were part of a coordinated program focused on Valens's new forum, and because that forum included three statues of Valentinian, it must have been completed before his death in 375. On this complex of buildings see Downey 1961, 403–7, 632–40.

35. See Downey 1961, 406 n. 57, on Malalas's confusing reference to these structures as βασιλικαί.

An 7 *Valentinum lavacrum* of Antioch (a. 370/78):[36] AM 31.1.2; Malalas 13.31 (p. 339); Michael Syrus *Chron.* 1.294 (Chabot)

An 8 *Cynegion* in Antioch (a. 370/78):[37] Malalas 13.31 (p. 339); cf. Michael Syrus *Chron.* 1.294 (Chabot)

An 9 Vaulting over the Parmenios (a. 370/78):[38] Malalas 13.30 (p. 339)

36. See Poccardi 1994, 1003–4, on the remains of baths.

37. See Downey 1961, 407–10. The hippodrome was also rebuilt in the fourth century, perhaps under Valens. See Humphrey 1986, 455–57.

38. See Downey 1961, 405, on the remains.

BIBLIOGRAPHY

PRIMARY SOURCES

Where the best text for a source remains the *Patrologia Graeca* or the *Patrologia Latina*, the source is not listed below. In these instances, the *PG* or *PL* volume and page number are cited in the notes together with the source reference. Translations are listed where they formed an important basis for translated passages in the text.

Agathangelos. *History of the Armenians*, trans. R. W. Thomson (Albany, N.Y., 1976).
Agathias. *De imperio et rebus gestis Iustiniani: CFHB* 2 and 2a (ed. R. Keydell, trans. J. D. Frendo, 1975).
Ambrose. *De fide: CSEL* 78 (ed. O. Faller, 1962).
———. *De obitu Valentiniani: CSEL* 73: 327–67 (ed. O. Faller, 1955); cf. *De consolatione Valentiniani*, ed. T. A. Kelly (Washington, D.C., 1940).
———. *Epistulae: CSEL* 82.1 (ed. O. Faller, 1968: books 1–6); *CSEL* 82.2 (ed. M. Zelzer, 1990: books 7–9); *CSEL* 82.3 (ed. M. Zelzer, 1982: book 10 and *Epistulae extra collectionem*).
———. *Expositio evangelii secundum Lucam: CCSL* 14 (ed. M. Adriaen, 1957).
Ambrosiaster. *Quaestiones veteris et novi testamenti CXXVII: CSEL* 50 (ed. A. Souter, 1908).
Ammianus Marcellinus. *Rerum gestarum libri qui supersunt*, ed. C. U. Clark, 2 vols. (1910; reprint, Berlin, 1963); cf. *Ammianus Marcellinus*, trans. J. C. Rolfe, 3 vols. (Cambridge, Mass., 1935–39).
Amphilochius. *Homilia in Vita Basilii*, trans. K. V. Zettersteén, *Oriens Christianus* 31: 67–98 (1934).
Asxarhac'oyc'. The Geography of Ananias of Sirak (Asxarhac'oyc'): The Long and Short Recensions, trans. and comm. R. H. Hewsen. *Beihefte zum Tübinger Atlas des Vorderen Orients*, B, 77 (Wiesbaden, 1992).
Athanasius. *Festal Letters* (Syriac), trans. W. Cureton, *The Festal Epistles of S. Athanasius* (Oxford, 1854).

————. *Festal Letters* (Coptic), *Lettres festales et pastorales en copte: CSCO.SC* 150–51 (ed. and trans. L.-T. Lefort, 1955).

Augustine. *De civitate dei libri XXII: CSEL* 40.1–2 (ed. E. Hoffmann, 1899–1900).

————. *Epistulae 1*–29*: CSEL* 88 (ed. J. Divjak, 1981).

Aurelius Victor. *Liber de caesaribus,* ed. F. Pichlmayr (Leipzig, 1961); cf. *Aurelius Victor: De Caesaribus,* trans. H. W. Bird (Liverpool, 1994).

Ausonius. *Decimi Magni Ausonii opera,* ed. R. P. H. Green (Oxford, 1999); cf. *Ausonius,* trans. H. G. Evelyn-White, 2 vols. (Cambridge, Mass., 1919–21).

Auxentius of Durosotrum. In *Dissertatio Maximini contra Arianos: CCSL* 87.1: xxi–xxii; 160–66 (ed. R. Gryson, 1982).

Barbarus Scaligeri. Chronica minora I: MGH.AA 9: 290–98 (ed. T. Mommsen, 1892).

Basil. *Lettres,* ed. and trans. Y. Courtonne, 3 vols. (Paris, 1957–66); cf. *St. Basil: The Letters,* trans. R. J. Deferrari, 4 vols. (Cambridge, Mass., 1926–34).

Buzandaran Patmut'iwink'. The Epic Histories attributed to P'awstos Buzand (Buzandaran Patmut'iwink'), trans. and comm. N. G. Garsoïan (Cambridge, Mass., 1989).

Cedrenus. *Historiarum compendium: CSHB* 34 (ed. I. Bekker, 1838).

Chronicon Edessenum: CSCO.SS 3.4.1 (ed. I. Guidi, 1903).

Chronicon miscellaneum ad annum domini 724 Pertinens: CSCO.SS 3.4 (ed. E.-W. Brooks, 1904).

Chronicon miscellaneum ad annum domini 846 pertinens: CSCO.SS 3.4 (ed. E.-W. Brooks, 1904).

Chronicon paschale: CSHB 16 (ed. L. Dindorf, 1832); cf. *Chronicon paschale, 284– 628 A.D.,* trans. M. Whitby and M. Whitby (Liverpool, 1989).

Codex Theodosianus. Theodosiani libri XVI cum constitutionibus Sirmondianis, ed. T. Mommsen (1905; reprint, Hildesheim, 1990); cf. *The Theodosian Code and Novels and the Sirmondian Constitutions,* trans. C. Pharr (Princeton, N.J., 1952).

Codex Iustinianus. Corpus iuris civilis, ed. P. Krueger, vol. 2 (1914; reprint, Berlin, 1954).

Codinus. *Patria Constantinopoleos.* In *Scriptores originum Constantinopolitanarum,* ed. T. Preger, pp. 135–289 (Leipzig, 1907).

Consularia Constantinopolitana. The Chronicle of Hydatius and the Consularia Constantinopolitana: Two Contemporary Accounts of the Final Years of the Roman Empire, ed. and trans. R. W. Burgess, pp. 211–45 (Oxford, 1993).

Consultatio Veteris Cuiusdam Iurisconsulti. In *Collectio Librorum Iuris Anteiustiniani in Usum Scholarum,* ed. P. Krueger, T. Mommsen, and G. Studemund, vol. 3 (Berlin, 1890).

De rebus bellicis, ed. R. I. Ireland (Leipzig, 1984), cf. *A Roman Reformer and Inventor,* trans. E. A. Thompson (Oxford, 1952).

Dio Cassius. *Historia Romana,* ed. L. Dindorf, 5 vols. (Leipzig, 1863–65).

Ephrem Syrus. *Carmina Nisibena: CSCO.SS* 218–19 (ed. E. Beck, 1961).

————. *Hymnen de Fide: CSCO.SS* 154–55 (ed. E. Beck, 1955).

————. *Sancti Ephraem Syri hymni et sermones,* ed. and trans. T. J. Lamy, 4 vols. (Louvain, 1882–1902); cf. *Ephrem the Syrian: Hymns,* trans. K. McVey (New York, 1989).

Epiphanius. *Panarion Haeresiarum,* ed. C. Holl and J. Dummer, 3 vols. (Berlin, 1915–85); cf. *The Panarion of Epiphanius of Salamis,* trans. F. Williams, 2 vols. (Leiden, 1987–94).

Epitome de caesaribus. In *Sexti Aurelii Victoris Liber De Caesaribus,* ed. F. Pichlmayr, pp. 131–76 (Leipzig, 1966).

Eunapius. *Historiarum Fragmenta.* In *The Fragmentary Classicising Historians of the Later Roman Empire*, ed. and trans. R. C. Blockley, 2: 2–150 (Liverpool, 1982).

———. *Vitae Sophistarum*, ed. I. Giangrande (Rome, 1956); cf. *Philostratus and Eunapius the Lives of the Sophists*, trans. W. C. Wright (Cambridge, Mass., 1921).

Eusebius. *Oratio de laudibus Constantini.* In *Eusebius Werke* 1, ed. I. A. Heikel, pp. 195–223 (Berlin, 1902); cf. *In Praise of Constantine*, trans. H. A. Drake (Berkeley, 1975).

———. *Vita Constantini: Eusebius Werke* 1.1 *Über das Leben des Kaisers Konstantin*, ed. F. Winkelmann (Berlin, 1975).

Eutropius. *Breviarium ab urbe condita*, ed. C. Santini (Leipzig, 1897).

Excerpta Valesiana, ed. J. Moreau (Leipzig, 1968).

Expositio totius mundi et gentium: SCh 124 (ed. and trans. J. Rougé, 1966).

Festal Index: SCh 317 (ed. and trans. A. Martin and M. Albert, 1985).

Festus. *The Breviarium of Festus: A Critical Edition with Historical Commentary*, ed. J. W. Eadie (London, 1967).

Firmicus Maternus. *Matheseos Libri VIII*, ed. W. Kroll and F. Skutsch (Stuttgart, 1968).

Gregory of Nazianzus. *De vita sua*, ed. and trans. C. Jungck (Heidelberg, 1974); cf. *Gregory of Nazianzus Autobiographical Poems*, trans. C. White (Cambridge, 1996).

———. *Discours 4–5: SCh* 309 (ed. and trans. J. Bernardi, 1983).

———. *Discours 6–12: SCh* 405 (ed. and trans. M.-A. Calvet-Sebasti, 1995).

———. *Discours 20–23: SCh* 270 (ed. and trans. J. Mossay, 1980).

———. *Discours 24–26: SCh* 284 (ed. and trans. J. Mossay and G. Lafontaine, 1981).

———. *Discours 42–43: SCh* 384 (ed. and trans. J. Bernardi, 1992).

———. *Lettres*, ed. and trans. P. Gallay, 2 vols. (Paris, 1964–67).

Gregory of Nyssa. *Adversus eos qui baptismum differunt: GNO* 10.2: 357–70 (ed. H. Polack, 1996).

———. *Contra Eunomium: GNO* 1–2 (ed. W. Jaeger, 1952).

———. *In laudem Basilii. Encomium of Saint Gregory of Nyssa on his Brother Saint Basil*, ed. and trans. J. A. Stein (Washington, D.C., 1928).

———. *In Meletium: GNO* 9: 441–57 (ed. G. Heil et al., 1967).

———. *Lettres: SCh* 163 (ed. and trans. P. Maraval, 1958).

———. *Vita Macrinae: GNO* 8.1: 370–414 (ed. V. Woods Callahan, 1952).

Himerius. *Declamationes et orationes cum deperditarum fragmentis*, ed. A. Colonna (Rome, 1951).

Historia acephala: SCh 317 (ed. and trans. A. Martin and M. Albert, 1985).

Historia S. Ephraemi. In *Sancti Ephraemi Syri hymni et sermones*, ed. and trans. T. J. Lamy, vol. 2 (Louvain, 1886).

Inscriptions of Roman Tripolitania, ed. J. M. Reynolds and J. B. Ward Perkins (Rome, 1952).

Itinerarium Alexandri ad Constantium Augustum, ed. A. Mai (Frankfurt am Main, 1818); cf. R. Tabacco. *Per una nuova edizione critica dell'Itinerarium Alexandri* (Bologna, 1992).

Itinerarium Antonini. In *Itineraria romana*, ed. O. Cuntz, vol. 1 (Leipzig, 1929).

Itinerarium Egeriae. In *Itineraria et alia geographica: CCSL* 175: 26–103 (ed. A. Franceschini and R. Weber, 1965).

Jacob of Edessa. *Chronicon: CSCO.SS* 3.4 (ed. E.-W. Brooks, 1905).

Jerome. *Chronicon: Eusebius Werke* 7, ed. R. Helm and U. Treu, 3d ed. (Berlin, 1984).

————. *Epistulae: CSEL* 54–56 (ed. I. Hilberg, 1910–18).

John of Antioch. *Historiarum Fragmenta*. In *Fragmenta historicorum graecorum*, ed. K. Müller, 4: 535–622 (Paris, 1868).

John Cassian. *Conlationes XXIIII: CSEL* 13 (ed. M. Petschenig, 1886).

John Chrysostom. *Ad viduam iuniorem: À une jeune veuve sur le mariage unique: SCh* 138 (ed. and trans. B. Grillet and H. Ettlinger, 1968).

————. *De incomprehensibilitate Dei: Sur l'incompréhensibilité de Dieu homélies I–V: SCh* 28 bis (ed. and trans. J. Daniélou, 1970).

John Lydus. *De magistratibus populi romani libri tres: On Powers, or, The Magistrates of the Roman State*, ed., trans. and comm. A. C. Bandy (Philadelphia, 1982).

John of Nikiu. *The Chronicle of John, Coptic Bishop of Nikiu*, trans. R. H. Charles (London, 1916).

Jordanes. *Getica: MGH.AA* 5: 53–138 (ed. T. Mommsen, 1882).

————. *Romana: MGH.AA* 5: 1–52 (ed. T. Mommsen, 1882).

Joshua the Stylite. *The Chronicle of Pseudo-Joshua the Stylite*, trans. and comm. F. R. Trombley and J. W. Watt (Liverpool, 2000).

Julian. *Epistulae leges poemata fragmenta varia*, ed. and trans. J. Bidez and F. Cumont (Paris, 1922).

————. *Oeuvres complètes*, ed. and trans. J. Bidez, C. Lacombrade, and G. Rochefort, 4 vols. (Paris, 1932–64).

Lactantius. *De mortibus persecutorum*, ed. and trans. J. L. Creed (Oxford, 1984).

Lazar P'arpec'i. *The History of Lazar P'arpec'i*, trans. R. W. Thomson (Atlanta, 1991).

Libanius. *Opera*, ed. H. Foerster, 12 vols (Leipzig, 1903–23); cf. *Libanius: Autobiography and Selected Letters*, trans. A. F. Norman, 2 vols. (Cambridge, Mass., 1992), and *Libanius, Selected Works*, trans. A. F. Norman, 2 vols. (Cambridge, Mass., 1969–77).

Malalas, Iohannes. *Chronographia: CFHB* 35 (ed. J. Thurn, 2000); cf. *The Chronicle of John Malalas*, trans. E. Jeffreys, M. Jeffreys, and R. Scott (Melbourne, 1986).

Marcellinus Comes. *Chronicon: MGH.AA* 11: 37–108 (ed. T. Mommsen, 1894).

Menander Rhetor, ed. and trans. D. A. Russell and N. G. Wilson (Oxford, 1981).

Michael the Syrian. *Chronique*, ed. and trans. by J.-B. Chabot, 4 vols. (1899–1924; reprint, Paris, 1963).

Moses Khorenats'i. *History of the Armenians*, trans. R. W. Thomson (Cambridge, Mass., 1978).

Narratio de imperatoribus domus Valentinianae et Theodosianae. In *Chronica minora* 1: *MGH.AA* 9: 629–30 (ed. T. Mommsen, 1892).

Notitia dignitatum, ed. O. Seeck (1876; reprint, Berlin, 1962).

Notitia urbis Constantinopolitanae. In *Notitia dignitatum*, ed. O. Seeck, pp. 227–43 (1876; reprint Berlin 1962).

Optatianus Porfyrius. *Carmina*, ed. J. Polara, 2 vols. (Milan, 1973).

Orphei Lithica. In *Orphica*, ed. E. Abel (Leipzig, 1885).

Orosius. *Historiarum adversum paganos libri VII: CSEL* 5 (ed. K. Zangemeister, 1882); cf. *Orose Histoire contre les païens*, ed. and trans. M.-P. Arnaud Lindet, 2 vols. (Paris, 1991).

Panegyrici Latini, ed. R. A. B. Mynors (Oxford, 1964); cf. *Panégyriques Latins*, ed. E. Gallatier, 3 vols. (Paris, 1949–55).

P Abbinaeus. The Abbinaeus Archive: Papers of a Roman Officer in the Reign of Constantius II, ed. H. I. Bell et al. (Oxford, 1962).

P Florentiae. Papiri fiorentini, ed. G. Vitelli (Milan, 1905).

P Graecae Magicae. Die Griechischen Zauberpapyri, ed. K. Preisendanz (Stuttgart, 1973).

P Lipsiae. Griechische Urkunden der Papyrussamlung zu Leipzig, ed. L. Mitteis (Leipzig, 1906).

P Oxy. The Oxyrhyncus Papyri, eds. B. P. Grenfell et al. (London, 1898–).

P Turner. Papyri Greek and Egyptian Edited by Various Hands in Honor of Eric Gardner Turner (London, 1981).

Parastaseis syntomoi chronicae. In *Scriptores originum Constantinopolitanarum,* ed. T. Preger, pp. 19–73 (Leipzig, 1907).

Passio Artemii. In *Philostorgius Kirchengeschichte,* ed. J. Bidez and F. Winkelmann, pp. 151–75 (Berlin, 1972).

Passio Sancti Sabae Gothi, ed. H. Delehaye, *AB* 31: 216–21 (1912); cf. *The Goths in the Fourth Century,* trans. P. Heather and J. Matthews, pp. 109–17 (Liverpool, 1991).

Passio sanctorum Innae, Rhimae et Pinae. ed. H. Delehaye, *AB* 31: 215–16 (1912).

Philostorgius. *Historia ecclesiastica: Kirchengeschichte,* ed. J. Bidez and F. Winkelmann (Berlin, 1972).

Procopius. *Opera omnia,* ed. J. Haury, 3 vols. (Leipzig, 1905–13).

Prosper Tiro. *Epitoma chronicon.* In *Chronica minora* 1: *MGH.AA* 9: 341–499 (ed. T. Mommsen, 1892).

Relatio Ammonii (Greek). In *Illustrium Christi martyrum lecti triumphi,* ed. F. Combefis, pp. 88–32 (Paris, 1660).

Relatio Ammonii (Syriac). In *The Forty Martyrs of the Sinai Desert and the Story of Eulogius from a Palestinian Syriac and Arabic Palimpsest,* ed. and trans. A. S. Lewis, pp. 1–14, Horae Semiticae 9 (Cambridge, 1912).

Res gestae Divi Saporis. In *Recherches sur les Res Gestae Divi Saporis,* ed. and trans. E. Honigmann and A. Maricq, Mémoires des lettres et des science morales et politiques de l'Académie royale de Belgique 47 (Brussels, 1953).

Rufinus. *Historia ecclesiastica.* In *Eusebii historia ecclesiastica translata et continuata,* pp. 957–1040 (ed. T. Mommsen, 1908); cf. *The Church History of Rufinus of Aquileia: Books 10 and 11,* trans. P. Amidon (Oxford, 1997).

————. *Opera: CCSL* 20 (ed. M. Simonetti, 1961).

Scriptores historiae augustae, ed. E. Hohl, C. Samberger, and W. Seyfarth, 2 vols. (Leipzig, 1997).

Socrates. *Historia ecclesiastica: Kirchengeschichte* (ed. G. C. Hansen, 1995).

Sozomenus. *Historia ecclesiastica: Kirchengeschichte,* 2d ed. (ed. J. Bidez and G. C. Hansen, 1995).

Suidas. *Lexicon,* ed. A. Adler, 5 vols. (1928–38; reprint, Stuttgart, 1967–71).

Sulpicius Severus. *Vie de Saint Martin: SCh* 133–135 (ed. and trans. J. Fontaine, 1967–69).

Symmachus. *Q. Aurelii Symmachi quae supersunt: MGH.AA* 6.1 (ed. O. Seeck, 1883).

Synesius. *Opere di Sinesio di Cirene: Epistole, operette, inni,* ed. and trans. A. Garzya (Turin, 1989).

Synodicon Vetus: CFHB 15 (ed. and trans. J. Duffy and J. Parker, 1979).

Tabari. *The History of al-Tabari,* vol. 5: *The Sasanids, the Byzantines, the Lakmids and Yemen,* trans. C. E. Bosworth (Albany, N.Y., 1999).

Tabula Peutingeriana, ed. E. Weber (Graz, 1976).

Tacitus. *Annales,* ed. C. D. Fisher (Oxford, 1906).

Themistius. *Orationes quae supersunt,* ed. G. Downey, 3 vols. (Leipzig, 1965–74).

Theodore Lector. *Historia ecclesiastica: Kirchengeschichte*, ed. G. C. Hansen (Berlin, 1971).

Theodoret. *Historia ecclesiastica: Kirchengeschichte*, ed. L. Parmentier and G. C. Hansen, 3d ed. (Berlin, 1998).

———. *Historia Religiosa: Histoire des moines de Syrie: SCh* 234–35 (ed. and trans. P. Canivet and A. Leroy-Molinghen, 1977–79).

Theophanes. *Chronographia*, ed. C. DeBoor. (1883; reprint, Hildesheim, 1963).

Vegetius Renatus. *Epitoma rei militaris*, ed. C. Lang (Leipzig, 1885); cf. *Vegetius: Epitome of Military Science*, trans. N. P. Milner (Liverpool, 1993).

Vita Isaaci. In *Acta sanctorum Maii* 7: 599–612 with supplement at F. Halkin, *AB* 66: 75–80 (1948).

Vita Nerses. Généalogie de la famille de Saint Grégoire illuminateur de l'Arménie et vie de Saint Nersès Patriarche des Arméniens, trans. J.-R. Emine. In *Collection des historiens anciens et modernes de l'Armenie*, ed. V. Langlois, 2: 19–44 (Paris, 1869).

Vie et miracles de Sainte Thecle, ed. and trans. G. Dagron, Subsidia Hagiographica 62 (Brussels, 1978).

Wilcken *Chrestomathie. Grundzuge und Chrestomathie der Papyruskunde*, ed. U. Wilcken and L. Mitteis (Leipzig, 1912).

Zonaras. *Epitomae historiarum libri XVIII*, ed. T. Büttner-Wobst (Bonn, 1897).

Zosimus. *Histoire nouvelle*, ed. and trans. F. Paschoud, 3 vols. (Paris, 1971–89).

SECONDARY SOURCES

Abel, E., ed. 1885. *Orphica*. Leipzig.

Abler, T. S. 1992. "Beavers and Muskets: Iroquois Military Fortunes in the Face of European Colonization." In *War in the Tribal Zone: Expanding States and Indigenous Warfare*, ed. R. B. Ferguson and N. L. Whitehead, 151–74. Santa Fe, N.Mex.

Adams, R. M. 1981. *Heartland of Cities: Surveys of Ancient Settlement and Land Use on the Central Floodplain of the Euphrates*. Chicago.

Adontz, N. 1970. *Armenia in the Period of Justinian: The Political Conditions Based on the Naxarar System*. Edited and translated by N. G. Garsoïan. Lisbon.

Agrell, S. 1936. *Die pergamenische Zauberscheibe und das Tarockspiel*. Lund.

Aleskova, B., and C. Mango. 1971. "Bargala: A Preliminary Report." *DOP* 25: 265–69.

Alföldi, A. 1926. "Die Donaubrücke Konstantins des Großen und verwandte historische Darstellungen auf spätrömischen Münzen." *ZN* 36: 161–74.

———. 1952. *A Conflict of Ideas in the Late Roman Empire: The Clash between the Senate and Valentinian I.* Translated by H. Mattingly. Oxford.

Alföldy, G. 1984. Review of *Latin Inscriptions of Chersonesus Tauric* by I. Sopomonik. *Gnomon* 50: 784–6.

Algaze, G. 1989. "A New Frontier. First Results of the Tigris-Euphrates Archaeological Reconnaissance Project." *JNES* 48.3: 240–81.

Alston, R. 1995. *Soldier and Society in Roman Egypt: A Social History*. London.

Amandry, M., et al. 1982. "L'affinage des métaux monnayés au bas-empire: Les réformes Valentiniennes de 364–368." *Quaderni ticinesi* 11: 279–95.

Amory, P. 1997. *People and Identity in Ostrogothic Italy, 489–554*. Cambridge.

Ando, C. 1996. "Pagan Apologetics and Christian Intolerance in the Ages of Themistius and Augustine." *JECS* 4: 171–207.

Andreotti, R. 1931. "Incoerenza della legislazione dell'imperatore Valentiniano I°." *NRS* 15: 456–516.

Aricescu, A. 1980. *The Army in Roman Dobrudja.* BAR-IS 86. Oxford.

Arjava, A. 1988. "Divorce in Later Roman Law." *Arctos* 22: 5–21.

———. 1996. *Women and Law in Late Antiquity.* Oxford.

Arnaldi, A. 1980. "I cognomina devictarum gentium di Valentiniano I, Valente e Graziano." *RIL* 114: 41–51.

Asche, U. 1983. *Roms Weltherrschaftsidee und Außenpolitik in der Spätantike im Spiegel der Panegyrici Latini.* Bonn.

Asdourian, P. 1911. *Die politischen Beziehungen zwischen Armenien und Rom von 190 v. Chr. bis 428 n. Chr.* Venice.

Atallah, N. 1996. "Nouvelles inscriptions grecques et latines du nord-est de la Jordanie." *Syria* 73: 15–22.

Athanassiadi, P. 1981. *Julian: An Intellectual Biography.* Oxford.

Austin, N. J. E. 1972a. "Ammianus' Account of the Adrianople Campaign: Some Strategic Observations." *AClass* 15: 77–83.

———. 1972b. "A Usurper's Claim to Legitimacy: Procopius in AD 365–366." *RSA* 2: 187–194.

———. 1979. *Ammianus on Warfare: An Investigation into Ammianus' Military Knowledge.* Collection Latomus 165. Brussels.

Austin, N. J. E., and N. B. Rankov. 1995. *Exploratio: Military and Political Intelligence in the Roman World from the Second Punic War to the Battle of Adrianople.* New York.

Azarpay, G. 1982. "The Role of Mithra in the Investiture and Triumph of Sapur II." *Iranica Antiqua* 17: 181–7.

Babut, E. 1912. *Saint Martin de Tours.* Paris.

Bagnall, R. S. 1985. *Currency and Inflation in Fourth-Century Egypt.* BASP Suppl. 5. Atlanta, Ga.

———. 1993. *Egypt in Late Antiquity.* Princeton, N.J.

Bagnall, R. S., et al. 1987. *Consuls of the Later Roman Empire.* Philological Monographs of the American Philological Association 36. Atlanta, Ga.

Baldini, A. 1979. "Su alcune costituzioni di Valentiniano I 'De operibus publicis' (364–365 d.C.)." *SDHI* 45: 568–82.

Baldwin, B. 1975. "The Career of Oribasius." *AClass* 18: 85–97.

———. 1978. "Festus the Historian." *Historia* 27: 197–217.

Balla, L. 1963. "*Savaria invalida:* Notes to the History of Pannonian Towns in the Time of Valentinian." *AErt* 90: 75–80.

———. 1989. "Contributions aux problèmes de l'histoire des Syriens et de leurs cultes dans la region danubienne." *ACD* 25: 85–90.

Banchich, T. M. 1985. "Eunapius on Libanius' Refusal of a Prefecture." *Phoenix* 38: 384–86.

Barb, A. A. 1963. "The Survival of the Magic Arts." In *The Conflict between Paganism and Christianity in the Fourth Century,* ed. A. Momigliano, 100–125. Oxford.

Barbieri, F. 1980. "Formule laudative imperiali nelle monete da Valentiniano a Teodosio (364–395)." *MGR* 7: 525–64.

Barceló, P. A. 1981. *Roms auswärtige Beziehungen unter der Constantinischen Dynastie (306–363)*. Regensburg.

Barkóczi, L. 1964. "The Population of Pannonia from Marcus Aurelius to Diocletian." *AArchHung* 16: 257–356.

Barlow, J. and P. Brennan. 2001. "*Tribuni scholarum palatinarum* c. A.D.: Ammianus Marcellinus and the *Notitia dignitatum*." *CQ* 51: 237-53.

Barnea, I. 1968. *Din istoria Dobrogei*. Vol. 2, part 2. Bibliotheca Historica Romaniae 4. Bucharest.

Barnes, T. D. 1972. "Some Persons in the Historia Augusta." *Phoenix* 26: 140–82.

———. 1976a. "Imperial Campaigns, A.D. 285–311." *Phoenix* 30: 174–93.

———. 1976b. "Victories of Constantine." *ZPE* 20: 149–55.

———. 1981. *Constantine and Eusebius*. Cambridge, Mass.

———. 1982. *The New Empire of Diocletian and Constantine*. Cambridge, Mass.

———. 1985a. "Constantine and the Christians of Persia." *JRS* 75: 126–36.

———. 1985b. "Proconsuls of Africa 337–392." *Phoenix* 39: 144–53, 273–4.

———. 1987. "Himerius and the Fourth Century." *CPh* 82: 206–25.

———. 1990a. "The Consecration of Ulfila." *JThS* 41: 541–45.

———. 1990b. "Literary Convention, Nostalgia and Reality in Ammianus Marcellinus." In *Reading the Past in Late Antiquity*, ed. G. Clarke, 59–92. Rushcutters Bay, Australia.

———. 1993. *Athanasius and Constantius: Theology and Politics in the Constantinian Empire*. Cambridge, Mass.

———. 1996. "The Military Career of Martin of Tours." *AB* 114: 25–32.

———. 1997. "The Collapse of the Homoeans in the East." *Studia Patristica* 29: 3–16.

———. 1998. *Ammianus Marcellinus and the Representation of Historical Reality*. Ithaca, N.Y.

Barnish, S. J. 1987. "Pigs, Plebeians and Potentes: Rome's Economic Hinterland, c. 350–600 A.D." *PBSR* 55: 157–85.

Barone Adesi, G. 1990. *Monachesimo ortodosso d'Oriente e diritto romano nel tardo antico*. Milan.

Barry, W. D. 1996. "Roof Tiles and Urban Violence in the Ancient World." *GRBS* 37: 55–74.

Bastien, P. 1988. *Monnaie et donativa au Bas-Empire*. Wetteren, Belgium.

———. 1992. *Le buste monétaire des empereurs romains*. Wetteren, Belgium.

Bavant, B. 1984. "La ville dans le nord de l'Illyricum." In *Villes et peuplement dans l'Illyricum protobyzantin: Actes du colloque organisé par l'École française de Rome (Rome, 12–14 Mai 1982)*. Collection de l'École française de Rome 77, 245–88. Rome.

Baynes, N. H. 1910. "Rome and Armenia in the Fourth Century." *EHR* 25: 625–43. Reprinted in *Byzantine Studies and Other Essays*, 186–208. London, 1955. Reprint Westport, Conn., 1974.

———. 1928. Review of *Geschichte des spätrömischen Reiches* by E. Stein. *JRS* 18: 217–225. Reprinted in *Byzantine Studies and Other Essays*, 317–20. London, 1955. Reprint Westport, Conn., 1974.

Bean, G. E., and T. B. Mitford. 1970. *Journeys in Rough Cilicia, 1964–1968*. Denkschriften der österreichischen Akademie der Wissenschaften 102. Vienna.

Beard, M., J. North, and S. Price. 1998. *Religions of Rome*. 2 vols. Cambridge.

Bedrosian, R. 1983. "The Sparapetut'iwn in Armenia in the Fourth and Fifth Centuries." *Armenian Review* 36: 6–46.

Bellamy, A. 1985. "A New Reading of the Namarah Inscription." *JAOS* 105: 31–51.

Béranger, J. 1948. "Le refus du pouvoir (Recherches sur l'aspect idéologique du principat)." *MH* 5: 178–96.

———. 1972. "Julien l'Apostat et l'hérédité du pouvoir impérial." *Bonner Historia-Augusta-Colloquium 1970*, 75–93. Bonn.

Berchem, M. van, J. Strzygowski, and G. L. Bell. 1910. *Amida: Matériaux pour l'épigraphie et l'histoire musulmanes du Diyar-bekr*. Heidelberg.

Berger, A. "Regionen und Straßen im frühen Konstantinopel." *Istanbuler Mitteilungen* 47 (1997): 349–414.

Bernand, E. 1990. "A propos d'une inscription grecque d'Eléphantine." *ZPE* 82: 179–81.

Bernardi, J. 1968. *La prédication des pères Cappadociens: Le prédicateur et son auditoire*. Montpelier.

———, ed. 1992a. *Grégoire de Nazianze. Discours 42–43*. SCh 384. Paris.

———. 1992b. "La lettre 104 de saint Basile, le préfet du prétoire Domitius Modestus et le statut des clercs." In *Recherches et tradition: Mélanges à Henri Crouzel*. Théologie historique 88, 7–19. Paris.

Bertinetti, M. 2000. "Il ponte di Valentiniano." In *Aurea Roma: Dalla città pagana alla città cristiana*, ed. S. Ensoli and E. La Rocca, 55-57. Rome.

Beschaouch, A. 1975. "Tremblement de terre et prospérité économique: Les années 365–370 en Afrique." *CRAI:* 101–11.

Bidez, J., and F. Winkelmann, eds. 1972. *Philostorgius Kirchengeschichte mit dem Leben des Lucian von Antiochien*. Die Griechischen Christlichen Schriftsteller der ersten Jahrhunderte. Berlin.

Biernacka-Lubanska, M. 1982. *The Roman and Early Byzantine Fortifications of Lower Moesia and Northern Thrace*. Translated by Lorraine Tokarczyk. Wrocław.

Bird, H. W. 1984. *Sextus Aurelius Victor: A Historiographical Study*. Liverpool.

———. 1986. "Eutropius and Festus: Some Reflections on the Empire and Imperial Policy in A.D. 369/70." *Florilegium* 8: 11–22.

———. 1988. "Eutropius: His Life and Career." *EMC* 32: 51–60.

———, trans. and comm. 1993. *: The Breviarium ab urbe condita of Eutropius*. Translated with an introduction and commentary. Translated Texts for Historians 14. Liverpool.

———. 1996. "Julian and Aurelius Victor." *Latomus* 55: 870–4.

Birley, A. 1988. *Septimius Severus: The African Emperor*. New Haven, Conn.

Biró, M. 1974. "Roman Villas in Pannonia." *AArchHung* 26: 23–57.

Bleckmann, B. 1995. "Bemerkungen zu den *Annales* des Nicomachus Flavianus." *Historia* 44: 83–99.

Blockley, R. C. 1975. *Ammianus Marcellinus: A Study of His Historiography and Political Thought*. Collection Latomus 141. Brussels.

———, ed. and trans. 1981–83. *The Fragmentary Classicising Historians of the Later Roman Empire: Eunapius, Olympiodorus, Priscus and Malchus*. 2 vols. Liverpool.

———. 1984. "The Romano-Persian Peace Treaties of A.D. 299 and 363." *Florilegium* 6: 28–49.

———. 1985. "Subsidies and Diplomacy: Rome and Persia in Late Antiquity." *Phoenix* 39: 62–74.

———. 1987. "The Division of Armenia between the Romans and the Persians at the End of the Fourth Century A.D." *Historia* 36: 222–34.

————. 1988. "Ammianus Marcellinus on the Persian Invasion of A.D. 359." *Phoenix* 42: 244–60.

————. 1989. "Constantius II and Persia." In *Studies in Latin Literature and Roman History 5* , ed. C. Deroux, 465–90. Collection Latomus 206. Brussels.

————. 1992. *East Roman Foreign Policy: Formation and Conduct from Diocletian to Anastasius.* Leeds.

Blois, L. de. 1986. "The Εἰς Βασιλεῖα of Ps.-Aelius Aristides." *GRBS* 27: 279–88.

Boer, W. den. 1972. *Some Minor Roman Historians.* Leiden.

Bogaers, J. E. and C. B. Rüger. 1974. *Der Niedergermanische Limes: Materialien zu seiner Geschichte.* Kunst und Altertum am Rhein 50. Cologne.

Bonamente, B. 1977. "La dedica del *Breviarium* e la carriera di Eutropio." *GIF* 29: 274–97.

Bookidis, N. and R. S. Stroud. 1997. *The Sanctuary of Demeter and Kore, Topography and Architecture.* Corinth: Results of Excavations Conducted by the American School of Classical Studies at Athens, vol. 18 pt. 3. Princeton, N.J.

Booth, A. D. 1978. "Notes on Ausonius' *professores.*" *Phoenix* 32: 235–49.

————. 1981. "The Chronology of Jerome's Early Years." *Phoenix* 35: 237–59.

Bowersock, G. W. 1976. "Limes Arabicus." *HSPh* 80: 219–29.

————. 1978. *Julian the Apostate.* London.

————. 1980. "Mavia, Queen of the Saracens." In *Studien zur antiken Sozialgeschichte: Festschrift F. Vittinghoff,* 477–95. Kölner historische Abhandlungen 28. Cologne. Revised and reprinted in *Studies on the Eastern Roman Empire: Social, Economic and Administrative History, Religion, Historiography,* 127*–40*. Goldbach, 1994.

————. 1983. *Roman Arabia.* Cambridge, Mass.

————. 1986. "Byzantium and the Arabs." *CR* 100: 111–17.

————. 1987. "Arabs and Saracens in the Historia Augusta." In *Bonner Historia-Augusta-Colloquium 1984–1985,* 71–80. Bonn.

————. 1990. *Hellenism in Late Antiquity.* Ann Arbor, Mich.

Bowersock, G. W., P. Brown and O. Grabar, eds. 1999. *Late Antiquity: A Guide to the Postclassical World.* Cambridge, Mass.

Bounegru, O. and M. Zahariade. 1996. *Les forces navales du Bas-Danube et de la Mer Noire aux Ier–VIe siècles.* Colloquia Pontica 2. Oxford.

Bradbury, S. 1994. "Constantine and the Problem of Anti-Pagan Legislation in the Fourth Century." *CPh* 89: 120–39.

Brandt, H. 1988. *Zeitkritik in der Spätantike: Untersuchungen zu den Reformsvorschlägen des Anonymus De rebus bellicis.* Munich.

Brauch, T. 1993. "The Prefect of Constantinople for 362 A.D.: Themistius." *Byzantion* 63: 37–78.

Braund, D. 1984. *Rome and the Friendly King: The Character of Client Kingship.* London.

————. 1994. *Georgia in Antiquity: A History of Colchis and Transcaucasian Iberia, 550 B.C.–A.D. 562.* Oxford.

Brennan, P. 1980. "Combined Legionary Detachments as Artillery Units in Late-Roman Danubian Bridgehead Dispositions." *Chiron* 10: 553–67.

Brennecke, H. C. 1988. *Studien zur Geschichte der Homöer der Osten bis zum Ende der homöischen Reichskirche.* Beiträge zur historischen Theologie 73. Tübingen.

Brockmeier, B. 1987. "Der große Friede 332 n. Chr.: Zur Außenpolitik Konstantins des Großen." *BJ* 187: 79–100.

Brown, P. 1992. *Power and Persuasion in Late Antiquity: Towards a Christian Empire.* Madison, Wis.

———. 1995. *Authority and the Sacred. Aspects of the Christianization of the Roman World.* Cambridge.

———. 1998. "Christianization and Religious Conflict." In *Cambridge Ancient History,* vol. 13: *The Late Empire, A.D. 337–425,* 2d ed., ed. A. Cameron and P. Garnsey, 632–64. Cambridge.

Bruggisser, P. 1987. "Gloria novi saeculi: Symmaque et le siècle de Gratien (Epist. 1.13)." *MH* 44: 134–49.

Brunt, P. A. 1974. "Conscription and Volunteering in the Roman Imperial Army." *Scripta Classica Israelica* 1: 90–115. Reprinted with additions in *Roman Imperial Themes,* 188–214, 512–513. Oxford, 1990.

Burgess, R. W. 1988. "Quinquennial Vota and the Imperial Consulship in the Fourth and Fifth Centuries, 337–511." *NC* 148: 77–96.

———, ed. and trans. 1993. *The Chronicle of Hydatius and the Consularia Constantinopolitana: Two Contemporary Accounts of the Final Years of the Roman Empire.* Oxford.

Burns, T. S. 1973. "The Battle of Adrianople: A Reconsideration." *Historia* 22: 336–45.

———. 1994. *Barbarians within the Gates of Rome. A Study of Roman Military Policy and the Barbarians, ca. 375–425 A.D.* Bloomington, Ind.

Bursche, A. 1996. *Later Roman-Barbarian Contacts in Central Europe: Numismatic Evidence.* Berlin.

Cagnat, R. 1914. *Cours d'épigraphie Latine.* 4th ed. Paris.

Calò-Levi, A. 1952. *Barbarians on Roman Coins and Sculpture.* New York.

Cameron, A. 1968. "Gratian's Repudiation of the Pontifical Robe." *JRS* 58: 96–102.

———. 1969. Review of *The Breviarium of Festus* by J. W. Eadie. *CR* 83: 305–7.

———. 1985. "The Date of the Anonymous *De rebus bellicis.*" In *Literature and Society in the Early Byzantine World,* no. 9, ed. A. Cameron. London.

———. 1999. "The Last Pagans of Rome." In *The Transformations of Vrbs Roma in Late Antiquity,* ed. W. V. Harris, 109–22. JRA-SS 33. Portsmouth, R.I.

Cameron, A., and J. Long. 1993. *Barbarians and Politics at the Court of Arcadius.* Berkeley.

Campbell, J. B. 1984. *The Emperor and the Roman Army, 31 B.C.–A.D. 235.* Oxford.

Canali de Rossi, F. 1999. "Il restauro del passaggio al Monte Croce Carnico sotto Valentiniano, Valente e Graziano." *Tyche* 14: 23–8.

Cappelletti, L. 1999. "Autonius Iustinianus *rector provinciae Samnitium* (post 375 d.C.?)." *Tyche* 14: 29–41.

Carrié, J.-M. 1986. "L'esercito: Trasformazioni funzionali ed economie locali." In *Società romana e impero tardoantico,* vol. 1: *Istituzioni, ceti, economie,* ed. A. Giardina, 449–88. Rome.

———. 1989. "L'état à la recherche de nouveaux modes de financement des armées (Rome et Byzance, IVe–VIIIe siècles)." In *The Byzantine and Early Islamic Near East,* vol. 3: *States, Resources and Armies,* ed. A. Cameron, 27–60. Princeton, N.J.

———. 1993. "Observations sur la fiscalité du IVe siècle pour servir à l'histoire monétaire." In *L'inflazione nel quarto secolo d.C.: Atti dell'incontro di studio, Roma 1988,* 115–54. Rome.

Carroll-Spillecke, M. 1993. "Das römische Militärlager *Divitia* in Köln-Deutz." *KJ* 26: 321–444.

Cazaru, M. 1972. "*Montes Serrorum* (AM 27.5.3): Zur Siedlungsgeschichte der Westgoten in Rumänien." *Dacia,* n.s., 16: 299–301.

Cazzaniga, I. 1958. "Note marginali al papiro berlinese 13927 (V–VI sec. a.c.): Un inventario di oggetti necessari per rappresentazioni sceniche." *SCO* 7: 7–19.

Çeçen, K. 1996. *The Longest Roman Water Supply Line.* Istanbul.

Cesa, M. 1984. "376–382: Romani e barbari sul Danubio." *StudUrb B3,* 57: 63–99.

———. 1985. "Osservazioni su Eunap. 43 M." *QUCC,* n.s., 19: 197–200.

———. 1994. *Impero tardoantico e barbari: La crisi militare da Adrianapoli al 418.* Biblioteca di Athenaeum 23. Como.

Chastagnol, A. 1962. *Les fastes de la préfecture de Rome au Bas-Empire.* Paris.

———. 1969. "La restauration du temple d'Isis au *Portus Romae* sous le règne de Gratien." In *Hommages à Marcel Renard,* vol. 2, 135–44. Collection Latomus 102. Brussels.

———. 1976. "Remarque sur les sénateurs orientaux au ive siècle." *AAntHung* 24: 341–56.

———. 1982. "La carrière senatoriale du Bas-Empire (depuis Diocletien)." In *Colloquio internazionale AIEGL su epigrafia e ordine senatorio, Roma, 14–20 maggio 1981,* vol. 1, tituli 4, 167–93. Rome.

———. 1986. "La législation sur les biens des villes au IVe siècle à la lumière d'une inscription d'Éphèse." In *VI Convegno internazionale dell'Accademia romanistica constantiniana,* 76–104. Perugia.

———. 1987. "Les quinquennalia de Valentinien 1er et Valens." In *Mélanges de numismatique offerts à P. Bastien,* 255–66. Wetteren, Belgium.

Chaumont, M.-L. 1969. *Recherches sur l'histoire d'Arménie de l'avènement des Sassanides à la conversion du royaume.* Paris.

———. 1976. "L'Arménia entre Rome et l'Iran. I. De l'avènement d'Auguste à l'avènement de Dioclétien." *ANRW* II.9.1: 71–194.

Chauvot, A. 1998. *Opinions romaines face aux barbares au ive siècle ap. J.-C.* Paris.

Chiabò, M. 1983. *Index Verborum Ammiani Marcellini.* Hildesheim.

Christensen, A. 1944. *L'Iran sous les sassanides.* 2d ed. Copenhagen.

Christie, N. 1996. "Towns and Peoples on the Middle Danube in Late Antiquity and the Early Middle Ages." In *Towns in Transition: Urban Evolution in Late Antiquity and the Early Middle Ages,* ed. N. Christie and S. T. Loseby, 71–98. Aldershot, UK.

Christol, M. and T. Drew-Bear. 1986. "Documents latins de Phrygie." *Tyche* 1: 41–87.

Chrysos, E. 1972. Τὸ Βυζάντιον καὶ οἱ Γότθοι· Συμβολή εἰς τὴν ἐξοτερικὴν πολιτικὴν τοῦ Βυζαντίου κατὰ τὸν δ' αἰῶνα. Thessalonika.

———. 1973. "*Gothia Romana:* Zur Rechtslage des Föderatenlandes der Westgoten im 4. Jahrhundert." *Dacoromania* 1: 52–64.

———. 1976. "Some Aspects of Roman-Persian Legal Relations." *Kleronomia* 8: 1–60.

———. 1997. "Conclusion: *De foederatis iterum.*" In *Kingdoms of the Empire: The Integration of Barbarians in Late Antiquity,* ed. W. Pohl, 185–206. Leiden.

Clauss, M. 1981. *Der magister officiorum in der Spätantike (4.–6. Jahrhundert).* Vestigia 32. Munich.

Cleremont-Ganneau, C. 1888. "Inscriptions grecques inédites du Hauran et des régions adjacentes." *Recueil d'archéologie orientale* 1: 1–33.

Cohen, H. 1862. *Description historique des monnaies frappées sous l'empire romain: Médailles impériales,* vol. 6. Paris.

Corcoran, S. 1995. "The Praetorian Prefect Modestus and Hero of Alexandria's *Stereometrica.*" *Latomus* 54: 377–84.

————. 1996. *The Empire of the Tetrarchs: Imperial Pronouncements and Government,* A.D. 284–324. Oxford.

Coşkun, A. 2000. "Ammianus Marcellinus und die Prozesse in Rom (a. 368/69-371/74)." *Tyche* 15: 63-92.

Courcelle, P. 1964. *Histoire littéraire des grands invasions germaniques.* 3d ed. Paris.

Cracco Ruggini, L. 1987. "Utopia e realtà di una riforma monetaria: L'*Anonymus De rebus bellicis* e i Valentiniani." In *Studi per Laura Breglia,* vol. 2: *Numismatica romana, medioevale e moderna.* Bullettino di numismatica suppl. al n. 4, 189–96. Rome.

Cramer, F. H. 1954. *Astrology in Roman Law and Politics.* Philadelphia.

Crow, J. G. 1986. "A Review of the Physical Remains of the Frontiers of Cappadocia." In *The Defense of the Roman and Byzantine East,* ed. P. Freeman and D. Kennedy, 77–91. BAR-IS 297. Oxford.

Crow, J., and Ricci, A. 1997. "Investigating the Hinterland of Constantinople: Interim Report on the Anastasian Long Wall." *JRA* 10: 235–62.

Crump, G. A. 1975. *Ammianus Marcellinus as a Military Historian.* Historia Einzelschriften 27. Wiesbaden.

Cunliffe, B. W. 1988. *Greeks, Romans and Barbarians: Spheres of Interraction.* New York.

Ćurčić, S. 1993. "Late-Antique Palaces: The Meaning of the Urban Context." *Ars Orientalis* 23: 68–90.

Curran, J. 1998. "From Jovian to Theodosius." In *Cambridge Ancient History,* vol. 13: *The Late Empire,* A.D. 337–425, 2d ed., ed. A. Cameron and P. Garnsey, 78–110. Cambridge.

Dagron, G. 1968. "L'empire romain d'orient au IVe siècle et les traditions politiques de l'hellénisme: Le témoignage de Thémistios." *T&MByz* 3: 1–242.

————. 1970. "Les moines et la ville: Le monachisme à Constantinople jusqu'au concile de Chalcedoine (451)." *T&MByz* 4: 229–76.

————. 1974. *Naissance d'une capitale: Constantinople et ses institutions de 330 à 451.* Paris.

————. 1978. *Vie et miracles de Sainte Thècle.* Brussels.

Dalman, K. O. 1933. *Der Valens-Aquädukt in Konstantinopel.* Istanbuler Forschungen 3. Bamberg.

Daly, L. J. 1971. "Themistius' Plea for Religious Tolerance." *GRBS* 12: 65–79.

————. 1972. "The Mandarin and the Barbarian: The Response of Themistius to the Gothic Challenge." *Historia* 21: 351–79.

Dauge, Y. A. 1981. *Le barbare: Recherches sur la conception romaine de la barbarie et de la civilisation.* Collection Latomus 176. Brussels.

Dean, L. F. 1916. "A Study of the Cognomina of Soldiers in the Roman Legions." Diss. Princeton, N.J.

Decret, F. 1979. "Les conséquences sur le christianisme en Perse de l'affrontement des empires romain et sassanide de Shapur I à Yezdegerd I." *RevAug* 14: 91–152.

De Dominicis, M. A. 1953. "Il problema dei rapporti burocratico-legislativi tra 'occidente ed oriente' nel basso impero Romano alla luce delle inscriptiones et subscriptiones delle costitutzioni imperiali." *RIL* 86: 331–487.

Delbrueck, R. 1933. *Spätantike Kaiserporträts von Constantinus Magnus bis zum Ende des Westreichs.* Berlin. Reprint, 1978.

Del Chicca, F. 1987. "Per la datazione dell' *Oratio* 3 di Simmaco." *Athenaeum,* n.s., 65: 534–41.

Delehaye, H. 1912. "Martyrs de l'église de Gothie." *AB* 31: 274–94.

Delmaire, R. 1989. *Les responsables des finances impériales au Bas-Empire romain (IVe–VIe s.): Études prosopographiques.* Collection Latomus 203. Brussels.

———. 1997. "Les usurpateurs du bas-empire et le recrutement des fonctionnaires (essai de reflexion sur les assises du pouvoir et leurs limites)." In *Usurpationen in der Spätantike,* ed. J. Szidat and F. Paschoud, 11–26. Stuttgart.

Demandt, A. 1970. "*Magister Militum.*" *RE Suppl.* 12: 553–790.

———. 1972. "Die Feldzüge des älteren Theodosius." *Hermes* 100: 81–113.

———. 1989. *Die Spätantike: Römische Geschichte von Diocletian bis Justinian, 284–565 n. Chr.* Handbuch der Altertumswissenschaft 3.6. Munich.

Demougeot, E.1969. "À propos des lètes gaulois du ive siècle." In *Beiträge zur alten Geschichte und deren Nachleben: Festschrift für Franz Altheim,* ed. R. Stiehl and H. Stier, 101–13. Berlin.

———. 1979. *La formation de l'Europe et les invasions barbares,* vol. 2: *De l'avènement de Dioclétien (284) à l'occupation germanique de l'Empire romain d'Occident (début du VIe siècle).* Paris.

Depeyrot, G. 1987. *Le Bas-Empire Romain économie et numismatique.* Paris.

———. 1995. "L'origine du metal des solidi de Valens (1)." *CahNum* 124: 33–8.

DeSalvo, L. 1979. "Ancora sull'istituzione della dioceses Aegypti." *RSA* 9: 69–74.

———. 1992. *Economia privata e pubblici servizi nell'impero romano: I "corpora naviculariorum."* Messina.

De Ste. Croix, G. E. M. 1981. *The Class Struggle in the Ancient Greek World: From the Archaic age to the Arab Conquests.* Ithaca, N.Y.

Devreesse, R. 1940. "Le christianisme dans la peninsule sináïtique, des origines à l'arrivée des Musulmans." *RBi* 49: 205–23.

———. 1945. *Le patriarcat d'Antioche depuis la paix de l'église jusqu'a la conquete arabe.* Paris.

De Vries, B. 1986. "Umm el Jimal in the First Three Centuries A.D." In *The Defense of the Roman and Byzantine East,* ed. P. Freeman and D. Kennedy, 227–41. BAR-IS 297. Oxford.

———. 1998. *Umm El-Jimal: A Frontier Town and Its Landscape in Northern Jordan.* vol. 1. Portsmouth, R.I.

Diaconu, G. 1975. "On the Socio-Economic Relations between Natives and Goths in Dacia." In *Relations between the Autochthonous Population and the Migratory Populations on the Territory of Romania,* ed. M. Constantinescu, S. Pascu, and P. Diaconu, 67–75. Bucharest.

Diaconu, G., et al. 1977. "L'ensemble archéologique de Petroasele." *Dacia* 21: 199–220.

Diesner, H.-J. 1968. "Protectores (domestici)." *RESuppl.* 11: 1113–23.

Dillemann, L. 1962. *Haute Mésopotamie orientale et pays adjacents.* Paris.

DiMaio, M. 1978. "The Transfer of the Remains of the Emperor Julian from Tarsus to Constantinople." *Byzantion* 48: 43–50.

DiMaio, M., J. Zeuge, and J. Bethume. 1990. "*Proelium Cibalense et proelium campi Ardiensis:* The First Civil War of Constantine I and Licinus I." *AncW* 21: 67–91.

Dodgeon, M. H. and S. N. C. Lieu, eds. 1991. *The Roman Eastern Frontier and the Persian Wars (A.D. 226–363): A Documentary History.* London.

Doignon, J. 1966. "Le titre *Nobilissimus Puer* porté par Gratien et la mystique littéraire des origines de Rome à l'avènement des Valentiniens." In *Mélanges d'archéologie et d'histoire offerts à A. Piganiol*, 1693–1709. Paris.

Downey, G. 1955. "*Philanthropia* in Religion and Statecraft in the Fourth Century after Christ." *Historia* 4: 199–208.

———. 1957. "Themistius and the Defence of Hellenism in the Fourth Century." *HThR* 50: 259–74.

———. 1961. *A History of Antioch in Syria from Seleucus to the Arab Conquests*. Princeton, N.J.

———, ed. 1965–74. *Themistii orationes quae supersunt*, 3 vols. Leipzig.

Drake, H.A. 2000. *Constantine and the Bishops: The Politics of Intolerance*. Baltimore.

Dressel, H. 1973. *Die römischen Medaillone des Münzkabinetts der Staatlichen Museen zu Berlin*, ed. K. Regling. Berlin.

Drew-Bear, T. 1977. "A Fourth-Century Latin Soldier's Epitaph at Nakolea." *HSPh* 81: 257–74.

Drijvers, J.W. 1999. "Promoting Jerusalem: Cyril and the True Cross." In *Portraits of Spiritual Authority*, ed. J.W. Drijvers and J.W. Watt, 79–95. Leiden.

Drinkwater, J.F. 1983. "The 'Pagan Underground', Constantius II's 'Secret Service' and the Survival, and the Usurpation of Julian the Apostate." In *Studies in Latin Literature and Roman History 3*, ed. C. Deroux, 348–87. Collection Latomus 180. Brussels.

———. 1999. "Ammianus, Valentinian and the Rhine Germans." In *The Late Roman World and its Historian: Interpreting Ammianus Marcellinus*, eds. J.W. Drijvers and D. Hunt, 127–38. London.

Duncan, G.L. 1983. "Coin Circulation on the Danubian *limes* of Dacia ripensis." In *Ancient Bulgaria: Papers Presented to the International Symposium on the Ancient History and Archaeology of Bulgaria, University of Nottingham, 1981*, ed. A.G. Poulter, 165–76. Nottingham.

———. 1993. *Coin Circulation in the Danubian and Balkan Provinces of the Roman Empire A.D. 294–578*. London.

Duncan-Jones, R. 1990. *Structure and Scale in the Roman Economy*. Cambridge.

———. 1994. *Money and Government in the Roman Empire*. Cambridge.

———. 1903. *Mission scientifique dans les régions désertiques de la Syrie Moyenne*. Paris.

Durliat, J. 1995. "L'approvisionnement de Constantinople." In *Constantinople and its Hinterland*, eds. C. Mango and G. Dagron, 19–34. Aldershot, UK.

———. 1990. *De la ville antique à la ville byzantine: Le problème des subsistances*. CEFA 136. Rome.

Dussaud, R. 1902. "Inscription nabatéo-arabe d'En-Namara." *RA* 2: 409–21.

Duval, N. 1987. "Le site de Gamzigrad (Serbie) est-il le palais de retraite de Galère?" *BSAF,* 61–84.

Duval, N., and V. Popović. 1977. "Horrea et Thermes aux abords du rempart sud." In *Sirmium VII*. Collection de l'École française de Rome 29.1. Belgrade.

Dyson, S.L. 1971. "Native Revolts in the Roman Empire." *Historia* 20: 239–74.

———. 1975. "Native Revolt Patterns in the Roman Empire." *ANRW* II.3: 138–75.

Eadie, J.W., ed. 1967. *The Breviarium of Festus: A Critical Edition with Historical Commentary*. London.

———. 1982. "City and Countryside in Late Roman Pannonia and the *Regio sirmiensis*." In *City, Town and Countryside in the Early Byzantine Era*, ed. R. Hohlfelder, 25–42. New York.

Edmondson, J. C. 1989. "Mining in the Later Roman Empire and Beyond: Continuity or Disruption?" *JRS* 79: 84–102.

Ehling, K. 1996. "Der Ausgang des Perserfeldzuges in der Münzpropaganda des Jovian." *Klio* 78: 186–91.

Elbern, S. 1984. *Usurpationen im spätrömischen Reich*. Bonn.

——. 1987. "Das Gotenmassaker in Kleinasien (378 n. Chr.)." *Hermes* 115: 99–106.

Ellis, L. 1996. "Dacians, Sarmatians and Goths on the Roman-Carpathian Frontier: Second–Fourth Centuries." In *Shifting Frontiers in Late Antiquity*, ed. R. W. Mathisen and H. S. Sivan, 105–25. Aldershot, UK.

Elmer, G. 1937. "Die Kupfergeldreform unter Iulianus Philosophus." *NZ*: 25–42.

Elton, H. 1996a. *Frontiers of the Roman Empire*. Bloomington, Ind.

——. 1996b. *Warfare in Roman Europe A.D. 350–425*. Oxford.

Enßlin, W. 1934. "Der konstantinische Patriziat und seine Bedeutung im 4. Jahrhundert." In *Mélanges Bidez*. Annuaire de l'Institut de Philologie et d'Histoire orientales 2, 361–76. Brussels.

——. 1948. "Valentinianus II." *RE* 14: 2205–32.

——. 1957. "Prokopius 2." *RE* 23.1: 252–56.

Er, Y. 1991. "Diversità e interazione culturale in Cilicia Tracheia: I monumenti funerari." *Quaderni storici* 76: 105–40.

Erdélyi, I. 1992. "Goten und Hunnen in Südrußland." *ZfA* 26: 11–16.

Errington, R. M. 1996a. "The Accession of Theodosius I." *Klio* 78: 438–53.

——. 1996b. "Theodosius and the Goths." *Chiron* 26: 1–27.

——. 1997. "Church and State in the First Years of Theodosius I." *Chiron* 27: 21–72.

——. 2000. "Ammianus and His Emperors." *Chiron* 30: 861–904.

Fasolino, M. 1976. *Valentiniano I: L'opera e i problemi storiografici*. Naples.

Fele, M. L. 1975. *Lexicon Florianum*. Hildesheim.

Festugière, A. J. 1959. *Antioche païenne et chrétienne*. Paris.

Fiebiger, O., and L. Schmidt. 1917. *Inschriftensammlung zur Geschichte der Ostgermanen*. Denkschriften der kaiserlichen Akademie der Wissenschaften in Wien, Phil.-hist. Kl., 60. Vienna.

Fiey, J.-M. 1977. *Nisibe, métropole syriaque orientale et ses suffragants des origines à nos jours*. CSCO 338. Louvain.

Fitz, J., ed. 1976. *Gorsium-Herculia*. Székesfehérvár, Hungary.

——. 1980. "Administration and Army." In *The Archaeology of Roman Pannonia*, ed. A. Lengyel and G. T. B. Radan, 125–40. Budapest.

——. 1983. *L'administration des provinces pannoniennes sous le Bas-Empire romain*. Collection Latomus 181. Brussels.

——. 1990. *Die Fundmünzen der römischen Zeit in Ungarn I*. Bonn and Budapest.

Fitz, J., and J. Fedak. 1993. "From Roman Gorsium to Late-Antique Herculia: A Summary of Recent Work at Tác (NE Pannonia)." *JRA* 6: 261–73.

Floriani Squarciapino, M. 1946–48. "Un nuovo ritratto di Valente." *BCAR* 72: 95–101.

——. 1949–50. "Ancora sui ritratti di Valente." *BCAR* 73: 97–99.

——. 1973–74. "*Albei Tiberis Ripas et Pontes Tredecim.*" *ArchClass* 25–6: 250–61.

Foerster, F. 1900. "Andreas Dudith und die zwölfte Rede des Themistius." *Neue Jahrbücher* 3: 74–93.

Fontaine, J., ed. and trans. 1967–69. *Vie de Saint Martin*. 3 vols. Paris.

Fontaine, J., G. Sabbah, and M.-A. Marié, eds. and trans. 1968–87. *Ammien Marcellin, Histoire.* 4 vols. Paris.

Forlin Patrucco, M. 1972. *"Domus Divina Per Cappdociam." RFIC* 100: 328–33.

Fortina, M. 1953. *L'imperatore Graziano.* Torino.

Foss, C. 1979. *Ephesus after Antiquity: A Late Antique, Byzantine and Turkish City.* Cambridge.

Fowden, G. 1978. "Bishops and Temples in the Eastern Roman Empire A.D. 320–435." *JThS* 29: 53–78.

———. 1982. "The Pagan Holy Man in Late Antique Society." *JHS* 102: 33–59.

———. 1991. "Constantine's Porphyry Column: The Earliest Allusion." *JRS* 81: 119–31.

———. 1998. "Polytheist Religion and Philosophy." In *Cambridge Ancient History,* vol. 13: *The Late Empire,* A.D. *337–425,* 2d ed., ed. A. Cameron and P. Garnsey, 538–60. Cambridge, 1998.

Frank, R. I. 1969. *Scholae Palatinae: The Palace Guards of the Later Roman Empire.* Papers and Monographs of the American Academy in Rome 23. Rome.

Frakes, R. M. 2001. *Contra Potentium Iniurias: The Defensor Civitatis and Late Roman Justice.* Munich.

Freeman, P., and D. Kennedy, eds. 1986. *The Defense of the Roman and Byzantine East.* 2 vols. BAR-IS 297. Oxford.

French, D. H. 1988. *Roman Roads and Milestones of Asia Minor.* BAR-IS 392. Oxford.

French, D. H., and C. S. Lightfoot, eds. 1989. *The Eastern Frontier of the Roman Empire: Proceedings of a Colloquium Held at Ankara in September 1988.* 2 vols. BAR-IS 553. Oxford.

Frendo, D. 1992. "Sasanian Irredentism and the Foundation of Constantinople: Truth and Historical Reality." *Bulletin of the Asia Institute* 6: 59–66.

Frere, S. 1987. *Britannia: A History of Roman Britain.* 3d ed. London.

Frézouls, E. 1983. "Les deux politiques de Rome face aux barbares d'après Ammien Marcellin." In *Crise et redressement dans les provinces européens de l'Empire (milieu du IIIe–milieu du IVe siècle ap. J.-C.):* Actes du Colloque de Strasbourg, décembre 1981, ed. E. Frézouls, 175–97. Contributions et travaux de l'Institut d'histoire romaine 3. Strasbourg.

Frye, R. N. 1984. *The History of Ancient Iran.* Handbuch der Altertumswissenschaft 3.7. Munich.

Fülep, F. 1977. *The Roman Cemeteries on the Territory of Pécs (Sopianae).* Budapest.

———. 1984. *Sopianae: The History of Pécs during the Roman Era and the Problem of Continuity of the Late Roman Population.* Budapest.

Funke, H. 1967. "Majestäts-und Magieprozesse bei Ammianus Marcellinus." *JbAC* 10: 145–75.

Gabriel, A. 1940. *Voyages archéologiques dans la Turquie orientale.* 2 vols. Paris.

Gagé, J. 1933. "La théologie de la victoire impériale." *RH* 171: 1–43.

Gager, J. G. 1992. *Curse Tablets and Binding Spells from the Ancient World.* New York.

Gain, B. 1985. *L'église de Cappadoce au ive siècle d'après la correspondance de Basile de Césarée (330–379).* Rome.

Gallay, P. 1943. *La vie de Saint Grégoire de Nazianze.* Lyons.

Garnsey, P. 1970. *Social Status and Legal Privilege in the Roman Empire.* Oxford.

Garnsey, P., and C. Humfress. 2001. *The Evolution of the Late Antique World.* Cambridge.

Garrido Gonzàlez, E. 1987. "Relación entre sociedad y ejército en el reinado de Valentiniano I visto a través de la legislación." *Latomus* 46: 841–46.

Garsoïan, N. G. 1967. "Politique ou orthodoxie? L'Arménie au quatrième siècle." *REArm* 4: 341–52. Reprinted in *Armenia between Byzantium and the Sasanians,* ed. N. G. Garsoïan, no. 3. London, 1985.

———. 1969. "'Quidam Narseus'—A Note on the Mission of St. Nerses the Great." In *Armeniaca: Mélanges d'études arméniennes,* 148–64. Venice. Reprinted in *Armenia between Byzantium and the Sasanians,* ed. N. G. Garsoïan, no. 5. London, 1985.

———. 1976. "Prolegomena to a Study of the Iranian Elements in Arsacid Armenia." *Handes Amsorya* 90: 177–234. Reprinted in *Armenia between Byzantium and the Sasanians,* ed. N. G. Garsoïan, no. 10. London, 1985.

———. 1980. "The Locus of the Death of Kings: Iranian Armenia the Inverted Image." In *The Armenian Image in History and Literature,* ed. R. Hovannisian, 27–64. Los Angeles. Reprinted in *Armenia between Byzantium and the Sasanians,* ed. N. G. Garsoïan, no. 11. London, 1985.

———. 1983. "Nerses le Grand, Basile de Césarée et Eustathe de Sébaste." *REArm* 17: 145–69. Reprinted in *Armenia between Byzantium and the Sasanians,* ed. N. G. Garsoïan, no. 7. London, 1985.

———, trans. and comm. 1989. *The Epic Histories attributed to P'awstos Buzand (Buzandaran Patmut'iwink').* Cambridge, Mass.

Gaudemet, J. 1956. "Le partage législatif dans la seconde moitié du ivème siècle." *Studi in onore di Pietro de Francisci,* 2: 319–54. Milan.

———. 1978. "Note sur une constitution de Valentinien Ier relative à l'incessibilité des fonds emphytéotiques." In *Festschrift für Franz Wieacker zum 70 Geburtstag,* ed. O. Behrends, 66–70. Göttingen.

———. 1979. *La formation du droit séculier et du droit de l'Église aux IVe et Ve siècles.* 2d ed. Paris.

Geary, P. "Barbarians and Ethnicity." In *Late Antiquity: A Guide to the Postclassical World,* ed. G. W. Bowersock, P. Brown, and O. Grabar, 107–29. Cambridge, Mass.

Genser, K. 1986. *Der österreichische Donaulimes in der Römerzeit: Ein Forschungsbericht.* Der römische Limes in Österreich 33. Vienna.

Giardina, A., trans. and comm. 1989. *Anonimo Le cose della guerra.* Milan.

Giardina, A., and F. Grelle. 1983. "La tavola di Trinitapoli. Una nuova costituzione di Valentiniano I." *MEFRA* 95: 249–303.

Giet, S. 1943. *Saint Basile: Une conscience aux prises avec les difficultés de l'heure.* Lyons.

Giglio, S. 1990. *Il tardo impero d'occidente e il suo senato.* Naples.

Gleason, M. W. 1995. *Making Men: Sophists and Self-Presentation in Ancient Rome.* Princeton, N.J.

Gnecchi, R. 1912. *I medaglioni romani.* Milan.

Gnoli, G. 1989. *The Idea of Iran: An Essay on Its Origins.* Rome.

Goffart, W. 1977. "The Date and Purpose of Vegetius *De re militari.*" *Traditio* 33: 65–100.

Goldsworthy, A. K. 1996. *The Roman Army at War 100 B.C.–A.D. 200.* Oxford.

Gömöri, J. 1986. "Grabungen auf dem Forum von Scarbantia (1979–82)." *AArch-Hung* 38: 343–96.

Gordon, C. D. 1949. "Subsidies in Roman Imperial Defence." *Phoenix* 3: 60–70.

Goudswaard, B. 1995. "A Late-Roman Bridge in the Meuse at Cuijk, The Netherlands." *AKB* 25: 233–41.

Graf, D. F. 1978. "The Saracens and the Defense of the Arabian Frontier." *BASOR* 229: 1–26. Reprinted in *Rome and the Arabian Frontier from the Nabataeans to the Saracens*, ed. D. Graf, no. 9. Aldershot, UK, 1997.

———. 1989. "Rome and the Saracens: Reassessing the Nomadic Menace." In *L'Arabie préislamique et son environnement historique et culturel. Actes du Colloque de Strasbourg 24–27 Juin 1987*, ed. T. Fahd, 341–400. Leiden. Reprinted in *Rome and the Arabian Frontier from the Nabataeans to the Saracens*, ed. D. Graf, no. 10. Aldershot, UK, 1997.

———. 1997. "The *Via Militaris* and the *Limes Arabicus*." In *Roman Frontier Studies 1995: Proceedings of the XVIth International Congress of Roman Frontier Studies*, ed. W. Groenman-van Waateringe et al., 123–33. Oxford.

Graf, D. F., and M. O'Connor. 1977. "The Origins of the Term Saracen and the Rawwafa Inscriptions." *Byzantine Studies* 4: 52–66.

Graf, F. 1997. *Magic in the Ancient World*. Translated by F. Philip. Cambridge, Mass.

Grattarola, P. 1986. "L'usurpazione di Procopio e la fine dei Constantinidi." *Aevum* 60: 82–105.

Grbic, M. 1936. "Bassianae, Yugoslavia." *Antiquity* 10: 475–77.

Greatrex, G. 1998. *Rome and Persia at War, 502–532*. Leeds, UK.

———. 2000. "The Background and Aftermath of the Partition of Armenia in AD 387." *AHB* 14: 35–48.

Green, R. P. H., ed. and comm. 1991. *The Works of Ausonius*. Oxford.

Grierson, P. 1962. "The Tombs and Obits of the Byzantine Emperors (337–1042)." *DOP* 16: 1–60.

Grierson, P., and M. Mays. 1992. *Catalogue of Late Roman Coins in the Dumbarton Oaks Collection and in the Whittemore Collections. From Arcadius and Honorius to the Accession of Anastasius*. Washington, D.C.

Griffith, S. H. 1986. "Ephraem, the Deacon of Edessa, and the Church of the Empire." In *Diakonia. Studies in Honor of Robert T. Meyer*, eds. T. Halton and J. P. Williman, 22–52. Washington, DC.

Grubbs, J. Evans. 1995. *Law and Family in Late Antiquity: The Emperor Constantine's Marriage Legislation*. Oxford.

Grumel, V. 1951. "L'Illyricum de la mort de Valentinien Ier (375) à la mort de Stilicon (408)." *REByz* 9: 5–46.

Güterbock, K. 1900. *Römisch-Armenien und die römischen Satrapieen im vierten bis sechsten Jahrhundert*. Königsberg, Germany.

Gutmann, B. 1991. *Studien zur römischen Außenpolitik in der Spätantike (364–395 n. Chr.)*. Bonn.

Gyeselen, R. 1989. *La géographie administrative de l'empire Sassanide: Les témoignes sigillographiques*. Paris.

Gwatkin, H. M. 1900. *Studies of Arianism*. Cambridge.

Haas, C. 1993. "The Arians of Alexandria." *VChr* 47: 234–45.

———. 1997. *Alexandria in Late Antiquity: Topography and Social Conflict*. Baltimore.

Haehling, R. von. 1977. "Ammians Darstellung der Thronbesteigung Jovians im Lichte der heidnisch-christlichen Auseinandersetzung." In *Bonner Festgabe J. Straub*, 347–58. Bonn.

———. 1978. *Die Religionszugehörigkeit der hohen Amtsträger des Römischen Reiches seit Constantins I: Alleinherrschaft bis zum Ende der Theodosianischen Dynastie (324–450 bzw. 455 n. Chr.).* Bonn.

Hahn, I. 1958. "Zur Frage der Sozialen Grundlagen der Usurpation des Procopius." *AAntHung* 6: 199–211.

Halkin, F. 1948. "Le synaxaire grec de Christ Church à Oxford." *AB* 66: 59–90.

Hall, J. M. 1997. *Ethnic Identity in Greek Antiquity.* Cambridge.

Hamblenne, P. 1980. "Une «conjuration» sous Valentinien?" *Byzantion* 50: 198–225.

Harhoiu, R. 1993. "Die Medaillone aus dem Schatzfund von Simleul Silvaniei." *Dacia* 37: 221–36.

———. 1997. *Die frühe Völkerwanderungszeit in Rumänien.* Bucharest.

Harl, K. W. 1996. *Coinage in the Roman Economy 300 B.C. to A.D. 700.* Baltimore.

Harries, J. 1988. "The Roman Imperial Quaestor from Constantine to Theodosius II." *JRS* 78: 148–72.

———. 1999. *Law and Empire in Late Antiquity.* Cambridge.

Hassall, M. W. C., ed. 1979. *De Rebus Bellicis. Part I: Aspects of the De Rebus Bellicis. Papers Presented to Professor E. A. Thompson.* BAR-IS 63. Oxford.

Hauschild, W.-D, trans. and comm. 1973–90. *Basilius von Caesarea: Briefe.* 3 vols. Stuttgart.

Hauser-Meury, M.-M. 1960. *Prosopographie zu den Schriften Gregors von Nazianz.* Bonn.

Häusler, A. 1979. "Zu den sozialökonomischen Verhältnißen in der Cernjachov-Kultur." *ZfA* 13: 23–65.

Heather, P. J. 1986. "The Crossing of the Danube and the Gothic Conversion." *GRBS* 27: 289–318.

———. 1991. *Goths and Romans, 332–489.* Oxford.

———. 1994. "New Men for new Constantines? Creating an Imperial Elite in the Eastern Mediterranean." In *New Constantines: The Rhythm of Imperial Renewal in Byzantium, 4th–13th Centuries,* ed. P. Magdalino, 11–33. Aldershot, UK.

———. 1995. "The Huns and the End of the Roman Empire in Western Europe." *EHR* 110: 4–41.

———. 1996. *The Goths.* Oxford.

———. 1997. "*Foedera* and *Foederati* of the Fourth Century." In *Kingdoms of the Empire. The Integration of Barbarians in Late Antiquity,* ed. W. Pohl, 57–74. Leiden.

———. 1998. "Senators and Senates." In *Cambridge Ancient History,* vol. 13: *The Late Empire, A.D. 337–425,* 2d ed., ed. A. Cameron and P. Garnsey, 184–210. Cambridge.

———. 1999a. "The Barbarian in Late Antiquity: Image, Reality and Transformation." In *Constructing Identities in Late Antiquity,* ed. R. Miles, 234–58. London.

———. 1999b. "The Creation of the Visigoths." In *The Visigoths from the Migration Period to the Seventh Century: An Ethnographic Perspective,* ed. P. J. Heather, 43–92. Woodbridge and Rochester.

Heather, P. J. and J. F. Matthews. 1991. *The Goths in the Fourth Century.* Translated Texts for Historians 11. Liverpool.

Heberdey, R. 1906. "Zum Erlaß des Kaisers Valens und Eutropius." *JÖAI* 9: 182–92.

Hedeager, L. 1987. "Empire, Frontier and the Barbarian Hinterland: Rome and Northern Europe from A.D. 1–400." In *Centre and Periphery in the Ancient World,* ed. M. Rowlands, M. Larsen, and K. Kristiansen, 125–40. Cambridge.

Heering, W. 1927. *Kaiser Valentinian I (364–375 n. chr.).* Diss. Jena. Magdeburg.

Heintze, H. von. 1984. "Eine Bronzebüstchen des Kaisers Gratianus." In *Vivarium. Festschrift T. Klauser,* 144–69. Münster.

Hellenkemper, H. 1980. "Zur Entwicklung des Stadtbildes in Kilikien." *ANRW* II.7.2: 1262–83.

Hendy, M. F. 1972a. "Aspects of Coin Production and Fiscal Administration in the Late Roman and Early Byzantine Period." *NC* 12: 117–139.

———. 1972b. "Mint and Fiscal Administration under Diocletian, His Colleagues and His Successors: A.D. 305–24." *JRS* 62: 75–82.

———. 1985. *Studies in the Byzantine Monetary Economy, c. 300–1450.* Cambridge.

Herzog, R., and P. L. Schmidt, eds. 1989. *Handbuch der Lateinischen Literatur der Antike,* vol. 5: *Restauration und Erneuerung: Die lateinische Literatur von 284 bis 374 n. Chr.* Handbuch der Altertumswissenschaft 8.5. Munich.

Heuss, A. 1954. "Alexander der Große und die politische Ideologie des Altertums." *A&A* 4: 65–104.

Hewsen, R. H. 1965. "Armenia According to Asxarhac'oyc'." *REArm* 2: 319–42.

———. 1988–89. "Introduction to Armenian Historical Geography IV: The *Vitaxates* of Arsacid Armenia. A Reexamination of the Territorial Aspects of the Institution (Part One)." *REArm* 21: 271–319.

———. 1990–91. "Introduction to Armenian Historical Geography IV: The *Vitaxates* of Arsacid Armenia. A Reexamination of the Territorial Aspects of the Institution (Part Two)." *REArm* 22: 147–83.

———. 1992. *The Geography of Ananias of Sirak (Asxarhac'oyc'): The Long and Short Recensions.* Beihefte zum Tübinger Atlas des Vorderen Orients, B, 77. Wiesbaden.

———. 1996. "An Ecclesiastical Analysis of the Naxarar System: A Reexamination of Adontz's Chapter XII." In *From Byzantium to Iran: Armenian Studies in Honour of Nina G. Garsoïan,* J.-P. Mahé and R. W. Thomson, 97–149. Atlanta, Ga.

Hild, F., and H. Hellenkemper. 1990. *Kilikien und Isaurien.* Tabula Imperii Byzantini 5. Denkschriften der österreichischen Akademie der Wissenschaften 215. Vienna.

Hill, S. 1996. *The Early Byzantine Churches of Cilicia and Isauria.* Birmingham Byzantine and Ottoman Monographs, 1. Aldershot, UK.

Höckmann, O. 1986. "Römische Schiffsverbände auf dem Ober und Mittelrhein und die Verteidigung der Rheingrenze in der Spätantike." *JRGZ* 33: 369–416.

———. 1993. "Late Roman Rhine Vessels from Mainz, Germany." *IJNA* 22: 125–35.

Hodinott, R. F. 1975. *Bulgaria in Antiquity: An Archaeological Introduction.* New York.

Hoffmann, D. 1969–70. *Das spätrömische Bewegungsheer und die Notitia Dignitatum.* 2 vols. Epigraphische Studien 7. Dusseldorf.

———. 1978. "Wadomar, Bacurius und Hariulf. Zur Laufbahn adliger und fürstlicher Barbaren im spätrömischen Heere des 4. Jahrhunderts." *MH* 35: 307–18.

Hoffmann, G. 1880. *Auszüge aus syrischen Akten persischer Märtyrer.* Abhandlungen für die Kunde des Morgenlandes 7.3. Leipzig.

Holman, S. R. 1999. "The Hungry Body: Famine, Poverty and Identity in Basil's Hom. 8." *JECS* 7: 337–63.

———. 2001. *The Hungry are Dying: Beggars and Bishops in Roman Cappadocia.* Oxford.

Honigmann, E. 1935. *Die Ostgrenze des byzantinischen Reiches von 363 bis 1071.* Vol. 3 of *Byzance et les Arabes,* ed. A. A. Vasiliev. Corpus Bruxellenses Historiae Byzantinae 3. Brussels.

Honigmann, E., and A. Maricq. 1953. *Recherches sur les Res Gestae Divi Saporis*. Brussels.

Honoré, T. 1986. "The Making of the Theodosian Code." *ZSS* 103: 133–222.

———. 1998. *Law in the Crisis of the Empire, 379–455 A.D.: The Theodosian Dynasty and Its Quaestors, with a Palingenesia of Laws of the Dynasty*. Oxford.

Hopwood, K. R. 1989. "Consent and Control: How the Peace Was Kept in Rough Cilicia." In *The Eastern Frontier of the Roman Empire*, ed. D. H. French and C. S. Lightfoot, 191–201. BAR-IS 553. Oxford.

———. 1999. "Ammianus Marcellinus on Isauria." In *The Late Roman World and Its Historian: Interpreting Ammianus Marcellinus*, eds. J. W. Drijvers and E. D. Hunt, 224–35. London.

Horden, P., and N. Purcell. 2000. *The Corrupting Sea: A Study of Mediterranean History*. London.

Houwink ten Cate, P. H. J. 1965. *The Luwian Population Group of Lycia and Cilicia Aspera during the Hellenistic Period*. Leiden.

Hübschmann, H. 1904. "Die altarmenischen Ortsnamen: Mit Beiträgen zur historischen Topographie Armeniens." *Indogermanische Forschungen* 16: 197–490.

Humbert, J. B., and A. Desreumaux. 1990. "Huit campagnes de fouilles au *Khirbet es-Samra* (1981–1989)." *RBi* 97: 252–69.

Humphrey, J. H. 1986. *Roman Circuses: Arenas for Chariot Racing*. London.

Hunt, E. D. 1982. *Holy Land Pilgrimage in the Later Roman Empire, A.D. 312–460*. Oxford.

Iluk, J. 1985. "The Export of Gold from the Roman Empire to Barbarian Countries from the Fourth to the Sixth Centuries." *MBAH* 4: 79–102.

Instinsky, H. U. 1952. "Zur Entstehung des Titels Nobilissimus Caesar." In *Festschrift für Rudolf Egger*, 98–103. Beiträge zur älteren europäischen Kulturgeschichte. Klagenfurt.

Ioniţă, I. 1966. "Contributii cu privire la cultura Sîntana de Mureş-Cerneahov pe teritoriul Republicii Socialiste România." *Arheologia Moldovei* 4: 189–259.

———. 1972. "Probleme der Sîntana de Mureş—Cernjakov Kultur auf dem Gebiete Rumäniens." In *Studia Gotica: Die eisenzeitlichen Verbindungen zwischen Schweden und Südosteuropa*, ed. U. E. Hagberg, 95–104. Stockholm.

———. 1975. "The Social-Economic Structure of Society during the Goths' Migration in the Carpatho-Danubian Area." In *Relations between the Autochthonous Population and the Migratory Populations on the Territory of Romania*, 77–89. Bucharest.

———. 1994. "Römische Einflüsse im Verbreitungsgebiet der Sîntana de Mureş-Cernjachov-Kultur." *Arheologia Moldovei* 17: 109–16.

Isaac, B. 1984. "Bandits in Judaea and Arabia." *HSPh* 88: 171–203.

———. 1992. *The Limits of Empire: The Roman Army in the East*. Rev. ed. Oxford.

———. 1998. "The Eastern Frontier." In *Cambridge Ancient History*, vol. 13: *The Late Empire, A.D. 337–425*, 2d ed., ed. A. Cameron and P. Garnsey, 437–60. Cambridge.

Ivanov, R. 1996. "Der *Limes* von Dorticum bis Durostorum (1.–6. Jh.)—Bauperioden des Befestigungssystems und Archäologische Ergebnisse 1980–1995." In *Roman Limes on the Middle and Lower Danube*, ed. P. Petrovic, 161–72. Belgrade.

Jacques, F., and B. Bousquet. 1984. "Le raz de marée du 21 juillet 365." *MEFR* 96: 423–61.

Jameson, R. 1913. *Collection R. Jameson*, vol. 2: *Monnaies impériales romaines*. Paris. Reprint, Chicago, 1980.

Janin, R. 1964. *Constantinople Byzantine: développement urbain et répertoire topographique.* 2d ed. Paris.

Johnson, M.J. 1991. "On the Burial Places of the Valentinian Dynasty." *Historia* 40: 501–6.

Johnson, S. 1983. *Late Roman Fortifications.* Totowa, N.J.

Jonge, P. de. 1977. *Philological and Historical Commentary on Ammianus Marcellinus XVII.* Translated by P. de Waard-Dekking. Groningen.

Jones, A. H. M. 1954. "The Date of the *Apologia Contra Arianos* of Athanasius." *JThS* 5: 224–7.

————. 1964. *The Later Roman Empire (284–602).* 3 vols. Oxford.

————. 1971. *Cities of the Eastern Roman Provinces.* 2d ed. Oxford.

Jones, A. H. M., J. R. Martindale, and J. Morris. 1971. *The Prosopography of the Later Roman Empire,* vol. 1: *A.D. 260–395.* Cambridge. Reprint, 1987.

Jones, C. P. 1987. "*Stigma:* Tatooing and Branding in Graeco-Roman Antiquity." *JRS* 77: 142–55.

Judeich, W. 1891. "Die Schlacht bei Adrianopel am 9. August 378." *Deutsche Zeitschrift für Geschichtswissenschaft* 6: 1–21.

Kahlos, M. 1997. "Vettius Agorius Praetextatus and the Rivalry Between the Bishops in Rome in 366-367." *Arctos* 31: 41-54.

Kajanto, I. 1965. *The Latin Cognomina.* Helsinki.

Kazanski, M. 1991a. "Contribution à l'histoire de la défense de la frontière pontique au bas-empire." *T&MByz* 11: 487–526.

————. 1991b. *Les Goths, Ier–VIIe siècles ap. J.-C.* Paris.

————. 1995. "Les tombes des chefs alano-sarmates au IVe siècle dans les steppes pontiques." In *La Noblesse Romaine et les chefs barbares du IIIe au VIIe siècle,* ed. F. Vallet and M. Kazanski, 189–205. Rouen.

Kelletat, D. 1998. "Geologische Belege katastrophaler Erdkustenbewegungen 365 A.D. im Raum von Kreta," In *Naturkatastrophen in der antiken Welt: Stuttgarter Kolloquium zur historischen Geographie des Altertums, 6, 1996,* ed. E. Olshausen and H. Sonnabend, 156–61. Stuttgart.

Kelly, C. 1998. "Emperors, Government and Bureaucracy." In *Cambridge Ancient History,* vol. 13: *The Late Empire, A.D. 337–425,* 2d ed., ed. A. Cameron and P. Garnsey, 138–83. Cambridge.

Kelly, J. N. D. 1975. *Jerome: His Life, Writings and Controversies.* New York.

————. 1995. *Golden Mouth: The Story of John Chrysostom—Ascetic, Preacher, Bishop.* Ithaca, N.Y.

Kempf, J. G. 1901. *Romanorum sermonis castrensis reliquiae collectae et illustratae.* Jahrbuch für classische Philologie, Suppl. vol. 26. Leipzig.

Kennedy, D., and D. Riley. 1990. *Rome's Desert Frontier from the Air.* Austin, Tex.

Kent, J. H. 1966. *The Inscriptions, 1926–1950.* Corinth: Results of Excavations Conducted by the American School of Classical Studies at Athens, vol. 8, pt. 3. Princeton, N.J.

Kent, J. P. C. 1956. "Gold Coinage in the Later Roman Empire." In *Essays in Roman Coinage Presented to Harold Mattingly,* ed. R. A. G. Carson and C. H. V. Sutherland, 190–204. Oxford.

————. 1957. "A Supposed Coin of Procopius." *NC* 17: 248.

————. 1959. "An Introduction to the Coinage of Julian the Apostate (A.D. 360–3)." *NC* 19: 109–17.

————. 1967. "Fel. Temp. Reparatio." *NC* 7.7: 83–90.

————. 1981. *The Roman Imperial Coinage*, vol. 8: *The Family of Constantine I*, A.D. 337–364. London.

Kettenhofen, E. 1982. *Die römisch-persischen Kriege des 3. Jahrhunderts n. Chr. nach der Inschrift Sahpuhrs I. an der Ka'be-ye Zartost (SKZ)*. Wiesbaden.

————. 1984. "Die Einforderung des achämenidenerbes durch Ardasir: Eine *Interpretatio Romana*." *OLP* 15: 178–90.

————. 1989. "Toponyme bei Ps-Pawstos." *Handes Amsorya* 103: 65–80.

————. 1995. *Tirdad und die Inschrift von Paikuli: Kritik der Quellen zur Geschichte Armeniens im späten 3. und frühen 4. Jh. n. Chr.* Wiesbaden.

Kienast, D. 1996. *Römische Kaisertabelle. Grundzüge einer römischen Kaiserchronologie*. Darmstadt.

Klein, K. K. 1952. "Der Friedensschluß von Noviodunum." *AAHG* 5: 189–92.

————. 1956. "Kaiser Valens vor Adrianopel (378 n. Chr.)." *Südostforschungen* 15: 53–69.

Klose, J. 1934. *Roms Klientel-Randstaaten am Rhein und an der Donau: Beiträge zu ihrer Geschichte und rechtlichen Stellung im 1. und 2. Jhdt. n. Chr.* Breslau.

Kneissl, P. 1969. *Die Siegestitulatur der römischen Kaiser: Untersuchungen zu den Siegerbeinamen des ersten und zweiten Jahrhunderts*. Göttingen.

Köhler, G. 1925. *Untersuchungen zur Geschichte des Kaisers Valens*. Diss. Jena.

Kondić, V. 1973. "Two Recent Acquisitions in Belgrade Museums: II, An Unrecorded Medallion of Valentinian I." *JRS* 63: 47–49.

Konrad, M. 1999. "Research on the Roman and Early Byzantine Frontier in North Syria." *JRA* 12: 392–410.

Krierer, K. R. 1995. *Sieg und Niederlage: Untersuchungen physiognomischer und mimischer Phänomene in Kampfdarstellungen der römischen Plastik*. Vienna.

Kropotkin, A. V. 1984. "On the Centres of the Chernyakhovo Tribes." *Sovetskaja arheologia* 3: 35–47.

Kurbatov, L. 1958. "The Revolt of Procopius." *Vizantiinski Vremmenik*, n.s., 14: 3–26.

Lacam, G. 1990. "A New Consular Solidus in the Name of Valens from the Mint of Antioch." *NC* 150: 237.

Ladner, G. 1976. "On Roman Attitudes toward Barbarians in Late Antiquity." *Viator* 7: 1–26.

Lallemand, J. 1963. *L'administration civile de l'Égypte de l'avènement de Dioclétien à la création du diocèse (284–382)*. Paris.

Lander, J. 1984. *Roman Stone Fortifications: Variation and Change from the First Century* A.D. *to the Fourth*. BAR-IS 206. Oxford.

Landesman, P. 2001. "The Curse of the Sevso Silver." *Atlantic Monthly* 288.4: 66–89.

Lane Fox, R.J. 1997. "The Itinerary of Alexander: Constantius to Julian." *CQ* 47: 239–52.

Langlois, V. 1867–69. *Collection des historiens anciens et modernes de l'Arménie*. 2 vols. Paris.

Lányi, V. 1969. "The Coinage of Valentinian in Siscia." *AArchHung* 21: 33–46.

————. 1972. "Die spätantiken Gräberfeldern von Pannonien." *AArchHung* 24: 53–213.

Lányi, V., ed. 1993. *Die Fundmünzen der römischen Zeit in Ungarn, II.* Bonn and Budapest.

Leadbetter, B. 1998. "'Patrimonium Indivisum'? The Empire of Diocletian and Maximian, 285–289." *Chiron* 28: 213–28.

Lee, A. D. 1993. *Information and Frontiers: Roman Foreign Relations in Late Antiquity.* Cambridge.

———. 1998. "The Army." In *Cambridge Ancient History*, vol. 13: *The Late Empire, A.D. 337–425*, 2d ed., ed. A. Cameron and P. Garnsey, 211–37. Cambridge.

Lehmann-Haupt, C. F. 1908. "Eine griechische Inschrift der Spätzeit Tigranakerts." *Klio* 8: 497–520.

———. 1910. *Armenien Einst und Jetzt.* Vol. 1. Berlin.

Lendon, J. E. 1997. *Empire of Honour: The Art of Government in the Roman World.* Oxford.

Lengyel, A., and G. T. B. Radan, eds. 1980. *The Archaeology of Roman Pannonia.* Budapest.

Lenski, N. 1995a. "The Gothic Civil War and the Date of the Gothic Conversion." *GRBS* 36: 51–87.

———. 1995b. "Valens and the Fourth Century Empire." Diss. Princeton.

———. 1996. Review of *Basil of Caesarea* by Philip Rousseau (Berkeley, 1994). *BMCR* 7: 438–44.

———. 1997. "*Initium mali romano imperio:* Contemporary Reactions to the Battle of Adrianople." *TAPhA* 127: 129–68.

———. 1999a. "Basil and the Isaurian Uprising of 375." *Phoenix* 53: 308–29.

———. 1999b. "Romanization and Revolt in the Territory of Isauria." *JESHO* 42: 413–65.

———. 2000. "The Election of Jovian and the Role of the Late Imperial Guards." *Klio* 82: 492–515.

———. 2002. "Were Valentinian, Valens and Jovian Confessors before Julian the Apostate?" *ZfaC* 6: 94–117.

———. "Isaac and Valens' Recruitment of Monks for Military Service." Forthcoming.

Leppin, H. 1996. *Von Constantin dem Großen zu Theodosius II: Das christliche Kaisertum bei den Kirchenhistorikern Socrates, Sozomenus und Theodoret.* Hypomnemata 110. Göttingen.

Leppin, H., and W. Portmann, trans. 1998. *Themistios Staatsreden.* Stuttgart.

Levick, B. 1965. "Two Inscriptions from Pisidian Antioch." *AnatStud* 15: 53–62.

Lewin, A. 1991. "Banditismo e *civilitas* nella Cilicia Tracheia antica e tardoantica." *Quaderni storici* 76: 167–84.

L'Huillier, M.-C. 1992. *L'empire des mots: Orateurs gaulois et empereurs romains, 3ᵉ et 4ᵉ siècles.* Paris.

Liebeschuetz, J. H. W. G. 1972. *Antioch: City and Imperial Administration in the Later Roman Empire.* Oxford.

———. 1990. *Barbarians and Bishops: Army, Church and State in the Age of Arcadius and Chrysostom.* Oxford.

———. 1994. "Realism and Phantasy: The Anonymous *De rebus bellicis* and Its Afterlife." In *The Roman and Byzantine Army in the East*, ed. E. Dabrowa, 132–39. Kraków.

Lieu, S. N. C. 1985. *Manichaeism in the Later Roman Empire and Medieval China A Historical Survey.* Manchester.

———. 1986. "Captives, Refugees and Exiles: A Study of Cross-Frontier Civilian Movements and Contacts between Rome and Persia from Valerian to Jovian." In *The Defense of the Roman and Byzantine East*, ed. P. Freeman and D. Kennedy, 475–505. BAR-IS 297. Oxford.

Lightfoot, C. S. 1986. "Tilli: A Late Roman *equites* Fort on the Tigris?" In *The Defense of the Roman and Byzantine East,* ed. P. Freeman and D. Kennedy, 509–29. BAR-IS 297. Oxford.

———. 1988. "Facts and Fiction—The Third Siege of Nisibis (A.D. 350)." *Historia* 37: 105–25.

———. 1990. "Trajan's Parthian War and the Fourth-Century Perspective." *JRS* 80: 115–26.

Lippold, A. 1991. *Kommentar zur Vita Maximini Duo der Historia Augusta.* Vol. 1. Beiträge zur Historia-Augusta-Forschung 3. Antiquitas 4. Bonn.

———. 1992a. "Kaiser Claudius II. (Gothicus), Vorfahr Konstantins d. Gr. und der römische Senat." *Klio* 74: 380–94.

———. 1992b. "Konstantin und die Barbaren (Konfrontation? Integration? Koexistenz?)." *SIFC* 10: 371–91.

Lizzi, R. 1996. "La politica religiosa di Teodosio I: Miti storiografici e realtà storica." *RAL* 9.7: 323–61.

LoCascio, E. 1999. "*Canon frumentarius, suarius, vinarius:* Stato e privati nell'approvvigionamento dell' *Vrbs.*" In *The Transformations of Vrbs Roma in Late Antiquity,* ed. W. V. Harris, 163–82. JRA-SS 33. Portsmouth, R.I.

Löhr, W. A. 1993. "A Sense of Tradition: The Homoiousian Church Party." In *Arianism after Arius: Essays on the Development of the Fourth-Century Trinitarian Conflicts,* ed. M. R. Barnes and D. H. Williams, 81–100. Edinburgh.

Loofs, F. 1898. *Eustathius von Sebaste und die Chronologie der Basilius-Briefe.* Halle, Germany.

MacCormack, S. 1975. "Latin Prose Panegyrics." In *Empire and Aftermath: Silver Latin II,* ed. T. A. Dorey, 143–205. London.

———. 1981. *Art and Ceremony in Late Antiquity.* Berkeley.

MacDonald, M. C. A. 1993. "Nomads and the Hawran in the Late Hellenistic and Roman Periods: A Reassessment of the Epigraphic Evidence." *Syria* 70: 303–413.

Mackensen, M. 1999. "Late Roman Fortifications and Building Programmes in the Province of *Raetia.*" In *Roman Germany: Studies in Cultural Interaction,* ed. J. D. Creighton and R. J. A. Wilson, 199–244. JRA-SS 32. Portsmouth, R.I.

MacMullen, R. 1963. "The Roman Concept Robber-Pretender." *RIDA* 10: 221–25.

———. 1980. "How Big Was the Roman Army." *Klio* 62: 451–60.

———. 1985. "How to Revolt in the Roman Empire." *RSA* 15: 67–76. Reprinted in *Changes in the Roman Empire: Essays in the Ordinary,* ed. R. MacMullen, 198–203. Princeton, N.J.

———. 1988. *Corruption and the Decline of Rome.* New Haven, Conn.

Maenchen-Helfen, O. J. 1973. *The World of the Huns: Studies in Their History and Culture.* Berkeley.

Magomedov, B. 1995. "La stratification sociale de la population de la culture de Cernjahov." In *La noblesse romaine et les chefs barbares du III*^*e* *au VII*^*e* *siècle,* ed. F. Vallet and M. Kazanski, 133–38. Rouen.

Maisano, R. trans. and comm. 1995. *Discorsi di Temistio.* Torino.

Malcus, B. 1967. "Die Prokonsuln von Asien von Diokletian bis Theodosius II." *OAth* 7: 91–160.

Mango, C. 1985. "Deux études sur Byzance et la Perse Sassanide." *T&MByz* 9: 91–118.

———. 1990a. "Constantine's Mausoleum and the Translation of Relics." *ByzZ* 83: 51–61.

———. 1990b. *Le développement urbain de Constantinople (IVe–VIIe siècles).* Paris.

———. 1995. "The Water Supply of Constantinople." In *Constantinople and its Hinterland,* eds. C. Mango and G. Dagron, 9–18. Aldershot, UK.

Mango, C., and R. Scott, trans. 1997. *The Chronicle of Theophanes Confessor: Byzantine and Near Eastern History, A.D. 284–813.* Oxford.

Mann, J. C. 1979. "Power, Force and the Frontiers of the Empire." *JRS* 69: 175–83.

———. 1983. *Legionary Recruitment and Veteran Settlement during the Principate.* London.

Mannino, V. 1984. *Ricerche sull "defensor civitatis."* Milan.

Mansion, J. 1914. "Les origines du christianisme chez les Goths." *AB* 33: 5–30.

Markwart, J. 1896. "Untersuchungen zur Geschichte von Eran, 5. Zur Kritik des Faustos von Byzanz." *Philologus* 55: 215–44.

———. 1901. *Eranshahr nach der Geographie des Ps. Moses Xorenac'i.* Abhandlungen der königlichen Gesellschaft der Wissenschaften zu Göttingen, 3. Berlin.

———. 1930. *Südarmenien und die Tigrisquellen nach griechischen und arabischen Geographen.* Vienna.

Martin, A. 1996. *Athanase d'Alexandrie et l'église d'Égypte au IVe siècle (328–373).* CEFR 216. Rome.

Martin, K. M. 1969. "A Reassessment of the Evidence for the *comes Britanniarum* in the Fourth Century." *Latomus* 28: 408–28.

Martindale, J. R. 1980. *The Prosopography of the Later Roman Empire,* vol. 2: *A.D. 395–527.* Cambridge.

Mattern, S. P. 1999. *Rome and the Enemy: Imperial Strategy in the Principate.* Berkeley.

Matthews, J. F. 1967. "A Pious Supporter of Theodosius I: Maternus Cynegius and his Family." *JThS* 18: 438–46.

———. 1973. "Symmachus and the Oriental Cults." *JRS* 63: 175–95. Reprinted in *Political Life and Culture in Late Roman Society,* ed. J. F. Matthews. London, 1985.

———. 1975. *Western Aristocracies and Imperial Court, A.D. 364–425.* Oxford.

———. 1984. "The Taxation of Palmyra: Evidence for Economic History in a City of the Roman East." *JRS* 74: 157–80.

———. 1989. *The Roman Empire of Ammianus.* London.

———. 2000. *Laying Down the Law: A Study of the Theodosian Code.* New Haven, Conn.

Mattingly, H. 1933. "Fel. Temp. Reparatio." *NC* 5.13: 192–212.

Mauss, M. 1921. "Une forme ancienne de contrat chez les Thraces." *REG* 34: 388–97.

———. 1990. *The Gift: The Form and Reason for Exchange in Archaic Societies.* Translated by W. D. Halls. Reprint, London.

May, G. 1973. "Basilios der Grosse und der römische Staat." In *Bleibendes im Wandel der Kirchengeschichte,* ed. B. Moeller and G. Ruhbach, 47–70. Tübingen.

Mayerson, P. 1963. "The Desert of Southern Palestine According to Byzantine Sources." *PAPhS* 107: 160–72. Reprinted in *Monks, Martyrs, Soldiers and Saracens: Papers on the Near East in Late Antiquity (1962-1993),* 40-52. Jerusalem, 1994.

———. 1976. "An Inscription in the Monastery of St. Catherine and the Martyr Tradition in Sinai." *DOP* 30: 375–9. Reprinted in *Monks, Martyrs, Soldiers and Saracens: Papers on the Near East in Late Antiquity (1962-1993),* 129-33. Jerusalem, 1994.

———. 1980a. "The Ammonius Narrative: Bedouin and Blemmye Attacks in Sinai."

In *The Bible World: Essays in Honour of Cyrus H. Gordon,* ed. G. Rendsburg et al., 133–48. New York. Reprinted in *Monks, Martyrs, Soldiers and Saracens: Papers on the Near East in Late Antiquity (1962-1993),* 148-63. Jerusalem, 1994.

———. 1980b. "Mavia, Queen of the Saracens—A Cautionary Note." *IEJ* 30: 123–31. Reprinted in *Monks, Martyrs, Soldiers and Saracens: Papers on the Near East in Late Antiquity (1962-1993),* 164-72. Jerusalem, 1994.

Mazzarino, S. 1951. *Aspetti sociali del quarto secolo: Ricerche di storia tardo-romana.* Rome.

———. 1974. "Sulla politica tributaria di Valentiniano I (a proposito di un' epigrafe da Casamari)." In *Antico, Tardoantico ed èra costantiniana I,* ed. S. Mazzarino, 299–327. Bari.

McCormick, M. 1986. *Eternal Victory: Triumphal Rulership in Late Antiquity, Byzantium and the Early Medieval West.* Cambridge.

McLynn, N. 1994. *Ambrose of Milan: Church and Court in a Christian Capital.* Berkeley.

———. 1997. "Theodosius, Spain and the Nicene Faith." In *Congreso Internacional La Hispania de Teodosio,* 1.171–78. Salamanca.

Meischner, J. 1992. "Das Porträt der Valentinianischen Epoche." *JDAI* 107: 217–34.

———. 1993. "Familie Valentinian gratuliert." *Istanbuler Mitteilungen* 43: 463–66.

Meslin, M. 1967. *Les Ariens d'occident.* Patristica Sorbonensia 8. Paris.

Meyer, H. 1980. "Die Frieszyklen am sogennanten Triumphbogen des Galerius in Thessaloniki: Kriegschronik und Ankundigung der zweiten Tetrarchie." *JDAI* 95: 374–444.

Meyer, M., and R. Smith. 1999. *Ancient Christian Magic: Coptic Texts of Ritual Power.* Princeton, N.J.

Mihăilescu-Bîrliba, V. 1980. *La monnaie romaine chez les Daces orientaux.* Bucharest.

Millar, F. 1977. *The Emperor in the Roman World.* Ithaca, N.Y.

———. 1982. "Emperors, Frontiers, and Foreign Relations, 31 B.C. to A.D. 378." *Britannia* 13: 1–23.

———. 1983. "Empire and City, Augustus to Julian: Obligations, Excuses and Status." *JRS* 73: 76–96.

———. 1988. "Government and Diplomacy in the Roman Empire during the First Three Centuries." *International History Review* 10: 345–77.

———. 1993. *The Roman Near East, 31 B.C.–A.D. 337.* Cambridge, Mass.

Milner, N. P., trans. with comm. 1993. *Vegetius: Epitome of Military Science.* Translated Texts for Historians 16. Liverpool.

Minor, C. E. 1979. "The Robber Tribes of Isauria." *AncW* 2: 117–27.

Mirković, M. 1971. "Sirmium—Its History from the First Century A.D. to 582 A.D." In *Sirmium: Archaeological Investigations in Syrmian Pannonia,* vol. 1, ed. V. Popović, 5–90. Belgrade.

———. 1993. "'Υπήκοοι und σύμμαχοι: Ansiedlung und Rekrutierung von Barbaren (bis zum Jahr 382)." In *Klaßisches Altertum, Spätantike und frühes Christentum: Adolf Lippold zum 65. Geburtstag gewidmet,* ed. K. Dietz et al., 425–34. Würzburg.

Mitchell, S., ed. 1983. *Armies and Frontiers in Roman and Byzantine Anatolia: Proceedings of a Colloquium held at University College, Swansea, in April 1981.* BAR-IS 156. Oxford.

———. 1993. *Anatolia: Land, Men and Gods in Asia Minor.* 2 vols. Oxford.

———. 1994. "Notes on Military Recruitment from the Eastern Roman Provinces." In *The Roman and Byzantine Army in the East,* ed. E. Dabrowa, 141–48. Kraków.

———. 1999. "Native Rebellion in the Pisidian Taurus." In *Organised Crime in Late Antiquity*, ed. K. Hopwood, 155–75. London.

Mitford, T. B. 1980. "Cappadocia and Armenia Minor: Historical Setting of the *Limes.*" *ANRW* II.7.2: 1169–1228.

———. 1986. "A Late Roman Fortress South of Lake Van?" In *The Defense of the Roman and Byzantine East*, ed. P. Freeman and D. Kennedy, 565–73. BAR-IS 297. Oxford.

Mitrea, B. 1957. "La migration des Goths reflétée par les trésors de monnaies romaines enfouis en Moldavie." *Dacia* 1: 229–36.

Mitteis, L., ed. 1906. *Griechische Urkunden der Papyrussamlung zu Leipzig.* Leipzig.

Mócsy, A. 1962. "Pannonia." *RE Suppl.* 9: 516–776.

———. 1970. "Murocincta." In *Adriatica praehistorica et antiqua: Miscellanea G. Novak dicata*, 583–776. Zagreb.

———. 1974. *Pannonia and Upper Moesia: A History of the Middle Danube Provinces of the Roman Empire.* London.

———. 1985. *Beiträge zur Namenstatistik.* Dissertationes Pannonicae 3.3. Budapest.

Mócsy, A., and T. Szentléleky, eds. 1971. *Die römischen Steindenkmäler von Savaria.* Amsterdam.

Momigliano, A. 1963. "Pagan and Christian Historiography in the Fourth Century." In *The Conflict between Paganism and Christianity in the Fourth Century*, ed. A. Momigliano, 79–99. Oxford.

Mommsen, T. 1862. "Verzeichnis der römischen Provinzen aufgesetzt um 297." *Abhandlungen der Berliner Akademie der Wissenschaften, phil.-hist. Kl.*, 489–518. Reprinted in *Gesammelte Schriften*, 5: 561–88.

———. 1880. "Zur Kritik Ammians." *Hermes* 15: 244–6. Reprinted in *Gesammelte Schriften*, 7: 389–91.

———. 1882. "Die Inschrift von Hissarlik und die römische Sammtherrschaft in ihrem titularen Ausdruck." *Hermes* 17: 523–44. Reprinted in *Gesammelte Schriften*, 6: 303–23.

———. 1884. "Protectores Augusti." *Ephemeris Epigraphica* 5: 121–41. Reprinted in *Gesammelte Schriften*, 8: 419–46.

———. 1889. "Das römische Militärwesen seit Diocletian." *Hermes* 24: 195–279. Reprinted in *Gesammelte Schriften*, 6: 206–83.

Mundell Mango, M., and A. Bennett. 1994. *The Sevso Treasure, Part One.* JRA Supplement 12.1. Ann Arbor, Mich.

Mutafian, C. 1988. *La Cilicie au carrefour des empires.* Paris.

Nagl, A. 1948a. "Valens 3." *RE* II.7.2: 2097–2137.

———. 1948b. "Valentinianus 1." *RE* II.7.2: 2158–2204.

Nagy, T. 1991. "Die Okkupation Pannoniens durch die Römer in der Zeit des Augustus." *AArchHung* 43: 57–85.

Nathan, G. S. 2000. *The Family in Late Antiquity: The Rise of Christianity and the Endurance of Tradition.* London.

Neri, V. 1985a. *Ammiano e il Cristianesimo: Religione e politica nelle "Res Gestae" di Ammiano Marcellino.* Bologna.

———. 1985b. "Ammiano Marcellino e l'elezione di Valentiniano." *RSA* 15: 153–82.

Nicasie, M. J. 1998. *Twilight of Empire: The Roman Army from the Reign of Diocletian until the Batttle of Adrianople.* Amsterdam.

Niculescu, G. A. 1993. "The Cremation Graves from the Cemetery of Tîrgsor (Third–Fourth Centuries A.D.)." *Dacia* 37: 197–220.

Nikolov, D. 1976. *The Thraco-Roman Villa Rustica near Chatalka, Stara Zagora, Bulgaria.* BAR-SS 17. Oxford.

Nixon, C. E. V. 1983. "Coin Circulation and Military Activity in the Vicinity of Sirmium, A.D.364–378, and the Siscia Mint." *JNG* 33: 45–56.

———. 1991. "Aurelius Victor and Julian." *CPh* 86: 113–25.

———. 1998. "The Early Career of Valentinian I." In *Ancient History in a Modern University,* ed. T. W. Hillard et al., 294–304. Grand Rapids, Mich.

Nixon, C. E. V., and B. Saylor Rodgers. 1994. *In Praise of Later Roman Emperors: The Panegyrici Latini. Introduction, Translation and Historical Commentary.* Berkeley.

Nöldeke, T., trans. 1977. *Geschichte der Perser und Araber zur Zeit der Sasaniden aus der Arabischen Chronik des Tabari.* Leiden.

Noreña, C. F. 2001. "The Communication of the Emperor's Virtues." *JRS* 91: 146–68.

Norman, A. F. 1958. "Notes on Some *Consulares* of Syria." *ByzZ* 51: 73–77.

———, trans. and comm. 1965. *Libanius Autobiography (Oration I).* Oxford.

———, trans. 1969–77. *Libanius Selected Works,* 2 vols. Loeb Classical Library. Cambridge, Mass.

———, trans., 1992. *Libanius, Autobiography and Selected Letters,* 2 vols. Loeb Classical Library. Cambridge, Mass.

Oaks, J. 1996. "The Birth Dates of Valentinian II and Valentinian III: A Correction to *PLRE* I." *Medieval Prosopography* 17: 147–8.

Oates, D. 1968. *Studies in the Ancient History of Northern Iraq.* London.

Oldenstein, J. 1993. "La fortification d'Alzey et la défense de la frontière romaine le long du Rhin au IV et au V siècles." In *L'armée romaine et les barbares du IIIe au VIIe siècle,* ed. F. Vallet and M. Kazanski, 125–33. Rouen.

Opelt, I. 1971. "Ein Edikt des Kaisers Valens." *StudClas* 13: 139–42.

Outtier, B. 1973. "Saint Éphrem d'après ses biographies et ses oeuvres." *Parole de l'orient* 4: 11–33.

Overbeck, B., and M. Overbeck. 1985. "Zur Datierung und Interpretation der spätantiken Goldbarren aus Siebenbürgen anhand eines unpublizierten Fundes von Feldioara." *Chiron* 15: 199–210.

Pabst, A., trans. and comm. 1989. *Quintus Aurelius Symmachus Reden.* Darmstadt.

———. 1986. *Divisio Regni: Der Zerfall des Imperium Romanum in der Sicht der Zeitgenossen.* Bonn.

Pack, E. 1986. *Städte und Steuern in der Politik Julians: Untersuchungen zu den Quellen eines Kaiserbildes.* Brussels.

Palade, V. 1980. "Éléments géto-daces dans le site Sîntana de Mureş de Birlad Valea Seaca." *Dacia* 24: 223–53.

Palanque, J.-R. 1944. "Collégialité et partages dans l'empire romain aux IVe et Ve siècles." *REA* 46: 47–64.

Parker, S. T. 1986. *Romans and Saracens: A History of the Arabian Frontier.* Winona Lake, Ind.

———. 1989. "The Fourth-Century Garrison of Arabia: Strategic Implications for the South-Eastern Frontier." In *The Eastern Frontier of the Roman Empire: Proceedings of a Colloquium Held at Ankara in September 1988,* ed. D. H. French and S. Lightfoot, 355–66. BAR-IS 553. Oxford.

———. 1997. "Geography and Strategy on the Southeastern Frontier in the Late Roman Period." In *Roman Frontier Studies, 1995: Proceedings of the XVIth International Congress of Roman Frontier Studies*, ed. W. Groenman-van Waateringe et al., 115–22. Oxford.

Parsi, B. 1963. *Désignation et investiture de l'empereur romain (Ier et IIe siècles après J.-C.).* Paris.

Paschoud, F., ed. and trans. 1971–89. *Zosime: Histoire nouvelle*, 5 vols. Paris.

———. 1975. *Cinq études sur Zosime.* Paris.

———. 1992. "Valentinian travesti, ou, de la malignité d'Ammien." In *Cognitio Gestorum: The Historiographic Art of Ammianus Marcellinus*, ed. J. den Boeft, D. den Hengst, and H. Teitler, 67–84. Amsterdam.

Paschoud, F., and J. Szidat, eds. 1997. *Usurpationen in der Spätantike.* Stuttgart.

Patsch, C. 1899. "Cibalae." *RE* 3.2: 2534–35.

Peachin, M. 1985. "The Purpose of Festus' Breviarium." *Mnemosyne* 38: 158–61.

Pearce, J. W. E. 1951. *The Roman Imperial Coinage.* Vol. 9: *Valentinian I–Theodosius I.* London.

Peeters, P. 1910. *Bibliotheca Hagiographica Orientalis.* Subsidia Hagiographica 10. Brussels.

Penella, R. 1985. "Did a Hilarius Govern Lydia in the Fourth Century A.D.?" *AJPh* 106: 509–11.

———. 1990. *Greek Philosophers and Sophists in the Fourth Century A.D.: Studies in Eunapius of Sardis.* Leeds.

Pergami, F. 1993. *La legislazione di Valentiniano e Valente (364–375).* Milan.

———. 1995. "Sulla istituzione del defensor civitatis." *SDHI* 61: 413–32.

Peters, F. E. 1978. "Romans and Bedouin in Southern Syria." *JNES* 37: 315–26.

Petit, P. 1955. *Libanius et la vie municipale à Antioche au ive siècle.* Paris.

———. 1957. "Les sénateurs de Constantinople dans l'oeuvre de Libanius." *AC* 26: 347–82.

Petrikovits, H. von. 1971. "Fortifications in the North-Western Roman Empire from the Third to the Fifth Centuries A.D." *JRS* 61: 178–218.

Petrovic, P. 1993. "Naissus: A Foundation of Emperor Constantine." In *Roman Imperial Towns and Palaces in Serbia*, ed. D. Srejović, 55–81. Belgrade.

Pietri, C. 1976. *Roma christiana: Recherches sur l'Église de Rome, son organisation, sa politique, son idéologie de Miltiade à Sixte III.* BEFAR 224. Rome.

Piganiol, A. 1972. *L'empire chrétien, 325–395.* Revised ed. Paris.

Pitts, L. F. 1989. "Relations between Rome and German 'Kings' on the Middle Danube in the First to Fourth Centuries A.D." *JRS* 79: 45–58.

Poccardi, G. 1994. "Antioche de Syrie: Pour un nouveau plan urbain de l'île de l'Oronte (Ville Neuve) du IIIe au Ve siècle." *MEFRA* 106: 993–1023.

Póczy, K. 1977. *Scarbantia: Die Stadt Sopron zur Römerzeit.* Budapest.

———. 1980. "Pannonian Cities." In *The Archaeology of Roman Pannonia*, ed. A. Lengyel and G. T. B. Radan, 239–74. Budapest.

Polascheck, E. 1925. "Zwei römische Münzchätze aus Wien." *NZ* 18: 127–29.

Pollard, N. 2000. *Soldiers, Cities, and Civilians in Roman Syria.* Ann Arbor, Mich.

Popović, V. 1971. "A Survey of the Topography and Urban Organization of Sirmium in the Late Empire." In *Sirmium: Archaeological Investigations in Syrmian Pannonia*, vol. 1, ed. V. Popović, 119–34. Belgrade.

————. 1993. "Sirmium: A Town of Emperors and Martyrs." In *Roman Imperial Towns and Palaces in Serbia*, ed. D. Srejović, 15–27. Belgrade.

Popović, V., and E. L. Ochsenschlager. 1976. "Der spätkaiserzeitliche Hippodrom in Sirmium." *Germania* 54: 156–81.

Portmann, W. 1989. "Die 59. Rede des Libanios und das Datum der Schlacht von Singara," *ByzZ* 82: 1–18.

Potter, D. S. 1990. *Prophecy and History in the Crisis of the Roman Empire: A Historical Commentary on the Thirteenth Sibylline Oracle.* Oxford.

————. 1992. "Empty Areas and Roman Frontier Policy." *AJPh* 113: 269–74.

————. 1994. *Prophets and Emperors: Human and Divine Authority from Augustus to Theodosius.* Cambridge, Mass.

Pouchet, R. 1992. "La date de l'élection épiscopale de S. Basile et celle de sa mort." *RHE* 87: 5–33.

Poulter, A. G. 1983. "Town and Country in Moesia Inferior." In *Ancient Bulgaria: Papers Presented to the International Symposium on the Ancient History and Archaeology of Bulgaria, University of Nottingham, 1981*, ed. A. G. Poulter, 74–118. Nottingham.

————. 1992. "The Use and Abuse of Urbanism in the Later Roman Empire." In *The City in Late Antiquity*, ed. J. Rich, 99–135. London.

————. 1995. *Nicopolis ad Istrum: A Roman, Late Roman, and Early Byzantine City. Excavations, 1985–1992.* London.

Preda, C. 1975. "Circulatia monedelor romane postaureliene in Dacia." *SCIV* 26: 441–86.

Prunaeus, J., ed. 1571. *Operum Gregroii Nazianzeni tomi tres.* Basel.

Rapp, C., and M.R. Salzman, eds. 2000. *Elites in Late Antiquity.* Arethusa 33.3. Baltimore.

Ratti, S. 1996. *Les empereurs romains d'Auguste à Diocletian dans le Breviaire d'Eutrope: Les livres 7 à 9 du Bréviaire d'Eutrope.* Paris.

Redgate, A. E. 1998. *The Armenians.* Oxford.

Reece, R. 1963. "Some Analyses of Late Roman Silver Coins." *NC* 7.3: 240–1.

Rémondon, R. 1955. "Problèmes militaires en Égypte et dans l'empire à la fin du ive siècle." *RH* 213: 21–38.

Rendić-Miočević, D. 1963–64. "Études d'onomastique illyrienne, II: Les noms romains Firmus, Valens, Maximus et leur apparition dans l'onomastique illyrienne." *ZAnt* 13: 101–10.

Richard, M. 1949. "Saint Basile et la mission du diacre Sabinus." *AB* 67: 178–202.

Ritter, A. M. 1966. *Das Konzil von Konstantinopel und sein Symbol.* Göttingen.

Robert, L. 1948. "Épigrammes relatives à des gouverneurs." In *Hellenica IV*, ed. L. Robert, 35–114. Paris.

————, ed. and trans. 1994. *Le martyre de Pionios, prêtre de Smyrne.* Revised by G. W. Bowersock and C. P. Jones. Washington, D.C.

Roberts, M. 1984. "The 'Mosella' of Ausonius: An Interpretation." *TAPhA* 114: 343–53.

Rolfe, J. C., trans. 1935-49. *Ammianus Marcellinus*, 3 vols. Loeb Classical Library. Cambridge, Mass.

Rott, H. 1908. *Kleinasiatische Denkmäler aus Pisidien, Pamphylien, Kappadokien und Lykien.* Leipzig.

Roueché, C. 1984. "Acclamations in the Later Roman Empire: New Evidence from Aphrodisias." *JRS* 74: 181–99.

————. 1989. *Aphrodisias in Late Antiquity*. London.

Rougé, J. 1958. "La pseudo-bigamie de Valentinien Ier." *CH* 3: 5–15.

————. 1966. "L'Histoire Auguste et l'Isaurie au IVe siècle." *REA* 68: 282–315.

————. 1974. "Justine, la belle Sicilienne." *Latomus* 33: 676–79.

————. 1987. "Valentinien et la religion: 364–365." *Ktèma* 12: 286–97.

Rousseau, P. 1994. *Basil of Caesarea*. Berkeley.

Rubin, Z. 1981. "The Conversion of the Visigoths to Christianity." *MH* 38: 34–54.

————. 1990. "Sinai in the Itinerarium Egeriae." In *Atti del Convegno internazionale sulla Peregrinatio Egeriae, 1987*, 177–91. Arezzo.

Rugullis, S. 1992. *Die Barbaren in den spätrömischen Gesetzen: Eine Untersuchung des Terminus Barbarus*. Frankfurt am Main.

Runkel, F. 1903. "Die Schlacht bei Adrianopel." Diss., Rostock.

Russell, D. A., and N. G. Wilson, eds. and trans. 1981. *Menander Rhetor*. Oxford, 1981.

Russell, J. R. 1987. *Zoroastrianism in Armenia*. Harvard Iranian Series, vol. 5. Cambridge.

Russi, A. 1991. "Attivitá giudiziaria ed edilizia pubblica a Luceria al tempo di Valentiniano I e Valente." *MGR* 16: 299–322.

Sabbah, G. 1978. *La méthode d'Ammien Marcellin: Recherches sur la construction du discours historique dans les Res Gestae*. Paris.

————. 1992. "Présences féminines dans l'histoire d'Ammien Marcellin: Les rôles politiques." In *Cognitio Gestorum: The Historiographic Art of Ammianus Marcellinus*, ed. J. den Boeft, D. den Hengst, and H. Teitler, 91–105. Amsterdam.

Sági, K. 1961. "Die zweite altchristliche Basilika von Fenékpuszta." *AAntHung* 9: 397–459.

Sahas, D. J. 1998. "Saracens and the Syrians in the Byzantine Anti-Islamic Literature and Before." In *Symposium Syriacum VII*, ed. R. Lavenant, 387–408. Rome.

Salamon, M. 1972. "La prétendue guerre populaire en Thrace et en Asie Mineure au temps de l'usurpation procopienne (365–366)." *Eos* 60: 369–79.

Saller, R. P. 1987. "Men's Age at Marriage and its Consequences in the Roman Family." *CPh* 82: 21–34.

Salway, B. 1994. "What's in a Name? A Survey of Roman Onomastic Practice from c. 700 B.C. to A.D. 700." *JRS* 84: 124–45.

Salway, P. 1981. *Roman Britain*. Oxford.

————. 1993. *The Oxford Illustrated History of Roman Britain*. Oxford.

Salzman, M. R. 1990. *On Roman Time: The Codex-Calendar of 354 and the Rhythms of Urban Life in Late Antiquity*. Berkeley.

Sangmeister, E. 1993. *Zeitspuren: Archäologisches aus Baden*. Freiburg am Breisgau.

Santos Yanguas, N. 1977. "Algunos problemas sociales en Asia Menor en la segonda mitad del siglo IV d.C.: Isaurios y Maratocuprenos." *HispAnt* 7: 351–78.

Saria, B. 1966. "Der Römische Herrensitz bei Parndorf und seine Deutung." In *Festschrift A. A. Barb*. Wissesnschaftliche Arbeiten aus dem Burgenland 35, 252–71. Eisenstadt.

Sartre, M. 1982. *Trois études sur l'Arabie romaine et byzantine*. Collection Latomus 178. Brussels.

Schäferdiek, K. 1979. "Wulfila: von Bishof von Gotien zum Gotenbischof." *ZKG* 90: 253–303.

————. 1988. "Das gotische liturgische Kalenderfragment—Bruchstück eines Konstantinopeler Martyrologs." *ZNTW* 79: 116–37.

———. 1992. "Das gotische Christentum im vierten Jahrhundert." In *Triuwe: Studien zur Sprachgeschichte und Literaturwissenschaft für Elfriede Stutz*, eds. K.-F. Kraft, E.-M. Lill, and U. Schwab, 19–50. Heidelberg.

Scharf, R. 1990. "Der *Comes sacri stabuli* in der Spätantike." *Tyche* 5: 135–47.

———. 1991. "*Seniores-Iuniores* und die Heeresteilung des Jahres 364." *ZPE* 89: 265–72.

Schenk von Stauffenberg, A., Graf. 1947. *Das Imperium und die Völkerwanderung*. Munich.

Schmidt, L. 1934. *Geschichte der deutschen Stämme bis zum Ausgang der Völkerwanderung: Die Ostgermanen*. 2d ed. Munich.

Schmitt, O. 1997. "Der 'Gotensieg' von Tomi: Verlauf und Hintergründe." *Historia* 46: 379–84.

Schnurbein, S. von, and H.-J. Köhler. 1989. "Der neue Plan des Valentinianischen Kastells Alta Ripa (Altrip)." *BRGK* 70: 507–26.

Schoo, G. 1911. *Die Quellen des Kirchenhistorikers Socrates*. Berlin.

Schulten, A. 1906. "Zwei Erlasse des Kaisers Valens über die Provinz Asia." *JÖAI* 9: 40–70.

Schurmans, C. 1949. "Valentinien I et le sénat romain." *AC* 18: 25–38.

Scorpan, C. 1980. *Limes Scythiae: Topographical and Stratigraphical Research on the Late Roman Fortifications on the Lower Danube*. BAR-IS 88. Oxford.

Seager, R. 1996. "Ammianus and the Status of Armenia in the Peace of 363." *Chiron* 26: 275–84.

———. 1997. "Perceptions of Eastern Frontier Policy in Ammianus, Libanius and Julian (337–363)." *CQ* 47: 253–68.

———. 1999. "Roman Policy on the Rhine and Danube in Ammianus." *CQ* 49: 579–605.

Seeck, O. 1906a. *Die Briefe des Libanius*. Texte und Untersuchungen zur Geschichte der altchristlichen Literatur 30. Leipzig.

———. 1906b. "Zur Chronologie und Quellenkritik des Ammianus." *Hermes* 41: 481–539.

———. 1912. "Gratianus 2." RE 7: 1831.

———. 1913. *Geschichte des Untergangs der antiken Welt*. Vol. 5. Stuttgart.

———. 1919. *Regesten der Kaiser und Päpste für die Jahre 311 bis 476 n. Chr.: Vorarbeit zu einer Prosopographie der christlichen Kaiserzeit*. Stuttgart.

Seyfarth, W., ed., trans. and comm. 1968–71. *Ammianus Marcellinus: Römische Geschichte*. 4 vols. Berlin.

Shahid, I. 1984a. *Byzantium and the Arabs in the Fourth Century*. Washington, D.C.

———. 1984b. *Rome and the Arabs: A Prolegomenon to the Study of Byzantium and the Arabs*. Washington, D.C.

Shanzer, D. 1998a. "The Date and Literary Context of Ausonius' *Mosella*: Ausonius, Symmachus, and the *Mosella*." In *Style and Tradition: Studies in Honor of Wendell Clausen*, eds. P. Knox and C. Foss, 284–305. Stuttgart.

———. 1998b. "The Date and Literary Context of Ausonius's *Mosella*: Valentinian I's Alamannic Campaigns and the Unnamed Office-Holder." *Historia* 47: 204–33.

Shaw, B. D. 1982–83. "'Eaters of Flesh and Drinkers of Milk': The Ancient Mediterranean Ideology of the Pastoral Nomad." *AncSoc* 13–14: 5–31.

———. 1984. "Bandits in the Roman Empire." *P&P* 105: 3–52.

————. 1990. "Bandit Highlands and Lowland Peace: The Mountains of Isauria-Cilicia." *JESHO* 33: 199–233, 237–70.

————. 1993. "The Bandit." In *The Romans*, ed. A. Giardina, 300–41. Chicago.

————. 1999. "War and Violence." In *Late Antiquity: A Guide to the Postclassical World*, ed. G. W. Bowersock, P. Brown and O. Grabar, 130–69. Cambridge, Mass.

Sheridan, J. 1998. *Columbia Papyri IX: The Vestis militaris codex*. Atlanta, Ga.

Sievers, G. R. 1868. *Das Leben des Libanius*. Berlin. Reprint, Amsterdam, 1969.

Sinclair, T. A. 1987–89. *Eastern Turkey: An Architectural and Archaeological Survey*. 3 vols. London.

Sirks, B. 1991. *Food for Rome: The Legal Structure of the Transportation and Processing of Supplies for the Imperial Distributions in Rome and Constantinople*. Amsterdam.

Sivan, H. 1993. *Ausonius of Bordeaux: Genesis of a Gallic Aristocracy*. London.

————. 1996. "Was Theodosius I a Usurper?" *Klio* 78: 198–211.

Smith, R. B. E. 1995. *Julian's Gods: Religion and Philosophy in the Thought and Action of Julian the Apostate*. London.

Smith, R. R. R. 1997. "The Public Image of Licinius I: Portrait Sculpture and Imperial Ideology in the Early Fourth Century." *JRS* 87: 170–202.

Snee, R. 1985. "Valens' Recall of the Nicene Exiles and Anti-Arian Propaganda." *GRBS* 26: 395–419.

Solari, A. 1932a. "Il consiglio di guerra ad Adrianapoli nel 378." *RFIC* 60: 501–5.

————. 1932b. "Graziano Maior." *Athenaeum* 19: 160–64.

————. 1932c. "Il non intervento nel conflitto tra la Persia e Valente." *RFIC* 60: 352–58.

————. 1932d. "La rivolta procopiana a Constantinapoli." *Byzantion* 7: 143–48.

————. 1933. "Strategia nella lotta tra Procopio e Valente." *RFIC* 61: 492–96.

Soproni, S. 1967. "Burgus-Bauinschrift vom Jahre 372 am Pannonischen Limes." In *Studien zu den Militärgrenzen Roms I: Vorträge des 6. internationalen Limeskongresses in Süddeutschland, 1964*, 138–43. Cologne.

————, ed. 1968. *Tabula Imperii Romani, L34: Aquincum-Sarmizegetusa-Sirmium*. Budapest.

————. 1969. "Über der Munzlauf in Pannonie zu Ende des 4. Jahrhunderts." *Folia Archeologica* 20: 69–78.

————. 1978. *Der spätrömische Limes zwischen Esztergom und Szentendré: Das Verteidigungssystem der Provinz Valeria im 4. Jahrhundert*. Budapest.

————. 1985. *Die Letzten Jahrzehnte des pannonischen Limes*. Munich.

————. 1989. "Militärinschriften aus dem 4. Jh. im Donauknie." *AArchHung* 41: 103–18.

Soraci, R. 1968. *L'imperatore Gioviano*. Catania.

————. 1971. *L'imperatore Valentiniano I*. Catania.

Sotiroff, G. 1972. "The Language of Emperor Valentinian." *CW* 65: 231–32.

Southern, P., and K. R. Dixon. 1996. *The Late Roman Army*. New Haven, Conn.

Speidel, M. P. 1977. "The Roman Army in Arabia." *ANRW* II.8: 687–730.

————. 1980. "Legionaries from Asia Minor." *ANRW* II.7.2: 730–46.

————. 1996a. "Raising New Units for the Late Roman Army: *Auxilia Palatina*." *DOP* 50: 163–70.

————. 1996b. "Sebastian's Strike Force at Adrianople." *Klio* 78: 434–37.

————. 1998. "The Slaughter of Gothic Hostages after Adrianople." *Hermes* 126: 503–6.

Spoerl, K. M. 1993. "The Schism at Antioch Since Cavallera." In *Arianism after Arius:*

Essays on the Development of the Fourth-Century Trinitarian Conflicts, ed. M.R. Barnes and D.H. Williams, 101–26. Edinburgh.

Srejović, D. 1985. "Felix Romuliana: Galerijeva palata u Gamzigrad." *Starinar* 36: 51–67.

———. 1992–93. "A Porphyry Head of a Tetrarch from Romuliana (Gamzigrad)." *Starinar* 43–44: 41–7.

———. 1993a. "Felix Romuliana—Galerius' Ideological Testament." In *Roman Imperial Towns and Palaces in Serbia*, ed. D. Srejović, 29–53. Belgrade.

———, ed. 1993b. *Roman Imperial Towns and Palaces in Serbia*. Belgrade.

Srejović, D., and C. Vasic. 1994. *Imperial Mausolea and Consecration Memorials in Felix Romuliana (Gamzigrad, East Serbia)*. Belgrade.

Staats, R. 1990. "Die römische Tradition im Symbol von 381 (n. C.) und seine Entstehung auf der Synode von Antiochien 379." *VChr* 44: 209–22.

Staesche, M. 1998. *Das Privatleben der römischen Kaiser in der Spätantike*. Berlin.

Stallknecht, B. 1969. *Untersuchungen zur römischen Aussenpolitik in der Spätantike (306–395 n. Chr.)*. Bonn.

Stancliffe, C. 1983. *St. Martin and His Hagiographer: History and Miracle in Sulpicius Severus*. Oxford.

Steigerwald, G. 1990. "Das kaiserliche Purpurprivileg in spätrömischer und frühbyzantinischer Zeit." *JbAC* 33: 209–39.

Stein, E. 1959. *Histoire du bas-empire*. Vol. 1: *De l'état romain à l'état byzantin (284–476)*. Translated by J.R. Palanque. Paris.

Stiglitz, H., M. Kandler, and W. Jobst. 1977. "Carnuntum." *ANRW* II.6: 583–730.

Straub, J. 1938. "Kaiser und Heer in spätrömischer Zeit." *GArb* 10: 7–8. Reprinted in *Regeneratio imperii: Aufsätze über Roms Kaisertum und Reich im Spiegel der heidnischen und christlichen Publizistik*, 64–69 (Darmstadt, 1972).

———. 1939. *Vom Herrscherideal in der Spätantike*. Forschungen zur Kirchen- und Geistesgeschichte, 18. Stuttgart.

———. 1943. "Die Wirkung der Niederlage bei Adrianopel auf die Diskussion über das Germanenproblem in der spätrömischen Literatur." *Philologus* 49: 255–86. Reprinted in *Regeneratio imperii: Aufsätze über Roms Kaisertum und Reich im Spiegel der heidnischen und christlichen Publizistik*, 195–214 (Darmstadt, 1972).

———. 1986. "*Germania Provincia*. Reichsidee und Vertragspolitik im Urteil des Symmachus und der Historia Augusta." In *Colloque genevois sur Symmaque à l'occasion du mille six centième anniversaire du conflit de l'autel de la Victoire*, ed. F. Paschoud, 209–30. Paris.

Swoboda, E. 1964. *Carnuntum: Seine Geschichte und seine Denkmäler*. 4th ed. Graz.

Sydow, W. von. 1969. *Zur Kunstgeschichte des spätantiken Porträts im 4. Jahrhundert n. Chr.* Bonn.

Syme, R. 1968. *Ammianus and the Historia Augusta*. Oxford.

———. 1971. *Emperors and Biography: Studies in the Historia Augusta*. Oxford.

———. 1974. "The Ancestry of Constantine." In *Bonner Historia-Augusta-Colloquium 1971*, 237–53. Bonn.

Szidat, J. 1995. "Staatlichkeit und Einzelschicksal in der Spätantike." *Historia* 44: 481–95.

Teitler, H.C. 1985. *Notarii and Exceptores: An Inquiry into the Role and Significance of Shorthand Writers in the Imperial and Ecclesiastical Bureaucracy of the Roman Empire (from the Early Principate to c. 450 A.D.)*. Amsterdam.

————. 1992. "Ammianus and Constantius. Image and Reality." In *Cognitio Gestorum: The Historiographic Art of Ammianus Marcellinus,* ed. J. den Boeft, D. den Hengst, and H. Teitler, 117–22. Amsterdam.

Teja, R. C. 1974. *Organización economica y social de Cappadocia en el siglo IV, segun los Padres Capadocios.* Salamanca.

Thelamon, F. 1981. *Païens et chrétiens au IVe siècle: l'apport de l'"Histoire ecclésiastique" de Rufin d'Aquilée.* Paris.

Thomas, E. B. 1964. *Römische Villen in Pannonien.* Budapest.

————. 1980. "Villa Settlements." In *The Archaeology of Roman Pannonia,* ed. A. Lengyel and G. T. B. Radan, 275–321. Budapest.

Thompson, E. A. 1947. *The Historical Work of Ammianus Marcellinus.* Cambridge.

————, trans. 1952. *A Roman Reformer and Inventor: Being a New Text of the Treatise* De rebus bellicis, *with a Translation and Introduction.* Oxford.

————. 1956. "Constantine, Constantius and the Lower Danube Frontier." *Hermes* 84: 372–81.

————. 1963. "The Visigoths from Fritigern to Euric." *Historia* 12: 105–26.

————. 1965. *The Early Germans.* Oxford.

————. 1966. *The Visigoths in the Time of Ulfila.* Oxford.

————. 1996. *The Huns.* Revised by P. J. Heather. Oxford.

Thompson, L. A. 1989. *Romans and Blacks.* Norman, Okla.

Thomson, R. W., trans. 1978. *Moses Khorenats'i: History of the Armenians.* Cambridge, Mass.

Todd, M. 1992. *The Early Germans.* Oxford.

Tomlin, R. 1972. "*Seniores-Iuniores* in the late Roman Field Army." *AJPh* 93: 253–78.

————. 1973. "The Emperor Valentinian I." Diss. Oxford.

————. 1974. "The Date of the 'Barbarian Conspiracy.'" *Britannia* 5: 303–9.

————. 1979. "Ammianus Marcellinus 26.4.5–6." *CQ* 29: 470–8.

————. 1998. "Christianity and the Late Roman Army." In *Constantine: History, Historiography and Legend,* ed. S. N. C. Lieu and D. Montserat, 21–51. London.

Tomovic, M. 1996. "Ravna—The Roman and Early Byzantine Fortification." In *Roman Limes on the Middle and Lower Danube,* ed. P. Petrovic, 73–80. Belgrade.

Tóth, E. 1973. "Late Antique Imperial Palace in Savaria." *AArchHung* 25: 117–37.

————. 1982. "Tetrarchiezeitliche Namensgebung von Iovia-Herculia in Pannonien." *AErt* 109: 55–72.

Toumanoff, C. 1963. *Studies in Christian Caucasian History.* Washington, D.C.

Toynbee, J. M. C. 1944. *Roman Medallions.* Numismatic Studies 5. New York. Reprint, 1986.

Treadgold, W. 1995. *Byzantium and Its Army, 284–1081.* Stanford, Calif.

Treucker, B. 1961. *Politische und sozialgeschichtliche Studien zu den Basilius-Briefen.* Munich.

Tritle, L. A. 1994. "Whose Tool? Ammianus Marcellinus on the Emperor Valens." *AHB* 8: 141–53.

Trombley, F. R. 1993. *Hellenic Religion and Christianization, c. 370–529.* 2 vols. Leiden.

Tudor, D. 1937–40. "Ein konstantinischer Meilenstein aus Dazien." *Serta Hoffilleriana. Vjesnik hrvatskoga archeoskoga drustva,* n.s., 18–21: 241–47.

————. 1974. *Les ponts romains du bas-Danube.* Bucharest.

Turcan, R. 1966. "L'abandon de Nisibe et l'opinion publique (363 ap. J.C.)." In *Mélanges d'archéologie et d'histoire offerts à A. Piganiol,* vol. 2, ed. R. Chevallier, 875–90. Paris.

Ulrich, J. 1995. *Barbarische Gesellschaftsstruktur und römische Außenpolitik zu Beginn der Völkerwanderung: Ein Versuch zu den Westgoten, 365–377.* Bonn.

Ulrich Bansa, O. 1949. *Moneta Mediolanensis.* Venice.

Urbainczyk, T. 1997a. "Observations on the Differences between the Church Histories of Socrates and Sozomen." *Historia* 46: 355–73.

———. 1997b. *Socrates of Constantinople: Historian of Church and State.* Ann Arbor, Mich.

Valensi, L. 1957. "Quelques réflexions sur le pouvoir imperial d'après Ammian Marcellin." *BAGB* 4.4: 62–107.

Vanags, P. 1979. "Taxation and Survival in the Late Fourth Century: The Anonymus' Programme of Economic Reform." In *Aspects of the De rebus bellicis: Papers Presented to Professor E. A. Thompson,* ed. M. W. C. Hassall and R. Ireland, 47–57. BAR-IS 63. Oxford.

Van Dam, R. 1986. "Emperor, Bishops, and Friends in Late Antique Cappadocia." *JThS* 37: 53–76.

Vanderspoel, J. 1995. *Themistius and the Imperial Court: Oratory, Civic Duty, and Paideia from Constantius to Theodosius.* Ann Arbor, Mich.

Van Millingen, A. 1899. *Byzantine Constantinople: The Walls of the City and Adjoining Historical Sites.* London.

Várady, L. 1969. *Das letzte Jahrhundert Pannoniens: 376–476.* Amsterdam.

Vatin, C. 1962. "Les empereurs du IVᵉ siècle à Delphes." *BCH* 86: 229–41.

Velkov, V. 1980. "Themistius as a Source of Information about Thrace." In *Roman Cities in Bulgaria: Collected Studies,* ed. V. Velkov, 171–98. Amsterdam.

———. 1983. "La Thrace et la Mésie inférieure pendent l'époque de la Basse Antiquité (iv–vi ss)." In *Ancient Bulgaria: Papers Presented to the International Symposium on the Ancient History and Archaeology of Bulgaria, University of Nottingham, 1981,* ed. A. G. Poulter, 177–93. Nottingham.

———. 1989. "Wulfila und die *Gothi minores* in Moesien." *Klio* 71: 525–27.

Vera, D. 1983. "La carriera di Virius Nicomachus Flavianus e la prefettura dell'Illirico Orientale nel iv sec. d.C." *Athenaeum* 61: 390–426.

Vetters, H. 1954–57. "Sueridas und Colias (zu Ammianus Marcellinus 31.6)." In *Antidoron: Festschrift M. Abramic.* Vjesnik za Archeologiju i Historiju Dalmatinsku 56–59: 127–30.

Viansino, J. 1985. *Ammiani Marcellini rerum gestarum lexicon.* Hildesheim.

Vincenti, U. 1991. "'Praescriptio fori' e senatori nel tardo impero romano d'Occidente." *Index* 19: 433–40.

Visy, Z. 1995. "Wachttürme an der Ripa Pannonica in Ungarn." *AAntHung* 36: 265–74.

Vogler, C. 1979. *Constance II et l'administration impériale.* Strasbourg.

Vorbeck, E., and L. Beckel. 1973. *Carnuntum: Rom an der Donau.* Salzburg.

Vulpe, R. 1960. "Les Gètes de la rive gauche du bas-Danube et les Romains." *Dacia* 4: 309–32.

Walker, D. R. 1978. *The Metrology of Roman Silver Coinage, Part III, from Pertinax to Uranius Antoninus.* BAR-SS 40. Oxford.

Wallace-Hadrill, A. 1981. "The Emperor and His Virtues." *Historia* 30: 298–323.

———. 1983. *Suetonius: The Scholar and His Caesars.* London.

Wanke, U. 1990. *Die Gotenkriege des Valens: Studien zu Topographie und Chronologie im unteren Donauraum von 366 bis 378 n. Chr.* Frankfurt am Main.

Wardman, A. 1984. "Usurpers and Internal Conflicts in the 4th Century A.D." *Historia* 33: 220–37.

Ward-Perkins, B. 1998. "The Cities." In *Cambridge Ancient History*, vol. 13: *The Late Empire, A.D. 337–425,* 2d ed., ed. A. Cameron and P. Garnsey, 371–410. Cambridge.

Warmington, B. H. 1977. "Objectives and Strategy in the Persian War of Constantius II." In *Limes: Akten des XI internationalen Limeskongresses, Székesfehérvar, 1976,* 509–20. Budapest.

Wellner, I. 1990. "Die Militärlager Aquincums in spätrömischer Zeit und im Mittelalter." In *Akten des 14. internationalen Limeskongresses in Bad Deutsch-Altenberg / Carnuntum, 1986,* 715–22. Vienna.

Wells, P. S. 1999. *The Barbarians Speak: How the Conquered Peoples Shaped Roman Europe.* Princeton, N.J.

Welsby, D. A. 1982. *The Roman Military Defence of the British Provinces in Its Later Phases.* BAR-IS 172. Oxford.

Wenskus, R. 1961. *Stammesbildung und Verfassung: Das Werden der frühmittelalterlichen gentes.* Cologne.

Wheeler, E. L. 1998. "Constantine's Gothic Treaty of 332: A Reconsideration of Eusebius *VC* 4.5–6." In *The Roman Frontier at the Lower Danube 4th–6th Centuries: Studia Danubiana Pars Romaniae Series Symposia I,* ed. M. Zahariade, 81–94. Bucharest.

Whitby, M., and M. Whitby, trans. and comm. 1989. *Chronicon paschale, 284-628* A.D. Translated Texts for Historians 7. Liverpool.

Whitehead, N. L. 1992. "Tribes Make States and States Make Tribes: Warfare and the Creation of Colonial Tribes and States in Northeastern South America." In *War in the Tribal Zone: Expanding States and Indigenous Warfare,* eds. R. B. Ferguson and N. L. Whitehead, 127–50. Santa Fe, N.Mex.

Whittaker, C. R. 1976. *"Agri Deserti."* In *Studies in Roman Property,* ed. M. I. Finley, 137–65. Cambridge.

———. 1994. *Frontiers of the Roman Empire: A Social and Economic Study.* Baltimore.

Wiebe, F. J. 1995. *Kaiser Valens und die heidnische Opposition.* Antiquitas 44. Bonn.

Wightman, E. M. 1971. *Roman Trier and the Treveri.* New York.

Wilkinson, J. trans. and comm. 1999. *Egeria's Travels.* 3d ed. Warminster, UK.

Williams, D. H. 1995. *Ambrose of Milan and the End of the Nicene-Arian Conflict.* Oxford.

———. 1996. "Another Exception to Later Fourth-Century 'Arian' Typologies: The Case of Germinius of Sirmium." *JECS* 4: 335–57.

Williams, S., and G. Friell. 1994. *Theodosius: The Empire at Bay.* London.

Winkelmann, F. 1966. *Untersuchungen zur Kirchengeschichte des Gelasios von Kaisareia.* SB Berlin, Literatur und Kunst, 1965, no. 3. Berlin.

Winter, E. 1988. *Die sassanidisch-römische Friedensverträge des 3. Jahrhunderts n. Chr.* Frankfurt am Main.

———. 1989. "On the Regulation of the Eastern Frontier of the Roman Empire in 298." In *The Eastern Frontier of the Roman Empire: Proceedings of a Colloquium Held at Ankara in September 1988,* ed. D. H. French and C. S. Lightfoot, 555–71. BAR-IS 553. Oxford.

Wirbelauer, E., and C. Fleer. 1995. *"Totius Orbis Augustus:* Claudius Mamertinus als *Praefectus Praetorio* der Kaiser Julian und Valentinian." In *Historische Interpretationen: Festschrift Gerold Walser,* ed. M. Wienmann-Walser, 191–201. Historia Einzelschriften 100. Stuttgart.

Wirth, G. 1975. "Alexander und Rom." In *Alexandre le grand: Image et realité*, ed. A. B. Bosworth, 181–211. Entretiens Hardt 22. Geneva.

———. 1984. "Jovian, Kaiser und Karikatur." In *Vivarium: Festschrift T. Klauser*, 353–84. Münster.

Wolf, P. 1952. *Vom Schulwesen der Spätantike: Studien zu Libanius*. Baden-Baden.

Wolfram, H. 1975. "Gotische Studien I–II." *MIÖG* 83: 1–32, 289–324.

———. 1976. "Gotische Studien III." *MIÖG* 84 (1976): 239–61.

———. 1977. "Die Schlacht von Adrianopel." *AAWW* 114: 227–50.

———. 1988. *History of the Goths*. Translated by T. Dunlap. Berkeley.

———. 1997. *The Roman Empire and Its Germanic Peoples*. Translated by T. Dunlap. Berkeley.

Woloch, M. 1966. "Indications of Imperial Status on Roman Coins, A.D. 337–383." *NC* 136: 171–78.

Woodman, A. J. 1977. *Velleius Paterculus: The Tiberian Narrative*. Cambridge.

Woods, D. 1994. "The Baptism of the Emperor Valens." *Classica et Mediaevalia* 45: 211–21.

———. 1995a. "Ammianus Marcellinus and the Deaths of Bonosus and Maximilianus." *Hagiographica* 2: 25–55.

———. 1995b. "The Fate of the *Magister Equitum* Marcellus." *CQ* 45: 266–68.

———. 1995c. "A Note Concerning the Early Career of Valentinian I." *AncSoc* 26: 273–88.

———. 1996. "The Saracen Defenders of Constantinople in 378." *GRBS* 37: 259–79.

———. 1997. "Ammianus and Some *Tribuni scholarum palatinarum* c. A.D. 353–64." *CQ* 47: 269–91.

———. 1998. "Maurus, Mavia and Ammianus." *Mnemosyne* 51: 325–36.

———. 2001. "Dating Basil of Caesarea's Correspondence with Arinetheus and his Widow." *Studia Patristica* 37: 301-7.

Zachhuber, J. 2000. "The Antiochene Synod of A.D. 363 and the Beginnings of Neo-Nicenism." *ZAC* 4: 83–101.

Zahariade, M. 1983. "Ammianus Marcellinus (27.5.2), Zosimus (4.11) si campania lui Valens din anul 367 împotriva gotilor." *SCIVA* 34: 57–70.

Zahariade, M., and A. Opait. 1986. "A New Late Roman Fortification on the Territory of Romania: The *Burgus* at Topraichioi, Tulcea County." In *Studien zu den Militärgrenzen Roms III: 13. Internationalen Limeskongresses, Aalen, 1983*, 565–72. Stuttgart.

Zeiller, J. 1918. *Les origines chrétiennes dans les provinces Danubiennes de l'Empire romain*. Paris. Reprint, Rome, 1976.

Zuckerman, C. 1991a. "Cappadocian Fathers and the Goths." *T&MByz* 11: 473–86.

———. 1991b. "The Early Byzantine Strongholds in Eastern Pontus." *T&MByz* 11: 527-53.

———. 1994. "Aur. Valerianus (295/305) et Fl. Severinus (333), commandants en Arabie, et la forteresse d'Azraq." *Antiquité tardive* 2: 83–88.

INDEX

THE TRANSFORMATION OF THE CLASSICAL HERITAGE

Peter Brown, General Editor